KU-202-709

Researching Society and Culture

Denzin
Lincoln

The Sage handbook of
Qualitative Research

Doing Psychological
Research

Nicky
Hayes

Researching Society and Culture

Second edition

Edited by Clive Seale

LEARNING
RESOURCES
CENTRE

SAGE Publications
London ● Thousand Oaks ● New Delhi

301·018

188407

ISBN 0-7619-4196-7   ISBN-13 978-0-7619-4196-5
ISBN 0-7619-4197-5 (pbk)   ISBN-13 987-0-7619-4197-2 (pbk)

© Clive Seale 1998, 2004
First published 1998
Reprinted 2000
Second edition 2004
Reprinted 2005, 2006

Apart from any fair dealing for the purposes of research or private study, or criticism or review, as permitted under the Copyright, Designs and Patents Act, 1988, this publication may be reproduced, stored or transmitted in any form, or by any means, only with the prior permission in writing of the publishers, or in the case of reprographic reproduction, in accordance with the terms of licences issued by the Copyright Licensing Agency. Inquiries concerning reproduction outside those terms should be sent to the publishers.

SAGE Publications Ltd
1 Oliver's Yard
55 City Road
London EC1Y 1SP

SAGE Publications Inc
2455 Teller Road
Thousand Oaks
California 91320

SAGE Publications India Pvt Ltd
B–42 Panchsheel Enclave
PO Box 4109
New Delhi 110 017

British Library Cataloguing in Publication data
A catalogue record for this book is available from the British Library

Library of Congress Control Number: 2003115336

Printed on paper from sustainable sources

Typeset by GCS Composition, Leighton Buzzard, Bedfordshire
Printed and bound in Great Britain by
Alden Press Limited, Osney Mead, Oxford

Contents

Acknowledgements

The Durkheim example in Chapter 2 was originally developed by Dr Norman Stockman (University of Aberdeen). Paul Acourt (Goldsmiths) gave helpful comments on Chapter 5. William Trochim gave permission for use of the picture in Figure 7.1. Workshop Exercise 17.2 was developed from original materials written by Nigel Fielding (University of Surrey). Workshop Exercise 24.3 was developed from original materials written by Lionel Sims (University of East London). Daniel Miller (University College, London) supplied the material for Exercise 17.3. Marion Garnett (Goldsmiths) supplied a data extract from her study used in Box 23.5. Patricia Taraborelli (University of Wales) gave permission for the use of the diagram in Figure 23.6. Basiro Davey (Open University) gave permission for use of the interview material in Box IV.7. Vikki Bell (Goldsmiths) provided the idea for Exercise 27.2. Table 25.1 is adapted from an original developed for teaching purposes by George Brown (Royal Holloway). Sara Arber (University of Surrey) gave permission for use of the material in Tables 26.1 and 26.2. Caroline Ramazanoglu (Goldsmiths) supplied guidelines for Exercise 14.1. Lyn Richards (QSR, Australia) gave permission for use of the screen shots of NVivo and the reproduction of the interview in Box IV.4. DRS Data and Research Services gave permission for the use of the questionnaire in Box IV.3.

We would like to thank all these people for allowing their ideas to be used in this book.

1

Introduction

Clive Seale

This second edition of *Researching Society and Culture* provides, like its predecessor, theoretically informed guidance to practising the key social research methods for investigating society and culture. It is a text in both methods and methodology, in which the importance of understanding the historical, theoretical and institutional context in which particular methods have developed is stressed. The contributors share a belief that social researchers do not just apply a set of neutral techniques to the issues which they investigate. Research is part of a dynamic, reflexive engagement with social and cultural worlds, and the way in which students learn 'methods' requires a continual awareness of this.

Many existing textbooks imply a 'toolbox' approach to research. This originated at a time when researchers were primarily committed to an idea of a social science modelled on the approach of natural sciences. Under this scheme, a view of methods as neutral tools for the objective investigation of social and cultural life is uncontroversial. Classically, this has been the approach of texts describing social survey work, the method primarily associated with a positivist social science. But, it seems, undergraduate and even some postgraduate courses, as well as publishing houses, have taken some time to shake off this legacy of the toolbox approach, in spite of the revolutions in social theory and methodology that have successfully challenged the once

dominant, quantitatively oriented social survey approach. Existing textbooks, even where they describe qualitative approaches, often reflect an uncomfortable degree of separation between the philosophy of social science, social theory and the actual practice of social and cultural research.

As well as presenting approaches in which the links between these areas are stressed, we wish in this book to help students to break free from divisive and stultifying disputes between rival camps associated with particular approaches. Divisions have often been over-emphasized as researchers have struggled to find the institutional and intellectual space to develop distinctive new approaches. A variety of theoretically informed qualitative approaches to social and cultural research have resulted from struggles with the old quantitative orthodoxy. Yet some of the most keenly defended distinctions and disputes have developed between those advocating different varieties of qualitative methodology. We believe that a considerable amount can now be done to bring these different traditions together, emphasizing the need for practising researchers to find what is of value in each approach.

Social and cultural research can be understood as proceeding as a series of *genres*. An analogy with schools of painting may help explain this. Convention has it that impressionism, cubism, fauvism, post-impressionism and so on describe particular approaches to fine art around the early years of the twentieth century. No one now tries to claim that one of these is more 'true' than another. At most, this is a matter of taste; beauty is a more dominant criterion than truth. Can we understand schools of social and cultural research in this way? Is a preference for numbers, for ethnography, interviews, discourse analysis, ethnomethodology or semiotic analysis simply a matter of taste? At one level, this is so. Nobody is forced to 'belong' to a particular school of social research, and aesthetic taste certainly enters the picture in explaining why some individuals come to be committed to particular approaches.

Yet there are also differences between fine art and research. Avoiding some of the furthest extremes of postmodern thought, some commitment to truth as well as beauty seems right to most practising social researchers (Silverman, 1997). A text reporting on a research project can be ugly or inelegant but nevertheless be true to the social or cultural world being analysed. Even with this modified position, though, the *genre* analogy holds some force. The greatest painters have made it their business to practise in a variety of genres during their careers, then breaking free from existing divisions and using their creative powers to generate new forms from the old ones. This is also true of the innovators in social and cultural research who draw upon a variety of influences, using their thorough familiarity with existing approaches, to deal with new research problems in creative ways. If this book can convey something of this spirit it will have succeeded.

This book outlines in a concise way the standard methods that a student beginning to learn how to do research will need to know: doing a literature review, the conduct of social surveys, interviews (both qualitative and quantitative), participant observation, coding and the basic procedures of statistical and qualitative data analysis, grounded theorizing, the writing of research proposals, ethical issues in research, validity and reliability concerns. However, the book is also more ambitious as it seeks to bring to a student readership knowledge and practice in methods hitherto the preserve of more advanced texts. Thus, there are chapters on discourse analysis, the analysis of visual images, archival and secondary analysis, and conversation

analysis. Several of these have arisen from revolutions in social theory that have occurred over the past 20–30 years. It is also our belief that one can only fully understand methods if one has an understanding of the historical and theoretical context from which they arise. To this end, there are chapters on the history and theoretical context of methods towards the beginning of the book. The book also contains some innovatory chapters on subjects that rarely appear in conventional methods texts: making and managing audio recordings, using the Internet for research purposes, doing a dissertation and what to do when things go wrong.

This is a book about **methodology** as well as methods. That is to say, it is a book which encourages you to think about the political, theoretical and philosophical implications of making particular choices of method when doing a research project. To this end, there are chapters on the relationship between research and social policy, research and social theory, the philosophy of social science and subject position and method. If the revolutions in social theory that have transformed our understanding of research methods have a common direction, it is towards an interest in the role of language in representing and creating social realities. Importantly, therefore, the book contains a chapter analysing the writing of social research itself. A heightened awareness of the rhetorical strategies used in social research writing enhances the **reflexivity** of social researchers; that is, their capacity to reflect upon what they are doing, and to recognize that social research is itself a form of intervention in the social and cultural world.

Although all the contributors are, or have been, members of the Department of Sociology at Goldsmiths College, the book is not solely addressed to sociologists. This is in part because of the nature of the department at Goldsmiths, which contains groupings of staff with backgrounds and interests in disciplines other than sociology: cultural studies, philosophy, literature, history, geography and anthropology, for example. But it is also because the old divisions between academic subjects that once were a guide to associated divisions in methods have now been broken down. Increasingly it is the case that sociologists have become interested in historical and cross-cultural perspectives, out of a belief that this is a valuable way to understand the present. Sociology, in some respects, has become a 'history of the present' just as anthropologists have become more interested in making their *own* cultures anthropologically strange. Additionally, anthropologists, geographers, students of cultural and media studies, historians, people involved in health studies, sociologists and others have increasingly come to recognize common interests and influences in social theory, and therefore in methods for investigating social and cultural life.

Organization of the book

At a more mundane level, this book addresses the practical constraint of undergraduate student finances at a time when it is unrealistic to expect all students to buy three or four texts for each of the courses they may study during a typical year. Under one cover, *Researching Society and Culture* offers the opportunity to learn how to practise the main varieties of method used by social and cultural researchers today. To this end, the final part contains a variety of practical exercises designed for use in workshops and discussion groups, all of which have been tried and tested with students by the contributors to this book. At the end of each chapter there is guidance on further reading which will allow a deeper understanding of the topic to develop.

Key terms are shown in **bold** type where a definition of the term is given in the text. Wherever possible, this occurs when the term is first used and sometimes such terms are defined more than once in the text, occurring in bold on each occasion. Every such occurrence of a key term is indexed at the end of the book, so that you can look up the definitions. Additionally, many of the more important key terms are explained in a separate glossary towards the end of the book. *Italic* type is used for emphasis and on some occasions where key terms are used, but not defined. If you need to know what these italicized words mean, you can use the index and glossary to find out.

However, it is inevitably the case that a book like this contains some variability in the level of language used in the chapters. Although both the contributors and the editor have tried to assume no previous familiarity with the topics discussed, learning this material is always going to feel a little like learning a new language. This variability is in part due to the fact that some of the ideas are more abstract and difficult than others, and this is especially so when the approach is explicitly seeking to generate a novel view of the social and cultural world, breaking with common-sense ideas. People sometimes express their feeling of strangeness about the language of social research by saying that it feels 'too technical', or that there is 'jargon' involved. We hope that you will find these feelings of strangeness reduce as you gain familiarity with the topics of the book.

The book is divided into four parts. Part I contains chapters on the context of research, involving discussions of philosophy, social theory, social policy, the politics of research knowledge, issues of truth and quality, ethics and research design. Additionally, there are chapters outlining the history of both quantitative and qualitative methods. This part is designed to give a broad background of the ideas and developments that either exercise an influence over, or are implied in the practice of, social and cultural research.

Part II contains chapters covering a full spectrum of the methods in use by social and cultural researchers, ranging from statistical and survey work to a variety of qualitative approaches, and ending with a chapter on how one can combine the lessons of the various chapters in the context of an integrated research project done for a student dissertation, and another on what to do if initial plans go wrong. These chapters give practical guidance on how to apply the methods in research projects, coupled with a continual awareness of the theoretical, ethical, political and philosophical implications of methodological decisions.

Part III contains three case studies in which the authors describe particular research projects (or in one case, a series of linked projects) that illustrate how various methods can be used in the context of research practice. These are designed to point you in the direction of developing your own personal research practice.

The book ends with the workshop and discussion exercises of Part IV, which are aimed at helping you become a methodologically aware research practitioner.

A number of features in the text of this second edition have been added to improve the clarity with which ideas are presented and give you pointers in how to explore particular topics further, using both conventional library sources and resources available on the Internet, which have improved and expanded enormously since the first edition. These include:

- Greater use of bullet points, figures and text boxes for the provision of key points, examples and illustrative material
- A glossary of key terms at the end of the book

- Web pointers, in most chapters, to indicate relevant Internet resources
- An associated website* for the book in which you will find reproduced:
  - Live links to the web pointers by chapter (regularly updated)
  - The glossary to the book
  - The workshop and discussion exercises in Part IV, together with extra resources not in the print edition (for example, downloadable data)
- References to further reading
- References at the end of each chapter to relevant readings from a Student Reader (Seale 2004) that contains a section of edited classic readings on methods and methodology**
- A list of the key concepts in each chapter

---

* The website for the book can be found at: www.rscbook.co.uk
or by visiting the Sage website www.sagepub.com/ or www.sagepub.co.uk and searching for 'Researching Society and Culture' where there is a link to the book's website. As web addresses sometimes change, links shown on the website are regularly updated.

**Seale, C.F. (ed.) (2004) *Social Research Methods: A Reader.* London: Routledge.

Part I: Research contexts

2

Selected issues in the philosophy of social science

David Lazar

CONTENTS

In this chapter I will first consider how we might gain knowledge of social life and what should count as knowledge in the social sciences. One approach for social researchers is to examine the possible implications of competing philosophies of natural science (for example, physics, chemistry, biology) for the social sciences. The arguments here are between those who claim that only *scientific* methods produce knowledge and those who claim that such methods are irrelevant to the subject matter of the social sciences. The former are **naturalists,** who argue that the methods of natural science are models for social science, and the latter are **interpretivists** (or *interpretive* social scientists), who claim that there is a sharp disjunction between the methodology appropriate in the two realms. Indeed, many of the latter group deny that what I am calling social science should be called 'science' at all. Naturalists argue that basic methodological principles (for instance, models of explanation) are shared between natural and social sciences, while interpretivists emphasize the *meaningfulness* of social life and the alleged irrelevance of natural scientists' modes of analysis and explanation. On this issue the philosopher Roy Bhaskar writes: 'Without exaggerating, I think one could call this question the primal problem of the philosophy of the social sciences' (1989: 66).

Secondly, I shall consider whether the particular social sciences (economics, sociology, psychology, politics, anthropology) produce anything that is true knowledge of some objective reality, rather than, say, ephemeral notions merely dictated by fashion or subjective pictures of social, psychological or economic reality. This problem is often referred to as the problem of **objectivity.** Because it is about the *status* of social scientific 'knowledge', it is one that no social scientist can avoid. For even if we try to avoid the issue, others in wider society will raise it and thereby question the validity of our methods and conclusions.

A sensitivity to the philosophical issues discussed in this chapter is essential for anyone who wishes to be able to evaluate social research results thoroughly. I have already said that we need to think about how we might gain knowledge and about the status of the results produced by research. The problem is that, all too often, researchers and readers of research reports are unconscious of the fact that any approach to research is based on often contentious philosophical assumptions about these matters. This chapter will enable you to discern such underlying assumptions, even when authors fail to make them explicit or are themselves unaware that they have made methodological decisions by default. It will also provide you with some explanations of key ideas to which other chapters frequently refer.

Philosophies of natural sciences and the social sciences

What is science, and is there an identifiable scientific method? What implications (if any) do the successes (and failures) of the natural sciences have for social science methodology? By **methodology**, I refer to the fundamental or regulative principles which underlie any discipline (for example, its conception of its subject matter and how that subject matter might be investigated). There are no straightforward answers to these questions. Major philosophers of science (for example, Kuhn, Popper, Feyerabend) have debated whether science is a *distinctive* kind of activity, and their contributions are discussed below. However, for many social scientists in the interpretive (or humanistic) tradition, the agreements or disagreements of philosophers about the nature of science and scientific method are of no relevance. For such theorists, the essential point of social science is to grasp *meanings* and complexes of meanings. We can, therefore, say that there are basically three streams in social science with respect to the above questions: *naturalists* who advocate the adoption of some preferred conception of science and scientific method as a model for the social sciences; *interpretive* social scientists, who reject the scientific model because they believe that the nature of human social life is not appropriately grasped by scientific methods; and *reconcilers*, who wish to bridge the divide between naturalism and humanism. In sociology, the work of Max Weber (1864–1920) is an example of such reconciliation. His ideas are discussed in more depth in Chapter 4.

Competing philosophies of science: Karl Popper

The examination of philosophies of science will enable us to understand the complex relationships between theory and observation and what it might mean for a social science to be modelled on the natural sciences. I will begin with the ideas of Karl Popper (1902–94) and then describe the rival views of Kuhn and Feyerabend.

First, Popper rejected **inductivist empiricism**. This is a view which claims that scientific theory has validity because it is rigorously derived from repeated observations. The **empiricist** view is that knowledge must be derived from observation. Accordingly, scientific knowledge is thought to be valid because it is a complex product of such innumerable, systematic and repeated observations. Scientific theories are claimed to be derived from observation by a process called **induction**. Inductive logic is believed by such theorists to enable us to move from the particular to the general, that is, from many observations to some kind of universal statement. But Popper argues both that inductive inference is an invalid form of inference and that scientific theories are not in fact derived from observation. Popper preferred a view of science based on *critical rationalism,* and argued that science consisted of conjectures and refutations.

His claim (Popper, 1963: ch. 1) that induction is not a logically valid method for deriving theories from observations is supported by his argument that theories are general and refer to all occurrences of a phenomenon in the past, present and future. But observation is always finite and we can never know whether the instances we have not observed (or which have not yet occurred) will resemble those we have. Therefore, induction cannot be a valid form of inference because even one counter-instance would refute the theory. Instead, Popper states, scientific progress is made possible because scientists seek theory with a greater scope and truth content, replacing empirically or theoretically discredited theories with better ones. For Popper what is crucial is that, although theories cannot be proved, they can be refuted, and the refutability of scientific theories is what demarcates real sciences from what he calls pseudo-sciences (for example, astrology).

His view that theories are not derived from observation is supported by his argument that theorizing is *prior* to observation. Popper believed that we cannot observe without theories. Incidentally, this is a common assumption of what Hesse (1972: 10–11) refers to as a 'post-empiricist' philosophy of science. It is a view, for example, which underlies the post-structuralist and post-modernist theories explained in Chapter 4. Sciences, Popper contended, are particularly sophisticated forms of theory but like all theory are problem-solving enterprises, that is, driven by speculative solutions to problems rather than by fact gathering. At this point, you need to understand that an **epistemology** is a specific theory of knowledge or, in the words of Williams and May, an answer to the question 'Where does our knowledge come from and how reliable is it?' (1996: 5). Popper advocates a **rationalist epistemology**, that is, he believes that knowledge is a product of mind actively organizing and making sense of our experience of the world. This is in contrast to an **empiricist epistemology**, which claims that knowledge and scientific theories of the world are derivable solely from empirical sense experience or observation.

We can understand why observation cannot be prior to theory by examining Popper's (1963: 44–5) argument about judgements of similarity. Popper contends that any generalization (and theories are very abstract generalizations) depends upon judgements of similarity. Say we wish to formulate a generalization about the connection between events of type A and events of type B. How do we know that particular events are all examples of As and others are all Bs? Only because we have theories (however low-level) which tell us which characteristics matter. That is, judgements of similarity are not possible purely on the basis of observation.

Popper is also a rationalist in a second sense in that he believed that theory choice in science can be *rationally justified* by reference to a universal set of criteria. As Newton-Smith states:

A rational model [of scientific change] involves two ingredients. First, one specifies something as the goal of science. That is, scientists are taken as aiming at the production of theories of some particular kind. For example, it might be said as Popper would that the goal of science is the production of true explanatory theories ... Second, some principle or set of principles is specified for comparing rival theories against a given evidential background. (1981: 4)

The principles Newton-Smith is referring to are, for instance, accuracy, explanatory scope, absence of internal contradictions or contradictions of other accepted theories, simplicity and fruitfulness in terms of new research findings.

In fact this led Popper to believe in the *unity of science* and he proposed a single model on which he felt scientific explanations could rest: the **hypothetico-deductive scheme** (Popper, 1957). Some philosophers of science (for example, Hempel, 1966) refer to this as the *covering law model of explanation*. According to this view, explanations consist of two elements, one general and one more specific. Together these elements form an explanation of what has to be explained. More precisely, one can **deduce** a statement describing the matter to be explained from the statements which form the explanation. This is shown in Box 2.1. You explain an event by showing that it can be *deduced* from a general *law* (or generalization or theory) together with *initial conditions,* these being statements that describe the relevant antecedent events. Let us examine a well-known sociological example to see whether this idea of a common scheme of explanation for all sciences is at all relevant to the social sciences.

Additionally, Popper can be characterized as a **falsificationist** rather than a **verificationist**. That is to say, he believed that science proceeded best if scientists tried to *disprove* rather than *prove* their hypotheses and theories. Trying to refute theories

rather than looking for confirmatory evidence was part of a generalized commitment to open debate for Popper. Thus 'Falsificationism ... is as much an attitude to research as a set of methodological procedures' (Smith 1998: 18). Chapter 7 follows through the application of falsificationism to research practice.

Competing philosophies of science: Thomas Kuhn

Kuhn differs from Popper in rejecting the rationalist view of scientific development: he does not accept that there is a set of (rationally justifiable) principles for the comparison of, and choice between, competing theories. He argues instead that mature sciences are characterized by **paradigms**. Scientific development is only possible if practitioners of the particular discipline share a whole way of working and an overall conception of what it is they are studying. Kuhn distinguishes two basic meanings of the term: 'paradigms [are] the entire constellation of beliefs, values, techniques, and so on shared by members of a given [scientific] community' (1970: 175) and they are a concrete puzzle solution or exemplar of how to solve a scientific problem.

He emphasizes that the paradigm is a shared view of the discipline and the world it seeks to investigate, as well as a set of methods for such an investigation. Thus for Kuhn, everyday science is *normal science* or science as it is practised within the confines of a paradigm. Normal science involves puzzle-solving activity within the disciplinary cognitive world of the paradigm. Characteristically, according to Kuhn, a lack of fit between the theory and the facts is a puzzle to be solved by developing a theory (or, if you like,

---

Box 2.1   Hypothetico-deductive scheme

LAW
(a generalization or theory which covers events and phenomena of this type)

INITIAL CONDITIONS
(statements that describe the circumstances in which the events take place)

EVENT(S) TO BE EXPLAINED
(statement describing what is to be explained)

Box 2.2   Durkheim's use of the hypothetico-deductive scheme

Emile Durkheim (1858–1917), in his work on *Suicide* (1897/1970), set himself the task of providing a sociological explanation for the wide variations in suicide rates in different sections of the population, revealed in official statistics. In particular, he found that Catholics showed lower suicide rates than Protestants. For Durkheim, suicide was a **social fact,** that is, a property of society rather than an aggregate of individual actions. He distinguished between types of suicide, one of which was *egoistic suicide*. Durkheim contended that certain states of religious society, of domestic life and of political society more effectively bind individuals to a group. For instance, he said that Catholicism was associated with greater social cohesion than was Protestantism. Durkheim claimed that egoistic suicide was the result of an excessive detachment of the individual from the group, writing: 'So we reach the general conclusion: suicide varies inversely with the degree of integration of the social groups of which the individual forms a part' (1970: 209). Greater social cohesion (argued to be provided by Catholicism) led to a lower suicide rate, and lower cohesion led to a higher suicide rate (argued to be characteristic of Protestantism). Thus Durkheim's explanation of the phenomenon of the suicide rate for egoistic suicide was cast in terms of the hypothetico-deductive scheme:

LAW: Suicide varies inversely with the degree of integration of the social groups of which the individual forms a part.

INITIAL CONDITIONS: Catholicism binds the individual into a more socially cohesive community than does Protestantism.

EVENT EXPLAINED: The suicide rate for Catholics is lower than that for Protestants.

---

articulating the paradigm) or reinterpreting the facts. Kuhn (1970: 146–7) therefore differs from Popper in claiming that everyday science is not, in practice, continuously critical of the paradigm.

Normal science is only possible when puzzle solving that stays within the boundaries of the paradigm is still feasible. But, ultimately, certain recalcitrant and significant anomalies appear which are not resolvable within these boundaries. If they are too important to be ignored by practitioners, the paradigm is in crisis. Kuhn believes that normal science is largely uncritical of basic assumptions within the relevant paradigm. It is only during a crisis of the paradigm that new, competing theories get the attention of the scientific community. There is then felt by some to be a need for a *paradigm shift*, a time of fundamental change. Change of paradigm can be so fundamental as to be thought of as **scientific revolution** (for instance, change from Ptolemy's earth-centred astronomy to Copernicus's sun-

centred astronomy). Indeed, the book in which Kuhn explains these ideas is called *The Structure of Scientific Revolutions* (1970).

For Kuhn, the essential feature of a scientific revolution is that the new paradigm and the old are *incommensurable*. Incommensurability means that there is no shared set of criteria of evaluation and there is a qualitative break between successive paradigms. Successive paradigms conceptualize the world which the discipline studies in starkly different ways and there is *no* universal set of principles that are accepted by adherents of both as criteria of evaluation applicable to each. This is why Kuhn sees scientific revolutions as being like a conversion experience rather than a rational process (as Popper would). It is an exchange of *belief* systems. The new paradigm becomes the conceptual and methodological basis of everyday scientific practice. Because of this, Kuhn might be said to reject the rationalist view of science. Indeed, some have accused him of **relativism**, that is, a belief that the terms 'truth' and 'falsity' have meaning only within a paradigm and that there is no reality outside the paradigm (relativism is also discussed later in the chapter).

In criticism, it should be noted that Kuhn's notion of the paradigm seems to deny that theoretical diversity is a feature of everyday science. Indeed, the theoretically disputatious state of all social sciences, despite the self-proclaimed scientific nature of certain perspectives in psychology and economics, would probably lead Kuhn to refer to such disciplines as inherently inferior because they are pre-paradigmatic. Other criticisms have been made by Paul Feyerabend, whom we shall examine below. Feyerabend is scathing about Kuhn's idea of normal science. He argues: 'Was there ever a period of normal science in the history of thought? No – and I challenge anyone to prove the contrary' (1981: 160). Like Popper, despite their disagreements, he believes that science is intrinsically disputatious.

Paul Feyerabend: the rejection of method

We have been trying so far to identify the characteristics of science and scientific method. Both Popper and Kuhn, despite their deep differences, believe wholeheartedly in the value of science. But Feyerabend has a deeply critical view of science.

Feyerabend claims that the history of science shows that there is no single scientific method. For him, however, a lack of rules is a matter for celebration rather than concern. In large measure, he is concerned to nourish the conditions for individual, as well as intellectual and theoretical, diversity. He develops a powerful **epistemological** argument for using a diversity of methods to gain knowledge. (An epistemological argument is a claim about how we might gain true knowledge of the world.) Feyerabend opposes the notion that there is one supreme method for doing this:

> the world we want to explore is a largely unknown entity. We must, therefore, keep our options open … Epistemological prescriptions may look splendid when compared with other epistemological prescriptions …

but who can guarantee that they are the best way to discover, not just a few isolated 'facts', but also some deep-lying secrets of nature? (1975: 20)

Feyerabend denies that the growth of science has, in fact, depended on one particular method: 'All methodologies have their limitations and the only "rule" that survives is "anything goes"' (1975: 296). Epistemological pluralism, or in his terms *epistemological anarchism,* he argues, is essential for science. He recommends that we might advance science by proceeding *counter-inductively.* This means, first, that it is often fruitful to adopt hypotheses that *contradict* well-established theories. He justifies this recommendation by stating that no theory ever 'agrees with all the known facts in its domain' (1975: 31). He argues that we are more likely to maximize the empirical content of scientific theories if we stand outside those that are widely accepted.

Feyerabend contends that it is a myth that science is characterized by scepticism and openness (as, for instance, argued by Popper). Science has, in his view, overpowered its opponents: *'But science still reigns supreme … its practitioners are unable to understand,* and *unwilling to condone,* different ideologies, because they have the *power* to enforce their wishes' (1975: 298). As I mentioned earlier, Feyerabend wishes to encourage diversity of thought: 'Science does not excel because of its method for there is no method; and it does not excel because of its results; we know what science *does,* but we have not the faintest idea whether other traditions could not do *much better.* So we must find out' (1978: 106).

The fundamental question for social and cultural researchers, however, concerns the value of these ideas of Popper, Kuhn and Feyerabend about natural sciences for philosophical understanding of the social sciences, and it is to this matter that we now turn. Should the social sciences seek laws (if such exist) of social development and of social life? Is the investigation of social life in its myriad forms (economic action and institutions, cultural production, political action and systems and so on) analogous to the study of the natural world, or is there fundamental discontinuity between these worlds?

Meaning and the social sciences

What primarily distinguishes human beings from organic and inorganic matter is that they consciously act and what they do has *meaning* for them. In social science there are those, for instance Durkheim, Parsons and Merton, who advocate a natural scientific approach to investigation in their disciplines (they are *naturalists)*, and those, like Geertz, Taylor and Schutz, who are deeply critical of this idea of a science of society because they focus on the meaningfulness of the subject matter of the social sciences (they are *anti-naturalists* or *interpretivists)*. Max Weber attempted to reconcile the two positions but, despite this, can be considered as the founder of *interpretive* social science because of the central importance he gave to the interpretive understanding of subjective meaning.

Let us start with the naturalists. Émile Durkheim argued that the study of social life could and should be scientific. For Durkheim, sociology was the study of **social facts.** He used this term to refer to a wide range of regularities of social life, for instance, to 'religious beliefs and practices, the rules of morality and the innumerable precepts of law' (1972: 73). Social facts, in Durkheim's view, could be identified by certain characteristics: they constrain individuals, are general throughout society and are independent of their individual manifestations. In *The Rules of Sociological Method* (1982: ch. 2), Durkheim outlined rules for the observation of social facts. He argued: 'The first and most basic rule is *to consider social facts as things*' (1982: 60). He was claiming *not* that social facts were no different from natural facts but rather that the sociological attitude should be like that of the natural scientist. In his view, social science ought to be a rigorously empirical discipline. Thus he wrote:

> He [the social scientist] must embark upon the study of social facts by adopting the principle that he is in complete ignorance of what they are, and that the properties characteristic of them are totally unknown to him, as are the causes upon which these latter depend. (1982: 245–7)

Durkheim contended that to achieve this empirical attitude, it was necessary to eradicate the influence of values and preconceptions and to observe what was there rather than substitute our prior notions for the thing we should be observing.

We now turn to an examination of the approach that emphasizes the *meaningfulness* of the subject matter of social science. Clifford Geertz characterizes this approach by emphasizing the centrality of *interpretation* rather than the methods appropriate to the natural sciences. He states in relation to the study of culture:

> Believing, with Max Weber, that man is an animal suspended in webs of significance he himself has spun, I take culture to be those webs, and the analysis of it to be therefore not an experimental science in search of law but an interpretive one in search of meaning. (1973: 3)

Similarly, Charles Taylor argues that interpretation is essential in the social sciences. He rejects the notion of the empiricist tradition that 'tries to reconstruct social reality as consisting of brute data alone' (1994: 181–211). Brute data are those that can (allegedly) be observed independently of interpretations. They are, therefore, according to the view Taylor criticizes, empirically established. To this view Taylor counterposes a conception of 'social reality as characterized by intersubjective and common meanings (1994: 199). He states:

> Common meanings are the basis of community. Intersubjective meaning gives a people a common language to talk about social reality and a common understanding of certain norms, but only with common meanings does this common reference world contain significant common actions, celebrations, and feelings. These are the objects in the world that everybody shares. This is what makes community. (1994: 197)

This demonstrates how the social sciences are inextricably bound up with interpretation because social science needs to be able to make sense of this subject matter. Now the problem with this for naturalists, who believe social sciences should be methodologically like natural sciences, is how one might test any purportedly valid interpretation.

Finally, let us briefly look at the views of Alfred Schutz (1899–1959). Schutz contends in his classic paper 'Concept and theory formation in the social sciences' that:

> The primary goal of the social sciences is to obtain organised knowledge of social reality. By the term 'social reality' I wish to understand the sum total of objects and occurrences within the social cultural world as experienced by the common sense of men living their daily lives among their fellowmen, connected with them in manifold relations of interaction. (1970: 5)

He criticizes those I have referred to as *naturalists* for not analysing basic features of the social world: 'Intersubjectivity, interaction, intercommunication and language are simply presupposed as the unclarified foundation of these theories' (1970: 6). For Schutz, *interpretive understanding* or **verstehen** (the German word for this) is not just a method in social science but the way in which everyday participants in the social world understand each other.

Weber's reconciliation of naturalism and the interpretive tradition

Weber makes clear that he wishes the study of social life to be *both* scientific and interpretive. He is emphatic that persuasive interpretation of social action is necessary but not sufficient:

> Every interpretation attempts to attain clarity and certainty, but no matter how clear an interpretation as such appears to be from the point of view of meaning, it cannot on this account claim to be the causally valid interpretation. On this level it must remain only a peculiarly plausible hypothesis. (1978, vol. 1: 9)

Accordingly, he asserts: 'verification of subjective interpretation by comparison with the concrete course of events is, as in the case of all hypotheses, indispensable' (1978, vol. 1: 10). Weber states clearly that both interpretation and scientific verification are essential:

A correct causal interpretation of typical action means that the process which is claimed to be typical is shown to be both adequately grasped on the level of meaning and at the same time the interpretation is to some degree causally adequate. If adequacy in respect of meaning is lacking, then no matter how high the uniformity and how precisely its probability can be numerically determined, it is still an incomprehensible statistical probability ... On the other hand, even the most perfect adequacy on the level of meaning has causal significance from a sociological point of view only insofar as there is some kind of proof for the existence of a probability that action in fact normally takes the course which has been held to be meaningful. (1978, vol. 1: 12)

The interpretive tradition has informed several approaches to social research, about which more will be found in Chapter 4. Broadly speaking, interpretivists tend to favour **qualitative** rather than **quantitative** methods. This is because, on the whole, researchers find that people's words provide greater access to their subjective meaning than do statistical trends. Weber's perspective, though, opens up possibilities for using both quantitative and qualitative methods in pursuing explanations adequate at the levels of both cause and meaning.

Can social science produce objective knowledge?

Social scientists, whatever their theoretical perspectives, are individuals with personal characteristics, are situated in a certain class, ethnic group, gender, religious group and live in a particular historical period. How, when each researcher is embedded in prejudices, values and specific cognitive frameworks, can we move, however tentatively, towards something that might be called *objectivity*? Both Weber and Durkheim were, although in different ways, convinced that a scientific way of studying social and cultural life could be constructed which would generate objective results, that is, conclusions that were not merely valid within a particular school of theory.

Four basic positions about the implications of initial value commitments and subjectivity for the achievement of objectivity can be described (see Box 2.3). Each will be considered in the section that follows.

Eradicating values: Durkheim's scientific approach

Durkheim wrote in *The Rules of Sociological Method* that:

> reflective thought precedes science, which merely employs it more methodically. Man cannot live among things without forming ideas about them … [B]ecause these notions are closer to us and more within our mental grasp than the realities to which they correspond, we naturally tend to substitute them for the realities, concentrating our speculations upon them. Instead of a science which deals with realities, we carry out no more than an ideological analysis. (1982: 60)

He was aware that our ideas are powerful influences on us because of the sentiments we attach to them. Our political, religious and other ideas, for instance, are connected to our fundamental values and moral notions. Therefore, between us and the reality which we seek to know stands a whole host of assumptions, preconceptions, ideologies and beliefs. This is true of natural science but even more so in social science. Durkheim believed that empirical detachment is a precondition for scientific knowledge: 'social phenomena are things and should be treated as such … they are the social *datum* afforded the sociologist. A thing is in effect all that is given, all that is offered, or rather forces itself upon our observation. To treat phenomena as things is to treat them as *data,* and this constitutes the starting point for science' (1982: 69).

Durkheim formulated rules that would help social scientists to achieve this goal. First, he described a *negative* rule: *'One must systematically discard all preconceptions'* (emphasis in original). The social scientist 'must resolutely deny himself the use of those concepts formed outside science and for needs entirely unscientific' (1982: 73). Secondly, he added a *positive* rule: we must attend to the 'inherent properties' of the phenomena. Initially, the only properties to which we have access are the external features, these are all we know of reality. He readily admits that such external properties may be insignificant but in this way we start correctly: our point of departure is the *real* rather than our ideas. Thus social scientists should attempt, through the rigorous application of these methodological procedures, coupled with the demand to expose their methods and findings to a critical scientific community, to achieve objectivity.

Values have a positive but limited role: Weber on facts, values and objectivity

Weber's starting point was that reality is infinitely complex and that what we see and know represents a specific way of organizing and selecting from an infinite number of sense impressions. Underlying human thought then is a *selective* standpoint. Therefore, the notion that we can construct

---

Box 2.3 Four positions about values and objectivity

1 Values can be eradicated *either* through a rigorous detachment on the part of the social scientist *or* by means of the critical role of the scientific community which independently evaluates research.
2 Values have a positive, but strictly limited, role in research.
3 Values and personal experience are the fundamental resource out of which we can fashion disciplines that truly reflect what social life is like for those who live it. Here the researcher's own emotions play an important role.
4 **Relativism:** the view that different theories construct their *own* conception of reality as well as criteria for evaluating claims to knowledge.

an objective science of society merely on the basis of observation is inconceivable for Weber.

According to Weber, we live in a world of irreconcilable values. There is no rational or empirical way to choose between values. How is science possible in a world of conflicting values? For Weber, the key point is to distinguish between determining the facts and making judgements of value: 'An empirical science cannot tell anyone what he *should* do – but rather what he *can* do' (1949: 54). There is no way to demonstrate the validity of values, even the value of science itself. The scientist must concern herself or himself with what *is* (what are the facts) rather than what may, from her or his point of view, be desirable. Weber knew that it was no easy matter to discard values and merely determine the facts. He contended that we cannot help but structure what we see according to our values. How, then, can Weber believe that anything objective can be produced by people studying social life? The answer is that he distinguishes between *relevance for value* and **value freedom.** He accepts that we study what has 'cultural significance' for us: this is relevance for value. Consequently, what we study and the concepts we use incorporate our values. But, and this is what makes objective social science possible, once we have decided on our topic and framework of analysis, it is the social scientist's responsibility to determine the facts in a value-free manner.

The uses of emotion

Stanley and Wise are feminist social researchers who examine 'the place of the personal within research' (1993: 150). They reject the notion of 'research as orderly, coherent and logically organized' (1993: 152). The researcher's self cannot be left behind when doing research. The conventional view treats theory as superior to experience but, in their view, researchers should not 'mistrust experience' (1993: 153) and should, indeed, challenge the 'power relationship between theory and experience' (1993: 162). Feminists contend the personal is political: 'We suggest that this insistence on the crucial importance of the personal must also include an insistence on the importance, and also the presence, of the personal *within research experiences* as much as within

other experiences' (1993: 157). Accordingly, they reject the goal of seeking objective descriptions based on the separation of researcher and researched. The researcher is a 'person' and, if one wishes to understand the oppression of women, one should start from 'the point of view of women's reality' (1993: 161). They assert that objectivity is 'an excuse for a power relationship every bit as obscene as the power relationship that leads to women being sexually assaulted, murdered, and otherwise treated as objects' (1993: 167).

This point of view might seem like a species of relativism, in that Stanley and Wise (1993: 171) work with the notion of 'partial' truths and many realities. In fact, though, Stanley and Wise give a privileged position to their versions of truth and reality. That is, that oppressed women's experiences and the theory derived from them are considered to be true and that **androcentric** (male-centred) theory and data collection distort reality.

Renato Rosaldo also rejects the idea that social scientists should cultivate detachment. Rosaldo (1989) discusses Weber's conception of value freedom and claims that the idea has been transformed since Weber from a 'demanding ethic' into an orthodoxy. Weber's notion of research is that research is driven by passion and yet the researcher needs to be cool-headed, but Rosaldo says that contemporary researchers take detachment to extremes. He tries to show how the emotional feelings of researchers about their subject of study are *resources* of knowledge. For instance, Rosaldo refers to the work of Briggs on the Inuit. Briggs, according to Rosaldo, 'used her own feelings, particularly depression, frustration, rage, and humiliation, as sources of insight into the emotional life among members of an [Inuit] group' (1989: 176). He states: 'My argument is that social analysis can be done – differently, but quite validly – either from close up or from a distance, either from within or from the outside' (1989: 188). Chapter 3 explores some of these arguments in greater depth.

Relativism: truths not truth

The **relativist** position is that there are only *truths* and no universal *truth,* versions of reality but no one reality. The point of departure is the well-known fact that cultures are diverse. We shall concentrate on *conceptual relativism*. In Daniel Little's words this means that

> Different cultures employ radically different conceptual schemes defining what exists in the world, how things are organized in time and space, what sorts of relation obtain among things, and how some things influence others ... [from this standpoint] it is not possible to give rational grounds for concluding that one such scheme is more congruent to reality than another. (1991: 203)

Peter Winch exemplifies a particularly radical version of conceptual relativism. He rejects the notion that science tells us what exists. He claims that 'the check of the independently real is not peculiar to science' (1970: 81). And he states in respect of the idea of God: 'The point is that it is *within* the religious use of language that the conception of God's reality has its place, though, I repeat, this does not mean that it is at the mercy of what anyone cares to say: if this were so, God would have no reality' (1970: 82). Like all relativists, Winch does not accept that reality exists outside cultures and languages: 'Reality is not what gives language sense ... both the distinction between the real and the unreal and the concept of agreement with reality themselves belong to our language' (1970: 82). Goodman (1982), another radical relativist, makes a similar point in arguing that social science can produce no single 'right' view of the world, but only one of many possible 'versions'.

However, *rationalists* – in the second sense of this term, referring to a belief in universal principles of theory choice, as introduced earlier in the discussion on Popper – reject conceptual relativism. Popper refers to the 'myth of the framework', this being the view that 'a rational and fruitful discussion is impossible unless the participants share a common framework of basic assumptions or, at least, unless they have agreed on such a framework for the purpose of the discussion' (1994: 34–5). Popper contends that it is in fact *differences* between frameworks which lead to fruitful dialogue. The opposite belief that frameworks are

incommensurable is one he wholeheartedly criticizes: 'The proponents of relativism put before us standards of mutual understanding which are unrealistically high. And when we fail to meet those standards, they claim that understanding is impossible' (1994: 334). Dialogue will be fruitful but we must not expect final agreement for that would be too much (1994: 37). Dialogue takes the form of mutual *criticism* from which both sides learn.

To resolve these problems Popper (1972) distinguishes three worlds: a world of physical objects; a world of states of consciousness; and a *third* world, the world of **objective knowledge.** This third world consists, for instance, of theoretical systems, problems and problem situations and critical arguments. This world effectively exists autonomously of individual scientists (1972: 111). This suggests, I think, that a focus on the people who produce knowledge might be inappropriate. Popper distinguishes his view from traditional epistemology, that is, traditional theories of knowledge. Traditional epistemology has studied knowledge and thought in the 'subjective sense', that is, from the point of view of an individual subject (1972: 108). Popper is claiming that knowledge, problem situations, criticism are 'out there' and develop effectively a momentum independent of individuals because the community of scientists (science being for him the most important form of knowledge) develops a world independent of the wishes of particular individuals. For instance, new problems which emerge from a theory are not 'generally intentionally created by us' (1972: 119). Thus a problem leads to a tentative theory, which in turn leads to a process of error elimination, so that we are left with a new problem. The new problem is not intentionally created but emerges in the third world. Popper argues 'that the study of the products is vastly more important than the study of the production of [knowledge]' (1972: 114). If one looks at knowledge this way, it is possible to believe in the feasibility of objectivity in a world of clashing theories.

Conclusion

If we wish to decide whether social sciences

Box 2.4   Web pointers for philosophy of social science

Social Science Information Gateway (SOSIG): philosophy of social science
www.sosig.ac.uk/roads/subject-listing/World-cat/philsoc.html

www.philosopher
www.philosopher.org.uk

Guide to philosophy on the Internet
www.earlham.edu/~peters/philinks.htm

Philosophy around the Web
http://users.ox.ac.uk/~worc0337/phil_index.html

Visit the website for this book at www.rscbook.co.uk to link to these web pointers.

---

might learn from the successes (and failures) of natural sciences, we must ask both what is science and what is scientific method. In this chapter, therefore, we examined three competing views of science. Popper is a rationalist in two senses. First, he stresses the priority of theory over observation and, secondly, he believes that theories share a common goal of seeking true explanations *and* universal criteria for the evaluation of opposed theories. Kuhn is a moderate relativist. He takes for granted the value of science but takes a relativist position about the incommensurability of paradigms which makes it difficult to see the history of science as rational progress towards truth. Feyerabend takes a radically relativist position, claiming that there is no one scientific method: epistemologically and methodologically, anything goes.

Popper argues that the common model of explanation for all sciences is the *hypothetico-deductive scheme*. But the key question is this:

should social scientists gear research to a search for laws? Or, to put it differently, are humans and their institutions governed by laws in the way many naturalists would claim? Do social scientists find the idea of a methodological unity of science, that is a common model of explanation for all sciences, helpful? Does, rather, the notion of a single model of explanation deny the validity of a rich variety of methods and associated theories which is, after all, the reality with which we are all familiar?

The interpretive tradition contends that the *meaningfulness* of the social world makes the application of scientific methods such as explanation by laws and causes inappropriate. Instead, the social sciences should seek to grasp the meanings that individuals and social groups give to their actions and institutions.

The possibility of objectivity was discussed from the point of view of those who believe that the influence of values and preconceptions can be

---

Student Reader (Seale, 2004): relevant readings

   3   Emile Durkheim: 'Laws and social facts'
   4   Walter L. Wallace: 'The logic of science in sociology'
   5   Thomas D. Cook and Donald T. Campbell: 'Popper and falsificationism'
  26   Paul Feyerabend: 'Against method'
  27   Thomas S. Kuhn: 'The structure of scientific revolutions'
  59   Renato Rosaldo: 'Grief and a headhunter's rage'
  67   Max Weber: 'Science as a vocation'
  71   Sandra Harding: 'Is there a feminist method?'

eradicated from research. The Weberian tradition is associated with the idea that values play a positive role in determining what it is worth investigating. However, there is a fundamental distinction in this tradition between stating value judgements and determining the facts. For feminists, values and experience are not something to be excluded from research or controlled but are, instead, a fundamental resource. Finally, relativism rejects the notion of a common objective reality and counterposes to the idea of truth the notion of truths, there being (allegedly) no rational basis for choosing one version of truth as *the* truth.

Further reading

Martin and McIntyre (1994) is a treasury of important articles in the philosophy of science. Hollis (1994) is an exceptionally good introductory text. Smith (1998) is a good introductory book, with excellent coverage of contemporary develeopments.

Key concepts

Androcentrism	Objectivity/objective knowledge
Empiricism	Paradigm
Epistemology	Qualitative/quantitative method
Falsificationism	Relativism
Hypothetico-deductive scheme	Scientific revolution
Induction	Social fact
Interpretivism	Value freedom
Methodology	Verificationism
Naturalism	*Verstehen* (intersubjective understanding)

3

Politics, identities and research

Suki Ali, Kirsten Campbell, Duncan Branley and Robert James

CONTENTS

What are the politics of research? Can research be value-free, objective and neutral? How does research address social inequalities? In this chapter we will explore the ways in which the production of knowledge can work to challenge or maintain forms of 'social difference'. The political concept of *identity*, whether collective or individual, has been central to transforming contemporary research, and this means that we must also understand knowledge itself as politically informed. This new understanding of knowledge impacts upon research in both theory and practice, and shows knowledge to be political.

In the first section, we outline some traditional approaches to social research and identify the concepts that inform them. These ideas have come from the *Enlightenment* project of scientific evaluation of the world in which we live, which is often understood as an attempt to 'conquer' Nature (see Chapter 4). The model of the omnipotent and powerful 'subject' of research investigating a passive 'object' of study has had a long history, as does the perceived division between the 'hard' and 'soft' sciences. In this model, physics exemplifies the 'hard' sciences and biology the 'soft' sciences, but research concepts such as 'truth' and 'objectivity' are the foundations of both as knowledges. By contrast, social sciences (sociology, psychology) are often seen pseudo-sciences relying on supposition and intuition. These kinds of hierarchies have been extensively discussed (Williams and May, 1996) and continue to be of importance when thinking about *epistemology* (theories of knowledge itself). This section looks at the ways in which social sciences have developed from *positivist* models of research, and how this impacts upon the production of knowledge about the social world.

In the second section we look at critiques of what has been termed **malestream** or **androcentric** knowledge made by feminists (Stanley, 1990) and other critical theorists who centralize the importance of social difference to research work. Using examples, we show how these challenges had a significant impact upon social research in general. We examine the methodologies that first emerged from **New Social Movements** in the 1960s and 1970s, which developed the concepts of identity and experience as sources of knowledge. We discuss the importance of the development of *standpoint theories* and how these theories remain influential in social research despite debates about their usefulness.

We go on to argue that many forms of social divisions require us to rethink the concept of identity and how it informs experience. We consider the use of the term *intersectionality* and how contemporary theories of identity and subjectivity can provide us with new tools for understanding the relations between 'subjects' and 'objects'. This theoretical approach insists that research processes are embedded in highly complex networks of *power*. Finally, we suggest new ways of researching that draw upon an understanding of methodology as the expression of a *politics of knowledge* and require ongoing engagement with the role of power in social research.

Traditional forms of knowledge

As researchers, we aim to learn something about social and cultural life. We want to understand what people do and why they do it. Researchers often claim to present a 'true' depiction of social life, which describes the nature of social action and the reality of the social world that shapes it. Traditionally, researchers have claimed that their description of social life is accurate because of their methods of research. They argue that certain ways of doing research enable us to uncover the truth of social life. In particular, researchers working in the *positivist* tradition (see Chapter 4) contend that scientific approaches to understanding the social world guarantee an accurate knowledge of social life. This model of research is often characterized as **empiricist**. As explained in Chapter 2, empiricism is an idea of knowing which argues that our senses – such as sight – provide us with accurate information about reality. The classical positivist model argues for a scientific knowledge derived from 'the facts of experience acquired by observation and experiment' (Williams and May, 1996: 15). This account of how we know the world has been very influential in shaping research in social science. Traditional models of social research assume that it is a science and should follow scientific positivist methods: to be a truthful description of social life

---

Box 3.1   Research within the traditional model

The preface to a (British) Home Office Research Study on the incidence of rape and sexual assault of women explains the purpose of the Home Office Research Studies:

> The Home Office Research Studies are reports on research undertaken by or on behalf of the Home Office. The RDS (Research, Development and Statistics Directorate) is part of the Home Office. The Home Office's purpose is to build a safe, just and tolerant society in which the rights and responsibilities of individuals, families and communities are properly balanced and the protection and security of the public are maintained.

> RDS is also part of National Statistics (NS). One of the aims of NS is to inform Parliament and the citizen about the state of the nation and provide a window on the work and performance of government, allowing the impact of government policies and actions to be assessed. (Myhill and Allen, 2002)

This Home Office Research Study frames itself in terms of neutral and objective social research. It draws on social survey questionnaire work in order to describe 'the state of the nation'. While acknowledging the difficulties of doing so in research areas such as sexual assault, it claims to provide an accurate representation of social life by using scientific methods of social research.

---

our research needs to be value-free, and that as researchers we need to be neutral observers of the social world.

Critical interventions
New Social Movements

The traditional view of social research came to be increasingly challenged by the anti-racist, feminist and gay liberation social movements in the 1960s and 1970s. Social movements arose around political ideas and actions focusing on inequalities based on categories of difference such as gender, class, 'race', ethnicity, sexuality and ability. These political interventions had a major impact upon research which was often based upon such distinctions. Their concepts of identity not only informed changes in politics and policy, but also epistemology.

Issues were raised in relation to three key areas:

1 that social research should not exclude the diversity of social experiences;
2 that social research should not reproduce the values of an oppressive society but should be **emancipatory** (in other words, it should contribute to setting people free from oppressive social relations);

3 and that for this reason we need to find new models of social research itself.

In this period, for example, the issue of gender became increasingly visible in social research because the emergence of the women's liberation movement (**second-wave feminism**) and the increasing numbers of women participating in higher education. Second-wave feminists first argued that traditional models of social research ignored the different social experience of women. Martin Hammersley (1992a), who is otherwise critical of feminist perspectives, admits that prior to its recognition of feminist arguments, sociology too often studied men's experiences of social life and either assumed that experience was true for all people or ignored women's social experience altogether.

These feminist interventions have been the most important development in social and cultural research during the twentieth century. Yet some early feminist thought has been criticized for being based upon the concerns of 'white, middle-class women' working in European and North American contexts. Simply including 'women' does not necessarily provide us with 'better' research. Such a strategy can obscure the differences between women as well as women and men. One type of difference between women that was often overlooked was that of 'race'. At this time, theorists such as Hazel Carby (1982) notably criticized much white feminist work for actually perpetuating and worsening racism.

This kind of intervention was part of a wider debate in Britain about so-called **identity politics**. In primarily urban locations, 'black' became a *political category* around which to organize, and up to the mid-1980s being 'black' often indicated being 'non-white' and/or disadvantaged by, and in relation to, the dominant white English ethnicity. For a short time Irish and Cypriot people were included as 'black' in local government policies in London. OWAAD (Organization of Women of African and Asian Descent) organized a hugely diverse group of women to find common ground and fight against racism, sexism and other forms of oppression and inequality (Bryan et al., 1985). However, many South Asians objected to being included in the term 'black' and chose for themselves the separate appellation 'Asian'. Underlying such debates were questions of 'authenticity' and 'hierarchies of oppression'. Despite early successes, OWAAD encountered much disagreement, especially around the issue of sexuality, and eventually folded in 1982 (Mason-John, 1995).

Sexuality had been less visible as a category for and within political movements such as second-wave feminism and Civil Rights. However, political interventions and campaigns encouraged the questioning of a range of power interests operating within society, and sexuality was a major source of inequalities. At this time homosexuality was still illegal for men, and not legally recognized at all for women. The gay liberation movement emerged in the context of struggles for social and political freedoms (see Box 3.2 below). However, the gay liberation movement was dominated by men, and came under fire for being sexist. Some argued that gay men had even more invested in patriarchy than other men. In addition, the women's movement was perceived as being predominantly heterosexist. This led to the development of *lesbian feminism,* with some heated debates about which should be the primary category of identity – being a woman or being a lesbian. These categories are of course not mutually exclusive, and indeed there may be other important factors, such as disability, which are of primary importance to researcher and researched (see below).

As these examples have shown, researching the social world requires us to think about the complexities of social identities. This is particularly important when undertaking **'cross-cultural' research**. This term can cover researching cultures, nations, or 'races' that are other than our own. In early models of anthropological work, for example, the role of the social scientist has been of 'civilized observer' of 'primitive peoples' (see Chapters 9 and 17). This kind of research furthered the work of colonialism and imperialism, as the more 'advanced' nations of the world sought to document and categorize 'Others' in ways that created hierarchical relations of power between entire peoples. Many of these projects used technologies of vision following the general principles of empiricism (see also Chapter 20). What they failed to do was acknowledge the authority of different ways of knowing the social world. So, for example, Caplan (1987) studied the ways in which sexualities are understood differently across cultural contexts. The examples above about taking on a homosexual identity may not be have been relevant to a culture in which homosexual practices were an accepted part of sexual life. However, cross-cultural research also raises the question of **cultural relativism** for researchers: should researchers, for example, accept local justifications for practices that they find difficult or 'aberrant'? Do we need 'to be one to know one'? (see, Fay, 1996). We explore this issue further below.

New methods for social research

The above discussion shows that identities, experiences and politics are central to how we understand the social world and therefore to social research. As researchers, we need to consider not only *what* we know, but also *how* we come to know it. These identities, experiences and politics have been used as resources to develop critical interventions into research practice. This approach argues that the methods we use in research reflect social values. Feminist social researchers, such as Stanley and Wise (1993), argue that we need

---

Box 3.2   The gay liberation movement in the United States

In the spring of 1969 the mayoral election campaigns in New York City led to a resurgence of the previously relaxed police raids on gay bars in the city (Jagose 1996). A raid on the Stonewall Inn led to rioting on the street 'with nearly a thousand persons participating, as well as several hundred cops' (Leitsch, 1969: 12). This has been described as the birth of gay liberation. However, this movement did not emerge from nowhere; its gestation had been long and created not only by gay men's resistance to oppression, but by following the example of the 'Black militants [who] provided a model of an oppressed minority that transformed their "stigma" into a source of pride and strength' (D'Emilio, 1981: 466). Gay liberation sought to politicize gay men so that they could overcome their oppression and a new politizised sense of self developed. Instead of being men who simply met other men for companionship and sex, an explicit social identity based on being openly gay appeared. Building on the feminist dictum that the personal is political, gay men started to make public statements revealing the truth about themselves that they were gay: 'coming out'.

---

understand the role that we play as researchers in the research process. **Reflexivity** (the capacity to reflect on our role in generating research knowledge) is crucial. Stanley and Wise argue that we should not try to remove the researcher from the research in a misguided attempt to remove the 'bias' of the researcher's values. Instead, we need to understand the political implications of our location as researchers.

Working from this position, feminist sociologists, such as Dorothy Smith (1987), have developed a *standpoint* model of research. Standpoint models assume that different social positions will produce different types of knowledge of the social world, because different social positions produce different social experiences. Patricia Hill Collins (1990) has developed this theoretical approach in relation to African-American women. Hill Collins argues that experience is a valid source of knowledge, and that we need to engage with the

---

Box 3.3   Research with families

In Britain and the United States, 'the family' was traditionally thought of in idealized terms as the heterosexual nuclear family, mother and father and 2.2 children. Writing in the 1980s, Errol Lawrence (1982) and Ann Phoenix (1987) have shown how this has the effect of pathologizing any kind of family that falls outside this norm. Concerns about the 'death of the family', the 'problem of single mothers' and the failures of absent fathers have hidden within them ethnocentric and class-biased values. Research had been generalized from 'white families', and analysed drawing on 'white', middle-class values and ideals. Research with 'black families' showed that:

- Black families more than any other 'racial' group are headed by single women. However, these women are also likely to be in full-time employment and supporting families. Concerns about mother-headed families and the stereotype of single mother as state scrounger were inaccurate and inappropriate in these cases.
- 'White feminists' have located the family at the heart of the reproduction of gender inequalities, but many black families consider them to be the primary source of support in a racist society.

---

experiences of socially oppressed and marginalized groups. She suggests that knowledge from these groups provides a fuller account of the social world because:

- they provide a more accurate account of the reality of social life, including oppressive social relationships; and
- they provide a better political account of the social world because they identify relations of domination.

We can identify two strands of standpoint research: identity standpoint and standpoint theory.

Identity standpoint, which is closely tied to identity politics as outlined above, argues that members of oppressed or exploited groups have different experiences of the social world to members of socially dominant groups. Membership of a group constitutes a personal identity. This identity shapes our experience and hence our knowledge of the social world. That experience can and should found a critical knowledge of the social world. bell hooks argues that '[i]dentity politics emerges out of the struggles of oppressed or exploited groups to have a standpoint on which to critique dominant structures, a position that gives purpose and meaning to struggle' (1994: 88). One example of this model in operation can be seen in research into families (Box 3.3).

Using the white, middle-class family as the norm provides a partial view of family life that has helped to contribute to forms of social discrimination. Research with marginalized social groups sheds light on a range of family forms, counteracts this imbalance and provides different kinds of knowledge to inform policy and practice. These developments, although important, can also be limited in their application as we discuss below.

Standpoint theory, as proposed by Sandra Harding, also argues that

> The experience and lives of marginalized peoples, as they understand them, provide distinctive problems to be explained or research agendas that are not visible or not compelling to the dominant groups. Marginalized experiences and lives have been devalued or ignored as a source of

important questions about nature and social relations ... It is valuable new questions that thinking from the perspective of such lives can generate. (1998: 151)

However, this approach also argues that we need to understand not only how our social standpoints reflect our experience of social life, but also how social structures produce those experiences. Standpoint is 'an objective position in social relations' (1998: 151), because social relations produce our understanding of who we are. As researchers, therefore, we need to identify *social groups* who are not dominant social groups, and begin our exploration of social life from their experience of it.

Although we have shown the importance of standpoint theory for social research, we must also be aware of its limitations in relation to the notion of 'social groups'. In the next section we outline the debates around standpoint theory and return to the example of research with families.

Debating standpoints

Standpoint theory shows us that we need to think differently about what social research *is*. It contends that we need to understand the research process not as the production of objective knowledge but as produced by knowers who are situated in the social world and whose knowledge reflects its values. These values are not a neutral frame for research but reflect a social world in which certain groups dominate and have powers over others. If social research reflects the social world that produces it, then it too will have a politics, putting the view of one group rather than another. Moreover, social research is political because it is sometimes used to justify certain social relations and not others, as can be seen in some research informing government policy.

There are a number of debates concerning standpoint research focusing upon the complexities of using the concepts of identity and experience. Most recently, the focus of these debates has been upon the question of 'difference', asking whether it is possible to describe ourselves as having one identity, or whether what we experience as identity is more complex. As we have highlighted, it can be problematic to speak of a 'woman's standpoint' when women are a diverse social group.

For example, Prathiba Parmar has criticized:

> political practice which employs the language of 'authentic subjective experience' [which] … has given rise to the self-righteous assertion that if one inhabits a certain identity this gives one the legitimate and moral right to guilt-trip others into particular ways of behaving … There has been an emphasis [in the women's movement] on accumulating a collection of oppressed identities in turn, which has given rise to a hierarchy of oppression. (1990: 126)

She claimed that this led women into leading 'ghettoized lives' and embracing a lifestyle politics 'unable to move beyond personal and individual experience'. To write inclusively about black women as if they were one homogeneous group is inadequate. Experience is not a unified category as it has different purposes and gives rise to different knowledges (Gray, 1997).

Similar problems are raised in relation to the notion of 'a social group', which standpoint theory relies upon. As researchers, we need to ask who speaks on behalf of an oppressed community, who comes to be counted as a member of a subordinated group and how those groups are defined in complex social processes. Many of these debates emphasize the constructed nature of identity and social groups. Researchers need to reflexively explain that construction rather than taking the existence of selves or communities for granted.

Emancipatory methods

In common with feminist and anti-racist projects, disabled people have produced an **emancipatory** paradigm for social research using notions of social identity. The basis for this starts with the **social model of disability** that identifies the disabling barriers inherent in societies as the major issue for disabled people rather than medically defined body differences. A statement that summarizes the social model succinctly, if crudely, is to say that disability is caused not by an inability to climb stairs, but by the fact that buildings have stairs at all. The roots of this emancipatory approach to research go back to a celebrated case in the history of the disabled rights movement (see Box 3.5).

Priestley (1997: 1) highlighted 'six principles' of the emancipatory research paradigm:

1 The social model of disability is a fundamental basis from which to start research.
2 Researchers must abandon claims to objectivity but instead work toward the empowerment of disabled people.
3 Research should be done only when it is actually useful or helpful to disabled people or in taking away disabling barriers.

Box 3.4   Research with families: further reflections

Returning to the example of the family (as in Box 3.3), we may then ask how the notion of 'black families' can be challenged. Although some black families are headed by single women, many are not. Do 'black' families automatically reproduce some kind of 'authentic black experience'? The answer to that must surely be 'no'. 'Black' is itself a heterogeneous category and although we can learn much about diversity from studying a range of family models across ethnicities, nations and cultures, we must be cautious about how these can be taken up as exemplars of an entire group. There may be huge variation within and across social groups such as 'white, working-class' that contradict simplistic and stereotypical accounts of the 'benefits of the extended family', or the 'problem of teenage mothers'. As with all other social categories, these terms need to be used in a thoughtful and considered way.

Box 3.5 Resisting the messages of 'objective' research

The residents of the Le Court Cheshire Home invited experts in group dynamics to help them in a struggle to gain greater control over their lives from restrictions imposed by the system operated by local managers and professionals in the social care field. Researchers from the Tavistock Institute were funded to undertake a three-year in-depth study (Miller and Gwynne, 1972). Disillusionment with the approach of the objective researchers began during the study and came to a head when the results were published. Despite categorizing the residents' experience within the institution as a 'living death', Miller and Gwynne (1972) recommended ways to try to make the 'death' a little more palatable rather than any wholesale changes in the system. The residents hit back at what they felt was a failure to listen to any of their views, a rejection of all of their criticisms and condemned social scientists as 'parasites' (Hunt, 1981). Some of the people from the Le Court Home went on to form the Union of the Physically Impaired Against Segregation (UPIAS) who declared:

> We … are not interested in descriptions of how awful it is to be disabled. What we are interested in is the ways of changing our conditions of life, and thus overcoming the disabilities imposed on top of our physical impairments by the way this society is organised to exclude us. (UPIAS, 1976: 4)

From this standpoint it was only a short step to see the criticism that much social research on disability had, by focusing on the 'awfulness' of disability or the methods of coping with this awfulness, perpetuated an oppressive mindset in researchers and done nothing to help disabled people. Attempts have since been made to produce a different and emancipatory paradigm for working with disabled people.

---

4 Let disabled people control the design and management of the research.
5 Ensure individuals' voices can be heard in the research as well as the common nature of the barriers imposed upon disabled people.
6 Use a variety of methods in collecting and analysing data.

Criticisms have come from within and without the disability movement that this misses out on what might be gained from researchers' expertise in creating and implementing research and tends to overestimate the capacity of research to have an impact on people's daily lives (Bury, 1996; Shakespeare, 1996). Other issues that have led to debate have been the role of disabled and non-disabled researchers working in the field, how both can maintain a self-critical, reflexive and enabling approach and how research language can be more accessible, particularly for those with

learning disabilities. Additionally, there is the question of whether disabling barriers in society should be studied or whether ways to empower individuals and groups of disabled people should be the focus. In spite of these questions, there have been many interesting and creative developments arising from the emancipatory model. Thus, in the field of mental health, user-led research has developed, an example of which is given in Box 3.6.

Yet the problems of conducting research with disabled people without 'parasitically' benefiting from their experience persists for some researchers, bringing home to us that these dilemmas are experienced at a personal level, not in the abstract. Mike Oliver, having been a leading light in developing 'social model' research, has stated (Oliver, 1999) that he is abandoning the field altogether, feeling that the person who gained most from his disability research was himself. Others, though, are more optimistic in their assessments of how

---

Box 3.6 User-led research in mental health

A report published by The Sainsbury Centre for Mental Health offers a new perspective on how mental health service users view their care in both hospital and the community.

The report, *Users' Voices*, summarizes four years of findings from an innovative research methodology, User Focused Monitoring (UFM). This breaks new ground in employing service users to both devise questions and carry out interviews. The approach encouraged responses from people with severe problems who have never previously had a voice.

'UFM has demonstrated the power and value of employing users at the heart of research,' said Dr Diana Rose, who developed the methodology. 'Not only is the process empowering for the user-interviewers but, crucially, you get different questions – about things that really matter to users. For example, we asked about dignity and respect in the giving of medication not just about how people could be persuaded or forced to take it.

'Equally importantly, the research shows that people with severe and enduring illness are able to give balanced, thoughtful and constructive views on how services can be improved.'

More than 500 users participated in the research which took place between 1996 and 1999 in seven sites spanning inner city London and rural areas. Interviews were conducted by users, many of whom had severe and enduring mental health problems themselves. Visits took place in people's homes, in supported housing and in a variety of care settings in both the statutory and voluntary sector.

(*Source*: press release from The Sainsbury Centre for Mental Health, 15/01/2001. See: www.scmh.org.uk)

---

emancipatory research has pushed researchers to work in more reflexive ways and has highlighted how the attitudes of people, particularly in the caring professions, can sometimes prevent disabled people from achieving control, dignity and power over their own lives.

Political standpoints

The example of user-led research shows that this type of political research can be difficult. Despite the best intentions of researchers, emancipatory processes and outcomes may be hard to achieve in practice. Another strategy for dealing with these complexities can be found in discussions about political standpoints. For theorists such as Donna Haraway, this standpoint is generated from a political position, which begins from an analysis of power relations and argues that certain social relations, meanings or actions are unjust, inequitable or oppressive. The disabled people who

took part in the user-led model of disability research exemplify an engagement with such an approach.

This strategy has led to the development of new concepts of social groups and identities as political and understandings of knowledge as partial. Haraway argues that rather than thinking of knowledge as universally applicable, we should understand it as *situated* and, in particular, that 'feminist objectivity means quite simply *situated knowledges*' (1991: 188). This 'opens the way to stronger standards of both objectivity and reflexivity. These standards require that research projects use their historical location as a resource for obtaining greater objectivity' (Harding, 1991: 163). This, then, is a radically different notion of objectivity to the one contained in traditional discussions (see Chapter 2).

Using the concept of situated knowledges in research requires us to consider the issue of **intersectionality**. This means, as we have

29

illustrated throughout this chapter, that identities themselves are shaped by a number of intersecting social differences. So, for example, one is not exclusively white, disabled or gay but can experience all of these aspects of identity together.

Thinking about social research being guided by the 'intersectionality' of social identities is one way of working for more emancipatory research outcomes. But it has been argued that this way of working leaves social categories intact and so can reinforce hierarchies of social difference. We might ask instead how is it that categories such as 'white' or 'man' can be eradicated. An approach which *de*-constructs these categories is often seen as being a more radical form of emancipatory practice. It encourages researchers who want to challenge social inequalities to look at more than simply intersecting axes of difference and instead to ask how can they be dismantled.

Returning to the example of 'the family', we have already noted that discussing 'the Asian family' is as problematic as 'the white, middle-class family'. An approach that foregrounds *intersectionality* would ask questions about geographic location, class, cultural practices, economic stability and so on. We could also ask how these factors *construct* 'the family' and explain the social practices which constitute it, rather than simply describe it. This kind of information would

enable us to *de*-construct these same features and then use this information to challenge the kind of 'conventional' wisdom that often informs inequitable policy and practice for families

As a result of work in which sexual identities were deconstructed (see Box 3.7) there was a marked shift from the earlier uses of 'lesbian' and 'gay' to denote critical research perspectives in this area. Instead, the term 'queer' became influential. This term was chosen to mark a break with what were seen as earlier **essentialist** notions of identity that understood it as having as fixed characteristics. **Queer theory** challenges the concept of constructed sexual identities based upon sexuality. This deconstructive approach to sexualities can also be seen other areas of social research.

Thus, the work of Paula Moya (2002) provides an interesting bridge between the more traditional and these *post-structuralist* models of research (see also Chapter 4). She engages with these issues of knowledge from a Chicana feminist perspective and revitalizes the argument that identities-based experiences have something 'objectively' useful to tell us about the social world we live in. Her term the 'politics of trans-figuration' (2002: 14) used in relation to theory indicates that minority groups play key roles in the production of knowledge and its potential for

---

Box 3.7 The deconstruction of sexual identities

In the 1980s and 1990s there were increasing numbers of academics researching lesbian and gay subjects. Attention was turned to the 'intelligibility' of categories of gender and sexuality, whose meaning and power were understood to reside in language, or systems of representation. For example, Wittig argued that '"woman" has meaning only in heterosexual systems of thought and heterosexual economic systems'(1992: 31 [first published in 1980]). The important work of Judith Butler built on this ten years later:

> Heterosexualization of desire requires and institutes the production of discrete and asymmetrical oppositions between 'feminine' and 'masculine', where these are understood as expressive attributes of 'male' and 'female'. (Butler, 1990: 17)

In this more critical view, what seems natural to common sense is an effect of ways of thinking about people. It understands gender and sexuality as mutually reinforcing and invented terms which classify people and so control them. In this sense, these identities are effects of power. They have no reality but are rather 'constructs'. These perspectives emphasized the power of language (such as the language of research reports) to shape experience.

Box 3.8   Web pointers for identities, politics and research

Feminist Review
www.feminist-review.com/

Feminist.com
www.feminist.com/

Centre for Disability Studies
www.leeds.ac.uk/disability-studies/

Queer theory
www.queertheory.com/

How to conduct anti-racist research online
www.crr.ca/en/MediaCentre/FactSheets/eMedCen_FacShtHowtoConductAnti.htm

Visit the website for this book at www.rscbook.co.uk to link to these web pointers.

---

transforming social relations. This political approach to knowledge production provides us with a way of thinking about differences that refuses essentialist notions of identity. This is a similar strategy to the concept of 'situated knowledges' we discussed earlier.

Conclusion

Throughout this chapter we have problematized the relationship between theories of knowledge, the politics that inform them and how they impact upon research methodologies. We have set out the terms of the debate as a dialogue between competing forms of knowledge about society and the implications these have for effecting social change. From critical interventions into traditional forms of research to what are sometimes called 'postmodern methods', we have explored how politics and identities are central to the production of social research. An understanding of diverse identities challenges simplistic notions of 'experience' as an unproblematic source of knowledge. We argued that as identities and experiences are shaped by a wide range of divisions and differences in society, our research processes must reflect this. We have suggested that a commitment to an engaged and critical form of reflexivity is the best way of engaging with this challenge.

The theorists and examples we have discussed throughout this chapter have shown that complex ideas underpin what can appear to be quite simple approaches to research. This means we can never take for granted our research practice or how it may be used by or impact upon others. Our attempts to produce 'better' knowledge about the social world cannot rest upon an uncritical acceptance of theoretical materials any more than it can for empirical data. We need to continue to engage with the challenging yet rewarding work of social research that incorporates the principle that all research is political.

Further reading

Caroline Ramazanoglu and Janet Holland (2002) provide an excellent introduction to the meaning and practice of feminist methodology. Jagose (1996) provides an introduction to queer theory. Barnes (2003) reviews, in a journal article, a decade of developments in 'disability studies'. The journal, *Disability and Society* is a good one to browse if you are interested in this area. Journals are also good sources for research that centralizes 'race' and ethnicity, for example, *Ethnic and Racial Studies*.

Student Reader (Seale, 2004): relevant readings

71 Sandra Harding: 'Is there a feminist method?'
72 Mary Maynard: 'Methods, practice and epistemology: the debate about feminism and research'
73 Les Back and John Solomos: 'Doing research, writing politics the dilemmas of political intervention in research on racism'
74 Martyn Hammersley: 'Hierarchy and emancipation'

Key concepts

Androcentric knowledge	Intersectionality
'Cross-cultural' research	Malestream knowledge
Cultural relativism	New Social Movements
Emancipatory research	Queer theory
Empiricism	Reflexivity
Essentialism	Second-wave feminism
Identity politics	Social model of disability
Identity standpoint	Standpoint, standpoint theory

4

Developments in social theory

Paul Filmer, Chris Jenks, Clive Seale, Nicholas Thoburn and David Walsh

CONTENTS

This chapter reviews the main ideas of a variety of social theories that seek to explain the distinguishing characteristics of social and cultural life, and which can guide the practising social researcher in formulating research problems and deciding on methods. The chapter reviews a variety of competing perspectives which have variously influenced social scientists over time. It will appear, at first, that Kuhn's depiction of social science as 'pre-paradigmatic', which we saw in Chapter 2, is fully justified. The differences between perspectives may seem impossible to reconcile, yet it is the key message of the final theoretical perspective reviewed in this chapter, *postmodernism,* that the very search for a single, unifying model of social and cultural life may be inappropriate. The notion of researchers pursuing a variety of *genres* (explained more fully in Chapter 1) may be more appropriate.

It will also become clear from reading this chapter that social theories, and the methods that can be located within them, are human products, with an institutional history and micro-politics of their own. 'Theory' can sometimes look as if it has a life independent of human agency, with the objective hardness of a *thing,* enshrined in textbooks that appear to give it a solid, fixed quality. Theories and models (the difference between which is explained in Chapter 5), then, are 'handed down' to new generations of students, who learn the truths of rival camps, and come to recognize familiar disputes. But social theory, if perceived to be the creation of particular human individuals, struggling to generate their own visions of the social world against the traditions 'handed down' to them in their time, is in fact much more fluid than this, and should be used and shaped by practising researchers, rather than mechanically determining their actions.

For example, it is sometimes put about that a particular philosophical position, theory or model (say, *positivism* or *functionalism*) inevitably entails the use of a particular set of methods (for example, statistical approaches). While such stereotypes always hold a kernel of truth, this book will help you see that these are links from which creative researchers often break free. Indeed, the logical connections between areas of theory (such as *symbolic interactionism*) and par-

ticular methods (such as ethnography) are often more a matter of appearance than reality, encouraged by the tendency of researchers to increase the legitimacy of their work by publicly avowing its theoretical location (see Hammersley, 1992c for an extended discussion of this feature of social research). In Chapter 5 of this book a more flexible approach to the use of social theory in thinking about research problems is outlined.

If there is one key development that stands out above all others in more recent trends in social theory, it is the change that has occurred in the view of language. Broadly speaking, there has been a shift from seeing language as *referential* (that is, that it refers to a reality existing beyond language) to seeing it as *representational* and *constructive* of reality. That is to say, the perception has increased that language is the means by which humans *socially construct* their worlds. This interest in the play of language runs through some of the more recent conceptions of ethnography (Chapters 17 and 29), and wholly informs the approaches of semiotics, discourse analysis and conversation analysis (Chapters 27 and 28). One of our key messages, though, is that language is clearly *both* referential and representational; it describes the world, and is limited in its possible descriptions by an externally existing reality, as well as generating new realities. This means that methods which often (though not always) draw upon the more common-sensical view of language as referential, such as classical social surveys and certain types of ethnography and interviewing, have a valuable role in investigating social and cultural life.

This is not just an abstract issue, or a matter of preference, but a political issue as well, and goes to the heart of the position of social and cultural researchers in society. This is illustrated by the issues raised in feminist thought (Chapter 3), where it is sometimes claimed that the realities of oppression and disadvantage are belittled by an approach to the social world that says all is a social construction, potentially to be swept away by some alternative construction. The typifying character of representational language in use, however, is clearly a feature of the experienced realities of disadvantage and oppression that are addressed by critical feminist theory and methods. The case of illness and suffering (with which some social researchers are concerned) also reminds us that the material conditions of our bodily existence give us a basic grounding in a reality that exists prior to language, and suggests a (literally) solid foundation for the existence of human need.

Those new to social theory will find this chapter easier to understand having first read Chapter 2, which explains many of the ideas underlying the theories reviewed. We have also done our best to explain words that are new, and to maintain a reasonable degree of linkage with more concrete phenomena to which concepts refer.

The Enlightenment legacy

The idea of a science of society can be said to have emerged in the eighteenth-century **Enlightenment**, a period in European history characterized by intellectual innovations, ranging across the arts, literature, science and engineering. The spirit of these times can be characterized as *progressive,* in that there existed faith in the power of reason and rationality to order and improve human affairs. Revolutions in America and France, and striking evidence of the power of science to transform the physical conditions of people's existence, combined to generate this sense of optimism, which was also associated with a growing rejection of religious authority.

Thinkers like Saint-Simon (1760–1825), Comte (1798–1857) and Spencer (1820–1903) developed this positive spirit in their social theories, to conceive of a social science that might guide the evolution of societies towards utopian forms, in which social affairs were regulated by the principles of reason.

Comte coined the term **positivism** or 'the positive philosophy' to indicate the broad direction of his views. As a philosophy of science, positivism is identified with **empiricism,** which, as was shown in Chapter 2, is a belief in the importance of observation and the collection of facts, assumed to exist prior to theories. Positivism is also a **naturalist** approach (in the sense used in Chapter 2), in that the methods of the social sciences are seen as appropriately modelled on that of the natural sciences. The aim was to discover 'laws' of society, that operate in a manner similar to the laws of na-

ture, so that just as technology successfully manipulated the physical world, a social technology could engineer rational changes in the social world.

Because the subject matter of social science was not distinguished from that of natural science, this new science paid little attention to the inner lives, the thoughts and feelings, of people (their **subjectivity**). Just as it made no sense for physicists to inquire into the inner thoughts of molecules, it made no sense for positivist social scientists to consider subjectivity. With Durkheim, subjectivity came to be of greater interest to social science, though in a particular, **deterministic**, way. Thus his study of suicide (described in Chapter 2) envisioned people's subjectivities (the emotions that led to suicide) as being determined in a law-like way by their degree of integration into larger social structures. It should be noted, however, that Durkheim's thought is by no means as simple as this brief outline suggests, and his writings on the meanings of religion (Durkheim, 1915) suggest a conception of the relationship between humans and their society that varies substantially from the over-determinism of which he has sometimes been accused. While he was by no means a straightforward positivist, he shared Comte's vision of the social scientist as potential social engineer, and his statements on method stress the discovery of causal laws and the use of statistical data.

Durkheim is also associated with the theory of **functionalism,** which involves the idea that society is a system of interrelated forces, all of which tend to combine to produce social stability. When used to explain particular social phenomena, functionalism can lead to some surprises, such as Durkheim's idea that a certain level of criminal behaviour was necessary for the maintenance of social order, a view that made him enemies in the French establishment of his time. Functionalism influenced both anthropologists and sociologists, but shares with Comte's positivism a tendency towards a deterministic view of people, which underplays their capacity to formulate their own plans of action independent of the influence of 'society'. Functionalism is most often associated with conservative thinkers such as Parsons, who stress the value of consensus and social order.

However, it is possible to understand both Marxism and functionalism as holistic theories, concerned with the structures and processes of societies in their entirety. Whilst both are concerned with social forces (which similarly determine human subjectivity), an important difference between them is that Marxism is primarily concerned with conflict, revolution and change.

The research methods that have often been associated with these theories are quantitative and statistical. In part this is because such methods are easily cast in a mould that imitates the natural sciences, generating *hypotheses,* measuring *social facts* and discovering the causes of events so that laws are generated. However, this is not exclusively so. Durkheim drew extensively on the qualitative research of early anthropologists for his study of religion, and functionalist anthropologists straightforwardly used the ethnographic method.

Additionally, the mere fact of quantification does not imply an adherence to all the tenets of positivism or functionalism. Counting regularities and their statistical analysis is, in practice, done by social researchers using the whole range of methods described in this book.

Realism and idealism

Returning briefly to concepts in the philosophy of science, it is helpful at this point to distinguish between **realism** and **idealism** (see Box 4.1).

Taking up Kant's idealist position, social science developed the **interpretive** tradition which argues that the social world is distinguished from the natural world. It is an **intersubjective** world of culture, consciousness and purposive action, in which relationships are organized through the ideas, values and interests of members of society, producing human action and interaction. With this comes a politics of critical, relativistic enquiry into society rather than a politics of social engineering.

Action theory

Weber (1864–1920) primarily established the interpretive tradition in social science, and his contemporary Simmel (1858–1918) developed it specifically in the analysis of culture. Weber focused on the place of subjectivity, consciousness and culture in social life because, he argued, the social world consists of the subjectively meaningful action of individuals, as opposed to the intrinsically meaningless world of objects, which is nature. Precisely because individuals give meaning to their actions they have a purposive character, so he constructed an **action theory** of society. Weber was drawing here on the legacy of nineteenth-century political liberalism, based on the supremacy of the individual.

For Weber, action becomes social – and through it society is produced – when individual actors orient their actions to one another, acknowledging shared beliefs, values and interests. Social institutions are reducible to interactions of this kind. Social research, then, involves interpretation, and social life cannot be reduced to explanation solely in terms of laws. Action cannot

---

Box 4.1   Realism and idealism

Realism: the view that the world has an existence that is independent of our perceptions of it, so that science is an attempt to explain in thought the things that act independently of thought. Realism is not the same as empiricism, but it has some similarities.

Idealism: the view that the world exists only in so far as people think it exists. If our thoughts change, then so does the world. Idealism entered social science primarily through the work of Kant (1724–1804). For Kant, mind introduces an order into sensory experiences, establishing their objective character. He proceeded further to argue that the mind also contained a world of values and freedom of action, distinct from the world of (mind-ordered) facts. Values were the determinants of human life which was ordered on the basis of reason and purposive actions.

Box 4.2   Weber on the origins of modern capitalism

Modern capitalism is typified by the highly rationalized organization of economic activity, depending on the calculative use of human and material resources to produce and sell commodities on a free market for profit. But, Weber argued, the rationalism and instrumentalism of capitalist economic activity was dependent on the emergence of particular cultural values, which he called the 'spirit of capitalism'. Protestantism, specifically its Calvinist Nonconformist form, introduced a new theology based on the doctrines of a calling, predestination and asceticism. Religious duty was a task to be performed through adherence to a work ethic as its moral foundation. Success in this, as measured by profit, was then seen as a sign of God's favour. Asceticism prevented the use of profit for enjoyment so it could only be ploughed back into economic activity. So Calvinism promoted the spirit of capitalism and legitimated its consequences, such as the unequal distribution of wealth.

---

be understood by external observation; the researcher must achieve a degree of empathy with the actor to get at its meaning. This is achieved not through an identification with the actor (in which the researcher tries to become the actor) but by grasping the actor's meaning. It is the latter that is crucial for the method of understanding, which Weber called **verstehen**, because it provides rational understanding as opposed to the emotional understanding which identification would produce. Such rational understanding is capable of empirical verification and therefore objective. And in this way it creates the possibility of a *science* of action.

Famously, Weber (1930) brought interpretive understanding to an analysis of the origins of modern industrial capitalism (see Box 4.2).

Weber demonstrated his arguments about the origins of capitalism through an analysis of historical materials, statistical data and theological and economic texts written by Calvinist theologians and capitalist businessmen. Although he used statistical data, they were insufficient on their own for his analysis. They had value for the explanation of social life only when translated into meanings. For this he engaged in the qualitative analysis of texts.

Simmel moved action theory on into a more specifically cultural analysis of social life. Primarily he demonstrated, in studies of a variety of topics taken from economic life, and aspects of the city in the modern world, how cultural organization influenced social consciousness, experience

and identity. Thus he wrote essays on money, religion, gender, capitalism and love to show how these reflected and influenced modern consciousness.

Action theory set up an alternative approach to that of functionalism and led to modifications of quantitative, positivist empiricism, shifting the emphasis towards various forms of qualitative research and analysis. First, social scientists moved from the investigation of *social facts* to examining a socially meaningful world of intersubjective action and interaction. Secondly, social enquiry was shifted from observation of the structural determination of social life to an understanding of subjectivity. Finally, as the social world is treated as a world of meaning and value, the values of the analyst come into play. Values decide the problem which the analyst seeks to investigate, the way the phenomena relevant to the investigation are conceptualized and the explanations that are finally arrived at. Weber argues that all socio-cultural inquiry is value-oriented in this way. Evidence, both experiential and factual, with which to test explanations, provides objectivity. Nor does a commitment to *verstehen* as a method preclude any interest in the causal explanation of action, though Weber rejects the positivist notion of general laws. For Weber explanations adequate at the levels of both cause and meaning are the ideal. The reconciliation between the two consists of showing how meanings are the motivational determinants of action and provide a basis for the legitimation of its consequences.

Symbolic interactionism

Action theory established itself in Europe on the basis of Kantian idealism. A similar theory based in the philosophy of **pragmatism** arose in the United States called **symbolic interactionism.** Pragmatism, in the work of Dewey and Peirce, argues that all animal behaviour (which includes human beings) is based upon a problem-solving adaptation to the environment, but whereas in animals this behaviour is instinctive, in human beings it is a matter of thought and reflection. Unlike animals, human beings are conscious and sentient creatures and their environment is a symbolic universe with which they engage in terms of their understanding as well as their senses.

Mead (1863–1931) brought the pragmatist perspective to bear on social behaviour, arguing that human social conduct has a symbolic character. What permits human beings to interact and form social relationships and society is their ability to understand one another's gestures and responses. This is because they share *symbols*, embodied in a common language which enables communication. Social relations depend on people's use of language to 'take the role of the other', understanding others as being like oneself and *vice versa*. The similarities with Weber's notion of intersubjective understanding are clear. The social world is a world of inter-communicative *symbolic interaction.*

Mead's views led him to a theory of the *self,* which he saw as constructed through interaction in which the individual internalizes the other's definition of his or her behaviour. Within the individual, self-formation is generated in terms of a dialogue between two parts, the 'I' and the 'me'. The 'I' consists of the physiological and psychic impulses that produce gestural behaviour in the individual but the 'me' is the response of the other which is internalized by the individual. So the self becomes a society in miniature, replicating internally the symbolic interaction of society. This is what provides for consciousness and inner experiences in human beings as they routinely think about and weigh up the possibilities of action. The self of individual human beings changes through life as they learn to take on new roles, incorporating new others, thus acquiring new definitions and meanings which lead to new forms of action.

So, as in action theory, human behaviour is neither mechanical nor explicable in terms of laws. Symbolic interactionists argue that human action can be investigated most effectively by gaining access to the meanings which guide it. This involves learning the culture or subculture of the people under study and means that the social world is best investigated in naturally occurring situations rather than under artificial conditions. This is sometimes described as the position of **naturalism.** Note that this is different from the earlier methodological use of the term 'naturalism', which in Chapter 2 was used to denote the position that the natural and social sciences should use the same methods, a view which symbolic interactionists would oppose. Symbolic interactionists are, in general, committed to field study based on participant observation and ethnographic analysis to describe what happens in social settings, how the people involved see their own

---

Box 4.3   Three uses of the term 'natural'

Naturalists: take the view that the methods of the natural sciences are appropriate to the study of the social and cultural world.

Naturalism/naturalistic: is sometimes used to refer to the claim of ethnographers to collect naturally occurring data.

To naturalize: refers to the process whereby matters that are in fact socially constructed and were once fluid and changeable come to be perceived as a part of the natural order and therefore fixed, inevitable and right. Social researchers often wish to 'denaturalize' phenomena (such as sexual identity for example) by exposing the human processes whereby they are constructed.

Box 4.4 *The Gold Coast and the Slum*

Zorbaugh's *The Gold Coast and the Slum* (1929) enquired into a district lying north of the business area. There were marked contrasts of social and living conditions there. For example, one part – the 'Gold Coast' – was a fashionable upper-class area, but behind that lay an area of 'hobohemia' that had become the final resort of the criminal and down-and-out. Zorbaugh's study described the varying ways of life of the inhabitants, to form a theory of city development and community.

---

actions, and the contexts in which action takes place (see Chapter 17 for a fuller description).

The Chicago School

The empirical programme of symbolic interactionism developed at the University of Chicago from the 1920s. Here, Park and Burgess created a large programme of research into urban life and culture focused mainly on Chicago itself. They applied anthropological methods to the study of various subcultures of the city. Box 4.4 describes a typical early Chicago School study.

The primary methods of the Chicago School were those of field research, interviews, life histories and ethnography based on participant observation. It established naturalism as the favoured approach to empirical research and produced a politics sympathetic to social and cultural relativism and to the less privileged, allying itself with the disempowered in society. As Becker (1967) (a leading inheritor of the symbolic interactionist tradition in Chicago) has put it, the question that the ethnographer must first ask is 'Whose side are we on?' before proceeding to engage in research.

Phenomenology and ethnomethodology

Phenomenology is a method of philosophical enquiry, involving the systematic investigation of consciousness, brought to the study of the social world by Alfred Schutz. **Ethnomethodology** is a term coined by the American Harold Garfinkel. The two approaches share a concern with **microsocial interaction** – that is interaction on a small scale, between individuals or within small groups. Both focused intensively on language as the fundamental resource for microsocial interaction. There were clear reasons for these concerns. The overdeterminism of Parsons's version of functionalism, as well as its political conservatism, had become problematic. For example, he defined the individual as a collectivity member performing a social role by assuming 'obligations of performance in [a] concrete interaction system … normatively regulated in terms of common values and of norms sanctioned by these common values' (Parsons et al., 1961: 42). This 'oversocialized' concept of the individual (Wrong, 1961) as one who has internalized the social system's determinations of action is a marginalization of individual subjectivity. It reflects a concern only with the *typical* characteristics of the individual, avoiding the investigation of particular individuals making choices on the basis of their unique biographies and the specific features of the situations in which they do so.

Garfinkel regarded as unjustified the criticisms that Parsons's concept of the individual as a collectivity member was of an oversocialized individual. But he wanted to explore how social actors were actively engaged in playing their social roles. Additionally, Garfinkel argued that people were actively engaged in producing social institutions and that the ordinary, everyday practices by which this was routinely accomplished showed the reality of society to be a **social construction.** Here, Garfinkel's views were comparable with those of Berger and Luckmann (1966), who had developed a related phenomenological perspective, expressed in their book *The Social Construction of Reality.* In this work they argued that from a stream of undifferentiated experiences people construct the phenomena of the world (objects, other people, social institutions). Such constructions will often then take on a hard **objectified** character, enabling them to 'act back' on consciousness. For example, in childhood we are taught the 'facts' of history, the 'truths' of ethical values and expected behaviour, as if they are naturally handed down from some supra-human source.

Phenomenology

Schutz developed Weber's concept of *verstehen* to create his own theory of social action. Social actors, Schutz proposed, were governed by a principle of **reciprocity of perspectives.** This involves two working assumptions that social actors hold about each other as necessary conditions of their interaction. The first is the assumption that each person makes about the other that, if they change places, each will perceive their situation in the same way as the other. The second is that each takes for granted that the differences in perspective that result from their unique biographies and different experiences are irrelevant to their present interaction, and that both will define their current interaction in the same way. As Schutz pointed out, these assumptions are 'idealizations' rather than always being true of all interactions. This is revealed when communication difficulties arise, which people, on the whole, try to avoid. Schutz thus provided Garfinkel with an account of the means by which social actors construct and sustain the reality of their interactions. People transcend individual subjectivity to construct an *intersubjective* world. In effect, they *produce common sense,* and they do so quite ordinarily and routinely – and so are able to take it for granted.

Schutz, like other interpretivists, argued that, unlike the natural world, the social world is intrinsically meaningful. He disagreed with the positivist view that tended to treat consciousness as determined by the natural processes of human neurophysiology. Husserl (1859–1938), who had reintroduced phenomenology to modern philosophy, had argued that such a perception, which involves seeing the natural and the social worlds as factual, is a **naive attitude** because it does not attend to the more fundamental process of the *social production* of both worlds. Psychology is charged

by Husserl with a particular neglect in this respect because of its naive support of this assumption of the **facticity** of the world. Husserl further argued that, unlike the objects of the natural world, those of the social world depend upon human recognition for their existence: they are objects that have a constructed character. Yet social actors **naturalize** the 'facts' of the world in the common sense of their naive (or 'natural') attitude, treating what Durkheim called social facts as if they were really 'out there'. Husserl shows, in effect, how it was that Durkheim could recommend that social facts should be treated as 'things'.

Schutz refers to everyday language as the 'typifying medium *par excellence* ... a treasure-house of ready made preconstituted types and characteristics, all socially derived, carrying along an open horizon of unexplored content' (1962: 14) These **first-order typifications,** as Schutz terms them, make intersubjectivity possible and communicable by enabling individuals to formulate their own subjectivity in terms that are understandable by others who are able in turn to relate it to themselves. This, Schutz argues, is the appropriate way to understand the activity of social scientists who limit the open qualities of first-order typifications by defining and thus attempting to fix the meaning of particular terms, thereby creating a new linguistic world of **second-order typifications.** Science can thus be differentiated from common sense, but the two share common materials, a feature which Garfinkel was to exploit.

Ethnomethodology

Ethnomethodology, as conceived by Garfinkel, involves investigation of the methods by which people make sense of their activities, both to themselves and to others. Drawing on the insights of phenomenology, social life is seen as a continual and routine accomplishment, particularly through the use of language. Thus ethnomethodologists speak of 'doing' things like walking, friendliness or sexual identity, to indicate the constructed nature of all human activity, including social science itself.

The concepts of **indexicality** and essential **reflexivity** summarize the ethnomethodological view of language, referring to the way in which the meaning of words depends on the context in which they are used, and their relationship to other words. Thus words 'index' meanings, rather than referring to fixed, permanent realities. Additionally, language is essentially *reflexive* on everyday actions, since in 'describing' those actions it makes them appear rational. Ethnomethodologists differ from Schutz in that they do not distinguish a world of scientific discourse from a world of everyday language. The work of Antaki and Rapley (1996) demonstrates this; they apply an ethnomethodological perspective to the social construction of facts in research interviews. They do so by using the method of *conversation analysis,* which is the most important research method to have emanated from ethnomethodology, and is described more fully in Chapter 28.

Structuralism

Structuralism shares with the interpretive theories reviewed so far a concern with the role of language in shaping social life, but is less interested in explaining social actions in natural settings. Instead, structuralist approaches can be seen as related to the determinism characteristic of functionalist theory, in that subjectivity is seen as being formed by 'structures' that lie beneath the surface of social reality. Structuralist approaches offer valuable insights for researchers interested in analysing cultural forms (such as art, literature, images or film). This has been particularly evident in *semiotic* analysis, described in Chapter 20.

Something of the flavour of structuralism is provided in the following quotation from Lévi-Strauss, a leading French structuralist:

The method we adopt, in this case as in others, consists in the following operations: (i) define the phenomenon under study as a relation between two or more terms, real or supposed; (ii) construct a table of possible permutations between these terms; (iii) take this table as the general object of analysis which, at this level only, can yield connections, the empirical phenomenon considered at the beginning being only one possible combination among others, the complete system of which must be constructed beforehand. (1969a: 84)

The idea here is that phenomena as diverse as myths, superstitions, kinship systems, restaurant menus and orchestral scores can be understood as surface phenomena of deeper **structures** that involve the systematic combination of elements. In Chapter 20 this is explained in detail in an analysis of Saussure's structuralist ideas about the elements that combine to create linguistic meanings.

Lévi-Strauss was interested in explaining human cognitive action, which he saw as the product of universal structures. Whatever the variability of its surface, Lévi-Strauss asserted that the human mind has always worked in the same way. Social action itself is, for the purposes of structuralist analysis, a surface manifestation of a series of deep master patterns, internalized at the level of cognition. Particular cultures then, are seen as manifestations of an unconscious, universal rule system.

Lévi-Strauss drew on Durkheim and his collaborator Mauss. Durkheim's 'social Kantianism' or 'soft idealism' was apparent in his later work (on religion, for example) where he appeared to contradict his early positivism and replaced his concern for social facts with an attention to the symbolic formations that bind human relations. Mauss had suggested that such 'collective representations' were general psychological dispositions common to all humankind.

Structuralism plays on the dichotomy between *essence* and *appearance,* suggesting a continuum between *depth* and *surface.* Lévi-Strauss (1969b) used a geological metaphor to develop this. He likens the formation of cultural phenomena to the layering, expanding, contracting and intruding of rock strata; each stratum appears unique but shares certain underlying elements with similar geological phenomena. Geologists understand such phenomena by the excavation of these strata to expose their patterns of interrelation. The pattern derives from the structure, so elements of a culture, as we experience them, are the surface patterns or manifestations of underlying structures at a deeper level. Because culture is based on deep structures the rules that order it may be only part of the unconscious of its members. Cultural symbols and representations are the surface structure and acquire the appearance of 'reality'.

Post-structuralism and postmodernism

Structuralism was the underlying orientation of much social and cultural research for an extended period until the late 1970s and early 1980s when the phenomenon of the 'post-' started to emerge. In the subsequent period post-structuralist and postmodern thought has come to play an important and influential part in the breadth of the social sciences. Whilst post-modernism and post-structuralism are terms that refer to diverse theories, methods and politics, it is possible to delineate a set of prominent concerns and directions in these approaches.

Post-structuralist thought is associated most closely with the French theorists who came to prominence at the time of the 1968 student and worker uprisings and the shift in understandings of culture, politics and power that these events marked. Derrida, Foucault, Deleuze and Guattari are probably the most influential figures, but a list of other theorists associated with this perspective would include Irigaray, Kristeva, Levinas, Lyotard and Spivak. At the centre of poststructuralist thought is a concern to comprehend life not as something composed of identities, objects and subjects, but of **difference**, complex relations, and instability. In this, post-structuralism is indebted to the work of Friedrich Nietzsche (1844–1900). In his diagnosis and critique of modern culture, Nietzsche posed a radical challenge to the identity-based thought that had dominated Western culture in the post-Enlightenment period. Modern European culture, he argued, has created an image of the world populated by discrete entities, with the rational human individual, or subject, at the core. Rather than start with identity, Nietzsche sought to show that identity was a *product* of modern values, and that it served to order, police and deny the creativity and potential of life, where life is conceived as a 'monster of energy', or a continuous process of change, disruption and becoming. Nietzsche was thus concerned both to trace the emergence of this model of identity (focusing in particular on the role of Christian morality), and to disrupt it towards an overcoming of identity that he named the 'overman'.

The post-structuralist critique of the subject,

and the methods and research possibilities that it can lead to, is well exemplified in the work of Michel Foucault, one of the most influential heirs to Nietzsche. Foucault's studies of sexuality, discipline, governmentality, ethics, health and madness are concerned with 'the different modes' by which human beings are *made* subjects (Foucault, 1982: 208). Foucault proposes that with the development of modernity and modern capitalism, a new regime of social power emerges that takes life itself as its object. This '**biopower**' operates not by *repressing* social activity, but by investing the life of populations and individuals (the human species and the human body) in a *productive* manner. Describing this form of productive power, Foucault writes:

> We must cease once and for all to describe the effects of power in negative terms: it 'excludes', it 'represses', it 'censors', it 'abstracts', it 'masks', it 'conceals'. In fact, power produces; it produces reality; it produces domains of objects and rituals of truth. The individual and the knowledge that may be gained of him belong to this production. (Foucault, 1977: 194)

Productive power operates through what Foucault calls '**discursive formations**', which are not exclusively linguistic (and this marks a break with structuralism), but 'thoroughly heterogeneous ensemble[s] consisting of discourses, institutions, architectural forms, regulatory decisions, laws, administrative measures, scientific statements, philosophical, moral and philanthropic propositions' (Foucault, 1980: 194). Following this framework, Foucault's research is oriented toward all the aspects of social and cultural life that serve to produce modern forms of identity, and their corresponding knowledges and truths. In the case of modern sexuality, for example, Foucault (1979) overturns the conventional interpretation that sexuality is a repressed essence of the self, and argues that it is a network of discursive formations that invest the body and the species in order to produce, control and govern the population. Foucault makes this case through a detailed historical study (or '**genealogy**') of the practices, institutions, techniques, experts, knowledges and subjects that

---

Box 4.5   *Discipline and Punish* (Foucault, 1977)

A genealogy of the practice of incarceration.

Specific topic: studies the actual practice of punishment, rather than theories of criminology or the prison as an institution.

Local knowledge: systematically works through penal reports by medico-legal and psychiatric experts published in journals of the nineteenth and twentieth centuries.

Subjugated knowledge: gathers data from discourses coming out of prisons, as well as discourses about prisons, and analyses where they converge and diverge.

Meticulous detail: studies the minute processes of incarceration.

Emergence: examines the myriad circumstances which allowed the practice of imprisonment to become accepted, and to seem normal. For example, the shift of power from above the social body to within it, and the architecture of surveillance (e.g. the Panopticon).

The manufacture of 'self-evident' truth: the dominant criminological discourse about the reform of criminals.

(*Source*: adapted from Moynagh, 2003:
www.stfx.ca/people/mmoynagh/445/more-445/Concepts/genealogy.html#examples)

---

take sexuality as their object, as sexuality develops from being the terrain of 'sin' (to be confessed, interpreted and channelled in the Christian confessional) to that of a deep, inner, private 'desire' (to be interpreted in terms of healthy and abnormal manifestions of the self). In Foucault, as in all post-structuralist research, it is important to recognize that the human subject is **decentred** from being the *agent* of social development to being a *product* of social relations. This decentring of the subject not only opens research to an analysis of the wealth of formations and regimes that produce human subjects in a myriad of changing ways, but also contributes toward the overcoming of the subject that is the rather Nietzschean political project of post-structuralism. Box 4.5 summarizes Foucault's genealogical study of incarceration.

Post-structuralist thought has certainly had a great influence on researchers who argue that we live in a '**postmodern**' world, but the theorists of postmodern culture are more diverse in theoretical and political orientation, and frequently diverge from post-structuralist concerns. In its most general sense, postmodernism is said to signify the end of the Enlightenment project, where reason was to triumph over faith, humankind was to become the measure of all things, nature was to be quelled and put to the service of humankind,

and time was to be measured in terms of a transition from darkness into light, a transition and an implicit theory of moral evolution that came to be known as *progress*. As such, Lyotard (1984: xxiv) argues in *The Postmodern Condition* that postmodernism marks a contemporary 'incredulity' toward all modernist '**metanarratives**', or grand explanatory schemes and projects of liberation. Instead, instability and uncertainty are introduced into knowledge claims and practices, and a more pragmatic and situated model of research is promoted. Beyond this, many theorists of postmodernism have focused on developments in contemporary capitalist culture, particularly on the forms of media image, commodity, self and meaning.

Media images are a central object of study for those interested in postmodernism. Importantly, the image tends to be analysed not in terms of the meaning or ideology encoded within it, but in terms of the intensities, affects and desires it arouses in the consumer, and the way this relates to new forms of self-hood, collective experience and control. For Baudrillard (2001), to take one of the more influential postmodern theorists, Western cultures have entered a time of '**hyperreality**' where the *signifier* and *signified* of structuralist interpretation (see Chapter 20) have been broken

43

apart, resulting in a culture of endless signs without referents. These signs (and the fascination and intensity that is invested in them) become more real than the real. For example, the consumers of Western media are said to experience the reality of events such as the 1991 Gulf War more in the decontextualized and highly mediated images of CNN than in any sense of the 'real' experience of the war in Iraq (that which one might conventionally see as the referent of the signifiers of war).

This postmodern culture of the image is interpreted by other theorists in terms of what Featherstone (1991) discerns as a generalized 'aestheticization of everyday life', where the boundaries between art and everyday life, high and low culture, and past and present, have broken down in a culture of depthlessness, sensory overload, and fluidity of the self. Media images and cultures of consumption are, however, far from the only objects of concern for those who conceive of contemporary societies in terms of the postmodern. Donna Haraway (1991), for example, has developed an influential materialist interpretation of contemporary culture in terms of the new 'cyborg' arrangements that have arisen from the boundary breakdowns between humans, animals and machines due to developments in technology, science and production since the Second World War. In Haraway's understanding of the cyborg we can discern three prominent areas of interest in contemporary social theory – technology, work and politics – and it is worth briefly considering these in order to emphasize the research possibilities of recent social theory.

Developing a theoretical framework not dissimilar to that of Foucault's 'discursive formations', Haraway argues that human relations with technology (especially in an era of informational and communicational machines) are best analysed not in terms of distinct human and technical entities, but as integrated arrangements, constantly being reassembled for particular ends. For example, the activity and social role of a garment worker in a Southern hemisphere export processing zone is best understood through interpreting the global network of production that he or she is part of at any one time. In this framework, research considers the agency of the collective whole (as it is made up of complex and divergent scientific, technological, linguistic, institutional, human, organic and architectural parts and forces), rather than that of an individual human actor. Such a concern to consider the complex interrelation of humans and technology (against *essentialist* understandings of the human subject – see Chapter 3) and the agency of non-human objects is evident in a number of contemporary theorists and researchers (for example, Deleuze and Guattari, 1988).

This understanding of human–machine relations has important ramifications for the interpretation of society and culture as a whole, but Haraway places an emphasis on the changes in the area of work and in global capitalist production – a field of research that has often been marginalized in postmodern thought. Haraway (1991: 166–7) argues that the cyborg condition is producing a new 'world-wide working class', a globalized

---

Box 4.6 Web pointers for social theory

The International Social Theory Consortium
www.cas.usf.edu/socialtheory/

Ashworth Program in Social Theory
www.ashworth-centre.unimelb.edu.au/

The Theory, Culture & Society Centre
http://tcs.ntu.ac.uk/home.html

Social Science Information Gateway (SOSIG): Schools and Theories
www.sosig.ac.uk/sociology/schools_and_theories/

Visit the website for this book at www.rscbook.co.uk to link to these web pointers.

'homework economy' and a 'feminization of work'. Here, new time arrangements (zero-hours contracts, flex-time and so on) and the global decentralization of production enabled by new communications technologies is said to be breaking down the old distinctions between home, factory, paid work and reproduction work, and leading to an intensification of work characterized by insecurity, vulnerability and 'poverty *with* employment'.

Just as Marx sought to discern both the constraining and liberating aspects of life in the capitalist mode of production, Haraway also looks for political possibilities in this cyborg condition. She argues that the global cyborg condition forces a movement away from the old models of liberation based on essentialist understandings of the human, and toward a politics based both on the new creative possibilities of relations between humans, animals and machines, and on temporary and particular sites of struggle and collective invention. Haraway (1991: 157) proposes, for example, that the cyborg condition forces feminism to break from an essentialist understanding of a unified global subject of 'woman', and 'embrace partial, contradictory, permanently unclosed' political alliances and collectivities that challenge oppression. Such an emphasis on a politics of invention rooted in particular experience and a critique of essentialism is also evident in the work of a number of recent theorists and researchers. Paul Gilroy (1993), for example, has developed a politics against racial thinking through an analysis of the hybrid cultural and political creations of transatlantic black populations.

In all of these theoretical concerns and research focuses, what is important to stress is the engagement they make with contemporary social, political, economic and cultural forms and arrangements. Theory, as Foucault once suggested, should be seen as a 'tool box' for critical and productive engagement with the world, as it seeks to open new sites for inquiry, research and politics.

Conclusion

This chapter has summarized developments in social theory, from early positivism, to functionalism, the interpretive tradition, and later structuralist, post-structuralist and postmodern perspectives. Each of these theories orient the researcher to different areas of social and cultural life, and are sometimes incompatible with each other. This is not to say, however, that social and cultural research cannot usefully draw upon a variety of theoretical perspectives. Indeed, as recent developments in social theory have shown, some of the most innovative theoretical work has maintained an openness to a variety of theoretical schools and perspectives. As an aid to making links between the social theory reviewed here and the practice of research, Chapter 5 demonstrates a variety of ways in which researchers can bring the two together.

Further reading

Collins (1994) is an exceptionally clear guide to the earlier strands of social theory reviewed in this chapter. May (1996) and Layder (1994) provide helpful guides to social theory, and Best and Kellner (1991), Lechte (1994) and Smart (1993) provide useful introductory guides to post-structuralism and postmodernism.

Student Reader (Seale, 2004): relevant readings

3   Emile Durkheim: 'Laws and social facts'
29   Alfred Schutz: 'Concept and theory formation in the social sciences'
47   David Silverman: 'Harvey Sacks: social science and conversation analysis'
49   Claude Lévi-Strauss: 'The structural study of myth'
51   Stuart Hall: 'Foucault and discourse'
62   Zygmunt Bauman: 'Intellectuals: from modern legislators to postmodern interpreters'
63   Madan Sarup: 'Postmodernism'

Key concepts

Action theory	Microsocial interaction
Biopower	Naive attitude
Determinism	Naturalism *(three kinds)*
Difference	Objectification
Discursive formations	Positivism
Empiricism	Postmodernism
Enlightenment	Post-structuralism
Ethnomethodology	Pragmatism
Facticity	Realism
Functionalism	Reciprocity of perspectives
Genealogy	Reflexivity
Hyperreality	Social constructionism
Idealism	Structuralism
Indexicality	Subjectivity
Interpretivism	Symbolic interactionism
Intersubjectivity	Typifications
Metanarrative	*Verstehen*

5

Research and social theory

David Silverman

CONTENTS

Until recently, the different social sciences seemed to vary in the importance that they attached to theory. To take just two examples, psychologists and anthropologists, for all their differences, seemed to downplay theory. In psychology, the benchmark was the laboratory study. For psychologists, the motto seemed to be: 'demonstrate the facts through a controlled experiment and the theories will take care of themselves'. Anthropologists were just as interested in 'the facts'. However, their most important facts were revealed in observational case studies of groups or tribes usually found in faraway lands. None the less, until recently, most English-speaking anthropologists followed psychologists in elevating facts above theories. This can be described as an empiricist approach in that facts are assumed to exist prior to the theories that explain them. In Chapter 2 there is a discussion of this empiricist vision which elucidates these points.

More recently, theory has become more important in both anthropology and psychology. Psychologists, for example, have become interested in discourse analysis (see Chapter 27). Anthropology has been particularly influenced by post-structuralist and postmodern theories (see Chapter 4) and theories of gender (see Chapter 3). By contrast, generations of British sociology students have long been made very aware of the primary importance attached to theory in their discipline. For instance, although undergraduate sociology courses tend to be split into three main areas (the 'holy trinity' of social theory, social structure and research methods), it is the course in social theory which is usually given the most prestige. Using the example of sociology, it is worth examining how far this elevation of theory is appropriate or fruitful.

Do we need theory?

The main complaint about courses in social theory heard from students relates to the complex and confusing philosophical issues which are raised and the use of impenetrable jargon. It may seem that students have to learn a new language before they can begin to ask properly accredited questions and, moreover, that this new language seems to be of doubtful relevance to the social or political issues which may have brought them to the subject in the first place.

Even if they can penetrate the jargon, students may be puzzled by discovering that, just as they have learned the ideas of one social theorist, the rug appears to be pulled out from under their feet by an apparently devastating critique of those ideas. So Durkheim, they learn, is a positivist (obviously disreputable) and mistakes society for a biological organism. And Marx's social theories are largely inappropriate to the age in which we live. As each succeeding theorist is built up, only to be torn down, people become understandably concerned about the point of the whole exercise.

The situation would not be so bad if theoretical ideas could be applied to research studies. But even brilliant contemporary syntheses of social theory (like those in the works of Anthony Giddens) seem to have an uncertain relationship to actual research. Moreover, when you open a typical research study, although you may see a passing reference to the kind of social theories you have learned about elsewhere, you will very likely find that theory is rarely used or developed in the study itself, except as some kind of ritual reference to add legitimacy to an otherwise 'factual' piece of research.

Does that mean that we do not need theory to understand social research? To answer that question let us take a concrete example from Eric Livingston (1987). Livingston asks us to imagine that we have been told to carry out some social research on city streets. Where should we begin? He sets out four 'data possibilities' for such a study: official statistics (traffic flow, accidents); interviews (how people cope with rush hours); observation from a tower (viewing geometrical shapes); observation or video at street level (how people queue or otherwise organize their movements).

As Livingston points out, each of these different ways of looking involves basic *theoretical* as well as methodological decisions. Very crudely, if we are attached to social theories which see the world in terms of correlations between *social facts* (see the discussion of Durkheim in Chapter 2), we are most likely to consider gathering official statistics. By contrast, if we think, like Weber, that social *meanings* are important, we may be tempted by the interview study. Or if we have read

---

Box 5.1   Doing research on city streets

Data	Theory
Official statistics	Social facts
Interviews	Meanings
Observation from above	Interactionism
or	or
Observation at street level	Ethnomethodology

(*Source:* Adapted from Livingston 1987)

---

about contemporary American theories like interactionism or ethnomethodology, we are likely to want to observe or record what people actually do *in situ* and elect the third or fourth options. But note the very different views of people's behaviour we get from looking from on high (the third option), where people look like ants forming geometrical shapes like wedges, or from street level (the fourth option), where behaviour seems much more complex.

The point is that none of these views of data is more real or more true than the others. For instance, people are not really more like ants or complex actors. It all depends on our research question. And research questions are inevitably theoretically informed. So we *do* need social theories to help us to address even quite basic issues in social research. Let me underline this point through an extended example.

Theory in the field: who are the Lue?

In this section, I will look in greater detail at a study by Moerman (1974) of a tribe living in Thailand. As an anthropologist, Michael Moerman was interested in learning how a people categorized their world. Like most anthropologists and Chicago School ethnographers (see Chapter 17), he used native informants who, when asked questions like 'How do you recognize a member of your tribe?', produced a list of traits which Moerman called **ethnic identification devices**.

You will recall that Moerman was troubled about what sense to read into the Lue's own accounts. His questions often related to issues that were either obvious or irrelevant to the respondents. As he puts it: 'To the extent that answering an ethnographer's question is an unusual situation for natives, one cannot reason from a native's answer to his *normal* categories or ascriptions' (1974; 66, emphasis added). So Moerman started to see that ethnic identification devices were not used all the time by these people any more than we use them to refer to ourselves in a Western culture. This meant that, if you wanted to understand this people, it was not particularly useful to elicit from them what would necessarily be an abstract account of their tribe's characteristics. So instead, Moerman started to examine what went on in everyday situations through observation.

However, it was not so straightforward to switch to observational methods. Even when ethnographers are silent and merely observe, their presence indicates to people that matters relevant to 'identity' should be highlighted. Consequently, people may pay particular attention to what both the observer and they themselves take to be relevant categorization schemes – like ethnic or kinship labels. In this way, the ethnographer may have 'altered the local priorities among the native category sets which it is his task to describe' (1974: 67). What, then, was to be done? A clue is given by the initially opaque subheadings of Moerman's article: 'Who are the Lue?', 'Why are the Lue?', 'When are the Lue?'

Moerman argues that there are three reasons why we should *not* ask 'Who are the Lue?' These are shown in Box 5.2.

> ## Box 5.2   Three reasons for not asking 'Who are the Lue?'
>
> 1 It would generate an inventory of traits. Like all such inventories it could be endless because we could always be accused of having left something out.
> 2 Lists are retrospective. Once we have decided that the Lue *are* a tribe, then we have no difficulty in 'discovering' a list of traits to support our case.
> 3 The identification of the Lue as a tribe depends, in part, on their successful presentation of themselves as a tribe.

As Moerman puts it: 'The question is not "Who are the Lue?" but rather when how and why the identification "Lue" is preferred' (1974: 62). He adds that this does *not* mean that the Lue are not really a tribe or that they fooled him into thinking they were one. Rather their ethnic identity arises in the fact that people in the area use ethnic identification devices some of the time when they are talking about each other.

Of course, some of the time is not all the time. Hence the task of the ethnographer should be to observe when and *if* ethnic identification devices are used by the participants being studied. Moerman neatly summarizes his argument as follows:

Anthropology [has an] apparent inability to distinguish between warm ... human bodies and one kind of identification device which some of those bodies sometimes use. Ethnic identification devices – with their important potential of making each ethnic set of living persons a joint enterprise with countless generations of un-examined history – seem to be universal. Social scientists should therefore describe and analyse the ways in which they are used, and not merely – as natives do – use them as explanations. (1974: 67–8)

You will see, in the introduction to Chapter 25, that it is possible to conduct causal enquiries into social phenomena such as the use of ethnic identification devices. In that chapter a statistical approach to investigating causation is outlined. Moerman preferred a qualitative approach to explaining 'Why are the Lue?', drawing on his observations of when the devices were used and

what his informants said about them. He suggests that they are used in order to provide the Lue with a sense of distinction and self-esteem in distinguishing themselves from 'hill' or 'jungle' people, whom they consider to be barely human, and 'officials' or 'townsfolk' who would otherwise be understood as insufferably superior. The Lue occupy a somewhat ambiguous position in a nation experiencing tensions between movement from a 'tribal' to a 'civilized' society and this gives added motivation for the display of characteristic labels of 'identity'.

Moerman's study can be understood as relating to broader theories of *anti-essentialism* and *social constructionism* now prevalent in contemporary social theory (see Chapter 4). It reveals that any empiricist attempt to describe things 'as they are' is doomed to failure. Without *some* perspective or, at the very least, a set of animating questions, there is nothing to report. Contrary to crude empiricists, who would deny the relevance of theory to research, the facts *never* speak for themselves.

Implications: theory and research

Moerman's research points to the way in which idealized conceptions of phenomena like 'tribes' can, on closer examination, become like a will-o'-the-wisp, dissolving into sets of practices embedded in particular settings. Nowhere is this clearer than in the field of studies of the 'family'. As Gubrium and Holstein (1987) note, researchers have unnecessarily worried about getting 'authentic' reports of family life given the privacy of the household. Thus researchers may be satisfied that they have got at the 'truth' of family life only when they have uncovered some hidden secret (for example, marital disharmony, child abuse), regarding public presentations as a 'false front'. This, classically, is the perspective of Chicago School ethnography, which often involved a sense of triumph in revealing matters hidden from view by official smokescreens. But this implies an idealized reality – as if there were some authentic site of family life which could be isolated and put under the researcher's microscope. Instead, discourses of family life are to be found largely in people's talk, in a range of contexts. Many of these, like courts of law, clinics and radio call-in programmes where people often reveal what they mean by the term 'family', are public and readily available for research investigation.

If 'the family', like a 'tribe', is present wherever it is invoked, then the worry of some researchers about observing 'real' or 'authentic' family life looks to be misplaced. Their assumption that the family has an essential reality looks more like a highly specific way of approaching the phenomenon, most frequently used by welfare professionals and by politicians.

As it turns out, finding the family is no problem at all for ordinary people. In our everyday life, we can always locate and understand 'real' families. In this regard, think of how social workers or lawyers in juvenile or divorce courts 'discover' the essential features of a particular family. Because we cannot assume, as these practitioners must, that families are 'available' for study in some kind of straightforward way, *how* we invoke the family, *when* we invoke the family and *where* we invoke the family must be central theoretical concerns for social researchers.

But, faced with a topic to study, like 'families' or 'tribes', how do we actually make the move towards a theoretically informed understanding? One way to develop theoretical understanding of observational data is to begin with a set of very general questions. Good examples of such questions are provided by Wolcott: 'What is going on here? What do people in this setting have to know (individually and collectively) in order to do what they are doing? How are skills and attitudes transmitted and acquired, particularly in the absence of intentional efforts at instruction' (1990: 32). Already here, we can see that Wolcott's questions are guided by a particular theoretical focus on people's knowledge and skills. This emerges out of a set of assumptions common to qualitative researchers informed by *interactionism* and *ethnomethodology* (see Chapter 4).

These assumptions are as follows:

1 Common sense is held to be complex and sophisticated rather than naive and misguided.
2 Social practices rather than perceptions are the site where common sense operates. Thus the focus is on what people are doing rather than upon what they are thinking. For example, researchers should study people talking to one another, having meetings, writing documents and so on.
3 'Phenomena' are viewed within such inverted commas. This means that, like Moerman and Gubrium, we should seek to understand how phenomena (such as ethnic identification devices or families) are produced through the activities of particular people in particular settings.

Of course, these are not the only kind of assumptions that may properly inform social research. Depending on our preferred theoretical framework, we might take a completely different position. For instance, researchers interested in the effects of social structure (as Durkheim was in his study of suicide) or feminists would argue that **social structures** (which Durkheim called *social facts,* as was shown in Chapter 2), such as social class, ethnic identity or family type, exist beyond face-to-face interaction. Many feminists would focus as much on what people were thinking (and feeling) as on what they were doing (see also Chapter 3). The issue, for the moment, is not which theoretical framework is 'best' or even most useful. Instead, I have been suggesting that *some* theory of human or social action necessarily informs any piece of social research. Given this, we always need to try to specify our theoretical assumptions rather than to use them unconsciously or uncritically. In this way the practice of research becomes more fully **reflexive**.

Theories, models and hypotheses

I have so far concentrated on showing how theories are used in social research through the use of

Table 5.1 *Basic terms in research*

Term	Meaning	Examples
Model	An overall framework for looking at reality	Ethnomethodology, feminism
Concept	An idea deriving from from from a given model	Social practices, oppression
Theory	A set of concepts used to define and/or explain some phenomenon	Ethnic identification devices, social construction
Hypothesis	A testable proposition	'Tribes invoke ethnic identification devices more frequently when threatened by external enemies'
Methodology	A general approach to studying research topics	Quantitative, qualitative
Method	A specific research technique	Social survey, conversation analysis

(*Source:* adapted from Silverman, 1993: 1)

concrete examples. But what precisely is a 'theory'? And how does it differ from a 'hypothesis'? Table 5.1 defines these and other basic terms in research.

As we see from the table, **models** provide an overall framework for how we look at reality. In short, they tell us what reality is like and the basic elements it contains. In social research, examples of such models are *functionalism* (which looks at the functions of social institutions), *behaviourism* (which defines all behaviour in terms of 'stimulus' and 'response'), *symbolic interactionism* (which focuses on how we attach symbolic meanings to interpersonal relations) and *ethnomethodology* (which encourages us to look at people's everyday ways of producing orderly social interaction).

Concepts are clearly specified ideas deriving from a particular model. Examples of concepts are 'social function' (deriving from functionalism), 'stimulus/response' (behaviourism), 'definition of the situation' (interactionism) and 'the

documentary method of interpretation' (ethnomethodology). Concepts offer ways of looking at the world which are essential in defining a research problem.

Theories arrange sets of concepts to define and explain some phenomenon, for example the nature of 'tribes' and 'families'. As we have already seen, without a theory these phenomena cannot be understood. In this sense, without a theory there is nothing to research. So theories provide the impetus for research. As living entities, they are also developed and modified by good research. However, as used here, models, concepts and theories are self-confirming in the sense that they instruct us to look at phenomena in particular ways. This means that they can never be disproved but only found to be more or less useful.

This last feature distinguishes theories from **hypotheses**. Unlike theories, hypotheses are tested in research. Examples of hypotheses, discussed in Silverman (1993), are: 'how we receive advice is linked to how advice is given';

'responses to an illegal drug depend upon what one learns from others'; 'voting in union elections is related to non-work links between union members'. As we shall see, a feature of many qualitative research studies is that there is no specific hypothesis at the outset but that hypotheses are produced (or induced) during the early stages of research. In any event, unlike theories, hypotheses can, and should be, tested. Therefore, we assess a hypothesis by its validity or truth.

A **methodology** is a general approach to studying a research topic. It establishes how one will go about studying any phenomenon. In social research, examples of methodologies are **quantitative** methodology, which uses numbers to test hypotheses and, of course, **qualitative** methodology, which tries to use first-hand familiarity with different settings to induce hypotheses. Like theories, methodologies cannot be true or false, only more or less useful.

Finally, **methods** are specific research techniques. These include quantitative techniques, like statistical correlations, as well as techniques like observation, interviewing and audio recording. Once again, in themselves, techniques are not true or false. They are more or less useful, depending on their fit with the theories and methodologies being used and the hypothesis being tested or the research topic that is selected. So, for instance, behaviourists may favour quantitative methods and interactionists often prefer to gather their data

by observation. But, depending upon the hypothesis being tested, behaviourists may sometimes use qualitative methods – for instance in the exploratory stage of research. Equally, interactionists may sometimes use simple quantitative methods, particularly when they want to find an overall pattern in their data.

The relation between models, concepts, theories, hypotheses, methodology and methods is set out schematically in Figure 5.1. Reading the figure anti-clockwise, each concept reflects a lower level of generality and abstraction. The arrow from 'findings' to 'hypotheses' indicates a feedback mechanism through which hypotheses are modified in the light of findings.

Let me now try to put flesh on the skeleton set out in Figure 5.1 through the use of some concrete examples. Imagine that we have a general interest in the gloomy topic of death in society. How are we to research this topic? Before we can even define a research problem, let alone develop a hypothesis, we need to think through some very basic issues. Assume that we are the kind of social scientist who prefers to see the world in terms of how social structures determine behaviour, following Durkheim's injunction to treat social facts as real things (see Chapter 2). Such a *model* of social life will suggest concepts that we can use in our research on death. Using such a model, we will tend to see death in terms of statistics relating to rates of death (or 'mortality'). And we will want

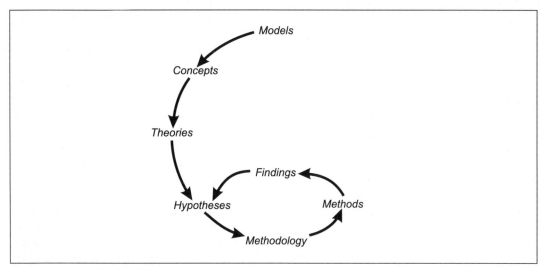

Figure 5.1   *Levels of analysis*

to explain such statistics in terms of other social facts such as age or social class.

Armed with our concepts, we might then construct a *theory* about one or other aspect of our topic. For instance, working with our assumption that death is a social fact, determined by other social facts, we might develop a theory that the rate of early death among children, or 'infant mortality', is related to some social fact about their parents, say their social class. From this theory, it is a quick step to the *hypothesis* that the higher the social class of its parents, the lower the likelihood of a child dying within the first year of its life. This hypothesis is sometimes expressed as saying that there is an *inverse* relationship between social class and infant mortality.

As already implied, a model concerned with social facts will tend to favour a quantitative methodology, using methods such as the analysis of official statistics or the use of large-scale social surveys based on apparently reliable fixed-choice questionnaires. In interpreting the findings of such research, one will need to ensure that due account is taken of factors that may be concealed in simple correlations. For instance, social class may be associated with quality of housing and the latter factor (here called an *intervening* variable) may be the real cause of variations in the rates of infant mortality. Multivariate analysis of this sort is discussed in Chapter 25.

This overall approach to death is set out schematically in Figure 5.2. Figure 5.3 sets out a very different way of conceiving death. For interactionist social researchers, social institutions are created and stabilized by the actions of participants. A central idea of this model is that our labelling of phenomena defines their character. This, in turn, is associated with the concept of **definitions of the situation** which tells us to look for social phenomena in the ways in which meaning gets defined by people in different contexts. The overall message of the interactionist approach is that 'death' should be put in inverted commas and hence leads to a theory in which 'death' is treated as a *social construct*.

Of course, this is very different from the social fact model and, therefore, nicely illustrates the importance of theories in defining research problems. Its immediate drawback, however, may be that it appears to be counter-intuitive. After all, you may feel, death is surely an obvious fact. We are either dead or not dead and, if so, where does this leave social constructionism?

Let me cite two cases which put the counter-argument. First, in 1963, after President Kennedy was shot, he was taken to a Dallas hospital with, according to contemporary accounts, half of his head shot away. My hunch is that if you or I were to arrive in a casualty department in this state, we would be given a cursory examination and then recorded as 'dead on arrival' (DOA). Precisely because they were dealing with a President, the staff

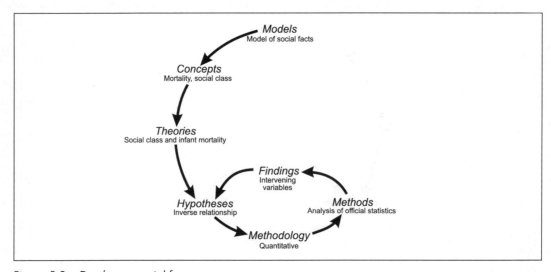

Figure 5.2   *Death as a social fact*

had to do more than this. So they worked on Kennedy for almost an hour, demonstrating thereby that they had done their best for such an important patient.

Now think of contemporary debates about whether or when severely injured people should have life-support systems turned off. Once again, acts of definition constitute whether somebody is alive or dead. And note that such definitions have real effects. Of course, such a constructionist version of death is just one way of theorizing this phenomenon, not intrinsically better or worse than the social fact approach. But, once we adopt one or another model, it starts to have a big influence upon how our research proceeds. For instance, as we have seen, if 'dead on arrival' can be a label applied in different ways to different people, we might develop a hypothesis about how the label 'dead on arrival' is applied to different hospital patients.

Because of our model, we would then probably try to collect research data that arose in such **naturally occurring** (or non-research-generated) settings as actual hospitals, using methods like observation or audio or video recording (see also the discussion of *naturalism* in Chapter 4). Note, however, that this would not rule out the collection of quantitative data (say from hospital records). Rather, it would mean that our main body of data would probably be qualitative. Following earlier research (for example, Jeffery, 1979; Dingwall

and Murray, 1983) our findings might show how age and presumed moral status are relevant to such medical decision-making as well as social class. In turn, as shown in Figure 5.3, these findings would help us to refine our initial hypothesis.

Generalizations and theory building

Theorizing about data does not stop with the refinement of hypotheses. In this section, I will show how we can develop generalizations out of successfully tested hypotheses and, thereby, contribute to theory *building*, an approach to social research that is discussed in depth in Chapter 18 on 'grounded theory.' First, we need to recognize that **case studies,** limited to a particular set of interactions, still allow one to examine how particular sayings and doings are embedded in particular patterns of social organization. We first caught sight of this earlier in this chapter when I mentioned how Moerman (1974) used his research in Thailand to suggest generalizations which included English-speaking societies.

A classic case of an anthropologist using a case study to make broader generalizations is found in Mary Douglas's (1975) work on a central African tribe, the Lele. Douglas noticed that an ant-eater that Western zoologists call a 'pangolin' was very important to the Lele's ritual life. For the Lele, the pangolin was both a cult animal and an anomaly. It

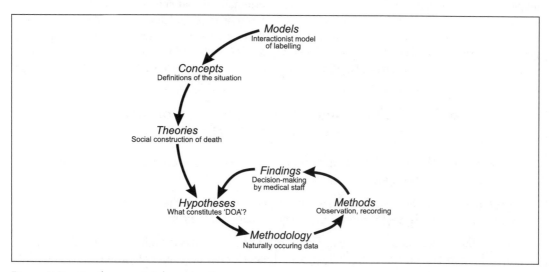

Figure 5.3   *Death as a social construction*

was perceived to have both animal and human characteristics. For instance, it tended to have only one offspring at a time, unlike most other animals. It also did not readily fit into the Lele's classification of land and water creatures, spending some of its time on land and some time in the water. Curiously, among animals that were hunted, the pangolin seemed to the Lele to be unique in not trying to escape but almost offering itself up to its hunter. Fortunately, Douglas resisted what might be called a 'tourist' response, moving beyond curiosity to systematic analysis. She noted that many groups who perceive anomalous entities in their environment reject them out of hand. To take an anomalous entity seriously might cast doubt on the **naturalized** status of your group's system of classification.

The classic example of the rejection of anomaly is found in the Old Testament. Douglas points out that the reason why the pig is unclean, according to the Old Testament, is that it is anomalous. It has a cloven hoof which, following the Old Testament, makes it clean, but it does not chew the cud – which makes it dirty. So it turns out that the pig is particularly unclean precisely because it is anomalous. Similarly, the Old Testament teachings on intermarriage work in relation to anomaly. Although you are not expected to marry somebody of another tribe, to marry the offspring of a marriage between a member of your tribe and an outsider is even more frowned upon. In both examples, anomaly is shunned.

However, the Lele are an exception: they celebrate the anomalous pangolin. What this suggests to Douglas is that there may be no *universal* propensity to frown upon anomaly. If there is

variability from community to community, then this must say something about their social organization. Sure enough, there is something special about the Lele's social life. Their experience of relations with other tribes has been very successful. They exchange goods with them and have little experience of war. What is involved in relating well with other tribes? It means successfully crossing a frontier or boundary. But what do anomalous entities do? They cut across boundaries. Here is the answer to the puzzle about why the Lele are different.

Douglas is suggesting that the Lele's response to anomaly derives from experiences grounded in their social organization. They perceive the pangolin favourably because it cuts across boundaries just as they themselves do. Conversely, the ancient Israelites regarded anomalies unfavourably because their own experience of crossing boundaries was profoundly unfavourable. Indeed, the Old Testament reads as a series of disastrous exchanges between the Israelites and other tribes.

Douglas, applying an historical and comparative method, moves from a single-case explanation to a far more general theory of the relation between social exchange and response to anomaly. Glaser and Strauss (1967) in their outline of grounded theorizing (see Chapter 18) have described this movement towards greater generality as a move from **substantive** to **formal** theory. In their own research on hospital wards caring for terminally ill patients, they show how, by using the comparative method, we can develop accounts of people's own awareness of their impending death (a substantive theory) into accounts of a whole range of 'awareness contexts' (formal

---

Box 5.3 Building theory from case study observations: Mary Douglas and the Lele

Observation 1: The Lele celebrate the pangolin, an anomalous animal. The Lele have good relationships with their neighbours.

Observation 2: In the Old Testament an anomalous animal, the pig, is regarded as unclean. The ancient Israelites were frequently at war with their neighbours.

Theory: The experience of crossing boundaries (as in relations with neighbours) can be generally good or bad and this influences whether anomalies are celebrated or shunned.

theory – see also Boxes 23.7 and 23.8).

Douglas's account of the relation between responses to anomaly and experiences of boundary crossing can also be applied elsewhere. Perhaps bad experiences of exchanges with other groups explains why some Israeli Jews and Palestinian Muslims are so concerned to mark their own identity on the 'holy places' in Jerusalem and reject (as a hateful anomaly) multiple use of the same holy sites?

In any event, Douglas's study of the Lele exemplifies the need to locate how individual elements are embedded in forms of social organization. In her case, this is done in an explicitly *Durkheimian* manner, which sees behaviour as the expression of a 'society' that works as a 'hidden hand' constraining and forming human action. Alternatively, Moerman's work indicates how, using a *constructionist* framework, one can look at the fine detail of people's activities without treating social organization as a purely external force. In the latter case, people cease to be 'cultural dopes' (Garfinkel, 1967) and skilfully reproduce the moral order.

How to theorize about data

Unlike Moerman or Douglas, most readers will not bring to their research any very well-defined set of theoretical ideas. If you are in this position, your problem will be how you can use data to think in theoretical terms. The list below is intended merely as a set of suggestions. Although it cannot be exhaustive, it should serve as an initial guide to theorizing about data. It can also be read in conjunction with the discussion of grounded theorizing in Chapter 18.

In carrying out your research, I suggest that you think about the following five issues.

1 Consider *chronology*: Can you gather data over time in order to look at processes of change? If not, it is worth searching out historical evidence that may at least suggest how your research problem came into being (see also Chapter 19).

2 Consider *context*: How are your data contextualized in particular organizational settings, social processes or sets of experiences? For instance, as Moerman shows, answering an interviewer's question may be different from engaging in the activity which is the topic of the interview. Therefore, think about how there may be many versions of your phenomenon.

3 Make use of *comparison*: Like Mary Douglas, who generated her theory by comparing how different groups treated anomalies, always try to compare your data with other relevant data. Even if you cannot find a comparative case, try to find ways of dividing your data into different sets and compare each. Remember that the comparative method is the basic scientific method.

4 Consider the *implications* of your research: When you are reporting your research, think about how your discoveries may relate to broader issues than your original research topic. In this way, a very narrow topic (for example, how the Lele perceive the pangolin) may be related to much broader social processes (for example, how societies respond to anomalous entities).

5 Be like the Lele and engage in *lateral thinking* if you can: Don't erect strong boundaries between concepts but explore the relations between apparently diverse models, theories and methodologies. Celebrate anomaly!

Conclusion

The philosopher of science Thomas Kuhn (1970) has described social science as lacking a single, agreed set of concepts (see Chapter 2). In Kuhn's terms, this makes social research preparadigmatic or at least in a state of competing paradigms. As I have already implied, the problem is that this has generated a whole series of social science courses which pose different approaches to research in terms of either/or questions. Classically, for example, qualitative methodology is thought to be opposed to quantitative.

Such courses are much appreciated by some students. They learn about the paradigmatic oppositions in question, choose A rather than B and report back, parrot fashion, all the advantages of A and the drawbacks of B. It is hardly surprising that such courses produce very little evidence of independent thought. This may, in part, explain why so many undergraduate social science courses actually provide a learned incapacity to go out and do research.

Learning about rival 'armed camps' in no way allows you to confront research data. In the field, material is much more messy than the different camps would suggest. Perhaps there is something to be learned from both sides, or, more constructively, perhaps we start to ask interesting questions when we reject the polarities that such a course markets? Even when we decide to use qualitative or quantitative methods, we involve ourselves in theoretical as well as methodological decisions. These decisions relate not only to how we conceptualize the world but also to our theory of how our research subjects think about things. Theory, then, should be neither a status symbol nor an optional extra in a research study. Without theory, research

is impossibly narrow. Without research, theory is mere armchair contemplation.

Further reading

A brief discussion of current theoretical ideas in qualitative research can be found in Silverman (2001), pp.70–8. An excellent book-length treatment is provided by Gubrium and Holstein (1997). Silverman (1998) offers an introduction to the work of Harvey Sacks, a key figure in constructionist theorizing. Relevant chapters by ten Have (on ethnomethodology and research practice) and Kendall and Wickham (on Foucault and research practice) are in *Qualitative Research Practice* (Seale et al., 2004).

Student Reader (Seale, 2004): relevant readings

29 Alfred Schutz: 'Concept and theory formation in the social sciences'
46 Udo Kelle: 'Theory building in qualitative research and computer programs for the management of textual data'
47 David Silverman: 'Harvey Sacks: social science and conversation analysis'
56 Alvin W. Gouldner: 'Toward a reflexive sociology'
64 Arthur W. Frank: 'Can we research suffering?'

Key concepts

Case study	Methods
Concept	Model
Formal theory	Reflexivity
Hypothesis	Substantive theory
Methodology	Theory

6

Research and social policy

David Silverman

CONTENTS

In my experience, researchers at the beginning of projects often make two basic errors. First, they fail to distinguish sufficiently between research problems and problems that are discussed in the world around us. The latter kind of problems, which I shall call **social problems,** are at the heart of political debates and fill the more serious newspapers. They are often the focus of social policies and researchers may find themselves commissioned by policy makers to address such problems in their research. However, I will be arguing that although social problems, like unemployment, homelessness and racism, are important, by themselves they cannot provide a researchable topic.

The second error to which I have referred is sometimes related to the first. It arises where researchers take on an impossibly large research problem. For instance, it is important to find the causes of a social problem like homelessness, but such a problem is beyond the scope of a single researcher with limited time and resources. Moreover, by defining the problem so widely, one is usually unable to say anything at great depth about it. It is often helpful instead to aim to say a lot about a little problem. This means avoiding the temptation to say a little about a lot. Indeed, the latter path can be something of a 'cop-out'. Precisely because the topic is so wide-ranging, one can flit from one aspect to another without being forced to refine and test each piece of analysis.

In the first section of this chapter I shall focus on the first of these errors – the tendency to choose social problems as research topics. However, in recommending solutions to this error, I shall imply how one can narrow down a research topic and thus deal with the second error. The second section of the chapter will consider a variety of roles that can be adopted by social researchers in relation to policy makers. Lastly, the chapter will illustrate some of these issues by describing my research in health care settings.

What is a problem?

One has only to open a newspaper or to watch the TV news to be confronted by a host of social problems. In the mid-1990s, the British news media were full of references to a 'wave' of crimes committed by children – from the theft of cars to the murder of old people and other children. There were also several stories about how doctors infected by HIV continued to work and, by implication, endangered their patients. The stories had this in common: they assumed some sort of moral decline in which families or schools failed to discipline children and in which physicians failed to take seriously their professional responsibilities. In turn, the way each story was told implied a solution: tightening up discipline in order to combat the presumed moral decline.

However, before we can consider such a cure, we need to consider carefully the diagnosis. Had juvenile crime increased or was the apparent increase a reflection of what counts as a good story? Alternatively, might the increase have been an artefact of what crimes get reported? Again, how many health care professionals actually infected their patients with HIV? I know of only one (disputed) case – a Florida dentist. Conversely, there is considerable evidence of patients infecting the medical staff who treat them. Moreover, why focus on HIV when other conditions like hepatitis B are far more infectious? Could it be that we hear so much about HIV because it is associated with stigmatized groups?

Apparent social problems are not the only topics that may clamour for the attention of the researcher. Administrators and managers point to 'problems' in their organizations and may turn to social scientists for solutions. It is tempting to allow such people to define a research problem – particularly as there is usually a fat research grant attached to it! However, we must first look at the terms that are being used to define the problem.

Let us imagine that a manager defines problems in their organization as problems of 'communication'. The role of the researcher is then to work out how people can communicate 'better'. Unfortunately, talking about communication problems raises many difficulties. For instance, it may assume that the solution to any problem is more careful listening, while ignoring power relations present inside and outside patterns of communication. Such relations may also make the characterization of 'organizational efficiency' very problematic. Thus administrative problems give no more secure basis for social research than do social problems. Of course, this is not to deny that there are real problems in society. However, even if we agree about what these problems are, it is not clear that they provide a researchable topic.

Take the case of the problems of people infected with HIV. Some of these problems are, quite rightly, brought to the attention of the public by the organized activities of groups of people who carry the infection. But social researchers should try to contribute the particular theoretical and methodological skills of their discipline, giving an initial research topic their own theoretical and methodological 'twist'. So:

- *Economists* can research how limited health care resources can be used most effectively in coping with the epidemic in the West and in the Third World.
- Sociologists using *social surveys* can investigate patterns of sexual behaviour in order to try to promote effective health education.
- Sociologists using *qualitative methods* may study what is involved in the 'negotiation' of safer sex or in counselling people about HIV and AIDS.

For instance, in my research on HIV counselling (Silverman, 1996), I used tape recordings and detailed transcripts, as well as many technical concepts derived from my interest in the qualitative method of conversation analysis (see Chapter 28). It is therefore usually necessary to refuse to allow our research topics to be totally defined in terms of the conceptions of social problems as recognized by either professional or community groups. Ironically, by beginning from a clearly defined social science perspective, we can later address such social problems with, I believe, considerable force and persuasiveness. I shall seek to show this later in the chapter.

Sensitivity and researchable problems

I have been arguing that it is often unhelpful for researchers to begin their work on the basis of a social problem identified by either practitioners or managers. It is a commonplace that such definitions of problems often may serve vested interests. My point, however, is that if social science research has anything to offer, its theoretical imperatives drive it in a direction that can offer practitioners, managers and policy makers *new* perspectives on their problems. Paradoxically, by refusing to begin from a common conception of what is 'wrong' in a setting, we may be most able to contribute to the identification both of what is going on and, thereby, how it may be modified in the pursuit of desired ends. The various perspectives of social science provide a sensitivity to many issues neglected by those who define social or administrative problems. I will discuss three types of sensitivity in turn: historical, political and contextual.

Box 6.1 Two examples of historical sensitivity

Example 1: In the 1950s and 1960s it was assumed that the *nuclear family* (parents and children) had replaced the *extended family* (many generations living together in the same household) of pre-industrial societies. Researchers simply seemed to have forgotten that lower life expectancy may have made the extended family pattern relatively rare in the past, and historical research has broadly confirmed that this was so (Laslett, 1979).

Example 2: Historical sensitivity helps us to understand how we are governed. For instance, until the eighteenth century, the majority of the population were treated as a threatening mob to be controlled, where necessary, by the use of force. Today, we are seen as individuals with 'needs' and 'rights', which must be understood and protected by society (see Foucault, 1977). But, although oppressive force may be used only rarely, we may be controlled in more subtle ways. Think of the knowledge about each of us contained in computerized data banks and the pervasive CCTV cameras which record movements in many city streets.

Historical sensitivity

Wherever possible, one should establish **historical sensitivity** by examining the relevant historical evidence when we are setting up a topic to research. This is a point dealt with at greater length in Chapter 19, which outlines the uses of historical and archival methods in social and cultural research. Box 6.1 gives two examples of the way historical sensitivity can offer us multiple research topics that evade the trap of thinking that present-day versions of social problems are unproblematic.

Political sensitivity

Allowing the current media scares to determine our research topics is just as fallible as designing research in accordance with administrative or managerial interests. In neither case do we use **political sensitivity** to detect the vested interests behind this way of formulating a problem. The media, after all, need to attract an audience just as administrators need to be seen to be working efficiently.

So political sensitivity seeks to grasp the politics behind defining topics in particular ways.

In turn, it helps in suggesting that we research how social problems arise.

Political sensitivity does not mean that social scientists argue that there are no real problems in society. Instead, it suggests that social science can make an important contribution to society by querying how official definitions of problems arise. To be truthful, however, we should also recognize how social scientists often need to accept tacitly such definitions in order to attract research grants.

Contextual sensitivity

This is the least self-explanatory and most contentious category in the present list. By **contextual sensitivity**, I mean the recognition that apparently uniform institutions like 'the family', 'a tribe' or 'science' take on a variety of meanings in different contexts. This is linked to ideas about identity and **anti-essentialism** discussed in Chapter 3, where we saw that social theorists and researchers have increasingly come to see personal identity as being constructed in interaction, rather than fixed.

Contextual sensitivity is reflected most obviously in Moerman's (1974) study of the Lue

---

Box 6.2   An example of political sensitivity

Barbara Nelson (1984) looked at how 'child abuse' became defined as a recognizable problem in the late 1960s. She shows how the findings of a doctor about the 'battered baby syndrome' were adopted by the conservative Nixon administration through linking social problems to parental 'maladjustment' rather than to the failures of social programmes.

Box 6.3   Lue 'ethnic identification devices'

The Lue claimed that these made them *different* from their neighbours, the Yuan:

- the use of mattresses and blankets
- the possession of a village 'spirit house'
- the singing of particular types of folk song

These, though, they shared with the Yuan:

- the use of pillows and mosquito nets
- working in cooperative labour groups
- using a rice pounder to make rice flour

tribe in Thailand (discussed more fully in Chapter 5). Moerman began with the anthropologist's conventional appetite to locate a people in a classificatory scheme. To satisfy this appetite, he started to ask tribespeople questions like 'How do you recognize a member of your tribe?'. He reports that his respondents quickly became adept at providing a whole list of *traits* which constituted their tribe and distinguished them from their neighbours, as well as others which they said they shared with their neighbours (see Box 6.3).

But Moerman began to feel that such a list was, in purely logical terms, endless. Perhaps if you wanted to understand this people, it was not particularly useful to elicit an abstract account of their characteristics, which Moerman called **ethnic identification devices.**

So Moerman stopped asking 'Who are the Lue?'. He came to believe that ethnic identification devices were not used all the time by these people any more than we use them to refer to ourselves in a Western culture. Instead, Moerman started to examine what went on in everyday situations. Looked at this way, the issue was no longer who the Lue essentially were but when, among people living in these Thai villages, ethnic identification labels were used and what were the consequences of invoking them. For example, a common cause for their display was the presence of strange, Western anthropologists asking the people to identify themselves! Curiously enough, Moerman concluded that, when you looked at the matter this way, the apparent differences between the Lue and ourselves were considerably reduced. Only an ethnocentric Westerner might have assumed otherwise, behaving like a tourist craving for out-of-the-way sights.

But it is not only such large-scale collectivities as tribes that are looked at afresh when we use what I have called contextual sensitivity. Other apparently stable social institutions (like the family) and identities (gender, ethnicity and so on) may be insufficiently questioned from a social problem perspective. For instance, commentators says things like 'the family is under threat'. But where are we to find the unitary form of family assumed in such commentary? And doesn't 'the family' look different in contexts ranging from the household, to the law courts or even the super-

market? Rather than take such arguments at face value, the researcher must make use of contextual sensitivity to discover how things actually operate in a social world where, as Moerman shows us, people's practices are inevitably more complex than they might seem.

One final point: the three kinds of sensitivity we have been considering offer different, sometimes contradictory, ways of generating research topics. I am not suggesting that *all* should be used at the beginning of any research study. However, if we are not sensitive to *any* of these issues, then we run the danger of lapsing into a 'social problem'-based way of defining our research topics.

What is the social scientist's role?

Even if we accept the argument above, we are still no clearer about the purpose of social science. To what ends are we attempting to be sensitive? The American sociologist Howard Becker puts this question very starkly: 'The question is not whether we should take sides, since we inevitably will, but rather whose side are we on?' (1967: 239). Not all social researchers would agree with Becker's call for moral or political partisanship. Perhaps responding to state apparatuses which are at best suspicious of the purposes of social science, many would go on the defensive. They might find it easier or more acceptable to argue that their concern is simply with the establishment of facts through the judicious testing of competing hypotheses and theories. Their only slogan, they would say, is the pursuit of knowledge. They would claim to reject political partisanship, at least in their academic work; they are only, they would say, partisans for truth.

I am not, for the moment, concerned to make a detailed assessment of either Becker's statement or the defensive response to it which I have just depicted. I believe both contain dangerous simplifications. As I shall later show, the partisans for truth are mistaken about the purity of knowledge, while Becker's rhetoric of 'sides' is often associated with a style of research which is unable to discover anything because of its prior commitment to a revealed truth (the plight of the underdog, the inevitable course of human history and so on). Curiously, both positions can be elitist, establishing themselves apart from and above the people they study.

For the moment, however, I want to stress a more positive feature of both arguments. Both recognize that no simply neutral or value-free position is possible in social research (or, indeed, elsewhere). The partisans for truth, just as much as the partisans of the 'underdog', are committed to an absolute value for which there can be no purely factual foundation. As Weber (1946, 1949) pointed out in the early years of this century, all research is contaminated to some extent by the values of the researcher. Only through those values do certain problems get identified and studied in particular ways. Even the commitment to scientific (or rigorous) method is itself, as Weber emphasizes, a value. Finally, the conclusions and implications to be drawn from a study are, Weber stresses, largely grounded in the moral and political beliefs of the researcher.

Using Weber's ideas, I develop below the position of the partisans for truth. To simplify, I refer to this as the position of the **scholar**. I retain the term **partisan** for those who claim their primary allegiance is to purely moral or political positions.

The scholar

In his two famous lectures, 'Science as a vocation' and 'Politics as a vocation' (Weber, 1946), Weber enunciated basic liberal principles to a student audience in 1917. Despite the patriotic fervour of the First World War, he insisted on the primacy of the individual's own conscience as a basis for action. Taking the classic Kantian position (see Chapter 2), he argued that values could not be derived from facts. However, this was not because values were less important than facts. Rather, precisely because 'ultimate evaluations' (or value choices) were so important, they were not to be reduced to purely factual judgements. The facts could tell you only about the likely consequences of given actions but they could not tell you which action to choose. For Weber, the very commitment to science was an example of an ultimate evaluation, exemplifying a personal belief in standards of logic and rationality and in the value of factual knowledge. Ironically echoing certain aspects of the 'Protestant ethic' whose historical emergence he himself had traced (see Chapter 4), Weber appealed to the scholar's conscience as the sole basis for conferring meaning and significance upon events.

Weber's appeal to Protestantism's and liberalism's 'free individual' was fully shared, 50 years on, by Norman Denzin (1970). Denzin at that time rejected any fixed moral standards as the basis for research. For example, it is sometimes argued that it is wrong for social researchers to observe people secretly (see Chapter 10 for a discussion of the ethics of this). Denzin did not agree. Nor was he prepared to recognize that research must necessarily contribute to society's own self-understanding. Both standards were, for him, examples of 'ethical absolutism' which failed to respect the scholar's appeal to his or her own conscience in the varying contexts of research. Denzin's stand was distinctively liberal and individualist: 'One mandate governs sociological activity – the absolute freedom to pursue one's activities as one sees fit' (1970: 332). What 'one sees fit' would take into account that no method of sociological research is intrinsically any more unethical than any other. Citing Goffman, Denzin argued that, since the researcher always wears some mask, covert observation is merely one mask among others. Denzin did suggest that the pursuit of research in terms of one's own standards should have certain safeguards. For instance, subjects should, wherever possible, be told of the researcher's own value judgements and biases, and should be warned about the kinds of interpretation the research may generate within

---

Box 6.4 Denzin's (and Lincoln's) position 30 years on

'The qualitative researcher is not an objective, authoritative, politically neutral observer standing outside and above the text ... Qualitative inquiry is properly conceptualized as a civic, participatory, collaborative project. This joins the researcher and the researched in an ongoing moral dialogue.' (Lincoln and Denzin 2000: 1049)

Box 6.5 Partisanship in a study of medical consultations

Howard Waitzkin, in his study of American medical consultations, had the laudable aim of relating 'the everyday micro-level interaction of individuals' to 'macro-level structures of domination' (1979: 601). For instance, when a doctor says 'good' after a patient has said he is now able to go back to work, Waitzkin argues that the doctor's comment reinforces a capitalist work ethic. Again, when a doctor's diagnosis appears to emphasize the mechanical workings of the body rather than the patient's personal experiences, Waitzkin once more interprets this in terms of the hidden hand of capitalism treating people simply as machines.

---

the community. But he was insistent that the ultimate arbiter of proper conduct remains the conscience of the individual researcher. (His position has changed quite significantly since 1970 – see Box 6.4.)

Weber and Denzin's liberal position seems rather unrealistic. Curiously, as social scientists they fail to see the power of social organization as it shapes the practice of research. For while Denzin acknowledged the role of pressure groups, he remained (at least in 1970) silent about the privileged authority of the scientist in society and about the deployment of scientific theories by agents of social control as mobilizing forms of power/knowledge.

The partisan

Unlike scholars, partisans (such as Lincoln and Denzin in the year 2000 – see Box 6.4) do not shy away from their accountability to the world. Instead, the partisan may seek to provide the theoretical and factual resources for a political struggle aimed at transforming the assumptions through which both political and administrative games are played. Box 6.5 shows an example of one such partisan study (described more fully in Silverman, 1985).

As Rayner and Stimson (1979) point out, Waitzkin's interpretations depend upon a mechanistic version of Marxism which reduces the doctor–patient relationship simply to an ideological state apparatus of the capitalist state. Knowing what he is going to find, Waitzkin treats his data largely as illustrative of a preconceived theory. Two things never seem to strike him.

- First, it is possible that what he finds is true but not necessarily caused by the factors in his theory. For instance, Strong (1979) suggests that doctors' use of the machine analogy in describing the body may be a feature of medical consultations in all industrialized social systems and not, as Waitzkin suggests, specific to capitalism.

- Secondly, he seems unaware that contrary evidence should be hunted down and followed up. For instance, Waitzkin notes – but makes nothing of – his own apparently contrary findings that women patients receive more information, while 'doctors from working-class backgrounds tend to communicate less information than doctors from upper-class backgrounds' (1979: 604).

Just as partisans do not seek to be surprised by their data, they tend to be elitist in regard to political change. Not surprisingly, Waitzkin (1979: 608) seeks to encourage 'patient education' to invite the questioning of professional advice. At the same time, he makes nothing of patients' self-generated attempts to challenge professional dominance. Waitzkin illustrates some of the more unfortunate consequences of the researcher adopting the role of the partisan. In the same way as the Bible advises 'seek and ye shall find', so partisans (Marxists, feminists, conservatives) often look and then find examples which can be used to support their theories.

We have seen, then, that neither the position of the partisan nor that of the scholar provides a satisfactory basis for social science. The partisan is often condemned to ignore features of the world which do not fit his or her preconceived moral or political position. The scholar goes too far in the other direction, wrongly denying that research has any kind of involvement with existing forms of social organization. Both positions are too extreme and thus fail to cope with the exigencies of the actual relationship between social researchers and society. The rest of this chapter is, therefore, devoted to describing a more pragmatic position that seeks to outline what social science can contribute to society.

Social science's contribution: a qualitative sociologist's experience

For the past 20 years, I have conducted qualitative research in a range of health care settings from outpatient clinics to AIDS counselling sessions (see Silverman, 1987, 1996). In this section, I will explain two practical contributions of my research in hospital clinics, namely:

- the revelation of surprising facts; and
- the possibilities for influencing health care practice.

Revealing surprising facts

Sometimes, in my own research, without any intellectual intent, I have revealed things opposed to what we might readily assume about how people behave. In work I was doing in a children's heart unit, in the early 1980s, we interviewed parents of child patients. Parents told us that one of the things that made their first outpatient consultations so difficult was that there were so many people in the room. This was a very serious occasion; for many parents their child would be given a sentence of life or death. They said it was confusing and intimidating because of the many doctors, nurses and sociologists present.

We found this quite convincing but used a problematic kind of measure to look at this further. We looked through our tape-recorded consultations where there were different numbers of people in the room and then we counted the number of questions asked by parents. Table 6.1 presents our findings. As you can see, our findings went against the common-sense expectation that the more people in the room, the fewer questions would be asked since the parents would have been, as they claimed, more intimidated. Based on its crude measures, Table 6.1 shows that, in our sample, parents asked more questions when there were five or more people in the room. I will not go into detail about what we made of this. But let me reassure you that we did not say that this meant that parents were wrong. On the contrary, there was evidence that parents were trying to behave responsibly and were appealing to the number of people present at the consultation as one way of depicting the pressures they were under. The numbers present thus worked not as a *causal* factor in determining parents' behaviour but as something which could subsequently be used to rationalize their guilt at not asking as many questions as they would have liked.

We started to develop policy interventions in relationship to what the parents were telling us. For instance, how could a context be created where parents could display their responsibility to medical staff who, unlike researchers, could not visit them in their own homes? In due course, at our suggestion, the hospital created an additional clinic which was held some weeks after the first hospital interview. Here children were not examined and parents were free to interview doctors. The intervention was liked by both parents and doctors. Doctors liked it because it provided a

Table 6.1 *Questions asked by parents by number of medical staff present*

	Number of consultations	Total questions	Average questions
1–4 medical staff	17	48	2.8
5+ medical staff	23	99	4.3

$p < 0.05$.

Box 6.6 Another example of discovering new facts

This arose from my research on three cancer clinics (Silverman, 1984). In this research, I looked at the practice of a doctor in the British National Health Service and compared it with his private practice. This study was relevant to a lively debate about the British National Health Service and whether there should be more private medicine. I showed that the private clinic encouraged a more 'personalized' service and allowed patients to orchestrate their care, control the agenda, and obtain some 'territorial' control of the setting. However, despite these 'ceremonial' gains, in the 1980s the NHS provided cancer patients with quicker and more specialized treatment. So the cancer study serves as an example of how researchers can participate in debates about public policy.

good opportunity to get to know families before they were admitted to the ward. Parents said that they felt under less time pressure because their child did not need to be examined and because, in the weeks that had passed since their first hospital visit, they had had time to work out what they wanted to know. Moreover, many mothers commented that they felt that their children had benefited as well because, while their parents spoke to the doctor, they could spend time in the hospital children's play-room. Consequently, the hospital now seemed a less frightening place to these children. So this is an example of a situation in which sociological research, by discovering new facts, has come up with a practical solution to an everyday problem.

Debating public policy

Returning to the two positions I outlined earlier, the scholar argues that research need never have any relation to public debates about social policy. By contrast, the partisan, while very interested in such debates, is likely to bring too many preconceptions to them. How have I tried to enter into such debates without limiting myself to the assumptions of either position? Box 6.7 shows an example of a finding from the same heart unit which we have already discussed.

In addition, the second type of consultations were longer and apparently more democratic than elsewhere. A view of the patient in a family context was encouraged and parents were given every opportunity to voice their concerns and to participate in decision making. In this subsample, unlike the larger sample, when given a real choice, parents almost always refused the test. It turns out that this smaller subsample was composed of parents of children with Down's syndrome, who had mental and physical disabilities in addition to

Box 6.7 Different approaches to parents' right to choose

At one point, we were looking at how doctors in the heart unit talked to parents about the decision to have a small diagnostic test on their children.

In *most cases*, the doctor would say something like: 'What we propose to do, if you agree, is a small test.' No parent disagreed with an offer that appeared to be purely formal, like the formal right (never exercised) of the Queen not to sign legislation passed by the British Parliament.

For a *subsample* of children, however, the parents' right to choose was far from formal. The doctor would say things to them like the following: 'I think what we would do now depends a little bit on parents' feelings'; 'Now it depends a little bit on what you think'; 'It depends very much on your own personal views as to whether we should proceed.'

Box 6.8   Web pointers for research and social policy
The Policy Studies Institute (UK) www.psi.org.uk/about/default.asp **The Brookings Institution (USA)** www.brook.edu/ **The Urban Sector Network (South Africa)** www.usn.org.za/index.htm **Institute for Research on Public Policy (Canada)** www.irpp.org/indexe.htm *Visit the website for this book at www.rscbook.co.uk to link to these web pointers.*

their suspected heart disease. Moreover, the policy of the consultant at this unit was to discourage surgery, all things being equal, on such children. So the democratic form coexisted with (and was indeed sustained by) the maintenance of an autocratic policy.

The research thus discovered the mechanics whereby a particular medical policy was enacted. The availability of tape recordings of large numbers of consultations, together with a research method that sought to develop hypotheses *inductively* (see Chapter 2), meant that we were able to discover a phenomenon for which we had not originally been looking. More importantly, from the point of view of our present concerns, the research underlined how power can work just as much by encouraging people to speak as by silencing them (see Foucault, 1977, 1979).

'Democratic' decision making and 'whole-patient medicine' are thus revealed as discourses with no intrinsic meaning. Instead, their consequences depend upon their deployment and articulation in particular contexts. So even democracy is not something that we must appeal to in all circumstances. In contexts like this, democratic forms can be part of a power play. As in the previous illustration, we had discovered a surprising fact. In this case, this fact was relevant to an important public debate about the care of disabled children.

Two practical consequences arose from the study of consultations with children with Down's syndrome. First, we asked the doctor concerned to

rethink his policy or at least reveal his hidden agenda to parents. We did not dispute that there are many grounds to treat such children differently from others in relation to surgery. For instance, they have a poorer post-surgical survival rate and most parents are reluctant to contemplate surgery. However, there is a danger of stereotyping the needs of such children and their parents. By 'coming clean' about his policy, the doctor would enable parents to make a more informed choice.

The second practical point, revealed by this research, relates to my earlier remark about the limits of reducing social problems to issues of 'poor communication'. In some respects, this doctor's 'democratic' style seems to fit the requirements of 'good communication'. However, as good practitioners realize, no style of communication is intrinsically superior to another.

Conclusion

In these examples, we see how social research can contribute to the community precisely by insisting on the relevance of its own social science perspectives and refusing to limit its vision to common-sensically defined 'social problems'. By pursuing rigorous, analytically-based research guided by its own sensitivities, we can contribute most to society.

Further reading

Silverman (2001) presents a more detailed

introduction to issues in research methodology, focused on qualitative methods. Hammersley (1995a) contains several relevant essays dealing with the relation between politics and social research. Silverman (1997) is a collection of essays on qualitative research methods with a chapter by Bloor on 'Addressing social problems through social research'.

Student Reader (Seale, 2004): relevant readings

67   Max Weber: 'Science as a vocation'
68   Carol H Weiss: 'The many meanings of research utilization'
70   Julienne Meyer: 'What is action research?'
71   Sandra Harding: 'Is there a feminist method?'
72   Mary Maynard: 'Methods, practice and epistemology: the debate about feminism and research'
73   Les Back and John Solomos: 'Doing research, writing politics the dilemmas of political intervention in research on racism'
74   Martyn Hammersley: 'Hierarchy and emancipation'

Key concepts

Contextual sensitivity	**Partisan** *versus* **scholar**
Ethnic identification devices	**Political sensitivity**
Historical sensitivity	**Social problems**

7

Validity, reliability and the quality of research

Clive Seale

CONTENTS

Discussions of the quality of social and cultural research often begin with the ideas of validity and reliability. These derive from the scientific (sometimes thought of as 'positivist') tradition. Thus **validity** refers to the truth-value of a research project; can we say whether the reported results are true? **Reliability**, on the other hand, concerns the consistency with which research procedures deliver their results (whether or not these are true). Thus we can ask whether a particular questionnaire, if applied on two different occasions to the same person, would generate the same answers. When the concept of reliability is applied to whole research projects, we are asking questions about their **replicability.** That is to say, if we repeated the research project exactly, would we get the same result again? In the scientific tradition, replicable studies using reliable research instruments have been considered essential preconditions for studies that produce valid or true knowledge. Many procedures and techniques have been devised in order to test validity and reliability and this chapter will demonstrate some of these.

However, the scientific discussion of validity and reliability makes assumptions that sit uncomfortably with many conceptions of qualitative social and cultural research. The interpretive tradition (see Chapter 4) comes in many guises, of course, but some forms of this research reject *realism* as an adequate basis for judging the value of research studies, substituting a variety of *idealist* philosophical conceptions, or indeed political conceptions of the value of research. Scientific discussions of validity and reliability are firmly rooted in the realist tradition. Here, the task of the researcher is to find something out about the world and report findings in an objective, value-free manner. If, however, research knowledge itself is treated as a *social construction*, it is hard to sustain a commitment to realism and objectivity. Other criteria must then be used to judge the quality or value of a research study. Perhaps, for example, the quality of a study can be judged according to whether it promotes insight, understanding or dialogue, or in terms of whether it gives voice to particular social groups whose perspective has been hidden from public view. This chapter will first introduce you to scientific conceptions of validity, reliability and replicability and will then show you how a variety of qualitative researchers in the interpretive tradition have approached the issue of judging the quality of their work. The chapter will conclude with some comments about how you may be able to use these discussions to inform your own research practice.

The scientific tradition

In this tradition validity is understood to have various components. These are indicated in Box 7.1.

Measurement validity

The **measurement validity** of questions in interviews and questionnaires can be improved by various methods (see Chapter 13 for an account of how to design questions for social surveys). The first and perhaps most common method is known as **face validity,** whereby the researcher thinks hard about whether the questions indicate the intended concept. The assessment of face validity may be helped by asking people with practical or professional knowledge of the area to assess how well questions indicate the concept, including their judgements of how comprehensively the various aspects of the concept have been covered.

Box 7.1 The components of validity

- *Measurement validity*: the degree to which measures (for example, questions on a questionnaire) successfully indicate concepts
- *Internal validity*: the extent to which causal statements are supported by the study
- *External validity*: the extent to which findings can be generalized to populations or to other settings

---

Thus a sequence of questions designed to indicate a person's health status might be assessed by a group of nurses or doctors (the term content validity is also sometimes used to describe such assessment by experts).

Criterion validity involves comparing the results of questions with established indicators of the same concept. Criterion validity can be **concurrent** or **predictive**. Concurrent criterion validity might, for example, involve comparing the results of an interview survey of people's health status with the results of a doctor's examination of the same people done at around the same time. If the interview results differ from the doctor's assessment, the interview would be judged to have poor validity. Predictive criterion validity involves comparisons with what happens in the future. For example, the validity of examinations at school in measuring academic ability might be judged by seeing whether these are good at predicting eventual degree results.

Construct validity evaluates a measure according to how well it conforms to expectations derived from theory. Thus, if we have reason to believe that health status is related to social class, we would expect our measure of health status to give different results for people from different social classes. The construct validity of certain questions may only be established after a series of studies and analyses in which researchers build up a greater understanding of how the questions relate to other constructs.

None of these methods of improving measurement validity is perfect. Argument about the face validity of indicators often reveals disagreement about the meaning of concepts. For example, what do we mean by 'health'? Although our indicator may agree with some external criterion, who is to say that the external criterion is valid? Thus a doctor's judgement about health status is not infallible; sometimes people get poor degrees for reasons other than their academic ability. Construct validity depends both on a theory being correct, and on other measures of other concepts in the theory being valid. If social class is not related to health, or if our measure of social class is itself not valid, then associations between health and social class cannot show the validity of our measure of health.

Internal validity

It is important to have valid measures if **internal validity** is to be sustained, but this is not the only necessary component. In order to prove that one thing (A) has caused another (B) three basic conditions must be met. First, A must precede B in time (the problem of **time order**). Secondly, A must be associated with B. That is to say, when the measure of A changes, the measure of B must also change. Thirdly, the association must not be caused by some third factor C (the problem of **spurious causation**).

Thus, in examining the hypothesis that people with a higher educational level (A) therefore subsequently achieve higher income levels (B) it is no good if a person's income is assessed before their education is complete (a time order problem). Additionally, there is unlikely to be a causal relationship if people with a high educational achievement do not differ from those with a low educational achievement in their incomes (in which case we would say that there is no association between the variables). Most difficult to establish in social research, however, is the issue of whether some third variable – such as parental social class (C) – is associated with both educational achievement (for example, rich parents send their children to private schools) and income (for example, a private income from family wealth). In this case, an apparent relationship between education and income may be spurious since both educational achievement and income have been affected by the third variable. Ensuring that causal statements are valid is a matter of research design and the adequacy of statistical analysis and will be covered in later chapters (particularly Chapter 25). The example in Box 7.2 will also help you understand the ideas involved.

External validity

In social survey work, done in the scientific tradition, external validity is ensured by representative *sampling*, techniques for which are described in Chapter 13. Since a researcher cannot study everyone in a population (unless they do a complete census of all members of that population), there is inevitably a degree of selection involved in choos-

---

Box 7.2 Connecticut traffic fatalities

The causal proposition
In 1960 the Governor of Connecticut announced that a police crackdown on speeding and drunk drivers had resulted in a dramatic reduction from the alarmingly high rate of traffic fatalities that had been evident in 1955.

Threats to internal validity
Campbell (1969) listed a number of 'threats' to this as a causal claim, including:

- *History*: For example, the weather might have been better in later years resulting in fewer accidents.
- *Maturation*: Drivers may have been getting more careful anyway.
- *Instability and regression*: Traffic fatality rates go up and down from year to year anyway: 1956 just happened to have a high number of fatalities. In subsequent years a 'regression towards the mean' was therefore pretty likely.
- *Testing*: Perhaps publishing the high 1955 death rate made people more careful when driving.
- *Instrumentation*: Perhaps the method for estimating number of deaths changed. For example, in 1955 death could have been recorded according to whether people resided in Connecticut, whereas in 1956 death might have been recorded according to place of death (or vice versa).
- *Selection*: This would occur, for example, if the population of Connecticut had undergone a change. Perhaps an economic boom produced an influx of young male drivers with cheap cars during the high fatality year.
- *Experimental mortality*: Perhaps fewer counties in the state returned death statistics in one year compared to the other.

---

ing people (or settings) to study. Representative sampling seeks to ensure that the people (or settings) studied are not unusual or atypical in any way, so that what is discovered about them may also hold true for others in the population. Usually, *statistical inference* is used to make a probabilistic estimate of the likelihood that a result in a randomly selected sample is a freak occurrence (see Chapter 24).

However, it is quite common for there to be shortcomings in the degree to which social and psychological research done from within the scientific tradition deals with external validity. This can be particularly evident in *experiments* where people are recruited as volunteers. An experimenter may discover that a group of volunteers behave in a certain way under experimental conditions, but if the volunteers are different from the people to whom the result is to be generalized, external validity may be poor. Additionally, an

experimental situation may not be very good at mimicking the conditions of real life.

Consider the traffic fatalities example (Box 7.1). Imagine that the problems of internal validity were overcome. As a complete census of Connecticut drivers, there would be no problem then in drawing conclusions about police influence on drivers' behaviour in Connecticut. But if drivers' attitudes to the police, or indeed police behaviour during crackdowns were different in other places, a different impact on driver behaviour might be experienced.

Reliability and replicability

A study can be reliable without being valid. Consider an archery target: arrows can strike it consistently (reliably) in the wrong place. Thus a measurement can be consistently wrong. At the same time, as the second target shows, a valid

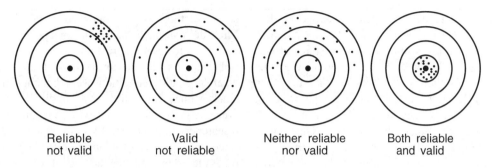

| Reliable | Valid | Neither reliable | Both reliable |
| not valid | not reliable | nor valid | and valid |

Figure 7.1   *The relationship between reliability and validity (Trochim, 2003)*

measure is not necessarily reliable if the object being measured is changing: perhaps the target is moving? Figure 7.1 shows these ideas in visual form. See if you can interpret the third and fourth targets.

In the realist, scientific tradition it is important to get consistent results when observations are being made, or questions are being asked. If different researchers use the same interview schedule it is no good if they get different results with the same person (assuming that the person has not changed their views between interviews). Similarly, if researchers applying a *coding scheme* (see Chapter 23) for analysing data disagree amongst each other about how to assign codes, it is hard to place much faith in their objectivity. For this reason questionnaires, interview schedules, measuring devices of various sorts and coding schemes are often subjected to tests of their reliability, sometimes involving **inter-rater** or **inter-coder reliability tests**. Thus a questionnaire designed to measure political preferences might be tested by being applied to the same group of respondents twice by different researchers. If the results are the same each time, even though different researchers have used it, the questionnaire is said to be reliable. If different researchers categorize the same qualitative answers from a survey in the same way, inter-coder reliability is said to be high.

More broadly, replicability is at stake when comparing different studies of the same problem that have used the same or similar methods. In the early days of scientific studies it was considered important to develop a style of research reporting so that other investigators could repeat studies and, hopefully, get the same results. This would then increase faith in the truth-value of the findings because they would be seen to have been replicated by other investigators. For this reason, accounts of method in research reports may be quite detailed.

The interpretivist tradition

It would be wrong to say that all qualitative, interpretivist approaches to research make a radical break with the conceptions of validity and reliability thus far outlined. Quite a lot of qualitative researchers pursue a broadly *realist* and scientific agenda, and so can often apply the ideas of internal and external validity and reliability to their work, though some modifications may be necessary. In other cases, though, particularly if associated with *idealist* and *social constructionist* perspectives, this is a greater problem and quite different notions of quality come into play. These reflect profoundly different conceptions about the purposes and status of the knowledge that researchers produce and ultimately relate to differing philosophical and political considerations. I will therefore first describe modifications and then radical breaks from the scientific tradition.

Modifications

Realist qualitative or interpretivist research often involves intensive study of single settings (*case studies*) or a small number of people. In *ethnography*, for example, a researcher may spend a considerable amount of time participating in the everyday life of a particular social group so that it can be studied in considerable depth (see Chapter 17). The advantage of doing this is often claimed to be that of **naturalism**; the capacity to reveal how people behave as they ordinarily ('naturally') go about their lives. This is felt to contrast with less naturalistic methods (such as inter-views) which temporarily extract people from their daily lives so that they can answer questions about events that they may not actually have to face in real life, or about which they may give misleading answers. Qualitative, exploratory interviews, though, are sometimes said to be superior to the structured ones favoured by survey researchers in the scientific tradition in that they allow the perspectives and priorities of individuals to be revealed, without imposition of the pre-conceptions of the researcher (see Chapter 14).

Both ethnographic method and qualitative interviewing are very time-consuming, though, and can normally only be applied to very few cases, settings or people. In other words, the *breadth* of a social survey may be sacrificed for *depth*, meaning that representativeness and therefore *external validity* may be seen as questionable. At the same time, an exploratory approach can reveal phenomena that have not been predicted in advance. Thus it can be said that quantitative research often establishes the prevalence of things already known about, whereas in-depth case study research can find things that no one has ever noticed before. Originality and discovery, then, might be seen as indicators of the quality of qualitative research, with external validity being of lesser importance. Some people (for example, Mitchell, 1983) have expressed this as **theoretical generalization**, contrasting this with the 'empirical generalization' of statistical studies. This is because, when a new phenomenon is discovered, its importance can only be judged by reference to its contribution to some existing body of knowledge, or 'theory'. Thus, discovering a black stone on a pebble beach may seem to be of no great importance in its own right, but if such a discovery is made in an area where geological conditions were thought to make black stones impossible, the finding acquires greater significance. This is why some qualitative researchers nowadays like to speak about 'theorizing' an area of inquiry: only when a finding is placed in a relevant theoretical context can it acquire significance, so a knowledge of social theory may be particularly important for qualitative inquirers. Chapter 5 discusses a variety of ways in which social theory can be incorporated into research practice.

Additionally, *internal validity* may take on a different meaning in interpretivist research. Causal inquiry has got itself a bad name in some qualitative research circles, being associated with a *deterministic* model of human agency that denies the capacity of people to exercise free will and fails to explore meaning-making activities in social life (see the discussion of *action theory* in Chapter 4). Yet causal statements are pretty much inevitable in any discussion of human social and cultural life. If you look closely at research reports they will always contain implied causal mechanisms. Box 7.3 contains an illustration of this. Additionally, not all statistical work is devoted to proving causality, but instead is descriptive. It is true to say, though, that proving the existence of causality is only very rarely an interest of qualitative researchers, so scientific notions of internal validity are not much use in assessing the quality of such studies.

Measurement validity, which has been shown to be an essential precondition for the *internal*

Box 7.3 Implicit causal reasoning in a qualitative study

'The general region from which the immigrant came was also important in the organization of Cornerville life. The North Italians, who had greater economic and educational opportunities, always looked down upon the southerners, and the Sicilians occupied the lowest position of all' (Whyte, *Street Corner Society*, 1981: xvii).

Whyte, in this passage of 'description', is proposing a causal relationship between region of origin and Cornerville pecking order. Further, he is suggesting that economic and educational differences between Italian regions influence this.

validity of statistical studies, might be seen quite straightforwardly as an important aspect of quality in qualitative research. Of course, measurement may not be something attempted by qualitative researchers (although they may sometimes count things), but the underlying issue in measurement validity is the adequacy of links between concepts and their indicators (**concept–indicator links**). These links are important in qualitative research too, and *grounded theory* is an approach that prioritizes the creation of good concept–indicator links. Chapter 18 describes grounded theory in depth but for the moment you should note that it is based on creating new concepts and ideas and the relations between them (in other words, *theory*) from observations of social settings. This contrasts with an approach that starts with theory and then seeks empirical examples. As a result, research reports based on grounded theorizing generally exhibit excellent links between concepts and the examples drawn from data. In this sense, qualitative researchers can be thought of as being concerned with a form of 'measurement validity'. A good qualitative report exemplifies concepts with good examples.

Yet there are recognizable difficulties in applying the scientific paradigm to qualitative research work. Various authors have therefore proposed modified schemes. Lincoln and Guba's (1985) account of quality issues in what they call 'naturalistic inquiry' (drawing on the meaning of *naturalism* that refers to the study of people in their normal, or 'natural' settings) is one such effort and is shown in Box 7.4.

These authors are critical of the notion of 'truth-value,' saying that it assumes a 'single tangible reality that an investigation is intended to unearth and display' (1985: 294), whereas the naturalistic researcher makes 'the assumption of multiple constructed realities' (1985: 295). In this respect they reveal a dissatisfaction with crude realism and appear to be moving towards a *social constructionist epistemological* position (see Chapters 2 and 4). They argue, then, that **credibility** should replace 'truth-value'. Through prolonged engagement in the field, persistent observation and *triangulation* exercises, as well as exposure of the research report to criticism by other researchers and a search for *negative instances* that challenge emerging hypotheses and demand their reformulation, credibility is built up.

Triangulation is a technique advocated by Denzin (1978) for validating observational data. Denzin outlines the following four types of triangulation.

1 *Data triangulation* involves using diverse sources of data, so that one seeks out instances of a phenomenon in several different settings, at different points in time or space. Richer descriptions of phenomena then result.
2 *Investigator triangulation* involves team research; with multiple observers in the field, engaging in continuing discussion of their points of difference and similarity, personal biases can be reduced.
3 *Theory triangulation* suggests that researchers approach data with several hypotheses in mind,

---

Box 7.4   Lincoln and Guba's translation of terms

Conventional inquiry	*Naturalistic inquiry*
Truth-value (Internal validity)	**Credibility**
Applicability (External validity)	**Transferability**
Consistency (Reliability)	**Dependability**
Neutrality (Objectivity)	**Confirmability**

to see how each fares in relation to the data.

4 *Methodological triangulation* is the most widely understood and applied approach. This, for Denzin, ideally involves a 'between-method' approach, which can take several forms but, classically, might be illustrated by a combination of ethnographic observation with interviews. Additionally, methodological triangulation is frequently cited as a rationale for mixing qualitative and quantitative methods in a study (see Chapter 22).

Negative instances are instances of data (sometimes also called 'deviant cases') that contradict emerging analyses, generalizations and theories. Discovery of these can have a variety of effects, sometimes leading to the abandonment of ideas, but more often to a deeper analysis that accounts for a wider variety of circumstances. An example of a negative instance found in a research study that extended an initial analysis produced by another investigator, is shown in Box 7.6.

Returning to Lincoln and Guba (Box 7.4), these authors also advise researchers to 'earmark' a portion of data to be excluded from the main analysis, returned to later once analysis has been done in order to check the applicability of concepts. But 'the most crucial technique for establishing credibility', they say, is through 'member checks' (1985: 314), showing materials such as interview transcripts and research reports to the people on whom the research has been done, so that they can indicate their agreement or disagreement with the way in which the researcher has represented them (this can also be called **member validation**).

'Applicability', in Lincoln and Guba's view, depends on generalizing from a sample to a population on the untested assumption that the 'receiving' population is similar to that of the 'sending' sample. The *naturalistic* inquirer, on the other hand, would claim the potential uniqueness of *every* local context. This means study of both sending and receiving contexts so that **transferability** is established. This is clearly quite demanding and, apart from *theoretical generalization* (see above), other conceptions of transferability in qualitative research are possible. For example, it can be argued that a very detailed or *thick* description of a setting can give a reader of a research report the vicarious experience of 'being there', in the same way as a good travel writer can facilitate armchair 'travelling' (Geertz, 1973, 1988). The reader is then well equipped to assess the similarity of the setting described in the research report to settings in which she or he has personal experience (see Chapter 17 for a discussion of thick description).

Box 7.5 An example of methodological triangulation

Rossman and Wilson (1994) describe a project to investigate the impact on school organization of state authorities' introduction of minimum competency tests in schools. This combined qualitative interviews with school teachers and other educationists in 12 school districts with a postal questionnaire of a larger sample. Analysis of the questionnaire results suggested that curricular adjustments were more common in school districts where teachers reported that their relationship with state educational authorities was 'positive'. The qualitative interviews sought and found corroboration of this. Thus, for example, in a district where no changes occurred in the curriculum, a local administrator said 'The state has become someone we have to beat rather than a partner to work with' (1994: 320–1). The authors go on to say:

'On the other extreme was a district that accepted the state's increased role in monitoring educational outcomes and worked hard to find creative instructional techniques to improve student performance. The qualitative descriptions of how these two districts responded to the state mandate corroborated and offered convergence to the quantitative findings' (1994: 321).

Box 7.6 Typifications and personal responsibility in hospital casualty departments

The initial generalization (Jeffery, 1979)
In hospital casualty departments, staff categorize patients as 'bad' if they have problems deemed to be trivial, or are drunks, tramps or victims of self-harm. On the other hand, if patients have problems which allow doctors to practise and learn new clinical skills, or test the professional knowledge of staff, they are categorized as 'good'.

The negative instance (Dingwall and Murray, 1983)
Children in casualty departments often exhibit the qualities identified by Jeffery as being those of the 'bad' adult patients, being uncooperative for example, or suffering from mild or self-inflicted injuries. Yet staff do not treat them harshly.

Reformulation of the generalization by Dingwall and Murray, (1983)
Labels applied by staff depend on a prior assessment of whether patients are perceived as being able to make choices (children are not, adults are, on the whole). Children are therefore generally 'forgiven' behaviour that in adults would be deemed reprehensible on the grounds that children are understandably irresponsible. Additionally, staff assess whether the situation is such that patients are able to make choices. Thus, some adults might be categorized as being present in casualty inappropriately, rather than being 'bad' patients if the events that led them there are not their 'fault' (for example, they had had poor advice to go to casualty from a person in authority).

To replace consistency, or *reliability* as conventionally conceived, Lincoln and Guba propose **dependability**, which can be achieved by a procedure which they call **auditing**. This involves 'auditors' scrutinizing the adequacy of an 'audit trail', consisting of the researchers' documentation of data, methods and decisions made during a project, as well as its end product. Auditing is also useful in establishing **confirmability**, Lincoln and Guba's fourth criterion, designed to replace the conventional criterion of neutrality or objectivity. Auditing is also an exercise in **reflexivity** which involves the provision of a methodologically self-critical account of how the research was done. The authors conclude by pointing out that the trustworthiness of a qualitative, naturalistic study is always negotiable and open-ended, not being a matter of final proof whereby readers are compelled to accept an account.

Lincoln and Guba's philosophical position is (at this stage in their writing) half-way between *realism* and *idealism*. As we saw, they are dissatisfied with the crude realism that they feel characterizes the conventional, scientific view of validity and reliability and, at some points, speak of 'multiple realities,' something which is normally associated with a *social constructionist*, idealist view (see Chapter 2). Another way of describing such half-way positions is Hammersley's (1992c) term: **subtle realism**. Here, there is recognition of the existence of a social world that exists independently of the researcher's mind, but also recognition of the impossibility of knowing this world in any final, certain sense. Research reports can only approach reality in various ways.

This subtle realist position, for Hammersley, leads to an emphasis on the **plausibility** and the *credibility* of research reports. In assessing the claims made in a research report Hammersley argues that we should first assess how plausible these are in the light of what is already known about the subject. If a research study contradicts existing knowledge we need quite compelling evidence in support of its claims. Credibility refers to the adequacy of the links between claims and evidence within the report. It is important to provide the strongest of evidence for the most important claims; lesser claims may need less stringent proof. Additionally, we may wish to assess the *relevance* of a research study for political, policy-related or practical concerns (see Chapter 6).

Hammersley has been described as a **post-positivist**, signalling his position as one who modifies 'positivist' or 'scientific' conceptions of validity and reliability in order to apply somewhat similar thinking to qualitative, interpretivist research work. Also within this post-positivist tradition can be placed the work of Becker (1970) and Glaser and Strauss (1967). A later writer who adopts a somewhat scientific conception of the quality of qualitative research is Silverman (2001). These authors represent a tradition that has advocated a number of practical ways in which the quality of qualitative research may be enhanced, listed in Box 7.7 along with references to fuller discussions. Some of these have been mentioned in this chapter or are explained more fully elsewhere in this book. Not all of these authors would agree on all of these things, and their discussions of them contain many subtleties and reservations that cannot be discussed fully here, but you can use the items as a guide to further exploration of these issues and techniques.

Radical conceptions

Lincoln and Guba occupy an interesting position in these debates because, even in their 1985 book, they sat rather uneasily in the *post-positivist* or *subtle realist* camp. In later work (Guba and Lincoln, 1994) they reveal a more radical position and it is worth examining the shift in their thinking that occurs here since it gets to the heart of the difference between the modified and the radical views.

As we saw, at one point they referred to 'multiple constructed realities' lying at the heart of their position, thus revealing themselves to be, at the philosophical level, occupying a *relativist* or *social constructionist* position (see Chapter 2). In this respect they differ from post-positivists like Hammersley, though by 1985 it seems they had not fully worked through the implications of this for research practice. Relativism, if applied to the truth status of research reports themselves, suggests that these are humanly constructed 'versions' of the world, perhaps written out of a commitment to certain value positions or political interests. This contrasts with a view of research as an objective report on the world. Instead, research reports are really no more than 'representations' of the social and cultural world and should be

---

Box 7.7 Ways of enhancing the quality of qualitative research

- *Triangulation* (Seale, 1999: ch. 5; see also Box 7.5)
- *Member validation* (Seale, 1999: ch. 5)
- Search and account for *negative instances* or deviant cases that contradict emerging ideas (Seale, 1999: ch. 6; see also Box 7.6)
- Produce *well-grounded theory* with good examples of concepts (Seale, 1999: ch. 7; Chapter 18 in this book)
- Demonstrate the *originality* of findings by relating these to current social issues or social theories (Seale, 1999: ch. 8; Mitchell, 1983; Chapters 5 and 6 in this book)
- *Combine* qualitative and quantitative methods (Seale, 1999: chs 8 and 9; Chapter 22 in this book)
- Use *low inference descriptors* that show the reader a very full account of observations made, reducing the extent to which the researcher's interpretations are involved in recording raw data, as in conversation analytic transcriptions (Seale, 1999: ch. 10; Chapter 28 in this book)
- Present a *reflexive account* of the research process so that the reader can see where the ideas and claims come from (Seale, 1999: ch. 11; Chapter 3 in this book)

assessed as 'partial truths' (Clifford and Marcus, 1986). Chapter 17 assesses the application of this view to ethnography, demonstrating that – particularly in the discipline of anthropology – a view of research as representation has led to a deeper understanding of the political uses of research knowledge. In the case of anthropology, for example, a view has emerged that is highly critical of the involvement of this (supposedly 'objective') discipline in supporting oppressive colonialist views.

Bauman (1987) is another writer who has thought deeply about the politics of research knowledge. He distinguishes between two positions on this, which can be broadly equated with those of *post-positivism* and *postmodernism*.

- One view of research knowledge, Bauman argues, is that it is an attempt to *legislate* on the truth, so that debates can be resolved once and for all. The researcher occupies a superior position, employing methods that provide a better, more authoritative view than those employed in everyday life.
- A second view, though, is that researchers are more like *interpreters*, who generate conversations between groups of people who may not yet have communicated. Thus a researcher or an intellectual, Bauman says, occupies a facilitative role in society, encouraging debate rather than ruling on the truth.

Research understood from this second perspective starts to lose its distinction from social commentary. The distinction between 'data' and 'theory' begins to break down, being revealed as a hangover from a past scientific age. Data, after all, is pre-constituted by the theories and values of the researcher so that it cannot be regarded as an objective account of reality (see Chapter 2). Rather than looking to the inner qualities of a research account in order to judge its quality, some say that it would therefore be better to examine the effects of a research study in society in order to see whether it is good or bad. In their 1994 book, Guba and Lincoln begin to outline this view by presenting a fifth criterion for judging the quality of naturalistic inquiry: **authenticity**.

In describing this Guba and Lincoln reveal a sympathy for political conceptions of the role of research that goes several steps beyond Hammersley's concern with political and practical *relevance* (see earlier). Authenticity, they say, is demonstrated if researchers can show that they have represented a range of different realities ('fairness'). Research should also help people develop 'more sophisticated' understandings of the phenomenon being studied ('ontological authenticity'), be shown to have helped people appreciate the viewpoints of people other than themselves ('educative authenticity'), to have stimulated some form of action ('catalytic authenticity') and to have empowered people to act ('tactical authenticity').

Of course, the view that fairness, sophistication, mutual understanding and empowerment are generally desirable is itself a value-laden position. It represents an attempt to pull back from the relativist abyss by founding research practice on a bedrock of political values. Attempts to implement 'democratic' values like this are not always appreciated by people who prefer to organize their lives and political systems according to alternative values. But it can be seen that Guba and Lincoln have travelled on a path beginning with a rejection of *positivist* criteria and the substitution of *interpretivist* alternatives. Dissatisfied with the limitations of these, *constructivism* has been embraced, introducing an element of *relativism*. Political versions of the value of research have then been imported to save facing the logical implications of relativism, which might end in a nihilistic vision and abandonment of the research enterprise.

This is a path that other qualitative researchers have trodden. Working together with Yvonna Lincoln, Norman Denzin has been influential in promoting political conceptions of the research enterprise, arguing that qualitative research has reached a moment in its development where postmodernist and constructivist influences have resulted in a 'crisis of legitimation'. They argue that

> The qualitative researcher is not an objective, authoritative, politically neutral observer standing outside and above the text … Qualitative inquiry is properly conceptu-

alized as a civic, participatory, collabora-tive project. This joins the researcher and the researched in an ongoing moral dia-logue. (Denzin and Lincoln, 2000: 1049)

This follows on from an earlier statement in which they say that a central commitment of qualitative researchers remains

> in the humanistic commitment of the quali-tative researcher to study the world always from the perspective of the interacting indi-vidual. From this simple commitment flow the liberal and radical politics of qualitative research. Action, feminist, clinical, con-structivist, ethnic, critical and cultural stud-ies researchers are all united on this point. They all share the belief that a politics of liberation must always begin with the per-spectives, desires, and dreams of those indi-viduals and groups who have been oppressed by the larger ideological, eco-nomic, and political forces of a society, or a historical moment. (Denzin and Lincoln, 1994: 575)

As a criterion for judging the quality of research it is immediately obvious that this is open to dis-pute. It is not difficult to imagine a well-conducted study that enabled people in positions of power to achieve their aims. The vision of society as no more than a system inhabited by oppressors and oppressed also seems naive (see also Hammersley, 1995). Research can at times be more relevant to

direct political projects, at others less relevant, but its quality is an issue somewhat independent of this.

Conclusion: how to use these discussions

As a practising researcher you may be wondering which of these conceptions suits you best. Are you going to commit yourself to a scientific vision in which you prioritize objectivity and replicability, or to a post-positivist position in which you retain some of this commitment in a modified form, or will you reject these in favour of a political con-ception of the research process? Clearly, the views of the various authors are often incompatible. It seems wrong to develop a measuring instrument that can be judged reliable and valid if the measur-ing instrument is really no more than an imposi-tion of a particular, value-laden vision of the world on oppressed people. It seems foolish to assess a research report solely according to its political consequences if its findings and claims are poorly supported with evidence, or if the analysis of evidence is clearly influenced by the researcher's values.

In these disputatious circumstances many re-searchers seem to feel that they must belong to one camp or another, to identify themselves as 'scien-tists', 'subtle realists' or 'radical constructionists' before they begin their research activities. In my view this is a mistake. Many of the disputes that exist at the level of methodological debate are sim-ply not resolvable by further discussion, but are a

---

Box 7.9 Web pointers for validity, reliability and quality

Research methods knowledge base
http://trochim.human.cornell.edu/kb/contents.htm

Measurement validity and reliability
www.lwc.edu/staff/dkelley/Socl345/validity/

Validity and reliability in quantitative research
www.qmuc.ac.uk/psych/RTrek/study_notes/web/sn3.htm

Reliability and validity in qualitative research
www.qmuc.ac.uk/psych/RTrek/study_notes/web/sn5.htm

Visit the website for this book at www.rscbook.co.uk to link to these web pointers.

matter of preference. Depending on the actual topic of the research and the problems that are seen to be central, certain considerations will always be more important than others. The personal biographical situation and local circumstances of researchers and their likely audiences are the main influences on how projects proceed and quality is judged. Exposure to methodological discussions such as the ones outlined in this chapter can help in producing generalized methodological awareness that can be helpful when actually carrying out a research project or intellectual inquiry. Thus a researcher who is aware of these debates is more likely than one who is not to produce a research study that is sophisticated. That is to say, it will be a study that is sensitive to a variety of ways in which it is

possible to proceed, show awareness of the consequences of particular decisions made during the course of the study, and the eventual report will demonstrate to a variety of potential audiences that something of value has been created.

Further reading

This chapter is a condensed and simplified version of a book on the quality of qualitative research which I wrote (Seale, 1999) and which is the best place to start in expanding your knowledge of this area. The book contains an account of validity and reliability in the quantitative tradition as well. There are relevant chapters by Gobo, Flybjerg and Seale in *Qualitative Research Practice* (Seale et al., 2004).

Student Reader (Seale, 2004): relevant readings

6   Thomas D. Cook and Donald T. Campbell: 'Validity'
25   R.C. Lewontin: 'Sex lies and social science'
35   Martyn Hammersley: 'Some reflections on ethnography and validity'
48   Anssi Peräkylä:'Reliability and validity in research based on tapes and transcripts'
62   Zygmunt Bauman: 'Intellectuals: from modern legislators to post-modern interpreters'
65   Patti Lather: 'Fertile obsession: validity after poststructuralism'
66   Thomas A. Schwandt: 'Farewell to criteriology'
79   Maureen Cain and Janet Finch: 'Towards a rehabilitation of data'

Key concepts

Auditing	**Member validation**
Authenticity	**Naturalism**
Concept-indicator links	**Plausibility**
Confirmability	**Post-positivism**
Construct validity	**Reflexivity**
Credibility	**Reliability**
Criterion validity (concurrent and predictive)	**Replicability**
Dependability	**Spurious causation**
External validity	**Subtle realism**
Face validity	**Theoretical generalization**
Inter-coder/inter-rater reliability	**Time order**
Internal validity	**Transferability**
Measurement validity	**Validity**

8

History of social statistics and the social survey

Fran Tonkiss

CONTENTS

This chapter describes the origins of statistical and survey methods for the investigation of social life. Focusing on developments in the nineteenth and early twentieth centuries, the discussion outlines how these techniques came to produce new kinds of knowledge about modern populations, recording, measuring and comparing a range of factors from poverty and disease to crime and race.

The discussion begins by looking at the emergence of statistics in the late eighteenth and early nineteenth century. Collection of social statistics was an important element in the project of a science of society. Many early statistical thinkers saw society as organized by 'laws' that could be quantified and predicted through research, and adjusted by rational and informed policy measures. From the outset, these methods of social investigation were closely tied to programmes of government and social reform. The central part of the chapter concerns the origins of the social survey in the massive poverty studies undertaken by Booth and Rowntree in late Victorian Britain, as these sought to develop more rigorous methods of social investigation and to produce sounder knowledge about the causes of poverty. The discussion goes on to look at the emergence of the survey at this time in the United States, before considering more recent developments in such fields as marketing, opinion polling, public policy and academic research.

Recent critical accounts of social research methods have emphasized that the forms in which we gather, record and analyse data about different social factors have important consequences for the way we define, interpret and understand social relations, social groups and social problems. The chapter concludes by considering these critiques in relation to traditions of quantitative social research.

The origins of social statistics

Surveys and social statistics developed in the nineteenth century as important new methods for gathering information about the population. This is not to say, however, that the idea of counting and categorizing groups of people or collecting information relating to their conditions of life was itself a new idea. Early demographic studies, for example, were developed during the seventeenth and eighteenth centuries in England, Ireland and Scotland by such figures as Graunt, Petty and King, and used to record distributions of population, mortality and property. This **'political arithmetic'** of population and wealth became central to debates concerning changing social and economic conditions, as exemplified in Britain by the fears over population growth stirred by Thomas Malthus's 1798 *Essay on Population* (see Box 8.1). Such arguments helped galvanize Parliament to legislate for the collection of the first census in Britain in 1801. The population by these means came to be thought about not just as a mass of people but also as a set of demographic variables that might be measured in terms of size, distribution and growth, and increasingly in terms of a plethora of local rates of disease, marriage, age, employment, wealth, birth, death and so on. By the end of the eighteenth century, Bulmer et al.

Box 8.1   Thomas Malthus (1798) on population growth

'The population of the Island [Great Britain] is computed to be about seven millions, and we will suppose the present produce equal to the support of such a number. In the first twenty-five years the population would be fourteen millions, and the food being also doubled, the means of subsistence would be equal to this increase. In the next twenty-five years the population would be twenty-eight millions, and the means of subsistence only equal to the support of twenty-one millions. In the next period, the population would be fifty-six millions, and the means of subsistence just sufficient for half that number. And at the conclusion of the first century the population would be one hundred and twelve millions and the means of subsistence only equal to the support of thirty-five millions, which would leave a population of seventy-seven millions totally unprovided for.'

(1991: 6) note, the term 'statistics' had become established in the English language to describe inquiries of this kind.

The early history of 'social accounting' reflects an emergent concern with the size, distribution and condition of people, property and wealth. However, the desire to enumerate was, until the nineteenth century, not matched by effective or systematic counting and recording techniques. The 1801 census itself was rather patchy in terms of its methods of collection and the information it sought to gather. It was not until later in that century that more organized methods of information gathering and recording were developed, and it is at this point that we can begin to speak of social statistics and the social survey 'proper'.

There are two important things to note about the early development of social statistics.

- First, such inquiry was greatly influenced by models derived from the natural sciences. Early statisticians followed the example of natural scientists in their conviction that fact gathering on a large scale might lead to the development of positive knowledge about the nature of society. Indeed, it was widely held that the systematic collection of numerical facts could be used to establish certain causal 'laws' that governed social life and helped to produce regular patterns of poverty, indolence and crime (see Hacking, 1990).
- Secondly, the development of social statistics frequently was tied to questions of government and social reform. The population debate of the eighteenth century, associated with the work of Malthus, is one significant example of a set of social and economic problems which statistics appeared capable of settling. Was the population growing or declining? Were the poorer classes outstripping other classes of society? Was the wealth of the nation increasing or decreasing? The 1801 census offered a rather crude but nevertheless *empirical* response to these questions, in that it was based on systematic data collection rather than on theory or speculation. Numerical facts were intended to provide a basis for politicians and reformers to make rational and informed decisions about economic and social policy.

The shortcomings of the 1801 census served only to reinforce the commitment to producing sound numerical information about social conditions. In a rapidly changing society marked by accelerating urbanization and industrialization, and by the growth of middle-class and working-class radicalism, it appeared increasingly important to members of the governing class to monitor both the condition of different groups in society and any 'trends' towards social and economic decline and disintegration.

The main forums for providing these analyses were the **statistical societies** that emerged in the first half of the nineteenth century. Such societies were formed in a number of cities, first in Manchester in 1833, and then in other cities including London, Bristol, Liverpool, Birmingham, Leeds, Belfast and Glasgow. A common set of concerns emerged in the statistical analyses that members of these societies undertook. In particular, the state of the working classes in terms of their size, housing and employment, crime and destitution, education (and truancy), sanitation, hygiene and disease, preoccupied Victorian social researchers. Such studies aimed both to produce factual knowledge about the extent and distribution of various social 'problems', and to establish the causal patterns that lay behind them. Rawson's 1839 *An Inquiry into the Statistics of Crime in England and Wales,* for example, aimed to show regularities in patterns and rates of crime across these countries. This research was based on analysis of census data together with statistics produced by the judicial system over a five-year period. Alongside crime statistics, the 'vital statistics' of health, illness and mortality were an important feature of the statistical movement. They are especially interesting in indicating the development of a clearly *social* approach to knowledge, linking issues of health and disease not only to physical causes but also to social and economic factors. William Guy's 1843 *An Attempt to Determine the Influence of the Seasons and Weather on Sickness and Mortality*, for instance, looked for correlations between patterns of illness and physical factors such as temperature, but also socio-economic factors such as occupation. William Farr's famous work on medical statistics, too, linked the incidence of cholera to population densities (see Kent, 1981).

The Statistical Society of London had a particularly close relationship to government, providing information directly to parliamentary committees. At the same time government departments were setting up their own statistical sections, such as in the Home Office and the Board of Trade, and in 1836 the General Register Office was established to centrally collate information on births, deaths and marriages. The most comprehensive statistical work at this time was in fact undertaken by government bodies, such as the royal commissions into the Poor Laws and the condition of the Irish poor, and within the factory inspection system.

By the middle of the nineteenth century, then, a speculative and often haphazard desire to produce statistical information had become organized into systematic measures to quantify the population and inform government policy, based on a belief that numerical facts provided the basis for rational and conclusive knowledge about social trends. It was a common conviction that statistical facts would 'speak for themselves', unaffected by the opinions or actions of the researcher. There are two objections to make here.

- The first is that the conclusions established by early social statistics often make it hard to distinguish between Victorian morality and scientific fact.
- This point touches on the second objection to be made to the idea that statistical facts might 'speak for themselves'. Such a notion fails to address the wider social context in which statistics are produced, and the way in which statistical knowledge is taken up and used.

Concerning the first of these points, Kent (1981) cites the case of the Reverend John Clay's 1839 study of the *Criminal Statistics of Preston,* which sought to establish the causes of crime and to analyse annual variations in local crime rates. The causal factors identified by Clay included such categories as drunkenness, idleness, intellectual weakness, the keeping of bad company and temptation (Kent, 1981: 23). While such causal links may be arguable (a relationship between alcohol and crime, for example, is strongly supported by modern criminal statistics), the framing of these categories appears to owe as much to a particular moral standpoint as to the self-evidence of numerical facts. The separation of facts from values in the collection and presentation of data was at best a rather shaky process, and is particularly questionable in light of the political uses which a great deal of social statistics served.

Concerning the second point, the realm of facts that researchers investigated was shaped by the broad political agenda of the day – especially in relation to concerns over the plight of the poorer classes and the unruliness of certain groups in society, with all the associated threat of social disorder. These statistical facts, moreover, were intended to serve political ends. However, while the collection of statistical data sought to establish certain correlations and causal patterns, it could not offer clear guides to policy. Nineteenth-century social statistics were firmly wedded to the concerns of government, yet they could not in themselves suggest the most appropriate ways to initiate social and economic reforms. If statistical facts could not *speak for themselves* independently of either the values of the researcher or the social context of their production, the extent to which they could *speak to* what were ultimately political problems was also rather limited. Information and quantification were not in themselves sufficient grounds for making decisions about the proper government of a modern population.

Exploring by numbers: the social survey in Britain

The concern with social and political problems that animated early social statistics also underlay the development of survey methods in the later part of the nineteenth century. The emergence of the social survey was a critical step forward for social inquiry, based on the first-hand collection of information geared to exploring specific questions, rather than the analysis of varied and sometimes slapdash statistical sources. The early social survey aimed not only to access direct knowledge of people's conditions of social life, but to explore these in a detailed and in-depth manner.

Booth

Charles Booth is a key figure in the development of the social survey as a distinct method for studying social life. Booth's classic study of the *Life and Labour of the People of London* was based on the systematic collection of original and extensive data on the conditions of the urban population. Booth, a wealthy industrialist who was disturbed by the poor conditions of working-class life in late Victorian Britain, began his investigations in 1886 and published them in 17 volumes in 1902. His vast study into the working classes of London was framed by two chief concerns with the social and economic state (the 'life' and 'labour') of this population: focusing attention on the living conditions of working-class families, and the occupation and income of their `breadwinners'. An in-depth study of this massive urban population was made possible not by surveying each house-

hold directly, but by interviewing the school board visitors who had access to each family with children in local schools. Their detailed knowledge of the households in their local district – including the details of their employment, rent and wages - was supplemented by further information obtained from local police, churchmen and district superintendents.

Booth was interested not simply in amassing numerical facts about the population as a whole, but in developing categories to define different social strata. On the basis of his investigations, Booth classified the people of London into distinct social classes, from the 'vicious' and 'semi-criminal' to the wealthy upper classes. He drew a **poverty line** which marked off the comfortable from those living in relative states of poverty. Booth's poor endured lives characterized by economic hardship, lacking in domestic comforts, with low or irregular earnings, while at the bottom end of

---

Box 8.2 Booth's social classes and street colours

Booth assigned a colour letter code to each street according to the social mix of its residents and its general living conditions. The following seven colours were used on his map:

Street Colour	Social Condition	Social Classes
Black	*Lowest class* Vicious, semi-criminal	A
Dark Blue	*Very poor, casual* Chronic want	B
Light Blue	*Poor* 18s. to 21s. a week for a moderate family	C, D
Purple	*Mixed* Some comfortable, others poor	C, D, E, F
Pink	*Fairly comfortable* Good ordinary earnings	E, F
Red	*Middle class* Well-to-do	G
Yellow	*Upper-middle and Upper class* Wealthy	H

As might be expected, black streets were mainly located in inner London areas, and yellow streets were largely located in the more prosperous outer suburbs.

(*Source*: Shepherd, I. (2000) *Booth's Street Colours.* http://mubs.mdx.ac.uk/Staff/Personal_pages/Ifan1/Booth/colours.htm)

his scale, the 'very poor' existed in a state of chronic want. While Booth's methods of classification were somewhat imprecise – a category such as 'loafers', for example, is one that is difficult to specify with any sort of precision, and is distinctly value-laden – his model is important in attempting to distinguish categories amongst the mass of 'the poor'.

Booth began his inquiries in the East End of London, which he took to represent the most destitute population in the city, and predicted that rates of poverty throughout London would tend to be lower than in this especially deprived area. This 'pilot' study recorded details of occupation, income and living conditions for each household in the local survey. Such a method produced an unwieldy mass of data, and in his larger-scale study of London Booth took the street rather than the household as the basic unit of analysis, defining each street in terms of the average condition of its residents. On this basis Booth produced a series of 'poverty maps' that sketched the geography of destitution and privilege across London, something like a street atlas of poverty and wealth (Box 8.2).

Booth's mammoth survey led to two major claims. The first concerned poverty as a moral problem, and specifically its potential threat to social order. Booth concluded that the urban poor did not represent so great a threat to social stability as was frequently imagined by the more feverish moralists of late Victorian times. Rather than constituting a danger to civilized life in the capital, London's poor – though struggling and often living in want – were for the most part respectable and orderly in their conduct and way of life. By dividing up his poor into different classes, Booth was able to demonstrate that the 'undeserving', disreputable or criminal poor made up less than 1% of the urban population.

Booth's second claim concerned the causes of poverty. In order to establish **causal relationships,** Booth took a sample of 4,000 families from his larger study, and analysed the immediate causes of poverty in these cases. The majority showed that poverty could be traced to conditions of employment, such as irregular or low earnings, rather than to moral or individual failings. Booth's systematic approach to social inquiry, while it did

stress economic rather than moral explanations of poverty, did not wholly escape the morality of his time. Some of his findings pointed to correlations between patterns of poverty and 'questions of habit': for example, in around 5% of cases, household poverty was linked to the presence of a 'drunken or thriftless wife'.

Booth's findings contain a further important claim, one that has been backed up by more recent inquiries into patterns of poverty. An unexpected outcome of his comprehensive survey was that rates of poverty throughout London, averaging around 31% for the whole city, were comparable to those Booth discovered in what he had assumed to be the extreme case of the East End. Across the capital, Booth found pockets of destitution and patterns of poverty, often alongside sites of relative privilege. While concentrated areas of material deprivation certainly existed in Victorian London – as they do in twenty-first-century London – Booth's findings indicate that the distribution of poverty was complex and was not reducible to certain poverty 'black spots'. This is in line with much more recent research that contests simplistic accounts of urban deprivation by demonstrating that not all residents of 'inner city' areas are poor, and that not all people living in poverty live in the 'inner city' (for example, Townsend et al., 1987). Booth's approach was distinctive and highly influential in showing the spatial distribution of poverty and wealth, alongside his concern with both structural and personal causal factors.

Rowntree

Booth's work greatly influenced the development of empirical social research into the causes and condition of poverty, and this focus was to define the social survey into the twentieth century. One of the most significant of these studies in Britain was Rowntree's survey undertaken in York and published in 1901 as *Poverty: A Study of Town Life.* Like Booth before him, Rowntree was a prosperous businessman who was concerned by Booth's 'problem of problems' – the persistence and severity of poverty in modern society. Rowntree set out to examine whether the patterns of poverty that Booth uncovered in London were matched by similar conditions in a smaller city such as York.

While Rowntree's study was deeply influenced by Booth's, it involved a number of significant methodological and analytic advances.

- First, Rowntree undertook a comprehensive house-to-house survey of every working-class family in York. Booth's reliance on school board visitors for his data, conversely, meant that his study was limited to only those wage-earning families with children of school age.
- Secondly, Rowntree enlisted interviewers to derive data directly from the survey population themselves, rather than relying on the accounts of informants such as Booth's school board visitors, clergymen and police.
- Rowntree's third critical innovation was to establish a more systematic model for the analysis of poverty and social class (Box 8.3).

In tracing the causes of primary poverty, Rowntree employed rather more rigorous categories than had Booth. He identified six major causal factors, listed in Box 8.4. Of these six immediate causes of primary poverty, Rowntree concluded that the majority of families in York living below the poverty line had a chief wage-earner who was in regular work, but who earned wages that were too low to support the basic physical needs of their family. Low wages, that is, rather than individual or moral failings – as well as circumstances such as illness or family size – constituted the major cause of primary poverty.

While the York study represented a critical advance in the survey as a technique of inquiry into social problems, Rowntree's methodology was not watertight and aspects of his analysis reflected a particular moral standpoint. Informants, who were frequently the wage-earners' wives, could not always be relied upon to know or accurately divulge their husbands earnings. Moreover, the procedure for classifying 'secondary poverty' involved rather subjective assessments of families' spending habits and the appearance of want. While the causal factors established for primary poverty created a picture of the respectable poor, Rowntree tended to attribute secondary poverty to such factors as drink, gambling and improvidence. In spite of this, the use of direct and comprehensive methods and of clear analytic categories marked Rowntree's approach as a clear advance in the development of survey research.

Bowley

In common with Booth's work, Rowntree's investigations were both extremely time-consuming and very costly. This is because they were **censuses** of the entire population covered, rather than **sample surveys** from which generalizations to the population are made on the basis of probabilities. A decade after the publication of these exhaustive urban surveys, an important innovation in social survey research was made in Bowley's study of the wage-earning class in Reading (Bowley and Burnett-Hurst, 1915). Bowley's distinction was to

---

Box 8.3 Rowntree's definitions of primary and secondary poverty

Rowntree distinguished between two basic forms of poverty:

- **Primary poverty** was said to exist where a family's income was insufficient to provide for the basic physical necessities of life – or what Rowntree called 'physical efficiency'.
- **Secondary poverty**, on the other hand, existed where family income would provide for basic physical necessities, but did not allow for any further expenditure. Rowntree's definition of 'physical efficiency' was stringent, allowing for the barest dietary needs of the family, together with a modest provision for rent, clothing and fuel.

Based on this calculation, Rowntree established that average weekly earnings for unskilled labourers in York were insufficient to provide for the essential physical needs of a family.

Box 8.4   Causes of poverty in Rowntree's study

1 Death of chief wage-earner.
2 Incapacity of chief wage-earner through accident, illness, or old age.
3 Chief wage-earner out of work.
4 Chronic irregularity of work (sometimes due to incapacity or unwillingness of worker to undertake regular employment).
5 Largeness of family, i.e. cases in which the family is in poverty because there are more than four children, though it would not have been in poverty had the number of children not exceeded four.
6 Lowness of wage, i.e. where the chief wage-earner is in regular work, but at wages which are insufficient to maintain a moderate family (i.e. not more than four children) in a state of physical efficiency.

(*Source*: Rowntree, S. (1901) *Poverty: A Study of Town Life* London: Macmillan. pp.119–20)

See also:
www2.arts.gla.ac.uk/History/ESH/rowntree/contents.html

---

make use of **sampling** techniques, selecting every twentieth building on the borough residential register, and excluding non-working-class households. This left Bowley with a sample of 743 wage-earning households, each of which was visited and surveyed. Additionally, Bowley developed methods for adjusting for non-response. Sampling techniques are explained in greater detail in Chapter 13.

Bowley took up Rowntree's definition of the poverty line, modifying it somewhat to reflect the changing dietary needs of children of different ages, and allowing rather more variation (and more meat!) in adult diets. This reliance on the earlier study – and Rowntree's own debt to Booth – indicates a move to greater *replication*, reference and comparison amongst surveys into social problems. Bowley himself undertook a second study in Reading a decade after his first (Bowley and Hogg, 1925), while a large-scale *New Survey of London Life and Labour* was published between 1930 and 1935 as a follow-up to Booth's pioneering work. Rowntree, meanwhile, administered two further surveys into working-class poverty in York (Rowntree, 1941; Rowntree and Lavers, 1951), which both modified his original poverty standard and rejected the earlier measurement of secondary poverty.

The social survey in the United States

The development of the social survey method in the United States reveals a similar concern with questions of poverty and conditions of urban life as was evident in the pioneering British studies. A central body of work in the US context was associated with the Settlement House movement, which developed from the 1880s along the model established in Britain by Toynbee Hall in London's East End (see Bulmer et al., 1991). These voluntary institutions provided places of residence, study and work in urban areas for reformers who wanted to investigate and address social conditions and problems in the modern city. One of the most influential of the American settlements was Hull House in Chicago, home to a number of key figures – especially women reformers such as Jane Addams and Florence Kelley – whose ideas and work were crucial to the development of research and reform in social policy and social welfare. The Hull House researchers had close links to academic sociologists at the University of Chicago, representing an important bridge between academic and reformist social research.

The surveys produced by researchers within the settlement movement focused on such issues

---

Box 8.5 Du Bois's method in studying 'The Philadelphia Negro'

Published in 1899, Du Bois's study detailed the living and working conditions of 4,000 black residents of Philadelphia's Seventh Ward. While undertaking the research, Du Bois and his family lived in what he described as the 'worst part' of the Seventh Ward district, and Du Bois conducted the detailed survey himself over the period of more than a year. The survey took in issues of occupation and income, family structures, housing conditions, education, political organization, community relations, crime and poverty.

---

as poverty, housing, labour conditions and juvenile justice (Bulmer et al., 1991: 28–9). The US survey movement was also distinguished by its interest in mapping the ethnic and racial geography of major cities. This early history meant that the US social survey was closely concerned with political debate, agitation and reform. At the same time, the connection and cross-over between reformist and academic social researchers meant that survey techniques emerged rapidly in the early decades of the twentieth century as a privileged method of inquiry within US social science – particularly via the developing influence of the Chicago School of sociology (see Chapters 4 and 9).

This relationship between academic research and social issues is clearly evident in the classic work of W.E.B. Du Bois on *The Philadelphia Negro* (see Box 8.5 and Chapters 9 and 29).

While Booth had understood poverty as the 'problem of problems' in late Victorian Britain, Du Bois saw the 'Negro problem' as the central issue of race and class in modern US society. Aspects of Du Bois's study, though, are strongly reminiscent of Booth's approach in London, as he divides the black population into different 'grades' or classes – from the 'vicious and criminal' to the black 'middle classes and those above' – and maps these groups as a social and spatial geography. While concerned with critical social and economic questions, however, Du Bois's study lacks the overt reformist impulses of the British poverty surveys and the work of the US settlement house movement. Du Bois was firmly committed to the principles of social science, and much of his text is couched in its neutral language (see Chapter 29 for a discussion of Du Bois's writing; see also Bulmer 1991). At the same time, the political and moral framing of the analysis is very interesting

and quite variable. Du Bois analyses the impact of racial prejudice on the opportunities and experience of his study population through in-depth case studies, but also takes a rather paternalistic tone on such issues as pauperism, crime and alcoholism. The overall effect, critically, is to assert that the black population in Philadelphia (and elsewhere) must be thought of in terms of different and specific social circumstances and forms of behaviour, rather than as an undifferentiated mass and a generalized 'problem'.

Later developments

The early decades of the twentieth century saw the consolidation of the survey method, as the innovation of sampling allowed it to be used more widely, and without the massive resources required by Booth or Rowntree. For a while, though, the topics investigated remained rather narrowly defined, so that in 1935 Wells was able to define a social survey as being a 'fact finding study dealing chiefly with working class poverty and with the nature and problems of the community' (1935: 1). The interests of people using social surveys became broader, though, as the growing discipline of town planning increasingly came to rely on surveys.

In the post-war period social surveys developed in four main institutional locations:

1 Market and audience research
2 Opinion polling
3 Government social surveys
4 Academic social science

The first of these will be familiar to anyone who has ever been stopped in the street to be asked about shopping preferences and the like. Market researchers generally have to work quickly, generating results in a matter of a few days or weeks, and on limited budgets. Special sampling methods such as *quota sampling* (see Chapter 13) have been developed to enable this. Opinion pollsters often work under similar constraints. Perhaps the most important contribution made by this type of survey work has been an appreciation of how question wording can affect response, leading to a reinforcement of the desire to standardize the wording of questions, and thus try to eliminate the influence of the interviewer whose rewordings might otherwise produce unreliable replies.

Most advanced industrial democracies have developed a range of official statistics and social surveys, reflecting the links between government and quantification of the population outlined earlier. Government social surveys have characteristic strengths in the selection of large, representative samples, and in the training of interviewers to ask standardized, structured questions. While official statistics have often been criticized for their sometimes limited analysis of the data that emerge, the availability of data sets generated by government social surveys in data archives offers an immensely valuable resource for social researchers interested in the **secondary analysis** of such data for their own purposes (Dale et al., 1988). Secondary analysis is discussed in more detail in Chapter 26.

The use made of the social survey in the fourth institutional location, academic social science, is very diverse. Researchers working within the disciplines of social policy and social administration offer examples that are closest to governmental aims, and in area studies such as health or educational research the method has proved useful. A helpful way to understand the range of social survey work in academic locations is to divide it into two types of survey: **descriptive** and **explanatory**.

- **Descriptive** social surveys are characteristic of an important strand of sociology, represented in the work of the University of Chicago School under Robert Park and Ernest Burgess, and the Institute of Community Studies (ICS) founded in Britain in the 1950s. ICS research-

ers used the social survey to give accounts of such topics as family and kinship in east London (Young and Willmott, 1957), widowhood (Marris, 1958) and the experience of social mobility (Jackson and Marsden, 1962). An offshoot of the ICS, the Institute for Social Studies in Medical Care (ISSMC), applied the descriptive survey approach to a variety of topics in health care (for example Cartwright, 1964). This tradition is characterized by the use of both quantitative and qualitative data, so that the broad picture shown by the statistical tables is supported by the selection of quotations taken from interviews, so as to provide numbers with a 'human face'. The descriptive tradition continues to the present day, for example in studies of death and dying (Cartwright and Seale, 1990; Seale and Cartwright, 1994; Young and Cullen, 1996). Chapter 34 describes work done within this tradition.

- **Explanatory** social surveys attempt the more ambitious task of explaining why events occur, and they do this by looking for *causal relationships*. Methods for doing this are explained in Chapter 25. They developed initially in the work of social scientists in the United States, shown most characteristically by Hyman (1955), Lazarsfeld and Rosenberg (1955) and Rosenberg (1968). The purpose of this type of analysis is to show how a variety of phenomena are determined by features of *social structure*. Classically, this was shown by Durkheim's analysis of the causes of suicide. An example from the American tradition is Hirschi and Selvin's (1967) attempt to discover the causes of 'juvenile delinquency', a phenomenon which they felt might be caused by a variety of social structural factors.

Explanatory data analysis of social survey data rests on the empiricist assumption that facts exist independently of theories. Theories exist to provide propositions and *hypotheses* which are then confirmed or refuted by the facts. This is, of course, the language of natural science, and is associated with the positivist enterprise of discovering regularities and laws underlying the dynamics of society, and determining variation in social phenomena.

In Chapter 4 we encountered the interactionist critique of the model of human social action that this type of analysis involves. Researchers who prefer qualitative research in 'natural' settings, rather than the 'artificial' setting of the survey interview, prioritize the investigation of how people actively *constitute* phenomena (such as suicide, or delinquency) in their everyday interactions. On the other hand, it has proved possible to generate causal analyses from social survey data that have greater adequacy at the level of meaning, exemplified in the work of Brown and Harris (1978) on the social origins of depression. This work is discussed in Marsh (1982) and also in Chapter 23 of this book.

Finally, the feminist critique of positivism and the scientific method developed in relation to the social survey from the early 1970s. This is seen most powerfully in the feminist critique of the structured interview, both in terms of the relationship it establishes between researcher and research subject, and as a means of accessing accounts (see Oakley, 1981 or Finch, 1984). But, as explained in Chapter 3, elements of the feminist critique of science have been more profound than this, pointing out the political implications of supposed 'value neutrality' and describing the stance of 'objectivity' as providing only limited access to knowledge about social life. None the less, feminist stances towards the quantitative social survey and its political uses are variable, so that it is claimed that social statistics, and indeed the experimental method (albeit with appropriate ethical safeguards) in social research, can provide a powerful source of facts and figures in the pursuit of feminist political objectives (Jayaratne, 1983; Oakley, 1989).

The politics of social surveys

Within contemporary social research, then, both the techniques and the value of quantitative approaches have been put into serious question. These criticisms have been directed on the one hand at the methodological claims of surveys and social statistics – in terms of their representativeness, their validity as a reflection of a complex social reality and the analytic usefulness of 'head counting'. On the other, the politics of

quantitative social research have been challenged in relation to the latter's assumed neutrality, its treatment of people as 'just numbers', and its tendency to impose categories of meaning on aspects of social experience (for a discussion of these related problems of 'method' and 'epistemology' in relation to survey research, see Marsh, 1984).

These arguments are compelling, but are not entirely new. An important strand of these critical challenges has involved a reappraisal of the historical tradition of survey research (Kent, 1981). A central argument here is that the kinds of investigation carried out by statistical societies, government inquiries and individual social explorers did much to 'make up' an image of society which reinforced the moral norms and political wisdom of their time, rather than to produce direct or value-free knowledge about the anatomy of modern society (see also Hacking, 1990). Accusing early social surveyors of being involved in politics, however, would hardly have constituted a challenge: the various institutional bodies and individual researchers were self-consciously engaged in producing knowledge that would inform public debate and policy. The social survey developed in the nineteenth century out of a perspective which held that the application of scientific method to the study of society could provide a basis for rational social reform. What remains in question is how clearly survey findings can provide directives for political action. Research into poverty, for example, was undertaken and taken up by political conservatives, reformers and radicals alike. The accounts provided by a conservative such as Booth and a reformer such as Rowntree suggest rather different solutions to the problem of poverty.

- Booth's studies, for example, confirmed him in his belief in individualism and minimal government measures to ameliorate social conditions, although he also favoured the removal of the poorest classes of society – whose lives 'were in every way wasteful' (Kent, 1981: 59) – to industrial camps or poorhouses.
- Rowntree, while inspired by Booth's methods, was a firm supporter of welfare measures and a public system of social security.

Box 8.6   Web pointers for the history of social statistics and the social survey

Thomas Malthus: 'An essay on the principle of population' (1798)
http://dspace.dial.pipex.com/town/terrace/adw03/peel/social/prindex.htm

Charles Booth online archive
http://booth.lse.ac.uk

Seebohm Rowntree: life and works
www.spartacus.schoolnet.co.uk/RErowntreeS.htm

History of statistics and probability
www.mrs.umn.edu/~sungurea/introstat/history/indexhistory.shtml
and
www.york.ac.uk/depts/maths/histstat/welcome.htm

History of the (UK) Census
www.statistics.gov.uk/census2001/bicentenary/history.html

Visit the website for this book at www.rscbook.co.uk to link to these web pointers.

These conclusions circulated within a larger set of social and political debates, which themselves shaped competing research agendas. Rowntree's 1951 study suggested that primary working-class poverty in post-war society had decreased to an almost insignificant level, and was in its turn challenged by the revival of the 'poverty debate' in the 1960s, galvanized by Abel-Smith and Townsend's (1965) research into *The Poor and the Poorest* in the 'affluent society' of late-twentieth-century Britain.

While survey research has clearly been linked to wider political debates, it might also be thought about in terms of the politics of social research itself. We have seen the way in which many Victorian surveys drew on and reinforced aspects of social morality in using such explanatory categories as idleness or improvidence. It took some time for social researchers to accept that categories of definition and measurement were not simply neutral, that they were an invention of the researcher rather than a characteristic of those being researched. Rowntree is a notable exception here in being profoundly aware of the static nature of statistical representation. A key argument within his original study was that there existed a 'life cycle' of poverty, such that those individuals

and families he identified as living in primary poverty were not simply stuck in a monolithic underclass. Rather, Rowntree argued that there were certain life and work stages – what he called 'poverty periods' – which were more likely to produce conditions of primary poverty. Childhood and old age were the most severe periods of poverty in the life cycle of the labourer, while working-class women frequently lived in primary poverty throughout the time that they were raising children. Such findings are strikingly in tune with established analyses of poverty current today.

Conclusion

The reappraisal of a historical tradition of survey research can provide valuable resources for thinking about the politics and methods of contemporary social research. This is not simply a question of understanding where our research traditions have come from – although this is a critical issue – but is also one of examining the claims and the internal critiques made by earlier social researchers. While certain methods and moralities may now seem rather unsophisticated, the enduring commitment of social researchers to producing useful knowledge about their society, as well as to processes of social and economic reform, suggest important guides for interrogating the aims and the orientation of much current social research.

Further reading

Moser and Kalton (1971: ch. 1) provides a clear introduction to the history of the social survey in Britain, and an overview of the various uses of survey methods. Abrams (1968) includes a useful introductory essay, together with primary extracts from social researchers including Rowntree and Bowley. Bulmer et al. (1991) provides an excellent coverage of the development of the social survey in Britain and the United States (and includes a chapter by Gorges on Germany). Kent (1981) is an extremely readable and comprehensive history of empirical social research (with a strong focus on quantitative methods), from the eighteenth century to the 1970s. Hacking (1990) is a fascinating critical account of the history of the social survey, using a range of examples from the fields of health, crime and so on.

Student Reader (Seale, 2004): relevant readings

15 Ian Hacking: 'The taming of chance'
25 R.C. Lewontin: 'Sex lies and social science' (a book review with subsequent correspondence from the book's authors and other readers of the review)

Key concepts	Poverty line
	Primary poverty
Causal relationship	**Secondary poverty**
Census	**Sample survey**
Descriptive and **explanatory** analysis	**Sampling**
Political arithmetic	**Secondary analysis**
	Statistical societies

9

History of qualitative methods

Clive Seale

CONTENTS

'Qualitative method' can be understood as the title of a social movement, a banner around which people in social and cultural research communities have mobilized, with a particular energy from the late 1960s onwards in Western (or at least Anglophone) social research. Alasuutari (2004) has suggested that the qualitative methods movement has been a convenient vehicle for the rediscovery and legitimation of approaches to human inquiry that were, in fact, quite prevalent (particularly in sociology) before the Second World War. This was before the American-led development of social survey methods under a scientific paradigm, arising from wartime experience and continuing into the 1950s and 1960s, which came to dominate methodological thinking and practice in human sciences at a time when faith in progress through the application of science was a widespread social value (see Chapter 8). People interested in more literary, interpretive approaches at that time felt considerably threatened by this scientific – some might say scientistic – orthodoxy and developed a **qualitative creation myth** (Seale, 1999) that contributed to the idea of a separation between qualitative and quantitative method and an amnesia about 'qualitative' research practice before the 1940s. In fact, the set of practices that came to be incorporated under the 'qualitative method' banner had been part and parcel of a general approach to scholarship and academic inquiry, in which quantitative–qualitative distinctions were relatively unimportant.

A properly historical analysis, then, will need to recover an appreciation of the role which qualitative work (although it may not have gone under that name) played in research activity from considerably further back than the past 40 years or so. In this chapter I will begin by discussing the early development of ethnographic method and the history of interviews, these being two key 'qualitative' methods in social research. In the second part of the chapter, consideration of developments from the 1960s onwards will incorporate an increasing diversity of qualitative research practice, the contemporary scope of which is represented in a number of recent collected volumes (for example, Denzin and Lincoln, 2000; Seale et al., 2004) as well as the present book.

Early history of ethnography

Ethnography might be said to have roots in the European 'discovery' from the fifteenth century onwards of new kinds of human beings living in the Americas (and later in the South Seas) whose very existence spelled trouble for biblical accounts of human descent and whose ways of life seemed to incorporate radically different behaviour and morality. Attempts to understand and explain these peoples and their behaviours from a European Christian point of view, subsequently from the vantage point of a colonial mentality, were made in accounts from missionaries, travellers, explorers, local administrators and the like. A key tension in these accounts – and it is one which in slightly different forms runs through today's methodological debates about ethnography (see Chapters 17 and 33) – lay in the difficulty in recognizing subjects of reports (the indigenous 'Other') as having a right to be regarded as equally human to the European observer. As Vidich and Lyman (2000) put it:

> How is it possible to understand the other when the other's values are not one's own? This problem arises to plague ethnography at a time when Western Christian values are no longer a surety of truth and, hence, no longer the benchmark from which self-confidently valid observations can be made. (2000: 41)

As these authors go on to show, ethnography from the early twentieth century onwards came to be professionalized as the discipline of social anthropology developed within universities, bringing with it the practice of spending a lengthy period of time (a year or more) living 'in the field' in some foreign land, the anthropologist's passage (and therefore his or her perspective) often being arranged through the good offices of some local colonial administrator. The paradigmatic case of this mode of qualitative knowledge production was Malinowski, whose writings addressed both the popular appetite for lurid tales from strange lands (one of his books was called *The Sexual Life of Savages*, 1929) and aspired to scientific respectability through the claim to have applied a rigorous method (see Box 9.1)

Box 9.1   Malinowski and anthropology

'Malinowski's *Argonauts of the Western Pacific* ... is [a] canonical text ... Published in 1922, it is conveniently taken as marking the beginning of British social anthropology and, more specifically, of establishing it as a discipline based on what he called "scientific ethnographic fieldwork." ... While others had undertaken anthropological fieldwork previously, Malinowski's was at the time of unusual length (two years in the Trobriands) and intensity – not merely "a sporadic plunging into the company of natives [but] being really in contact with them" (1922: 7) as he put it. Moreover, in *Argonauts* he presented this personal experience as a "scientific" approach, capable of going beyond amateur accounts of "native peoples" by providing "concrete statistical documentation" (1922: 24) ... The calculated positioning between the literary and the scientific, and the academic and the popular, and the play between depicting difference and illuminating humanistic universalism (showing how Trobriand practices were not so strange as they might at first appear), was undoubtedly crucial to Malinowski's success in putting British social anthropology on the map.' (MacDonald, 2001: 61–2)

Malinowski placed methodological claims considerably to the fore in his writing (advocating his method as 'scientific' and trumpeting his occasional reliance on 'statistics', for example). But anthropological writing in the early part of the twentieth century was in general characterized by a lack of the kind of methodological self-consciousness, involving self-doubt about the authority of the writer to report objectively on witnessed ways of life, prevalent nowadays. Very few direct quotations from respondents are presented in the classic ethnographies of this time, fieldworkers being trusted to summarize reliably and accurately the views of the people studied, with no suspicions aired about the likely role of the observer's interpretations in forming such summaries. Immersion in the field itself gave the author the necessary credibility and the intensity and commitment involved in this was therefore stressed in the few methodological accounts that were thought necessary (see Box 9.2 for an example).

Denzin and Lincoln (2000), commenting on the anthropological work that arose from the efforts of early academic pioneers such as Mead and Malinowski, have argued that this period in

---

Box 9.2   Margaret Mead's account of her immersion in 'the field'

'This account is the result of six months' concentrated and uninterrupted field work. From a thatched house on piles, built in the centre of the Manus village of Peri, I learned the native language, the children's games, the intricacies of social organization, economic custom, and religious belief and practice which formed the social framework within which the child grows up. In my large living-room, on the wide verandas, on the tiny islet adjoining the houses, in the surrounding lagoon, the children played all day and I watched them, now from the midst of a play group, now from behind the concealment of the thatched walls. I rode in their canoes, attended their feasts, watched in the house of mourning and sat severely still while the mediums conversed with the spirits of the dead. I observed the children when no grown-up people were present, and I watched their behaviour towards their parents. Within a social setting which I learned to know intimately enough not to offend against the hundreds of name taboos, I watched the Manus baby, the Manus child, the Manus adolescent, in an attempt to understand the way in which each of these was becoming a Manus adult.' (Mead, 1942: 15–16: first published in 1930)

---

the development of qualitative research can be characterized as its **traditional moment** and that four beliefs and commitments characterized ethnography at this time:

1   Commitment to objectivism
2   Complicity with imperialism
3   Belief in monumentalism (i.e. the report would contribute to a museum-like repository of knowledge)
4   Belief in the timelessness of the culture studied

Denzin and Lincoln make these points in the context of a book that seeks to outline how subsequent **moments** in the history of qualitative research have involved questioning all these things. Their reading of history, then, is perhaps led by a particular 'creation mythologizing' agenda; things may not have been as extreme as they portray. One of Malinowski's themes, in fact, was the time-*boundedness* of the cultures he studied, which he felt he was capturing in print before they changed. Some ethnography contributed to critiques of crudely imperialist mentalities. Nevertheless, the points made by Denzin and Lincoln convey features of early ethnography that are useful in understanding later developments, since the people leading these have often shared this reading of history.

Ethnography as it developed in the discipline of sociology, most famously in the work of Chicago School ethnographers (see Chapter 4), can similarly be understood as 'othering' members of the large, culturally diverse urban communities that had formed in American cities by the end of the nineteenth century. An important precursor to Chicago School ethnographies had been the work of W.E.B. Du Bois (see Chapter 29), whose work in documenting the lives of the Philadelphia Negro population (Du Bois, 1899/1996) relied on large-scale survey and statistical work (see Chapter 8) but is nevertheless commonly understood as an 'ethnography' in the original sense of that word, which is to map the characteristics of a nation or ethnic group. This work was profoundly influenced by a desire to contribute to the uplift of the Negro population by the surrounding Quaker community. As Vidich and Lyman (2000) observe, this study exhibits a 'tone of noblesse oblige,' a

---

Box 9.3   Finding a sponsor in fieldwork – an account by W.F. Whyte

[At first] I was completely baffled at the problem of finding my way into the district ... I was still a stranger ... In a sense, my study began on the evening of February 4, 1937, when the social worker called me in to meet Doc ... I began by asking him if the social worker had told him about what I was trying to do.

'No, she just told me that you wanted to meet me and that I should like to meet you.'

Then I went into a long explanation ... Doc heard me without any change of expression, so that I had no way of predicting his reaction. When I was finished, he asked: 'Do you want to see the high life or the low life?'

'I want to see all that I can. I want to get as complete a picture of the community as possible.'

'Well, any nights you want to see anything. I'll take you around. I can take you to the joints – gambling joints – I can take you around to the street corners. Just remember that you're my friend. That's all they need to know. I know these places, and, if I tell them that you're my friend, nobody will bother you. You just tell me what you want to see, and we'll arrange it.'

The proposal was so perfect that I was at a loss for a moment as to how to respond to it ... that was our beginning. At the time I found it hard to believe that I could move in as easily as Doc had said with his sponsorship. But that indeed was the way it turned out. (Whyte, 1955: 289–93)

reminder of 'the paternalistic benevolence underlying this first ethnographic study of a community' (2000: 48).

Chicago School ethnography (see Chapter 4) under Park and Burgess ditched an explicitly Christian mission while retaining a generally humanistic moral agenda. It used qualitative (and sometimes quantitative) methods to document the lives of a variety of (usually, but not always urban) social groups living in relative degrees of visibility from the vantage point of educated, mainstream American society. Perhaps the most famous of these studies was William Foote Whyte's account of *Street Corner Society* (originally published in 1943). This was an account of Italian Americans in Boston, widely regarded as an exemplary application of qualitative method and, in particular, participant observation. In the 'Methodological Appendix' to this book Whyte outlines in detail his journey into this field, emphasizing his initial innocence and eventual inclusion through the offices of his 'sponsor' Doc (see Box 9.3). As Geertz (1988) has observed, such accounts of entry into the field (Mead's in Box 9.2 is another) have been an important way of persuading readers of the authenticity and exceptional insight of the reports that then emerge, convincing the reader of the claim to have 'been there'.

Early uses of the qualitative interview

The identification of the 'qualitative interview' as a particular type only became necessary in post-war social research. Before the 1940s people just interviewed. Researchers were influenced by the examples of early survey researchers such as Booth (see Chapter 8) whose interviewers had questioned proxy respondents about the circumstances of families living in particular streets rather than members of those families. They were also influenced by the kind of 'case work' information-gathering strategies employed by social workers with their clients. The self-completion *questionnaire* or the *schedule* of the census enumerator were perceived to be different exercises. It was only with the post-war development of the large scale survey involving sampling that the *structured interview* really began to develop as a separate mode of face-to-face questioning.

A typical mode of interviewing on many social research projects in the United States or the UK in pre-war years, then, would have involved the researchers themselves, who would approach respondents on the basis of their being likely to know a lot about a particular area of life. The respondents might therefore be considered key informants or gatekeepers, rather than members of a sample representing some population. This is much the same way in which a journalist nowadays treats interviewing. Such key people were typically asked for their views in a manner that was relatively loosely structured, resulting in qualitative anecdotes and opinions summarized according to the developing research interests of the investigator. Frequently the interviewee would have been a person of higher social status than the investigator, so presentation of a loosely structured research agenda allowed the respondent a degree of freedom to raise topics of personal interest, appropriate for the requirements of conversational deference (see Platt, 2000 and the advice to interviewers in Box 9.4).

Alternatively, informal interviews as a part of ethnographic investigations would be treated as conversations with a purpose – somewhat for-

---

Box 9.4   Advice to interviewers in 1929

'An interview is made for the purpose of securing information ... about the informant himself, or about other persons or undertakings that he knows or is interested in. The purpose may be to secure a life history, to corroborate evidence got from other sources, to secure ... data which the informant possesses. [It] ... may also be the means of enlisting the informant's cooperation ... in the investigation, or ... advice ... in the procedure to be followed ... If the student is not acquainted with the informant, some method of introduction through a mutual acquaintance should be secured.' (Odum and Jocher, 1929: 366–7)

mal extensions of the kind of informal interactions that arose more naturally during fieldwork (Warren, 2002). Nowadays, the terms *life history* or *case study* might be used to describe such work (see Chapter 14). Again, the interviewer would most likely have been the researcher, with questioning during the interview being informed by first hand knowledge of the underlying research questions.

Developments in the survey field from the 1940s onwards meant that the approach to interviewing which until then had been predominant became separately identified as the 'qualitative interview', involving a different kind of knowledge and conception of the research subject from the 'norm' of scientific survey research. Although structured forms of interviewing arose in part from the demands for standardization of information for the purposes of statistical analysis (see Chapter 13), in addition large-scale surveys required the employment of 'hired hand' interviewers. These people would not know much about the purpose of the investigation, so could not be relied upon to question respondents appropriately in a loosely structured 'qualitative' format. Thus the roots of the quantitative–qualitative divide which ran through methodological thinking in post-war years developed.

Post-war developments

The dominance of the social survey and quantitative work in social research during the 1950s meant that those employing qualitative methods, whose claims to legitimacy drew on a literary rather than a scientific tradition, frequently felt marginalized. If qualitative method had a place in the social survey it lay in preliminary developmental work for designing questionnaire items, or in the highly limited format of the occasional open-ended question within structured interview formats. Truly interpretive qualitative work had little to offer research funding bodies mesmerized by a scientific vision.

This began to change with the development within sociological ethnography of a rhetoric of justification that addressed scientific concerns about rigour and proof and culminated in the writings of Glaser and Strauss (1967) on *grounded theory* (see Chapter 18). A classic article here is Howard Becker's 'Problems of inference and proof in participant observation' (1958), and the collection of his methodological writings (Becker 1970) encapsulate the spirit of this time, which Denzin and Lincoln (2000) call the **modernist** phase in the development of qualitative method.

Becker's 'Problems of inference and proof' pointed out, for the sake of those readers schooled in thinking about research problems from a *hypothetico-deductive* point of view, that participant observers do not just test hypotheses but discover them in the course of research. Having thus symbolically introduced the reader to what might have seemed a new way of thinking, Becker then addresses issues of truth and validity from a realist point of view, going so far as to recommend the use of *quasi-statistics* (a term taken from the writings of the leading social survey researcher of the time, Paul Lazarsfeld (Barton and Lazarsfeld, 1955)). Box 9.5 shows the relevant passage.

In assessing the truth-value of participant observation data, Becker argues, the observer must be aware that people sometimes provide misleading stories, or behave in atypical ways, so that checking veracity must involve collecting many items of information and types of evidence if a generalization is to be adequately supported (this is reminiscent of the concept of *triangulation* – see Chapter 22). The researcher should be aware of the *reactive* effect that his or her presence may have on people's behaviour and seek to adopt an unobtrusive, non-directive role as far as possible in order to avoid this. *Negative instances* (or *deviant cases*) should be sought for in data collection and in sorting through collected data, so as to challenge and improve emerging theory (this concept is explained more fully in Chapter 7). This rigorous, self-critical approach to inference and proof in qualitative work means that:

> the technique consists of more than merely immersing oneself in data and 'having insights'. The discussion may also serve to [make] qualitative research ... become more a 'scientific' and less an 'artistic' kind of endeavour. (Becker, 1970: 38)

As grounded theory, which emerges from a very similar set of concerns, is treated at chapter length elsewhere in this book I will not discuss it fully here, except to say that the historical antecedents of this work should be appreciated, and can be elucidated by saying something about the personal biographies of the two key authors of grounded theory. While Strauss had worked closely with Becker on an ethnographic observational study of medical student culture (Becker et al., 1961), from which the ideas in '*Problems of inference and proof*' were developed, Glaser had worked in Columbia University, an institution also associated with the development of the *elaboration paradigm* for the causal analysis of quantitative survey research data (see Chapter 25). In important respects grounded theorizing shares common ground with this statistical approach: both, for example, stress the continual cycling back and forth between theory construction and examination of data. Both see data analysis as a matter of generating falsifiable theoretical arguments, whose complexity and scope develops through the discovery of negative evidence.

In Denzin and Lincoln's (2000) periodization of the history of qualitative method the modernist phase began with Becker's '*Problems of inference and proof*' and ended with grounded theory, although they detect (as do I) a continuing interest in doing qualitative research using modernist principles in much present-day qualitative research practice. Indeed, the authors reviewed have continued to write influential texts on qualitative methods (Becker, 1998; Strauss and Corbin, 1990). Following the modernist phase, though, is what Denzin and Lincoln call the moment of **blurred genres**, which fell roughly between 1970 and 1986, in which arose methods influenced by a wide variety of philosophical positions, social theories and political views. These included, for example, feminist method, phenomenology, ethnomethodology and conversation analysis, critical and neo-Marxist perspectives. Structuralist and semiotic methods also began to influence researchers as the discipline of cultural studies grew in importance. Before exploring some of these, though – and they are all covered quite fully in other chapters in this book – it is instructive to examine what was happening to the qualitative interview during this period.

The qualitative interview and the 'interview society'

Silverman (1997) has argued that nowadays we live in an **interview society**, by which he means that interviews have become increasingly common in the kind of world we have been living in for the past 30–40 years or so and are central to the ways in which we make sense of our lives. Three conditions have led to this:

1   Individual selves (rather than religious or collectivist ideologies) are seen as the appropriate sources of subjectivity. Psychology is thus used to 'explain' experience.

2   A 'technology of the confessional' has arisen, whereby techniques for gathering personal narratives have become very widespread (for example, the 'confession' to a policeman, a priest, a psychotherapist, a journalist, a research interviewer).

3   Everyone has become familiar with the aims and methods of the interview, so that they know the behaviour appropriate to both interviewer and interviewee (see Box 9.6 for an example of what happens when this familiarity is not established).

Box 9.5   Quasi-statistics in participant observation

'Participant observations have occasionally been gathered in standardized form capable of being transformed into legitimate statistical data. But the exigencies of the field usually prevent the collection of data in such a form as to meet the assumptions of statistical tests, so that the observer deals in what have been called "quasi-statistics". His conclusions, while implicitly numerical, do not require precise quantification.' (Becker, 1970: 31; first published 1958)

Box 9.6   An interview occurring outside the 'interview society'

Evans-Pritchard (1940) presents this extract from his fieldwork with Nuer people in southern Sudan to demonstrate his difficulties in gaining information by the interview method:

I: Who are you?
Cuol: A man.
I: What is your name?
Cuol: Do you want to know my *name*?
I: Yes.
Cuol: You want to know *my* name?
I: Yes, you have come to visit me in my tent and I would like to know who you are.
Cuol: All right. I am Cuol. What is your name?
I: My name is Pritchard.
Cuol: What is your father's name?
I: My father's name is also Pritchard.
Cuol: No, that cannot be true. You cannot have the same name as your father.
I: It is the name of my lineage. What is the name of your lineage?
Cuol: Do you want to know the name of my lineage?
I: Yes.
Cuol: What will you do with it if I tell you? Will you take it to your country?
I: I don't want to do anything with it. I just want to know it since I am living at your camp.
Cuol: Oh, well, we are Lou.
I: I did not ask you the name of your tribe. I know that. I am asking you the name of your lineage.
Cuol: Why do you want to know the name of my lineage?
I: I don't want to know it.
Cuol: Then why do you ask me for it? Give me some tobacco.

(*Source:* Evans-Pritchard, 1940: 12–13)

From the late 1960s, when there were widespread social upheavals in the United States, Britain and other 'Western' countries where social research is commonly done, a particular form of qualitative interviewing emerged that was in tune with the spirit of the times. This spirit involved an intense celebration of individualism, often with a highly **romantic** tinge; young people in particular sought more authentic, self-fulfilling lives and there was a widespread sense of rebellion against established authority and life-plans based on obligation, duty and tradition. Science and rationality were associated with authority and control; instead, aesthetic experience, emotionality and personal freedom were embraced. At the same time an egalitarian ethic spread, based on a perception of a common humanity that levelled people previously perceived to be naturally occupying positions in what came to be seen as unequal, hierarchical social relations.

Developments in social research methodology reflected these currents in wider society and 'qualitative research' became the banner headline and social movement to which I referred at the outset of this chapter. A concomitant distrust and stigmatization of quantitative work developed as this became associated with excessive rationality, control and hierarchy. The qualitative interview was a key symbol here, becoming a vehicle for social researchers to participate in the more general romantic celebrations of individualism and attempts to erase inequality and difference.

Box 9.7 contains a quotation from a textbook that reflects such a version of qualitative interviewing. Note that this comes from a book published in the early 1980s; methodology textbooks are often a little 'behind the times'. Also, methodological fashions rarely completely die out: the conception of qualitative interviewing reflected in Taylor and Bogdan's book has currency for many contemporary researchers, in much the same way as modernist versions of qualitative research remain attractive to numerous research practitioners in spite of attempts by new 'fashion leaders' to move things on (see Box 18.6 in Chapter 18).

The Taylor and Bogdan quote can be analysed now from a discourse analytic point of view (see Chapter 27) as a very particular rhetorical *construction* of its subject, done in part by 'othering' alternative modes of doing research. The 'robotlike data collector' is imagined, presented as a person who is not only inflexible, 'formal' and static (as opposed to the 'flexible', 'dynamic' and informal qualitative interviewer), but one who imagines that he or she is simply the user of a 'tool', 'schedule' or 'protocol' that is external to themselves. The qualitative interviewer is both egalitarian and understanding, concerned to elicit the unique perspective that each person is imagined to possess. The identification of a person (the qualitative researcher) as being themselves 'the research tool' is designed to disrupt the expectations of the reader (after all, 'tools' are not 'people' but 'things') and impress a new wisdom. Wisdom, too, is evoked in the final sentence which is deliberately reminiscent of Zen or other 'Eastern' philosophies of life that became popular alternatives to Western rationality in the 1970s.

Silenced in this discourse on the qualitative interview is recognition that post-war concern with democratic and egalitarian values was in fact attached to ideals of progress through the application of rationality and science. The development of the Welfare State and the National Health Service in Britain was a realization of this. Yet in this extract these have become ideologically separated, indeed constructed as antagonistic to one another. Additionally, appreciation of the ingenuity, creativity and rigour that the survey research tradition had developed in relation to question wording and technique as well as the commitment of many survey researchers to the complex business of learning how to ask good questions is suppressed through a process of stigmatization.

Feminist researchers such as Oakley (1981) participated in developing romantic visions of qualitative interviewing, attaching the humanistic interest in subjectivity and the interviewee's right to be heard to a more explicitly political agenda (see Chapter 14 for further discussion of this). Qualitative interviews were advocated as giving voice to otherwise silenced groups (such as women) and for a while became a preferred method for many feminist researchers. The qualitative approach, as Reinharz (1992) has pointed out, 'is an antidote to centuries of ignoring women's ideas altogether or having men speak for women' (1992: 19).

Topicalizing the interview

At the same time as romantic impulses were gathering pace, though, an alternative perspective on the analysis of talk was developing from the

---

Box 9.7 A romantic conception of the qualitative interview

'In stark contrast to structured interviewing qualitative interviewing is flexible and dynamic ... By in-depth qualitative interviewing we mean repeated face-to-face encounters between the researcher and informants directed towards understanding informants' perspectives on their lives, experiences or situations as expressed in their own words. The in-depth interview is modeled after a conversation between equals, rather than a formal question-and-answer exchange. Far from being a robotlike data collector, the interviewer, not an interview schedule or protocol, is the research tool. The role entails not merely obtaining answers, but learning what questions to ask and how to ask them.' (Taylor and Bogdan, 1984: 77)

viewpoint of *ethnomethodology* and *conversation analysis* (see Chapter 28). This qualitative method initially took as its object of inquiry talk occurring in a variety of settings, including phone conversations, courtrooms, medical consultations, news interviews and the like. It was made possible by the technological development of the portable cassette tape recorder which enabled close transcripts to be made and examined in detail. The emphasis here was on analysing the co-construction of meaning in talk, so that the world that speakers referred to (what they had seen, what they had experienced, their inner lives) was treated as being of secondary importance to the worlds, or versions of the world constructed in interaction. When eventually applied to interview material (for example, Antaki and Rapley, 1996; Holstein and Gubrium, 1995), this approach treated the interview as a site for the observation of behaviour. Thus the interview occasion was a **topic** in its own right, rather than a **resource** for discovering and authenticating things occurring outside the interview (as the romantic version had treated it). For this reason, for example, ethnomethodologists and feminist social researchers often parted company. (In later years, these fixed positions have been loosened: Oakley (1989) has rediscovered the value of quantitative, scientific method; feminists have found it possible to explore their concerns through conversation analysis (Kitzinger 2000).)

Ethnomethodology (which began in the work of Harold Garfinkel in the 1960s – see Chapter 4) developed a research programme and approach that was rigorously empirical, scientific and observational, distinguishing fact from value and committed to producing single, authoritative readings of social reality. In these respects (though on many other points there were differences) ethnomethodologists shared much with the 'positivist' quantitative research practice that the qualitative alternative aspired to replace. Yet feminist and other politically informed research practice, conversation analysis, humanistic interviewing, action research, naturalistic ethnography and other approaches developed and flourished together from the late 1960s into the 1970s and beyond. Denzin and Lincoln's (2000) characterization of this period as being one of **blurred genres** is designed to convey the diversity and

sometimes irresolvable differences that arose between different modes of qualitative research during this period. The term also refers to the blurring of boundaries that all of this involved between scientific and literary traditions.

The rise of constructionism

Gathering pace in the 1980s, but only really developing fully in the 1990s and beyond, social and cultural research practice influenced by **constructionist epistemologies** (see Chapter 4) represents a fourth important phase in the development of qualitative research in Anglophone countries (though not necessarily elsewhere, for which see below). These perspectives took as their starting point the philosophical view that all knowledge – not just that of research participants – is socially constructed. That is to say, research reports themselves are particular *versions,* constructing realities that, if another person had written the report, might have been very different. Considerable attention was paid to the role of researchers themselves in creating knowledge, therefore, both in the decisions made about what questions to ask and how to ask them and in the writing of research reports themselves. **Auto-ethnography** developed, in which researchers used their own experiences and responses to events as sources of evidence about social processes. The social construction of knowledge was also recognized as having a political aspect, reflecting power relations, for example between Western or white or middle-class or male researchers and the 'researched'. Chapter 3 outlines some implications for researchers of these considerations. Denzin and Linclon term this fourth 'moment' in the history of qualitative research the **crisis of representation**.

Perhaps the single most important work heralding the shift towards more exclusively constructionist perspectives on research practice was the collection of writings edited by Clifford and Marcus (1986) called *Writing Culture.* In one piece within this collection, for example, a contributor (Tyler, 1986) puts forward a radical vision of his position in relation to traditional ethnography, arguing that science is now an archaic mode of consciousness which has not led to successful universal laws. The postmodern ethnography that he now aspires to produce would involve cooperatively evolved text, a pastiche of fragments of discourse allowing both reader and writer a fantasy of possible worlds, in the manner of some poetry. The experience of reading such texts, claims Tyler, should transport people into a sacred world, allowing them to return to the everyday world with refreshed visions. Polyphony and dialogue are the ideals, with problematic status accorded to the voice of the author. Ethnographic discourse 'evokes' rather than 're-presents'. The old scientific rhetoric, using words like 'objects', 'facts', descriptions', 'inductions', generalization', 'verification', 'experimentation' and 'truth' can now be substituted with a vision of writing as a magical act, where there is no consensus, only fragmentation.

This spirit resulted, for some but by no means all of the qualitative research community, in the production of a variety of **experimental texts**. These included the use of drama and poetry (see Box 9.8) to present the 'results' of research, or attempts to delete the 'presence of the author' by presenting relatively unedited passages of talk from interviewees with little or no accompanying commentary.

Less radically, Fontana (2002) summarizes postmodern approaches to interviewing in a way that encapsulates a range of contemporary qualitative research sensibilities (Box 9.9). Note that many of the items on Fontana's list express concerns similar to those current in the 1970s, even down to the ritualized 'othering' of survey interviewing in item 4, where the 'faceless number' image might be compared with Taylor and Bogdan's 'robotlike' (see Box 9.7). The concern with representation (item 3), with new modes of reporting (item 6) and with the context of electronic media (item 7) are, however, new developments.

Writing a history

It is a commonplace amongst professional historians that the form a historical account takes will be influenced by – and to some extent will 'construct' – present-day concerns. Another, cruder way of putting this is that all history is biased by the point of view of the historian. There is no doubt that the history of qualitative method that I am writing here is influenced by my personal methodological experience and preferences. It is instructive to reflect a little on the version of history presented in

---

Box 9.8   An example of experimental writing

Richardson (1997) presented the 'result' of interviewing a middle-aged woman as a piece of poetry, an extract of which is:

So, the Doctor said, 'You're pregnant,'
I was 41. John and I
had had a happy kind of relationship,
not a serious one.
But beside himself with fear and anger,
awful, rageful, vengeful, horrid,
Jody May's father said,
'Get an abortion.'

I told him,
'I would never marry you.
I would never marry you.
I would never.'

(*Source*: Richardson 1997: 133)

> ## Box 9.9 Postmodern sensibilities and interviewing
>
> 1 The boundaries between, and respective roles, of interviewer and interviewee have become blurred as the traditional relationship between the two is no longer seen as natural.
> 2 New forms of communication in interviewing are being used, as interviewer and respondent(s) collaborate together in constructing their narratives.
> 3 Interviewers have become more concerned about issues of representation, seriously engaging questions such as, Whose story are we telling and for what purpose?
> 4 The authority of the researcher qua interviewer but also qua writer comes under scrutiny. Respondents are no longer seen as faceless numbers whose opinions we process completely on our own terms. Consequently, there is increasing concern with the respondents' own understanding as he or she frames and represents an 'opinion'.
> 5 Traditional patriarchal relations in interviewing are being criticized, and ways to make formerly unarticulated voices audible are now centre stage.
> 6 The forms used to report findings are now hugely expanded. As boundaries separating disciplines collapse, modes of expression from literature, poetry and drama are being applied.
> 7 The topic of inquiry – interviewing – has expanded to encompass the cinematic and the televisual. Electronic media are increasingly accepted as a resource in interviews, with growing use of e-mail, Internet chat rooms, and other electronic modes of communication.
>
> (*Source:* adapted from Fontana, 2002: 162–3)

the highly influential *Handbook of Qualitative Research* (Denzin and Lincoln, 2000), on which I have drawn to some extent in forming the account given here. This book ambitiously attempts to set new directions for qualitative research and it does so at least in part by presenting a **progress narrative** in which the author's own preferred direction influences their presentation of the history of qualitative method.

This is particularly evident in considering the use of the **moments** device to summarize historical periods (Box 9.10). In a first edition of the *Handbook* (Denzin and Lincoln, 1994) only the first five were identified. Note how the more recent 'moments' occupy far shorter periods than the earlier ones. An impression of developments gathering pace is thereby created.

The moments device itself creates an idea of linear development in which each successive phase replaces the previous one. Denzin and Lincoln try to address this by pointing out that traces of earlier moments may persist in contemporary research practice, but it is instructive to consider what might have happened had they chosen a less

> ## Box 9.10 Denzin and Lincoln's (2000) seven 'moments'
>
> 1 Traditional period (1900–50)
> 2 Modernist phase (1950–70)
> 3 Blurred genres (1970–86)
> 4 Crisis of representation (1986–90)
> 5 Triple crisis (1990–95)
> 6 Post-experimental (1995–2000)
> 7 The future

linear model around which to arrange their history and instead opted for a **centrifugal** model, in which a central dominant orthodoxy persisted at *all* periods of time. This dominant orthodoxy at the centre would have involved a broadly *realist* research practice, addressing some of the issues important in the scientific tradition of social research which 'qualitative' researchers share with their 'quantitative' counterparts, as well as drawing on strengths in the tradition of literary scholarship particularly appropriate to interpretive work. With a centrifugal rather than linear model, the diversity, creativity and subtlety of work done at chronologically earlier times might then have been less subject to the stigmatizing 'othering' implied by being out of fashion. Practising researchers might then have been more free to learn from the example of the past rather than imagining that only the new is good. This might have placed chronologically recent developments like experimental writing and radically political versions of qualitative research practice towards the outer edge of a spinning wheel, a less comfortable place to be than a vanguard position at the head of a linear, progressive social movement.

Other developments

The metaphor of a centrifuge or spinning wheel, rather than a linear development of 'moments', allows us, too, to understand the place of some important recent developments in qualitative research practice that do not come at the 'right' time for a linear version of history. Computer-assisted qualitative data analysis, for example, became popular from the mid-1980s onwards as researchers increasingly found personal computers were within their budgets (Fielding and Lee, 1991). These developments were associated initially with the continuing popularity of (modernist moment) grounded theorizing. John Seidel's software program. The Ethnograph was a pioneer here. Now in its fifth release, this program was based on a simple code-and-retrieve logic (see Chapter 23) and proved immensely popular in the 1980s because it automated many of the tasks qualitative data analysts had had to do laboriously by hand. Later software (NUD*IST, ATLAS.ti, NVivo, for example) developed capacities beyond

those of coding and retrieval to incorporate a greater variety of analytic practices. While the image of computers may, for some, provoke thoughts of science and rationality – matters which, as we have seen, certain romantic impulses within the qualitative research community have at times rejected – in fact, these programs have proved useful in doing research from a variety of analytic viewpoints and epistemological positions. They are, after all, basically electronic filing cabinets or card indexes and these are devices which scholars from many traditions have long found useful.

Conversation analysis, as has already been noted, is significantly out of step with postmodern and constructivist sensibilities, yet it has thrived as a subgenre within qualitative research throughout the 1980s, 1990s and beyond. More recent developments that have been transforming qualitative research practice in recent years include the increasingly widespread use of *focus groups* (see Chapter 15). These herald a new spirit of cooperation between academic social researchers and market researchers, who have long used this method (Ereaut, 2004) within a commercial environment. Focus groups at least in part replace the reliance of policy makers on gauging public opinion via large-scale surveys of opinion polling, suggesting some shift of balance from quantitative to qualitative.

Other developments worth mentioning are the growth in qualitative data archiving (see Chapters 19 and 26), the accessibility of which has been enhanced by the possibility of remote access across the Internet and the increasing tendency for transcripts to be stored in electronic form. Like the portable cassette recorder in the 1970s and the dissemination of the personal computer in the 1980s, the growth of email- and Internet-based research (Chapter 21) seems set to transform certain qualitative research practices in the future, examples of technology-driven (rather than theoretically conceived) methodological development.

Finally, from the 1980s on, as appreciation of the rich variety and strength of qualitative perspectives developed, it became less necessary to actively maintain the qualitative creation myth so important to the Romantics of the 1960s and 1970s. This led to active attempts to deconstruct the qualitative–quantitative divide and to promote mixed methodological practice (Bryman, 1988; Brannen, 1992b; see also Chapter 22). While this form of research practice still has some way to go before the prejudices and stereotypes of earlier generations can be fully overcome, it suggests that the future of qualitative social research lies not in some seventh 'moment' in qualitative research, but in renaming 'qualitative research' as 're-search'.

Anglo-American dominance

Pertti Alasuutari, a Finnish qualitative research practitioner, reports the anecdote in Box 9.11 from when he prepared an English language edition of his textbook *Researching Culture: Qualitative Method and Cultural Studies* (Alasuutari, 1996)

Alasuutari goes on to observe that this is partly because English has increasingly become the international language and partly because the economics of textbook marketing include the simple fact that the United States is the biggest single market for academic books. Additionally, social science writers – even when writing in languages other than English – make an automatic assumption of familiarity with American and British places, personalities and popular events, whereas

the same things in other countries are not assumed to be internationally as well known. This reflects the general promulgation of these in international media. This means that researchers working outside the English-speaking centre have to see their own practice as if it were on the periphery. One thing that this has led to, in Alasuutari's view, has been the representation of the preferences of a very small, 'practically all-American' group of qualitative researchers as if it were the cutting edge, through such mechanisms as the Denzin and Lincoln (2000) *Handbook*.

Uwe Flick (1998) points out the problems that this then creates for non-English traditions. Describing the German qualitative research experience, he points out that in the early 1970s German researchers drew heavily – indeed 'imported' – many of the ideas and methods of American research practice. From the late 1970s onwards, though, German researchers diverged, producing work that was methodologically original along different lines from the Anglo-American stream. In particular the *narrative interview* (Schütze, 1977) and *objective hermeneutics* (Oevermann et al., 1979) were developed, influencing a generation of German qualitative researchers, most of whom published their work in German. Writers like Alasuutari and Flick represent the exception

---

Box 9.11   Illustration of Anglo-American dominance

'My publisher expressed a concern about the fact that in the book, there were plenty of references to studies that had been published in Finnish:

> At a basic level, the proportion of Finnish work cited in the text will not be helpful to British, American or other readers, to whom this literature will not be readily available or familiar ... Would it be possible to rework the text as you go along so that references of this kind are replaced by references to examples which are fairly well-known in the English language literature? I am not asking you to completely empty the text of any Finnish connection, but to ensure that the overall balance makes the English language reader feel at ease with the presentation.

'The request was quite understandable, and I did change several research examples into work that had appeared in "internationally" published books or journals. In some cases, having to build my point around a new research example probably did good to the text, in some other cases I was not pleased with the quality of research I found and thought that that the original research example was better and more interesting. Yet I grudgingly had to promote a piece of research basically only because it had been published in English.'
(Alasuutari, 2004)

rather than the rule, in that they both read and write in English as well as their own languages. One future for qualitative research may be the further development of productive communication between English- and non-English-speaking traditions.

Conclusion

Qualitative research, like quantitative research, has a rich and varied history. This chapter has sought to indicate something of the diversity of qualitative research practice, showing that methodological principles and prescriptions, as well as research techniques, arise from human activity and social relations as much as any other area of knowledge. They were not handed down from on high, but were invented by people, the product of personal and political struggles over ideas, signs of their times. One of the points I have emphasized is that an historical account is inevitably partial, and this one is no exception. In particular, linear progress narratives may be unhelpful ways of writing histories. This chapter will, I hope, contribute towards a deeper understanding of the historical roots of the particular social practices we choose to call 'methods'.

Further reading

Apart from the accounts given by authors drawn upon for this chapter (for example, Denzin and Lincoln, 2000; Atkinson et al., 2001) the following recommendations can be made. Abrams et al. (1981) contains several readings about the history of qualitative method in Britain before 1980. Platt (1996) provides a history of sociological methods in America before 1960. Seale et al. (2004) provide an edited collection of a full range of qualitative research practice, including many authors drawn from outside the Anglo-American circuit. Seale (2004a) presents a book of classic readings taken from the history of both quantitative and qualitative research.

Key concepts

Anglo-American dominance
Autoethnography
Centrifugal *versus* **linear** *model of history*
Constructionist epistemology
Interview society

Moments in history
   Blurred genres
   Crisis of representation
   Modernist
   Traditional
Progress narrative
Qualitative creation myth
Romantic conception of research

10

Ethics and social research

Suki Ali and Moira Kelly

CONTENTS

Ethical issues are often difficult to define and harder still to work with, yet all social research involves ethical decision making. This may become relevant in the formulation of a research question, when sampling, gaining access to data or research respondents, whilst collecting data, when analysing data or at the writing up stage, even when engaging with audiences and publishing findings. In this chapter we will explain why ethical considerations are important to social research, provide a historical introduction to the inception of ethical guidelines, and go on to consider specific points in the research process at which ethics may play a significant role. Both conventional conceptions of research ethics and contemporary reflections on research ethics as they relate to power relations will be considered.

Why do we need research ethics?

Many people consider ethics to be a small part of the research process, one that may not even be relevant to their work at all. For example, in the past it has been usual to think about ethics predominantly in relation to social research with *people*, concentrating on the ways in which people are affected by their participation in research. Conventionally, and associated with the idea that research involves the pursuit of objective truths, it has been thought that the social researcher has certain obligations and responsibilities in considering the effects of such truths on both respondents and wider communities. In this kind of model, ethical practice is akin to a form of professional practice. Ethics here are centred on *procedural issues* and especially on the principle of *informed consent*. The emphasis on correct ethical procedures contains the danger that somewhat prescriptive codes of practice are formulated which may allow researchers to think that as long as certain procedures are followed, research practice is automatically 'ethical'.

In recent years, the way we think about ethics has changed and the topic has opened up, with its relevance becoming much wider. *Post-structuralist* ways of thinking about the social world have challenged the idea that objective, knowable truths are uncovered by expert researchers (see Chapter 4). One of the most influ-

ential interventions into research ethics has come from feminist researchers who have challenged the idea that ethical practice *per se* can ensure non-harmful research practice. They have shifted emphasis onto the role of power relations at all levels of knowledge production, from *epistemology*, through research relationships, to the dissemination of findings. If we think about research in this larger way then the links between power, politics and research ethics become clearer.

We can see, then, that ethical considerations may be closely aligned to both *moral* and *political* considerations in research work. More importantly, what is considered to be ethical in research has changed over time and may be highly influenced by the researcher's own theoretical, moral or political approach to his or her research. Whatever approach that may be, ethics will play a part. Even epistemological frameworks can be informed by ethical considerations. In the next section we outline the historical developments which led to contemporary *medical* research ethics, and how these have given rise to the development of key ethical principles of practice for researching culture and society.

What are research ethics?

Ethics is the branch of philosophy, said to have been initiated by Aristotle, which takes human action as its subject matter (Finnis, 1983). This can mean opinions about human action, opinions about right human action, right opinions about human action, or all of these topics. Ethics in this classic sense is about practical knowledge and the application of theory to human activities. As Homan says, 'Ethics is the science of morality: those who engage in it determine values for the regulation of human behaviour' (Homan, 1991: 1).

We are all aware of the moral debates that are discussed on a daily basis in the media on topics such as euthanasia, civil disobedience and genetic engineering. Much of this debate is related to the *regulation* and *legality* of these activities. Social and cultural researchers, too, are interested in the values that may regulate the conduct of research. The decisions we make at different stages in our research may have ethical implications even though we may not be aware of them. Even when deciding on a topic for study we are making a choice about a population to investigate and this may have ethical implications.

Influences on the ethics of social research

Contemporary research ethics has developed from the numerous philosophical debates that have gone on since the time of Aristotle. A central issue in ethics is the relationship between the individual and the social world. In research we need to consider how the imposition of the research on individuals (with their consent or otherwise) can be balanced with the benefit of making the world a better place to live in.

The complexity of human conduct means that there are no absolutes in practice: there is no single ethical theory which accounts for all possible contingencies. Differing philosophical perspectives may be presented as opposing perspectives. **Utilitarian** theory has been influential in thinking about the ethics of empirical research, with philosophers such as Bentham and Mill arguing that certain actions can be justified in terms of their contribution to the greater good. A research project may therefore be justified on the basis of its potential benefit to society, even if it may cause harm to an individual. Other philosophers, such as Rawls, argue that the rights of the individual in terms of their freedom to choose (for example, whether to take part in research) will always come first. Thus there is a tension between activities (such as research) that aim to improve the world in which we live and the rights of the individual.

The philosophical arguments of writers such as Mill and Rawls were not originally couched in terms of research practice, but were more general reflections on the nature of morality. However, they are still highly relevant to the conduct of a research project, potentially influencing decisions about what and how to study. In fact, achieving a balance between respecting the rights of the individual and making the world a better place often underlies contemporary discussions of research ethics. The role of such ethical debate, then, is to help decide on an appropriate course of action, but should never be reduced to a straightforward application of ethical principles regardless of context:

Box 10.1 Two medical ethics scandals

Nazi experiments
The importance of protecting human beings from invasive medical treatments was highlighted during the post-war Nuremberg trials. The trials of 23 doctors revealed that many people held in concentration camps had been made to participate in dangerous medical experiments, such as exposure to extreme temperatures, often with fatal results. This led to the Declaration of Helsinki produced by the World Medical Association in 1964, which was to safeguard against future atrocities of this nature. This was revised for the fifth time in 2000 (Christie, 2000). It sets out international standards for conducting medical research with human subjects (Singer and Benetar, 2001).

The Tuskegee experiment
In the Tuskegee experiment between 1932 and 1972 the US Public Health Service denied effective treatment to 399 African Americans who were in the late stages of syphilis, a disease which can involve tumours, heart disease, paralysis, insanity, blindness and death. The men were not told of the disease from which they were suffering and were, for the most part, illiterate and poor. The aim was to collect information at autopsy so that the effects of the disease in black sufferers could be compared with those in whites. In practice, the results of the study did not contribute to the control or cure of the disease. In 1997 President Clinton issued a public apology for these government-sponsored actions to the few remaining survivors (Jones, 1993).

The applied ethics model assumes that moral problems come neatly labelled and categorized and that their pre-assigned categories match those in the norms. But norms are not self-applying. Considerable moral work gets done in deciding how a situation is to be characterized, and that moral work can determine how issues are resolved. (Hoffmaster, 1994: 1157)

Medical research ethics

Emphasis on the ethical aspect of social research has increased significantly in recent years. It has taken a lead from developments in medical research ethics that have taken place since the end of the Second World War, which have been fuelled by some ethical scandals (see Box 10.1). The practices of the Nazi doctors could be seen as an extreme case, but dangerous medical research practices did not end with the Nazis. In the Tuskegee experiment people were experimented upon without full knowledge of the procedures to be undertaken, causing them harm. The controversy surrounding Tuskegee led to a tightening up of regulations concerning research ethics in the United States (Benetar and Singer, 2000).

Although there is considerable debate within medicine regarding ethical research practice, a number of principles are commonly regarded as fundamental. These have been set out by Beauchamp (1994: 3):

1 **Beneficence** (the obligation to provide benefits and balance benefits against risks)
2 **Non-maleficence** (the obligation to avoid the causation of harm)
3 Respect for **autonomy** (the obligation to respect the decision-making capacities of autonomous persons)
4 **Justice** (obligations of fairness in the distribution of benefits and risks)

These principles also underlie the development of social research ethics. They are not rules in themselves but are generally used as reference points for the development of ethical guidelines.

Whereas the ethics of medical research are often seen in terms of balancing risks against potential benefits this is not always seen as useful in social research (Kelman, 1982). Concern with harms and benefits in medical research generally refer to physical responses to treatment. In social research such harms and benefits are harder to predict and therefore to 'balance' against risks. However, it can be taken that we have a moral obligation to avoid actions that reduce the well-being (broadly defined) of others or that may inhibit their freedom to express and develop themselves.

Our primary concern is with protecting and enhancing the well-being of research participants and of others who are, or may in the future be, affected by the research. We therefore have an obligation to minimize the risk of harm caused by the research and to forgo research that carries unacceptable risks. (Kelman, 1982: 87)

Ethical practice in social research

Despite the increasing regulation and monitoring of social research, ethical practice in effect comes down to the 'professional' integrity of the individual researcher. The history of social research, like that of medical research, contains examples of questionable ethical practice (see Box 10.2) and regulation (in the form of codes of ethical practice, requirements for research ethics committees and the like) is partly a response to these incidents. In addition, feminist researchers have argued that, from a political standpoint, researchers need to pay attention to issues of power in knowledge production and that this is a matter of ethics. This has resulted, in particular, in a focus on research relationships and issues of hierarchy.

Relationships with research participants

It is commonly argued (for example, by the British Sociological Association, 2002) that research relationships wherever possible should be characterized by trust and integrity. If researchers work at gaining the trust and respect of the populations they study they are likely also to gain the trust of the wider community. Poor ethical practices cause potential harms to those studied and also muddies

---

Box 10.2   Examples of ethically dubious social research

Example 1:   Milgram (1974)

In an experiment done in 1963 Stanley Milgram was interested in why people were willing to harm other people if they thought they had been ordered to do so. The defence that 'we were only obeying orders' had been used by many who had perpetrated war crimes and other cruelties in the Nazi era. Pretending that he was trying to see if punishment affected people's capacity to learn, unwitting research subjects were required to administer electric shocks to other 'subjects' if these people gave incorrect answers to questions, sometimes to the point at which people screamed and begged for mercy. The shocks, though, were not real and the people receiving the shocks were actors. Milgram was able to demonstrate that many people are willing to suspend moral doubts if authority over them is strong enough.

Example 2:   Humphrey (1970)

Laud Humphrey studied homosexual encounters in public toilets by acting as a lookout ('watchqueen'), not telling the people he studied of his true identity (although he did gain the trust of some after disclosing his purpose). As a covert researcher he could not interview men without revealing his identity, so he wrote down the car licence plate numbers of the men and found out where they lived. Changing his appearance he then interviewed them a year later in their homes on the pretext of carrying out a survey on a different subject. His study contributed to the de-stigmatization of such men who at the time were harassed by police authorities, overcoming stereotypes that they were predatory in relation to non-homosexuals, for example.

---

the waters for future efforts to undertake research in those populations.

These issues are often particularly acute when conducting ethnographic research (see Chapter 17). Indeed some feminist researchers have argued that, although ethnography allows better knowledge of many research areas than other methods such as surveys, as well as involving less hierarchical relationships between researcher and researched, it also opens up greater potential for harm because of a deeper level of personal involvement and better access to otherwise hidden aspects of people's lives (see Stacey, 1988 and Skeggs, 1994). However, other methods (for example, qualitative interviews) also involve these problems, if to a lesser degree, and these concern both the nature of developing relationships in the field and what happens to respondents after researchers have left. This is especially relevant when researching sensitive issues, such as sexual abuse.

Managing ethical involvement with participants involves two main areas of concern: issues of *privacy* and *confidentiality* and of gaining *informed consent*. We will take each in turn.

Privacy, confidentiality and data protection

Most research studies involve an invasion of privacy at some level, even if this is as simple as being stopped in the street for a consumer survey. Invasion of privacy can be viewed both as a harm in its own right and also as a condition that subjects people to the possibility of harm by depriving them of the protection that privacy offers. The harms that may result from unwitting disclosure of personal information are both *foreseeable* and *unforeseeable* harms and the researcher has a duty to protect people from both (Kelman, 1982).

In response to the increased potential for distributing personal information collected as part of a research study, policies and laws on data protection have developed. For example, the 1998 Data Protection Act in the UK sets out eight principles of good practice, saying that stored personal data (which includes both facts about and opinions expressed by people) must be:

• Fairly and lawfully processed
• Processed for limited purposes
• Adequate, relevant and not excessive
• Accurate
• Not kept longer than necessary
• Processed in accordance with the data subject's rights
• Secure
• Not transferred to countries without adequate protection

(See: www.dataprotection.gov.uk/)

Care regarding data protection needs to be taken at all stages of research though particular sensitivity may be required at different stages. Note that unless the data sample is *self-selected*, such as through an advertisement, decisions on samples require the researcher to find out personal details even before subjects are recruited to the study.

Researchers usually explain to people, when approaching them about participation in a study, why they have been selected and how their name has been obtained. The potential participants may be assured at this point that the information they give will be confidential and that care will be taken to ensure that they will not be identified in a final report. Participants may also be assured that no information which could be used to identify them will be made available without their agreement to anyone outside the agency responsible for conducting the research. These promises, if made, mean that data must usually be 'anonymized', so all identifying names and places are taken out. This also protects other people and institutions to whom research participants may refer. The participant is likely to be told who will see the data in its original form (usually the research team). It is not always possible to ensure confidentiality or to do all of these things and, if so, it should normally be made clear that this is the case so that consent to participate is given on this basis.

On a practical level, it is also usual that researchers store data in a way that is secure and promotes confidentiality. Each research participant may be given a code number, included on any transcripts or questionnaires. Data may be kept in a locked filing cabinet or secure computer file in a locked room. It may be destroyed when it is no longer needed or, if deposited in an archive (see Chapters 19 and 26), may be subject to varying levels of availability depending on the nature of the subject and the promises made to original participants.

Problems in maintaining confidentiality may arise when studying topics where the populations are small or easily distinguishable. For example, in a study of women chief executives in the motor industry the numbers are likely to be small and it may therefore be difficult to maintain confidentiality even if pseudonyms are used. This issue is not easily subsumed under a procedure or rule. However, if it looks likely that confidentiality or anonymity will not be assured and the participant refuses to waive this right then the information they give you cannot be made public. Sometimes, in these cases, respondents are given the opportunity to delete particular segments in research reports, or there is restricted access to the final report.

In some instances confidentiality may not be an issue. Some respondents may even be proud and pleased that their personal story is going to be shown to a wider public. Additionally, a researcher can go back to respondents and attempt to re-negotiate confidentiality agreements if they feel that circumstances have changed. Feminist researchers, as well as others, have argued that research participants have a moral right to see interview transcripts and other kinds of data in order for them to assess whether their words or actions have been fairly represented. This can make for a more equal research relationship between researcher and researched (see, for example, Maynard and Purvis, 1994).

Informed consent

Following the Declaration of Helsinki (see Box 10.1), **informed consent** has been viewed as a focal point in any discussion of research ethics, in either natural or social science. Individuals are felt to have the right to know what is happening to them. Gaining informed consent is a procedure that aims to support the principle of individual autonomy and is widely agreed to be a safeguard for the rights of human subjects participating knowingly and voluntarily in research. The aim is to ensure that research participants are able to decide for themselves what is in their best interest and what risks they are prepared to take. In order for consent to be 'informed', the reason for the study, the requirements of participants and potential risks and harm need to be explained in appropriate detail and in terms meaningful to participants.

Potential research participants can be given information about the study both verbally and through an information sheet. Enough information needs to be given for the person to decide without overwhelming them with detail or specialist jargon. One way of presenting information in an accessible way is to include a number of questions and answers. Questions a potential participant may need to have answered could include:

- Why do you think I am suitable to take part in this research?
- How did you get my name/find out that I was suitable for the study?
- Why is this study important?
- How will the study be done?
- What does the study involve?
- Will this study benefit me?
- Are there any risks or hazards involved?
- Will people be able to find out my details because of this study?
- What if I change my mind or don't want to be involved?

The research participant may be assured that they can stop participating at any time for any reason. Researchers, particularly if they are doing social surveys, are often under pressure to maximize response rates. However, it is important that this does not become coercion or lead to participants being misled. Ideally, written consent will be provided through a **consent form** signed by the participant and the researcher. This may say that the participant has been informed about the study and what is required, that they understand the information collected will be confidential and that they can withdraw from the study at any time. Two copies may be signed, one kept by the researcher and one by the participant.

Although informed consent is considered the ideal in terms of respecting the autonomy of the potential research participant, it is also sometimes appropriate to study populations where this is not possible. For example, people with serious mental impairment may be unable to understand the purpose of a research study; people engaged in illegal or stigmatized activities may not want a researcher around them. If we believe in the value of social research it is important to learn about those populations who would be excluded if informed consent were always to be required in advance from individual participants. The issues this raises will be discussed further later in this chapter.

On the whole, practical arrangements for gaining informed consent are straightforward, particularly in interview studies, which may be one reason why they are so popular. However, there are some situations in which it is difficult to gain informed consent. For example, in studying a community or institution using methods such as observation it will usually be difficult to gain consent for each piece of data collected. Thus, if a public meeting is being observed it will be unwieldy to get written informed consent as described above beforehand from each person who may say something. One way around this is to provide information leaflets, posters or a verbal announcement about the research so that people can say if they do not want to be included. Another possibility is to gain consent from key figures and ensure they know what the research entails. Many organizations that fund research require that representatives of those studied are included in planning and advising on the conduct of the research. This may be considered to be linked to the issue of consent in that researchers are then increasingly accountable to research participants.

Covert research

There are situations where those researched are not informed about the study and consent is not sought prior to their participation in the research. **Covert** methods can range from misrepresenting the research to respondents at the outset, bugging or taping conversations, covert image collection

---

Box 10.3   Examples of covert research

Example 1:   In research on the National Front, Nigel Fielding (1981) used a combination of overt and covert methods. He gained consent for the study from the Front's 'head office', but in his participation in the activities of local groups he did not reveal his true status, displaying instead an attitude that appeared sympathetic to the aims of these groups and participating in events such as marches.

Example 2:   In research on the use of the Internet by white supremacist groups, Les Back had to use a pseudonym to access much of the material. He reasoned that giving his real name and revealing his identity as a researcher would have resulted in danger to himself and lack of cooperation from research participants. (Ware and Back, 2001; see also Back's article at: www.unesco.org/webworld/points_of_views/back.shtml)

(such as videoing and photographing) and covert participant observation. Investigations of white supremacist organizations, for example, have often involved covert methods (see Box 10.3). Researchers may inadvertently use a form of covert method by using informal discussions which they later report in research, or by video-taping or photographing in public places. However, it is more likely that the issue of sustained covert participant observation raises serious ethical considerations (as it did in Humphrey's study – see Box 10.2).

There are many reasons for avoiding the use of covert methods if possible. Homan (1991) argues that covert methods:

- Flout the principle of informed consent
- Help erode personal liberty
- Betray trust
- Pollute the research environment for other researchers
- Are bad for the reputation of social research
- Discriminate against the defenceless and powerless
- May damage the behaviour or interests of subjects
- Are invisibly reactive, suggesting, for example, support for the aims of the group studied
- Are seldom necessary
- Have the effect of confining the scope of research

Additionally, Homan says that if covert methods are used too readily the habit of deception may spread to other spheres of human interaction as they may become habitual in the everyday life of the person doing the research. They also place the covert researcher in conditions of excessive strain in maintaining the cover.

Given this litany of objections is covert research ever justifiable? The answer to this is by no means unanimous, but seems to be a cautious 'yes'. Under certain circumstances secrecy may be the only way to collect data that is not 'contaminated' by the presence of the researcher, and if it does not harm respondents it may be justifiable. For example, in psychological experimentation it is often the case that small children may be observed in a controlled environment without their knowledge in order to assess their behaviour. It is argued that if they knew there was an adult watching them play that they would be likely to alter their actions and a 'true' representation of their behaviour would be impossible to obtain. In these circumstances, too, it may be considered that parental consent is adequate. For those studying people engaged in actions deemed illegal or anti-social, who may wish to conceal their actions from researchers, as in the case of the groups concerned in Box 10.3, concerns about harming the interests of the groups involved (if not the individuals concerned) may be less pressing than in other research situations.

As a rule of thumb, from an ethical perspective, covert research should be avoided unless it is ab-

---

Box 10.4 Making assumptions about 'vulnerability'

Valerie Hey's work with frail elderly people shows how the assumption of 'vulnerability' (implied also in the choice of the word 'frail') can have a *disempowering* effect on the autonomy of respondents. In her article about researching decision making processes and community care, she argues that, in many cases, what might be considered by some as *incomprehension* of the purposes of research was in fact a form of *resistance* within the research process. Hey writes that we should not therefore conflate specific difficulties with gathering material from elderly people with mental and physical *incapacity*. Instead, we should respect people's accounts as thoughtful, perhaps strategic and certainly competent. This is part of Hey's commitment to ethical practice and awareness of political aspects to research processes in which power relations are held constantly under scrutiny.

---

solutely essential. Where possible, too, where covert observation or deception has been involved in collecting information it is desirable to inform those involved that they have participated in the research, and sometimes to negotiate consent at that stage.

Vulnerable groups

Working with **vulnerable groups** is likely to raise ethical dilemmas for the researcher. Vulnerable groups can loosely be defined as those who are at particular risk in society and from the research process in particular. These groups may include children, elderly people, people with learning disabilities, homeless or sick people and disenfranchised groups such as refugees. In all these cases, the vulnerability of the group is connected to issues of relative disempowerment within the social setting. However we should be careful not to present an overdetermined and constrained view of what constitutes disempowerment in the research setting, as Valerie Hey's (1994) research has demonstrated (Box 10.4).

In addition to the 'conventional' groups outlined above, it may be that the kind of research being conducting actually places people in a position of vulnerability. So if, say, you were interested in studying racism within a workplace, you might find that announcement of the research topic itself creates difficulties. It could suggest new racial or ethnic categorizations of co-workers to people in the organization who had previously not thought of their colleagues in this way.

Research with children

During the past 10 years there has been a shift in emphasis from research 'on' children to research 'with' them. This shift has implications for the ethical conduct of research since it emphasizes that children are competent and knowledgeable respondents (see, for example, Alderson, 1995). Research with children can give a particular focus to ethical issues that are common to all social research, though there are some age-specific issues too. Ethical guidelines for research with children have become increasingly important with the recognition of the high levels of abuse of children within families and institutional settings such as school and church. Researchers working with children must therefore be particularly aware of the potential abuse of power relationships between adult researchers and children. Anxieties about abuse have led to attempts to regulate researchers by means of police checks on criminal records. Although many researchers may be tempted to circumvent this requirement by using personal contacts, they ought to ask themselves whether this is right. Finally, legal considerations may come into play: adults in schools are considered to be *in loco parentis* (responsible in the place of parents if left 'in charge' of the child) and researchers left on their own with children may be held responsible if the child has an accident.

Informed consent has a particular resonance in work with children. Do children really always understand the implications of taking part in research? Can they be said to fully consent to the

---

Box 10.5 What do children make of guarantees of confidentiality and privacy?

The following excerpt is from research notes made in 1998 by Suki Ali in a study of 'mixed-race' identities:

> I was talking to Marita today for the first time in a one-on-one interview. She is a very bright child in Year 4 in ******* School. I began with my 'blurb' about the research and what it was about and then asked her if she would like to take part in this next stage. I explained (I thought) that the interview would be confidential and explained what that meant. That it would be between us and not for other people to know what had been said and so on. She said 'sort of like a secret' and I said 'yes'. It was a key theme with the children that what they said should not be reported back to the teachers or to their parents.
>
> Later in the interview she said 'If the interview is confidential, why are you taping it?'. It was an excellent question, because if confidential meant 'secret' it was indeed rather risky to be taping it! If it was only me who would use the information, and nobody else would hear what she had said, why tape it? I had to then re-think the way I explained 'confidential' and that it meant that she would not be identified but that what she said may be used in the research. I emphasized that it would be done in such a way that would be respectful of what she had said but would not get her into trouble.

---

process? Do they understand confidentiality? As we have seen, this is one of the key areas of ethical research practice and yet one of the hardest to be sure about in relation to both children and adults (see Box 10.5).

One of the most obviously difficult and disturbing aspects of work with children is what to do if a child discloses abuse of some kind. Teachers are legally required to report this to the relevant specialists within the school. But the researcher who may have already promised confidentiality may find themselves with an ethical dilemma. Some schools will indeed be clear about the way that they will expect the researcher to respond, but in many cases decisions have to taken in the first instance by the researcher. This brings to the fore issues of trust, privacy and confidentiality that can also occur – if more rarely – in research studies done with adults.

Ethical issues in data analysis

Some researchers may assume that once they have got through the difficulties of setting up a research project, working out a suitable question, accessing their sample and collecting data, that they are now into an area that has no ethical implications – data analysis. In many cases that may be true, or at least be limited to some quite straight-forward decision

making. In other cases, it may be that urgent ethical issues arise at this stage (Box 10.6).

Both Mauthner and Song in Box 10.6 are clear that there are no easy answers to this kind of dilemma. They call for a rigorously *reflexive* approach to analysis (see Chapter 3), and a recognition that whilst one account may be 'true' and the other 'false' they are both important contributions to the research. The processes of analysis and choice can also reflect the greater power and authority of the researcher, but with careful and thoughtful analysis, can add depth and richness to research.

These more obvious and understandable examples can be brought back to the issue of knowledge production more generally and questions of *epistemology*. Data analysis of all sorts involves decisions about which lines of analysis to pursue and which to put to one side. Choosing not to go down a particular route may have ethical implications: decisions made at this stage may 'silence' certain voices and give undue prominence to others. Thus the production of knowledge itself has to be understood as an ethical endeavour. Lorraine Code (1991) writes that objectivity and ethics in research are linked in a complex relationship which requires us to question who can know, and what they can know. Her work focuses on the exclusion of women from

---

Box 10.6 Examples of ethical issues when analysing contradictory accounts

Example 1: Melanie Mauthner (1998) interviewed sisters about their relationships with each other, leading to some difficult questions about voicing and making public some very personal issues. In some cases one sister gave information that she did not want shared with the other. The interpretation of this material was potentially compromised by trying to hold back the confidential parts.

Example 2: Miri Song (1998), also working with siblings, discusses the problems of being given competing accounts of the same relationships and events. She describes the difficulties with holding on to 'oppositional accounts' without 'stirring up trouble' or producing 'false' or one-sided accounts.

---

particular kinds of knowledge work such as science, but is relevant to all kinds of marginal and 'vulnerable groups' who are not afforded status as competent knowers. She therefore argues for a form of knowledge production that is *responsible* and therefore ethical. Doucet and Mauthner (2002) have elaborated on this, arguing that in order to 'know well', to 'know responsibly' and to hold to what they call **epistemic responsibility**, researchers do not just need to have good research relationships but should be clear that reflexivity and the ethical practice that it entails requires a strong engagement with social, institutional and political contexts as well as intellectual frameworks. These deeper-level ethical issues come into stark relief not only at the stage of data analysis, but at the point at which research studies are published.

Ethical issues in publishing research

Considerable ethical issues arise when writing and publishing research. There can be pressure from all sides to produce particular findings or present them in a certain way. This can be exerted by funders, other members of the research team or participants. An interesting example of this is described by Punch (1986) who details his experience of undertaking a PhD study on a progressive school in England, in which the sponsors (the school's trustees, alumni and staff) were at best ambivalent throughout its course. The central problem was his difficulties in getting his sponsors to allow him to publish it at all.

Problems may arise in research teams where team members with less power may feel under pressure to go along with interpretations of the data they do not agree with. Regarding participants, in order to undertake research in the first place, a relationship usually needs to be built with those who are to be 'researched'. This can be either individuals or a community or organization. This may place the researcher in the position of having to present negative findings or represent the population under study in an unflattering way. This means that it is especially important not to mislead participants at any stage.

Box 10.7 The duty of confidentiality can suppress important findings

Baez (2002) describes a study where participants reported instances of discrimination on the basis of gender and race. However, despite Baez feeling that there was a strong need to highlight this in the analysis, the small numbers of ethnic minority members in the population studied would mean that they would be identifiable. The individuals refused to waive their right to confidentiality, leaving Baez frustrated that the discriminatory practice highlighted by his research could not be challenged.

Additionally, the need to maintain confidentiality at publication stage can cause ethical tensions if important points are therefore suppressed (Box 10.7). Here the researcher can be caught between two ethical obligations: to publish the findings of research that may improve society, conflicting with an obligation to protect the rights of research participants.

Ethics committees

There are a number of sources of advice and information concerning research ethics, including ethical committees based in institutions such as universities and hospitals, and professional guidelines on research ethics. Obligations to get ethical approval for studies are sometimes seen as bureaucratic impositions. However, they can also be (and we would argue should be) treated as occasions for helpful advice. Most universities these days have ethical committees to review research proposals of staff and students, whereas even 20 years ago these were less common. Health services research is very commonly subject to the requirement that formal ethical approval be obtained before contacting potential participants and, sometimes, before seeking funding for research. This reflects the history of ethical debates, which as we have seen, have been highly influenced by events in medical research

studies. The growth of formal ethical scrutiny may appear restrictive, but can also contribute to greater transparency.

It may come as a surprise, too, to learn that good research design is often considered by formal research ethics committees to be a legitimate matter for comment and evaluation. Choice of research methodology and design would not appear to be intrinsically ethical, but it is generally viewed as ethically problematic to involve someone in a study that has been poorly designed. This may mislead participants, who are led to believe that they will give their time and talk about perhaps sensitive issues in order to contribute to the greater good, when in fact the design does not work or the data they give is not used in the end for whatever reason.

Conclusion

The central ethical issue for much social and cultural research is how the rights of participants (and researchers) are to be balanced against the potential benefits to society. The various facets of ethical practice we have discussed return, for the most part, to this issue. Ethical conduct requires attention to quite broad epistemological and political issues as well as matters pertaining to research relationships at the time a study is conducted. We have also argued that, at the end of the day, ethical

---

Box 10.8   Web pointers for research ethics

The Internet Encyclopedia of Philosophy – use it to look up entries on utilitarianism, Bentham, Mill, Rawl etc.
www.utm.edu/research/iep/

Bioethics resources on the Web – contains useful links to other sites on research ethics
www.nih.gov/sigs/bioethics/internationalresthics.html#research

Office for Human Research Protections (US Department of Health and Human Services)
http://ohrp.osophs.dhhs.gov/index.html

'Surveys in social research' – the website for a book by David De Vaus. Follow the links associated with his Chapter 5 for guidelines issued by research organizations
www.social-research.org/

Visit the website for this book at www.rscbook.co.uk to link to these web pointers.

practice depends upon the integrity of the researcher. Advice is often available from ethical committees. Guidelines exist to protect both the rights and safety of the research participants and the researcher (as well as the institution or subject discipline they represent). However, sticking rigidly to advice or guidelines cannot ensure that research is ethical: decisions still need to be made throughout the course of the research that demonstrate sensitivity to the local context of a project, for which the researcher takes ultimate responsibility. As Beauchamp comments, 'There is no such thing as a simple "application" of a principle so as to resolve a complicated moral problem' (1994: 11).

Further reading

Homan (1991) provides an excellent overview of research ethics considerations for social researchers. Mauthner et al. (2002) is a collection of writings, grounded in research practice, which consider the broader issues of epistemology and research ethics. Beauchamp et al. (1982) is a useful reader covering many of the topics arising in social research ethics. Renzetti and Lee (1993) provide a good review of the issues involved in researching sensitive topics. Ethical guidelines are produced by professional organizations, (such as the British Educational Research Association (BERA) and the American Sociological Association (ASA). Use the web pointers to access these.

Student Reader (Seale, 2004): relevant readings

69   British Sociological Association (BSA) and Council for American Survey Research Organizations (CASRO): 'Research ethics: two statements'

Key concepts	*In loco parentis*
	Informed consent
Autonomy	**Justice**
Beneficence	**Non-maleficence**
Consent form	**Utilitarianism**
Epistemic responsibility	**Vulnerable groups**

11

Research design and proposals

Moira Kelly

CONTENTS

This chapter describes the process of designing a social research project. The emphasis is on the pragmatics of developing research that works, or in other words produces analysis that adds to what is already known, is rigorous, relevant and accessible to the audiences you wish to reach. The key tool used in all research design is the research proposal. After an initial discussion of the importance of developing skills in research design, guidelines are provided on what a research proposal should contain, and why.

From theory to practice

Becoming a social scientist as opposed to someone with a degree in a social science is demonstrated by the ability to apply the knowledge gained during academic study to researching human life. As Weber (in Gerth and Mills, 1948) points out, unlike art 'scientific work is chained to the course of progress' (p. 137). As social scientists we aim to build on what is already known. In the same way that medical practice is defined by the application of medical knowledge in the treatment of illness, the craft of the social *scientist* is research (see, for example, Becker, 1998). To refer to Weber again, we need as social scientists to achieve a balance between creativity and passion for a topic with rigorous scientific endeavour:

> Ideas come when we do not expect them, and not when we are brooding and searching at our desks. Yet ideas would certainly not come to mind had we not brooded at our desks and searched for answers with passionate devotion. (Weber in Gerth and Mills, 1948: 136)

This can be taken here to apply to the relationship between creativity and practice in empirical social research. Practical skills in effective planning and application of the methodologies described in this text are valued by employers of social science graduates. Such skills are also increasingly emphasized by institutions who fund research. For example, the main social research funding body in the UK, the Economic and Social Science Research Council (ESRC), states that its activities (as a research funding body) should 'advance knowledge and provide trained social scientists who meet the needs of users and beneficiaries' (ESRC, 2003).

Part of the training expected by institutions such as the ESRC is a hands-on understanding of research design and process. Social science students, whether undertaking undergraduate or postgraduate courses, are expected to carry out at least one research project. This is where the emphasis shifts from education to training, as students are required to develop and demonstrate skills in designing, carrying out and writing up research.

Research design formats

The key principles of any **research design** are threefold.

1 There should be a *clearly conceived question*, problem or hypothesis.
2 The methods proposed should be likely to produce *robust data analysis* which will *address the research problem*.
3 The approach taken should be in line with *ethical research practice* (see Chapter 10).

At a basic level, research design can be viewed as an integrated map of your research project. In order to design a research study decisions have to be made about theoretical and methodological approaches to the research problem. This means that researchers need to be aware on some level of the possible application of a range of methodologies as they are often expected to justify their selected approach in relation to the suitability of alternative designs. Although the principles of research design are the same for any study, the form your particular project will take will be influenced by the decision to use quantitative or qualitative methods.

Quantitative

The two main designs in quantitative social research are the *survey* and the *experiment*. In both of these designs the approach is largely *deductive* (see Chapter 2), with possible relationships between variables being identified before data collection starts. This means that assumptions are made about the data based on evidence from previous research. These relationships are often presented in the form of a **hypothesis**. This is a statement specifying the relationship between two or more variables. The hypothesis is accepted or rejected depending upon there being a statistically significant difference between the variables. For example, a survey design might aim to see if the following statement is true: 'Men commit more crime than women'. This has implications for the data to be collected. Surveys can be *cross-sectional*, *longitudinal* or form a *time series*. These terms are explained in Chapter 25 (see Box 25.2).

The *validity* and *reliability* of the data must be considered at the design stage (see Chapter 7). This may involve specifying a sample size sufficient to perform the statistical analysis necessary to answer the research question. For example, I would need to ensure a large enough sample of both sexes in a survey of gender differences in crime in order to perform the appropriate tests of *statistical inference* (see Chapter 24). In **experimental designs** the aim is to see whether an intervention is effective or not. An example is given in Box 11.1.

Experimental designs can be highly complex. For example, they may involve **random allocation** of respondents to intervention and control groups, so that potential *spurious variables* (see Chapter 25) that may influence the relationship between the intervention and the outcome are controlled for. Or they may involve **blinding**, where either the people allocated to groups, or the researchers administering an intervention, or indeed both of these, are unaware to which group the people have been allocated. This prevents people, and experimenters, from allowing this knowledge to unconsciously influence the outcome of the experiment. Such procedures, though, are often impractical or unethical in social and cultural research. For this reason *quasi-experimental* designs, in which control over spurious variables is exercised at the analysis stage, may be used. Chapter 25 discusses these elaborations of experimental design in more detail.

Experimental designs originated in laboratory settings but are now also commonly used to measure the effectiveness of social interventions. In non-laboratory settings this type of research design is generally known as **evaluation**. You should know, though, that in recent years, there has been a growing interest in the contribution of qualitative designs to evaluation research (Pawson and Tilley, 1997).

Qualitative

In contrast to quantitative research, qualitative designs are often based on *induction* (see Chapter 2). This means that efforts are made to avoid assumptions about what the research findings might look like before the data are collected and analysed. Given the inductive model, some qualitative researchers may be resistant to setting out a formal structure at the start. However, even the most avowedly 'unstructured' qualitative researc incorporates some elements of design. For

---

Box 11.1   Example of an experimental design

The intervention: The introduction of close circuit television (CCTV) in a selected number of neighbourhoods in order to reduce vandalism.

The hypothesis: Neighbourhoods with CCTV will have less vandalism than those which have no CCTV.

The research design: Variables indicating the level of vandalism are measured *before* the CCTV is introduced and again *after* a given amount of time, both in neighbourhoods where CCTV is introduced (the **intervention** sites) and areas where it is not (the **control** sites). The data are then compared to see if the level of vandalism is significantly reduced following the intervention.

example, an ethnographic study of vandalism in a community might be proposed. This entails the specification of a topic and a research site.

Design formats that are more sensitive to qualitative research are beginning to develop. This has been stimulated by researchers in certain academic disciplines, which were traditionally dominated by quantitative methods, having become more convinced of the need for a range of research methodologies to address social problems. The perceived value of qualitative research has consequently been increased. From another perspective, though, qualitative researchers are increasingly expected to demonstrate how they will achieve rigour in terms of the *reliability* and *validity* of their findings. This means that the procedures used to analyse the data and address issues of reliability and validity should ideally be set out in the research design. Such procedures would also need to be set out in regard to the ethnographic study of vandalism referred to above. This involves setting the standards by which your research will be judged and assuring the quality of your study. As Najman et al. (1992) comment:

> Whether the research is qualitative or quantitative, cross-sectional or longitudinal, exploratory or confirmatory, the same criteria are used to judge its contribution – and it is only through the creative and insightful use of methods which address these criteria that we can expect to improve the quality of our contribution to knowledge. (p. 155)

The design formats reviewed here – survey, experimental and qualitative – are necessarily discussed in very general terms. You will find more detailed accounts of these in other chapters of this book, and two possible designs involving a survey and qualitative interviews are described in more detail later in the chapter.

The research proposal

Peer review and critical appraisal

The key tool in research design is the research proposal. The main reason for writing a proposal is to present your research design for critical appraisal.

This may be informal, such as discussing your research with peers. This is the 'friendly' version of peer review. It can be valuable to receive comments from others at various stages when designing a study. These can be from a supervisor or tutor, fellow student, colleague, experts in the field, or increasingly a representative of the population to be studied. Presenting ideas to someone for comment at an early stage helps to develop them. Comments may reinforce some areas, and highlight areas not presented clearly or which need more work, or aspects which are untenable in some way. Feedback can be on theoretical or practical issues which are both important. For example, there is a need to know that the research question has been well constructed, but also that it is possible to gain access to the data needed to answer it.

Research proposals may be also formally reviewed or assessed as part of a course of study, as an application for funding or for ethical committee approval. Presentation of the research design for critical appraisal means that the audience for your research is a central consideration from the start. The proposal is also a link to the social scientific community and to a wider community who may have an interest in your research.

It cannot be assumed that the audience to which your design is presented will be passive; they may well want to influence your study. A key issue in research design is the way in which the research problem is defined and, as is argued in Chapter 6, social and cultural researchers need to resist the temptation to accept the definitions of social problems offered them by policy makers. It is important that we as social scientists use our skills and knowledge to define the research problem. Although we can use common-sense concepts up to a point, we cannot expect such concepts to do the analytical work of theoretical concepts. The research design stage is often the point at which such issues are decided and this will influence the conduct of the research. If you are clear about what you are doing and why, it is much easier to communicate this to others. Presenting the design in a proposal forces researchers to sort out their ideas and make them accessible to others at an early stage. This may seem like hard work but communicating our research to others is an essential part of the job. It also enables us to define the research on our terms, as social scientists.

The research proposal as design tool

The need to produce a proposal in a particular format to satisfy the requirements of others may at times seem like a constraint. However, writing a proposal is also an important part of the process of designing research. It enables the researcher to set out the study from beginning to end so that the different elements that need to be included can be considered. It can be used to develop ideas and consider different methods, meaning that the initial draft of the proposal may look quite different from the final version. We often see things more clearly when we write them down. Drafting a research proposal allows you to design the study that you would like to do within the constraints you have, such as time, access to the population you are interested in and competence in particular methods.

Proposals for quantitative research could be said to be relatively straightforward, with information fitting into certain categories. Standards used in quantitative research have to some extent influenced expectations for qualitative research proposals. This can present a challenge for those proposing to carry out exploratory qualitative studies in which it may be counter-productive to pre-specify everything at the proposal stage. When using qualitative methods there is therefore the need to be creative and flexible in putting ideas

across, especially if the audience is used to receiving proposals for quantitative work. The most important thing is to be clear about what you are doing and why.

Writing a research proposal

The start of a research project is a time when you can think quite broadly about topics and methods. Later on you will need to focus in and be more specific about your design. So, where do you begin? You may already have an idea that you wish to investigate, or may need to think of one that is feasible. The beginning is not usually a blank page: researchers have normally already done some work in developing their ideas, having probably done some reading, with notes on this that can be used. Think about what you know about your idea, and what you would like to know. A researcher might want to see if findings from a study in one area can be replicated in another. For example, one could apply a research design used to investigate people in another country to the UK context. Bell (1999) suggests drawing up a list of questions you are interested in at this stage. For example, let us imagine that the topic concerns students' experience of paid employment. Some possible questions related to this topic are given in Box 11.2

Writing down such questions is the first part of drafting a proposal. It can be seen how one topic can generate a wide range of possible research questions. To develop the project requires moving beyond the stage of jotting down questions, and

---

Box 11.2   Possible questions for a study of students' experience of paid employment

1   What is the proportion of students who work for pay and is this increasing?
2   How many hours a week do students work on average in paid employment?
3   What factors influence them working, for example class, age, sex, geographical region, ethnic group?
4   What types of jobs do they do?
5   How does having to work affect their studies?
6   Does working while a student increase their chance of getting future work?
7   What sort of jobs do they do?
8   How do they feel about having to work?
9   How does working affect the social aspect of student life?

structuring the project so that what you are planning to do, why you are planning it, and how you intend to do it are clear. Krathwohl (1988) suggests that **signposts** in the way a proposal is presented are helpful. These may be subheadings indicating main areas to be included. I will use one such sequence of subheadings now, to explain what can usefully be placed under each.

Title

This should describe briefly what the project is about. For example:

Employment patterns in full-time under-graduates: proposal for a survey of students in London

In this title information is provided on the subject area, target audience and where it will be carried out. Your name and the names of any others involved if it is a collaboration should also be stated with the title.

Background or introduction

It is then important to introduce the subject and supply some background information. Social science covers all aspects of social life, and uses a wide range of theoretical perspectives and methodologies. Potential readers may need to be able to understand your proposal without necessarily having a thorough knowledge of the particular field. Similarly they may not be an expert in the methodological approach chosen. The main aim of a reader may be to appreciate the nature and feasibility of the study, rather than to gain in-depth knowledge of the subject and methodology.

Continuing the example of a hypothetical study of students and paid employment, I would now write about the following things:

One reason for choosing this is the continuing debate about funding for higher education in the UK. State funding has been cut and there is a lot of media coverage on the hardship faced by students, suggesting that an increasing number of students have to work part time in order to support

themselves. I would like to explore this phenomenon, to see if this is really the case, to what extent it is happening, and what effects it is having on students who have to work to help support themselves. For example, it may affect the time that students have to study, thus producing poorer examination results, or it may affect their social lives in adverse ways.

An introductory statement would point out all of this, but do so quite briefly, in order to give the reader a quick preview of the problems addressed by the research project.

Literature review

Following the introductory statement, it would be important to undertake a brief review of the relevant literature (which would be expanded in the main research report). The literature review is important because one of the first things a reader will want to know is whether this research has been done before. Any major research in the field needs to be described. It can then be shown how the project will add to current knowledge. Librarians can advise on a range of resources which may be helpful. A major source of relatively up-to-date information can be accessed through the Internet and computer databases that contain abstracts of recently published research. Chapter 12 contains more detailed guidance on this aspect of doing research.

The literature review will reflect whether the study is aiming to influence social *policy* or social *theory*.

One way of taking forward my proposed study of students is to include reference to current and previous higher education *policy* in the literature review. This emphasizes the policy relevance of my research.

Alternatively, I could discuss literature with a strong social *theory* perspective, such as *interactionist* studies [see Chapter 4] of the meanings students attach to paid employment while studying full time.

Thus, the type of literature explored here will have a bearing on the eventual use of the findings of your study. It is a good idea to highlight recent publications from both theory and policy. Most contemporary social research is expected to discuss policy implications on some level and many policy makers now understand the value of social theory in providing novel ways of seeing social issues. The literature reviewed may therefore need to include reference to both of these.

The extent of the literature review at the proposal stage will depend on the nature of the study, the time available, and to whom it will be submitted. Funding bodies will send a proposal out for peer review, so you need to ensure you have included research by any key people in the field. On the other hand, it is important to be selective in your reading, and stick to the things that are directly relevant to your research. This is a skill in itself. Finding and exploring the literature can be very time-consuming. If you have time, you may wish to contact people who are currently working in the field who can give you an idea of any work in progress.

A qualitative research proposal may involve a less comprehensive literature review at this stage, as data analysis may inform which literature is relevant. For example, if you are undertaking an exploratory study of students and paid work, you could assume that working is found to be stressful and undertake an extensive review of the literature on student stress. However, it may be that your data analysis indicates that students find working a positive experience which enables them to make friends outside college and gives them money to go out. In this case it would be better to review some of the relevant literature at the proposal stage, but allow the data analysis to inform a more extensive literature review. However, you will need to ensure that you build in time at the data analysis stage of the project to do this.

Aims and objectives

Now that the relevance of the area to be investigated has been highlighted, the research problem needs to be defined more precisely. How specific

the research problem is made at this stage will depend on what is to be discovered. You may wish to set up a *hypothesis*. For example, one could try to see whether the following statement is true:

> Full-time undergraduate students who are in paid employment are more likely to experience psychological stress than those who do not work.

On the other hand, a research problem for a quantitative or qualitative study could be:

> To describe the effects of paid employment on the lives of undergraduate students.

This type of research problem allows greater flexibility in terms of what the findings will be.

A number of **objectives** may be drawn up which describe what you need to do to achieve your aim, and thus address your research problem. For example, in relation to the second research problem stated above, an objective could be:

> To undertake a survey of full-time undergraduate students to describe the patterns of undergraduate employment in London.

This would include the number of students who work, their income, the number of hours worked per week, factors influencing the decision to take up or not take up work, their perceptions of the effects of the work upon their studies, and their examination results.

Objectives should be clear and it should be easy to decide whether they have been achieved or not. Definitions of the research problem or hypothesis and objectives are, as previously stated, an important part of a proposal. It is therefore important to spend some time working these out. In exploratory research the objectives may need to be quite broad. It is not uncommon for inexperienced researchers to get carried away with the methodology or idea and lose sight of whether the method will achieve the objectives. It is advisable to check them against each other regularly when developing your proposal. Pragmatic factors such as the time available may influence your research problem and objectives. It is tempting to set an

135

impossible research task. However, as suggested in Chapter 6, it is advisable to undertake detailed analysis of a small amount of data, or 'say a lot about a little', rather than carry out a superficial analysis of a large amount of data.

Methods

The way in which aims and objectives will be achieved will be set out in this section. An explanation of the *methods* to be used (for example, a survey based on random probability sampling, or discourse analysis of interview transcripts) and an explanation of why these methods are the most appropriate will be needed. For example, I could say:

> In order to ascertain patterns of part-time employment in students a survey of a random sample of 100 undergraduates in one university will be undertaken.

Alternatively I could propose that:

> Unstructured interviews with five working and five non-working students will be carried out. A comparative analysis of interview transcripts will be carried out, using discourse analysis, to explore how the students construct the meaning of employment and studying in their lives.

The methods section should also include other information about how the research will be carried out, including the sampling, recruitment of respondents, establishing access to the field and, in quantitative studies, what variables you intend to include in the analysis. The emphasis here will be influenced by the method. For example, a survey of students could be through face-to-face interview, a postal questionnaire, or telephone interview. Therefore I need to specify how I will carry out the survey. In a study using discourse analysis of interview transcripts, I need to set out what form the interviews with students will take, such as how I introduce the topic, and what areas will be covered.

Data analysis

A short summary of how you intend to analyse the data should be included. This is relevant to both quantitative and qualitative research. For example, you need to include the key variables you will use for subgroup analysis such as age, sex, ethnic group. Any statistical data analysis packages you plan to use should be stated (for example, SPSS). Methods of qualitative analysis should also be included where possible, and any qualitative data analysis computer programs specified (for example, NVivo). How you will ensure the *reliability* and *validity* of your findings should be clarified here and in the methods section (see Chapter 7).

For example, in a postal survey of students, I might seek to establish trust in reliability and validity by saying that I will:

> pilot the questionnaire with a small group of students before sending it out to the main sample. I will check to see whether any of the questions are ambiguous and interpreted differently by different people.

Statistical methods that will be used to ensure that findings from the survey are valid and reliable can also be stated. Statistical methods can be used to assess the likelihood of findings coming about through chance because a sample has been studied rather than the whole population. In order to use such statistics you need to ensure that you have included enough people in your sample. Methods of sampling and statistical inference are are explored further in Chapters 13 and 24.

Reliability and validity are also important in qualitative research though, as you saw in Chapter 7, it is sometimes felt necessary to modify quantitative criteria for establishing these things in qualitative studies. The broad principles, though, are often the same, and frequently involve ensuring consistency and accuracy in the way the data are collected and analysed. In a study involving open-ended interviews with students I might say that I plan to:

> use a short topic guide with all the interviewees, but also to use open-ended questions which will allow any new topics which I had not initially incorporated to be added to the topics included.

I would state that:

> In order to maximize the reliability of the findings all interviews will be transcribed and a number of categories produced based on an initial reading of the transcripts. Each interview will then be systematically analysed using these categories. Written analysis will be supported through extracts from the data.

Ethical issues

Social researchers are expected to take ethical issues into account when developing a proposal. This includes attention to ethical principles regarding the treatment of research participants, which are discussed in Chapter 10. The amount of attention to ethical issues required depends upon the sensitivity of the study proposed. For example, ethical issues surrounding interviews about sexual health are likely to be much more sensitive than interviews about work patterns. It is important that no harm, physical or psychological, will come to anyone taking part in your research.

Ethical issues in social research are not always clear-cut, but a key one is the preservation of confidentiality and the privacy of people involved. For example, in my proposed study I need to consider how I will ensure that individual students will not be identifiable when I present my findings. I also need to consider how I will gain consent from the students I want to interview. One possibility would be to state that I will:

> give all potential interviewees a letter with information about the study and its purpose, and ask them to sign a consent form. I will ensure that the interviews will be identifiable only by myself through a coding system.

The integrity of the research design is also an ethical issue in itself. As a researcher you have a responsibility to the participants. If you go ahead with a faulty design you will have misled your research participants and wasted their time. The strength of the research design is therefore also an ethical consideration.

Some organizations that sponsor or fund research require that under certain circumstances (for example, research involving human or animal participants) formal approval from a research ethics committee is gained from the outset. This is particularly common in health-related research. If this is the case, a letter indicating approval by such a committee may need to be attached to the proposal.

Dissemination and policy relevance

Dissemination of research findings is an issue that is receiving increasing emphasis, especially from bodies that fund research. Social and cultural research findings are used in two main ways: application to social policy, and building social theory. Social scientists have been criticized in the past for not sharing their research findings with those who may use them. Some funding bodies now require that applications for funding include plans for communication and details of how findings will be shared with users.

Continuing my hypothetical example, I might say that the research:

> will contribute to knowledge about the effects of employment on academic standards and student welfare.

I could argue that it has policy relevance, in that the research:

> will provide direction for the development of support services for students and will contribute to policy debates about levels of government financial support for students from government.

The study could also contribute to the development of social theory. For example, I could argue that:

Box 11.3   Budget outline from a research proposal

	Year 1	Year 2	Year 3	Total
A Staff				
Research and clinical supervision				
PLUS research associate:	31,488	33,128	34,138	98,754
Starting salary RA1A pt 10				
Secretarial support:	6,632	6,808	6,999	20,439
Clerical 3.1, 40% (2 days p.w.)				
Subtotal	38,120	39,936	41,137	**119,193**
B Accommodation, office support				
Photocopy/paper/printing	1,500	2,500	2,850	6,850
Telephone and postage	750	950	1,100	2,800
Computer consumables	300	250	350	900
Audio tapes/batteries	200	300	350	850
Interlibrary loans/external reports	300	150	350	800
Miscellaneous office supplies	400	500	600	1,500
Subtotal	3,450	4,650	5,600	**13,700**
C Travel, conferences etc.				
Travel to interviews, focus groups, London-based	200	500	500	1,200
Travel to interviews etc., non-London, day visits	750	1,250	1,000	3,000
Travel to interviews etc., incl. overnight stays	1,250	3,500	2,000	6,750
Travel to meetings/conferences for dissemination	750	1,750	5,600	8,100
Subtotal	2,950	7,000	9,100	**19,050**
D IT				
Laptop computer for mobile data gathering	1,250			1,250
Specialist tape recorder for focus groups	150			150
Subtotal	1,400	0	0	**1,400**
E Other				
Costs of transcription		2,000	4,000	**6,000**
			Total	**159,343**

> discourse analysis of interview transcripts will contribute to new understandings of how people construct narratives of self-identity in relation to work and studying.

Additionally, I might say that:

> A report will be written and submitted to the National Union of Students and the university Student Welfare Department, and it is planned to submit a paper to the next Sociology Association conference.

References and appendices

Any references to other studies made in the text should be listed at the end of the proposal. Referencing should be done according to a standard system such as the **Harvard referencing system** (see: www.ex.ac.uk/Affiliate/stloyes/harv.htm and Chapter 30 in this book), which requires standard information about books and articles to be presented in a particular order (for example, author, date, title, publisher). Place any appendices after the references, in the order in which they have been mentioned. Appendices will include any relevant papers you intend to use, such as questionnaires, topic guides and consent forms.

Resources

Formal applications for funding will usually require detailed budget breakdowns. An example of a typical budget for a study involving a survey, qualitative interviews and focus groups, is given in Box 11.3. A proposal should show that plans have been tailored so that they are feasible within budgetary limits. Resources can be anything you need for the successful completion of your study,

including money, personnel, training in computer-based analysis of statistical or qualitative data, equipment or time. Let us imagine that in my study I had planned to send a postal questionnaire to all the 2,000 full-time undergraduate students at my university. I have managed to gain a small grant from an interested organization for postage and printing of questionnaires. However, taking into account all the postage and printing costs, I can survey only 500 students. Similarly, in the study involving unstructured interviews I need to visit interviewees in their homes, which means that I need a budget for travel. This, together with other factors such as the time involved in travelling, has prompted my decision to limit the number of interviews I will undertake.

Schedule or timetable

It is valuable to have some form of structured timetable for a project. We often set ourselves unrealistic timescales for projects, for example by under-estimating how long it will take to gain access to the people we need to interview, or by not foreseeing that we may need to send out a second questionnaire to increase our response rate. For example: in considering my hypothetical project I realize that I need to allow time to negotiate access to student names and addresses through the university. The time available is 32 weeks from start to finish. I have been advised that it will probably be easiest to contact students during term time, so I need to take this into account in my plan. Box 11.4 shows a plan for the qualitative interview study.

Box 11.5 shows the same thing for a survey proposal. It can be seen that a longer time has been allowed for data analysis in the qualitative study. This will include time to explore relevant

---

Box 11.4   Timetable for a qualitative interview study

Proposal to be submitted to university ethical committee	Week 2
Contact university for names and addresses of students	Week 6
Begin interviews	Week 8
End interviews	Week 15
Complete data analysis	Week 23
First draft sent to others for comments	Week 26
Submission of final report	Week 32

Box 11.5   Timetable for a survey

Proposal to be submitted to university ethical committee	Week 2
Contact university for names and addresses of students	Week 6
First draft of literature review completed	Week 8
Questionnaire ready for piloting	Week 10
Complete pilot questionnaire	Week 12
Send out questionnaire	Week 14
Inputting of data completed	Week 22
Data analysis completed	Week 25
First draft sent to others for comments	Week 26
Submission of final report	Week 32

---

literature. The plan for the survey study follows similar lines, but has more structure.

Revising the proposal

A proposal will start off as an outline and usually require several revisions. Each section mentioned here affects the others. For example, your time schedule will influence the method you have chosen, which has been influenced by your research problem. You need to make sure that all aspects of the proposal look as if they will work in relation to each other. It is useful to think in terms of how the human body functions. If we undertake strenuous physical exercise like running a marathon, we will need to drink a lot more fluid than usual in order not to become dehydrated and to last the course. We thus need to plan ahead and to make sure we have access to fluid along the way. The main thing to check is that the method will enable you to achieve your objectives. Researchers tend to be over-ambitious in the amount they

set out to do. Feedback from others may be useful here. Alternatively, they may suggest new lines of inquiry, whose practical implications need to be thought through.

As discussed earlier, relevant audiences for your research need to be considered at an early stage. It is important to present work in a way that is accessible to other people. Strunk and White (1979) provide a useful guide, based on examples, on how to develop a good writing style. They suggest that 'the approach to style is by way of plainness, simplicity, orderliness, sincerity' (1979: 69). We all develop our own personal writing styles over time. It is valuable to ask others for their comments. For example, did they understand the reason for carrying out the research from the proposal? It is easy to get very wrapped up in the subject and think that, because we are convinced of the particular value of our research, others will be too. The way in which the proposal is presented can enable the reader to appreciate what you are planning to do. Box 11.6 shows an extract from

---

Box 11.6   The elements of style (Strunk, 1918)

... the expression *the fact that* should be revised out of every sentence in which it occurs. [For example:]

owing to the fact that [should be replaced with]	since (because)
in spite of the fact that "	though (although)
call your attention to the fact that "	remind you (notify you)
I was unaware of the fact that "	I was unaware that (did not know)
the fact that he had not succeeded "	his failure
the fact that I had arrived "	my arrival

(*Source:* www.bartleby.com/141/strunk5.html#13)

Strunk's *The Elements of Style* (1918), which is available in full on the Internet.

Ideally, a research proposal should be concise. This may seem impossible considering the amount of detail given here about what to put into a proposal. This is where revision and writing style is important. The reader will want to see easily what you are proposing, whilst at the same time have their attention held by the content. Krathwohl (1988) suggests that the proposal should be easy for the reader to skim. Dividing the proposal up using some of the headings discussed here will help with this. Effective use of language is important. For example, where possible use short, simple sentences.

Managing your research project

Producing a research design constitutes your study as a *project,* which implies that all the various aspects will be integrated. It provides the template for how you will manage your project. Researchers are accountable for the conduct of their research and need to demonstrate that they know what they are doing and that the project is likely to work as intended. This may seem daunting, but, as discussed earlier, you do not have to go it alone. It is often useful to access advice and support from peers when planning and conducting research. Feedback from friendly peers can help to prepare you for later appraisal by less sympathetic audiences. Critical appraisal works as a form of

quality control in the wider research community and is a feature of all research. However, whilst it is important to be open to the comments and advice of others, at the same time you need to make the research your own. You are the one who will have to describe and explain your rationale, and use the methods set out in the proposal. You therefore have to take responsibility for it.

Collaborating with others and submitting joint proposals for funding are common, which is another reason for getting used to sharing research ideas with peers. Collaboration might also include seeking advice from someone with particular expertise. For example, when undertaking quantitative research it is common to get advice from someone with statistical expertise at an early stage. Although it is not usual in research projects undertaken for a course of study, research is often undertaken by a team, sometimes including a range of different disciplines. Larger research projects usually have an advisory or **steering group** which is set up to discuss the study design and progress. If you are part of a research team it is important that all team members are clear about the research design and agendas are made explicit. One way of doing this is to ensure that there is clear documentation of how all decisions are made and of how the research progresses.

As we all know, even the best laid plans can go off course. A common problem when collecting quantitative or qualitative data is unforeseen difficulty in recruiting the samples proposed. The

---

Box 11.7   Web pointers for research design and proposals

Useful links for researchers – see section on 'Developing proposals' for links to sites on how to write successful research proposals
www.leeds.ac.uk/sddu/Res_links.htm

Follow the links to articles by Bottorff and Sandelowski on writing qualitative research proposals
www.nova.edu/ssss/QR/text.html

***The Elements of Style* by Strunk (1918) – a guide to using good English**
www.bartleby.com/141

Systems for referencing citations
www-mugc.cc.monash.edu.au/glib/style/systems.htm

Visit the website for this book at www.rscbook.co.uk to link to these web pointers.

---

likelihood of such problems will be minimized if time is taken to prepare the design at the start. If your study does not go according to plan, given accurate recording of the process of the research, it will be possible to learn from the experience and share that learning with others. Additionally, solutions may be available more easily than you expect if you are prepared to re-think your original aims so that failing to fulfil original plans is turned into a *strength* of a newly conceived project. Chapter 31 contains advice on how you can do this, together with some fully worked examples.

Conclusion

A research design is a way of ordering a study before data collection begins, and is developed through the process of drafting a research proposal. The main features and benefits of research design are summarized in Box 11.8.

Learning to design research and write proposals is part of the professional development of social scientists. Designs can be simple or detailed depending upon the scale of the study. A proposal for a small-scale study will usually be quite short, with maybe only a couple of sentences on some sections discussed here. All the areas covered should be at least given some thought. A proposal should be as short as possible, whilst at the same time containing all the necessary information the reader will need to appreciate what you plan to do and why.

Further reading

Bell (1999) and Denscombe (2002) are good basic guides to carrying out a research project from start to finish. Punch (2000) is a helpful text on writing research proposals. Strunk and White (1979), first published in 1919, is an interesting and helpful little book on how to write well, containing lots of useful examples of good and not so good writing style.

Box 11.8   Features and benefits of research design

- Sets up the research as an integrated 'project' with a start and end point
- Research idea is conceptualized
- Research problem is defined
- Theoretical framework is described
- Methodological framework is described
- Sets out standards for judging the quality of the study
- Resources required are stated – for example, time, costs
- Enables peer review and assessment
- Provides a template for the conduct of the research

Student Reader (Seale, 2004): relevant readings

2 C. Wright Mills: 'On intellectual craftsmanship'
7 Ray Pawson and Nick Tilley: 'Go forth and experiment'
78 Ann Oakley: 'Who's afraid of the randomised controlled trial? Some dilemmas of the scientific method and "good" research practice'

Key concepts	Signposts
	Steering group
Dissemination	
Evaluation	Experimental designs
Harvard referencing system	Blinding
Hypothesis	Control group
Objectives	Intervention group
Research design	Random allocation

Part II: Doing research

12

Doing a literature review

Duncan Branley

CONTENTS

What does it mean to 'do' a literature review? Feelings of apprehension when faced with an apparently overwhelming mass of information are understandable. Where do you begin? How do you make sense of it all? One approach is to treat it like eating an elephant (or a tree, if you are vegetarian): choose somewhere and take a bite. Chew it properly and, once you have swallowed, have another bite. Eventually the elephant (or tree) will be gone. This chapter will show you how to begin and help you to feel confident in taking your first bite. It will then take you through the stages of doing a literature review and will highlight the many useful research skills you will acquire as you do your own literature review. It is an academic exercise, but one that has many direct benefits for your research work both in terms of content and analytical skills. We will look at three broad areas in turn: research questions, finding references then managing them and your notes. We will finish with some comments on writing.

Getting started: research questions

Getting started with a literature review is also rather like walking through the door into a noisy party. You probably have practical knowledge of how parties tend to work, so you make your way to the kitchen where it is likely that you will be able to get a drink. Similarly, whether you are a student or an established researcher, you know that there are places where you can get informa-tion that is going to help you: libraries and the Internet. Importantly, there are also people you can ask too: librarians, academic staff and other students or researchers.

When you are choosing your drink at the party you might go for something you always have (staying in your 'comfort zone'), something familiar but with a slight twist (perhaps mixing an unusual combination) or you might decide to try something completely new. It might be that you limber up with something familiar and then ex-periment once you have relaxed a bit. To make these decisions you are drawing on your accumu-lated knowledge of drinks both from direct experience and from what others have told you. You are unlikely to be indulging in a substantial literature review until at least the last year of your undergraduate studies, more often in postgraduate research, so by this time you will have acquired quite some knowledge about your subject and should be able to choose an area in which you are interested and about which you may well have some questions in mind. Chapters 5 and 6 contain some helpful guidance on how to incorporate theoretical and policy-related concerns in the formulation of research questions.

You must decide on your research questions (no matter how provisionally) before you begin. If you have no questions in mind, you will read with little focus and at the end will feel that you have achieved little. Not being clear and focused with a literature review will itself thwart your broad research aims.

Box 12.1   First brainstorm

Before you set off for the library write down:
- The general area that you want to research
- What you know about it already:
  - who did or said what, when and how
  - what differences and similarities there are between these
  - some hunches about why
- What you do not know and want to know – and why this is important or interesting
- Where you might be able to find this information
- A vocabulary of the specific words used in your area – include synonyms and antonyms
- Possible theoretical models for constructing and arguing your case
- The practical research skills you might need to use if you are doing empirical research

Formulating your research questions

It is important to realize that your first definitions of your research questions will not constrain you completely – you will keep refining your questions for much of your research project as you encounter new ideas, produce new data and have new thoughts. But you need to start somewhere so that you have got ideas in play that you can question and explore. One good way to get going is to do a 'first brainstorm' (see Box 12.1). The product of this is a working document that will form the basis of your research questions, will guide your reading and help you develop your argument. There may be gaps and you may not see how things can be made to relate at this stage, but if you know everything now, why do the research?

You now need to develop your brainstorming in the library in order to situate your ideas in a broader context. In the general reference section read up on the areas and questions you have noted in your initial plan. Look for discipline-specific and biographical dictionaries or encyclopaedias. Your aim at this stage is to fill out your initial knowledge and hunches and so to make your research questions more researchable, in other words, better defined. You will find that you gradually revise your initial plans. If you make a note of these changes this can be useful later when you come to write up the 'natural history' of your research project.

Finding literature: where to search

When you start reading references will be made by authors to other sources, some of which will look like useful leads to follow. Each of those will, in turn, introduce you to other works. As you read you will make connections, guided by your research questions. Think of meeting people at a party: it does not have to be a passive or random process, but something you partly direct.

Library catalogues

Sometimes when browsing in the library you will come across other relevant books, but you should not rely on this informal approach when conduct-

ing a literature search. Academic knowledge is organized by librarians and 'information scientists' in the form of catalogues, these days usually searchable in computerized databases. A **database** is a structured way of holding related information. It can be a manual system in a book, on cards or an electronic system on a computer – what is important is that it is explicitly structured. So an address book is a manual database. It has different places for different types of information: names, streets, cities, postcodes and telephone numbers. Putting a telephone number where you would normally put a name is confusing when you try to retrieve it. The structure is there to help you find those specific bits of information quickly and accurately – and also to see gaps where you might want to complete the information later.

Each bit of information has an appropriate place, and in computer jargon these are known as **fields**. The content of the fields, which belong together (for example, one person's contact details), is known as a **record**. All of the records together constitute the database (for example, all the people in your address book). Figure 12.1 shows a simple database with three fields and two records. Notice the regular structure: if a telephone number were missing it would be immediately apparent. (Compare this with the *data matrix* shown in Chapter 23, Box 23.1)

	Field 1 *Name*	Field 2 *Address*	Field 3 *Telephone*
Record 1	A Person	1 London	123
Record 2	A N Other	2 London	456

Figure 12.1 *A database with three fields and two records*

A big advantage of computerized databases is that they enable you to enter information once and use it many times without having to re-enter it. For instance, you can produce mailing labels instead of having to write out lots of addresses by hand.

Library catalogues are specially designed databases for holding bibliographic records (known as **references**), that is, the details of the books, journals etc., which the library owns. There are fields for the author's name, the title of the publication, the date of publication, the publisher etc. Libraries rarely catalogue individual (and separately authored) items in collections such as journals, conference proceedings or chapters in books like this one you are reading now. If you are looking for an article contained in a journal or an edited collection you need to look for the main title of the book or journal in the catalogue.

It is useful to have an understanding of how the library of your university is organized to help you both in searching and in retrieving resources. The two leading classificatory systems in the English-speaking world are the **Dewey Decimal system** and the **Library of Congress system**. They are hierarchical, working from general disciplinary headings to ever more precise headings. Dewey uses numbers, the Library of Congress uses letters. Thus resources about social groups can be found at 305 (a subsection of 300 Social Sciences) in the Dewey system and at HQ-HT (subsections of H Social Sciences) in the Library of Congress system (Hart, 2001: 13–14). Knowing this you can browse through a library catalogue at specific subdivisions to see what they hold of relevance to you before visiting the library itself (and also see what might be on loan).

Bibliographic indexes

To find references to articles in a range of journals or chapters in books, discipline-related **bibliographic indexes** are published. Most are available over the Internet, are constantly updated and are searchable by anyone authorized to do so (there may also be quarterly hard copies and CDs). They are available by paying a subscription to the index publishers and hence access is normally restricted to students and staff of a subscribing university. Ask your university library staff which indexes they have subscriptions for and what you need to do to get access to them.

Many of the indexes will have **abstracts** of the articles provided either by the authors or by specialist abstracting staff at the index publishers. These short summaries are a guide to the issues the article addresses, how they are addressed and, if appropriate, some conclusions or results. They will help you decide whether or not the article in question is going to be of any use to you. They

may also suggest new terms or ways of thinking about your research questions before you have even read the article. Keep in mind your core research questions, though, so that you do not get distracted by each exciting new tangent or you will never get your project finished.

Other sources

Apart from library catalogues and bibliographic indexes there are other resources you may want to search, depending on your research project. Most major academic conferences and theses will be included in abstracts and indexes, although there are specific sites for theses and dissertations (see Box 12.4). The Internet as a resource is discussed in Chapter 21. You may want to consult official publications or government statistics – resources for accessing these change and are increasingly online so it is best to talk to your university librarian or an academic adviser to point you at relevant resources in the first instance. Reports by non-official organizations (for example, major charities) are known as **grey literature** and an online database for searching these exists (see Box 12.4). Newspapers and magazines often enable you to search some part of their archives online. Hart (2001) discusses this in detail over several chapters, but your first port of call should be your university librarians who will tell you just which sources they have subscriptions to and may have suggestions for the best way of locating useful materials.

Finding literature: how to search

Keywords and search terms

Book or article titles are not always a good guide to their contents, and abstracts are not always available. Fortunately library cataloguers and third party abstracters and indexers use a system of **keywords** (over and above the library classification systems discussed above and independent of the vagaries of book titling) to classify the contents of the work. The keywords are agreed terms used consistently whenever a work deals with a particular concept: listings of them are known as **control lists**. The actual keywords may not be used in the work at all, but a synonym will have been. For instance, works on sexual orientation might use any of the terms 'homosexual', 'gay' or 'queer', but all of the works might be found only under 'homosexual' and not under the other two terms. Control lists can function like a thesaurus, enabling you to broaden or focus your search terms.

Your preparatory work and initial library explorations will provide you with a good range of terms which map out different facets of your research questions. Ensure that you have grouped all such related **search terms** together and have shown how you think groups of terms relate to other groups; this will enable you to stay on top of your searching.

With card catalogues the degree of cross-referencing between cards varies. You are often limited to searching for particular authors or for works catalogued at a particular point in the classification system. With printed indexes and abstracts look up each of the terms in your vocabulary list and note the references that appear to be relevant. It might be that you come across other concepts, which you had not thought of at first; incorporate these into your search plan.

Computerized searching, using the 'search' or 'find' commands common on websites, works on the principle of pattern matching, looking for a specified sequence of characters (letters, numbers, punctuation or other things you can enter through you keyboard). If you tell a computer to search for 'rabbit' in a document, it will find every instance of that word. A word processor normally searches the document currently on screen. With a web browser you can either search the page currently onscreen through your browser's 'Find' command or search either the current website (or a number of other sites) with a search box on the web page itself (see Chapter 21 for guidance on using *search engines*). Most library catalogues can be searched using a web browser (see Figure 12.2).

With a database you can tell the computer exactly in which field to look. So if you want to find all works in your a library catalogue by Foucault, you type 'Foucault' in the author field box. If you want to find all works with 'power' in their title, you use the title field and you can even combine them (see Figure 12.2). Different library cata-

logues will have different fields which you can search, but most will have at least title, author, subject/keyword. When the results from your search appear on screen, you may often see a summary of all the search terms, known as a **query** (for example, 'author = Foucault AND subject = power'). You can often search in every field at once too, if you want to find, for example, all books authored by *and* about Foucault, though this might produce too many results.

Wildcards, truncating and other variations

The term you are searching for is often a complete word and so by default most database searches will only look for complete words rather than just the sequence of characters (for instance, searching for 'ant' would not find 'fondant', 'mordant', 'antonym' etc). If you find you get odd results, check the online help for 'complete words' or something similar.

If there are alternative spellings of a word, you may want to search for both of them at once. Perhaps you want to find a book by Alfred Smith, but cannot remember if that is the correct spelling of his surname or if it is Smyth. One solution is to use **wildcards**. These are characters which can stand in for any other character(s); when the computer does the search it substitutes all possible characters. Which wildcards work can vary with the database you are using so you will need to check the online help.

For a single character you can often use a question mark to stand in: so you would enter 'Sm?th' as your search term. One word of warning: a wildcard can be replaced by any character, so you might also find Smath, Smeth, Smoth and Smuth and other, perhaps unexpected, combinations. Entering 'cent??' would return both 'center' and 'centre'; entering 'col*r', in many systems, would return 'color' and 'colour', since * used as a wildcard usually stands for any number of characters.

An associated search concept is **truncation**. This is where you limit the number of specific characters you search for rather than using a whole word to find a range of related terms. Often you will need to append a multiple character wildcard (*) at the end of the text pattern you have

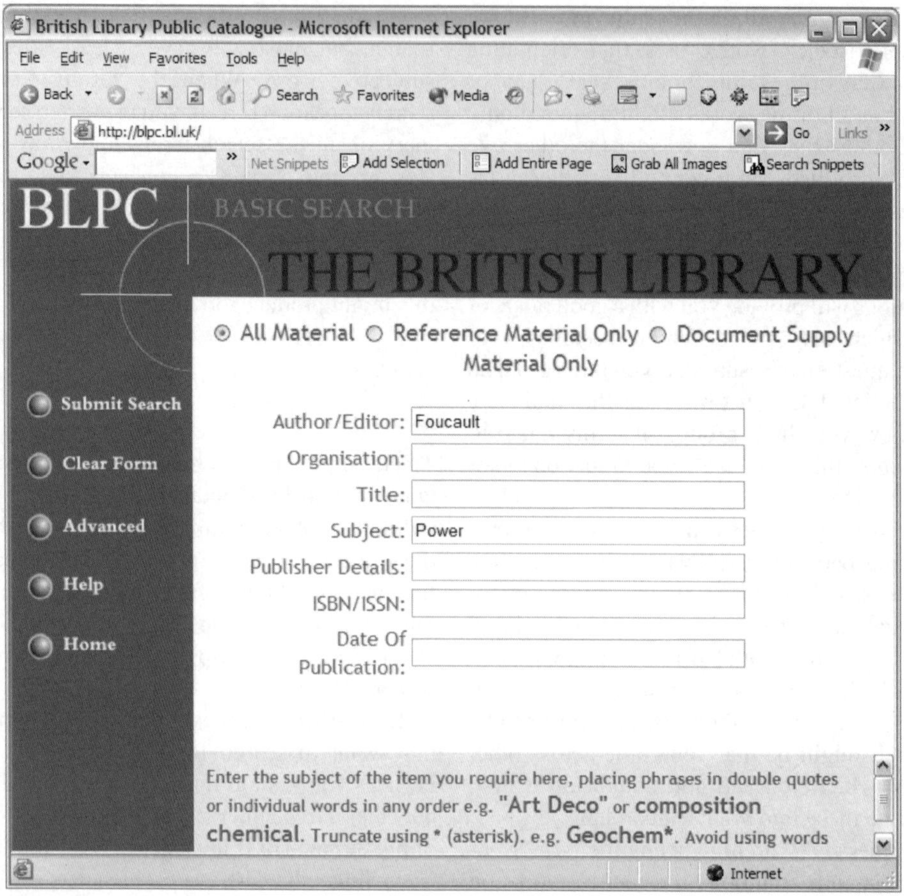

Figure 12.2   *Searching a library catalogue*

entered, and you need to ensure that you have enough of a text pattern to exclude words you do not want found. For example, searching for 'theol*', would find 'theology', 'theological', 'theologian', but not 'theodicy', 'theodolite', 'theogony' or 'theosophy'. Sometimes this is referred to as 'right-truncation'.

Often *capitalization* will be ignored. If you are entering everything in lowercase and not getting the results you might expect, check the online help to see whether searching is 'case-specific'. If it is, then try searching for 'Foucault' instead of 'foucault'. Sometimes the database will include simple *plurals* automatically ('gloves' still contains the pattern 'glove' – though if you are limited to searching for a whole word then this will not work). If you are searching in a language other than English, perhaps German, you might

want to search for both Erlass and Erlaß and similarly ä (ae), ö (oe) or ü (ue). With other letters bearing diacritical marks, it might be best to search both with and without, for example, citta and città, manana and mañana or sante and santé. To do just one search you could use the single character wildcard (?) to substitute for the possibly accented character or you could combine the search terms as discussed in the next section.

Combining search terms: Boolean logic and proximity operators

Often if you search for just one term you will get far too many references in your results; or if you have used a particularly specialist term, you may get too few. There are standard techniques for combining search terms which enable you to narrow or widen your search; however, their implementation can differ between databases. Consult the online help to see how search terms are combined for the database you are searching. If you understand the principles involved, you should be able to understand the explanation in the online help, even if different terms are used. The name given to this system of logical relationships is derived from the work of a British mathematician called George Boole and so is known as **Boolean**. You will see in Chapter 23 that Boolean logic is also used in software for qualitative data analysis.

When searching for two terms in the database fields there are three common ways of combining them and a fourth which you may occasionally find. In the diagrams in Figure 12.3 the left hand circle represents the set of results searching for the term 'Foucault' and the right hand circle that for 'power'. The shaded area represents the results of combining the searches using the operator described (and in bold).

Once you understand the logic behind these you will be able to create complex searches not only on bibliographic databases, but on the Internet and in data analysis too. The main problem at first tends to be the rather strict use of OR and AND which can seem contrary to everyday use in English. If you were to say to yourself 'I want everything about Foucault and power,' you might use 'and' to mean 'everything about Foucault *and* everything about power'; to formulate this using strict Boolean terminology you would need to use 'OR'.

You could use 'Alfred Smith OR Alfred Smyth' and should get similar results to using the single character wildcard (?). In fact it is more precise as you will not get the extra results if other words meet the pattern 'Sm?th'. Similarly using 'colour OR color' will not also find 'collar', 'colander' and 'collator' that using the multiple character wildcard (*) would. But sometimes there are keying errors and using wildcards will enable you to find things that have not been correctly entered into a database.

You can also use wildcards within elements of combined search terms. A search for 'foucaul* AND powe*' would find 'Foucauldian analyses of the powerful' as well as 'Foucault's concepts of power'.

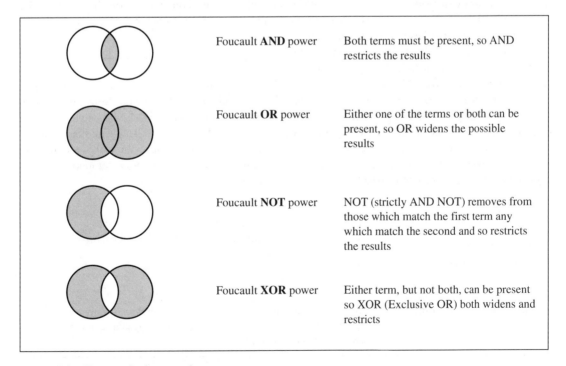

	Foucault **AND** power	Both terms must be present, so AND restricts the results
	Foucault **OR** power	Either one of the terms or both can be present, so OR widens the possible results
	Foucault **NOT** power	NOT (strictly AND NOT) removes from those which match the first term any which match the second and so restricts the results
	Foucault **XOR** power	Either term, but not both, can be present so XOR (Exclusive OR) both widens and restricts

Figure 12.3   *The main Boolean search operators*

If you are searching the abstracts in an index, there may be occasions when one term is at the beginning and another at the end and they are not related conceptually at all. You can control your searches by combining your search terms on the basis of how close the terms are within what is being searched using **proximity operators**. Figure 12.4 outlines the main relationships in increasing order of restrictiveness. The terms in capitals are common expressions for these relationships.

The methods of controlling searching using combination and proximity operators in catalogue and index database systems vary, so you should consult the online help for the exact syntax, now that you understand the principles behind the relationships.

Ordering of combined searches

Sometimes when combining search terms, the order in which the search is done is important. Rather than trying to learn or figure out each database's rules, it is easier to force the program to do the searches in the order you want. You can often do this using parentheses. The golden rule here is that the program will work out whatever is within parentheses first and then work with that result. You can enclose parentheses within other parentheses (known as **nesting**), but are unlikely to need to for a literature search although you might when searching the Web. You are only likely to need to create complex queries for a literature search if you have to used terms which are *homographs* because of a specialized usage in your area of research (for example, 'fair' can mean 'a market' or 'beautiful' or 'just'; 'queer' can vary subtly in meaning according to whether it is used within philosophy or within studies of sexuality).

Examples of the effect of parentheses on the results generated are shown in Figure 12.5, with the shaded area showing the results returned when combining the search terms Foucault (left), power (right) and sexuality (bottom) in different ways. The first column shows the results of the combination within parentheses and the second combining these results with the term outside of parentheses. These are meant as examples to get you thinking about how your terms relate and are not exhaustive. An important thing to notice is that after the results for the search term in parentheses have been found, it is *these* results which are combined with the next level of search terms, *not* the search terms which produced them. For instance, in '(Foucault AND power) OR sexuality' there could be some results which were excluded in resolving the parentheses because they did not contain both Foucault and 'power', but which when the results are combined with 'sexuality' using OR are then included again because they contain 'sexuality'.

Although this discussion of the mechanics of preparing search terms can be applied to any form of search, you need to be careful when you are not searching well-constructed databases, but the Internet generally (for which see Chapter 21).

Organising your search

It is important that you keep track of what you have searched for so that you do not waste time repeating searches needlessly. It is a good idea to plan your searches and to have a number of alternative resources that you can search should one become unavailable to you temporarily. You should note:

NEAR or WITHIN	Terms must be close to each other (WITHIN controls the maximum number of characters or words between the terms)
BEFORE or AFTER	Terms must be in a specified order (alternatives are PRECEDE or FOLLOWED BY)
NEXT, WITH or ADJACENT	Terms must be immediately next to each other with no intervening terms. You can also search for an exact phrase by putting it in inverted commas: 'Fine chocolate'

Figure 12.4 *Proximity operators*

(1) Work out parenthesis	(2) Apply additional term to results

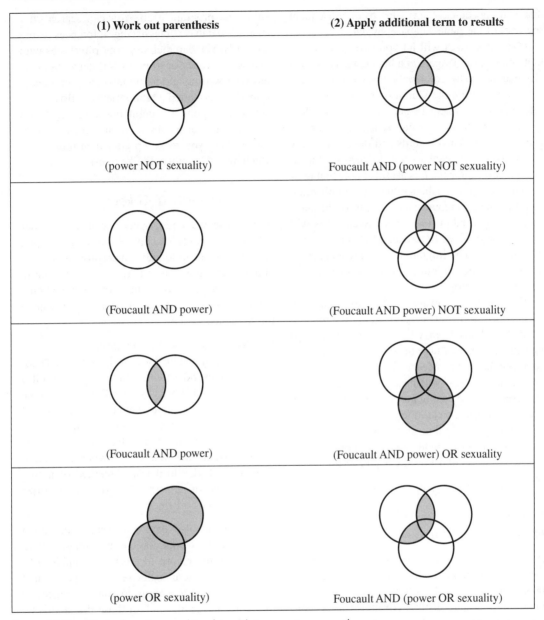

Figure 12.5 *Effect of nesting combined search terms using parentheses*

- Which resource you have searched.
- Which search terms you have used – including any restrictions on dates.
- When (date, time and how long) and where you did the search.
- How many results or 'hits' you have got.
- Any initial thoughts or follow-up activities needed, including any problems encountered, which you need to resolve.

If you have downloaded or emailed results to yourself rather than printing them out (which often you cannot do directly), give the file or the email a title which summarizes much of the above. For instance, 'soc-abs-identity-03-04-20-37.txt' would tell you that the files contained the results of your search of *Sociological Abstracts* for the term identity on 20 April 2003 which had 37 hits. The date portion is ordered year-month-day so that you can quickly sort files from subsequent searches of the same database, by date.

Many databases will let you save a search so that you can run it again at a later date. They may also enable you to search only those records added since you last did the search (hence keeping that information). Other resources run an **alert service**, which stores your search and runs it against newly added records and then emails any hits to you. This enables you to keep on top of current developments. It is useful to note that individual journal publishers often run publication alert systems to announce the contents of the latest issue of a journal or new books. Such alerts will often come out long before an article or book has been added to a bibliographic database and can be useful if a particular journal or author is central for your research project.

You should be aware of the time delays in publishing too. It can take 3–4 years for a book to reach the shops from when it was written and journal articles can take up to 2 years from first submission. If you need to be aware of current developments, you will need to keep abreast of conferences and seminars where people often present drafts of articles or chapters on which they are working. You will need to network with others working in your field and monitor relevant websites and email lists (see Chapter 21 for advice on this).

Managing the results of your literature searches

As you get results from your searches you need a system to organize them. You could just have a notebook into which you write everything by hand, but there are distinct advantages to a more structured approach. Researchers used to (and many still do) record their references on small note cards which are filed in boxes. More technically advanced and more flexible are easy-to-use bibliographic software programs such as *EndNote* (http://www.endnote.com/) or *RefWorks* (http://www.refworks.com/), which enable you not only to keep your references organized, but also to import downloaded search results, sometimes to save directly when searching a bibliographic database or even to search bibliographic databases from

within the program itself. You can search your personal database, classifying references using keywords. You can then use your references with your word processor to insert formatted citations into your writing and to automatically produce a properly formatted bibliography. Box 12.2 summarizes point by point the advantages and disadvantages of handwritten and software solutions to help you make up your own mind as to which method you would like to use.

What information to keep

A major use of a bibliography is to enable a reader to locate and consult a copy of the work to which you refer, so keep as full a record of the bibliographic details as you can. You may also want to keep information for your own organizational purposes, which will not appear in the printed bibliography, such as:

- Where you found the reference.
- Where you obtained a copy. Library and class-mark is useful should you need to consult a work again. If it was by inter-library loan, note which library supplied it and their reference. If you own a copy, perhaps note the ISBN in case you lose it and need to replace it.
- How useful each item was for your research. It is a good idea to devise a method of noting usefulness of items so that you can prioritize study of the core ones.

You should also devise a system for taking notes from the works you consult either on your cards or in the record in the bibliographic software. It can be useful to devise a system of content keywords which you apply to your references so that you can readily find all those that address a particular aspect of your research questions. You may find that the précis or abstract supplied by indexes is an adequate summary, but you should try to make it your own if possible. At any rate, *avoid* the practice of highlighting parts of the text with highlighter pen or other markers, as the effort of making your own summary is a much better method of ensuring that the main points are understood by you. Highlighting can also be an extremely antisocial habit since placing marks on library books spoils them for other readers.

Box 12.2 Comparison of manual and computerised methods for managing results of literature searches

Handwritten cards

Bibliographic software

Low level technology: pen and card

Computer access

Readily portable

Not as easily portable

No training requirement

Need to learn software

Need to decide on organizational principles: types of information, keywords etc.

Inbuilt bibliographic organization – though you need to decide just how you will use it

Need to order cards manually and consistently

Computerized records automatically ordered – and re-ordered in many different ways. You can also add keywords to help in classifying the contents of the references

Bibliographic data entry: freeform – write whatever you like, wherever you like

Bibliographic data entered into structured fields – gaps highlighted – encourages completeness

Commentary/critique: again entered freeform

Commentary/critique entered into freeform notes or abstracts field as part of the record

Sorting requires intense manual effort each time

Can sort easily, quickly and comprehensively each time

Retrieving data requires an efficient manual system – selecting on new criteria would demand a trawl through all cards (again)

Retrieve records based on content comparisons on any field or combination of fields. Highly flexible and focused. The computer trawls through the cards far more quickly and comprehensively than a human could. Can save selection criteria to re-run again

Each time a bibliography has to be produced in a slightly different format it has to be edited – with room for human error. If re-using previously entered references, you need to ensure that they contain all relevant bibliographic data, which might be a problem if your bibliography has expanded. Also bibliographic styles can and do differ from journal to journal

Bibliographies can be produced in a wide range of pre-defined formats and *ad hoc* ones can be produced – always from the latest version of your database. Can keep track of which records appeared on which bibliographies through the use of keywords, if writing shorter articles, which do not need a full bibliography

In-text citations need to be located, typed and kept track of as you are working and then at the end you need to type a full and accurate bibliography

In-text citations can be entered by using the program in conjunction with your word processor to search and copy the reference and then a formatted bibliogrpahy produced on the basis of all of your citations

Handwritten cards	Bibliographic software
Footnote/endnote entries need to be typed in each time. Subsequent occurrences need to be monitored for shorter versions/*op cit.* etc.	The bibliographic content of footnotes/endnotes can be copied directly from the program to your word processor as you work. There can be two different formats: one for the first occurrence and another for later ones
References from online or CD-ROM bibliographic databases must be written manually onto cards or physically pasted on from print-outs	References can be downloaded (i.e. saved electronically) and brought directly into your database without your retyping. You can also label records with their source when imported. For most standard sources importing is more or less automatic. Unusual ones can have formats devised for them, though sometimes it might be easier to key the references in directly, which you can do
Copies of your note cards are difficult to manage to avoid disaster should fire (or some other catastrophe) occur. Photo-copying is expensive and duplicating everything by hand is too laborious	Copies of computer files can be left in a number of locations easily and cheaply. The only issue is ensuring that you know the age of each version of your data (use the file date). Regular back-ups are essential

An overview of bibliographic software

Bibliographic programs are fairly similar so you will not be locked into using a particular one for ever and the skills you will acquire are largely generic and so transferable. Further, you can easily exchange data between different bibliographic software programs.

Different reference types

Bibliographic or **reference management** software programs are like a personal library catalogue. They are structured databases with separate fields for each part of a bibliographic reference. However, they differ in that you need to be able to store in one database information not only about books and journals as published, but also about the articles in journals and chapters in collections. This is significant because the *fields* required for books differ slightly from those for articles, which in turn differ slightly from those

for chapters in books of collected chapters. These records have many fields in common, but some will only be relevant to one specific type of reference. For instance, the book record type has just one field for the publication title, whereas the article record type has a field for the article title and a separate field for the publication title.

To accommodate such differences bibliographic databases contain different types of *record* within the same database. These may even include such things as newspapers, films, computer programs and works of art. For each different reference type the field names change appropriately. For instance, in the preceding list of reference types 'author' becomes 'journalist', 'director', 'programmer' or 'artist'. This flexibility improves accurate recording of references.

Importing references

You can enter references by typing in each one yourself. However, because the data in library catalogues and indexes and abstracts are already held in a structured way it is relatively simple to copy the data from them into your personal database. This is known as **importing references**. There are four main ways of doing this. Three require you to search using the database's search form and then to (1) save the results on a floppy disc and import them, (2) email them to yourself and import them or (3) click on a button to save directly into your personal database. The final method is to (4) search from within your personal bibliographic software itself. Each of these is discussed below.

The first two require more work by you. Once you have run your searches and selected those you want to retain (often by ticking to mark your choice), you can then choose either to download to a file or to email them to yourself (see the earlier discussion concerning naming files or emails). You will often have the option to specify how much information is downloaded. It is best to download as much as possible – you can always discard it later if you do not need it. If you have not downloaded it and need it later, you will have to redo the search, which can waste precious time. If you have emailed them to yourself, you will then need to save the text of the email as a plain text file – in effect producing the file as if you had been able to download directly to file. Sometimes you cannot download to file and are forced to email, at other times it might be more convenient for you. You then need to import the references in your file into your bibliographic database.

Importing is done by matching each field in the source database with those in your database (often called *mapping*): the contents of the author field in the source should go into the author field in your database. Personal bibliographic software provides special **import filters** to facilitate this. There are numerous database producers who in turn license several large database vendors to market their databases to universities and other research institutions. Each producer and vendor has their own proprietary structure for organizing the data they supply. For each producer and vendor combination there will be a different filter to ensure that the data go into the correct fields. You need to know which database you have been searching and which supplier has provided access

to select the appropriate filter. They are often named explicitly so this should not alarm you.

Box 12.3 shows an example of a reference found through a search and ready to import. Figure 12.6 shows the *import filter* which enables the importing of this record into EndNote.

Notice two-letter tags followed by a colon in the source file (Box 12.3) and the column headed Tag in the filter (Figure 12.6). Each tag is searched for by EndNote in the source file. When a match is made, the text which comes after it is put into the field indicated in the Field(s) column.

If you do not know the provider or the database, you will need to try to find as close a match as possible. See which filters use the same sort of tags as your downloaded references and try that. You may need to ask your library or IT support staff for assistance, if you are using software supported by your institution. If that is not available, most programs have technical help available by email and also have email discussion fora which are frequented by experienced users who are willing to help.

The two other ways of getting references into your personal database without retyping them are easier. However, at the time of writing not all library catalogues, indexes or abstract databases have the facility to click a button to save directly into your personal database instead of emailing or saving and importing.

The fourth and final method will actually do the searching from within your personal bibliographic software itself, connecting using an Internet standard called Z39.50. Once you have run your search you can choose which records to copy to your permanent personal database from all the hits you have found. This has the advantage that you do not have to learn all the nuances of different database searches. But it is a two-edged sword: you cannot usually do as focused a search as you could were you using the search tool specifically designed for the database in question. Sometimes you may also find that the same search done both ways will bring up slightly different sets of results. This is because of the sometimes different ways the databases are indexed to make them accessible via Z39.50. To check what you need to do to search in this way, you should consult the online help of the database, looking for

'Z39.50'. EndNote uses the same search box for all searching (including your own database) and connects to the external database using a 'connection file'.

You can use Z39.50 as a very quick way of entering all of the books on your shelf into your personal database. Connect to a large academic library (for example, the British Library) and enter the ISBN for each book in turn. The full bibliographic record will be returned very quickly since you are searching for something very precise in a specific field. It is a lot faster than typing in the whole reference manually, though you will need to check that it has been downloaded correctly, especially as regards capitalization and author names.

Writing and citing references in your personal bibliographic database

Using EndNote while you are writing in your word processor is one of the most productive benefits of this sort of technology. When you want to cite a work either in-text or in a footnote or endnote, you click on a button in your word processor which switches you to your bibliographic program and enables you to search the reference(s). You select one and a temporary link to your bibliographic database is inserted in your word processed document. You can save your document and continue working on it for as long as you need to: those temporary links will remain in place.

Eventually you will need to produce a hard copy of your work with the citations and bibliography formatted correctly. Again at the click of a button you tell the program to format them – and you can select just which bibliographic format to use. Look at the bibliographies in three books from different publishers and notice how varied their layouts are. For instance, it is fairly standard to have the first-named author first, but there is variety in how the name is shown: 'first name initials, surname', 'surname, first name initials' or

---

Box 12.3 Extract from a search on PsycInfo (abstract cut short)

Search History
* #1 gay identity (51 records)
Record 1 of 5 in PsycINFO 1999-2001/04

AN: 2001-16989-002
MT: Print-Paper
DT: Journal-Article
TI: Jewish gay men's accounts of negotiating cultural, religious, and sexual identity: A qualitative study.
AU: Coyle,-Adrian; Rafalin,-Deborah
AF: U Surrey, Guildford, England
SO: Journal-of-Psychology-and-Human-Sexuality. 2000; Vol 12(4): 21-48
JN: Journal-of-Psychology-and-Human-Sexuality
SI: Special Issue:
PB: US: Haworth Press Inc.
IS: 0890-7064
PY: 2000
URLP: http://www.haworthpressinc.com
XURL: URL; URL-PUBLISHER (URLP)
LA: English
AB: Research on the construction of lesbian and gay identity has represented this process as carrying considerable potential for intrapsychic and interpersonal stress and conflict. This paper reports findings from a qualitative study of 21 19–67 yr old Jewish gay men in Britain. Participants were ...

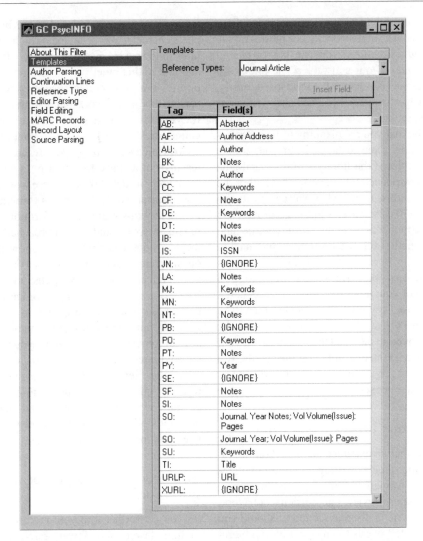

Figure 12.6   *The template in EndNote's PsycInfo import filter*

simply 'surname, initials'. There will be variety with all the other elements as well. Notice that the format of citations (in-text or within footnotes and endnotes) can vary between publishers too. A common style in the social sciences and humanities is the 'name-date' system where reference is made in brackets in the text to the author's surname and the year of publication (as in this book). Sometimes the specific pages are cited or superscript numbers in the text point to footnotes or endnotes, which give variously detailed bibliographic references.

There are several hundred formats with such apparently minor differences between them. Some disciplines have preferred **reference styles** and some have become *de facto* standards such as that recommended by the American Psychological Association, known as the APA style. Other common ones include Harvard, Chicago and the Modern Languages Association (MLA) style. It may be that your institution or department has regulations about which style you should use. When submitting a book or article for publication, you will need to follow the advice of the publisher. There are no hard and fast rules from the point of view of ensuring that your references enable people to consult the works you cite, other than ensuring that once you have selected a style to work with you should be consistent in its application throughout a single work. Since bibliographic databases are structured you can get formatted references out of your software at the click of a button. You can also change the style just as easily. With the help of a manual you can also write your own styles.

It may be that you are planning to visit a reference library at some distance from your home. You have explored the library's online catalogue and have downloaded into your database all of the references you are interested in. You can produce a listing of all the books and journals, ordered by their class numbers together with volume and issue information for articles, rather than having to consult the library catalogue again. Alternatively you may be writing and want to pull together all of your notes on a section of a chapter. If you have used keywords judiciously, you will be able to select just the relevant references by searching your database and then printing out your notes along with the full bibliographic details. You can then think about and plan your work away from the computer screen.

Writing your literature review

Putting together an extended annotated bibliography is not the same as writing a literature review. Sometimes a formalistic concern with how to construct a literature review can deaden your work. Should you write a discrete section or should you use your limited words to engage with the literature throughout your work? Different disciplines have different conventions here (see also Chapter 29). For example, journal articles in more 'scientific' traditions will tend to separate the literature review from the rest of the text; 'results', too, may be strictly separated from commentary or discussion of their significance. In more 'literary' traditions, or theory-oriented writing, these things are much more interweaved (see Swales, 1990 for an account of these conventions and their history).

Although you are writing to demonstrate that you know the body of work which relates to your research questions, you want to do more than just provide a series of stark signposts. If you were a host at a party, you would not simply point people out to a new arrival with a bald, disinterested summary. Rather you would pick those bits of someone's character and behaviour which you feel may interest the new arrival so that they will want to go and talk to that other person. So too with a literature review. You are demonstrating why you find various bodies of work interesting or productive for your research questions and you are trying to communicate your keenness to your readers.

You are also *situating* your research questions, teasing out a space for them by a close engagement with the detail of some core work and using a less central work to give a broader context. Frequently this will take the form of demonstrating that no other study has approached the topic in the way that you propose, or show that certain questions remain unanswered. If you have written a research proposal, much of this writing will have been done at an earlier stage in order to justify the project, so much of the advice in Chapter 11 is also relevant to the writing of a literature review in a final report. Realizing how your research is situated does not happen all at once after reading all of the literature. Rather you read with your research questions in mind, testing them against existing work, reformulating and devising new questions when something novel strikes you or when you make new connections.

How much is enough – or when to stop reading?

As you get further into your research you'll start finding fewer and fewer references to new sources. It is unlikely that you will ever be intimately acquainted with all of the works in any one field – there is too much published to achieve that and you are likely to have only a finite amount of time, and so have to prioritize. You will also need to consider the relevance of older literature: it may have been subsumed or superseded by later works. You should be guided by both your evolving research questions and any advisers you may have for your project in determining which are the most important studies to be working with. At some point you have to focus on producing something rather than holding on, expecting to have absolutely the last word. One way to get to this point is to imagine that you are engaged in a conversation with the works you have found. You are never going to meet *everyone* who might have something interesting to say, but if you have got a good coverage of the main people you can position yourself effectively to demonstrate the significance of your arguments.

You may feel anxious at the premium placed on originality. Be assured, it is unlikely that something will be published completely unexpectedly which alights on just the same questions as yours. If you have done a systematic literature search and monitored developments in your area through academic networks, you will be aware who is working in broadly the same area as you. If someone is working in an area close to your interests, that may well be a strength, not a problem: it shows that others think it is an area of significance and it may give you someone with whom to explore some of the more arcane areas.

At some point you need to stop reading and to review all that you have covered. Frequently people engaged in an empirical research project will want to write a draft literature review before becoming too involved in data collection, returning to it later for revision. Although this can be a very helpful strategy, be aware that the experience of fieldwork can change ideas about the significance of particular research questions, so that the relevance of early literature reviews is placed in doubt. Some of your early writing will contain interesting ideas, but will undoubtedly require revision as your research questions evolve. Tying your final writing together into a coherent argument, although never easy, should be more straightforward if you have focused on your research questions for the duration of your project and put other interesting ideas to one side to pursue once you have completed the current project.

Conclusion

The experienced sociologist Howard Becker advises a variety of methods for avoiding the

---

Box 12.4   Web pointers for doing a literature review

Library of Congress gateway to library catalogs
www.loc.gov/z3950/

The British Library Public Catalogue
http://blpc.bl.uk/

University of London Library – links to online indexes and other resources, including journal databases
www.ull.ac.uk/

Index to Theses (UK)
www.theses.com/

Online Dissertation Services (USA)
www.umi.com/hp/Products/Dissertations.html

The European Association for Grey Literature Exploitation
www.kb.nl/infolev/eagle/frames.htm

ABYZ News Links – gateway to news media
www.abyznewslinks.com/

EndNote
www.endnote.com/

RefWorks
www.refworks.com

Visit the website for this book at www.rscbook.co.uk to link to these web pointers.

trap of 'conventional ideas [becoming] the uninspected premises of their research' (1998:7), including trying to develop research questions initially *before* a detailed examination of the literature. Of course, all of your previous study will contribute to formulating those initial questions, but they will still have a roughness and energy which you should not lose under the weight of the literature. Counterbalancing this, Becker stresses that it is not productive to reinvent the wheel: asking research questions that have already been answered is pointless. Rather he describes producing research as akin to making a table: you do not have to make all the parts from scratch to make your very own table, but should use those prefabricated bits which have been tried and tested to enable your creative efforts to shine through on the other bits (Becker and Richards, 1986: 141–2). He concludes his chapter with advice which seems perfect for ending this one: 'Use the literature, don't let it use you' (Becker and Richards, 1986: 149).

Further reading

Becker and Richards (1986) provides a helpful guide, written from the point of view of experienced researchers, to the writing of research reports in general, including literature reviews. Hart's books (1998, 2001) are more focused on the literature review *per se*, giving detailed guidance on finding materials and writing creative literature reviews.

Student Reader (Seale, 2004): relevant readings

2   C. Wright Mills: 'On intellectual craftsmanship'
28   John M. Swales: 'Episodes in the history of the research article'

Key concepts

Abstracts
Alert service
Dewey Decimal library classification system
Grey literature
Library of Congress library classification system

Bibliographic indexes
    Boolean searches
    Control lists
    Database
    Fields

Keywords
Nesting
Proximity operators
Query
Record
Search terms
Truncation
Wildcards

References
    Import filters
    Importing references
    Reference management
    Reference styles

13

Doing social surveys

Alice Bloch

CONTENTS

This chapter explains the basic techniques for designing and carrying out a social survey. It will focus on the formulation of research aims, on different types of social surveys and designing questionnaires, including *operationalizing* concepts, developing indicators, questionnaire content, question wording and sampling techniques.

Defining the research aim and objectives

The first step when designing a social survey is to clarify the research aim and objectives. The starting point when deciding on the research aim is to review any relevant literature on the topic (see also Chapter 12). Often when reviewing the literature, researchers will notice unanswered questions or gaps in knowledge that could be explored in their own research. In classical social surveys research aims and objectives can often be formulated as precise statements called **hypotheses** whose truth or falsity can be tested by collecting relevant data. Box 13.1 illustrates aims, objectives and a sample of hypotheses from a particular study.

The aims and objectives of a social survey emerge from the theoretical concerns of an academic discipline as set out in the literature, from the concerns of policy makers or from the personal interests of the researcher. Policy-orientated research, as shown in Chapter 6, is often commissioned by policy makers, especially government departments, who either require research to inform the direction of policy or to analyse or evaluate the impact of policy initiatives. The above example incorporates both policy and theoretical concerns. For example, objective 1 would find out the barriers to the labour market from the refugee perspective and the findings could inform policy so that barriers could be alleviated. Objective 5 is informed by theoretical debates that highlight differences between different subgroups of refugees. Objective 5 will test these theories within the context of the proposed research.

The five objectives and the hypotheses shown in Box 13.1 contain a list of *phenomena* (for example job satisfaction, ethnic group, pay and employment aspirations) *all* of which in an *interactionist* or *constructionist* perspective would be seen as variably constituted across different social settings. For example, 'ethnic group' may be something that is created through the use of language, or in interaction (as was shown in the discussion of Moerman's study of Lue *ethnic identification devices* in Chapter 5). An awareness of this variation will inform the design of questionnaires and the interview process to ensure sensitivity to variations in social context.

Gathering information

A social survey is a type of research strategy associated with the production of social statistics.

Box 13.1   Aims, objectives and hypotheses in a study of refugees and asylum seekers

Aim: To examine the participation of refugees and asylum seekers in the UK labour market

Objectives:
1   To examine the barriers experienced in gaining access to employment
2   To compare levels of pay obtained by refugees in employment and other ethnic groups
3   To ascertain levels of job satisfaction among those who are working
4   To examine employment aspirations
5   To explore differences by country of origin, gender and length of time in Britain

Examples of *hypotheses*:
1   Female refugees will experience greater barriers to employment than male refugees
2   Job satisfaction will increase with length of time resident in Britain
3   Country of origin is more important than gender in predicting levels of pay

The key characteristic of a social survey is that the same information is collected from all cases in the sample. A case, otherwise known as a **unit of analysis**, is not restricted to an individual person. A case can be an institution, such as a school or hospital, a local authority, a country, a newspaper article or one of a series in public records. For the purposes of survey research a unit of analysis is the unit from which, or about which we obtain information.

While the unit of analysis and, as we shall see, the method of data collection can vary in survey research what makes a survey unique is that the same data is collected from each case and so variations between cases can be measured. The fact that all cases are asked the same questions, or to put it another way, are measured on the same variables, is the essential point that distinguishes the quantitative social survey from qualitative interviewing and ethnographic work.

Main methods of data collection

The three techniques used most often to collect data in survey research are face-to-face interviews, the self-completion questionnaire and telephone interviews.

Face-to-face interviews

Face-to-face interviews are carried out by an interviewer who has either **an interview guide** or an **interview schedule** (also called a **questionnaire**). An interview guide is associated most often with qualitative work (see Chapter 14). Such qualitative interviews are usually **non-standardized**: an interviewer works to a set of topics that must be covered, though the exact order in which questions are asked and the wording of questions can vary. Such interviews allow for flexibility, greater depth and more sensitivity to contextual variations in meaning than is generally the case in classical survey research using a *standardized* interview or questionnaire.

Survey research geared to producing quantitative data is often associated with the use of **standardized** interview schedules. Using an interview schedule means that the wording and order of questions is the same for each respondent. Wording the questions in the same way is called standardizing while asking questions in the same order is called **scheduling**. By using a standardised interview schedule researchers try to give respondents the same stimulus and therefore minimize the variation in the interview process. The aim is to ensure, as far as possible, that the variation between responses can be attributed to actual variations between interviewees rather than any variability in the interview process.

Interviews can also be **semi-structured**. Using this format, part of the interview is structured with a set of questions asked sequentially while other parts are unstructured and are designed to explore the views of the interviewee in detail. Semi-structured interviews gather a combination of quantitative and qualitative data. The qualitative component will need to be coded into categories to be made amenable to statistical analysis. The use of semi-structured approaches reflects the fact that qualitative material can be of great interest in a social survey. Chapter 23 on coding makes it clear that qualitative material of all types can be usefully quantified if this furthers the aims of a research project.

Using face-to-face interviews as a means of data collection has a number of advantages and disadvantages. The main advantages are as follows:

- The presence of an interviewer allows for complex questions to be explained, if necessary, to the interviewee.
- Interviews can generally be longer than when self-completion techniques are used as interviewees are less likely to be put off by the length or to give up half way through.
- There is more scope to ask unstructured questions since respondents do not have to write in their answer and the interviewer can pick up on non-verbal clues that indicate what is relevant to the interviewees and how they are responding to different questions.
- Visual aids can also be used in the face-to-face situation.
- The interviewer can control the context and the environment in which the interview takes place. For instance, the interviewer can make sure that the questions are asked and therefore answered in the correct order and that the inter-

view takes place in an appropriate setting which is conducive to accurate responses.

There are however, disadvantages with face-to-face approaches.

- The cost associated with face-to-face interviews can limit the size and geographical coverage of the survey.
- Interviewers can introduce bias which will affect the reliability of responses. Such bias might emerge from the way in which questions are asked, or in the personal characteristics of the interviewer, or in respondents' wish to give socially desirable responses. For instance, there tends to be an over-reporting of voting activity and of participation in voluntary activities in data gathered through interviews.

Postal, Web and email surveys

Postal, Web and email surveys use **self-completion questionnaires** that often follow a standardized format. With surveys delivered by these means, questions need to be simple and easy to understand and the questionnaire has to be clear and easy to complete because no interviewer is available to assist the respondent. Such surveys can be especially useful when respondents need time to gather information or consider their answers. For example, a survey of pay levels among university employees by gender would require complex information so a self-completion survey would provide respondents with time to check their records before answering.

Surveys using self-completion questionnaires have some distinct advantages over face-to-face interviews but also some disadvantages. The main advantages are as follows:

- They are cheap to administer. The only costs are those associated with printing or designing the questionnaires, their postage or electronic distribution.
- They allow for a greater geographical coverage than face-to-face interviews without incurring the additional costs of time and travel. Thus they are particularly useful when carrying out research with geographically dispersed populations.

- Using self-completion questionnaires reduces biasing error caused by the characteristics of the interviewer and the variability in interviewers' skills.
- The absence of an interviewer provides greater anonymity for the respondent. When the topic of the research is sensitive or personal it can increase the reliability of responses.

The main disadvantages of self-completion surveys are:

- Questionnaires have to be short and the questions have to be simple as there is no opportunity to probe or clarify misunderstandings.
- There is no control over who fills out the questionnaire and the researcher can never be sure that the right person has completed the questionnaire.
- Those with low levels of literacy or poor access to email or the Internet are unlikely to complete a questionnaire, meaning that they are excluded from the study.
- Response rates tend to be low and it is difficult to know the characteristics of those who have not filled in the survey and how their non-response will affect the findings.

Response rates in self-completion surveys tend to be maximized when respondents have an interest in the subject of the research and are therefore motivated to complete the questionnaire. In addition, response rates can be increased by sending out reminder letters and emails and follow-up postings of the questionnaire, though this does mean that the fieldwork element of such surveys can be lengthy (see below for more on response rates).

Telephone interviews

Telephone interviews using interview schedules are becoming increasingly efficient with developments in computer technology. **Computer Assisted Telephone Interviewing** (CATI) systems are available and these provide clear instructions for the interviewer, display the interview schedule and allow electronic recording of responses as they are given. This cuts out the **data**

entry part of survey research – that is transferring the responses from the interview schedule to the computer – because responses are recorded directly onto the computer (see Chapter 23 for more on preparing such data for analysis). This makes CATI quick and cheap to use. There are other advantages associated with telephone interviews:

- Because the researcher does not have to travel, interviews can take place over a wider geographical area.
- There are fewer interviewer effects – that is, the personal characteristics of the researcher will be less obvious than in face-to face situations and are therefore less intrusive.
- The physical safety of the interviewer is not an issue.
- Telephone interviews are subject to greater levels of monitoring because supervisors can unobtrusively listen in to interviews to ensure that they are carried out correctly.

But telephone interviewing has disadvantages too:

- Questions have to be simple and interviews need to be kept short because they tend to have higher break-off rates where people refuse to continue than face-to-face interviews.
- It can be difficult to ask sensitive questions on the telephone.
- There is no opportunity to use visual aids or to pick up so easily on the non-verbal responses of interviewees.
- There are some groups that are under-represented in telephone surveys. These include people without phones (often due to poverty), older people and people who are disabled or sick.

Questionnaire design

There are a number of stages in the process of designing a questionnaire for social survey work. The researcher needs to clarify the key concepts to be used in the research and to develop indicators for these. That is to say, **concept-indicator links** need to be established. Another way of putting this is to say that the researcher needs to **operationalize** the concepts so that they become

measurable phenomena. The structure of the questionnaire, the question order, the format of questions and the precise wording also need to be worked out. In all of this, the concern is to construct a questionnaire that has good *measurement validity* (see Chapter 7).

Concepts and indicators

The objectives of the survey shown in Box 13.1 contain a number of *concepts*. These include barriers to employment, pay, ethnic group, job satisfaction and employment aspirations. Because statistical social surveys depend on the ability to assign numbers to the characteristics of people or social settings, concepts have to be turned into measurable phenomena. Some concepts are easy to measure. Pay, for instance, could be measured in the number of dollars, pounds or other units of currency received each year. Therefore the *concept* of 'pay' is measured by the *indicator* 'money'.

Some concepts are more difficult to operationalize and are **multi-dimensional** – that is, they are made up of more than one component. Barriers to employment, job satisfaction and employment aspirations are all multi-dimensional concepts. Other concepts, such as ethnic group, might vary according to time and context. The starting point when operationalizing a concept is usually some conceptual work accompanied by a review of the relevant literature to see how others have used the term. Thinking first about the concept 'ethnic group', a researcher would need to find a way of categorizing different ethnic groups in order to allow comparisons between groups. One approach would be to use the same ethnic classifications as government studies such as the Census or the Labour Force Survey. Another approach would be to decide on categories that fit the objectives of the particular study. When thinking about multi-dimensional concepts such as job satisfaction, the researcher would need to think about all the dimensions that make up the concept. It might include, for example, levels of pay, opportunities for promotion, managerial responsibility, flexible working hours, workplace relations, amount of paid holiday and access to training. The researcher would need to design questions that

167

indicate each of the dimensions of the concept 'job satisfaction'.

At this point, it may be helpful to see how other researchers have measured the concept. Resources for this purpose are readily available on the Internet. For example, a visit to the Question Bank website (http://qb.soc.surrey.ac.uk/) led to links resulting in the question shown in Box 13.2. A variety of questions indicating the concept 'ethnic group' could be collected and compared to see which method suits the researcher's purpose.

Measurement

Once the dimensions of a concept have been decided, the next stage in the process of questionnaire design is to devise meaningful and accurate indictors for measurement. Measurement involves the assignment of numbers to categories that group together things considered to be alike. By definition, a **variable** has to have more than one category otherwise there would be no variation. Therefore, the key characteristic of measurement is that it relies on the possibility of variation. Variables can be either **categorical** or **numerical**.

Categorical variables

Categorical variables are those variables that are made up of a set of attributes that form a category but do not necessarily represent a numerical scale or measure. There are two levels of measurement with categorical variables: **nominal** and **ordinal**. Box 13.3 defines these with examples.

There are two key rules for devising categorical

Box 13.2   A question to indicate ethnic group

To which of these ethnic groups do you consider you belong?

SHOW CARD

White
1   British
2   Any other White background (Please describe)

Mixed
3   White and Black Caribbean
4   White and Black African
5   White and Asian
6   Any other Mixed background (Please describe)

Asian or Asian British
7   Indian
8   Pakistani
9   Bangladeshi
10 Any other Asian background

Black or Black British
11 Caribbean
12 African
13 Any other Black background

Chinese or other ethnic group
14 Chinese
15 Any other (Please describe)

(*Source:* Office for National Statistics 2003:
www.statistics.gov.uk/harmony/document.asp)

Box 13.3   Types of categorical variable

Nominal level variables assign numbers to the classification of characteristics but there is no inherent ordering or ranking in the classification. Examples of nominal level variables are *religion*, *ethnic group*, *sex* and *marital status*. We know that people in different categories differ from one another but it is not meaningful to place the categories in order, or to rank one above the other.

Ordinal variables are those where there is an *order* between different categories. However, it is not possible to quantify the exact difference between categories. Ordinal level variables are often attitudinal or have a time dimension. For example, a scale asking how often a student visited the library might have four categories 'daily, weekly, monthly, less than monthly'. The researcher can rank the frequency of visits but not in exact numerical terms.

---

variables. The categories must be *mutually exclusive* and they must be *exhaustive*. For the categories to be mutually exclusive, each one must be distinct and no respondent should be able to put themselves in more than one category. In the case of religion, if the categories were: Catholic, Muslim, Jewish, Christian, Hindu, Sikh then a Catholic respondent could place themselves in either the Catholic or the Christian categories. For categories to be exhaustive, they must cover the range of variation in the variable. Using the religion example, there are some religions such as Buddhism missing and so there would need to be additional categories.

Numerical variables
Numerical variables differ from categorical variables because numbers are used to represent each unit of the variable and the numbers carry

mathematical meaning. There are two levels of numerical variables: **interval** and **ratio**.

Order, format and general content of questions

At the beginning of any questionnaire should be an introduction that clearly states the purpose of the study, who is carrying out the research and what will be done with the information. An introduction for a face-to-face interview might be as follows:

> 'I am carrying out an interview about the employment and training needs of refugees in Lewisham. The study is being carried out by Goldsmiths College, University of London and aims to make sure that the services provided locally are more suitable

---

Box 13.4   Types of numerical variable

Interval level variables specify both rank order and the distance between numeric categories but not the absolute magnitude. An example would be the Fahrenheit scale because the categories are separate and ordered and the points on the scale can be determined mathematically.

Ratio scales build on the attributes of the other scales because they also have a true zero point so they can provide information about the magnitude of an attribute. Examples are height, weight and age. Often ratio variables are grouped and therefore turned into ordinal variables. With age, for example, instead of asking people their exact age, the variable is often put into groups (under 18, 18–24, 25–30 etc.). The level of measurement therefore depends on how the question is asked and the level of detail required.

---

for the needs of different refugee communities. Everything you say is confidential and at no time will you be individually identified. The information you provide will be used to write a report showing how to improve services for refugees in Lewisham.'

Order

There is evidence to suggest that the order in which you ask the questions affects both the answers and the response rate. The first few questions in a questionnaire should always be easy to answer, obviously relevant to the stated purpose of the survey and they should be interesting so the

---

Box 13.5   Structured, closed questions from a survey of refugees and asylum seekers (Bloch, 2002)

1 Are you currently working or studying towards any qualifications?
Yes   [1]
No (go to Q4)   [2]

2 What qualifications are you studying for?
Higher degree (including PGCE)   [1]
Postgraduate diploma   [2]
Degree level qualification   [3]
Diploma in higher education   [4]
Access Course   [5]
HNC/HND   [6]
ONC/OND   [7]
BTEC, BEC or TEC   [8]
Nursing or other medical qualification   [9]
A-level or equivalent   [10]
NVQ   [11]
GNVQ   [12]
AS-Level   [13]
GCSE   [14]
City and Guilds   [15]
YT Certificate/Modern Apprenticeship   [16]
Other (*please specify*)   [17]
Don't know   [18]

3 Who is paying for the course?
Employer   [1]
College   [2]
Government/Local authority   [3]
Self   [4]
Relative   [5]
Other (*please specify*)   [6]
Course is free   [7]
Don't know   [8]

4 Since living in Britain, have you obtained any formal qualifications?
Yes   [1]
No (go to Q7)   [2]

---

interviewee is keen to be interviewed. If the opening question is personal, sensitive or one to which the respondent does not know the answer it may make her or him reluctant to carry on.

Think of questions in clusters and sequentially. Group all the questions relating to one aspect of the research together and make sure that one question leads directly to another. For example, there is no point in asking someone about their university degree if you have not first established whether or not they have one.

Format

In survey research, as we have seen, the response format can vary from a **structured** or **closed** format to an **unstructured** or **open** format. A closed or structured format is where the questions are developed in advance and respondents are presented with a number of alternative answers from which they select one or more responses. An example of closed format questions that proceed sequentially, taken from a survey of refugees and asylum seekers in Britain, is shown in Box 13.5.

Note the use of a *filter* for respondents who answer 'No' to question 1 because the next two questions are not relevant to them. Also, note that the questions are *pre-coded* (see Chapter 23).

In contrast, an open-ended question is one in which the interviewee or respondent formulates his or her own answer. Open-ended questions are used most often in qualitative research but they can also be used in survey research and are often used in conjunction with a closed question as a mechanism for obtaining detail about a subject including the reasons why people hold the view they do or general feelings or motivations about a topic. Using questions from a survey of refugees and asylum seekers in Britain, Box 13.6 illustrates the way in which closed and open-ended questions can be used in the same questionnaire.

Note that in Question 3, where the fixed choice response is 'other', respondents are asked to specify their answer further. The data collected in the 'other' category will be *post-coded* to enable quantification (see Chapter 23).

Box 13.6   Closed and open-ended questions from a survey of refugees and asylum seekers (Bloch, 2002)

1 Since living in Britain, have you been involved in any voluntary work?
Yes   [1]
No (go to Q10)   [2]

2 Are you involved in voluntary work at the moment?
Yes   [1]
No (go to Q5)   [2]

3 What sort of voluntary work are you involved in?
Advice/advocacy   [1]
Administration/clerical work   [2]
Interpretation/translation   [3]
Management committee   [4]
Teaching   [5]
Driving   [6]
Befriending   [7]
Fundraising   [8]
Other (please specify)   [9]

4 What are your reasons for doing voluntary work?

Content

When thinking about the content of a questionnaire the researchers should ask themselves three questions, the first two of which are relevant to the assessment of the *face* or *content validity* of the questionnaire (see Chapter 7).

- *First*, is the questionnaire relevant to the subject of the research? All questions should be relevant to the research.
- *Secondly*, does the questionnaire cover everything? A questionnaire needs to be comprehensive. The researchers need to ask themselves whether anything that is important to the research is missing because it is very difficult to go back and ask people for additional information if you discover at a later date that an important question has not been asked.
- *Thirdly*, are the question topics understandable and do they have meaning for all the interviewees? For example, when asking questions, researchers have to consider whether or not the interviewee will understand the question and whether she or he will possess the necessary information or knowledge to answer the question.

Question wording

When constructing questions, there are some key principles to be followed. Questions have to be simple, clear and as short as possible. One of the ways to ensure that questions 'work' is to carry out a **pilot study**. By piloting or testing questions, researchers can find out if some questions are ambiguous, open to different interpretations or if respondents feel uncomfortable answering them. Some of the most obvious problems with question wording or the things to be aware of are listed below.

- Is the question *double-barrelled*?
- Is the question *leading*?
- Is the respondent likely to have the *necessary knowledge* to answer the question?
- Is there a *prestige bias*?
- Is the *frame of reference* clear?

A **double-barrelled question** is one that asks more than one thing and should therefore be divided into separate questions. An example would be the question 'Are you satisfied or dissatisfied with your lecturers in social research methods and social theory'? The respondent might be satisfied with one lecturer but not the other, but the wording of the question does not enable separate responses to be given.

Leading questions are those that direct the respondent towards a certain answer. Leading questions might start with statements like 'Don't you agree that' and 'Isn't it the case that'. These questions should be avoided because it will mean that the responses given might not be the real views of respondents but those directed by the researcher. An example of a leading question might be 'Don't you agree that the government should provide resources to cut hospital waiting lists?'.

Researchers should ensure, as far as possible, that respondents have the *necessary knowledge* about the subject of questions in order to answer them. It cannot be assumed that interviewees will voluntarily admit a lack of knowledge. Consider this question: 'Do you agree or disagree with the government's policy on supporting asylum seekers?' The interviewee may not know what the policy is, so researchers need first to establish whether people know what the policy is and only secondly to ask those who know for their views.

Prestige bias occurs when respondents distort their answers to impress the interviewer or fool themselves. Areas of activity that are often *over-reported* because of prestige bias include voting activity, reading books, contributing to charity and helping family and friends. Conversely some other areas are commonly *under-reported,* such as drinking alcohol and smoking.

Finally, the **frame of reference** of a question needs to be clear. For instance, the question 'How many hours do you study?' does not provide a temporal frame of reference. Is it asking respondents how many hours they study each day, each week, each month or even each year? For the question to work, the framework has to be clear and specified by the researcher. Researchers should also avoid terms like 'often' and 'regularly' because they are too vague and mean different things to different people.

Sampling

Social researchers sample because it is very rare that they have either the time or the resources to carry out research on the whole population that could be potentially included in a study. The application of **sampling theory** enables researchers to take a random selection or sample of the population and from that to make generalizations about the whole of the population. Sampling aims to provide good estimates about the nature of the whole population from a limited number of cases. Using a statistic called the **standard error**, researchers are able to measure the precision of the sample in relation to the population as a whole. The standard error decreases with increasing sample size, indicating a sample that is improving in precision.

As we have seen, the **population** of a survey may not always be individuals. The relevant population could be made up of schools, hospitals, small businesses, local authorities, newspapers and so on. When the population to be studied consists of individuals it might be the population of a particular town, university students, refugees, people living in residential care homes, homeless people, people claiming disability benefits and so on. A researcher designing a sample needs first to define the relevant population to be sampled from.

The way in which a sample is then designed will depend on the research goals. However, researchers need to consider whether or not they can generalize their findings to a wider group or population and the confidence with which they can do that. A sample which accurately reflects the *whole* population is called a **representative sample**. There are two broad types of sampling method: **probability** and **non-probability sampling**. A probability sample – which is generally regarded as more likely to provide representativeness – is one in which each person in the population has a known (usually equal) chance of being selected. A non-probability sample is one in which some people have an unknown, or no chance of being selected. When organizing a probability sample the way in which a known chance of selection is assured is to list all members of the relevant population. Such a list of the population is called a **sampling frame**.

Sampling frames

A number of sampling frames exist and are accessible to researchers. Samples of the whole UK population include the electoral register, telephone directories and the Postcode Address File (PAF), though they all have limitations in their coverage. The electoral register, for example, may under-represent people who frequently move house, while those who do not register to vote will not be included. Printed telephone directories are incomplete because they do not cover mobile phones, not everyone owns a land-line telephone and some people choose not to have their number listed anyway. The PAF is more up to date and has greater coverage of the population than the electoral register and has the advantage of being available electronically. However, because the file used for sampling is the 'small user file', which lists addresses receiving less than 25 items of post each day, included in the file are businesses that receive few items of post while private households that receive large amounts of post are excluded. The PAF is therefore not a full and accurate list of the population, though it is more accurate than many alternatives.

There are also sampling frames available for specific populations. For instance, there are lists available that cover institutions like the directories of universities, schools, colleges and penal institutions. There are directories that cover professional groups such as the medical directory, registers of nurses, psychologists and osteopaths. In addition, it is possible to gain access to lists other groups. For example, universities keep lists of students, schools keeps registers of pupils, employers keeps records of employees, the Department for Social Security keeps records of benefit claimants. Some lists are more accessible to social researchers than others. Some lists are in the public domain while others are protected and remain confidential. For some groups in the population sampling frames are not available and the way in which researchers compile sampling frames or carry out research with these groups is explored when considering *non-probability* sampling techniques.

Probability sampling techniques

There are three types of probability sampling methods:

- simple random sampling
- stratified sampling
- cluster sampling

All three approaches rely on the availability or the ability to compile a complete and accurate sampling frame. Once a sampling frame has been obtained, all the elements should be numbered and the size of the sample decided upon. The most basic type of probability sample is the **simple random sample.**

Simple random sampling (SRS)

In order to draw a sample using this approach, the researcher can use the lottery method, a table of random numbers or a systematic approach. The lottery method is akin to drawing numbers out of a hat. All elements of the population would be placed in a hat and the number required for the sample would then be drawn out. For example, if the population was 5,000 general practitioners (family doctors) and the sample size was 500, then the names of all 5,000 doctors would be placed in a hat and 500 would be drawn out. Here, each doctor in the population would have an equal, known chance of being selected: 1 in 10.

When the population is large the lottery method is unrealistic because it requires each member of the population to be listed separately, and random numbers or *systematic sampling* are used instead. Random numbers are generated by computers (see, for example, http://www.random.org/) which, if each member of the population has been given a unique number, can then be matched with the same number in the sampling frame for inclusion in the study.

To obtain a **systematic sample** the researcher needs to calculate a **sampling fraction** by dividing the required size of the sample by the population. If a sample of 500 doctors were required from a population of 5,000 then the sampling fraction is 10. Starting with a randomly selected doctor with a number below 10, the researcher then selects every tenth person on the list. If you began with number 4 then you would select cases 4, 14, 24, 34, 44, 54 and so on to be included in the sample. With systematic samples you need to be sure that there is no inherent ordering to the lists as this would distort the sample. For example, if male and female doctors' names alternated so that every even number was a male and every odd number was a female, the sampling strategy just outlined would generate a sample consisting of men only.

Stratified sampling

A **stratified sample** is more accurate, and therefore more representative of the population than a

---

Box 13.7   Stratified sampling: an example

The study: Of different levels and conditions of employment among university lecturers by ethnic group.

Stratifying factor: Ethnic group.

Procedure: List members of one ethnic group first, then list members of another ethnic group and so on until all of the members of the population are listed. Number each person in the list. Use a sampling fraction to select people for the sample.

Disproportionate stratification: If the sampling frame describes the general UK university lecturer population it is likely that the majority of the sample would be 'white' because the majority of the population falls into the 'white' category. Using disproportionate stratified sampling techniques would ensure that different ethnic groups were included in the sample. Here, a smaller sampling fraction is used for smaller groups in the population, giving them a greater (but still known) chance of being selected.

simple random sample, but also more complex. Each member of the population is divided into groups or *strata* and then a simple random sample is selected from each stratum. The strata are generally variables that the researcher wants to ensure are represented in the sample. Box 13.7 illustrates this.

Cluster sampling and multi-stage cluster sampling

Cluster sampling is particularly useful when the relevant population is widely dispersed because it economizes on the time and costs incurred by travel. If, for example, a researcher wanted to interview university students it would be more efficient first to sample (randomly) a group of universities from a list of all universities. Then students in the selected institutions could be selected. As well as travel savings this would have the added advantage of only requiring listings of students for selected universities. A random sampling procedure based on the whole population of university students would mean assembling a very large list of all students in the country.

Sometimes cluster sampling occurs in more stages than this, in which case it is called **multi-stage cluster sampling**. For example, the first stage might be to select several school districts or local education authorities (the first stage). Then, from lists of the schools in each selected area, a sample of schools would be chosen (the second stage). Then, from lists of the pupils in those schools, a random sample of pupils would be chosen (the third stage).

The accuracy of cluster sampling depends on how representative of the population the clusters chosen are. If a sample of 1,000 students was required, 200 students could be interviewed at five different universities, 100 students at 10 universities, 50 students at 20 universities, 10 students at 100 universities and so on. The researcher has to decide on the trade-off between a highly clustered sample and more variety. The smaller the number of clusters the more likely that the sample will lack variation. The larger the number of clusters the more representative of the population the sample will be.

Maximizing response rates

Researchers set out to maximize **response rates** among those selected for inclusion in a study using probability methods. The higher the response rates the more representative the sample is of the population. Generally face-to-face interviews have higher response rates than postal surveys though this will depend on the topic of the research. Self-completion surveys can achieve

Table 13.1   *Breakdown of a face-to-face interview sample*

Response category	Number	Percentage
Total addresses issued	**1972**	
Non-eligible addresses	223	11
Of which		
No trace of address	50	22
Business	76	34
Institution	2	1
Empty/boarded up	86	39
Other	9	4
Eligible addresses	**1749**	
Of which		
Successful interviews	1164	67
Refusals	310	18
Non-contacts (after four calls)	186	11
Not interviewable (e.g. away, on holiday, language difficulty, ill)	89	5

Source: adapted from Bloch and John, 1991

high response rates where the subject of the research is of interest to respondents. Table 13.1 shows the response to a survey using face-to-face interviews where sampling was done using the Postcode Address File. Table 13.2 shows response rates from a postal survey.

The reason stated most often for non-response among successful contacts eligible for the survey was refusal to participate. Generally, government surveys achieve higher response rates than other surveys because of perceptions about their importance. However, skilled interviewers can encourage participation and increase response rates though it is unethical to pressurize people into participating (see Chapter 10). The second reason was non-contact. Non-contact can be reduced by increasing the number of call-backs to each address and by varying the times of the day and days of the week that calls are made to increase the likelihood of finding the respondent at home. Some respondents cannot be interviewed because they are too ill, old and frail or there might be a language barrier. Excluding some of these groups from a survey might bias responses and steps can be taken ensure their participation. For example, interviews can be carried out using community languages to ensure that those with less fluency in English can participate.

The responses to the postal survey shown in Table 13.2 were based on three contacts with each respondent: an initial letter and questionnaire, a follow-up letter and then an additional follow-up letter and questionnaire. A response rate of 67% would generally be considered high for a postal survey.

In a probability sample survey the response rate should always be reported. Where known, information about the reasons for non-response and the characteristics of non-responders should be provided so that likely bias can be assessed.

Non-probability sampling techniques

It is not always possible to carry out a random sample of the population and it is not always desirable. Non-probability techniques are associated with qualitative work (as in *theoretical sampling* and *qualitative interviewing* – see Chapters 14 and 18), pilot work to test survey instruments, market research or when a complete and accurate sampling frame cannot be compiled. They are often used to access groups whose activities are normally 'hidden' from public or official view. The main types of non-probability sampling techniques used in survey research are **quota sampling** and **snowball** or **network** sampling.

Quota samples

Market researchers tend to use quota sampling techniques because they are relatively quick and cheap to carry out. Using this method interviewers must find interviewees who fit specified criteria, such as age and sex, and often the quotas used in the sample mirror the population. Typically people are stopped in the street and asked their age and if they fit the requirements of the quota the interview proceeds if the potential respondent agrees to participate.

Quota samples have the advantage of being cheap as there are no costs associated with

Table 13.2 *Breakdown of a postal survey sample*

Response category	Number	Percentage
Total number in sample	**851**	
Not eligible (gone away, died, not known)	75	9
Total eligible	**776**	
Of which		
Completed questionnaires	519	67
Returned but not filled out or incomplete (refusals, too ill etc.)	44	6
No reply	213	27

Source: adapted from Bloch, 1992

obtaining or compiling a sampling frame and there are no call backs if a potential respondent is not at home first time. They are often also cheap because street sampling means that interview time is very short since you cannot keep people talking on the street for very long. The main problem with quota samples is that they there are inherent biases. The quotas are usually obtained on busy shopping streets so frequent shoppers are over-represented and people who work outside the town centre are under-represented. Also, because quotas are not based on probability it is impossible to work out the standard error and therefore assess how representative the sample is.

Network or snowball sampling
Network or snowball sampling is used to obtain a sample when there is no list of the population available. In snowballing, respondents are obtained through referrals among people who share the same characteristic. This approach is used most often when the survey population is hidden or when there is no available sampling frame, such as drug users. Because this technique relies on personal recommendations by people whom the respondent knows the legitimacy of the researcher may be felt to be assured and it is therefore a use-ful way to tap into people who are involved in a network that might otherwise be wary of participating in social research.

The main problem with snowball techniques is that there is a possibility of interviewing people within one network which means that they might have similar experiences and this will bias the survey findings. Also, more isolated members of a group will not be included in the study. One way around this is to try to find multiple starting points for snowballing so that access to more than one network is obtained.

Conclusion

This chapter has reviewed the basic techniques used in survey research, from defining the aims of the research through to different types of social surveys, designing questionnaires, including operationalizing concepts, developing indicators, questionnaire content, question wording and sampling techniques. Carrying out a survey requires the researcher to make decisions at each stage of the process. When reporting on a survey it is important to be able to justify the decisions that were made in the design and the fieldwork stages. This chapter should assist you in understanding how to do this.

Box 13.8   Web pointers for survey research design

Surveys in Social Research
www.social-research.org/

Bill Trochim's Research Method Knowledge Base site:
http://trochim.cornell.edu/kb/survwrit.htm
http://trochim.cornell.edu/kb/intrview.htm
http://trochim.cornell.edu/kb/sampling.htm

Perseus Survey Solutions (a commercial web survey company)
www.perseusdevelopment.com/

Question Bank Resources
http://qb.soc.surrey.ac.uk/docs/resources.htm

Computer Assisted Telephone Interviewing
www.gesis.org/en/methods_consultation/CATI/

SurveyWiz (a free program to create a web-based survey), by Michael Birnbaum
http://psych.fullerton.edu/mbirnbaum/programs/surveyWiz.HTM

Visit the website for this book at www.rscbook.co.uk to link to these web pointers.

Further reading

De Vaus (2002a) is a popular and well-written guide to doing social surveys, taking the reader through all of the stages described in this chapter and including quantitative data analysis. A website is associated with the book and you will find links to most topics concerned with social survey research there: http://www.social-research.org/. Moser and Kalton (1971), although old, is still the most comprehensive and in-depth guide to all aspects of doing social surveys.

Student Reader (Seale, 2004): relevant readings

8 Barry Hedges: 'Sampling'
9 Sir Claus Moser and Graham Kalton: 'Questionnaires'
10 Herbert H. Hyman with William J. Cobb, Jacob J. Feldman, Clyde W. Hart and Charles Herbert Stember: 'Interviewing in social research'
11 A.N. Oppenheim: 'Attitude scaling methods'
12 Kim Sheehan and Mariea Hoy: 'On-line surveys'
21 Julius A. Roth: 'Hired hand research'
22 Aaron V. Cicourel: 'Fixed-choice questionnaires'
23 Cathie Marsh: 'The critics of surveys'
24 Hanneke Houtkoop-Steenstra: 'Quality of life assessment interviews'
25 R.C. Lewontin: 'Sex lies and social science'

Key concepts

Variables
Categorical variable
Interval level variable
Nominal variable
Numerical variable
Ordinal variable
Ratio scale
Variable

Questions and questionnaires
Closed question
Computer Assisted Telephone Interviewing (CATI)
Double-barrelled question
Frame of reference (of a question)
Interview guide
Interview schedule
Leading question
Non-standardized interview
Open question
Prestige bias
Questionnaire
Scheduling
Self-completion questionnaire
Semi-structured interview
Standardized interview

Structured questionnaire
Unstructured questionnaire

Sampling
Cluster sampling
Disproportionate stratification
Multi-stage cluster sampling
Population
Probability and non-probability sampling
Quota sampling
Representative sample
Sampling fraction
Sampling frame
Sampling theory
Simple random sampling
Snowball or network sample
Standard error
Stratified sample
Systematic sample

Other
Concept-indicator links
Data entry
Hypothesis
Multi-dimensional concept
Operationalization
Response rate
Unit of analysis

14

Qualitative interviewing

Bridget Byrne

CONTENTS

Box 14.1   Successful interviewing

'To interview successfully requires skill. But there are many different styles of interviewing, ranging from the friendly, informal, conversational approach to the more formal, controlled style of questioning, and good interviewers eventually develop a variation of their method which, for them, brings the best results and suits their personality. There are some essential qualities which the successful interviewer must possess: an interest and respect for people as individuals, and flexibility in response to them; an ability to show understanding and sympathy for their point of view; and, above all, a willingness to sit quietly and listen. People who cannot stop talking themselves, or resist the temptation to contradict or push an informant with their own ideas, will take away information which is either useless or positively misleading. But most people can learn to interview well.' (Thompson, 1988: 196)

What are qualitative interviews?

Interviews are most importantly a form of communication, a means of extracting different forms of information from individuals and groups. The interactive nature of their practice means that interviewing is a highly flexible but also somewhat unpredictable form of social research. In everyday life, there are many different forms of interviews, or conversations in which information is being elicited and/or shared with groups or individuals (see Box 14.2)

All of us will have experienced at least some of them and we are also familiar with reading the results of journalistic interviews, and perhaps also published 'conversations' between academics, as well as watching televised interviews. We are also familiar with conversational forms, which would not be considered as formal interviews, where we share with greater or lesser depth our feelings and views with friends, relatives, lovers and also perhaps counsellors and therapists. This experience tells us that the kind of talk we do, or information and opinions we share, varies widely depending on the context, our mood and the nature of the encounter (see Chapter 28 for an account of how to analyse conversations). It also varies depending on how familiar the form of encounter is to us – this is likely to be affected by our gender, class and cultural backgrounds.

Therefore in thinking about interviewing as a tool of social research, we need to be aware of the many different variables which will affect the outcome. These will include who is doing the interviewing, who is being interviewed, the location in which the interview takes place and the form of questioning. These factors need to be thought about before and during research, but they are also worth bearing in mind when reading research based on interviews. Does the researcher give you a sense of the interview content and context, have they answered these questions for you and have they taken them into account in the analysis of their interview material?

Box 14.2   Interviews in everyday life

Market research surveys
Doctors' consultations
Job or university interviews
Immigration interviews
Interviews to receive welfare or social security
Journalists' interviews
Television interviews
Therapeutic interviews

Social research interviews range from the formal *questionnaire*-based interviews at one end of the spectrum to totally open-ended interviews that might begin with a single prompt such as 'tell me about your life'. The term **qualitative interview** generally refers to in-depth, loosely or *semi-structured* interviews and these have been referred to as 'conversations with a purpose' (Burgess, cited in Mason, 1996: 38). They are often used to encourage an interviewee to talk, perhaps at some length, about a particular issue or range of topics. This distinguishes them from the classical tradition of social survey work represented by the sort of interviews done by Booth and Rowntree, as well as later social survey organizations such as the UK Office for National Statistics, and the increasing number of telephone and street surveys conducted for marketing purposes (see Chapter 8). As you saw in Chapter 13, survey-based interviews tend to rely more on *closed questions* which follow a *structured* format in the form of a *questionnaire* and are designed to elicit specific information or 'facts' from the interview subjects.

In a questionnaire-based survey, the aim is to *standardize* the interviews in order to claim direct comparability between interviews with different people and to interview enough people so that the results could be held to be statistically representative of a particular population. The intention, therefore, is that the interview should be neutral (that is to say, not influenced by the words, actions or position of the interviewer) and generalizable (and therefore often quantifiable). The emphasis is on **data collection** and it is based on a particular *epistemological* position taken in the classical survey research tradition. Here, the social world is assumed to have an existence that is independent of the language used to describe it. In contrast to this *realist* approach, an *idealist* account would see interview data as presenting one of many possible representations of the world. This latter approach tends to view the interview as a process of **data generation** rather than collection. In qualitative interviews, the researcher is often regarded as a co-producer of the data, which are produced as a result of an interaction between researcher and interviewee(s) (Mason, 1996: 36).

There are many different forms which qualitative interviewing can take. These range from interviews following an interview schedule of topics or themes to be covered in a loosely planned order, to an invitation for the interviewee to talk on whatever they feel is relevant. Qualitative interviewing may not only be one-on-one interviewing. It can also include **focus group** discussions that bring together a group of interviewees to discuss a particular topic or range of issues. In these contexts, the interactions between participants can generate different data than would have emerged in a one-on-one interview. Chapter 15 gives a full account of focus group research.

Whilst qualitative interviews are often undertaken as a result of a particular *epistemological* position taken by the researcher (as will be explored below), they are also a flexible resource which may be used in conjunction with other research techniques. So, for example, in-depth interviews may be used to explore in more detail with specially selected interviewees questions that have also been covered in a wider questionnaire-based survey. Equally, focus groups or one-on-one interviews may be used as a part of an ethnographic approach. This raises the question of why one would choose to use qualitative interviews and what they offer the researcher.

Box 14.3 Focus group interviews

'The method is particularly useful for allowing participants to generate their own questions, frames and concepts and to pursue their own priorities on their own terms, in their own vocabulary. Focus groups also enable researchers to examine people's different perspectives as they operate within a social network. Crucially, group work explores how accounts are articulated, censured, opposed and changed through social interaction and how this relates to peer communication and group norms.' (Barbour and Kitzinger, 1999: 5)

What the qualitative interview has to offer

Qualitative interviewing is particularly useful as a research method for accessing individuals' attitudes and values – things that cannot necessarily be observed or accommodated in a formal questionnaire. Open-ended and flexible questions are likely to get a more considered response than closed questions and therefore provide better access to interviewees' views, interpretations of events, understandings, experiences and opinions. Therefore, this approach tends to be used by those who come from an *ontological* position which values people's knowledge, values and experiences as meaningful and worthy of exploration. However, as we shall see below, few researchers believe that in the course of an interview, you are able to 'get inside someone's head'. What an interview produces is a particular *representation* or *account* of an individual's views and opinions.

One of the reasons why qualitative interviewing is a particularly suitable method for accessing complex issues such as values and understanding is that it is a flexible medium and, to a certain extent, allows interviewees to speak in their own voices and with their own language. Thus, qualitative interviewing has been particularly attractive to researchers who want to explore voices and experiences which they believe have been ignored, misrepresented or suppressed in the past. Feminists, for example, have used qualitative interviewing as a way of 'giving voice' to women's experiences and much oral history is concerned with capturing voices and experiences 'from below'. As we shall see later, this raises important questions about the dynamics of power in the interview and research process.

A further advantage of using qualitative interviewing as a research method is its flexibility in allowing research topics to be approached in a variety of ways. Issues that might be of a sensitive nature, for example, experiences of violence, or which interviewees may be reluctant to talk about (or unconscious of) such as racism or other forms of prejudice, can be approached with sensitivity to open up dialogue and produce fuller accounts. This again raises questions of power and ethics in the research process (see below).

Perhaps the most compelling advantage of qualitative interviewing is that, when done well, it is able to achieve a level of depth and complexity that is not available to other, particularly survey-based, approaches. The non-standardized interview enables the researcher to become attuned to subtle differences in people's positions and to respond accordingly, both at the time of interviewing and in the subsequent analysis.

The epistemological status of interviews

As we have seen, whilst qualitative interviewing offers particular advantages for researchers, it also raises epistemological, methodological and ethical issues for social researchers. However, it is also worth noting that many of these questions would also apply to other research methods.

Epistemological questions raised by qualitative interviewing centre around the status of the material produced:

- What can interviewees tell us and what do they not tell us?
- How do we assess and analyse the interview data?

How we answer these questions depends

Box 14.4   What qualitative interviews offer

Access to attitudes and values
Flexibility
Exploration of suppressed views
Sensitive issues can be broached
Achieve depth
Reflect complexity

largely on where we stand on the distinction between data *collection* and data *generation* mentioned earlier. In a *realist* approach, where the social world is assumed to have an existence independent of language, accounts given by interviewees are assessed according to how accurately they reflect this real social world. Thus, in this classical tradition, interviews are expected to act as a resource, providing real 'facts' about the social world. Thus interview data are scrutinized for **bias** – for the extent to which they present a distortion of the truth. In contrast, the *idealist* position takes the interviewee's account as one possible version of the social world. Here, the interview tends to be treated more as a social event in its own right, as a **topic** rather than a **resource**. In this approach, the researcher might be interested in analysing, for example, how the speaker uses various rhetorical strategies in order to achieve particular effects, or how the speaker is using particular **discursive repertoires** in their account (see Box 14.5 and Chapter 27).

In practice, researchers are often using interview material both as resource and a topic. Interviews are often analysed both for *what* interviewees say about their lives and experiences (the interview as *resource*) and for *how* the information is communicated and the accounts are told (the interview as *topic*). Therefore it is not always possible to completely sidestep issues of 'truth' and reliability. Analysis of accounts is likely to need to take into account some notion of how accurate the account is. If, for example, something is being misrepresented – a number or period of years being over-estimated – why does this happen? Why are certain things remembered more than others? Why is it more difficult to talk about certain subjects than others? As Luisa Passerini argues:

> There is no 'work of memory' without a corresponding 'work of forgetting' … So often forgetting indicates suffering, be it of the woman who 'does not remember' her housework because she has never been allowed to consider it important, or the silences of those who do not want to speak about the daily oppression of fascism and the massacres of nazism. (Passerini, 1983: 194)

Box 14.5 Discursive repertoires of whiteness

Ruth Frankenberg interviewed white women in the United States in order to explore their experiences of living in a racially hierarchical society. She identified different 'discursive repertoires', or ways in which race was spoken and written about in the United States. The dominant discourse was one of 'colour-blindness', or what Frankenberg named 'colour evasion': a way of thinking about race which 'asserts that we are all the same under the skin; that, culturally we are converging; that, materially, we have the same chances in U.S. society; and that – the sting in the tail – any failure to achieve is therefore the fault of people of color themselves' (Frankenberg, 1993: 14).

Thus, Frankenberg is interested in identifying when her respondents were using this kind of discourse, as where interviewee Ginny Rodd said:

> 'To me, they are like me or anyone else – they're human – it's like I told my kids, they work for a living like we do. Just because they are Black is no saying their food is give to them [sic]. If you cut them, they bleed red blood, same as we do.' (1993: 143)

Frankenberg contrasts these kinds of statements with those who she saw as drawing on a discourse of 'race cognizance', as in the words of interviewee Chris Patterson:

> 'When I look back, I think of myself as such a naïve white girl. Not even just naïve – naïve by isolation, by separation. Also coming from the white, privileged class … Means you don't have to look at anything else. You are never forced to until you choose to, because your life is so unaffected by things like racism.' (1993:161)

This 'work of forgetting' may be more interesting to the researcher than what is remembered, but interviews can only ever offer a partial view into the process.

Questions of power, difference and ethics

The interactive nature of the interview process can be the basis of many of its advantages as a research tool in that it allows for flexibility: the researcher can adapt in response to the reactions and responses of the interviewee. Whilst the nature of communication means that we can never be sure that two people's understandings of terms and concepts is exactly the same, the qualitative interview offers the possibility of exploring the interviewee's understanding in a more meaningful way than would be allowed by a less flexible survey questionnaire. However, the nature of interaction during interviews also raises some of the most critical questions that need to be dealt with by qualitative researchers.

Janet Holland and Caroline Ramazanoglu characterize interviews as 'stylized social events' and argue that 'differences such as age, class, gender, ethnicity and religion impinge on the possibilities of interaction and interpretation, and so on how the social world is known' (Holland and Ramazanoglu, 1994). This underlines the need to acknowledge and address difficult questions of **reflexivity**. Reflexivity involves critical self-scrutiny on the part of researchers, who need, at all stages of the research process, to ask themselves about their role in the research. Reflexivity involves a move away from the idea of the neutral, detached observer that is implied in much classical survey work. It involves acknowledging that the researcher approaches the research from a specific position and this affects the approach taken, the questions asked and the analysis produced. In the immediate context of the interview, reflexivity involves reflection on the impact of the researcher on the interaction with the interviewee.

Feminist researchers have been particularly alive to these questions. Ann Oakley wrote an influential critique of traditional standardized, structured interviews where these were based on the idea of a detached and neutral researcher who maintains control of the interview. Instead, Oakley argued that it

> becomes clear that, in most cases, the goal of finding out about people is best achieved when the relationship of the interviewer–interviewee is non-hierarchical and when the interviewer is prepared to invest his or her own personal identity in the relationship … Personal involvement is more than just dangerous bias – it is the condition under which people come to know each other and to admit others into their lives. (Oakley 1981: 41, 58)

Thus Oakley advocates the proffering of friendship and exchange within the interview process. However this may not always be possible or even desirable for either party involved. As Jane Ribbens points out, in some situations, the attempt of the researcher to place herself and give personal information may be seen as an imposition rather than as a welcome offer of friendship: 'After all, is not part of the research exchange that I have expressed an interest in hearing about the interviewees' lives?' (Ribbens 1989: 584). In addition, there is a risk that it is assumed that only women researchers should interview women respondents if they are to gain authentic accounts (see also Chapter 3). This overlooks other differences which may influence the interaction, such as age, social class and ethnicity. Thus in her article 'When gender is not enough: women interviewing women', Cathy Riessman contrasts her experience of interviewing middle-class Anglo women with that of interviewing working-class Puerto Rican women. Riessman (1987: 190) found that in the interviews between an Anglo researcher and Puerto Rican interviewees, the interview 'was hindered by a lack of shared cultural and class assumptions'.

Some might therefore argue that there should always be 'race', gender and class **matching** between respondents and researchers. However, exactly matching all the characteristics of respondents and interviewers is likely to be very difficult and would restrict many research projects. Ann Phoenix, reflecting on her research experience on two studies – one on young mothers and the other on social identities in young people – argues:

> [p]rescriptions for matching the 'race' and/ or gender of interviewers and respondents are … too simplistic … If different types of accounts about 'race' and racism are produced with black and white interviewers this is in itself important data and may be good reason for using interviewers of both colours whenever possible since it illustrates the ways in which knowledges are 'situated'. (Phoenix 1994: 49, 66)

Reflexivity in research requires that the impact of *both* similarities and differences on the research processes be examined. The impact of the social positioning of the researcher needs to be thought through and will be more significant to some research topics than others. For example, it might be more important to match gender when interviewing women about domestic violence. Questions about racism are likely to produce different responses depending on the racial identity of both interviewers and interviewees; being aware of when matching occurs or does not occur might be important in interpreting responses on such a research study.

The research relationship raises other ethical questions that need to be addressed (see also Chapter 10). Thus it is important to protect respondents from harm in the research process as well as to consider questions of *disclosure*, *consent* and *anonymity*. **Informed consent** should be obtained from interviewees wherever possible. This can be verbal, but should ideally be written, where interviewees are able to keep a copy of the agreement they have signed, including a statement about any questions of the copyright of the interview. It should also be clear to interviewees that they can stop the interview at any point if they want to. Depending on the research subject, it might be important to consider the extent to which interviewees are capable of giving informed consent. Do they understand the concept of research and what you are doing? Are they able to think through the implications? Should a third person be giving consent for them? This is particularly relevant to conducting research with children, but may also apply to others.

It is usual to offer anonymity to research respondents. But ensuring anonymity is not always a straightforward process. This is particularly true when dealing with in-depth biographical material which might be recognizable to friends and family unless some details are changed. Measures may also need to be taken in the recording and labelling of data to ensure that anonymity is preserved. Researchers need to think about where and how they will record and store their data during the research and writing up process. It is important to separate the interview material from the real names of the interviewees at an early stage, for instance on the labelling of tapes and transcriptions.

British Sociological Association (BSA) guidelines on the ethical conduct of research studies state that 'Sociologists have a responsibility to ensure that the physical, social and psychological well-being of research participants is not adversely affected by the research' (www.britsoc.org.uk/about/ethic.htm). It should be clear that research should not inflict harm on interviewees, but in some cases, the subject matter may be such that it is difficult to predict what is going to cause distress, and how much distress will be caused by taking part in an interview. Discussing violence, trauma, accidents, illegal activity and mistakes might all cause distress to interviewees. Researchers should ask themselves at all times if they are pushing too far in the questioning. In addition, they need to be aware that the interviewee might be saying too much – or things that they will regret disclosing. If you build up a good rapport with your interviewee it may start to feel like a counselling session, a role which the researcher is not necessarily trained to undertake.

Doing qualitative interviews

This section will examine some basic questions that need to be addressed when undertaking research using qualitative interviewing. These include:

- Whom do you interview (including how many people and how you contact them)?
- Where do you interview them?
- What do you ask them?
- How are you going to record the interviews?

Box 14.6   Ethical issues in interviews about sexual abuse

In one study of the experience of sexual abuse, the researcher, Catherine Kirkwood, asked her respondents what they felt about the interview process. Of the 16 interviewed, three felt that the interviews pushed them too deeply into the emotional responses to abuse, leading to nightmares for two of them and a third being unable to finish the interviews (Kirkwood, 1993: 34–5).

Some people are clearly more vulnerable than others and some subjects more difficult to deal with, and careful consideration should be given to the likely impact of interviews on respondents.

- How will they be analysed?

Answering all of these questions requires forward planning and in particular will depend on establishing a clear sense of *why* you are conducting the interviews in the first place.

Why interview?

Before you can plan your research, you need to have as clear a sense as possible about why you are proposing to undertake the research in a particular way and what you hope to achieve by it. This involves having at least a preliminary idea of how you will analyse your material (although in qualitative research this will often be a flexible process and subject to change). You can ask yourself:

- Is your aim to use the interview as an exercise in data *generation* or data *collection*? Related to this is the issue of whether you will be treating the interview as *topic* or *resource* – or both.
- Are interviews the best way of conducting the research or are there other sources which would be more efficient ways of getting the information? Perhaps you should be pursuing the interviews in conjunction with other sources for your research.
- Is your aim to test or develop theoretical propositions?
- What kinds of comparisons are you likely to want to make?

The different answers that you have for these questions should help you frame both *whom* you should interview and *how* you plan and conduct the interviews themselves.

Whom do you interview?

Qualitative interviewing is, by its very nature, relatively time-consuming compared to survey interviewing. Tom Wengraf argues that semi-structured interviews are 'high-preparation, high-risk, high-gain, and high-analysis operations' (Wengraf, 2001: 5). The time involved limits the possibilities for covering large samples and this is one reason why few attempts are made to achieve *random* or *probability* samples in qualitative interviews, although they may be conducted in conjunction with wider representative samples (see Chapter 13 for a discussion of sampling in survey research). So whilst the aim may not be statistical generalization, there is still the need to consider who should be interviewed in order to achieve a good understanding of the issue under research.

As with more stringent versions of sampling, you need to begin by identifying the wider population from which you will select your interviewees. For instance, are you interested in researching the experiences of black women under 20? Or of social workers who work in fostering and adoption? Or the whole population of people who live in a particular area of a large city? What is your particular interest in this population and how does it relate to your research? You will then need to make a selection of research subjects or interviewees from this broader population. In order to do this, you need to establish a relationship between the selection and the wider population. There are several different types of relationship which can be established. These are outlined in Box 14.7.

Additionally, *theoretical sampling* is a common approach to selecting of individuals for qualitative interviews. Here, people are selected

---

Box 14.7 Three possible relationships between sample and population

1 A *representative* relationship (as in *probability* sampling). This requires the selection of a sample which is representative of the total empirical population that the study refers to. It requires knowledge of the nature of the total population – so that proportions of social characteristics such as age, gender, ethnicity, class in the wider population can be mirrored in the sample. This requires the use of statistical conventions to enable you to argue that the general patterns discovered in the sample are representative of the wider population. As mentioned above, whilst this approach can be used in qualitative interviewing, it is not common.

2 A relationship designed to provide a close-up, detailed or *meticulous view of particular* experience. This could be as narrow as selecting the life and narrative of a particular person for scrutiny, or a small set of people. This approach allows for the in-depth examination of a particular set of social processes in a particular context. However, you need to be able to argue how this narrow example relates to a wider population and how the interviewees do, or do not, compare with each other.

3 A relationship that covers a *relevant range* of people in relationship to a wider population, but is not designed to represent it directly. This does not mean an *ad hoc* sample, but involves a strategy of selection which ensures that a relevant range is covered.

(*Source:* adapted from Mason, 1996: 91–2)

---

according to how likely it is their interview will contribute to the development of an emerging theory. The relationship of this to some population is generally not known. Theoretical sampling is discussed in depth in Chapter 18. Roger Hewitt's experience in a study of processes of racism is helpful in showing how sampling decisions can be made in a qualitative interviewing study (Box 14.8)

The size and nature of your sample will depend partly on how it is designed to relate to the wider population (and the nature of that wider population). It will also be affected by the *resources* available to you. Identifying and gaining the coop-

---

Box 14.8 Sampling in a study of racism

'We were concerned to build up a picture not simply of racial attitudes but of how young people who expressed racist opinions made the move into perpetrating racist acts. While we regarded understanding the experience of victims as central, it was the *perpetrators* of racist actions who were the major focus of our attention. At the same time, we were anxious to find out about those people who formed the social and family network of perpetrators. What did they think about racism and racist attacks? How did people in any neighbourhood allow harassment to go on? Who knew about it? What did they say to each other about it? This was part of what we called 'the social basis of racist action'. We believed that perpetrators of racist harassment probably did not behave in a social vacuum. It was somehow either allowed or even encouraged by others, and there was something in the local community that allowed it to happen.

'In order to investigate the social basis of racist action, we interviewed as many young people as well as adult professionals including youth and community workers, teachers and the police. We attended community groups and other such meetings, talked to a wide range of adults in different neighbourhoods and interviewed both boys and girls – in groups in schools and youth clubs.' (Hewitt, 1996: 2)

eration of interviewees and conducting the interviews themselves are all time-consuming processes. But they are likely to be outweighed by the time spent listening to and annotating or transcribing the interviews and analysing the results. You should start out with a target number of interviewees which you think is suitable for your project. This may include target numbers of different people who have the required characteristics to supply the range of people whom you want to interview. It might be helpful to set up a table of target interviewees who fulfil certain criteria (as in *quota sampling* – see Chapter 13). However (to introduce an element of theoretical sampling) this should be used flexibly by allowing for the development of new criteria and selection strategies as the research proceeds. For instance, you may realize after a while that there is a different group who provide a 'negative' comparison to those who form the bulk of your interviewees. It may be important to investigate this group. Or you may decide to follow up fewer interviewees but do so in more depth than originally planned, or conversely, increase your target number of interviews.

Once you have outlined your target selection, you then need to find the people and get them to talk to you. This can be a nerve-racking process, but it is often surprising how willing people are to give you their time if approached in the right way. You need to think about how to contact potential interviewees. Are there organizations which will give you access to a certain population or specific ways of contacting them? For instance, if your target group is social workers working on adoption and fostering, are there professional bodies you can approach to help you find interviewees? Can you identify the agencies in which they work and approach them directly? Are there professional journals or magazines which also might help you locate interviewees? But you also need to think about how the route taken for your approach to interviewees may influence whom you eventually interview. For instance, if you wanted to interview fathers who bring up single-headed families, you could contact the campaign groups that represent them. However, the men that are involved in these groups may have characteristics that are not shared by other men in similar situations. For instance, they might tend to have

different class characteristics, or be more unhappy with their situations. In this case, if you were concerned to represent a full range of fathers in this position, you would need to develop alternative strategies for contacting single fathers who had different characteristics.

Sometimes getting access to interviewees requires going through intermediaries or *gatekeepers* (see also Chapter 17). For instance, if you want to interview elderly people, you might choose to approach a nursing home or social group for pensioners. You will need to get the permission of the head of the nursing home or group organizer. You will also want to ensure that the gatekeepers are not putting pressure on people to participate, and try to judge whether being introduced in a particular way by a person perhaps in authority may affect the interviewees and what they say.

As is shown in Chapter 13, another method of finding interviewees is to *snowball*, where you ask people you have interviewed to suggest friends or colleagues to interview. This can be a very successful method of making contacts, but it is likely only to introduce you to people who are similar to those you have already interviewed. It can be helpful to get a sense of networks or the ways in which people in similar situations use the same *discursive repertoires*. However, it is not likely to enable you to cover people across a range of differences (there is a tendency for people to know and introduce you to others who are broadly similar to themselves). In addition, it makes you dependent on your interviewees' choices of whom you should talk to. They may have different selection criteria from you – for instance, suggesting people with unusual experiences where you want to interview more 'normal' cases.

However you contact your interviewees, you have to remain *reflexive* during this process, which is likely to happen over a period of time. You need to be aware of how your sample is developing and how it compares with your targets. Are there reasons for your changes to original plans? If certain people are particularly difficult to reach, can you find new approaches (see Chapter 31 on what to do 'When things go wrong')? If you are finding it difficult to find interviewees this may *add* to your understanding of what you are trying to research. For example, it is often hard to find people for interviews about the experience of certain illnesses (for example, HIV/AIDS) whereas others are conditions that people are more happy to discuss (for example, heart disease). This may reflect the fact that some conditions attract more social stigma than others.

Where do you interview?

The setting in which you interview may also make a difference. For instance, you could get different responses from teenagers if you interview them in a classroom rather than a familiar café. You should therefore give some thought to *where* the interviews are conducted. Ideally, you need a space where you and the interviewee (or group) will be relaxed, able to talk and be undisturbed. This can sometimes be difficult to achieve. Often inter-

views are conducted in people's own homes as this is most convenient for them. However, this can have implications for privacy if other family members are around. On the other hand, meeting in public places or at workplaces may influence the tone of the resulting interview in certain ways. Clearly, interviewing focus groups requires more space and a place where everyone is able to gather as well as, ideally, some refreshments on hand.

What do you ask?

Qualitative interviews can be experienced by the interviewee as very similar to an informal conversation. However, this does not mean that they are totally unstructured or unplanned. Like sampling, the conduct of the interview needs to be planned, but it must also be responsive and, as the quotation from Paul Thompson in Box 14.1 suggests, it is a

---

Box 14.9   Example of an interview topic guide

1   First trying marijuana
2   Circumstances surrounding first contact
3   State of being following first contact
4   Conditions for continual use
5   Conditions for curtailment or stoppage
6   Present situation
7   Current attitudes towards usage

Expansion of section 5:
5   Conditions for curtailment or stoppage
  A   Why did you decide to stop or cut down?
  B   What was happening to you at this time? (e.g. were you still in school, working, etc?)
  C   Was the drug still relatively accessible to you?
  D   Did your decision to stop have anything to do with what was taking place in your life career? (That is, was the usage of marijuana on a regular basis becoming too great a risk in moral, social, or legal terms?)
  E   Did any particular person or persons influence your decision to stop or cut down? Who, and how did they influence you?
  F   (To be asked of those who have *stopped completely*) Since having given up marijuana, have you felt any strong yearning to try it again or resume your use of it? Tell me about it (times, occasions, places, etc., in which yearning is experienced). How do you handle these feelings when you get them – what do you tell yourself or do in order to resist the desire?

(*Source:* quoted in Lofland, 1971: 78–9)

skill that needs to be learned. The key to a good interview is to adjust your approach so that the interviewee is encouraged to talk, but crucially to talk about subjects that you are interested in researching.

Different researchers and research projects will adopt different approaches to qualitative interviewing. At one end of the spectrum would be conducting interviews with reference to a relatively structured topic guide, such as that in Box 14.9 which is taken from a study of people who had ceased using marijuana.

At the other extreme is the *single question induced narrative* approach developed by Tom Wengraf (2001). Wengraf aims to elicit stories from the interviewee with a single question such as 'tell me the whole story of your life' and no further questions except for clarification. Clearly, this is appropriate for some research projects, but not all.

Most qualitative interviewing falls somewhere between the single question and the relatively structured topic guide. They will involve the researcher having planned in advance the way in which he or she intends to introduce and open the interview and a range of topics which they hope to cover. Qualitative interviewing is a skilled process as you need to develop the ability to listen carefully to what you are being told at the same time as you consider how to take the interview forward and what your next question will be. You also need to be aware of body language and other non-verbal signals that you are being given, as well as to attend to your means of recording the interview, either by taking notes or by making sure the recording equipment is still working. Juggling all these tasks takes practice.

As should be clear, conducting interviews is not the same as merely taking part in a conversation. It needs a different kind of listening and different responses. You need to take more care not to interrupt your interviewee's speech than you might in a normal conversation. Qualitative interviews generally concentrate on open-ended or 'non-directive' questions which require more response than a simple 'yes' or 'no'. There are various ways to encourage your interviewees to carry on talking or expand on what they are saying. Sometimes simply not rushing in with another

question will give them time to reflect on what they have said and say some more, especially if you are giving encouraging semi-verbal cues such as 'uh-huh' and nodding encouragement. You can also repeat statements back to the interviewer in the form of a question. For example, if someone says 'When I was young, I didn't have much of a relationship with my sister,' you can ask them again as a question 'You say you didn't have much of a relationship with your sister?' as an encouragement to further talk about this topic.

In some cases, qualitative interviews may be covering quite sensitive material, or issues that the interviewees do not particularly want to talk about. It is important to raise sensitive issues in ways that make interviewees still feel comfortable about discussing them. This may involve using indirect questions. For example, rather than asking a white interviewee directly about their own attitudes – 'What do you think of black people?' – it might be more productive to ask more general questions such as 'Do you think there is a problem of racism in this country?' Interviews may also place researchers in a disturbing position where they have to respond to statements and opinions with which they disagree or even find offensive. There is no single appropriate response to these situations. You may need, for example, to weigh up your ethical and political desire to combat prejudice wherever you encounter it with a desire to maintain a good relationship with your interviewee. On the other hand, sometimes a more combative response may produce a discussion which is useful for your research (see Back, 1996; Wetherell and Potter, 1992: 99)

How do you record interviews?

You need to think about how the interview material will be recorded and transcribed. This may depend in part on the form your analysis will take. For example, do you need exact transcription of the interviews (more important perhaps for *discourse* and *conversation analysis*)? Or will more summary notes be sufficient for your analysis? Will you be using a computer programme to help you code your data? In this case, you will need to have all your material in electronic form and this has important implications for the amount of time that the analysis will take.

The need to concentrate on what the interviewee is saying and how to respond and adapt to this is easier if you do not have to take notes of what is being said as you go along. This means that audio recording of interviews is often desirable, although it requires specific consent from the interviewee and may not be suitable in all cases. Recording also entails more post-interview work as you will need to listen again to the interview and perhaps transcribe it (see Chapter 16 for a full account of making and managing audio recordings for research purposes).

Whether the actual interview is recorded electronically or not, it is wise, once the interview is over, to make field notes of the encounter. Often these will record aspects of the interaction and your sense of the interview, not otherwise included in your interview notes or transcript. This can be very helpful in reminding you of important things when you analyse the material (Box 14.10).

How do you analyse interviews?

This section is short. Many chapters in the rest of this book guide you in doing this, since the considerations that apply to the analysis of qualitative interviews are really no different (and no less complex) than those that apply to other kinds of qualitative material. Thus, an interview might be analysed as a part of a project in which *grounded theory* is being generated (Chapter 18), for *conversation analytic* purposes (Chapter 28) or

qualitative content analysis or *discourse analysis* (Chapter 27). Combining qualitative with quantitative analysis (Chapter 22) may be appropriate; coding schemes are very likely to be involved, and possibly computer software (Chapter 23).

The distinction between analysis of interview material as a *topic* or a *resource* is a key one in understanding different approaches. Here, the basic decision is whether to 'read' interviews as a report of experience (the *resource* approach) or whether to treat them as events in their own right, so that they become occasions that are observed (the *topic* approach). This distinction was also discussed in the section earlier on the epistemological status of interviews.

Conclusion

This chapter has reviewed both practical considerations of qualitative interviewing and methodological issues that concern the underlying epistemological and political considerations that lie behind the use of this kind of material for research purposes. It should have equipped you both to do and to think about qualitative interviews. If you use this method, it is important to keep a note of all the decisions you make in planning and undertaking the interviews. This will help you when you come to writing up your research and providing a rationale for the way you have proceeded.

Finally, consider whether it is appropriate to have any follow-up with your interviewees. This

---

Box 14.10 Writing field notes after the interview

Janet Holland and Caroline Ramazanoglu stressed the importance of field notes to accompany interview data in their work on young people's sexualities:

> Obviously the text of a transcript does not reveal all that went on in the interview: language was not the only thing exchanged. Body language, non-verbal exchanges, distress and laughter are all part of that interchange, and all need to be taken into account in understanding and interpreting what the young women and young men were trying to communicate about their sexualities. (Holland and Ramazanoglu, 1994: 141)

They feel that these field notes helped analysis by reminding them about each interview.

> Since no researcher can gain more than a glimpse of other people's lives through accounts given in an interview, much of the 'skill' of interview-based research lies in what sense we make of the interview after the subject has gone – how we interpret our interview texts. (Holland and Ramazanoglu, 1994: 126)

Box 14.11   Web pointers for qualitative interviewing

Forum Qualitative Research – Click on 'Search' then search for the term 'Interview'
www.qualitative-research.net/fqs/fqs-eng.htm

Martin Ryder's qualitative research site – follow the links on interviewing
http://carbon.cudenver.edu/~mryder/itc_data/pract_res.html

Oral History Society (UK)
www.oralhistory.org.uk/

Oral History Association (USA)
www.dickinson.edu/organizations/oha/

Visit the website for this book at www.rscbook.co.uk to link to these web pointers.

---

might involve sending out a letter which tells them the results or progress of your research or even giving a workshop or presentation where you explain the results of your research to a group of respondents and give them a chance to comment on what you have found.

Further reading

Denzin (1989) gives an overview of a variety of approaches to qualitative interviewing. Silverman (2001) presents a sophisticated discussion of different ways of approaching the analysis of qualitative interview data. Scott (1984) gives a feminist account of interviewing. Gubrium and Holstein's *Handbook of Interview Research* (2002) gives a comprehensive, up-to-date and authoritative account of a wide range of approaches to interviewing.

Student Reader (Seale, 2004): relevant readings

10 Herbert H. Hyman with William J. Cobb, Jacob J. Feldman, Clyde W. Hart and Charles Herbert Stember: 'Interviewing in social research'

36 Howard S. Becker and Blanche Geer: 'Participant observation and interviewing: a comparison'

37 Sue Jones: 'Depth interviewing'

38 Ann Oakley: 'Interviewing women: a contradiction in terms?' (and a subsequent exchange with Joanna Malseed

79 Maureen Cain and Janet Finch: 'Towards a rehabilitation of data'

Key concepts	**Informed consent**
	Matching
Bias	**Reflexivity**
Data collection *versus* **data generation**	**Topic** *versus* **resource**
Discursive repertoires	

15

Using focus groups

Fran Tonkiss

CONTENTS

This chapter examines the use of focus groups within social and cultural research. It considers the different ways in which researchers use focus groups, their relationship to other methods of inquiry, issues involved in selecting and running focus groups, and their strengths and weaknesses as a research method. The aim of the chapter is both to outline some key methodological debates about the use and value of focus groups, and to consider certain practical questions that arise in using the method.

What is a focus group?

A focus group is, quite simply, a small group discussion focused on a particular topic and facilitated by a researcher. Focus groups originated in market research during the 1920s, and have been used within social science since at least the 1940s (see Kitzinger, 1994; Merton, 1987). There has, however, been increasing interest since the 1980s in the use of focus groups across different fields of social, cultural and policy research. These include media and communications research (especially audience studies), sociology and social psychology, policy consultation and evaluation, organizational studies, environmental studies, health research, and research into public attitudes. In the policy field, focus groups have featured in recent strategies to promote user involvement in public services, or to create forms of deliberative democracy or citizens' juries that allow people access to government debates and decision-making processes. In all of these contexts, focus groups offer a distinctive method for generating qualitative data on the basis of group interaction and discussion.

This interactive quality is the key feature of focus group research. The unit of analysis is the group, rather than the individuals taking part in the discussion. Focus groups in this sense are not simply a means of interviewing several people at the same time; rather, they are concerned to explore the formation and negotiation of accounts within a group context, how people define, discuss and contest issues through social interaction. Underlying this approach is an assumption that opinions, attitudes and accounts are *socially* produced – shaped by interaction with others – rather than

being discretely formed at the level of the individual (see Lunt and Livingstone, 1996: 90). Moreover, the group context makes visible *how* people articulate and justify their ideas in relation to others. Whereas a survey questionnaire can elicit what someone says they think about a specific topic, and an interview can describe how an individual accounts for their views, group discussions show how such accounts emerge through a communicative process. Beyond their status as a practical strategy for generating data, then, focus groups involve a stronger methodological assertion that the group context is important (and not just handy) for exploring the way social and cultural knowledge and meanings are produced.

The 'focus' of the group discussion can take different forms, and be more or less structured. To focus the interaction researchers might use:

- A fixed schedule of questions
- A *topic guide* of themes for discussion
- A group exercise
- Visual cues (such as video clips, advertisements, press reports or photographs)

Focus groups typically (and ideally) involve six to ten people – small enough to allow all the members to participate, but large enough to capture a variety of perspectives and enable people to bounce ideas off each other. While many research projects are based on a number of one-off groups, others involve a series of sessions with the same groups of people. Discussions are usually audio- or video-taped, allowing researchers to concentrate on guiding the discussion, and for the data to be transcribed for analysis. Before looking more closely at the practical conduct of focus groups, we can consider the range of contexts in which researchers use them.

How are focus groups used?

Focus groups are used in a number of different research settings:

- In *media and communications studies* to explore issues of audience reception
- In *consultation or evaluation research* to examine user demands and responses to services and agencies

- In *organizational research* to look at staff or members' views and opinions
- more generally, in the *interpretive study* of social and cultural attitudes on a range of issues

In these ways focus groups are relevant both to applied social research with a strong policy or practical orientation, and to theoretical research that seeks to explore social and cultural meanings, knowledge and discourses. Focus groups are effective both as an independent method for generating data, and in conjunction with other techniques of data collection. Where focus groups are used together with other methods, we can think about this relationship on two levels:

- *Level 1:* focus groups provide a *tool* of research design, refining and clarifying the concepts and language used within a study, or helping to evaluate and interpret research findings.
- *Level 2:* focus groups can be used at the *core* of a research project, combining with other methods to produce different forms of data within a multi-method approach to social and cultural research.

Focus groups initially were used within social science as a supplement to quantitative research methods. Merton (1987) describes the use of focused interviews to aid in the interpretation of experimental and survey data. Feeding results back to research participants in a group discussion allowed them to account for their responses in a qualitative manner. The earliest example of a focus group involved Paul Lazarsfeld in 1941 (see Box 15.1).

Whereas the experimental design could *indicate* people's responses, the group discussion was used to help *interpret* them. In recent years focus groups have been developed as a 'stand alone' method, but they continue to have value as an element of research design, or when used with other approaches. At the start of the research process, for instance, focus groups can help researchers to *operationalize* their core concepts: that is, to define and clarify the main themes that the research aims to investigate, and how these might be studied. Focus groups are valuable for exploring meaning in terms of participants' own understanding and terminology. For this reason, they can shed light on how respondents make sense of research problems or topics, helping to spell out key terms, issues and questions.

Focus groups and quantitative research

It follows that this qualitative method for exploring social meanings works well in tandem with quantitative research (see also Chapter 22 for an overview of mixed methods research). Focus groups play a useful role in survey design, clarifying and defining the key research concepts, ensuring that the language used in the survey is likely to be understood by respondents, and even generating attitude statements for questionnaires. An example is given in Box 15.2.

Box 15.1   The first focus group in social research

The first focus group [in social research] took place at the Office of Radio Research at Columbia University in 1941. Paul Lazarsfeld asked Robert Merton to help him tabulate audience response to radio shows. In Lazarsfeld's original experiment, the audience pressed different coloured buttons to indicate when they had either a positive or negative response to a radio show. Merton added depth to this process in that at the end of the radio show, audience members (as a group) were asked why they responded positively or negatively at particular moments in the show. In this context, the first focus group was conducted.

(*Source*: www.slis.ualberta.ca/cap02/kristie/history_of_focus_groups.htm)
(See also Lunt and Livingstone, 1996 and Merton, 1987 for an account)

Box 15.2   Focus groups used to inform the design of a survey

In a study on public trust in voluntary organizations, focus group research was used in conjunction with a large-scale attitude survey, where the survey items were based on the statements of the groups themselves (Tonkiss and Passey, 1999: 264–5). In this case, focus group research took place prior to the quantitative survey, exploring how different groups of people understood and talked about the slippery concept of 'trust' before attempting to measure wider public attitudes towards it.

Kitzinger describes an innovative combination of focus groups with surveys in her research on media coverage of AIDS (see Box 15.3). The focus group stage of the project was concerned with media 'effects' – how people consume and respond to media messages. Kitzinger and her colleagues were interested in using focus groups to explore the communicative processes through which knowledge is organized and opinions formed.

Knowledge about the topic, it was found, was shaped by values and personal experience as well as by information (and misinformation). A focus group of gay men, for example, placed 'male homosexuals' at lower risk than 'people who have sex with many different partners of the opposite sex', accounting for this assessment on the basis that gay men would be more likely to practise safer sex than would straight people with multiple sexual partners. Kitzinger comments that while other groups (including doctors, for instance) shared this knowledge about many gay men's awareness of safer sex, this did not necessarily inform those groups' collective assessment of risk. Moreover, these framing values and knowledges did not simply operate on an individual level; the

group processes showed how attitudes were collectively shaped, both in confirming and hardening attitudes (around homophobia within certain groups of men or adolescents, for example), or in working out ideas and contesting assumptions (about the risk status of lesbians, for instance) (Kitzinger 1994: 164–6).

Focus groups and interviews

Focus groups also have a dual relation to *interview* methods (se Chapter 14), providing both a tool in research design and a complementary method of data collection. At the stage of developing or piloting research, one or more focus groups can help researchers to formulate qualitative interview schedules: defining terms, raising themes for inclusion in a topic guide, clarifying the wording or order of questions, or assessing participants' understanding of key concepts and language. This is especially useful when researchers know what it is they want to study, but are less certain how their ideas can be turned into a relevant and meaningful set of questions. In an extended manner, the two methods can be used in conjunction with each other in the body of the re-

---

Box 15.3   Focus groups in a study of media coverage of AIDS

The exercise:

1 Individual participants first completed a questionnaire, rating different categories of people on a scale of risk in relation to AIDS.

2 This exercise was then repeated in a group context: using a 'card game' format, the groups were asked collectively to allocate these same social categories to one of four levels of risk. Working in a group made it necessary for people to discuss and negotiate their risk assessments, and here researchers were able to observe the modes of reasoning, the assumptions and at times the misconceptions behind people's responses.

(*Source:* Kitzinger, 1994)

---

search. Individual interviews can be valuable when different perspectives emerge from focus group discussions, or if potentially sensitive or contentious issues are at stake. This cuts in different ways: in certain contexts, group discussions may encourage people to speak with greater openness than they would in a one-on-one interaction with a researcher; in others, the group context can be inhibiting. It will depend on the nature of the topic, the research design, and the make-up of the groups. Furthermore, where group discussions are used to open up topics in general ways – exploring a range of views using topic guides or visual cues, for example – individual interviews can be used to examine responses in greater depth or to draw out contrasting views and accounts.

The difference between focus groups and individual interviews, however, is not simply a question of openness versus confidentiality or of generality versus detail. The two methods produce distinct forms of data, and it can be argued that they are premised on quite separate models of social action and meaning. A strong form of this argument holds that 'much individually based interview research is flawed by a focus on individuals as atoms divorced from their social context' (Morley, 1980: 33), when knowledge and opinions in fact are mediated by communication, and actors are irreducibly social. Focus group research, in this reading, does not seek to access individual opinions or even individual accounts, but is concerned with accounts that emerge through interaction. Its method of producing data is therefore suggestive of 'real' social processes. As Lunt and Livingstone (1996: 94) point out, of course, interviews are no less 'social' than are focus groups, but one-on-one and group interactions are different contexts for the production of meaning and the shaping of discourse, and the data that result will reflect these differences in ways researchers should attend to in their analysis.

Focus groups and ethnography

This interactive nature of focus group data is interesting in relation to a further approach to social and cultural research: *participant observation* or *ethnography* (see Chapter 17). The two methods share a number of practical and methodological features – including their use in the study of organizations and groups, their common emphasis on social meanings and communicative processes, and their concern with collective dynamics. The data produced by these two 'interactionist' methods are, though, rather different from each other. Focus groups can in a practical sense supplement observation methods, allowing researchers to elicit information or explore attitudes that are not easily accessible through observation alone. In this sense they add to the repertoire of methods that ethnographers draw on in field research (which include interviews or documentary analysis for example), but in a way that appears especially well-suited to a larger concern with social interaction and collective meanings.

In a stricter methodological sense, however, focus groups are an artificial intervention into a 'natural' observation setting, involving the researcher in a directive relation with their research subjects and with the process of data production. Just as focus groups can be seen as more realistic than individual interviews, then, they can be seen as less **naturalistic** than observation. Approached in less purist mode, however, focus group techniques provide a valuable ethnographic tool, and can prove particularly useful for field research in organizations where the researchers' access to different actors and exchanges is subject to practical constraints. Focused group discussions can enable the researcher to examine issues that are not always or easily observable 'in the field', and moreover to define these issues in terms of members' own understandings and concerns.

Focus groups and data analysis

This final point – the emphasis on members' understandings – indicates why focus groups are often seen as beneficial at the data analysis stage. With their emphasis on shared and contested meanings, focus groups can help researchers to explore the findings that emerge from surveys, interviews or observations. Their use here has the twin merits of adding interpretive weight to the researcher's own analysis, and seeking to integrate respondents' views and feedback in a participatory research process. Focus group work can be particularly valuable when results are puzzling (helping to dig deeper into inconsistencies or disagreements in responses) or surprising (helping to account in different ways for anomalies or blindspots). While this use of focus groups as an analytic tool echoes their early use in social science research, using focus groups to reflect on preceding stages of the research process is not only a convenient or consultative means of interpretation, but can add further layers to the research.

In an inventive piece of research with over one hundred children in a secondary school in East London, Jenny Pearce (2003) used a range of methods to explore young people's relationship to local spaces, and to related issues of safety and danger (see Box 15.4).

In Pearce's study the group context was important. It facilitated discussion, helping the children work through their ideas together, and easing the potentially intimidating dynamic of work with an adult researcher. The focus groups, then, did not simply help Pearce make sense of the data from children's charts and maps. Rather they generated a richer store of data about the young people's spatial practice and how they accounted for it, as well as involving them in a sustained and inclusive discussion about issues of race, gender, safety and danger in a way that took their voices seriously.

The different uses of focus groups described in this section indicate some of the tensions that underpin approaches to the method.

- On a *basic level*, focus group research is a practical means of generating data quickly and reasonably conveniently – you can get six or ten people's views all at once rather than having to interview them separately.
- On a *further level*, the focus group is a valuable tool of research design – helping you clarify your key concepts, refine your terminology, construct your questions; or of data analysis – aiding interpretation and seeking to reflect the understanding of research participants themselves.
- On a more *advanced level*, however, stronger methodological claims can be made for the focus group as a means of generating qualitative data. From this perspective, focus groups capture the inherently interactive and communicative nature of social action and social meanings, in ways that are inaccessible to research methods that take the individual as their basic unit of analysis.

Viewed on these terms, focus groups have moved some distance from their origins as a supplement to more orthodox social research techniques, to their current status as a distinctive method of

---

Box 15.4   Focus groups and children's use of space

- Pearce began by asking children in classes to draw maps and make lists of the places they used in their local area, noting in a few words what they did there, when they went, who they went with, and how they felt.
- From these basic charts, Pearce constructed a topic guide organized around the places listed most often by different groups of children (categorized by age, gender and self-defined ethnicity), also including places mentioned as important by a smaller number of respondents.
- In focused group discussions her young participants were able to explore the meanings, uses, perceived safety and danger of these places. They moved from the simple naming of places on maps and charts (park, mosque, shops, stairwells, etc.) to a richer discussion of how they made and claimed space for themselves. They discussed how they caused disruption in their local areas or kept themselves and others safe; how racism, gender and cultural differences shaped their everyday use of space.

(*Source*: described in Pearce, 2003)

social and cultural inquiry in their own right.

In the following sections, I consider some of the practical issues involved in using the focus group method, beginning with the question of how to go about selecting groups of participants.

Sampling and selection

Focus groups are a means of generating qualitative data so as to explore different perspectives on a topic, rather than to access representative or generalizable views about it. Even so, issues of selection remain critical. Focus group researchers adopt a range of approaches to the selection of participants, and debates in this area reflect and add to more general questions about sampling in qualitative research (see Lunt and Livingstone, 1996; Krueger and Casey, 2000). In particular, there is the issue of selecting *individuals* for a method that is concerned with the analysis of *groups*. This has implications for the status of the data that emerge from focus group discussions, and how far these data can be taken to reflect either individual opinion or general social attitudes. In the discussion that follows, I review different approaches to sampling and selection that a focus group researcher might adopt, from those which follow a more standard *survey* logic, to the use of *theoretical sampling* as a strategy for generating data (see also Chapters 13 and 18).

Random sampling

Random sampling is fairly uncommon in focus group research, given its association with larger-scale and quantitative studies (see Chapter 13). In some cases, however, researchers will be able to take a random sample of the population of interest. When researching a clearly defined organization, for instance, one might use random sampling to select groups of employees in a workplace, students within a university, or people registered with a medical practice. The purpose of such research, however, is unlikely to be simply a broad measure of satisfaction within an organization, or the highlighting of general problems or concerns. If that were the case, it would be easier and more reliable to use a survey instead. Focus groups offer evaluation and organizational research some-

thing different. The detailed nature of focus group data provides scope for greater insight into an issue. Why do different people say they are happy or unhappy with the service they get from their doctor? What do they say they want and what do they think might be done about it? Even where focus group research employs random sampling, it is not primarily for the purpose of generalizing from individual responses to external populations. This is because focus group research does not provide access in any systematic way to individual responses, but rather to *interactive discussions*. For evaluation research, then, focus groups might be more time-consuming, more expensive and less clear-cut than surveys, but they can involve respondents in consultations that attempt to negotiate different views and work through issues collectively. Group discussions help to explore the reasons behind people's responses, suggest alternatives and solutions, and feed user, client or staff views into processes of evaluation, planning and change.

Purposive sampling

While research within organizations offers potential for random sampling, focus group research more often is based on **purposive sampling**: where participants are selected on the basis of having a significant relation to the research topic. This works in different ways. In market research, for example, it might simply involve using a form of **quota sampling** – selecting a given number of men and women, of age groups, of income brackets or occupational types, to participate in focus groups that will be broadly *reflective* (if not strictly representative) of the population of interest, or that will provide an array of market views. The logic of selection is similar in the case of policy research into different groups' views about various issues or initiatives (middle-income voters, or rural voters, or young people, or women). The researcher here might be less interested in selecting groups that mirror the wider population, than in groups with a key relation to the topic.

The selection of focus groups, if rarely aiming to be representative, is often guided by these wider social debates. Social and political attitudes – as large-scale surveys, studies of electoral behav-

---

Box 15.5 Selecting people for focus groups in two studies

Study 1: Evaluating policy initiatives
The British government commissioned a series of focus groups in the late 1990s on policy proposals for work, childcare and welfare that were targeted at different groups of women voters, rather than at the electorate as a whole. The aim was not to generalize (even to women voters), but to elicit a range of responses, and accounts for those responses, through focused discussions. Different groups of women were chosen according to *age*, *marital* and *employment status*, reflecting the rationale that women in different situations were likely to have different relationships to questions of childcare, welfare and family-friendly work practices.

Study 2: Researching media audiences
In his classic study of television audiences, Morley (1980) used focus groups divided up in terms of *education, social class* and *political affiliation* to compare the various ways in which members of different social groups interpret and respond to current affairs messages.

---

iour, patterns of newspaper readership and common sense all suggest – tend to be shaped by people's age or life-stage, their social class, their gender or ethnic background, their family status. Such knowledge can aid in the selection of focus groups.

- A researcher interested in attitudes towards the *legalization of cannabis*, for example, might decide that *age* is a significant factor in selecting focus groups on the topic.
- Similarly, a focus group researcher looking at *public trust in the police service* might use *ethnic background* as a key selection criterion.

In these instances, the selection of focus groups is framed by broader public debates and social research knowledge about the topics under study. The aim of the research, however, will not be to 'prove' in either case that younger people are more likely to favour legalization, or that black people are less trusting of the police. Focus groups do not allow researchers to *measure* different responses and then generalize these to a larger population, but rather to explore how selected groups of individuals define, talk about and account for given issues. In these two examples, age and

ethnicity respectively are being used as **break characteristics**: that is, categories that distinguish groups from each other. This is one of the central criteria researchers use in selecting members of focus groups.

As well as defining groups in terms of distinctive characteristics, researchers might apply **control categories** that remain stable across groups. For example, say a researcher is interested in using focus groups to investigate attitudes towards abortion. Box 15.6 shows two different approaches to selecting members of the focus groups for this study. In the first approach, gender is a 'control' category: all groups in the study have a common gender mix. In the second approach, gender is used as a 'break' characteristic: as a criterion which differentiates groups within the study.

Let us consider the other decisions the researchers have made in selecting these contrasting samples.

- *Both researchers* agree that age is likely to be a relevant characteristic, and have divided their groups into broad generational ranges or life-stages. Notice that the age groups are quite clearly delineated by ten-year intervals, so as to mark out distinct age differences.

Box 15.6   Two approaches to selecting focus groups in a study of attitudes towards abortion

Approach 1: Gender is a **control category** (All groups include the same gender mix – for example, women only or men only or the same number of men and women in each group)

Groups	Age	Voting last election
Group 1	18–25	Progressive
Group 2	18–25	Conservative
Group 3	35–50	Progressive
Group 4	35–50	Conservative
Group 5	60+	Progressive
Group 6	60+	Conservative

Approach 2: Gender is used as a **break characteristic**

Groups	Age	Gender
Group 1	18–25	Female
Group 2	18–25	Male
Group 3	35–50	Female
Group 4	35–50	Male
Group 5	60+	Female
Group 6	60+	Male

- The *first researcher* has decided that attitudes towards abortion potentially reflect general social and political attitudes, and so has chosen *voting behaviour* as a simple proxy for indicating 'progressive' or 'conservative' attitudes. (This criterion of selection reflects a general practice in social research of using voting behaviour as a fairly blunt instrument for indicating wider social and political attitudes – newspaper readership is another standard proxy for social attitude.)
- The *second researcher* has decided that groups of men and women might talk differently about the topic of abortion, and so has used *gender* to divide groups.

In each case it is important to note that, while the researcher is interested in using focus groups to explore attitudes towards abortion, the design of the groups is already based on a number of assumptions about how those attitudes might be shaped.

Homogeneity and knowing other members

A standard argument within focus group methodology is that group members should be *homogeneous* in respect of the relevant selection criteria, but unknown to each other (Krueger and Casey, 2000; Morgan, 1997). This is so as to avoid established relations of power, disagreement or consensus being brought into the research setting, where assertive voices are more likely to direct the group discussion and where it might be difficult for individuals to dissent from an apparently collective view. In practice, however, there are many research contexts where focus group members are likely to be known to each other. This is clearly the case where participants are recruited from within organizations or associations – employees in a workplace, members of a voluntary group, trade union or political association, residents on an estate, students on a course, users of a service and so on.

On another level, however, this is not simply a practical question about how researchers access their participants. The question of how groups are constituted opens up larger methodological debates about the distinctive nature of the research method. For some critics, the textbook view that participants should be homogeneous in terms of certain social characteristics, but unfamiliar to each other, is evidence of a survey logic that sees the focus group as somehow typical of wider social categories (see Lunt and Livingstone, 1996: 87). Alternative approaches select focus groups not as quasi-experimental subsets of larger social groupings, but as actual groups or networks in their own right (see Box 15.7).

Philo's (1990) study of television influence at the time of the 1984–5 miners' strike in Britain provides a further interesting twist to this sampling issue, reflecting a half-way position between selecting according to existing networks and using key social variables (Box 15.8).

One notable finding of Philo's study was that his participants could reproduce the language and themes of news coverage months after the end of the strike. This emerged via an exercise he asked groups to carry out where they were given a set of pictures taken from actual television coverage and asked to write a news story using these images. This was followed up by individual questionnaires and interviews about participants' opinions and sources of information, and at times by further group discussions. Given his interest in whether people believed or rejected what they saw on the television news, Philo's research was designed on the principle that such beliefs are mediated socially rather than formed individually: 'group processes are important' for such research, he contended, 'since our culture and beliefs are, after all, the product of collective thought and action' (Philo 1990: 22).

This rationale for selection can be seen as a form of **theoretical sampling**, where participants are selected with the aim of developing conceptual insights in relation to the topic (see also Chapter 18). Focus group research that aims to develop analysis at a critical level can adopt a theoretical sampling approach designed in a quite directive way to access certain kinds of knowledge. Box 15.9 shows the groups selected in Passey's (1999) research on civil society and community, which used a theoretically informed sampling strategy to explore attitudes towards these themes amongst diverse groups in the UK population. Here, the aim of the research was not to reflect 'general' public views, but to explore ideas in terms of a diverse range of social positions, involving critical issues of social inclusion and exclusion, group identification, difference, locality and belonging. In certain of these cases group members would have been well-known to each other, in others they would be less familiar.

Box 15.7 Selecting members of existing social networks

In her study of women's consumption of popular romance, for example, Janice Radway (1987) convened focus groups using a network of readers based around a local bookshop. The group discussions examined how these women's readings of popular fiction were framed in terms of a social network or interpretive community, rather than simply being a matter of private (and passive) consumption. What is more, the focus group format could itself be seen to reproduce the discursive quality of the women's social network, thereby enhancing the claims of the researcher to have produced *naturalistic* data.

Box 15.8   Selection of focus group participants in a study of television influence

The study: An exploration of how various groups understood the nature and origins of violence during the 1984–5 miners' strike in Britain. Previous content analysis had suggested that news coverage over-reported the incidence of violence during the strike, and tended to associate violence with pickets rather than with police.

Selection of participants: Philo selected his groups on the basis that they should be both 'natural' – existing outside the research project – but also reflect differences in social background. He rejected 'artificial' groups based on such *break characteristics* as age, gender or class on the grounds that this is 'not the sort of group in which people usually meet or talk about television programmes' (Philo, 1990: 23). The study involved 169 people from various regional locations, occupations and special interest groups, including:

- Senior police officers from southern England
- Trade unionists from Scotland
- Printworkers and transport workers from London
- Solicitors from southern England and from Scotland
- Groups of retired people
- Mothers of small children

Running focus groups and analysing the interaction

Like other forms of research, the quality of the data generated by focus group research will depend on the quality of the research design, but execution – how effectively the researcher runs the focus group – is particularly important in this case. Focus group research is distinctive in allowing participants to work through and re-define key research concepts and questions in an interactive way; furthermore, they provide a 'mechanism for placing the control of this interaction in the hands of the participants rather than the researcher' (Morgan, 1993: 17–18). This also means that group discussions can be hard for researchers to manage. Running focus groups therefore requires the researcher to draw on certain skills, such as:

Box 15.9   Theoretical sampling groups in a study of civil society and community (Passey, 1999)

The seven focus groups convened for this study included:

- A group of unemployed men participating in an employment and training scheme in rural Cornwall in South-West England
- A group of residents of a hostel for homeless people in Belfast in Northern Ireland
- Members of a community centre in North Wales (Welsh speakers)
- A group of non-working mothers living on an council estate in Jarrow in Northern England
- A group of African-Caribbean men in Hackney in London, also participants in an employment and training scheme
- A group of Polish immigrants in West London, linked to a Polish community centre
- A group of professionals in South-East England

- Facilitating interaction and discussion
- Enabling space for different group members to make their views known
- Keeping the group discussion focused around the core themes
- Dealing with dominant or inappropriate voices
- Sustaining a pace of discussion that ensures key topics are covered without constraining or rushing the talk

The skills required in running focus groups, then, are rather different from the skills called upon in other kinds of social research, including individual interviews and surveys. In many respects they are closer to the range of skills needed to run a seminar, chair a meeting, or convene a jury.

While it is important for the researcher to be able to observe interactions within the focus group so as to direct the flow of discussion, it can be difficult for the researcher to record the process (the recording of talk for research purposes is discussed in Chapter 16). Focus groups are routinely audio- or video-taped – as in other research contexts, with the permission of the participants. Researchers can make basic notes during the group interaction, or use flipcharts or whiteboards as a way of facilitating the discussion which then provide a set of research notes. Researchers might consider having colleagues act as an observer and note-taker, although the advantage of this in terms of recording data needs to be balanced against the effect a non-participant might have on the flow of the group discussion. In any case, it is important to make the role of any researcher (including the facilitator) quite clear to the group members before the discussion starts.

One of the most basic practical issues involved in running focus groups is getting six to ten people together at the same time and in an appropriate space. Whereas interviewers often arrange times and locations for their meetings at the convenience of their participants, focus groups researchers need to bring participants together in a common place. It is good practice to pay the travel costs (and, if relevant, the childcare costs) of participants, and focus group researchers frequently offer refreshments, which also help to promote a relaxed and social atmosphere. Researchers will need to arrange a room which is private, quiet,

comfortable and accessible. The duration of focus groups varies, but a rule of thumb would be to allow around two hours for the whole process, and participants should be informed in advance of how long the researcher expects the session to last. Researchers will also need to make judgements about including breaks, both for the benefit of the participants and to make sure different themes are covered.

Particular issues of confidentiality and anonymity arise in the group setting. In general, individuals should not be identifiable outside the discussion context, and taped records should only be heard or seen by people directly involved in the research. As well as outlining to participants the purpose and nature of the research in advance of the meeting, sessions usually begin with an opening statement to the group, outlining the research aims and who is doing (or funding) it. This is an opportunity to reiterate the researcher's position on confidentiality and anonymity, and to agree ground rules for the discussion, falling into two main areas:

- *Practical:* addressing the need to record the session so as to keep track of what people say; explaining the role of the researcher in guiding the process but allowing participants to take up the discussion in their own terms; stressing the importance of turn-taking and not talking over one another so as to make the discussion clear; encouraging people to voice their own opinions.
- *Ethical:* such as seeking agreement within the group over the use of offensive language, allowing for others' opinions and voicing disagreements in a reasonable way, and maintaining confidentiality outside the group.

In addition to setting up the terms clearly, researchers will need a strategy for closing the session, facilitating the discussion so as to allow the talk to 'wind down' in a fairly smooth way at the end.

There are no special techniques for analysing focus group material, which rather draws on the range of methods common to qualitative data analysis. However, analysis does need to attend to the distinctive nature of the data that emerge from focus group discussions. This, to re-state an argument made earlier, is interactive data, where the group discussion (rather than the individual discussants) is the unit of analysis. One cannot simply read off individual opinions from collective exchanges; neither can one easily translate from the specific group context to any wider social groupings represented by the participants. For many researchers, this is the particular strength of focus group methods, allowing the data to capture something of the situated communicative processes through which social meanings are made and reproduced. For this reason, focus group data often are well-suited to techniques of *discourse or conversation analysis* (see Chapters 27 and 28). These methods are concerned with how language is used to create and secure meanings, how competing accounts are negotiated and how speakers draw on certain interpretive repertoires in making their arguments within a given discursive context.

Conclusion

Focus groups have developed from a practical supplement to other research methods into a technique of social and cultural inquiry based on distinct methodological claims. Their relative strengths and weaknesses, too, range from the practical to the methodological. Focus groups:

1 Are a fairly easy method of data collection, which can be undertaken on a small scale by researchers with limited resources.
2 Are good at accessing respondents' own

definitions and understandings, and at giving them a significant degree of involvement within the research process.
3 Work well with other research methods – either in multi-method approaches to data collection, or in terms of refining research problems and interpreting data produced by other methods.
4 Generate data on the basis of social interaction and communication; in this sense, they reflect the social and cultural processes through which meaning, opinions and attitudes are shaped.

Problems in using focus groups also are practical and methodological in character, and tend to mirror the advantages of the method:

1 Researchers have less control over the data that emerge than they have with individual interviews or surveys. The potential gain to the participants, in this sense, can be seen as a loss of power on the part of the researcher.
2 Focus groups do not meet conventional standards of reliability in social research, and are an insecure basis for generalization. It follows that any claims a researcher makes in terms of developing insights into social attitudes cannot be matched by systematic claims as to the representativeness of these attitudes. Focus group researchers can only explore a range of views, and analyse how respondents account for and negotiate these views.
3 While focus groups seek to reproduce the

Box 15.10   Web pointers for focus groups

Focus groups: an overview
www.slis.ualberta.ca/cap02/kristie/

Jacob Nielsen: *The Use and Misuse of Focus Groups*
www.useit.com/papers/focusgroups.html

Anita Gibbs: 'Focus groups', in issue 19 of *Social Research Update*
www.soc.surrey.ac.uk/sru/SRU19.html

Carter McNamara: *Basics of Conducting Focus Groups*
www.mapnp.org/library/evaluatn/focusgrp.htm

Visit the website for this book at www.rscbook.co.uk to link to these web pointers.

interactive nature of 'real' social processes, they are not in themselves naturally occurring interactions, and offer no guarantee as to what people say, or how they interact, outside the research context.

These are valid problems. However, for many social researchers they are outweighed by the value of focus groups on a range of fronts: in clarifying and refining concepts; in accessing information that is not available through observation; in placing communication and interaction at the centre of the research process; and in exploring attitudes, opinions, meanings and definitions on participants' own terms.

Further reading

Krueger and Casey (2000) and Morgan (1997) are two standard and very useful textbooks on the use of focus groups in social research; Barbour and Kitzinger (1999) bring together a range of interesting chapters on the politics, theory and practice of focus groups. For article-length discussions, see Lunt and Livingstone (1996) for a valuable overview of the role of focus groups in media and communications research, and Kitzinger (1994) for an interesting account of how focus groups were used together with questionnaires and interviews in a project exploring perceptions of risk in relation to HIV/AIDS.

Student Reader (Seale, 2004): relevant readings

39 Jenny Kitzinger: 'The methodology of focus groups: the importance of interaction between research participants'

Key concepts

Naturalism	**Break characteristics**
Purposive sampling	**Control categories**
Quota sampling	**Theoretical sampling**

16

Making and managing audio recordings

Duncan Branley

CONTENTS

Much social research involves recording interviews, focus groups or naturally occurring talk. This chapter looks at making recordings and their subsequent incorporation into a research project with an eye to smoothing the technicalities of the processes of transcription and analysis. Sometimes you may want to transfer recordings you have made onto a computer as audio files, at others you may want only to transcribe them, producing textual computer files. You may need to be careful to preserve anonymity in a recording. The ethics involved in terms of storage and use, as well as how to manage the strangeness that people can feel when being recorded and the effect of this on how they behave, will not be dealt with in detail (Chapter 10 discusses research ethics and Chapters 14 and 15 qualitative interviews and focus groups).

Thinking about the purposes of your recordings should help you decide how to proceed with recording and whether or how to transcribe. Ask yourself, then:

- *Are you producing original material which you would like or are obliged to deposit in an archive?* If so, you will need to consult the archive staff for advice on the formats in which they need your data. This will probably be digital, but they may well require in addition a range of information about your data (metadata). You should derive an awareness from this chapter to be able to understand their requirements and to ask them more informed questions.
- *Do you want to put your recordings on the Web or publish them on a CD?* The discussion in this chapter focuses on making sound recordings for research purposes where the quality of recording can be lower than materials intended for broadcasting, which results in a smaller file size. This chapter will also explore how the confidentiality and anonymity of digital recordings and transcriptions can be maintained.
- *Are you doing an in-depth, qualitative exploration or are you trying to get an overview for a time-pressured piece of commissioned research?* Much academic research is fairly long-term, but the skills outlined in this

chapter will be of use to you for shorter timescales and tighter deadlines too. I will be looking at partial transcription as well as full transcription, but will not be giving details of specialist transcription for conversation analysis, which is covered in Chapter 28.

Overview of audio recording technologies for research

It is important at this stage to draw some distinctions. The most obvious meaning of the term 'recording' is using a microphone with a device such as a cassette player or a Minidisc to record sounds. These produce a recording on **removable media** (cassettes or Minidiscs) which can be played back on any device similar to that used for the recording. Cassette recordings are *analogue* and Minidisc recordings are *digital* (see below for further details). Neither of these recordings can be used directly on a computer; you need to connect the equipment to a computer, start recording using the computer's sound card and playing the cassette or Minidisc in 'real' time. The computer will create a standard computer sound file, which you can then use with audio software.

You can also create files that can be used on a computer directly either by recording directly into a computer or by using a **digital recorder**. A digital recorder works in a similar way to a cassette or Minidisc recorder, except that it produces digital files which are immediately usable on a computer (unlike the digital files produced by Minidiscs). You can transfer these as computer files rather than having to play them, which can save significant amounts of time. At the time of writing digital recorders are in their infancy, but they are likely to become more attractive as they become more robust and cheaper.

The next section explains both the background and the technical terms which are used in working with sound. How and what you decide to record is an interpretative process which already transforms your material into data for your research, so it could be important methodologically as well as practically to make informed technical choices.

Principles of recording and working with sound

There are specialist terms which are used in this chapter and in audio equipment manuals which need explaining. This section is not an exhaustive exploration of the physics of sound, but it should give you enough information to follow the discussion and to know which settings to use when recording and when processing sound on a computer. There are websites with more detail listed at the end of the chapter.

What is sound?

Sound is a form of energy which moves through air (or other media). It is felt as vibrations by our ears, which convert it into an electrical signal, which is then interpreted by our brains: in short, hearing! Similarly, microphones convert the vibrations they sense into electrical signals, which are recorded by audio technologies. These audio technologies can reverse the process too by using the recordings to produce sound as vibrations through speakers. Sound moves in waves, which vary in shape and size and which correspond to variation in pitch and volume when heard by us. Sounds also happens in time, which means that graphs of waves over time can be plotted (**waveforms**). A simple note has a simple pattern (Figure 16.1); however, even a single word is composed of many different simpler sounds in combination and so its waveform looks a lot more complex (Figure 16.2).

Two features of sound waves which are important to understand are:

- **Frequency**: how many times the wave goes up and down (oscillates) per second is measured in Hertz. The symbol for Hertz is Hz and 1,000 Hertz is known as a kilohertz (kHz). The lower the number of Hertz, the lower the pitch of the sound.
- **Amplitude**: the size of the wave determines the loudness. With a recorded sound amplitude can be increased by an amplifier, if necessary.

The human ear cannot hear all sounds – only those within a certain range, and this narrows as we get older. Good hearing for an adult is between 20 Hz at the lower end (for example, the lowest notes on a piano) and 16,000 Hz or 16 kHz (above the level at which we can identify specific sounds). A child has a wider range: 16 Hz-20 kHz. Most conversation takes place in the range 250 Hz to 8,000 Hz (8 kHz), known as the 'mid-range'.

Your recording equipment needs to be able to pick up most of this. Speech recording microphones normally work best between 200 Hz and 10 kHz, but can go wider. Minidiscs can record between 20 Hz and 20 kHz, whereas cassette tape has a range of 60 Hz to 13 kHz. (Check the specifications in your recorder's handbook: it will be labelled 'frequency response' or something similar.) You need to remember that you are probably not producing a musical masterpiece where optimum sound quality is essential, but a recording of speech to work with analytically. So both cassette and Minidisc can cope.

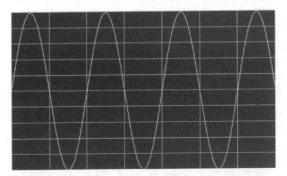

Figure 16.1 *A simple sound waveform (Source:* http://www.howstuffworks.com/analog-digital.htm)

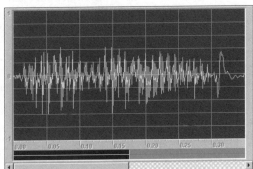

Figure 16.2 *Sound waveform for 'Hello' (Source:* http://www.howstuffworks.com/analog-digital.htm)

How is sound recorded?

There are two ways of recording what is converted to an electronic signal by microphones: analogue and digital.

Analogue recording creates an exact replica of the sound wave (an analogue) inscribed magnetically on a tape. The magnet moves very quickly, mimicking the shape of the waveform. It goes through a number of mechanical processes to achieve this. Each of the components as well as the quality of the tape can introduce some interference ('noise') which can affect the quality of the recording. When the sound is played the sound waveform is reproduced exactly as the microphone sensed it and the recording equipment recorded it.

Digital recording works differently: it takes a series of regularly spaced snapshots of the shape of the sound wave (which is continuous) and represents each of them separately as a numbers (digits). This is known as **sampling**. There are two factors affecting the closeness of the shape of the snapshots to that of the underlying waveform: the number of samples taken (**sampling rate**) and the size of the difference between the snapshot unit of measure (**sampling precision** or **resolution**). As the number of samples taken within a specific time period increases and/or the sampling precision increases, the approximation to the original sound wave becomes increasingly accurate. This is important because our ears might hear 'jaggedness' in a digitally produced sound if it is too different from the shape of the original sound wave.

Figure 16.3 shows how increasing the sampling rate and precision (each block is one sample) will produce a pattern closer to the original sound wave (the line). At a sampling rate above our upper hearing level of about 16–20 kHz, the human ear cannot detect the difference between an analogue recording and a digital one. A CD is recorded at over twice this level. (Although some particularly sensitive people claim to 'feel' the difference, for our practical research purposes we can ignore this level of finesse.)

Converting from analogue to digital

If you want to convert an analogue recording to digital, one of the easiest ways is to use the built-in **analogue to digital converter (ADC)** on your computer's soundcard by connecting your sound source to the computer, pressing 'play' on the sound source and telling your computer to record the sound it receives. This is discussed in detail below.

When digitally recorded sound (such as on CD or Minidisc) is played through speakers or headphones it is converted from digital to analogue using built-in software on your sound system or computer. This is the opposite to the above and so is called a **digital to analogue converter (DAC)**. You can play an analogue recording directly since it is already in the right format and does not need converting.

You would be forgiven for thinking that you can move all digital sound files from a recording medium directly onto a computer and *vice versa*. However, the large corporations which invest in audio research and development and produce consumer electronics have concerns about intellectual property (particularly as regards the music

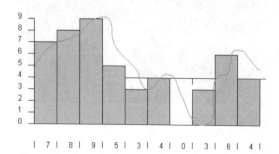

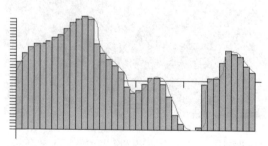

Figure 16.3 *Digital sampling approximating an analogue sound wave*
(*Source:* http://www.howstuffworks.com/analog-digital.htm)

Box 16.1   Some digital recording measuring terms

Sampling rate: measured in terms of how many samples are taken in a single second: a CD is sampled at 44,100 per second.

Sampling precision: each of these 44,100 samples per second is represented in numbers which computers can use called bits (binary digits). The two levels of sampling precision you are likely to encounter are *8 bit* or *16 bit*. With 8 bits you can represent 256 different sound levels; with 16 bits the figure is far higher: 65,536. This means that 16 bit recording can produce a more detailed and nuanced sound.

Channels: the number of signals you are recording. *Stereo* records the sound waves from two signals; monoaural (*mono*) only one. This may be of significance if you are recording a group of people speaking (for example, a focus group), where having separate channels recorded might help you to discern what a quieter person is saying. You would probably need to have a stereo microphone for this to work.

File space: the sampling rate, sampling precision and number of channels directly affect how much computer space a sound wave file occupies. Computer files are measured in kilobytes (KB) or megabytes (MB). A byte is another way of saying 8 bits (so 16 bits = 2 bytes). A kilobyte is 1,024 bytes and a megabyte is 1,024 × 1,024 = 1,048,576 bytes (less than the capacity of a floppy disk).

You can calculate the amount of space needed to store a sound file by multiplying the elements as follows:

samples per channel per second × bytes per sample × channels × time in seconds = bytes needed

You would probably convert the time into hours and minutes and the space into megabytes. So one *minute* of stereo sound at CD quality needs:

44,100 samples/channel/second × 2 bytes per sample × 2 channels × 60 seconds = 10,584,000 bytes

which is 10,336 KB = 10.1 MB – a large file indeed. One hour would take sixty times this: 606 MB. A one minute 8 bit mono file at half the sampling rate down would be smaller by a factor of 8:

22,050 samples/channel/second × 1 byte per sample × 1 channel × 60 seconds = 1,323,000 bytes

which is 1,292 KB = 1.3 MB – still fairly large, but it would fit on a floppy disk.

---

industry) and so try to control ways of duplicating sound files. Unfortunately this causes a slight hiccough when we want to use a Minidisc for recording research material. The only way to get Minidisc recordings onto a computer in a format usable and editable on the computer is to connect the Minidisc player to the soundcard and press play. This may seem counterintuitive since you are playing a digital recording through an analogue output and then letting the computer record it again digitally. This is because the Sony copyrighting mechanism built into the Minidisc format (ATRAC, see below) means that you cannot access the recordings directly. If there were software available to play ATRAC files on a computer, you would be able to download far more quickly using a digital connection such as a USB port.

With the humbler analogue cassette you can

only get the file onto a computer by playing it (in real time). This may not be a problem for either method since, if you connect a speaker to the computer at the same time, you can listen to your recordings another time, increasing your familiarity with them, which should help in your analysis.

Compressing digital audio files

You can control the size of the sound file produced by manipulating the settings discussed above when you use a digital recorder, record directly or re-record the original recording on Minidisc or cassette onto your computer. Large files of raw digital data can be used on computers (most often as WAV files on a PC and AIFF files on a Mac), but smaller files put less of a strain on your computer. So there are programs available which can **compress** these files (that is, delete some of the digits produced by the sampling) without a loss of quality discernible to the human ear, producing smaller files and thus making storage and retrieval easier. They are tailored to the hearing capabilities of the human ear (based on 'psychoacoustic principles') and can produce recordings which are more than good enough for interviews for research.

One of the most common is *mp3,* which reduces the amount of space needed by a factor of between 10 and 14. Although patented by a German company called Fraunhofer, an mp3 file is readily produced from a WAV file on a computer using freely available software. They can be played on most computers with suitable software installed and on several portable players. There are some digital recording devices which record directly into mp3 too. At the time of writing these are not well enough established to recommend them, but they look very promising for the future.

RealAudio has a similar compression rate. Files can be produced using RealAudio's free Helix Producer software, but they are really only for listening to on computers (typically over the Web).

Minidisc uses a compression system called ATRAC which has a reduction factor of about five times. It compresses as it records. Minidisc files have special copyright features which mean that they can be stored, but not be played on computers (they need to be downloaded to a Minidisc player

to hear them). This is not an issue in the recording of research encounters since once we have recorded them we have to play them on our Minidiscs and record them on our computers (see above).

How much space is needed to record speech digitally?

You need to be able to marry up how much sound information is being produced with how much space you have to record it. The main consideration here is the quality of the recording you need, which will be informed by your theoretical attitude to the material. If you are adopting a *conversation analytic* approach, your recording time may well be fairly short and the level of detail you aim to produce in your transcription will be fairly high; you will want a high-quality recording. If you aim to treat your recordings as a *resource* from which to extract information (rather than closely analysing the language used as a *topic* in itself) your quality requirements will be lower.

To capture sound digitally and to be able to play it back you need to ensure that the sampling rate is just above double the highest frequency you want to record. This is based on the 'Nyquist Theorem' which you may see mentioned. In summary, this means that you need to have a sample for each of the upper and lower parts of a complete wave oscillation for the highest frequency, so the number of times you must do it is two times the highest frequency. If you did not do this, you could introduce distortion, known as **aliasing**. Most recorders and sound processors such as a telephone have limits to the frequency they can record and filter out frequencies above this to avoid aliasing. For the filter to work there needs to be a margin above the highest frequency. CDs are sampled at 44.1 kHz; half of this is 22.05 kHz, which leaves a margin of 2.05 kHz above the upper limit of what a child's ear can hear, that is, 20 kHz.

The main implication of this for when you convert your sound into digital files on your computer is that there is no point sampling at much above double the rate of your sound source. If you do, all you are doing is creating a larger file than you need to: you cannot improve the quality of your sound source by increasing the sample rate. Earlier we learnt that although the maximum frequency our ears can discern is 20 kHz, most of the intelligible part of conversation takes place between 250 Hz to 8,000 Hz (8 kHz). To record this you need to capture the oscillations (both up and down) when you sample. So to capture the *upper* end of the adult conversation range you need to sample at 2 × 8,000 = 16,000 per second (remember that the number of Hertz is the number of oscillations per second) plus a bit of room. The next level up on your audio software will probably be 22,050 Hz, though if you have a long interview and will be pushed for space you could sample at 16,000 Hz with a minimal reduction in quality as far as research purposes are concerned.

The equipment you use will have its own limits too. Microphones work best up to about 10 kHz and so should be able to capture most of the sound in normal conversation. If you are recording speech directly into the computer you will be fine at either 16 kHz or 22.05 kHz. If, however, you are transferring a recording from cassette or Minidisc, then you are constrained by how much they have been able to record themselves. Minidiscs can record up to 20 kHz and cassette recorders up to 13 kHz (but you do need to check your recorder's specification – look for something like 'frequency response'). So reasonable models of both of these should capture normal speech perfectly well. If you are recording telephone interviews, it is important to realize that not all of the frequencies in speech are transmitted, limiting the upper frequency to 3.4 kHz, so set the sampling rate at 8 kHz.

Whether you use 8 bit or 16 bit sampling precision will depend not only on your methodological objectives, but also on the number of participants: better quality will enable you to discern different speakers more easily. If it is just you and the participant, then you may still want high quality to ensure you do not lose the richness of your material. Similarly, recording in stereo can help differentiate speakers in a focus group, but also might help you get more of a sense of the expressive qualities of a speaker's voice. There is not a wrong or right way to do this – it should be informed by your methodological decisions. If in doubt, record at a higher quality since you cannot repeat an interview, but you can always re-sample your sound file on a computer later. 16 bit stereo may not be necessary for recording interviews for academic research – it will take up four times as much space as an equivalent period of 8 bit mono recording.

What are the advantages of digital recordings?

Converting an analogue recording to digital may sound like a lot of bother – you may prefer to put your cassettes into a foot pedal controlled transcribing machine and type directly into your word processor. However, there are some distinct advantages:

Sound quality

Cassettes, even good quality metal ones, tend to record the mechanical noise produced by the recorder and the medium ('hiss') as well as the words you want. This can give you a higher than desirable number of inaudible sections and hence slow down your transcription. If you re-record this into a computer, you can use software to reduce the hiss and so render sections audible. Digital recordings (for example, Minidisc) record far less extra noise and so are far easier to work with. Re-recording this onto a computer needs to be done at a high enough sampling rate to preserve this quality differential.

Box 16.2 Suggested recording levels for usable research recordings

	Sampling rate	Sampling precision	Channels
Speech	16,000 or 22,050	8 bit or 16 bit	Mono or stereo
Telephone	8,000	8 bit	Mono

Copies

Once you have your interview data you need to look after them. If you have digitized the data, you can readily make an additional copy for off-site storage on a CD. If your data is not confidential, it is far easier to share a digitized recording either via CD or over a network. If the data are confidential in parts, you can make a 'clean' copy with identifying information silenced. There is no degradation when you copy digital recordings since you are only copying the numbers in the computer file, which represent the sound sample. If the copying does not work, the file will not work. It is all or nothing – usually all!

If you use a compression programme (such as mp3) to make a digital sound file smaller, each time you do it some of the base digital information is lost. Because of psychoacoustic principles this is not that noticeable the first time, but if you compress an already compressed file, the quality will be progressively lessened. There should be no need to do this since you can copy a digital file in exactly the same way that you copy any other computer file. Each time you make copies of analogue cassettes the quality degrades from the original. Unless you are using very high quality hardware and media, the copies may soon become very difficult to work with.

With both formats, it is advisable to keep your master copy pristine and to work with copies of it. Then if disaster should happen, you can always make another copy to work with. If you have improved a digital file by reducing the amount of interference, then keep this copy as an improved master too.

Storage

It is far easier to store digital copies than analogue cassettes – though you do need to have digital equipment to play it on, which tends to be more expensive than a cassette player. You may have an institutional policy about the length of time you should retain the actual recordings after a research project has finished and then destroy them. Even if not, you need to devise a system to track all copies of your material, so that you can ensure there is no unauthorized access. Materials will differ in their degree of sensitivity.

Media degradation

When an analogue cassette tape itself degrades over time, sound quality is lost. Digital recordings do not seem to degrade, though you need to be aware of the potential for file formats to change over time. If a file format does change, the new one is normally 'backwards compatible' – meaning that it should be able to read information in the older format. However, it may be sensible not to record directly into a compressed format such as mp3, but rather to use a raw audio file format first and then convert to mp3 to make it easier to work with (smaller computer files are usually easier to work with).

Choosing and practising with your recording equipment

Whichever method of recording you use, you should practise using your equipment so that you can work out any quirks. Once you have familiarized yourself with the basic technicalities of your recorder (that is, which buttons to press, when), practise recording the types of speech you want to record with some friends. Follow the suggestions made later in this chapter. You will only get one go at making the recording. In the unlikely event that you do suffer a total equipment failure, you should write down as much as you can remember about the research encounter. You may still be able to make something interesting of the time you have spent with your participant(s).

As mentioned in the introduction, there is a wide range of devices that can be used to record interviews: I shall only be looking at cassette recorders, micro-cassette 'dictaphones' and Minidisc recorders. The reason for this is that they are relatively easy to obtain since they are well-established products designed for the 'consumer market' (you may well have one already) and supplies for them are similarly easy to obtain. If you are doing fieldwork, it is best to work with technology that could be replaced without too much trouble and cost. Their ubiquity also may reduce the recording awkwardness that may occur in an interview situation. Professional or broadcast kit would be far more expensive and is overkill for recording speech in interviews – unless, of course, you are doing particular linguistic work. Even for this, the quality of digital recording on Minidisc may well be more than good enough.

Digital recorders, which record directly into standard digital audio files, are improving in quality and reliability all the time and may well be sufficiently well developed in a couple of years to make them the recorder of choice. You may also want to record directly into a computer. No matter how the technology changes, the broad principles will remain the same for the near future. If you are being very cautious you may decide to take both a Minidisc and a cassette recorder into a field situation as backup in case of problems, so it is worth being aware of the pros and cons of each.

Here are the functions you should look for when choosing your recording equipment and media to use with it.

All recorders

- When you are interviewing you want to concentrate more on the interview rather than worrying about your recording equipment. So a light to show you that recording is actually happening would be a reassuring feature to look out for.

- You should be able to pause recording if you need to – perhaps at the request of the participant.

- Also there should be a connection for an external microphone – built-in ones are rarely of sufficient quality. It is best if there is a microphone-in connection; if there is only a line-in connection, the signal produced may not be loud enough (see the section on 'Connecting a sound source to a computer' for explanation of these terms).

Dictaphones

- Dictaphones are convenient for recording notes for yourself but are not good enough quality to record interviews you will be working with closely. They often record only in mono and the micro-cassettes are not high quality. However, because of their portability and ease of working they can be useful if you serendipitously happen across something you want to record for your research when you are otherwise unprepared.

Cassette recorders

- There are four different types of cassette tape differentiated by what they are made of, with recording quality improving as the number gets higher. Type 0 is rare. Most tapes you can buy are either Type 1 (standard ferric oxide or 'normal bias') or Type 2 ('chrome' or its full chemical name chromium dioxide, CrO_2). There is a type 4 ('metal'), but not all cassette recorders can use it to record; all machines should be able to play it though. Metal cassettes require more power too, so may drain your batteries more quickly. Your best bet is to use Type 2 or II (Chrome). Sometimes the recorder's manufacturer will have made tapes that work best with the idiosyncrasies of their machine. As long as you do not buy the cheapest of the cheap, your recordings should be fine for research purposes.

- Turning the tape over may be a distraction to your interviewee. The longer the tape, the longer the period you can go without turning over, but this is counterbalanced by a diminution in quality. Using a tape of no more than 90 minutes length is a good idea; a C60 would be even better. Do not scrimp on the cost of your cassettes.

- A tape counter, while not vital on the recorder, would be useful for initial analysis in the field.

Minidisc

- Minidisc has better quality recording than a consumer-level cassette recorder, mainly as a result of there being less mechanical noise or hiss. There is also a longer uninterrupted recording time (74–80 minutes). A C60 cassette would need to be turned over each 30 minutes. Further, there are now long play functions on some models (MDLP) which can double or quadruple the time available (possibly allowing five hours of uninterrupted recording, if your batteries can survive).

- It may be worth looking for a model that is able to synchronize the external microphone so that recording starts and stops automatically when sound is detected. You should be able to set the level of noise which triggers this. Finally, it is desirable to be able to set the recording level (see below).

- You do need to be careful with a Minidisc in two ways. First, if they are jolted when recording they can jump, leaving you with blank sections. The way to avoid this is to put the recorder on a flat surface and leave it alone until you need to replace the Minidisc itself. Carrying in a pocket or bag can sometimes cause skipping too. The second area you need to be careful about is when you stop recording – it is often a two-stage process (stopping recording and then saving the recording onto the disc). You must not switch the power off until it has completely finished otherwise you may lose your recording (often the recording unit will turn off itself when it has finished saving the recording).

Microphone

- External microphones usually produce better results than the built-in ones and will have the most noticeable effect on the quality of your recordings. There are two common types. **Unidirectional** microphones (sometimes called 'cardioid') are designed to record most of the noise coming from in front, with progressively less coming from the sides and none from the back. These can be useful in an environment where there is a lot of background noise. The second type is **omnidirectional** which does not discriminate in the direction of the sound source. Some are specifically aimed at recording speech, by focusing on the mid-range frequencies and are not sensitive to and thus do not record some background noise.
- A plug-in-power microphone takes its power from the recorder and may be recommended by the manufacturer. Check the manual for guidance. Some microphones will require their own batteries.

Practical advice on recording in the research situation

This section aims to work as a checklist for you at different stages of the recording encounter.

Preparation before arriving at the research situation

All recorders

- Check batteries or other power supply – and carry spares. It may be worthwhile using brand new (and so full powered) batteries to start each interview.
- Have spare media – unwrapped and with the labels fixed so that you can write on them immediately after finishing.
- Possibly have a spare recorder too.
- Have a checklist of how to use the recorder based on your experimental learning earlier on. Carry the instruction book with you. You will know how to use it, but knowing you have this with you will reassure you and enable you to present yourself as a competent researcher!

Cassette recorders and dictaphones

- Wind to beginning of recordable section on the tape.

Setting up in the recording situation

Acoustics

Sound goes from a speaker in all directions, both towards and away from the microphone. In a room with hard surfaces (walls, floors, ceilings and furniture) some of the sound is reflected back and reaches the microphone a little later than that which arrived directly. This can create an echo effect or at least sound as though someone is talking to you from the end of a long corridor. Acoustic specialists calculate this delay as 'decay time', but for research purposes there are practical rules of thumb which should optimize the situation in which you are working. You can reduce the effect by reducing the extent of hard reflective surfaces, such as by being in a room which has soft furnishings such as carpets, curtains and fabric on chairs to absorb the sound rather than reflecting it. You should also try to be in as small a room as possible, which reduces the delay between the original, direct sound and the reflected sound hitting the microphone. Sitting in the corner of a room rather than the middle can aid this further because you are closer to the reflective surfaces. If you have the opportunity before you begin recording, test out different positions to see how they affect the quality of your recording.

Another source of problems is background noise. When we are in an environment our brains can filter out noises extraneous to those we are attentive to. A microphone, however, will pick up everything. Some of this background noise you can remove. For instance, you can turn off computers and other electrical equipment; if the lights are buzzing you may not need them all on or may be able to replace them with a quieter lamp. This is low-level constant noise in the immediate environment. There may be other noise intrusions from outside (adjacent rooms, corridors, busy roads). You may be able to change the room to reduce this. A third source of noise is your own and your participants' interaction with the room: check to see if chairs or tables squeak when adjusting position (try them out … roll around on that leather sofa!). When you have reduced such noise as much as possible, it is a good idea to record the environment without talking to get a base level of noisiness from the room. This is useful because later on you can specify this recorded background noise pattern to your sound software so that it can remove it from sections with both background noise and speech leaving only the speech.

One final source of noise is that from eating and drinking. If at all possible, at least avoid eating during your recording work (unless of course that is the focus of your work).

Microphone

- Check that your external microphone is properly connected. Not only in the right jack, but also fully inserted.
- Position the microphone as close to interviewees as possible without being too intrusive. The closer it is the louder the sound it picks up and the less background noise it will pick up. About 30 cm is optimal, though anything up to 1m away should produce good enough results. In acoustic jargon this is known as the **critical distance** and varies from room to room. It is calculated from the volume of the room and the

decay time (hence suggesting being in as small a room as possible, with soft furnishings). The more sensitive a microphone you have, the further away it can be from the speaker. However, it will also pick up more background noise.

- If you are conducting a focus or discussion group, place the microphone in the middle to pick up all sounds – a stereo one can be useful for discriminating between differently positioned speakers. Some stereo microphones can be separated and positioned differently, although when one person is talking the other part of the microphone might pick up a lot more background noise if they are more than the critical distance away. This is more of a concern for producing broadcast quality sound, but it is as well to be aware of it for research recordings.
- It is usually best to position your microphone on a stand to reduce the rustle that can be recorded if you continue to hold it. Further, this can naturalize the microphone and make your participants feel less strange than if you were to keep pointing a microphone towards their face for an extended period. Sometimes the surface you place it on can cause vibrations that will be recorded, so introduce some fabric or padding to absorb these.

Recording

Check the recording level

- The recording level will amplify the signal from the microphone. You want to make the recorded signal as loud as you can without causing the loudest bits to be 'clipped' – that is, distorted. Clipping means that the top and bottom of the waveform exceed the amplitude boundaries and so appear flat rather than rounded. When played back it sounds like popping or crackling. On some recorders (for example, standard cassette recorders) this will be fixed, but on many Minidiscs you should be able to set this yourself, although the unit can do this automatically too.
- If you can adjust the recording level, test it just before you begin recording the whole interview

and adjust it if you exceed the guidelines in the manual. You and your participants may well have quieter or louder voices within a particular environment. Tell your participants what you are doing and ask them so say a few brief words so that you can gauge the correct level. If you are in a group situation, it is useful for later identification to get each person in turn to say their names and a short sentence at this stage. This is useful even if you have an assistant in the room noting down the names of each successive speaker.

Monitor the recorder

- From time to time check that the recorder is still working. A quick glance at a light is easier and less disruptive than a close examination of the recorder, hence the advice to include it on your wish list. However, the liquid crystal displays on many consumer recorders are often clear enough if you know what you are looking for. If you have done your preparation properly, you should not have problems with the batteries.

When you stop recording

Do not stop recording until the interview is really finished

- You may get some really interesting material towards the end. You are in control of when you stop recording, so do not stop too soon. You may be saying thank you when a participant says something they had forgotten or had been unsure of saying. If they say it after you have told them you are stopping recording, this may be deliberate on their part. You should check with them that you can include that in the interview and possibly ask them if you could record some more discussion on that. Your ethical position in relation to the participant must be clear here.

When finished, prevent over-writing by disabling media

- Once you have finished recording make sure that your media cannot be overwritten by acci-

dent. For Minidiscs – slide the write-protect tab; for cassettes – click the tabs out.

Label the recordings so that you know what is on them later

- Labeling with the date, time and sequence, if you have more than one tape or Minidisc for a research encounter, are the minimum. You may want to label using a system to preserve anonymity. Work this out in advance or you will get confused.

Recording telephone interviews

Sometimes you will not be able to talk to people in person, but may be able to have a conversation or interview them on the telephone. Much of the advice remains the same, but there are some further constraints, of which you should be aware.

First, you need to get your participant's explicit permission to record the conversation. This is for both ethical and legal reasons. The ethical reasons are the same as those for recording any research encounter. The legal framework aims to control the covert recording of people's private telephone conversations ('tapping'), including by criminal investigators. The precise law varies from jurisdiction to jurisdiction, so you need to take advice from your institution before recording telephone calls.

Secondly as mentioned above, the signal on a telephone line does not represent the full range of frequencies even in the mid-range of conversation. Rather only frequencies between 400 and 3,400 Hz are transmitted. This is so that the telephone companies can transmit as efficiently as possible – to send the full range of the human voice would take up a lot more space and be a lot more expensive. For this reason, the sound which you manage to record on the telephone will sound 'thinner' than that recorded face-to-face.

The final constraint is that you need some extra equipment to record telephone conversations. You could use a loudspeaker telephone and a standard microphone, but the quality would not be very good and there would be a large differential between your voice and that of the person on the other end of the telephone line. The solution is to use an adaptor connected to your telephone using the standard telephone connections (called an RJ-11 connector). This presumes you are using a standard, not a mobile or cell telephone. Box 16.3 explains how to connect an adaptor

Transferring your recordings onto computer

If you are using a digital recorder which enables you to transfer audio files to a computer then this stage is relatively easy: you connect the recorder to the computer and download the files. If you have recorded onto a computer, you do not even have to do that! When you want to record onto a cassette or Minidisc, you connect a microphone or other sound source and press record. However, you are doing the reverse: you have a recording which you want to get into the computer. You could play it through speakers and record through a microphone connected to the computer. How-

ever, this would drastically reduce the quality of the recording. Far easier is to connect directly to the computer. Transferring is a four-step process:

1 Connect the line-out or headphones socket on your cassette recorder or Minidisc to the line-in or microphone socket on your sound-card.
2 Tell your computer which input you are using and close off the others to reduce interference noise.
3 Start some software to record.
4 Start playing the source and this will record in real time.

Connecting a sound source to a computer

You need to keep in mind what is producing the sound and what is recording it – then you should make the right connections. You want to get the sound out of the cassette or Minidisc player and

---

Box 16.3   Connecting a telephone adaptor

There are two ways of connecting such an adaptor: between the telephone line and the telephone or between the telephone and the handset. In most modern telephones both of these will be connected to the telephone using an RJ-11 connector. If you have been able to connect your computer's modem to your telephone line to connect to the Internet, you have all the skills you need! You will get better quality recordings if you use an adaptor that goes between the telephone and the handset because the signal from the sound of your voice and that of the person at the other end of the line will be balanced. If you use an adaptor that goes between the telephone and the line, your voice will sound rather loud and that of the other person rather quiet. Additionally, a telephone line adaptor may not work with more sophisticated telephones such as PBX, multi-line Key or ISDN since they can have different wiring; however, most of these sorts of telephones use a standard handset cord and so should be able to use adaptors designed for use between the telephone and the handset.

Once you have connected the telephone to the adaptor, you can then connect your recording device. Some have a standard 3.5 mm (1/8 inch) jack which you can treat as though it is a microphone and connect it to a cassette or Minidisc recorder or directly to a computer sound card. Others you can only connect directly to a computer sound card. Stockdale (2002) suggests that there could be problems with this should you lose power or your computer crash in the middle of your interview. To insure against this he uses a 'Y' splitter (a connector with a 3.5 mm plug which then splits in two in the shape of a 'Y' with 3.5 mm plugs at the end of each split) and sends one line to the computer and the other to a Minidisc recorder (powered by batteries). If all goes well, then you have your recording already digitized on your computer. If there is a problem, you should have your recording on Minidisc and can transfer it to the computer later.

Sound	*Symbols*	*Words*	*Soundcard Colours*
OUT (From your recorder)	⊙	(HEAD)PHONES, EAR	
	⊻ ←⊙ Arrow out of curves	LINE-OUT	Green
IN (Into your computer)	⫰⟫ ⫰	IN MIKE, MICROPHONE	Pink
	⊻ ⊙→ Arrow into curves.	LINE-IN	Blue

Figure 16.4   *Sound jack symbols and labels*

into the computer. You do this by inserting a cable into your player and another into the sound card of your computer. The connection points or jacks on the player are probably fairly obvious; those on a computer are often at the back near where you connect your mouse, keyboard and screen. If you have a laptop, they may be on one side rather than at the back. Sometimes these will be colour-coded, but almost always they will have a symbol next to the relevant jack. Both computer sound cards and devices such as cassette and Minidisc players can both play and record, and so have jacks for getting sound in and out. Figure 16.4 shows some common symbols and words used to identify these jacks.

To make the connection you need a **miniplug cable** with a 1/8 inch or 3.5 mm stereo plug (two black rings – see image in Figure 16.5) at each end. This carries an analogue signal only, but will be more than fine for speech recordings. One end goes into the output jack of your cassette player or Minidisc as your sound source, the other end goes into one of the computer's IN jacks. If you have

both types of connection on either your sound source or sound card, you should test each one to see if there is any difference in the level of sound recorded by recording and playing back a few seconds of your material. If you want to monitor the sound as you are recording, connect speakers or headphones to your computer's sound card line-out or headphone jacks.

Setting up recording volumes

I illustrate this process using a Windows PC. The principles will be very similar on other platforms such as Apple Macintosh or Linux. The Windows Play or Recording Controls control the volume of the signal on the computer sound card. For recording from an external source you need to ensure that you have the correct input jack activated on the Recording Control. If you are not getting any sound, this is the first thing to check. Double-click on the volume button (speaker icon) on the Windows toolbar or access it via the Control Panel – look for the Sounds option. This will bring up either the Playback Volume or the Recording Control (shown in Figures 16.6 and 16.7) – you switch via the Options menu.

You need to ensure that the jack you have connected to your sound source is ticked in the Recording Control (you can only have one source selected at a time). For instance, in Figure 16.6 the connection is to the Line In jack.

Figure 16.5   *A stereo miniplug cable*

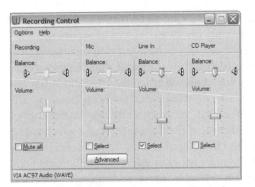

Figure 16.6   *Windows Recording Control*

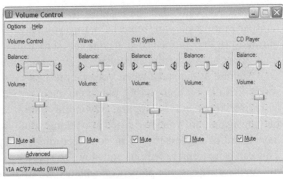

Figure 16.7   *Windows Playback Volume Control*

You also need to set the volume level on the sound source. The volume of both the sound source and the sound card level affects the loudness of the sound file. If it is too loud, it will distort ('be clipped'); too quiet, you will not hear it. Test it. Try to play your sound source with the volume as high as possible without distorting and then adjust the Recording Control volume until you find a balance that works well for your material.

Sound recording software

You need to run some software to create a blank sound file into which you record – otherwise it would be like trying to record without a cassette or Minidisc inserted; that is, you would be playing the sound, but not recording it on the computer. You may have your own software which came with your sound card or CD drive or you may have acquired specially designed audio software. The generic principles and settings are similar, but I use free software called *Audacity* (see Box 16.4).

With this software you can improve your recordings, making quiet parts louder, creating silences where people are identified and you want to keep their names off the recording and removing hiss.

Transcribing

Often in social research transcriptions are made of recordings. There are several ways of transcribing both in terms of the mechanics and what is actually written on the page. Different approaches may be suitable for varying styles of research and at different stages in conducting research. Seale and Silverman (1997) have shown how transcribing the same observed medical interview in two different ways enables different interpretations to be made about the meaning of exchanges within the interviews. Conversation analysts argue that a naturalistic, reportage style of transcription normalizes the exchange, but can leave the meaning of some utterances ambiguous (see Chapter 28). The important thing here is to recognize that transcription is not a neutral process, but is, in effect, part of your analysis. You select what you hear with the notation you use to record it. Even the conventions of conversation analysis may be a particular construction of reality. Taylor argues that they function to give an impression of scientific objectivity which undercuts their constructed nature (2001: 36).

If you are working to a tight deadline, you may not have the time to transcribe. However, you may be able to listen to your recordings a few times to familiarize yourself with the main points and perhaps to select small sections to transcribe in full for presentation with your analysis. This may be a useful technique in the field too, where you may want to reflect on your work and adapt it to explore more interesting things that have come up in the course of doing the field research. You can create such a summary in a word processor or in a notebook, by entering the tape counter number or the time elapsed from the beginning of the recording to the point of interest. If you are using qualitative data analysis software such as NVivo (see Chapter 23), then you can create a *proxy document* for just this purpose which has tape counts or elapsed time entered in already and you just make your comments at the relevant point.

221

This process can also be useful for initial familiarization with your material before you begin transcription proper so that you can start to think about how you might analyse.

If you are at the stage when you want to transcribe in full you can simply play your tape or Minidisc, repeatedly stopping, rewinding and playing again until you have typed everything you have heard of interest to you in your recordings. This can be extremely tedious and slow. To speed this up there are cassette players on which you can set an automatic rewind period and which you can control using a foot-pedal leaving your hands free to carry on typing. These are known as **transcribing machines**. If you have not transferred your

recording to digital audio files on a computer this is probably the fastest way of transcribing.

If, however, you have got your recordings as an audio file on your computer, you can use another software application to play the audio file and transcribe it within the same application. This enables you to synchronize your transcription with the sound files clause by clause which speeds up the checking of the transcription enormously. The synchronization effect is similar to reading the sub-titles on a foreign-language film. Once you have created your transcription you can export the transcription to qualitative data analysis software or web pages. There are not many programs which have these facilities, but I use another free

---

Box 16.4   Web pointers for audio recording

Glossary of recording terms, by Bruce Bartlett
http://tapeplus.com/glosofrecter.html

An approach to recording, transcribing and preparing audio data for qualitative analysis
www2.edc.org/CAEPP/audio.html

Guide to good practice: creating digital audio resources
www.pads.ahds.ac.uk:81/GGP_Audio

How analog and digital recording works
http://entertainment.howstuffworks.com/analog-digital.htm

Visual guide to sound card connections
http://geraldtomyn.tripod.com/digan.htm

Microphones and how to use them
www.shure.com/support/technotes/

Audacity: free software to create sound files
http://audacity.sourceforge.net/beta.php?lang=en

Also download the LAME add-on to create mp3s from the sound files you create:
http://mitiok.free.fr/

An initial guide to using Audacity is available at
http://homepages.gold.ac.uk/duncan/

Transcriber: a tool for segmenting, labelling and transcribing speech
http://www.etca.fr/CTA/gip/Projets/Transcriber/

You can download an initial guide to using Transcriber and the NVivo Export file to use with Transcriber from:
http://homepages.gold.ac.uk/duncan/

Visit the website for this book at www.rscbook.co.uk to link to these web pointers.

---

one called *Transcriber* (see Box 16.4).

Conclusion

Creating good audio recordings, transcribing and managing them is an important set of skills for researchers. As you have seen, this can get pretty technical, but if you get to grips with the technical side of recording sound you will find the acuity of your analysis improves considerably as you are able to hear and analyse finer details of talk. You will also save a lot of time and frustration that will otherwise arise, dealing with recordings that did not record, or segments of recording that are too bad to hear adequately. This chapter has been aimed at guiding you through the main concepts, procedures and equipment available today for making good quality recordings at a level appropriate for research purposes.

Further reading

This is a topic rarely covered in methods texts. Relevant texts include ten Have (1999), who has a helpful chapter that covers both audio and video recordings, and Lomax and Casey (1998), who discuss the impact of video recording for research purposes on research participants.

Student Reader (Seale, 2004): relevant readings

58 Paul Atkinson: 'Transcriptions'

Key concepts

Aliasing
Amplitude
Analogue and **digital** recording
Analogue to digital converter (ADC)
Channel
Critical distance
Digital recorder
Digital to analogue converter (DAC)
File compression

Frequency
Miniplug cable
Removable media
Sampling
Sampling precision or **resolution**
Sampling rate
Transcribing machines
Unidirectional versus **omnidirectional**
   microphone
Waveform

17

Doing ethnography

David Walsh

CONTENTS

Box 17.1 A definition of ethnography

'[Ethnography is] a particular method or set of methods which in its most characteristic form ... involves the ethnographer participating overtly or covertly in people's daily lives for an extended period of time, watching what happens, listening to what is said, asking questions – in fact, collecting whatever data are available to throw light on the issues that are the focus of research.' (Hammersley and Atkinson, 1995: 1)

The definition in Box 17.1 describes the essence of ethnography, showing it to be based in what is known as **participant observation.** This makes the researcher, as participant observer, the primary research instrument. Ethnography, then, contrasts with 'scientific' methods of social science research which, based upon a universalistic model of science, emphasize its neutrality and objectivity, attempting to generate data untouched by human hands. Ethnography belongs to the theoretical tradition which argues that the facts of society and culture belong to a different order from those of nature (see Chapters 2 and 4).

Theoretical foundations

Anthropologists developed ethnography to become their primary and almost exclusive method. Faced with non-Western societies that largely possessed an oral culture, anthropologists were encouraged by a perception of their diversity to take an attitude of **cultural relativism,** whereby the values and institutions of any given society were seen to have an internal logic of their own.

Any attempt to judge other societies as inferior or superior, in this view, is condemned as **ethnocentric.** Eventually this attitude was to lead to the view, amongst some, that rationality itself was simply a value position promoted by Western societies. Anthropologists took the view that society and culture could only be studied from inside by the immersion of the researcher in the society under study.

Later, sociologists pursuing *action theory* and *symbolic interactionism* came to use the method, as you saw in Chapter 4. It is, however, in *phenomenology* that we can see the most evocative conception of the ethnographer's role. Phenomenology, as was explained in Chapter 4, focuses on the inter-subjective constitution of the social world and everyday social life. Schutz (1964), in a seminal essay on *The Stranger,* shows how a social group has its own cultural pattern of life – folkways, mores, laws, habits, customs, etiquette, fashions and so on – that, as far as its members are concerned, are taken for granted, are habitual and almost automatic (see Box 17.2).

Schutz's stranger provides a model for the ethnographer using participant observation. The

---

Box 17.2 Members and strangers

Members living inside the culture of their group treat it as simply how the world *is* and do not reflect upon the presuppositions on which it is based or the knowledge which it entails. But the *stranger* entering such a group does not have this insider's sense of the world, and instead finds it strange, incoherent, problematic and questionable. Yet the stranger can become a member of the group through *participation,* becoming transformed into an insider, inhabiting it in the same taken-for-granted way as existing members. At the same time, being a stranger creates an attitude of objectivity because the stranger must carefully examine what seems self-explanatory to the members of the group. The stranger knows that other ways of life are possible.

(*Source*: summary of Schutz, 1964)

---

ethnographer tries to treat the familiar world of 'members' as **anthropologically strange,** to expose its social and cultural construction. This is particularly demanding when a researcher is studying a group with which he or she is familiar, but represents an ideal attitude of mind for the researcher to pursue nevertheless.

Constructionism is the view that society is to be seen as socially constructed on the basis of how its members make sense of it and not as an object-like reality (see also Chapter 4). It is latent in *symbolic interactionism* but more apparent in *phenomenology.* It has now become the primary theoretical foundation of contemporary ethnography. Indeed, one can see *ethnomethodology* as forming a part of this constructionist approach. Ethnomethodologists, though, are less interested in how people *see* things than more conventional ethnographers, and are more interested in how people *do* things, particularly in their uses of language. Chapter 28 shows how the method of *conversation analysis* has arisen from these concerns. Although such approaches share a view that the subject matter of social and cultural research is different from that of the natural sciences, they are nevertheless characteristically committed to a *realist* and scientific view of the world.

However, an altogether different version of ethnography has also emerged out of constructionism which urges a radical break with all ideas of objective scientific inquiry. This position involves not simply seeing ethnography as a revelation of social construction but seeing ethnographic research as *itself* participating in the construction of the social world. Bauman (1987) has summarized this by distinguishing a traditional form of social research which is legislative, in that the ethnographer rules some accounts of the world true and others false, and a newer form that is more genuinely interpretive. This view involves seeing social research as one possible interpretation amongst many (see also Chapter 7 for a discussion of this distinction). The American anthropologist Clifford Geertz (1973) has played an important part in forming this different sense of ethnography. Geertz argues that:

man [*sic*] is an animal suspended in webs of significance he himself has spun and I take

culture to be those webs, and the analysis to be therefore not an experimental science in search of law but an interpretive one in search of meaning. It is explication I am after, construing social expressions on their surface enigmatical. (1973: 5)

This leads Geertz to the view that the task of ethnography is to produce its own distinctive form of knowledge, which he calls **thick description**. Although the ethnographer continues to use the same techniques of data collection as conventional ethnographers, the focus of analysis turns much more to seeing culture as a system of *signs*. Here, the ethnographer comes close to doing a *semiotic* analysis (see Chapter 20). The easiest way to understand this is to imagine the ethnographer as being like a literary critic attempting to understand the organization, construction and meaning of a literary text. The ethnographer then finds a whole web of cultural structures, knowledge and meanings which are knotted and superimposed on to one another and which constitute a densely layered **cultural script.**

Famously, Geertz analyses the many layers of meaning involved in Balinese cockfights in a demonstration of this approach. He sees the event of a cockfight as an example of a cultural script being written, or enacted. Through an intensive and dense description of a cockfight, Geertz makes broader cultural interpretations and generalizations. Yet Geertz understands his own analysis of the various meanings of the event as a reflexive interpretation of it, rather than an objective description. This, of course, raises the issue of *validity.* If ethnographers are simply in the business of introducing new texts into a society and culture that is little more than an interplay of 'texts', we must give up any notions of science or truthfulness. As was shown in Chapter 4, this is Foucault's position, suggesting that the 'human sciences' are 'regimes of truth'.

There have been some very interesting deconstructions of ethnographic writing (reviewed in detail in Chapter 29). These emphasize that ethnographers are story-tellers and, like all such, create narratives of tragedy, irony and humour which make their writing a literary activity. They use the same fundamental resources of literature and the same sorts of recipes and material in conveying arguments and persuading readers that their accounts are plausible reconstructions of social actors and social scenes.

But it seems wrong for social researchers wholly to accept this postmodern discourse, to abandon all forms of realism as the basis for doing ethnography, and to accept that all is textuality and construction. It could be argued that this takes *reflexivity* too far and shuns the empirical too much. The rhetorical strategies of ethnographic writing should be acknowledged, but this cannot be the end of the story. The social and cultural world must be the ground and reference for ethnographic writing, and reflexive ethnography should involve a keen awareness of the interpenetration of reality and representation.

Doing ethnography

Quantitative research committed to a *positivist* vision of the unity of science (the philosophical term for this is **naturalism** – see Chapter 2) attempts to establish correlations between objectively defined variables as a basis for explanation. This proceeds through a research design that is organized as a logically sequential and separate series of stages, beginning from theory and going through hypothesis generation and data gathering to hypothesis testing. Frequently, one-off interviews or questionnaires are used. Ethnography departs from this. First, ethnographers study people in their natural settings (also said to be **'naturalistic'**, somewhat confusingly), seeking to document that world in terms of the meanings and behaviour of the people in it. It places in doubt the variables that quantitative research analyses, examining instead their sociocultural construction. Secondly, it does not follow the sequence of deductive theory testing because it is in the process of research itself that research problems come to be formulated and studied. Often these prove to be different from the problems that the ethnographer had initially intended to study. Theory is often *generated* rather than solely tested. Indeed the 'discovery of grounded theory' during fieldwork has been the subject of much debate in the literature on ethnography (Glaser and Strauss, 1967) and is discussed in

Chapter 18.

Ethnography is distinctive in three ways.

- First, as stated above, there are *no distinct stages* of theorizing, hypothesis construction, data gathering and hypothesis testing. Instead the research process is one of a constant interaction between problem formulation, data collection and data analysis. The analysis of data feeds into research design; data collection and theory come to be developed out of data analysis and all subsequent data collection is guided strategically by the emergent theory.

- Secondly, ethnography brings a *variety of techniques* of inquiry into play involving attempts to observe things that happen, listen to what people say and question people in the setting under investigation. So it involves, as McCall and Simmons put it:

  > genuinely social interaction in the field with the subject of study ... direct observation of relevant events, some formal and a great deal of informal interviewing, some counting, [the] collection of documents and artifacts, and open-endedness in the directions the study takes. (1969: 1)

- Thirdly, *the observer is the primary research instrument*, accessing the field, establishing field relations, conducting and structuring observation and interviews, writing field notes, using audio and visual recordings, reading documents, recording and transcribing and finally writing up the research.

So ethnography has a large constructional and reflexive character. It is essentially the observer who stands at the heart of ethnography and of its open-ended nature.

The observer position

Observation, inquiry and data collection depend upon the observer gaining access to the appropriate field and establishing good working relations with the people in it. They need to be relationships that are able to generate the data the research requires. The identity that the observer assumes determines the success of this.

A first issue is whether to take an **overt** or **covert** role in the setting. This, in turn, very much depends on the situation and on the **gatekeepers** who control access to it. Gatekeepers are the sponsors, officials and significant others who have the power to grant or block access to and within a setting. Sometimes, the ethnographer is faced with situations in which relevant gatekeepers are unlikely to permit access, so that covert or secret research is the only way of studying them. This has been done, for example, in studies of the police (Holdaway, 1982), religious sects (Shaffir, 1985), organized crime (Chambliss, 1975) and right-wing political movements (Fielding, 1981). Here, the observer seeks to present himself or herself as an ordinary, legitimate member of the group. This may solve the problem of access and observation as long as the covert role can be maintained, but successful maintenance produces major problems of an ethical and practical kind and a massive problem if the cover is 'blown'. Normally, then, totally covert research is rare in ethnography. More commonly the researcher lets some people know about the research and keeps others in the dark or only partially informed about the purposes of the research. Some ethnographers argue on ethical grounds that the researcher should always adopt a completely overt role in which the purposes of the research and its procedures are explained to the subjects under study. But Hammersley and Atkinson (1995) argue that, whereas deception should be avoided if possible, telling the whole truth about research may not be wise or feasible. Since research problems will change over the course of fieldwork, what the researcher can say about aims is often little more than speculation. Additionally, to produce too much information ahead of time may influence the behaviour of the people under study in such a way as to invalidate the findings.

Generally, then, a series of potential observer roles are open to the ethnographer. Junker (1960) identifies four.

First, there is the *complete participant*. This entails complete covert research. Although it seems to carry the attraction of generating a complete knowledge of the situation, apart from the problems outlined above it produces others too. It can place a severe restriction on the character of the data collected because the observer, as a completely participating member of it, becomes hedged in by the expectations of the role he or she has adopted. So many lines of inquiry will be missed and optimal conditions for data collection may not be available. Finally, it carries the risk of 'going native', where the observer abandons the position of analyst for identification with the people under study.

Secondly, Junker describes the role of the *complete observer*. Here the researcher simply observes people in ways that avoid social interaction with the observed, as Corsaro (1981) did in a study of nursery school children in the classroom which involved observing them through a one-way mirror. This reduces the possibilities of people reacting to being observed (known as **reactivity**) or of 'going native', but introduces the potential problem of *ethnocentrism* instead, in which the observer, by not interacting with the people under study, cannot get at their meanings and so imposes an alien framework of understanding on the situation. Moreover it places severe limits on what can be observed, although it can be a valuable supplement to other forms of ethnographic research.

The third role is that of the *participant as observer*. Here, the observer and the people being studied are aware that theirs is a field relationship, which minimizes the problems of pretence. It

---

Box 17.3   Four roles in participant observation

1   Complete participant
2   Complete observer
3   Participant as observer
4   Observer as participant

(*Source*: Junker, 1960)

involves an emphasis on participation and social interaction over observing in order to produce a relationship of rapport and trust. The problem is that it carries the danger of reactivity and of going native through identification with the subjects of study, unless the intimacy created in social interaction is restrained by attempts to maintain the role of the stranger on the part of the observer.

The fourth role is that of the *observer as participant.* Here the balance is in favour of observation over participation. This prevents the researcher from going native but restricts understanding because limited participation in social activities heightens the possibilities of superficiality, so that important lines of inquiry may be missed or not pursued, things go unobserved and the activities of participants are not properly understood. Typically most overt ethnography takes up a position somewhere between the third and fourth roles. Overt observer roles can never be entirely fixed and can and do change (the opposite is true if research is covert). Indeed, changes in the observer's role in the field over the course of fieldwork may be vital in producing new information, generating new data and creating new and fruitful problems and lines of inquiry that extend the scope of the research. In the end, however, the best observational position for the ethnographer is that of the *marginal native,* which will be described later in the chapter.

Beginning an ethnographic study

Although ethnography does not work with a logically sequential research design that compartmentalizes it into distinct stages it does have phases and activities that give it a **funnel structure** in which the research is progressively focused over its course. At the start of this funnel the researcher will be involved in formulating ideas about the sort of problem to be investigated. In ethnography, however, what the researcher initially sets out to investigate may change over the course of fieldwork, as problems are transformed or emerge in the field. The process of observation itself establishes problems and the possibilities of inquiry into them. Yet all ethnography begins with some problem or set of issues, which some call **foreshadowed problems,** that

are not specifically formulated hypotheses and which can have many sources. As is shown in Chapter 11, the requirement to write a research proposal may be the opportunity to lay out the nature of such foreshadowed problems. At the same time it is important not to let such an exercise close down avenues of inquiry that deviate from the proposal. One of the strengths of ethnography is its open-ended nature.

To begin with, the ethnographer needs to consult relevant *secondary sources* on the problems and issues under consideration, which can range from allied research monographs and articles through to other sources like journalistic material, autobiographies and diaries and even novels (see Chapter 12). But the focusing of research problems cannot really be started until initial data have been collected. As Geer says, one begins with early working hypotheses but ultimately goes on to generate 'hypotheses ... based on an accumulation of data ... [that] ... undergo a prolonged period of testing and retesting... over the period of [research]. There is no finality to them. They must be refined, expanded and developed' (1964: 152). Even at the early stage theory enters into the selection of research problems, as was shown in Chapter 5. Moreover, the initial consideration of foreshadowed problems has to begin a process that moves between the immediate empirical situation and an analytical framework.

However, the research problem is very much shaped by the nature of the setting chosen for study. Choice of setting may have arisen on an opportunistic basis. For example, a natural disaster may have occurred, or the researcher may come across the reconstruction of an organization, or the replanning of a city, or may find an entry opened through personal contacts. In choosing a setting the researcher may then need to 'case' it, with a view to assessing its suitability and feasibility for research purposes. This will involve assessing the possibilities for access to it, collecting preliminary data on it, interviewing relevant participants and finding potential gatekeepers. Finally, the practical issues of the time and money needed to do research will need to be considered.

It is important that the setting is a *naturally occurring* one, although it need not be geographically self-contained. It can be one that is constituted and maintained by cultural definitions and social strategies that establish it as a 'community'. For example, a study of green political movements would be like this. It may be necessary to go outside the setting to understand the significance of things that go on within it.

If the setting is a single case, this can pose problems of representativeness and therefore of the *external validity* of the study (see Chapter 7). This, though, can be circumvented by selecting on the basis of intrinsic interest and theoretical usefulness. Sampling *within* settings also occurs so it is important to make decisions about what to observe and when, whom to talk to, and what to record and how. Here three dimensions of sampling are relevant:

1 *Time:* attitudes and activities may vary over time so a study may have to represent this.
2 *People:* people vary so a range of types should be investigated.
3 *Context:* people do different things in different contexts so a variety of these will have to be studied. Such **contextual sensitivity** is vital to ethnographic study.

Access

Initial access to the field is essential but is also an issue to be resolved throughout the whole of the data collecting process. There are numerous aspects to the problem. At a first level, gaining access to a situation is an entirely practical matter which entails using the ordinary interpersonal resources, skills and strategies that all of us develop in dealing with the conduct of everyday life. But access is also a theoretical matter in ethnography because, as Hammersley and Atkinson (1995) argue, the discovery of obstacles to access can help one to understand the social organization of a setting, showing, for example, how people respond to strangers.

'Public' settings (for example, the street, a beach), although seeming to offer no difficulties of access, are, in fact, difficult for research. This is because deliberate and protracted observation can place the observer in a potentially deviant position, perhaps appearing as someone loitering with the intent to commit a crime. More typically, access to 'private' settings is governed by gate-

keepers who are not always easy to identify, though common sense and social knowledge can provide the vehicles for doing so. In formal organizations the gatekeepers will be key personnel in the organization, but in other settings the gatekeepers may be different. Whyte's (1943) classic study of slum ghetto life and its gang structure depended on his finding and being befriended by 'Doc', a leading gang leader, who provided the **sponsorship** through which the ghetto was studied. But whoever the gatekeepers are, they will be concerned with the picture of their community, subculture, group or organization and may want it and themselves painted in a favourable light. This, in turn, means they are likely to keep sensitive things hidden. They may also prevent the study of mundane matters because they take them for granted and see them as uninteresting.

Access affects the accuracy of ethnographic study because it determines how and where fieldwork can be organized. Relations with gatekeepers can either be facilitative, because friendly and cooperative, or the reverse and so obstructive. But even facilitative relations with gatekeepers will structure the research since the observer is likely to get directed to the gatekeeper's existing networks of friendship, enmity and territory. It may not be possible for the observer to become independent of the sponsor so the observer can be caught in a variety of webs of client–patron relationships in which all kinds of unsuspected influences operate. The observer must find a way of using this to get relevant information. For example, Hansen's (1977) study of a Catalonian village in Spain became possible only when he accepted aristocratic sponsorship and worked with the aristocrat–peasant hierarchy since the assumptions and interactions of village life were based on this.

Gatekeepers will have expectations about the ethnographer's identity and intentions, as will other people in the field. Hammersley and Atkinson (1995) argue that it is particularly important as to whether the host community sees the researcher as an expert (and thus a person to be welcomed because he or she is helping to sort things out) or a critic and very unwelcome. On the other hand, if the researcher is defined as an expert this may conflict with the cultivated naivety involved in being a stranger. Moreover, even with a friendly gatekeeper, the researcher will be faced with the fact that not everything is equally available to observation. People will not or cannot divulge everything, or may even be unwilling to talk at all. So access to data is a recurrent problem that only subtle negotiations with gatekeepers and careful manoeuvring of the researcher into a position to get data can resolve. This requires patience and diplomacy.

Internet ethnographies pose unusual access issues to consider, which centre not so much on the difficulties of gaining access, but on the consequences of access that, initially at least, seems almost too easy. Christine Hine explains the thinking behind this in Box 17.4. Chapter 21 explores these issues in more detail.

Field relations and observation

Essentially ethnography entails a learning role in which the observer is attempting to understand a world by encountering it first-hand. Once access to a setting has been achieved, the success of observational work depends on the quality of the relations with the people under study.

First the researcher needs to consider the initial responses of people in the field and how to gain their trust. People will inevitably try to place the researcher within their own experience because they need to know how to deal with him or her. If they know nothing about research, they are likely to be suspicious and wonder if the researcher is acting as some kind of agent or spy for an outside body. For example, Kaplan (1991) reports that the New England fishermen she studied thought she was a government inspector at first. On the other hand, if people are familiar with research and so view the researcher in a favourable light, there may be a mismatch between their expectations of what a researcher should do and the eventual research product. This can lead to a challenge to the legitimacy of the research and the credentials of the researchers. For example, Keddie (1971), although originally welcomed by teachers to do research within classrooms, was denounced later by them when her findings conflicted with their claims not to have streamed pupils in their mixed-ability curriculum. In the face of this the researcher needs to create a professional front.

But this raises a second issue in field relations, concerning **impression management** by the researcher. What is needed is a impression that facilitates observation and avoids producing obstacles. This, in turn, will require dress that is familiar to the people in the setting and the

---

Box 17.4   Access in virtual ethnographies

'What makes using the Internet a sensible thing to do?... answers to this question can fruitfully draw on a reflexive perspective on the experiences of the ethnographer both on-line and off-line ... Recently, the Internet explosion has provided an apparently natural "field" for ethnographers. ... The accessibility of the Internet attracts ethnographers to a field site which lives on the desk top, and a community which can apparently be joined without complex rituals and access negotiations. This very accessibility, however, tends to focus attention on the on-line community, to the exclusion of links with off-line lives, identities and activities. It also tends to leave unquestioned the status of the Internet as a communication medium and as a technology.' (Hine, 1998)

Box 17.5   Issues in conducting relations in the field

- Gaining trust and managing initial responses
- Impression management
- Awareness of the consequences of non-negotiable characteristics
- Dealing with marginality
- Deciding when to leave

cultivation of demeanour, speech and habits that fit. The researcher must be able to create different self-presentations for different settings. Above all, the researcher must establish a large degree of ordinary sociability and normal social intercourse. Without this, pumping people for information can become threatening. Most anthropological field studies show that the researcher must meet local customs and decorum before research can be done at all. Yet the researcher must prevent sociability, rapport and trust from deteriorating into exploitation or 'going native'. This means some degree of frankness and self-disclosure on the part of the researcher is needed. This is not easy. The researcher will have to suppress some things as he or she will have to interact with people whose views he or she disagrees with but cannot challenge. Rapport, then, is a delicate matter to be decided by progressive initiation into the field.

Thirdly, the researcher will not be able to negotiate all aspects of his or her personal front and these non-negotiable characteristics of identity will have to be monitored for their effects on the research. Such characteristics are largely the *ascribed* ones of gender, age, ethnicity and race which tend to be institutionalized in society in terms of style and expected forms of social interaction. In the early stages of research, the researcher will simply be like any other stranger in the setting who watches and asks questions to make sense of it. But gradually the researcher will establish a version of himself of herself as a naive participant. In doing this, he or she must retain a self-conscious position in which incompetence is progressively substituted by an awareness of what has been learned, how it has been learned and the social transactions that inform the production of knowledge. Complete participation in the situation is impossible; such immersion would risk going native, and so a degree of **marginality** in the situation is needed to do research. Marginality is a poise between a strangeness that avoids over-rapport and a familiarity that grasps the perspectives of people in the situation. Thus the researcher can be understood to be a *marginal native*. This position creates considerable strain on the researcher as it engenders insecurity, produced by living in two worlds simultaneously, that of participation and that of research. The researcher will

be physically and emotionally affected by this.

Finally, the researcher has to take a decision as to when to leave the field. This can be decided on the basis of the necessary data having been collected. Glaser and Strauss (1967) offer the concept of **theoretical saturation** to indicate the state of affairs that suggests that it is time to leave the field (see also Chapter 18). As a part of their scheme for generating theory they say that saturation occurs when no new ideas are generated by empirical inquiry, after the researcher has made strenuous efforts to find instances in the field which might contradict, or help develop further, the emergent theory. Leaving the field will have to be negotiated, as it entails closing relations with participants that may have been firmly established and which they may not wish to relinquish.

Interviewing

Interviewing has a particular character in ethnography. Some ethnographers, following the dictates of *naturalism,* argue that people's accounts should always be unsolicited, so as to avoid the *reactivity* of formal interviews. But interviewing may be the only way of collecting certain data, in which case the researcher needs to decide whom to interview. People in the field may select themselves and others as interviewees because the researcher has used them to update himself or herself on events. Or again gatekeepers may try to select interviewees, either in good faith or to manipulate the research. The researcher may have to accept both because access to data is not available otherwise. The researcher may consider that conventional notions of representativeness should dictate the selection of interviewees. Alternatively, informants may be selected on the basis of their particular value to the investigation: people who are outsiders, naturally reflective, or who have strong motives to reveal inside stories for a variety of personal reasons. Another principle may be that based on *theoretical sampling* (see Chapter 18): the selection of informants whose information is more likely to develop and test emerging analytical ideas.

Largely speaking, *depth interviews* are done (Chapter 14), requiring active listening on the part of the researcher to understand what is being said and to assess its relation to the research. The ethnographic analysis of interviews should focus on the context in which the interview occurred. All of the considerations about the analytic status of interview data raised in Chapter 14 apply.

Documents

Most settings in contemporary society are literate and much of everyday life in them is organized around the production and use of documents. These are a valuable resource for ethnographic study. Official statistics, for example, are documents. But from an ethnographic point of view they are often understood in terms of their social production rather than their truth. Another kind of key document is the official record. Records are central to work in large organizations and are made and used in accordance with organizational routines. Such records construct a 'privileged' reality in modern society because they are sometimes treated as the objective documentation of it. But like official statistics, such records should be interpreted by the ethnographer in terms of how they are written, how they are read, who writes them, who reads them, for what purposes, with what outcomes and so on.

Yet other documents, too, of a literate society are relevant for the ethnographer. Fiction, diaries, autobiographies, letters, photographs and media products can all be useful. These can be a source of sensitizing concepts and suggest foreshadowed problems largely because they recount the myths, images and stereotypes of a culture. But as accounts biased by social interests and personal prejudices such documents can be used only to sensitize the ethnographer and open up potential worlds for scrutiny. (Approaches to the analysis of texts are described in Chapter 27.)

Recording data

The typical means for recording observational data in ethnography is by making **field notes** which consist of fairly concrete descriptions of social processes and their contexts and which set out to capture their various properties and features. The initial principle of selection in this will be the foreshadowed problems of the research,

and in the beginning of inquiry this requires a wide focus in selection and recording. The systematic *coding* of observations into analytical categories comes later (see also Chapter 23). The central issues for making good field notes concern:

- *What* to write down,
- *How* to write it down
- *When* to write it down

In terms of *when,* field notes should be written as soon as possible after the events observed. Leaving this to a later point produces the problem of memory recall and the quality of the field notes deteriorates. But note taking has to fit in with the requirements of the setting under study, so the researcher must develop strategies for doing this. Buckingham, for instance, who adopted a secret observational role in a hospital by posing as a terminally ill patient, told anyone who inquired that he was 'writing a book' to explain his note-taking activities (Buckingham et al., 1976).

As to *how* to write down observations, field notes must be meticulous. This raises simultaneously the issue of *what* to write down. As social scenes are inexhaustible, some selection has to be made. At the beginning this must be wide, but as research progresses the field notes need to be relevant to emerging concerns. This requires focusing on the concrete, the detailed and the contextual. So the researcher should try to record speech verbatim and to record non-verbal behaviour in precise terms. Notes can then later be inspected in the secure knowledge that they give an accurate description of things. Field notes should also, wherever possible, record speech and action in relation to who was present, where the events occurred and at what time. Final analysis of data will draw on this knowledge of context. With interviewing, audio recording and with observation, visual recording can be used as an additional and valuable aid (see Chapter 16). But audio and visual recording are still selective and so is the transcription of tapes. This is partially resolvable by following the now well-established rules of transcription that conversation analysis has produced (see Chapter 28). But to transcribe at this level of detail is really only practicable for very short extracts. Documents can be collected and photocopied but they too will involve note taking in terms of indexing, copying by hand and summarizing. In all, the primary problem of recording is always the same: as literal data are reduced, more information is lost and the degree of interpretation is increased.

Additionally, the researcher should write down any analytical ideas that arise in the process of data collection. Such **analytic memos** identify emergent ideas and sketch out research strategy. They provide a reflexive monitoring of the research and how ideas were generated. Ultimately analytic memos may be best assembled in a fieldwork journal which gives a running account of the research.

All data recording has to be directed towards the issue of storage and retrieval. This usually begins with a chronological record, but then moves to the conceptualization of data in terms of themes and categories to create a coding system that actively fosters discovery (see Chapter 23). This provides an infrastructure for searching and retrieving data, providing a basis for both generating and testing theory. Here, computers often prove useful.

Data analysis and theorizing

In ethnography the analysis of data can be said to begin in the pre-fieldwork phase with the formulation and clarification of research problems. It continues through fieldwork into the process of writing up reports. Formally it starts to take place in analytic memos and fieldwork journals but, informally, it is always present in the ideas and hunches of the researcher as he or she engages in the field setting and seeks to understand the data being collected.

The fragmentary nature of ethnographic data introduces problems. Checking the *reliability* of a particular interpretation may be difficult because of missing data. *Representativeness,* the typicality of crucial items of data, may be hard to establish. It may not be possible to investigate comparative cases in order to demonstrate *validity.* The generation of theories may not be the main aim of the researcher: many early Chicago School ethnographers (see Chapter 4), for example, were

theory-free, at least in the explicit sense. The procedures of *coding,* whereby devices like *typologies* or *careers* may be developed, is the start of generating theory from data. Thus ideally theories are *grounded* in the data. Highly abstract theorizing, where concepts are not exemplified with data extracts, goes against the spirit of most ethnography.

In the funnel structure of this type of research, the initial task in the analysis of fieldwork data is to establish some preliminary concepts that make analytic sense of what is going on in the social setting. These can arise in a variety of ways. One is a careful reviewing of the corpus of the data in which the researcher seeks patterns to see if anything stands out as puzzling or surprising, to see how data relate to social theory, organizational accounts or common-sense expectations, and to see whether inconsistencies appear between different people's beliefs in the setting or between people's beliefs and their actions. Concepts can be generated in terms of *observer categories* derived from social theory, or from *folk categories,* terms used by participants in the field. But this initial conceptualization cannot be anything but sensitizing, a loose collection of orienting categories which gives a general sense of reference and guidelines in approaching the field.

The second stage is to turn such *sensitizing* concepts into *definitive* concepts, a stable set of categories for the systematic coding of data. These will refer precisely to what is common to a class of data and will permit an analysis of the relations between them. Glaser and Strauss (1967), describing the 'discovery of grounded theory', argue that the method for this in fieldwork should be that of **constant comparison** in which an item of data that is coded as a particular category is examined and its similarities with and differences from other items in the category are noted. In this way categories can be differentiated into new and more clearly defined ones and subcategories established. So this method, through its systematic sifting and comparison, comes to reveal and establish the mutual relationships and internal structure of categories. An example of the use of the constant comparative method is given in Chapter 18.

The discovery of grounded theory supplies a logic for ethnographic research, helping it gain scientific status. But whether this process of systematization is an entirely *inductive* and exclusively data-based method of theory generation, as Glaser and Strauss argue, is problematic. If the role of theory in structuring observation is recognized (see Chapter 2), then theory, common sense and other various assumptions precede theory generation, so grounded theory has a constructive character and not simply a data-based one. Whatever level of systematization takes place in the direction of theory construction, it is of value only if it offers a revealing purchase on the data.

Validation and verification

Ethnographic research has produced two suggested forms of validation: respondent or 'member' validation and triangulation. These are both discussed in Chapter 7 so will not be discussed at length here, except to point out some limitations of these techniques. **Member validation** consists of the ethnographer showing findings to the people studied and seeking verification in which the actors recognize a correspondence between the findings and what they, the actors, say and do. Thus verification is largely reduced to a matter of authenticity. But there are problems with this. Actors may not know things; they may not be privileged observers of their own actions or consciously aware of what they do and why. They may have an interest in rationalizing their beliefs and behaviour and so reject the ethnographic account of these, or indeed they may have no interest at all in the ethnographic account! So respondent validation cannot be a simple test of ethnographic findings, but it can be, as Bloor (1983) argues, a stimulus to generate further data and pursue new paths of analysis.

On **triangulation** it is worth noting the experience of West (1990), who used triangulation in a study of what mothers said to him in interviews about medical consultations. West wanted to know whether the accounts given in interviews were true or not. He therefore observed actual consultations and compared these with the interview accounts. Broadly speaking, he found the mothers' criticisms of the doctors to be supported. But this method of triangulation has its problems too. West's validation exercise is potentially limitless, as the next question to ask is whether his observations were true. At most, if different data tally, the observer can feel a bit more confident in his or her inferences, but can hardly conclude that a final truth has been reached.

Indeed, if we apply the perspective of constructionism to ethnographic writing itself (as was suggested earlier in the discussion of theoretical foundations for ethnography) the whole issue of the 'validity' of the method becomes more complex. Ethnographers in recent years have become very interested in this perspective on their own work and have experimented with a variety of reporting forms that attempt a more self-aware approach towards ethnographic authority. Chapter 29 covers these issues in more detail.

Box 17.6   Web pointers for ethnography

Laura Zimmer-Tamakoshi's 'Anthropologist in the Field' website:
www.melanesia.org/fieldwork/tamakoshil/

How to do ethnographic research: a simplified guide
www.sas.upenn.edu/anthro/CPIA/methods.html

Ethnography (journal site) – use the search facility on the following site to find this journal
www.sagepub.co.uk

Forum Qualitative Social Research – use the search facility with the words 'ethnography' and 'participant observation'
www.qualitative-research.net/fqs/fqs-eng.htm

Visit the website for this book at www.rscbook.co.uk to link to these web pointers.

Conclusion

Ethnography presents both problems and opportunities for social and cultural research because of its largely qualitative character and its essential basis in the participant observer as the research instrument itself. The problems are not entirely analytical but are ethical too. The fact that ethnographic research depends on building up relations of rapport and trust with people in the field, whilst using this to generate and collect data from them, raises issues of manipulation, exploitation and secrecy. These are maximized in covert research but exist even in overt research because of the degree to which the researcher must withhold disclosure about his or her activities in order to maintain sociability in the situation and to gain access. These ethical considerations also affect the publication of research. There may be political implications which damage the people whose lives have been investigated. Yet ethnography, through participant observation of the social and cultural worlds, opens out the possibility of an understanding of reality which no other method can realize.

Further reading

Hammersley and Atkinson (1995) is the best textbook-length introduction to doing ethnography. Atkinson et al. (2001) is an edited collection that outlines a broad range of approaches to doing, writing and reading ethnography. Coffey (1999) discusses the researcher's position in relationship to both ethnographic fieldwork and writing.

Student Reader (Seale 2004): relevant readings

29 Alfred Schutz: 'Concept and theory formation in the social sciences'
30 William Foote Whyte: 'First efforts'
31 Buford H. Junker: 'The field work situation: social roles for observation'
32 Barney G. Glaser and Anselm L. Strauss: 'Theoretical sampling'
33 John Lofland: 'Field notes'
34 Clifford Geertz: 'Being there'
35 Martyn Hammersley: 'Some reflections on ethnography and validity'
36 Howard S. Becker and Blanche Geer: 'Participant observation and interviewing: a comparison'
43 Robin Hamman: 'The application of ethnographic methodology in the study of cybersex'
57 James Clifford: 'Partial truths'
58 Paul Atkinson: 'Transcriptions'
59 Renato Rosaldo: 'Grief and a headhunter's rage'
61 John D. Brewer: 'The ethnographic critique of ethnography'

Key concepts

Analytic memos	Funnel structure
Anthropological strangeness	Gatekeepers
Constant comparison	Impression management
Constructionism	Marginality
Contextual sensitivity	Member validation
Cultural relativism	Naturalistic
Cultural script	Overt *versus* covert role
Ethnocentricism	Participant observation
Field notes	Reactivity
Foreshadowed problem	Sponsorship
	Theoretical saturation
	Thick description
	Triangulation

18

Generating grounded theory

Clive Seale

CONTENTS

In Chapter 7 it was shown that many researchers feel that establishing good links between concepts, ideas or theories and the things that they refer to is an important aspect of the quality of research reports. It was pointed out that this concern to ensure good **concept–indicator links** is one that is shared by both qualitative and quantitative researchers. Grounded theorizing is a set of techniques which emphasize the creation of theoretical statements from the inspection of data, largely gathered in qualitative observational studies of the sort described in the previous chapter on ethnography (Chapter 17). The participant observer using a grounded theory approach cycles between episodes of data collection and data analysis, the one informing the other, so that the eventual research report is very likely to exhibit good concept–indicator links.

Box 18.1 gives an example of a theory that is well-grounded in data. Wiener's research project involved interviews with people with rheumatoid arthritis as well as observation of their care. From close inspection of their accounts and the observational data, she found that the concept of 'normalization' summarized a broad range of experiences. Normalization was itself related to another concept, 'justifying inaction'. At every point in describing these concepts Wiener was able to show the reader what they meant by giving examples drawn from the interviews or observations.

In this chapter I will give an account of the main procedures involved in research using grounded theory as well as say something about the historical context in which this approach arose, explaining why it has gained such popularity. I will also assess some of the criticisms that can be made of the method.

The discovery of grounded theory

The original ideas of grounded theory were outlined by Glaser and Strauss (1967), arising from their work together on a research project that involved analysing the treatment of people dying in American hospitals. Grounded theory needs to be understood in its historical context, since it was fundamentally a reaction to a *positivist,*

Box 18.1   Grounded theory in a study of people with rheumatoid arthritis

How the analysis was done:

Analysis of field data was conducted in the following manner: indicators in the data (descriptions by the arthritic, or observations by the researcher, of an action, episode or event) were coded into categories and their properties. For example, all descriptions of behavioral attempts to continue a normal life were initially coded as *normalization* and then broken down into categories of normalization, such as *covering-up, keeping up* and *pacing.* Concepts which have been dictated by the data, and thus coded, can then be interrelated ... and can be carried forward in the writing ... one can carry forward a concept such as *covering-up* to demonstrate its relationship to another concept such as *justifying inaction,* but one cannot constantly carry forward a description such as 'When I walk, I walk as normally as possible' and demonstrate its relationship to another description such as 'My husband doesn't really understand'... It is intended that conceptually specifying behavior will strengthen its applicability as a guideline for health professionals ...(Wiener 1975: 97)

An extract from the report:

A successful repertoire for covering-up and keeping-up may at times turn out to be a mixed blessing. Relationships generally remain normal, but when the arthritic cannot get by, it is harder to *justify inaction* to others ... This problem is increased when others have stakes in the arthritic's remaining active, as was the case with a young mother whose condition worsened when she tried to keep athletic pace with her husband and son: 'My husband really doesn't understand. He is very healthy and he thinks there is some magic formula that I'm not following – if I would just exercise, or have people over.' (Wiener, 1975: 100)

verificationist approach which was then very dominant in American social research, threatening to overshadow the work of qualitative researchers with an approach that was almost exclusively quantitative and statistical. In this dominant approach, data was collected in order to test the truth value of theoretical propositions. Instead, grounded theorists favoured an approach that emphasized the *inductive* generation of theory from data. The scheme had an almost revolutionary appeal for a sociological 'proletariat' of qualitative research workers, keen to overthrow the twin domination of their field by 'theoretical capitalists' and big-time, government funded quantitative survey research work, represented for Glaser and Strauss in the 1960s by the work of theoreticians such as Talcott Parsons or the quantitative methodologist Paul Lazarsfeld, who, with others, developed the *elaboration paradigm* (see Chapter 25). In fact, Glaser had previously worked with Lazarsfeld and echoes of the elaboration paradigm can be found in the original book on grounded theory.

Theoretical sampling and theoretical saturation

A commitment to continual re-examination of data in the light of developing arguments is the principle feature of grounded theorizing. It is important to note that this extends to the collection of data as well. Too often, researchers go and do some qualitative interviews and then say that they have 'analysed them using grounded theory'. This is incorrect, since grounded theorizing involves collecting data in episodes punctuated by periods of data analysis; it cannot occur if data collection takes place at a single point in the research process.

The concept of **theoretical sampling** is designed to describe this. It modifies the principle (which at the time was well established by Becker (1970) and others) of searching for *negative instances* (see Chapter 7). Glaser and Strauss showed that this could be used in theory construction rather than (as in Becker) purely as a test of theory. Here, a difference becomes apparent with the elaboration paradigm whose authors, for practical reasons, could not envisage frequent returns

to data collection so that a relatively rapid cycling between fieldwork and data analysis might occur. Large scale social survey work does not permit very much repetition of expensive data-gathering exercises if a researcher discovers a key question has not been included in an interview schedule, thus limiting the exploratory potential of such work. The qualitative researcher, though, is more fortunate in this regard and Glaser and Strauss were able to exploit this very fully. They advocated that through theoretical sampling, a researcher might extend and broaden the scope of an emerging theory. Such sampling involves choosing cases to study, people to interview, settings to observe, with a view to finding things that might challenge the limitations of the existing theory, forcing the researcher to change it in order to incorporate the new phenomena. Box 18.2 shows Glaser and Strauss outlining this aspect of their method.

(An illustration of theoretical sampling from Glaser and Strauss's work on 'awareness contexts' is given in Boxes 23.8 and 23.9 in Chapter 23. You may like to study it before proceeding.)

This process of theoretical sampling is, of course, potentially limitless, since it comes up against the general problem of *induction,* which concerns the ever-present possibility that a further case will exhibit properties that force some further changes in a theory. Undaunted, Glaser and Strauss propose a typically pragmatic solution by describing a state of **theoretical saturation**, also shown in Box 18.2.

Constant comparison

In addition to the strategy of theoretical sampling and the recognition of theoretical saturation, the third core idea of grounded theorizing is that of the method of **constant comparison**, which is used as a systematic tool for developing and refining theoretical categories and their properties. If applied rigorously, it can aid in taking researchers beyond common sense reporting of participants' categories so that a study becomes genuinely relevant at a theoretical level. The method is not a loosely structured free-for-all, in which researchers glance impressionistically through their field notes looking for anecdotes that support their

Box 18.2   Theoretical sampling and theoretical saturation (Glaser and Strauss)

Theoretical sampling:

Theoretical sampling is the process of data collection for generating theory whereby the analyst jointly collects, codes, and analyzes his data and decides what data to collect next and where to find them, in order to develop his theory as it emerges. This process of data collection is *controlled* by the emerging theory ...The basic question in theoretical sampling (in either substantive or formal theory) is: *what* groups or subgroups does one turn to *next* in data collection? And for *what* theoretical purpose? In short, how does the sociologist select multiple comparison groups? The possibility of multiple comparisons are infinite, and so groups must be chosen according to theoretical criteria. (1967: 45, 47)

Theoretical saturation:

The criterion for judging when to stop sampling the different groups pertinent to a category is the category's *theoretical saturation. Saturation* means that no additional data are being found whereby the sociologist can develop properties of the category. As he sees similar instances over and over again, the researcher becomes empirically confident that a category is saturated. He goes out of his way to look for groups that stretch diversity of data as far as possible, just to make certain that saturation is based on the widest possible range of data on the category ... The adequate theoretical sampling is judged on the basis of how widely and diversely the analyst chose his groups for saturating categories according to the type of theory he wished to develop. The adequate statistical sample, on the other hand, is judged on the basis of techniques of random and stratified sampling used in relation to the social structure of a group for groups sampled. The inadequate theoretical sample is easily spotted, since the theory associated with it is usually thin and not well integrated, and has too many obvious unexplained exceptions. (1967: 61, 63)

preconceived ideas. Instead, it is a rigorous strategy for producing thoroughly saturated theoretical accounts.

The method of constant comparison proceeds in four stages, shown in Box 18.3

First, incidents in data are coded into categories so that the different incidents that have been grouped together by the coding process can be compared. Very quickly, this begins to generate ideas about the properties of the category. An example taken (and somewhat modified) from the work of Glaser and Strauss (1964) can be given.

As they observed nurses in hospital wards they noticed that when a patient died nurses commonly would reflect on the death, expressing sentiments such as 'He was so young', 'He was to be a doctor', 'She had a full life' or 'What will the children do without her?' These moments were coded as *social loss stories* by Glaser and Strauss, indicating that some calculation was being made of the degree to which the death represented a loss. As they looked at these different incidents, they gathered that this category had certain properties. For example, age, social class and parental status

Box 18.3   Four stages of the constant comparative method

1   Code data into **categories** so that items with shared characteristics are placed together. (*Example of a category:* the 'social loss story'.)
2   Integrate categories and their **properties**. (*Example of properties:* age and education, which interact to influence the kind of social loss story told.)
3   Reach theoretical saturation.
4   Write the theory.

appeared to influence the calculation of social loss.

The second stage of the constant comparative method involves the integration of categories and their properties, noting for example, how properties interact. From detailed inspection and comparison of instances, it became clear that age and education interacted, so that educational level was very important in calculating social loss if the person who died was a middle aged adult; for a very elderly person, though, educational level was of little importance. Additionally, at this second stage, the interaction of different categories is noted. Glaser and Strauss found that nurses sometimes lost their composure and wept when certain patients died, but did not do so in other cases. This, established through constantly comparing different instances, related to whether a social loss story constituted a successful rationale for the death. Death could be understood as a welcome relief in some cases, but a dreadful tragedy with which nurses identified in others.

The third stage is represented by theoretical saturation, discussed earlier, in which no new properties of categories appear, and no new interactions occur. Theoretical sampling will appear to have exhausted all such possibilities. The fourth stage, writing the theory, is then relatively straightforward, since categories and their interactions provide chapter headings or titles of papers, properties provide section headings and the coded data provide plentiful illustrative examples, which may even be counted so that the reader may assess the generality of the phenomena described. Theories developed in this way will, in the first instance, be *substantive*, in that they explain the immediate phenomena of interest to the researcher. However, they may be thought generalizable to other related settings, in which

case their potential scope is considerably broadened. Thus, as a substantive theory, the idea of the social loss rationale may only be applied in the sort of health care settings in which the theory was developed. But in a *formal* extrapolation, it might be applied more generally to the relationships between professionals and their clients. Thus, it can be hypothesized that all professionals involved in the provision of human services (social workers, teachers etc.) may calculate the social value of their clients according to their age, social class, educational background and so on, and vary the quality of their service to suit this perceived social value. Glaser and Strauss therefore distinguish between **substantive** and **formal** theories.

Later developments and disagreements

Both Glaser and Strauss have produced further book-length statements about the grounded theory approach (Glaser, 1978, 1992; Strauss, 1987; Strauss and Corbin, 1990). Of these, Strauss and Corbin (1990) is perhaps the best known, being a distillation of years of experience in supervising students and other researchers applying the original grounded theory approach, which in the 1967 book was expressed in language at times difficult to apply. The Strauss and Corbin volume has more the feel of a textbook to it, focusing on showing researchers how to apply a well-established method by applying some well-tried procedures.

Strauss and Corbin are also significant in introducing three distinctive ways of coding data (see Box 18.4).

In **open coding**, the researcher is involved in naming and categorizing phenomena through close examination of data. Without this first basic analytical step, the rest of the analysis and com-

---

Box 18.4   Coding in grounded theory

1 *Open coding*
   Marking instances of data according to emerging analytic themes
2 *Axial coding*
   Exploring the interconnections of coding categories
3 *Selective coding*
   Core categories are identified

---

munication that follows could not take place. During open coding the data are broken down into discrete parts, closely examined, compared for similarities and differences, and questions are asked about the phenomena as reflected in the data. Through this process, one's own and others' assumptions about phenomena are questioned or explored, leading to new discoveries. (Strauss and Corbin, 1990: 62)

Subsequently, **axial coding** becomes relevant, according to Strauss and Corbin. This involves intensive work with a single category, examining how it connects with other categories and seeking to explore its 'conditions, contexts, action/ interactional strategies and consequences' (1990: 96). The third type of coding activity Strauss and Corbin called **selective coding**, and this they associate with the point at which a fully fledged theory emerges. Taking a single 'core category' (such as 'awareness contexts' (Glaser and Strauss, 1966) or 'dying trajectory' (Glaser and Strauss, 1968)), all other categories and their properties are regarded as subsidiary to the core. Strauss and Corbin give an example from Corbin's (1987) work (see Box 18.5).

To call these three things 'coding' is something of a sleight of hand, as it is clear that only the first constitutes 'coding' as it was conceptualized in the 1967 book. Axial and selective 'coding' are in fact further elaborations of open codes, through a method of constant comparison. The book has a rather programmatic, formulaic feel to it and tends, according to Glaser (1992) in a critical response, to encourage an unwelcome degree of preconception. Glaser argues, too, that there is too much stress on verification in Strauss and Corbin, thus returning to one of the central issues of the original work on grounded theory. Indeed, a number of critics of grounded theorizing (Hammersley, 1995b; Hammersley and Atkinson, 1995; Rose, 1982) have noted both that theory *verification* should be regarded as important to qualitative researchers, and that Glaser and Strauss failed to recognize in their own work strong elements of theory *testing*. Glaser's main point of disagreement, though, concerns the over-technical, rule-following behaviour which is expected of researchers following the Strauss and Corbin text. He prefers to stress the centrality of the idea of constant comparison as containing the simple central idea of grounded theorizing:

> Strauss' method of labelling and then grouping is totally unnecessary, laborious and is a waste of time. Using constant comparison method gets the analyst to the desired conceptual power, quickly, with ease and joy. Categories emerge upon comparison and properties emerge upon more comparison. And that is all there is to it. (Glaser, 1992: 43)

Limitations and criticisms of grounded theory

A number of criticisms of grounded theorizing have emerged, some of which simply point out limitations in its applicability to all kinds of research problems, others of which suggest radically different conceptions of the research process and are not so easily addressed.

Limited applicability?

In the latter category is the point made by Brown (1973), who observes that grounded theorizing is

---

Box 18.5 An example of selective coding

In Corbin's (1987) study of the approach of women with chronic illness towards their pregnancies she found that the women played an active part in managing pregnancy risks. The core category which eventually emerged was that of *protective governing*, in which women were understood to be continually monitoring the risk status of their pregnancies, taking cues from a variety of sources including signs and the reactions of others. A variety of categories of action emanated from protective governing, including at times a trusting and cooperative relationship with health care staff, but at others a withdrawal from this relationship in order to 'save their babies'.

---

an inappropriate methodology for certain types of research problem. Brown, for example, was interested in unconscious processes at work in the connection between social factors and mental disorder, inferring the existence of these by demonstrating causal links that could be explained by no other means. Clearly, such things cannot be observed directly. Brown also notes that the study of certain types of long-term historical process would not be feasible with a grounded theory approach. For example, grounded theory could not be used to investigate the influence of economic recession on workers' willingness to strike, or the impact of warfare on the suicide rate. Thus he argues:

> [Grounded theory] may only be profitable in a fairly limited range of circumstances. The type of material best given to the development of grounded theory ... tends to involve relatively short-term processes, sequences of behaviour that are directly observed or can be easily reported upon, and behaviour which has a repetitive character. Something missed can often be observed again. (1973 :8)

In defence of grounded theory, though, we can say that Brown's points relate not so much to the

analytic methods described by Glaser and Strauss – the method of constant comparison, theoretical sampling and so on – but more to the common dependence of grounded theory on observational and interview data. In fact there is no logical reason why other types of data cannot be included in the approach. Comparative analysis, using historical records that relate to large scale societal developments, for example, has a distinguished history in social research (Llobera, 1998), though its practitioners will rarely have conceptualized their methods in terms of grounded theory.

Modernist assumptions?

A more radical critic is Denzin who, in reviewing a book by Strauss (1987) in which grounded theorizing was once again outlined, wrote the words contained in Box 18.6. This review does not so much criticize the approach as claim that it is now old-fashioned, with a variety of *postmodernist* approaches now being 'in'.

Denzin roots his criticism in the view that the modernist assumption of an empirical world that can be studied objectively by qualitative methods is no longer sustainable. He makes the apparently democratic point that the scientific emphasis on theories generated by

---

Box 18.6   Denzin's review of Strauss's (1987) book *Qualitative Analysis for Social Scientists*

'... this book marks the end of an era. It signals a turning point in the history of qualitative research in American sociology. At the very moment that this work finds its place in the libraries of scholars and students, it is being challenged by a new body of work coming from the neighboring fields of anthropology and cultural studies. Post-Geertzian anthropologists (Marcus, Tyler, Clifford, Bruner, Turner, Pratt, Asad, Rosaldo, Crapanzano, Fischer, Rabinow) are now writing on the politics and poetics of ethnography. They are taking seriously the question "How do we write culture?" They are proposing that postmodern ethnography can no longer follow the guidelines of positivist social science. Gone are words like theory, hypothesis, concept, indicator, coding scheme, sampling, validity, and reliability. In their place comes a new language: readerly texts, modes of discourse, cultural poetics, deconstruction, interpretation, domination, feminism, genre, grammatology, hermeneutics, inscription, master narrative, narrative structures, otherness, postmodernism, redemptive ethnography, semiotics, subversion, textuality, tropes.' (1988: 432)

researchers gets in the way of paying close attention to the theories people use in everyday life. He also claims that Strauss's modernist demand to make generalizations across cases gets in the way of a detailed focus on the individual characteristics of particular cases, observing that 'By making qualitative research "scientifically" respectable, researchers may be imposing schemes of interpretation on the social world that simply do not fit that world as it is constructed and lived by interacting individuals' (1988: 432).

Over-reliance on coding?

Somewhat linked to the postmodernist critique of grounded theory are the points made by Coffey, Holbrook and Atkinson (1996), who object to the narrow analytic strategy imposed by a heavy reliance on coding as a first step. This, they feel, is particularly encouraged by computer software for the analysis of qualitative data, based on a code-and-retrieve logic (see Chapter 23). Some approaches to qualitative analysis, say these authors, do not involve the coding and retrieval approach of grounded theorizing. Thus, they argue that *discourse analysis* (Potter and Wetherell 1987), or the analysis of formal narrative structure (for example, Riessman 1993), depend more on the thoughtful teasing out of the subtle and various meanings of particular words, or on a global perception of whole structures within data, that are otherwise fragmented and decontextualized if discrete segments are coded and grouped with others under invented categories (see Chapter 27 for an account of these methods).

Coffey et al. (1996) propose instead an approach to data analysis and representation that is consistent with postmodern sensibilities. This depends on the use of 'hypertext' links, which preserve data in their original form, allowing the 'reader' or user to leap from one link to another in an exploration of data that is open-ended, akin to the experience of the original producers of the data themselves. They equate grounded theorizing with an attempt to impose a single, exclusive interpretation of data, and advocate their hypertext alternative as allowing a much more open-ended presentation, recognizing multiple meanings which both actors and readers may bring to instances of text.

Against this, Kelle (1997) has pointed out that the equation of coding with grounded theorizing, and indeed with the imposition of singular interpretations, is somewhat forced. He argues instead that two broad possibilities exist for data analysts who wish to identify similarities and differences between particular text passages, and that these had been in existence in various branches of scholarship (including biblical hermeneutics) for hundreds of years, before becoming an issue for social scientists. On the one hand are *indexes*, such as an author or subject index in a book. 'Coding' of the sort described by Glaser and Strauss might equally well be termed 'indexing', in this sense. On the other hand, *cross references* can be constructed, of the sort Coffey et al. describe in their advocacy of hyperlinks, whereby textual passages are linked together. A King James Bible contains such devices, so that a teaching of Jesus in one of the Gospels is linked with the Old Testament passage to which Jesus refers.

Kelle then observes that in biblical scholarship 'techniques for indexing or cross references are used similarly by all interpreters ... whether they take into account or not the polyvocality and diversity of biblical authors ...' (1997: 2.4). The distinction between the two, made by Coffey et al., which equates indexing with univocality and cross-references with polyvocality is, Kelle argues, therefore unsustainable (see Chapter 4 for an account of *polyvocality*). This diversion into the deeper reaches of the scholarly tradition is helpful in addressing some issues raised by postmodern critics of grounded theorizing.

Conclusion

Many qualitative researchers are attached to the ideas of grounded theorizing and do not wish to dismiss these as inconsistent with contemporary sensibilities or to opt, wholesale, for the postmodern alternative à la Denzin. Grounded theory emerged at a time when scientific conceptions of qualitative research were rather dominant and literary, postmodern conceptions had not yet taken off. More technical explanations

---

Box 18.7 Web pointers for grounded theory

The Grounded Theory Institute
www.groundedtheory.com/

Grounded theory: doing it as part of public discourse
www.habermas.org/grndthry.htm

Grounded theory: a thumbnail sketch
www.scu.edu.au/schools/gcm/ar/arp/grounded.html

Visit the website for this book at www.rscbook.co.uk to link to these web pointers.

---

of the procedures involved are sometimes unwelcome reminders of this, but the spirit that lies behind the approach can be simply explained, and does not have to be attached to a naively realist epistemology, or indeed to an oppressive urge to force readers to regard its products as true for all time. It demands a rigorous spirit of self-awareness and self-criticism, as well as an openness to new ideas that is often a hallmark of research studies of good quality.

Further reading

The best place to start in finding out more is the original book on grounded theory by Glaser and Strauss (1967). I have written a more extended outline of the method as Chapter 7 in Seale (1999). In addition, you can see how researchers have actually used the approach by reading a book edited by Strauss and Corbin (1997) called *Grounded Theory in Practice* which contains reports of studies written by leading researchers using grounded theory.

Student Reader (Seale, 2004): relevant readings

32   Barney G. Glaser and Anselm L. Strauss: 'Theoretical sampling'
44   Anselm L. Strauss and Juliet Corbin: 'Open coding'
46   Udo Kelle: 'Theory building in qualitative research and computer programs for the management of textual data'

Key concepts

	Concept–indicator links
Axial coding	Constant comparison
Open coding	Substantive and formal theories
Selective coding	Theoretical sampling
Categories and properties	Theoretical saturation

19

Doing historical and archival research

Ben Gidley

CONTENTS

Doing archival or historical research is not a 'method' in the way that, say, doing ethnography is. Instead, we are talking about using a particular type of data – data generated in the past, stored in archives – which can be researched using a variety of methods. This chapter will show you what kinds of data are available in archives, tell you how to gain access to archives and introduce you to methodological issues relevant to their use.

Sources

The first matter to consider in approaching historical and archival research is the different types of available *source material*. Each of these can be used in different ways, depending on what our research question is. The types of historical source we can use include *primary* and *secondary* sources, and *oral* and *documentary* sources. In the first section of this chapter we will see what these different types of sources are, which will also allow us to get to grips with the basic terminology used in this field of research.

Primary and secondary sources

The most common distinction made between types of historical source is that between primary and secondary sources (Box 19.1).

Primary and secondary sources have different strengths and weaknesses. Just because someone witnessed something, we should not see it as a completely accurate account; the witness might have some particular motive for highlighting certain aspects of their experience rather than others. This might make the primary source 'unreliable', but it remains interesting to social researchers because of what it reveals about the way that the account was produced.

Oral and documentary sources

Another key distinction is between *oral* and *documentary* sources (Box 19.2).

Oral sources can be used in a huge variety of ways. To give a couple of examples, anthropologists Richard and Sally Price have worked

---

Box 19.1   Primary and secondary sources

Primary sources are actual records that have survived from the past, which may include *texts*, such as letters or diaries, or *material* artefacts like articles of clothing or shards of bone, *visual* artefacts such as photographs, *audio-visual* sources, such as film or tape recordings. These were produced in conditions of *proximity* (in time and space) to the events described.

Secondary sources are accounts created by people writing at some *distance* in space or time from the events described. For example, a historical textbook, written by someone one who did not experience or witness the events being described, is a secondary source. But it will draw on primary sources, on the recollections or reports of those who actually did experience of witness the events.

Box 19.2   Oral and documentary sources

Oral sources are the memories of people who lived through a historical moment, as related out loud, usually to an interviewer some time after the event. These are generally recorded and transcribed.

Documentary sources are written sources – personal letters, diaries, scrapbooks, memoirs, legislation, newspaper clippings, business accounts, marriage contracts. These might have been produced at the time of the events described, or some time later.

---

intensively with the oral history of the Saramaka Maroons – descendents of runaway slaves in Suriname, South America – culminating in their book *Two Evenings in Saramaka* (1991), which records verbatim two long sessions of Maroon story-telling, while historian Jerry White, in his books *Rothschild Buildings* (1980) and *The Worst Street in North London* (1986) present a complex picture of the recent history of two tiny neighbourhoods in London. Many of the methodological issues that concern oral history are similar to those concerning qualitative interviews in general (see Chapter 14).

Documentary sources will often have survived because they were kept in someone's personal collection, in a file somewhere, or an archive. There is a vast range of documentary sources, some personal, like diaries or letters, some official, like police reports or council memos, some corporate, like a company's accounts. Some documentary and primary sources have been digitized or put on microfilm or microfiche, or collected and printed in anthologies and sourcebooks. When using these, you should be aware that you are looking at something different from the original documentary sources.

Public and private, internal and external

Sometimes a distinction is drawn between documents for *internal* consumption – like a memo between two civil servants – and documents for *external* consumption – like a report those two civil servants wrote for publication. Related to this distinction is whether the document is publicly accessible today, regardless of whether it was intended for public consumption. In this sense, documents can be categorized into four further types (Scott, 1990):

- *Closed* – such as top secret espionage reports
- *Restricted* – documents which a researcher must get special permission to access
- *Open-archival* – something held in an archive like the UK Public Record Office (PRO), which can be consulted by anyone who goes there

- *Open-published* – something fully in the public domain because it has been published, which today includes documents published on the web

In making these sorts of distinctions, it is important to remember that the category into which a document falls might change over time. For example, the British government keeps secret documents 'closed' for a set period of time before making them accessible in the PRO. The way the PRO works is bound by the Official Secrets Act, and if you are researching politically sensitive topics – like the IRA or the Communist Party – you may come up against the restricted or closed data.

Why might I use archival sources?

Social research is often thought of in terms of researchers engaging directly with members of society – with methods such as interviews and participant observation. Archival research, on the other hand, is often seen as dry and dusty work, associated with other disciplines like history. However, as John Scott points out (1990), some of the classic texts in social science have been based on documentary or archive research:

- *Durkheim's* seminal work on *Suicide* (see Chapter 2) was based on an analysis of official records.
- *Weber's* research on religion that led to studies like *The Protestant Work Ethic*, was based on historical material.
- *Marx's* great texts, like *Capital*, were based on an analysis of government records archived in the British Museum.

There are a number of reasons why you might want to use archival and documentary sources to research society or culture. These are outlined in Box 19.3 and examples of each are given below.

The only means of access

Most obviously, the archive might be the best or only way of *accessing* the data that exist on your research question. 'Data on the phenomenon you

---

Box 19.3 Reasons for using archival sources

Archives may:

1 be the only means of access
2 allow a glimpse 'behind the scenes'
3 allow for *triangulation*
4 allow us to trace the *genealogy of ideas*
5 provide access to marginalized voices

---

are interested in may simply *not be available in other forms'* (Mason, 1996: 73). There may be no witnesses left alive or willing to talk or available to you.

For example, in my own research, I set out to examine East London Jewish radicals in early twentieth-century London, to find out how they understood their sense of identity and belonging. I originally contemplated oral history interviews, but as I began to focus on a historical period over 80 years earlier, I realized that I would not be able to interview many people involved in this milieu and turned to archival sources.

A glimpse behind the scenes

Archives can give you a glimpse behind the scenes. We can think of the insights archives offer in terms of Erving Goffman's analogy of 'frontstage' and 'backstage' identities, which he developed in his classic book *The Presentation of Self in Everyday Life* (1959). Goffman contrasted the 'official stance' of an organization or team or its members, visible in their 'frontstage' presentation, to their 'backstage' or 'off-the-record' performances. 'Backstage', Goffman suggested, conflicts, contradictions and ambiguities are more often expressed.

An example of this can be found in Clive Harris's work, which draws meticulously on official documents from the Public Record Office. He examined the racialization of black people in twentieth-century Britain, working closely on the text to trace the emergence of black identities within official discourses. He writes that:

The documentation ... clearly demonstrates the extent to which racism permeated the culture of the British establishment long before the introduction of formal immigration control ... [It] is drawn extensively from government archives only recently made available to scrutiny. (Harris, 1991: 2)

He shows that, even when the official 'frontstage' pronouncements of senior civil servants seemed not to use racist language, in their minutes and memos to each other, when they presented their 'backstage' identities, they frequently used a language that racialized black people.

Another reason why the glimpse behind the scenes that the archive allows provides a useful research tool is that we can see the workings that led to particular policies or practices emerging. For instance, using official archives we can see the discussions that went on behind the scenes before decisions were made, or we can see how particular languages or phrases came into use. An example of this is given in Box 19.4.

Triangulation

Many archives provide great opportunities for *triangulating* data (see Chapter 7). A government archive on conscientious objectors during a war – such as can be found in the Home Office files of the PRO – includes not just the government's view of the issue, but a wealth of materials which provide other perspectives. There might be, for example, pacifist leaflets, police transcriptions of speeches given at anti-war meetings, clippings from newspapers of different persuasions, notes of delegations made to ministers by anti-conscription groups. Sources such as these can be compared with the official views to provide a

---

Box: 19.4   Behind the scenes of MI5

This example comes from the government files of Vernon Kell, the first head of what was to become MI5 – who took the codename 'K', a name said to have led James Bond's creator Ian Fleming to call 007's boss 'M'.

During the First World War, Kell was involved in deciding which foreigners should and should not be interned in camps to protect public safety. He wrote a circular to the police that certain enemy aliens should be exempted from the internment 'because, although subjects of an alien power, they are assumed on racial or political grounds to be friendly' (PRO HO 45/19881/338498/2).

In the Home Office files, we can see a civil servant, Troup, amending this to read: 'because, although *technically* subjects of an alien power, they have been *ascertained* to be on *racial* grounds friendly to the allies and hostile to the enemy' (PRO HO 45/19881/ 338498/2; emphasis added)

In these changes, we can see the emergence of a way of thinking that contrasted the 'technical' subjecthood of empires with a 'racial' belonging to nation-states. This way of thinking is interesting because it was to inform the British government's support of the creation of a mosaic of 'racial' nation-states in Europe at the end of the war, and because it is the first time that 'racial' criteria were used in Britain as part of immigration control.

---

more reliable account of the moment. Similarly, when looking at recent history, documentary sources can be triangulated against oral sources.

The genealogy of ideas

Historical research allows us to trace the **genealogy of ideas** or institutions that are important today. Geoff Pearson (1983), for example, traced the way in which discussions of criminality and violence had been conducted over the years. He was able to question the idea that we are living in a time of exceptional criminality and violence compared with 'the good old days' by examining texts from the past that revealed identical 'respectable fears' being expressed in every generation.

Marginalized voices

Archives are useful because they provide access to voices that have been marginalized in previous historical literatures. Clive Harris, whose work was mentioned earlier, concludes his article on his archival research by saying:

No apologies are offered for not trying to document … the lives of the victims of racism. That I leave to others. What I have

aimed to do is shift attention to those structures of power which have proved so resistant to change, and thereby examine the micropolitics of the different institutions within the state in order to disclose the way in which techniques and practices were codified to secure the exercise of social control and domination. Only in this way can the silences of history be made to speak and fractured narratives restored. (1991: 28–9)

In other words, there is an ethical or political reason to work with archival material.

How to access an archive: practical issues

How you go about using an archive will depend on your research question. In general, though, it is advisable to begin with a *preliminary investigation*. This means finding out about the archives that may be useful in answering your research questions. You can go about this in several ways.

- *Secondary sources* on topics similar to yours will often have drawn on primary sources which you might also find useful. Check their references to find what these were.

- There are a number of guides to primary sources available. These range from the very general to the very specific (see 'Further reading' at the end of this chapter).
- Once you have located the archives you want to use, they will have **indexes**, sometimes in printed form, sometimes electronic. As more and more indexes are being digitized, they are becoming easier to search, for instance using keywords or dates.
- Major archives like the UK Public Record Office publish leaflets and guides to the sorts of materials they have.

Once you have conducted a preliminary investigation, you can begin to gather your data. A few practical issues arise at this point, some of which might be obvious, others less so.

- *Find out when the archive is open!* Specialized archives are notorious for having peculiar opening hours.
- *Consider how you want to take notes.* Many archives charge a lot for photocopying or are very particular about what you can copy – this is because of their duty to preserve documents. Many do not allow you to use a pen when taking notes; this is the case in the PRO and the Rare Manuscripts room of the British Library, both of which require you to use a pencil. Some provide power sources for laptop computers; others do not let you carry a bag.
- *Plan timings for your visits.* There is only so much time you can spend doing archival research in one go. If you are looking at hand-written documents, this can strain your eyes, as can working with microfiche or microfilm.

Methodological debates

In approaching historical documents, we can identify two broad ways of working. These are exactly parallel to the distinction made between *topic* and *resource* in discussing the status of material derived from qualitative interviews (see Chapter 14) and relate to the broad distinction between *realism* and *idealism*

that was introduced in Chapter 2.

The realist approach to archival work involves gathering as great a volume of texts as possible and scouring them for details of 'who,' 'when,' 'where' and 'what' – to use texts as *evidence*, as a representation of reality. This approach has often taken the documents themselves at face value – seeing them as a research *resource*. This approach reflects a decision made at the *epistemological* level (that is, in terms of the theory of knowledge and truth involved). The problem with it, from an idealist or *social constructionist* point of view, is as follows: just as ethnographic interviews are never completely transparent windows into present social reality, archived documentary sources are never perfect windows into the past. Rather, they are socially produced. As David Silverman has written:

> people who generate and use such documents are concerned with how accurately they represent reality. Conversely, ethnographers are concerned with the social organisation of documents, irrespective of whether they are accurate or inaccurate, true or biased. (1993: 61)

Atkinson and Coffey make a similar point when they describe documents as 'social facts': produced, shared and used in socially organized ways, not transparent representations of realities (1997: 47)

The social constructionist approach sees archived texts as *topic* rather than *resource* – as realities in themselves rather than a way of accessing some other reality. This approach is not concerned with the accuracy of the descriptions given in the documents, but in their social organization. That is, how are different discourses (and the different identities which emerge from them) produced?

These different approaches imply different ways of attending to *how* documents are produced. Those who see documents in a realist manner – as a window onto social reality – might be concerned about issues of authenticity, for example. Those who see documents from a constructionist perspective would be concerned, in contrast, to analyse the various ways in which social reality is constructed in documents. We will look at some of these issues here.

Issues of validity and reliability

If archived texts are to be used as *evidence*, as they are from a realist viewpoint which takes them to be a means of accessing past social realities, a number of issues of validity and reliability arise. Archives are *partial:* certain documents are archived whilst others are not. For example, the views of a managing director are more likely to survive in a company's archive than the views of a receptionist, while a managing director's views that come to be considered embarrassing might be shredded. Because of this, it is possible to argue that archival data is insufficiently reliable and valid.

Scott (1990: 6) suggests that we should judge an archived document by four criteria:

- *Authenticity:* is it genuine?
- *Credibility:* is it undistorted?
- *Representativeness:* is it typical of its kind?
- *Meaning:* is the evidence clear and comprehensible?

On one level, authenticity is a key issue for archival research. Documentary sources can, for example, turn out to be fakes (see Box 19.5).

Among the scholars who showed that the 'Hitler diaries' were fake was David Irving. Irving came to greater prominence in 2000, when he sued historian Deborah Lipstadt and her publisher Penguin Books for libelling him. In her book *Denying the Holocaust: The Growing Assault on Truth and Memory* (1993), Lipstadt had alleged that Irving had persistently and deliberately misinterpreted and twisted historical evidence to minimize Hitler's culpability for the Holocaust, which Irving claimed was defamatory. The judge eventually ruled against Irving. Box 19.6 shows some comments made after the case was decided. This example points to how seriously we must take issues of reliability and validity if we want to use documents as evidence of some reality that exists outside the documents.

Producing documentary realities

You can see from the last comment from the historian David Cesarani that he had a slightly different view of the trial than the other commentators. He argued that it was important for historians to take part in public debates, but expressed doubts about translating historical argument to a court of law. He argues that context and circumstance are central to the way that social scientists must use historical data. In support of this more constructionist view of documents Atkinson and Coffey write:

> Texts are constructed according to conventions that are themselves part of a documentary reality. Hence, rather than ask whether an account is true, or whether it can be used as 'valid' evidence about a research setting, it is more fruitful to ask ourselves questions about the form and function of texts themselves. (1997: 61)

Box 19.5 The case of 'Hitler's diaries'

In 1983, the German magazine *Stern* bought what it believed to be Adolf Hitler's war-time diaries. Although a number of historians – most significantly Hugh Trevor-Roper – accepted the authenticity of the diaries, they turned out to be forged. For example:

- The notebooks in which the 'diaries' were written were of post-war manufacture, and contained threads that were not made before the 1950s.
- The monogram on the front of one diary read 'FH' rather than 'AH'.
- The texts of the diaries contained historical inaccuracies and anachronisms.
- The ink used was chemically modern, and tests showed that it was recently applied to the paper.

Box 19.6   Comments on the David Irving holocaust denial case

'It was a struggle for truth and for memory.' Deborah Lipstadt (quoted in Busfield, 2000)
'No objective, fair-minded historian would have serious cause to doubt that there were gas chambers at Auschwitz and that they were operated on a substantial scale to kill hundreds of thousands of Jews.' (The judge, quoted in Busfield, 2000)

'This wasn't a trial about what happened in the second world war, it was a trial about Irving's methodology ... A serious historian has to take account of all the evidence. Irving does not do this; he fabricates.' (Richard Evans, historian and witness in the court case, quoted in Moss, 2000)

'Evidence in history is not like evidence in court ... In a court of law, context and circumstance are the least important evidence; they may be deemed inadmissible, not real evidence. The court wants physical evidence, a fingerprint that no one can argue with, but in history context and circumstance matter a great deal.' (David Cesarani, quoted in Moss, 2000)

And Silverman writes similarly about official files:

> Like all documents, files are produced in particular circumstances for particular audiences. Files never speak for themselves. The ethnographer seeks to understand both the format of a file (for example, the categories used on blank sheets) and the processes associated with its completion. (1993: 61)

There are three main aspects of archived documents to which we should attend in thinking about how they construct social and cultural meanings:

- The relationships between documents (their **intertextuality**)
- The **genre conventions** according to which they are written
- Their actual material production

Box 19.7   Intertextuality: relationships of sequence and hierarchy

A **relationship of sequence** might be the order in which documents were intended to be read or the order in which they were produced. For example:

- A memo replying to another memo
- The 'Matters Arising' section of a set of minutes which refers back to the minutes of the previous meeting
- The sequence in which two documents are filed or archived

Relationships of hierarchy between documents are not so straightforward, but here are some examples:

- Who in an organization *writes* a document, to whom it is *sent*, who has *the right to correct* it, who *reads the summary* of a document and who *summarizes* it, who has to *act* on it

These things depend on the formal and informal division of labour in an organization, a hierarchy which is inscribed in the documents.

Intertextuality and genre

Documents are related to each other *intertextually* in two key ways: there are relationships of *sequence* and relationships of *hierarchy*. These are shown in Box 19.7.

Atkinson and Coffey (1997: 55) use the term **intertextuality** to talk about the relationships between documents. This term comes from literary theory and refers to the hidden connections between texts, the way texts echo within other texts, whether explicitly or implicitly. The examples of 'Matters Arising' in minutes or a memo responding to another memo are examples of an *explicit* relationship between documents, as would be a citation of a newspaper report in a government file. *Implicit* relationships between documents might include shared conventions or style.

As Atkinson and Coffey note, documents are also often marked by the use of characteristic *registers* or **genres**, by which we can recognize what type of document we are looking at. We can easily recognize a set of corporate minutes, for example, by the way they are set out – and the same goes for a menu, a trial transcript, a set of medical notes, a diary, and so on. To say that documents share a genre is to say that they may follow prescribed formats, or have particular conventions and assumptions built into them. For example, in the minutes of a meeting, 'Matters Arising' always comes near the beginning and 'Any Other Business' near the end – just as the soups and

starters section of a menu comes before the list of desserts and coffees. The conventions of documentary genres include not just the order they are set out in but also the language they use. Official documents, for example, often use the passive voice and the third person ('it is felt that' rather than 'we feel') and often avoid expressing explicit opinions, emotions or beliefs. These characteristics of the linguistic register of documents may give them **facticity**, the sense of neutral, objective truth that we associate with bureaucracy. Another term for this is to say that official documents often **naturalize** the categories with which they deal, making these seem 'natural' and therefore unquestionable. This is a very different usage of the term 'natural' from *naturalistic* (used to describe the advantages of studying people in their natural settings – see Chapter 17) and *naturalism* (used to indicate the view that the natural and social sciences are unified at the level of methodology – see Chapter 2).

As well as the linguistic register, non-textual elements, like layout, also follow genre conventions. To follow the same example, official documents often use bullet points, lists and tables and rarely use extravagant typefaces – again reinforcing the sense of facticity and authority.

Genre also helps determine what is *excluded* from the text. Thus Casement (Box 19.8) put in his diary facts about his sex life and his daily expenses, as well as his emotional reactions to the atrocities he was witnessing; he did not put these

---

Box 19.8 Achieving facticity in documents

Anthropologist Michael Taussig (1987) has worked from various archival sources on the rubber terror in the Putamayo in Colombia in the early twentieth century – including the reports of Roger Casement, the British Consul-General in the Putamayo, there investigating atrocities committed in the rubber trade, as well as the edited versions of those reports produced by Casement's superior, the Foreign Secretary, Sir Edward Grey. Taussig describes the way in which the publication of stories in print and their repetition in legal spaces 'facilitated shifts in reality involved in the metamorphosis of gossip into fact and of story into truth' (1987: 33). He describes the shift in the mode of description between Casement's informants in the Putamayo, Casement's write up of their stories and finally the editing of Casement's report by bureaucrats back in Whitehall. Taussig suggests that Casement's report (in contrast to his diary) and Grey's editing exemplify 'what we could call the "objectivist fiction", namely, the contrived manner by which objectivity is created, and its profound dependence on the magic of style to make this trick of truth work' (1987: 37).

in his official reports. Diaries rarely record the number of times the diarist visits the bathroom in a given day. Menus rarely record the amount of fat or vitamins in a dish, while frozen food packaging is required to. Minutes do not record every comment made at a meeting but they will record the decisions reached – thus preserving the dominant or prevailing opinions for future archival researchers, but not necessarily the marginalized or minority ones.

Another example of archival research which treats the texts as research topics in themselves and works to unpack the official document's naturalizing 'trick of truth' is Karl Marx's work. Marx's use of documents as evidence is in many ways characteristic of how archives can be read critically to research society and culture. Box 19.9 shows how he approached official documents relating to laws regulating factory work.

When Marx speaks of 'listening' to the Inspectors, he is suggesting that the official texts produced by the Inspectors - supposedly neutral and objective - had a *voice*, a particular register, to which we can listen, in order to produce a critical understanding of the social reality the reports described and sought to naturalize. Marx's method involves taking the official categories, the analytical boxes into which the government inspectors place the phenomena they observe, and shows how these categories are *produced*, shows the human stories of suffering and struggle which shape these categories. The apparently commonsense official categories of 'full-time,' 'half-time' and 'the working day', he reveals, were produced socially, and carried particular cultural and historical baggage, which can be traced by tracing the *genealogies* of these terms.

The production of documents

What Taussig and Marx alert us to is that we cannot take the formats of official texts for granted: they are not *natural* but are *culturally constructed*.

Box 19.9   Official documents in Marx's *Capital*

The documentary material
The chapter in *Capital* called 'The Working Day' largely consists of a close reading of the body of official documentation relating to the Factory Acts. The Factory Acts were a series of laws passed in nineteenth-century England regulating the length of the working day and the conditions of labour within factories. A key provision of the first Factory Act, which was passed in 1850, was the creation of a small army of Factory Inspectors, who enforced the terms of the Act, collating reports on conditions which were passed to the government. 'Let us listen for a moment to the factory inspectors,' Marx writes.

Children depicted as units of time
The Inspectors write about workers as 'full-timers' and 'half-timers'. Under the provisions of the Factory Acts, children under 13 were only allowed to work six hours a day, and it is these children who are being described when the Inspectors speak of 'half-timers'. Marx comments: 'The worker is here nothing more than personified labour-time. All individual distinctions are obliterated in that between "full-timers" and "half-timers".'

Constructing the 'working day'
The category of the working day itself, which seems to have a common-sense meaning, is far from natural and obvious, but is likewise produced socially. As Marx puts it: 'the working day is not a fixed but a fluid quantity.' He argues that it was the struggle of the workers to reduce the length of the working day, and the struggle of capital to keep it long, that produced the definitions of the working day that are then inscribed in the law through things like the Factory Acts.

Box 19.10   Studies of the way documents are produced

- Garfinkel (1967) examined the way in which death certificates are written
- Sudnow (1965) looked at how crime records are generated through plea bargaining.
- Cicourel (1968) studied the way records were assembled on 'juvenile delinquents' in the American criminal justice system.
- David Silverman has looked at how a UK local government organization's selection interviews constituted a file (Silverman, 1975, Silverman and Jones, 1976)
- Dingwall (1977) looked at how health visitors produce their notes and how these are filed.
- Latour and Woolgar (1986) examined the way scientific facts are produced.

We must *learn* to produce documents like these – and *learn* to read them. A number of studies since the 1960s have highlighted the social processes at work in the production of particular types of document (see Box 19.10). These sorts of studies, rather than being concerned with whether the files were 'true' or 'false', have used files to reveal the social conditions of their own production. This sort of work makes us go beyond the actual documents and files themselves to the social context in which documents are produced, filed and archived.

The production of archives

To understand the growth of archives themselves, it is appropriate to delve into their history.

First, the archive is intimately connected to the *law*, to the state and its power. Derrida (1996) excavates the etymology of the word 'archive', tracing its Greek roots in the *arkheion*, the home of the 'archons', the magistrates. Official documents were stored in the home of the archons, who had the right to make law, to act as the guardians of the law, to keep and interpret the archive.

Secondly, the archive is intimately connected with the *modern nation-state* and its monopoly on law and the violence of law: 'archives, libraries and museums help to store and create modern "imagined communities" ... archives construct the narratives of nationality' (Brown and Davis-Brown, 1998: 20).

Third, the archive is intimately connected with the development of capitalist forms of power. Thus, in *Capital*, Marx used government archives to find a wealth of detail on the life and work of the proletariat – but he recognized that the production of these documents, this detail, was tied to administrative practices such as the Factory Acts, which were passed between 1831 and 1853, that is, contemporary with the Public Record Office, which was inaugurated in 1838. In other words, the production of the documents Marx read was intimately tied to the political will and class interests of the British capitalist state. At the level of the specific workplace, production of knowledge was tied to workplace discipline, to the practice of supervision.

Box 19.11   Nation-states and approaches to archiving

'[The shared features of archives can be traced to the] enlarged systems of surveillance, first established in the Europe of the eighteenth and nineteenth centuries as states adopted more bureaucratic forms of administration. Central to such systems were practices of "moral accounting", whereby a state initiated a system for monitoring the activities of its members through the policing of the population ... Administrative records therefore are not, and never were, merely neutral reports of events. They are shaped by the political context in which they are produced and by the cultural and ideological assumptions that lie behind it ...' (Scott, 1990: 60–2)

The supervisor thus embodied the authority of capital, and documents representing factory rules and regulations, such as attendance registers and time sheets, became both symbols and instruments of his authority. Supervision, so crucial to the working of capitalist authority, was thus based on documents and produced documents in turn. (Chakrabarty, 1989: 68)

Once we think of archives as socially produced within particular historical and cultural contexts, we can start to pay attention to different features of the archive. These include:

- The technologies which are used to produce files
- The way in which documents are filed (their **serialization**)
- The way in which bits of files go missing

Technologies

Working with archives, it is important to pay attention to the changing technologies involved. Changing technologies of printing, typing and reproduction affect the way in which files are produced – but so did the invention of the ballpoint

---

Box 19.12 The file of May Peters

The file is ordered chronologically in reverse, so that the civil servant consulting it only needs to read the top document in the file, the most recent, and summarize that. With each successive summary, the stories deposited in the earlier layers – allegations, rumours and hearsay – gain the status of facts.

1 In the bottom, earliest, file, from 1918, a right-wing MP, Sir Henry Page-Croft, passes on an anonymous note about May Peters to the Home Office, accusing her of receiving money from the Soviet government, of fomenting strikes and practising free love.

2 The MP's letter, passing on 'confidential' information that was already second-hand (from an 'informant'), was then passed to the CID, who found absolutely no evidence for the allegations whatsoever.

3 None the less, the Home Office kept the file, and added press cuttings about the husband, Jacob Peters, which support the myth that he (who *was* an active Bolshevik in London who returned to lead the Cheka) was 'Peter the Painter', a Lithuanian terrorist involved in a 1911 gun battle known as the Siege of Sidney Street.

4 When, a couple of years later, Mrs Peters found herself in Russia, divorced by her husband under Bolshevik marriage law, she applied to return to Britain, and the file was again consulted. A typed minute from a civil servant this time adds some more allegations, that she was a member of a 'notorious' socialist group 'from which she was threatened for expulsion for immorality' – and adds that she sends her daughter to modern dance classes, which 'can scarcely be taken as proof she has renounced her ways'.

5 Despite the CID dismissal of the 1918 allegations, the new version was accepted as true and later civil servants clearly stop reading the earlier documents in the file, relying on the later summaries.

6 May Peters continued to apply for re-entry to Britain through the 1920s, with no success.

7 The last document in the file is dated 1930, when the story stalls abruptly, and the file was placed in the Public Record Office, closed to public access until 1971.

(*Source:* Public Record Office: HO/45/24700)

---

pen. The invention of carbon paper, and later the mimeograph and more recently the photocopier means that multiple versions of the same document can be preserved. Paper clips are a relatively recent invention, and the staple even more so; these affect how files are kept together or not. The shredder has had a profound impact on what is archived, as have digitization and electronic memos.

Serialization

When documents are archived, they are filed in particular orders; we can call this process **serialization**. The post-colonial theorist and historian Ranajit Guha describes serialization as one of the ways in which the archive brings off its appearance of coherence. 'Historians know all too well how the contents of a series in an official archive or a company's record room derive much of their meaning from the intentions and interests of the government or firm concerned' (1997: 37). Richard Harvey Brown and Beth Davis-Brown also underline the political structures underlying the way that archives are serialized or classified:

> classifications never emerge solely from the material to be classified since our ways of defining the material itself are shaped by the dominant intellectual or political paradigms through which we view it ... Insofar as categorical systems appear to organize their relevant material 'correctly', all their ideological functions are thereby more disguised and, hence, all the more powerful. (1998: 25)

I came across a good example of this in my own research, when reading a Home Office file on a woman named May Peters, the wife of a Bolshevik named Jacob Peters. The changing meanings in a sequence of case notes is given in Box 19.12. In this file, we can see what Taussig calls the archive's 'trick of truth' at work: hearsay and rumours acquiring the status of fact through sounding like truth, through the use of specific modes of writing and filing.

Fragmentation

At the same time as clerks and archivists arrange files in particular orders, documents go missing, are accidentally or deliberately destroyed and so on: a process Guha (1997) calls **fragmentation**. In the file on May Peters, for example, some of the police reports which discredited the allegations against her have disappeared, so that we will never know the 'truth' of her story. Fragmentation can come about quite innocently, from the effects of damp weather or war-time bombing, through fires or floods, or through clerical error.

Conclusion

Serialization and fragmentation, as May Peters's story shows, mean that what we find in the archive are the *traces* of various past events. The Marxist historian E.P. Thompson, when describing his work, spoke of his task as rescuing working class rebels of the late eighteenth and early nineteenth century 'from the enormous condescension of posterity' (1966: 12). Foucault, whose key works are based on archival research, collected together fragments from prison archives. He wrote of giving a chance to

> these absolutely undistinguished people to emerge from their place amid the dead multitudes, to gesticulate again, to manifest their rage, their affliction ... [I wanted to present] lives that survive only from the clash with a power that wished only to annihilate them or at least obliterate them, that come back to us only through the effect of multiple accidents. (2000: 163).

We can assemble some of the fragments of the lives of people like May Peters, both tracing the way they were *constructed* in the archive – through processes like serialization, genre and so on – but also by hearing something of their voices across time.

Further reading

Scott (1990) is a good general guide and gives a

Box 19.13   Web pointers for archives

Archive directories

ArchiveHub
www.archiveshub.ac.uk/repositories.shtml
Links the archival holdings of UK universities and colleges.

The Historical Manuscripts Commission's ARCHON database
www.hmc.gov.uk/archon/archon.htm
This is a directory of archives in the UK, many pretty obscure and small.

The Historical Manuscripts Commission's National Register of Archives
www.hmc.gov.uk/nra/

UNESCO Archives Portal – follow the link to 'Archives por
www.unesco.org/webworld

Access to Archives
www.a2a.pro.gov.uk/
The A2A database contains catalogues of archives held across England and dating from the 900s to the present day.

Individual archives

The British Library
www.bl.uk/
The British Library, near King's Cross Station in London, is the biggest collection of published material in the UK, with everything from medieval manuscripts to contemporary scientific documents.

The Public Record Office
www.pro.gov.uk/
This is the official archive of the British government, located at Kew in South West London. It contains the records of every branch of the government, from the police records of the Jack the Ripper investigations to War Office records on military service.

London Metropolitan Archive
www.cityoflondon.gov.uk/leisure_heritage/libraries_archives_museums_galleries/lma/index.htm
Located in Farringdon, Central London, this collection contains municipal and business archives from London's past.

Modern Records Centre
modernrecords.warwick.ac.uk/
At Warwick, this archive includes both major and offbeat collections of original sources for British political, social and economic history, with particular reference to labour history, industrial relations and industrial politics. There are, for example, the papers of trade unions, Labour politicians and pressure groups.

Audio-visual archives

British Universities Film and Video Council
www.bufvc.ac.uk/
Resources on academic research using film and video.

National Film and TV Archive
www.bfi.org.uk/collections/

National Sound Archive
www.bl.uk/collections/sound-archive/cat.html
Oral history interviews, musical recordings, drama and literature, dialect recordings and wildlife sounds.

On-line archives
Here are just a few examples of the many digitized archives that can be accessed directly from the World Wide Web. A directory of on-line collections can be found at www.unesco.org/webworld/digicol/. The Humbul Humanities Hub, at www.humbul.ac.uk/, also provides links to various primary sources on the Web.

The Charles Booth On-Line Archive
http://booth.lse.ac.uk/
Charles Booth was one of the founders of British quantitative and qualitative research in the late nineteenth and early twentieth centuries. Based at the London School of Economics, this site includes digitized versions of his notebooks and famous 'poverty maps'.

Qualidata
www.qualidata.essex.ac.uk/
Based at Essex University, Qualidata archives various qualitative data sets, such as Peter Townsend's 1950s studies on care of older people in institutions, Paul Thompson's 1970s life-history interview studies and Goldthorpe et al.'s *The Affluent Worker* (1969). A similar resource for the Arts and Humanities is at www.ahds.ac.uk/.

National Digital Archive of Datasets
http://ndad.ulcc.ac.uk/
NDAD contains archived digital data from UK government departments and agencies. The system provides open access to the catalogues of all its holdings, and free access to open datasets following a registration process.

sunSITE Digital Collections
http://sunsite.berkeley.edu/Collections/
The University of California at Berkeley hosts a number of digital collections.

Visit the website for this book at www.rscbook.co.uk to link to these web pointers.

quick history of the UK Public Records Office and of the Official Secrets Act. Additionally, the following guides to archives are available. These are helpful resources to aid with getting started and knowing where to look:

Anon (1985) *National Inventory of Documentary Sources in the UK and Ireland.* Cambridge: Chadwyck-Healey.

Cornish, G.P. (1986) *Archival Collections of Non-Book Materials.* London: British Library.

Drake, M. and Finnegan, R. with Eustace, J. (eds) (1997) *Studying Family and Community History Nineteenth and Twentieth Centuries. Sources and Methods: A Handbook.* Cambridge: Cambridge University Press.

Foster, J. and Sheppard, J. (1994) *British Archives: A Guide to Archive Resources in the UK.* Basingstoke: Macmillan.

Kitchling, C.J. (ed.) (1997) *Surveys of Historical Manuscripts in the United Kingdom: A Select Bibliography.* London: HMSO.

Mortimer, I. (ed.) (1999) *Record Repositories in Great Britain.* London: Royal Commission on Historic Manuscripts.

Munby, L.M. (ed.) (1994) *Short Guides to Records.* London: Historical Association.

Olney, R.J. (1995) *Manuscript Sources for British History: Their Nature, Location and Use.* London: Institute of Historical Research.

Student Reader (Seale, 2004): relevant readings

41 Ken Plummer: 'On the diversity of life documents'
42 Martyn Hammersley: 'Qualitative data archiving: some reflections on its prospects and problems'

Key concepts

Facticity
Fragmentation
Genealogy of ideas
Genre conventions
Intertextuality

Naturalize (as in making something seem natural)
Oral versus **documentary sources**
Primary versus **secondary sources**
Relationships of sequence versus **relationships of hierarchy**
Serialization

20

Using visual materials

Suki Ali

CONTENTS

Introduction

In social and cultural research visual and spoken means of communicating are generally regarded as secondary to written methods. Yet we live in a society where visual images have proliferated and our ways of seeing and our experiences of and responses to visual spectacles are central to our understanding of who we are and where we belong. Vision should be, as Gillian Rose (2001) has argued, distinguished from **visuality** if we are to appreciate the *socially constructed* nature of what and how we see. Ways of seeing are not neutral matters of biology, but are structured in various ways that create social differences. Our visual experience plays a central role in identity formation, although this is of course dependent on us being able to see and is an 'ablist' understanding of the role of the visual. We can think of the field of vision as a transparent or neutral space with the job of 'visual culture' being to fill this space. Our analysis of visual culture in all its forms should attempt to reveal this illusion, and to make clear how this space is socially differentiated. In order to do this we need to recognize visuality as open to change over time. For example, technological advances that allow us to manipulate images make the relationship between what we see and what we know increasingly uncertain.

Studying the visual aspects of culture and society has become increasingly important, particularly in the fields of cultural studies and media and communication studies. While vision and visuality have always been at the heart of other disciplinary traditions such as fine art, art history, drama or film studies, the growing interest from social and cultural researchers more generally reflects shifts in social theory. In the move from *structuralist* to *post-structuralist* theory (see Chapter 4) it has become commonplace to think of all forms of representation as 'textual' in the broadest sense. This has meant that visual images in the form of photographs, films, bodies, sculptures, buildings and so on have all come to be regarded as 'texts' and worth analysing as cultural artefacts that can be 'read'. This chapter will guide you through key methods that use visual materials in research.

The range of visual materials that can be used for research purposes is very broad. Before deciding which to use, it is wise to consider the range of things that might be done with visual images. This is linked to the important question of *why* one would wish to use such materials for research purposes rather than using other, more traditional kinds of data. For example, one type of image that has proven very popular for research purposes is the advertisement, particularly print media advertisements. Consider the ways in which such material might contribute to a research investigation. You could:

1 Investigate the **production** of the advertisement itself – the author or artist, the industry.
2 Analyse the site and advertisement itself – its position on the page, composition, hidden messages and so on, so that the research study becomes an investigation of **representation**.
3 Assess **consumption** by the 'audience' for the advertisement. This might involve conducting a *focus group* to discuss the image (see Chapter 15).
4 Look at other people's use of visual materials as research and assess what role it plays in the research process, what 'job it does' (Rose, 2001).

Taking these four areas alongside a consideration of *modalities* in relation to the image provides a comprehensive research agenda. Modalities include visual technologies, compositional aspects and the whole spectrum of the social context.

In this chapter we will be mostly concerned with using representations but in addition will draw on methods (such as focus groups, surveys, ethnography) that are covered in other chapters in this book. Before considering the way images can be used in research, let us consider the kinds of visual materials that are available to you as a researcher, and some of their potential uses.

Visual materials for research

A convenient way of classifying images is to separate *moving* from *still* images. Of course, it is possible to analyse stills from film, video and television, and indeed many people do so. With computer software and animation techniques it is also possible that photographs and drawings can be turned into moving images. In addition, it is important to be aware of possible variations in *production* between 'human-made' and 'natural' images, and between simple chemical and **analogue** technologies (video and photography) and **digitally manipulated** media (digital recording and *post-photography*). Visual research now deals with increasingly mind-boggling amalgamations of the two – for example, 'real' images being digitally enhanced, and films interspersing images of 'real' people with 'computer-generated' material to name but two. Despite this blurring of boundaries, associated with the growing complexity of technology for producing images, there are nevertheless some methods of analysis that are associated with particular materials and thus make traditional distinctions useful.

Moving images

Film and television have long been resources for social scientists. The development of film technologies was linked to other scientific advances and in the early years of film there was an overlap between scientific uses of film and film as entertainment. Visual technologies and the magic of moving images of science were fed into entertainment and popular culture. Increasingly, though, the scientific 'truth' of film has been questioned, particularly in an age where digital technology allows for the enhancement and manipulation of initial footage.

In early anthropological work *documentary* film was a crucial way of recording the lives of 'others'. As with critiques of written ethnographies (see Clifford and Marcus, 1986 and Chapters 17 and 29 in this book), critiques of visual anthropological ethnographies (for example Harper, 1998) suggest that these films inevitably recorded a *partial* version of the truth. The power relations of production and dissemination favoured the anthropologist who could choose what to record and where and how to present it. Although there is debate about the extent to which such films in fact furthered imperial and colonial stereotyping (see Hallam and Street, 2000), it remains the case that these films helped to create and maintain ideas of 'primitive' versus 'civilized' people and making the notion of 'otherness' seem 'natural'.

Entertainment films, from Hollywood and Bollywood blockbusters to those produced by small 'art-house' independents, have been of interest to researchers for a number of reasons. There is considerable debate about whether films simply reflect or create problems in society. Films themselves have been scrutinized, addressing such key social issues as gender stereotyping, violence, sexual explicitness and racism. Psychoanalytic theory (see below) as well as other methods have been used to investigate viewers' subjectivities and spectatorship. Other research may look at audiences.

Television is a medium that can be distinguished from cinema chiefly by the relatively private nature of the viewing experience. Many of the interests in film are relevant to discussions of television. *Content analysis* (see Chapter 27) has been extensively used to understand this medium and distinctions between different media genres has been important. Thus soap operas, TV documentaries, serial dramas, news and current affairs all possess their own conventions of visual presentation. In addition to such studies of *representation*, studies of *production* and *consumption* have been important too. Ethnographies of newsroom activities, for example, can focus on how producers select certain images rather than others; investigation of audience response to television, viewing patterns and the like allows assessment of forms of identification and interpretation by viewers. Work has been done with children as audiences in relation to violence, with cross-cultural readings of soap operas, and with gendered patterns of family viewing. *Videos* can also be used by researchers and interesting work has been done on short promotional films in music that allow an assessment of the interpretive work done by spectators.

Still images

As with moving images, still images fall into many subcategories which often overlap. An important source of images for researchers has been the *photograph*. As a visual technology that emerged in the nineteenth century at a time of increased interest in the classification and study of humanity, its early history is associated (like that of anthropological film) with the documentation of *otherness* so that photography has played a role in producing and maintaining social divisions. Much of this work involved scientists using photography to classify humanity into 'groups' or 'types' and the camera was used in this way by biologists, psychiatrists, anthropologists, philanthropists and historians. In addition to its scientific role, it became the preferred way for the middle classes to document the family. The camera was seen as an artistic tool as well. In fact, many painters bemoaned the 'death of the artist' that photography appeared to herald. There is still some debate today about the status of photography as art, and as a result of technological developments that allow for the digital enhancement of images, we are now entering the age of **post-photography** (Lister, 1995).

Documentary photography and photojournalism are important areas for research investigation. In such cases images are often used in place of text, not simply as illustrations to written pieces. Certain visual images have made an enormous impact on public consciousness, recording and helping shape perceptions of key historical moments. It is often key *still* images from newspapers (rather than moving images) that are said to capture the most devastating events and eras and come to represent them forever. This power of the image means that the way they were produced, how and where they are reproduced, and how they may affect people involved are all areas that concern us as researchers. They reflect concerns with the burden of representation (Tagg, 1988).

Advertising images, as mentioned earlier, are some of the most popular for analysis. Many studies explore the links between consumption and identification with advertising images. By analysing examples such as car advertisements we can consider the issues of identity and social class, gender and 'race'. Advertisements for ordinary domestic products such as soap powders and daily foods are fertile territory for considering representations of families and gender relations. Perfumes

and alcohol adverts often highlight issues about sexuality and gender. Adverts in magazines and newspapers are easily accessed and cheap to use. Like television and film, they are a major part of daily life in Western countries and are exported around the world. This makes them a rich source of socially relevant data.

Domestic photography has been described by Bourdieu (summarized by Krauss, 1990) as 'an agent in the collective fantasy of family cohesion, and in that sense the camera is a projective tool, part of the theatre that the family constructs to convince itself it is together and whole' (Krauss, 1990: 19). It is only in the past decade or so that ordinary family snaps have been treated to systematic analysis by researchers. In part this reflects an increasing interest in autobiographical and biographical work (frequently also investigated by means of qualitative, *life history* interviews – see Chapter 14). Family photographs, portraits, often follow quite strict conventions and even 'family snaps', although apparently informal, also show recognizable or generic features. Additionally, as Holland has pointed out: '[T]he personal histories they record belong to narratives on a wider scale, those public narratives of community, religion, ethnicity and nation which make private identity possible' (Holland, 1991: 3). It is this combination of the distinct personal narrative and its intersection with wider social history that makes them useful tools for research. As historical documents, they may also be useful in facilitating *memory work* (see below).

Other sources of still visual images include *painting, drawings* and *graphics*. These kinds of images may range from the 'high culture' of traditional forms of fine art, to cartoons or children's finger paintings. Of course, the lines between these are increasingly blurred in contemporary visual culture, so that 'high' and 'low' distinctions may make little sense (see Figure 20.1).

Archives (see also Chapter 19) can be a useful source of visual materials, sometimes accumulated from family records but also from other sources. Eric Margolis (2000) has looked at archival materials in the United States to explore the ways in which gender and 'racial' difference has been constructed through school photographs (see also discourse analysis below). Margolis looked at

Figure 20.1 *Mona with burger: high or low culture? (Source: www.ninjaburger.com/fun/ creativity/art/mona-lisa-with-ninja.jpg)*

two 'virtual' archives that have been used as resources for teachers and students searching for primary source documents for history and social studies projects. What is important about this work is that it shows that the production of the archive itself – the choice of images, location, cataloguing, absences and inclusions – produces biased views of the history of education in the United States. He also analyses the images themselves for the work they do in this process. In his article, Margolis uses only one or two sources, several images as samples, and multiple methods of analysis to provide an extremely rich research project (described in further detail later in this chapter).

Methods for analysing visual materials

There are several different methods for analysing visual images. These need not be used exclusively and indeed it is becoming more popular to use a combination or 'mixed-methods'. In this

section I outline the main approaches to this before briefly considering ways of investigating *consumption.*

Psychoanalytic theory

This method is often used with work in film studies and focuses as much on audiences as upon representations, though this is approached through the study of representations themselves rather than by questioning members of audiences. There is an emphasis on desire, sexuality and subjectivity which means that psychoanalytic approaches are interested in emotional states and the role of the unconscious. Particular scenes may be looked at in great detail and the scene's spatial organization (the **mis-en-scène**) is subject to considerable analysis. Screen ratios, frames and planes, multiple images, focus, angles, point of view, camera movements and so on are all investigated for the work they do in creating the 'gaze' of both protagonists and spectators.

Laura Mulvey (1975) wrote an influential text on 'the male gaze', arguing that both male and female spectators must identify with male protagonists in order to gain pleasure from viewing. Although there are critiques of her work she and other feminist film analysts have shown how films can be 'phallocentric' and fetishize women. Lola Young (1996) used psychoanalytic theory in her work on 'race' and sexuality in the cinema to great effect. She uses these techniques of visual analysis with a selection of British films made from the 1950s through to 1987. She scrutinizes how black women are portrayed in the earlier films and looks at continuities and discontinuities in later films (see Box 20.1). Young's work shows the need to make a gendered and racialized use of psychoanalytic ideas and she criticizes other theorists for their failure to do this.

Other work in cultural studies has drawn on psychoanalytic theory to analyse still images. Kobena Mercer's work on Robert Mapplethorpe's series of photographs of black male (nude) bodies is exemplary of the genre. (See www.ocaiw.com or www.masters-of-photography.com for collections of Mapplethorpe's photographs.) Mercer uses the images to explore issues of racialization and sexuality (see Box 20.2).

Box 20.1   A psychoanalytically informed study of the film *Mona Lisa*

Lola Young's (1996) reading of the film *Mona Lisa* shows how it is that even without a significant number of black protagonists, racial differences are maintained. The two central characters are a white, male middle-aged newly released ex-convict, and a young, black, female prostitute. Young argues that the man, George, shows a 'phobogenic' response to black men – that is, he fears them. But he develops a relationship with the woman, Simone. Black people in the film are connected to low moral standards, and despite George's 'romanticization' of Simone, the relationship fails. Young discusses the commodification of black female sexuality, and the need to control the body of the Other demonstrated in the film. She suggests that Simone's body is in fact only there to service white men, and she is the object of the white male gaze. Simone's sexuality is pathologized in a number of ways, including her relationship with another young woman. Even though George is a working-class man, he holds a position of relative power over Simone, despite both of them occupying a sordid and dangerous underworld. Young concludes that the film should also be understood as arising at the time of Thatcherism in which a rampant form of individualism and neo-colonial conquering of 'foreign markets' harked back to older forms of colonial and imperial acquisition.

Box 20.2   Kobena Mercer's (1994) reading of Mapplethorpe's photographs

Mercer's analysis considers a range of photographs Mapplethorpe made during the 1980s. His choice of images include some nudes, some portraiture and a famous image 'Man in a Polyester Suit', which is a cropped image starting mid-chest and stopping at mid-thigh level. The trouser zipper is open to allow the man's penis to be outside the fabric.

All of these images are problematic for Mercer. He argues that Mapplethorpe facilitates the imaginary projection of certain racial and sexual fantasies about the black male body. The black nude is presented as an aesthetic object to be looked at and this is achieved through 'specific visual codes brought to bear on the construction of visual space' (1994: 174). The conventional nude is the white female body, and Mapplethorpe substitutes the black man. Mercer suggests Mapplethorpe is constructing a white, gay male gaze which embraces a colonial fantasy of black male sexuality and otherness. Sexual mastery is conveyed by the fact that only one male appears at a time, disallowing a collective identity.

Mercer describes how Mapplethorpe uses several camera codes to achieve these effects: sculptural, feminized *objet d'art* portraiture, cropping and lighting. The latter facilitates a view of black skin as a sexual fetish. In all he suggests, then, that there is a form of racial fetishism involved in looking at these images. He draws on the Freudian concept of splitting used by feminist analyses of gender fetishism and adapts it to discuss the 'Man in a Polyester Suit'. Despite Mapplethorpe's intentions, Mercer argues, the images are problematic and ambivalent. In Mercer's reconsideration of this article he argues that he may have overlooked the 'polyvocal' quality of Mapplethorpe's work – that is, that it can be read in many ways. In addition, Mercer later stresses the homoerotic nature of the imagery which undermines traditional forms of masculinity. Mapplethorpe did succeed in challenging the status quo of white, heterosexist masculinist cultural space with these images. Mercer concludes that they had significant political impact on 'readers'.

Content analysis

Content analysis is described more fully in Chapter 27 where its application to the analysis of written and spoken texts is emphasized. I will not repeat the detail of that discussion here. As you will have gathered by now, though, a **text** in the broadest sense includes more than just words; it incorporates images as well as material artefacts such as clothes, hairstyle, buildings, architectural plans, maps and so on. All of these things both reflect social processes and help construct perceptions of the social and cultural world. Content analysis, then, can be applied to the kinds of visual material discussed in this chapter. For example, a content analyst interested in gender in soap operas might ask questions like these.

- How prevalent in soap opera are sexist images of women?
- How often are women depicted in soap operas as mothers, as opposed to sex objects, workers or mainstays of the community?
- To what extent do women characters become less important in soap operas as they get older?

Cantor and Pingree (1983) studied soap operas with these and other questions in mind. The content analyst might aim to identify instances of 'sexist images' or roles in which women might be portrayed, and count the number of cases in a well-defined sample. The controlled and replicable counting of elements within a range of images should allow comparison and generalization across a field, so that one could speak about the role of women within a clearly defined population of images (for example, all soap opera, or American versus Mexican soap opera).

Trends over time can also be identified. For example, an analysis of samples drawn from a particular soap opera once a month from 1960 to 1997 might reveal much about changing representations of women not only in that soap opera, or soap operas in general, but by extension across much popular televisual culture. The point of such exercises is descriptive, but often takes the form of statements either about the accuracy with which the media represent aspects of the world, or about the kind of world to which viewers are exposed.

Box 20.3 describes a study using content analysis to understand trends in advertising. There are many advertisements (indeed, they may have become increasingly important) in which the very small amount of text is memorable and crucial.

Box 20.3   Content analysis of advertisements

Leiss et al. (1990), in *Social Communication in Advertising*, aimed to investigate how certain features of advertising changed over the twentieth century. Specifically they were interested in looking at how new communicative strategies had altered the ways in which representations of people, products and their relationship had changed over time.

To this end, they took a sample of advertisements for several product types (smoking products, cars, clothing, food, personal care items, alcohol products and corporate advertisements) that appeared in two Canadian magazines, one primarily directed at men, the other at women, over the period 1910 to 1975.

Amongst other things they wanted to see whether advertising had come to rely more on visual than verbal techniques. This is obviously a complex interpretive issue involving questions about the structure and meaning of a vast range of images. The authors get round this by measuring the proportion of space, in square inches, taken up by text versus image in every advertisement in their sample. Of course, the measurement of image space gives a very crude sense of the 'importance' of image versus text, paying no attention for example to the structural position (as opposed to size) of each, or of the importance that the text might have in actual readers' understandings of these advertisements.

(*Source:* adapted from Slater, 1998)

One can also think of advertisements in which the text *is* an image: for example, logos like Coca-Cola are both words and images. This illustrates a key tension in content analysis, where objectivity and the avoidance of interpretive ambiguity or unreliability may have to be traded off against in-depth contextual understandings of individual images.

Semiotic analysis

Semiotic analysis involves a greater reliance on personal interpretations of the researcher and is less concerned with objectivity and generalizability. It is based on the view that the meaning of an image (or indeed of a word, since semiotic theory can also be applied to these) is derived from its *interrelation* with other images. As Slater (1998) has pointed out:

> Where content analysis is all method and no theory, hoping that theory will emerge from observation, semiotics is all theory and very

little method, providing a powerful framework for analysis and very few practical guidelines for rigorously employing it. Above all, semiotics is essentially preoccupied with precisely that cultural feature which content analysis treats as a barrier to objectivity and seeks to avoid: the process of interpretation. (1998: 238)

Saussure's (1974) structural linguistics (see Chapter 4) forms the theoretical background to semiotic analysis. He argued that a system of **signs** generated the meanings of linguistic units. Thus, the meaning of a word such as 'flower' does not come from the things that this word describes, but from the relationship which this word has with other words, such as 'tree' or 'vegetable'. Different cultures and languages have different ways of representing the world, so that the English may have many different words for 'rain' (drizzle, fine mist, sheets, buckets) whereas people in a drier country or more stable weather conditions may make fewer distinctions. These then become the

---

Box 20.4   Saussure's method: concepts and distinctions underlying semiotics

1   **Diachronic analysis:** looks at the arrangement of elements in a system at a single point in time (for example, the items on a restaurant menu). This is the focus of semiotic analysis and
    is distinct from:
    Synchronic analysis: examines the historical development of languages, as in the discipline of *etymology*, which looks at how the meanings of words change over time. This is not of great interest to semioticians.
2   Language (**langue**): the system of signs
    is distinct from:
    Speech (**parole**): individual instances of the use of language resources to make particular utterances or speech acts.
3   Reality is **bracketed** so that the relations between words or signs and the *things* that these refer to (their **referents**) are treated as arbitrary.
4   A **sign** comprises two components: a **signifier**, which is the sound or the image of a word like 'cat', and a **signified**, which is a concept that we attach to the signifier ('four-legged furry beast that meows'). There is nothing immutable about this relationship, which is purely a *convention* that members of the same linguistic culture 'agree' to use. This can be seen in the fact that 'tom' can also signify cat, and that 'cat' can also be used to signify 'catamaran'.

(*Source:* adapted from Slater, 1998: 238)

---

mode of thought in which people in that linguistic culture operate, so that it may be hard to appreciate the distinctions made in other cultures and languages. Box 20.4 gives further details of Saussurian concepts and distinctions.

The meaning of a sign arises from the relationship between signifier and signified, *not* from the relationship between sign and referent (which is 'bracketed out' for analytic purposes). Understanding that a conversation about cats is about four-legged animals is based on 'linguistic context', our conversation sets up a relationship for the linguistic elements.

Recognition of the conventional basis of sign systems has quite profound consequences for our knowledge of the world. As Slater (1998) puts it:

Not only is the sign I use not determined by its referent, but my sense of what is out there in the world – my sense of the referent – is clearly structured by words and images through which I come to represent the world. Language as a system of difference *constructs* or *produces* our idea of the objective world, of referents. Languages do not neutrally reflect or mirror or correspond to the objective world, but rather different languages produce a different sense of the world. (Slater, 1998: 239; emphasis added)

Our view of the world depends less on the actual way things in the world are arranged, more on the means that we use to perceive and represent the world. Thus semiotic theory is a **social constructionist** approach to theories of knowledge (see also Chapter 2).

Although Saussure was a linguist and he intended his system, first, to be relevant to the analysis of words, it was clear to him that semiotic theory could be applied more widely. Indeed, a variety of objects can be thought of as 'signs'. Roland Barthes (1977, 1986) is one of the best-known semioticians to extend the ideas of Saussure to a wide variety of objects serving as signs. Barthes went on to consider what he regarded as higher orders of meaning, which he called **codes** or ideologies. The concept of code involves a further distinction, between **denotation** and **connotation**. Denotation refers to the basic

Figure 20.2 *Salute (Paris Match)*

factuality of an image for example. Does it appear to be a flower? Connotation, on the other hand, is more interesting: a rose may have connotations of beauty or romantic love. Thus flowers may form a part of more general codes or ideologies. Box 20.5 shows how Barthes applied these distinctions to the analysis of the photograph in Figure 20.2.

Barthes's understanding of the connotations of this image may reflect as much his personal biography and preferences as anything else. One of the strengths of semiotic analysis lies in the detailed analysis of elements of visual images in context; however, one person's analysis may differ from another's. The **polysemous** nature of interpretive analysis of this sort reflects the fact that different people will have different 'readings' and is a central part of discourse analysis

Discourse analysis

Chapter 27 focuses exclusively on discourse analysis, so this section provides only an overview of how it relates to the analysis of images. Many researchers have become interested in

Box 20.5 Semiotic analysis of the *Paris Match* cover

Denotation: the figure is male rather than female, black not white, young not old. The cap is a uniform, not a matter of personal choice. The young man is saluting someone or something. The caption and text shows us that the magazine is French. This is what the picture is *of*, at a basic descriptive level.

Connotation: ideological meanings are 'coded' in the image. The picture does not actually show the French flag, but it is connoted by the way the young boy has his eyes raised and focused on the middle distance. At the time, Algerians were fighting to be freed from French colonial rule. The image 'argues' that nevertheless colonial troops are loyal to France, which may be a racially diverse 'nation' but is nevertheless unified in its Frenchness. Thus the photograph is a sign that acts as a signifier in ideological systems of meaning about colonialism, nationalism and patriotism.

Barthes argued that images like this were a part of 'mythologization', by which he meant something similar to *naturalization*: they help create an assumption that it is natural for colonial subjects to feel loyalty to France. Something that is in fact a convention, an ideologically informed, partial version of the world, is made to look neutral and acceptable.

(*Source:* adapted from Slater, 1998, describing analysis in Barthes, 1986)

investigating the intentions of image *producers* as well as the multiple readings made by different audience members – the *consumers* of images. Hall (1980), for example, argues that consumers sometimes accept but also sometimes resist the dominant messages intended by image producers. Thus producers may **encode** certain meanings, but consumers will **decode** them in a variety of sometimes unexpected ways. However, for the most part, it is possible to look for both **preferred** readings (what the producer intended) and other individual and collective readings made by spectators by using a discursive approach. Although individuals can read texts/images in multiple ways they often do so by drawing on a range of discourses that are 'out there', so in order to find an image 'racist' or 'sexist' you will probably have an understanding of that term. You may also have different opinions about the same image depending on where it is located and so on. This forms the basis for much feminist media analysis (see for example van Zoonen, 1994).

We can see how Margolis (2000) used a broadly discursive framework in the example of the history of education archives. He analysed the historical context in which the images were shot, the way the archive was put together, the organization of the index, the choice of images, the images themselves and so on. Margolis not only provides the marginal groups but makes visible the invisible category of whiteness. The archive is as revealing in its absences as it is in what it includes. (See Figure 20.3.)

Margolis points to the framing of the first two photographs in the imposing doorway (a gateway to learning), the white children being carefully posed to create an image of obedience and order. The swords at the boys' sides and white dresses of the girls emphasize the production of gender. Children at Indian schools (the third photograph) were dressed in European clothes and their hair was cut. The photograph shows how overtly these children were disciplined into conforming to white American values. Margolis tells us that these children were not allowed to speak their own language, and were forced to assimilate. By drawing on the wider discourses of ethnic and ablist segregation he can demonstrate how the archive itself, as well as the images contained within it, function to further segregate marginal groups.

'School Girls', created between 1900 and 1905 (Detroit Publishing Co. American Memory, Library of Congress)

School Boys', created between 1900 and 1905. Note says, 'Students holding swords at their sides' (Detroit Publishing Co. American Memory, Library of Congress)

Very early class of young boys with flags at the Albuquerque Indian School, c.1895 (National Archives and Record Center, Still Picture Branch (NWDNS), National Archives)

Figure 20.3   *'Race', gender and ability in school photographs*

Photo elicitation

Photo elicitation is a straightforward way of using images in conjunction with other methods. It is most commonly used in the context of interviews or focus groups (Chapters 14 and 15). Most often researchers use photographs that they already own or chose specifically for the purpose of eliciting comments on a subject. In this case the choice of images is an important part of the research process. Some authors offer clear guidelines for how to proceed and what kind of questions should be asked.

For example, you may want to use images like the ones in Figure 20.3 in relation to discussions of gender, ethnicity and education. Here are some choices and questions you would need to make and ask in setting up the process.

- You could structure your work around individuals or focus groups of same or mixed sex. Think about how this choice would make a difference to the project.
- Would you conduct only one session or follow up with further work?
- What kind of questions could you ask? Would you ask directly about the image or the text or the participants' responses to it?
- What difference would age, sex or ethnicity make to the reading of the image? How could you ascribe different responses to these differences?

This is an interpretive approach and although you can ask supplementary questions about how someone responds to an image, you cannot know for sure why this is different from someone else. However, using discourse analysis (as above and Chapter 27) you could reveal some of the discursive formations that participants draw on to make sense of the image. Or you could apply a psychoanalytic analysis to the participants' fantasies or desires in relation to the image.

Memory work

This is often used seen as a form of photo-elicitation but has its roots in a quite different process. Feminists have developed methods that have been used very successfully to encourage autobiographical recollection. Here, photographs taken by interviewees themselves, or held in their own collections, can help facilitate memory work. This process involves not only recollection but the production of new memories. The kinds of questions that can be useful with family photographs are as follows:

- What does the photo represent to you? How do you feel when you look at it?
- Who is in it? Who is not in it?
- Who took the picture?
- What do you remember about the picture being taken?
- What do you remember about the time it was taken, the event?
- Can you describe anything in the picture that is important to you, and explain why? (From Kuhn, 1995)

Again, these are not exhaustive. They do show that the kind of questions you ask are more likely to engage the respondents with the emotional responses to the image, and are more flexible and open-ended than a more formal photo-elicitation method. The questions are deliberately vague so that the respondents can lead the research processes themselves into the areas that are important to them. This spontaneity can help to reduce the rigidity of the interviewer/interviewee positions in keeping with feminist research principles. Consideration for the respondents helps to minimize power relations between researcher and researched.

Making images

For students in many areas of the social sciences, the possibilities for submitting images for assessment may be somewhat limited. Practical courses in art and media, of course, require the production of images. But in most cases, although images can be submitted as illustrations, or as part of appendices to show the role they played in the research process, they require further textual explanation. None the less, the process of making images can provide a creative way into researching topics as well as presenting the results of research. On the one hand, the researcher can make images; on the other, research participants can make images.

Creating a documentary is one of the most obvious ways a researcher can produce images for research purposes. It can be that the researcher sets out to make a visual record of an event, situation or process. With colleges and universities providing technologies it is possible to make a film or video as well as photographs. However, you could ask research participants to do the same, and in this way would get a different perspective of the same thing. British television is now saturated with the 'video diary' which purports to give participants a 'say' in programmes. Ironically of course, as with 'reality TV', what we as viewers get to see is a highly edited version of the whole film and so meaning can still be controlled by the producers. This is something to be aware of when working with participants in your research. Another factor to consider is time and cost. Making films and videos and processing photographs can take a lot of time in the post-production phase, time that needs to be generously factored into the overall project. None the less, this can be a very rewarding way of working.

Rather than using existing images for photo elicitation, you can ask people to create their own images, perhaps by drawing, painting, photographing or choosing to create images from a series of other images (collage). This is a fairly simple and cheap way of encouraging research participants to become creatively involved in the research. There are numerous examples of taking this kind of approach with children. An example is in Box 20.6.

Box 20.6   Getting children involved in producing visual images for research

My own research with children (Ali, 2003) involved a number of visual methods. One of them required the children, aged 8–11 years old, to take pictures with throw-away cameras. The children used the cameras to show what 'family' and 'home' meant to them. In many cases, the results were not as expected. I accumulated numerous pictures of objects rather than people. These included some of doors, cars, gardens, pets and so on. By using a form of memory work with the children I still accumulated a fascinating wealth of data. The children reported enjoying using the cameras and that they felt they had some role in the research process.

Box 20.7   Web pointers for using visual images

International Visual Sociology Association
http://sjmc.cla.umn.edu/faculty/schwartz/ivsa/

Haddon on-line catalogue of archival ethnographic film footage 1895–1945
www.isca.ox.ac.uk//haddon/HADD_home.html

Semiotics for beginners, by Daniel Chandler (article)
www.aber.ac.uk/media/Documents/S4B/semiotic.html

Visual methods in social research, by Marcus Banks
www.isca.ox.ac.uk//vismeth/

Visit the website for this book at www.rscbook.co.uk to link to these web pointers.

Conclusion

Many of the methodological considerations that concern the use of visual images in social and cultural research are the same as they are for other kinds of research material. This chapter has sought to give you a guide to some of the main ways in which researchers have found it helpful to incorporate such materials in their work. Visual research has, historically, played a secondary role to research involving talk, text and numbers, but is growing in importance. If you combine this introductory account with some of the recommended further reading, you may find yourself re-orienting your own research plans towards exploiting more fully the potential of visual methods.

Further reading

Rose (2001) and Pink (2001) both provide good general outlines of the subject. *Visual Studies* and the *Journal of Visual Culture* both engage with the whole range of visual methods. Chandler (2001) gives a good introduction to semiotic analysis. Leiss et al. (1990) provide an excellent comparison and outline of both semiotic and content analysis, showing the application of this to the study of advertisements.

Student Reader (Seale, 2004): relevant readings

14 Robert Philip Weber: 'Content analysis'
40 John Collier Jr and Malcolm Collier: 'Principles of visual research'
50 William Leiss, Stephen Kline, Sut Jhally: 'Semiology and the study of advertising'

Key concepts

Analogue *versus* **digitally manipulated media**
Bracketing
Codes
Consumption, production and representation
Denotation and **connotation**
Diachronic *versus* **synchronic analysis**
Encoding and **decoding**
Langue and **parole**

Media genres
Mis-en-scène
Otherness
Photo elicitation
Polysemy
Post-photography
Referents
Signifier and **signified**
Signs
Social constructionism
Text
Visuality

21

Using the Internet

Pamelah Odih

CONTENTS

Global electronic communication makes possible a new kind of relationship between language, society and technology. Commenting on this, Cerulo has written:

> Recent developments have touched issues at the very heart of sociological discourse – the definition of interaction, the nature of social ties, and the scope of experience and reality. Indeed, the developing technologies are creating an expanded social environment that requires amendments and alterations to ways in which we conceptualize social processes. (Cerulo, 1997: 49)

Using the Internet, space can be traversed in almost no time. Previously distant things now form part of our daily lives as boundaries become permeable to information and communication. This offers unprecedented opportunities to social and cultural researchers which this chapter will describe. First, though, I shall discuss the history of the Internet since this helps to explain some of the key features and terminology that you encounter today when you use this medium.

Origins of the Internet

The beginning of the Internet proper is conventionally dated to the 1960s, when the US government established an experimental project designed to connect computer networks across the United States as part of its Cold War military and economic imperatives (Thomas and Williams, 1999). It was assumed that distributed networks of computers connected in a labyrinthine matrix (as opposed to a centralized configuration of communication terminals) were less easily disabled in the event of enemy attack (Cairncross, 1997). The electronic transfer of information in binary form, across networked computers, was also more economically viable. Unlike a telephone call which operates via a 'circuit-switch' (i.e. messages sent across a circuit established for the duration of that call), an electronic message is transformed into micro-fragments which need not take up an entire circuit and allow for an efficient and cheap use of transmission capacity.

By the 1970s the numbers of hosts attached to the Internet was increasing at a vast rate. Innovations in computer technology had also precipitated a veritable revolution in machine types, formats and operating standards. But their capacity to send information was constrained by the development of sophisticated **protocols** or rules inscribed using particular syntaxes, that enable computers to receive and decipher electronic information. In 1971 a fundamental innovation in the operating standards (protocols) for connecting computers was to overcome incompatibilities in the deciphering of electronic messages (Cairncross, 1997). The invention of the *Transmission Control Protocol* (TCP) provided the initial foundation in which electronic data could be sent over the Internet.

The transformation of the Internet from a network of computers to the popular cultural craze of the contemporary era was precipitated by the invention of the **World Wide Web** (WWW). A key figure in the invention of the World Wide Web is the computer scientist Tim Berners-Lee (2002), who, with his colleagues in the late 1980s, invented a program that allowed the creation, editing and browsing of Internet pages in colour, multi-media and data text form. They called this programme the World Wide Web (WWW). It was based on a unique text formatting system entitled **Hypertext Markup Language** (HTML), which enables documents with HTML tags to be displayed identically on any computer worldwide (Sherman and Price, 2001).

The ingenuity of **hypertext** is essentially its cross-referencing capacity. Computer users can navigate a page by clicking on a word or phrase colourfully highlighted. Having clicked on the **hyperlink** the user is presented with related information stored on a different computer in another part of the world. HTML therefore provides Internet texts with a unique *intertextuality*. In contrast with traditional browsing along linearly ordered bookshelves, Internet pages encourage users to 'follow a web-like non-linear search in which most "pages" emphasize eye-catching designs and attention-grabbing movement' (Sudweeks and Simoff, 1999: 32). Hypertext also allows the Internet user to create

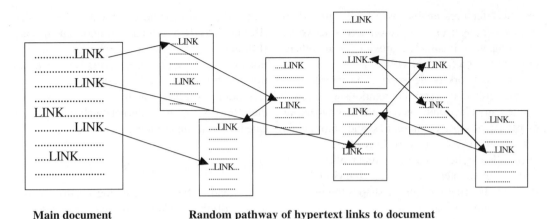

Main document   **Random pathway of hypertext links to document**

Figure 21.1   *Non-linearity and hypertext*

non-linear, random paths through the electronic document **(Figure 21.1)**. The implications of hyperlinks for the practice of research will be discussed in more detail later.

Tim Berners-Lee combined the ingenuity of HTML with the invention of **Hypertext Transport Protocol** (HTTP) to enable the rapid location and automatic retrieval of electronic documents regardless of their Internet location (Berners-Lee, 2002). This is why every web address has http:// inscribed at the beginning. When http:// is combined with a domain name it creates a **Uniform Resource Locator** (URL), which is the unique address of a particular file on the Internet. These

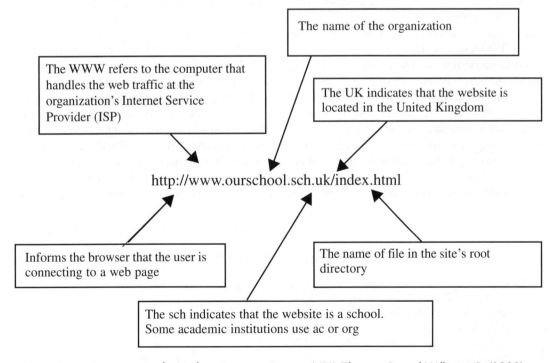

Figure 21.2   *Components of a Uniform Resource Locator (URL) (Thomas, B. and Williams, R. (1999) The Internet for Schools. Plymouth: Internet Handbooks. p. 62)*

technical features enable users to be linked to millions of pages of information across networks and computers. Figure 21.2 provides an annotated description of a fictitious URL.

As a 'network of networks', the Internet has been described as 'a series of relations which constitute an electronic geography', connecting dispersed groups, communities and individuals (Poster, 2000: 205). The world it offers has also been called 'cyberspace' or 'virtual reality' (Hine, 2000). This chapter discusses how the virtual reality of the Internet profoundly shapes the practice of social and cultural research.

Using the Internet to gather information

The World Wide Web is only one of many ways of gaining access to the Internet. Box 21.1 lists additional Internet interfaces.

The wide geographical spread of the Internet means that it can be treated as an expansive national and international information archive. A traditional information search is restricted by the physical location of the required information, something that is bypassed on the Internet. Proximity and access to the library or institution storing relevant information are no longer problems. The resulting immediacy of access to information on-line has precipitated a change in search strategies. Bradley (2001) has pointed out that traditional searching strategies are motivated by a 'just-in-case' model in which stores of information are accumulated and kept readily on hand in case required. By contrast, instant on-line access encourages the adoption of 'just-in-time' search strategies in which information is not stored locally but rather is 'retrieved as and when

required to meet the needs of a specific enquiry' (Bradley, 2001: 5). But it is important to apply skill and technique when searching for information on-line. A useful starting point is to decide on the specific on-line database relevant to your subject inquiry, yet these can be very complex. I will therefore discuss such Internet databases and indicate how you can use them.

Web directories and search engines

Users tend to begin by clicking on the 'search' button of their WWW browser and using the default search engine. In so doing they neglect a multitude of on-line databases available to the Internet user. **Web directories** are excellent resources for obtaining a detailed overview of a subject. Examples of web directories include Yahoo! (www.yahoo.co.uk) and Looksmart (www.looksmart.com). These are collections of links to web pages and sites arranged by subject area by catalogue editors who collect site information submitted by specialist authors and organize this information hierarchically, with major subject areas divided into smaller more specific subcategories. Directories allow you to use hyperlinks to move from topic to subtopic and ultimate end document. Figure 21.3 illustrates this, showing that it is similar to the approach used in a library classification scheme.

The subject headings and subheadings of web directories guide the user through the vast mass of information relevant to their topic area. The tree-like architectural design of web directories is particularly advantageous when the user has little knowledge of a subject area. Most web directories also offer an internal search device that allows the

---

Box 21.1   The variety of Internet interfaces

- Email
- Internet mailing lists
- Forums and bulletin boards
- Web directories
- Search engines
- Chatrooms
- Usenet and newsgroups

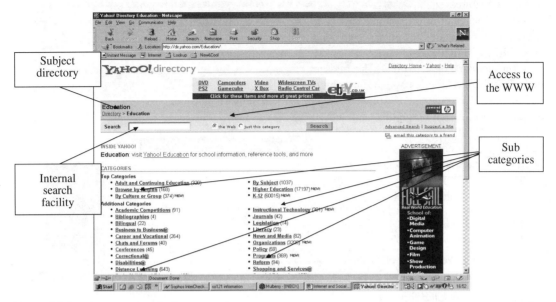

Figure 21.3   *Annotated web directory*

user to bypass browsing through subcategories and gain material in the more specialized recesses of the directory. Some web directories, such as Yahoo!, will also return results drawn from the Web to supplement its internal results.

Whilst directories are powerful tools for finding information by category, they lack the comprehensive coverage of **search engines**. Search engines use a variety of information retrieval techniques to allow access to information located throughout the open cyberspace of the Internet. Web directories provide a context-based framework for detailed structured browsing. Sites are submitted by experts and assigned to appropriate categories. Search engines, on the other hand, are full-text indexes. Sherman and Price (2001: 19), in trying to encapsulate this difference, say that 'web directories are similar to a table of

contents in a book; search engines are more akin to an index'. Figure 21.4 shows an annotated image of a search engine.

As a **full-text index**, search engines will locate matching keywords as they appear throughout any document located on the web (Sherman and Price, 2001: 21). But when a user searches the Web using a search engine they are actually searching an *index* of retrieved web pages and not the entire Web itself. Search engines are geared towards rapid retrieval: this would be impossible if they attempted to search the billions of pages that constitute the Web in real time.

Therefore, whenever a searcher enters a keyword into a search engine an *index* is searched. This has been created and stored in a large electronic database, having been generated by the activities of 'crawlers' or 'spiders', which

---

Box 21.2   Some useful web directories

- World Wide Web Library – http://vlib.org/
- Internet Public Library – www.ipl.org/ref
- Social Science Information Gateway (SOSIG) – www.sosig.ac.uk
- Excite – it supports a directory format, divided into topics – www.excite.com
- Looksmart, a manually compiled directory with over 300,000 sites – www.looksmart.com

---

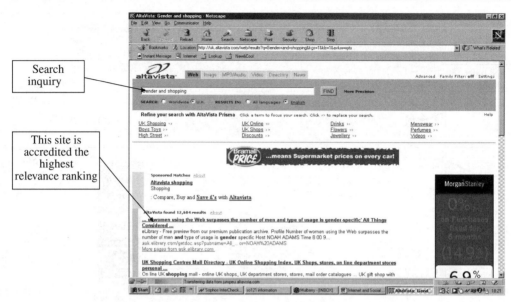

Search inquiry

This site is accredited the highest relevance ranking

Figure 21.4 *Annotated search engine*

regularly search and index new on-line sites, as well as changes to existing pages. When search engine users type in selected keywords, the engines return every indexed web page, which includes that keyword. Unless the keywords are selected skilfully the user may be deluged with information, though there are some features of search engines which help with this. For example, search engines provide 'relevance rankings' of the results obtained during an on-line search.

Mailing lists, newsgroups and chatrooms

Whilst a significant number of Internet users spend time on-line scouring information archives, for vast numbers the Internet is an opportunity to interact with others and exchange information.

Mailing lists, newsgroups and chatrooms are used extensively for the purposes of on-line social interaction. In technical terms newsgroups, mailing lists and chatrooms operate by using *email*. Indeed, email was one of the first implementations of Internet communication. Email as a form of communication is *asynchronous*: that is, unlike the telephone for example, it does not depend on the recipient's immediate availability to operate (Whittaker, 2002: 35), and has therefore gained wide acceptability.

Early electronic mail networks had significant drawbacks when it came to transferring information between individuals and managing large email address books. These complications where overcome with the development of software applications which automated the essential subscribing, announcing, and archiving operations

---

Box 21.3 Types of search engine

There are two distinct types of search engine: **free-text** and **meta-search**.

Free-text search engines enable the searcher to retrieve information about a topic area by simply typing in any number of words, phrases, numbers or letters, deemed relevant. An example of this kind of search engine is Google: www.google.com

Meta-search engines enable multi-threaded or parallel searching of several search engines simultaneously. An example of this kind of search engine is Search.com: www.search.com

---

Box 21.4   Three popular mailing list managers

- LISTSERV   www.lsoft.com
- ListProc   www.sourceforge.net/projects/listproc/
- Majordomo   www.greatcircle.com/majordomo

---

associated with the management of a **mailing list** (Stein, 1999).

In order to subscribe to a mailing list, the user has first to locate a list which matches their subject interests (the simplest place to begin a mailing list search is Topica at www.liszt.com). Having selected a list the user subscribes by sending an emailed command to the computer, which manages the mailing list.

Newsgroups are based on a similar operational logic to mailing lists. *Usenet* (the system of newsgroups available through the Internet) enables the distribution of postings to widely dispersed **bulletin boards,** which are accessed by a large number of newsgroup servers (a useful and comprehensive search engine for locating newsgroups is www.groups.google.com). Figure 21.5 shows a typical newsgroup reader page.

Doing Internet research

Web directories, search engines, email, news-groups and the other Internet tools reviewed so far all offer social and cultural researchers unprecedented opportunities to locate and exchange relevant information and resources. A rather different approach to the relevance of the Internet for research purposes concerns its uses as a site of study and a means of recruiting and communicating with research participants. Doing Internet research of this sort offers significant advantages over traditional 'face-to-face' methods, but also introduces important differences and restrictions. The sections that follow discuss these, starting with ethnographic approaches, then turning to the conduct of on-line surveys.

Ethnography and conversation analysis on the Internet

Christine Hine (2000) has summarized the significance of the Internet for the conduct of ethnographic research. She says that in traditional

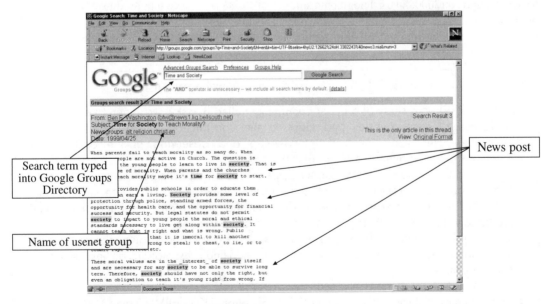

Figure 21.5   *A typical newsgroup reader page*

ethnography 'travel ... becomes a signifier of the relationship between the writer and readers of the ethnographic text ...' (2000: 45). Thus classical ethnographies are replete with linguistic clues, strategies and procedures, which provide authentic evidence of the author having travelled to the new cultural context. For instance, Schutz's (1964) concept of the 'stranger' is predicated on the researcher entering into a spatial context that is culturally 'strange' (see Chapter 17 for an account of traditional ethnographic method). Axiomatic to the significance of 'travel' is the reliance on a concept of culture as located in a bounded physical space: the street corner, a school or a doctor's surgery. More recently, though, critical ethnographers have questioned the representational pursuit in traditional ethnographic texts of fixed cultural spaces. Theoretical developments have drawn attention to ethnographic objects as located within 'translocal' or 'inter-visible' cultures (for example, Rosaldo, 1989). The rhizomatic architecture of the Internet draws attention to the limitations of traditional ethnography's reliance on physically bounded places.

Additionally, the asynchronous nature of Internet communication (see earlier) changes the nature of interaction with research participants. As Hine says, 'on the Internet ... you can be intimate with people who are not there any more, or who have yet to arrive' (2000: 84). Ethnographic study of the Internet, too, raises questions about the relationship between **on-line** and **off-line** realities.

For example: are they congruent? Does the Internet offer freedoms that are unavailable to people in their 'real' lives? Box 21.5 summarizes a study in which this was a central preoccupation.

The specialized nature of on-line communication presents additional methodological challenges for ethnographers, as well as new opportunities for conversation analysts (see Chapter 28). Communication on-line has similarities to speech in its notion of turn-taking, but the absence of paralinguistic clues (facial expressions, bodily gestures and so on) is a significant difference. The complex message structure of *chatroom* dialogues provide interesting examples of these distinctions. Conversation analysis shows how conversations are achieved through the adherence to linguistic rules, turns, strategies and goals. Figure 21.6 presents excerpts from chatrooms. Compare these with the examples of transcribed face-to-face talk in Chapter 28. The conversational structure appears more random and somewhat chaotic as numerous geographically dispersed people type in their conversations. This is partly because of the absence of pauses between turns and other non-verbal cues which are essential to achieving turn-taking in face-to-face conversation. Additionally some 'speakers' can simply type faster than others so can maintain a thread more easily. There is also a propensity for people to create a disturbance in the temporal flow of a conversation by randomly entering and leaving a chatroom. The anonymity means that on the one hand people can

---

Box 21.5   Studying a cybercommunity

Kendall (1999), in a study of a cyber community called Bluesky, was keen to explore the significance of race, gender and class to the construction of on-line and off-line communities. Her study involved interviewing and observing on-line and off-line interactions between members of the Bluesky group.

She found that although on-line forums appeared to offer participants a greater degree of choice in their presentations of self, these relative freedoms were nevertheless constrained so that, for example, the gender roles that participants inhabited in 'real life' were largely repeated in their parallel cyber self-presentations.

Additionally, members' off-line presentations of self were used to authenticate their on-line performances. Participants sometimes defined on-line presentations as 'less real' than off-line identities.

See also: www.rochester.edu/College/FS/Publications/KendallMUD.html

say whatever they want (and, of course, this may involve presenting false fronts and stories), and at the same time commitment to keeping one's interlocutor happy may be less strong than in face-to-face interaction. Despite this, even the most cursory perusal through chatroom conversations provides one with an important sense that meaning is being negotiated, so that these are potentially valuable sites for the study of interaction.

In the first excerpt in Figure 21.6, for example, the users nicknamed Sats and BETTE negotiate their respective responses to the announcement, by an additional member of the group, that he/she

---

Excerpt 1

Kiki - I was working as a key stage one teacher but my school was underfunded and as a result I am now unemployed
Kiki - I am currently a supply teacher in England hoping to emigrate to new Zealand or Australia
Sats - logged off …
Kiki - Hello
Sats - bye bette
BETTE - logged off
BETTE - need coffee need to make a pot ..neighboor is coming over for a facial soon..bbl
Kiki - logged on.
Sats - man I am so behind here
Sats - she has another job?
BETTE - thunder but your new better ;job should start soon
Sats - u sorry to hear that
Sats - yes I thought it would be great since the kids will be at home
quilter - logged off
BETTE - bye quilter
quilter - got to go too, must Fly … bye pecos
BETTE - sats what a great job
Sats - bye all who are leaving
U w baggy eyes - wow sats that is great as of tomorrow I am unemployed also
BETTE - bye pecos

Excerpt 2
<Cliff_Hanger> Jack wheres jill??
<@Jack> i ate jill
<Cliff_Hanger> oh .. u hate her .. i c
<@Jack> heh
<Cliff_Hanger> why didnt ya then put her in the well
<Fire-Lady> ouch
<Floppy_SA> wanna get a job
<@Jack> Floppy_SA hush
<Floppy_SA> helloooo
<@Jack> Floppy_SA seems next in line for a kick
<Fire-Lady> yep
*** a—PiousSheep has joined #chat-world
*** Torii18f^ has joined #chat-world
<Cliff_Hanger> Floppy.. u gonna get formatted soon..
<Fire-Lady> sry was on the phone
<@Jack> hey thats my line Fire-Lady

Figure 21.6 *Excerpts from chatroom discussions*

is soon to be unemployed. On entering the discussion the user nicknamed Kiki uses the employment discussion thread as a means of introducing him/herself to the group. This is a group of teachers chatting and some of the contributions (Kiki's for example) demonstrate conventionally 'good' grammatical structure. In the second excerpt, a more diverse set of people are chatting and there is more use of shortened words, jokes and *non sequiturs*. As in face-to-face talk, different social groups employ different communication styles.

On-line surveys

Social surveys (see Chapter 13) usually involve deriving the same information from each member of a sample of individuals who represent a given population. The Internet provides easy access to a globally dispersed population of users and therefore has great potential for doing survey research. Additionally, it may be able to reach people who are difficult to access by conventional methods. For example, people with hearing difficulties may be more adequately 'interviewed' by email than face to face; a student at Goldsmiths College, London recently completed a study of hearing impairment by this method. Coincidentally, she herself had profound hearing loss, suggesting that there can be advantages for researchers with disabilities too in using this means of doing surveys. But, like on-line ethnography and conversation analysis, on-line surveys are not without problems.

Clearly, when using the Internet for social survey research, methodological issues are raised about *sampling* bias, representation and therefore *generalization*. These methodological concerns are highlighted by Coomber (1997). Internet users tend to fit a specific demographic profile, which he describes as 'white, male, first world residents, relatively affluent and relatively well educated in comparison to any more general population' (1997: 5.1). This may not be a problem if the subject of the survey concerns computer usage, but is a major problem if the population of interest contains groups that are significantly disadvantaged in Internet access.

Even if the population of interest can be confined to Internet users, there may be issues to consider if one is wanting to draw up a representative sample. There is no comprehensive list (or *sampling frame*) of Internet users. The propensity for Internet users to have multiple accounts with Internet Service Providers and multiple subscriptions to on-line facilities compounds these problems – a researcher cannot know whether a person has been included twice or more under different identities. For these reasons Mann and Stewart (2000: 78) advocate the use of *purposive* or theoretically informed sampling strategies (see Chapter 13) rather than seeking representativeness when conducting on-line survey research, or indeed to do case study research on cyber-communities instead, thus turning to more ethnographic methods.

Nevertheless, good sampling strategies are available to the on-line researcher, including for example the creative use of mailing lists and newsgroups (see Box 21.6).

Access to an organization's mailing list will also require detailed communication and liaisons with gatekeepers. Organizations increasingly circulate information through the use of **intra-nets** and mailing lists. Intra-nets are closed communication systems, like a mini-Internet facility but confined (usually by means of a password) only to

---

Box 21.6 Sampling in on-line surveys

Fisher et al. (1996), in their study of how citizens are using the Internet to participate in civil life, targeted a range of representative USENET newsgroups and LISTSERV mailing lists. A stratified sample was applied, to select political and non-political groups.

These researchers provide useful suggestions of how to increase the representativeness of such an on-line sample, finding it to have been valuable to communicate in detail with the mailing list's managers. Communication provided access to valuable software used to screen mailing list subscribers and identify where responses originated.

authorized members of an organization, thus providing a valuable sampling frame and vehicle for distributing survey material. Internet etiquette as well as practical considerations necessitate that researchers gain consent from both the organization's gatekeepers and list users prior to distributing survey materials.

Additional methodological considerations, specific to Internet-based survey research, relate to the formatting of self-administered standardized questionnaires. In an emailed survey, the questionnaire is emailed to respondents as part of the text of a conventional email message. Text-based **email surveys** require no facilities and expertise beyond the respondent's generic, everyday emailing skills and capabilities (Mann and Stewart, 2000: 67). Text-based emails are therefore convenient for the respondent, but the textual format of the conventional email presents significant problems for the researcher. Although respondents are asked to use a particular format when typing their replies, there is little guarantee that they will adhere to the guidelines; they may alter its format either accidentally or by intention. Any alterations to the emailed questionnaire will significantly disrupt the survey's chances of having gathered the standardized information across respondents.

Mann and Stewart (2000: 68) describe how researchers have used email systems that can understand HTML as a means of overcoming these problems. HTML uses standard text characters, which allow the questionnaire to be sent as the text of an email. The respondent is not able to alter the format of the HTML-based emailed questionnaire, because it is encoded with HTML commands designed to restrict any changes to the format. The ability of an email system to read HTML commands provides the researcher with a wealth of design possibilities, which distinguishes the HTML-based emailed questionnaires from text-based questionnaires (see Figure 21.7).

HTML-based email questionnaires combine the benefits of standardized questionnaire formats with the direct response of emails (Mann and Stewart, 2000). But, these benefits are predicated on whether the potential respondents have access to an email system, which can interpret HTML. This potential problem is overcome with the use of Web-based surveys. Indeed, **web surveys** combine the advantages of HTML-based email surveys with the accessibility of the World Wide Web. Recent years have seen a proliferation of companies specializing in web survey software. These software programs assist in the construc-

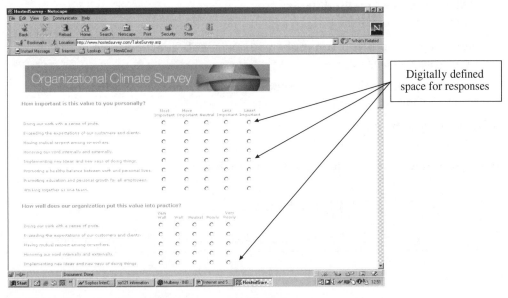

Figure 21.7 *Example of a web-based survey questionnaire*

tion of web-based social surveys, providing visually attractive graphical interfaces.

The graphical interface will often consist of a self-completion questionnaire, which respondents can complete on-line at a terminal. Preferably the survey software programme will provide access to a secure server, which will store the data received from completed questionnaires. Alternatively, a storage program could be established on the hard disk of a desk-top computer. These procedures enable web-based surveys to overcome the restrictions Internet Service Providers place on bulk mailing.

In summary, on-line social surveys require methods for data collection designed with specific regard to the unique architecture of the Internet. Cyberspace contains many points of difference with both the bounded communities of realist ethnography and the representative sampling frames of social surveys. On-line research brings up unique methodological opportunities and special considerations.

Conclusion

The first part of this chapter examined the challenges presented by the Internet as an informational resource for social research. On-line search facilities were described as offering the researcher instantaneous access to quantities and varieties of material unavailable by conventional means. The second part introduced the Internet as a site for doing social research, considering both ethnographic and survey-based approaches. It became clear that enthusiasm for the new opportunities provided by the Internet needs to be tempered by careful analysis of the advantages and disadvantages of this new medium when compared with conventional methods for doing equivalent tasks.

Further reading

Bradley (1999) provides a helpful advanced guide to users of the Internet searching for information. Mann and Stewart (2000) and Hine (2000) provide excellent accounts of doing on-line qualitative research and Jones (1999) has collected a series of such studies together in a single volume. De Vaus (2002a) provides further guidance on the conduct of Internet surveys.

Box 21.7   Web pointers for doing on-line research

WebSM: Web Survey Methodology
www.websm.org/topics.html

CreateSurvey – where you can make your own web questionnaire
www.createsurvey.com/

Cybersociology Magazine – for qualitative research concerning the Internet
www.socio.demon.co.uk/magazine/

HTML ethnography links
www.ethnoweb.com/loros/links.htm

The Cardiff hypermedia ethnography research team
www.cf.ac.uk/socsi/hyper/

See also Boxes 21.2, 21.3, 21.4 in this chapter.

Visit the website for this book at www.rscbook.co.uk to link to these web pointers.

Student Reader (Seale, 2004): relevant readings

12 Kim Sheehan and Mariea Hoy: 'On-line surveys'
43 Robin Hamman: 'The application of ethnographic methodology in the study of cybersex'

Key concepts

Bulletin boards
Email surveys
Full-text index
Hyperlink
Hypertext
Hypertext Markup Language (HTML)
Hypertext Transport Protocol (HTTP)

Intra-nets
Newsgroups
On-line and **off-line**
Protocols
Search engines
Uniform Resource Locator (URL)
Web directories
Web surveys
World Wide Web

22

Combining qualitative and quantitative methods

Neil Spicer

CONTENTS

Social and cultural researchers often emphasize differences between qualitative and quantitative methods. Qualitative methods tend to be linked with *interpretivism* and *postmodernism* while quantitative methods tend to be linked to *positivism* (see Chapters 2 and 4). However, focusing on the *differences* between these approaches reinforces their apparent incompatibility. In this chapter I want to suggest a number of ways in which the qualitative–quantitative divide might be destabilized so as to open up the possibilities for combining qualitative and quantitative methods within a single research project. I will use the term **combined methods research** to mean research that combines *both* qualitative and quantitative methods.

I will start by looking at the differences between qualitative and quantitative research and suggest that these can be over-emphasized and that considerable overlap between the two approaches can be found in the practice of social research. In addition to concerns of methodology, pragmatic and political considerations legitimately influence whether qualitative or quantitative methods or both are used in a research project. Methodological assumptions therefore should not be seen as dictating your decision whether to use qualitative or quantitative social research methods, or to combine them.

In the second half of the chapter I will look more closely at four possible approaches to combined methods research in practice, although the list is by no means definitive. The four approaches that I will be looking at are:

- The **triangulation** of methods. Triangulation implies combining more than one method in looking at a particular research question to cross-check results for consistency and enhance confidence in the research findings.
- The use of **multiple methods**. In contrast to triangulation, *multiple methods* entails exploring different facets of a broad research question or addressing a research question from a number of different perspectives.
- Combining methods to **generalize**. Quantitative methods can usefully be used to establish *generalizations* from predominantly qualitative studies (see also Chapter 7).

- The **facilitative** combination of methods. Qualitative and quantitative methods can be used sequentially. By this I mean the use of qualitative methods to *facilitate* or inform primarily quantitative research and *vice versa*.

Arguments for combining qualitative and quantitative methods

Revisiting the qualitative–quantitative divide

There are arguments both for and against combined methods research. A key question relates to the *differences* between the approaches to qualitative and quantitative research and whether these differences matter. Critics of combined methods research argue that the assumptions behind qualitative and quantitative methods are fundamentally different both in terms of *what we are able to know* and *how we can know it* (issues of **epistemology**) together with assumptions about the *nature of the social world* (issues of **ontology**). It could be argued that this makes the approaches incompatible:

> [this view holds that] ... research methods are ineluctably rooted in epistemological and ontological commitments ... the epistemological positions in which the two [qualitative and quantitative] methods are grounded constitute *irreconcilable views* about how social reality should be studied. (Bryman, 2001: 445; emphasis added)

But are the assumptions underlying qualitative and quantitative methods really mutually exclusive? Bryman (2001) suggests that the linkages between ontological and epistemological assumptions and research methods are rarely as deterministic, fixed and dualistic in practice as they are sometimes imagined to be. Hammersley notes in relation to the conventional qualitative–quantitative divide that: 'the distinction is ... misleading in my view because it obscures the breadth of issues and arguments involved in the methodology of social research' (1992b: 39). He argues that qualitative and quantitative methods

---

Box 22.1   Some commonly proposed differences between approaches

Quantitative	*Qualitative*
Positivist	Interpretivist/postmodernist
Artificial	Naturalistic
Deductive	Inductive
Objectivist	Constructionist/subjective
Structured	Exploratory
Theory testing	Theory generating
Controlling	Subjective

---

often share more common ground in practice than the conventionally held dichotomy would suggest. Recognizing this destabilizes the distinction between the two approaches and therefore their apparent incompatibility (Philip, 1998).

The view that qualitative research involves the study of people in *naturally occurring* settings (*naturalism*) is sometimes used to contrast this approach with quantitative research (see Box 22.1). Quantitative research is then associated with studying *artificial* settings established especially for the purpose of research in which extraneous variables are controlled for as they would be in a natural science experiment (see Chapter 25). This distinction, however, overly caricatures research in practice. Whilst ethnographic research may be closer to capturing 'naturally occurring' settings than other methods, it is inevitable that there will be **reactivity** among research participants, in other words they will alter their behaviour as a result of their awareness that they are participating in research. Likewise, whilst unstructured interviews or focus groups tend to be more informal in style, giving them the appearance of 'naturally occurring' conversations, they are not normal situations. As with ethnographic methods, reactivity will inevitably occur in that interview participants are conscious that they are taking part in interviews and adjust the way they talk accordingly. Furthermore, it is important to remember that *all* research, whether qualitative or quantitative, is part of the social world that it is studying (that definitely does not conform to laboratory standards), which, it could be argued, makes the distinction between

'artificial' and 'naturally occurring' irrelevant (Hammersley, 1992b).

A further example of the way in which the differences between the two approaches tend to be characterized is that quantitative research entails constructing hypotheses and subsequently testing them through empirical research (in other words a **deductive** process). Qualitative research, on the other hand, implies an **inductive** process in which theory is derived from (or 'grounded' in) empirical data. However, quantitative research, rather than a linear process of hypothesis testing, is often very much more exploratory than is generally appreciated; unexpected patterns, interconnections between concepts and ideas may emerge from the data during the analysis stage that were not conceived during the design stage of a research project. Conversely, qualitative methods such as unstructured interviews and ethnographic methods, are inevitably based on pre-formulated theories or 'hunches' (whether they are made explicit or not). Hence, research, whether qualitative or quantitative, tends to be an *iterative* process, as Hammersley puts it: 'all research involves both deduction and induction in the broad sense of those terms; in all research we move from ideas to data as well as from data to ideas' (1992b: 48).

In addition to epistemological and ontological concerns, more pragmatic factors such as the institutional context in which research is done, researchers' skills and the views of research funders influence which methods are chosen (Brannen, 1992b). For example, the current preference of qualitative methods in many social science departments in academic institutions may

---

Box 22.2 Feminism and the qualitative–quantitative divide

The feminist approach to social research in particular emphasizes the political motivations for conducting research using qualitative methods (see Chapter 3). More recently, a number of feminist scholars have been influential in re-establishing the profile of *quantitative* as well as *combined methods* research.

In a debate edited by Hodge (1995), 'Should women count?', which appeared in *Professional Geographer*, it was argued that quantitative methods can make gender inequalities more visible. They can therefore be used to inform and influence policy makers with a view to affecting social change and to challenge discrimination. A feminist geographer who took part in this debate summarized the advantages of using quantitative methods in combined methods research:

> quantitative methods can contribute by describing and analysing the broad contours of difference, by providing a basis for informed policy making and progressive political change, by identifying people and places for in-depth study, and by situating [qualitative] research in a broader context. (McLafferty, 1995: 436)

---

not encourage the creative use of quantitative methods. Conversely, some policy makers may not recognize the value of qualitative research. Box 22.2 shows how some feminist researchers have sought to use combined methods to give their research a greater chance of influencing policies.

Whilst I have suggested that there are more similarities between qualitative and quantitative approaches than the divide usually implies, I do not want to lose sight of the differences. These differences can be put to good use in combined methods research. **Postmodernism** in social research implies diversity, both in terms of embracing multiple truths and that there are, and should be, multiple standards by which the human and social world can be understood (this is known as **epistemological relativism**). Postmodernism offers the opportunity to adopt a *diversity* of methodological assumptions and methods in generating knowledge of the human and social world within a single research project. Philip (1998), for example, who argues in favour of combined methods research, says that:

> employing a range of methodological strategies means that the researcher does not necessarily privilege a particular way of looking at the social world ... I would suggest that such [postmodernist] diversity encompasses methodological plurality as well as postmodernism encouraging dif-

ferent voices to be heard and facilitating the exploration of different truths. (Philip, 1998: 261)

In a similar vein, Bryman suggests that the *differences* between qualitative and quantitative methods should be the *rationale* behind their combination within a single research project:

> quantitative and qualitative research are different, otherwise there would be no point in even discussing the possibility of combining them. They each have distinctive characteristics that make the possibility of combining them especially attractive. (Bryman, 1992: 75)

Revisiting quantitative methods

The claim that the use of quantitative methods in a *positivistic* framework has a monopoly in gaining knowledge of the human and social world contradicts the idea of *epistemological relativism* that I suggest should guide the adoption of combined qualitative and quantitative research. There are four important areas to revisit in considering the use of quantitative methods.

First, it is important to recognize the *rhetorical devices* that reinforce the authority of quantitative research writing and conceal the influence of researchers' subjectivity. This concealment reproduces the myth that social research can be done objectively. It is, however, worth remembering that the use of rhetoric is not unique to quantitative research; its use in qualitative research writing, in particular ethnographic writing, is now widely recognized (see Chapter 29).

Secondly, we should also recognize that quantification can be consistent with *humanistic* approaches that are more usually associated with qualitative methods:

> the humanistic approach to quantification is pragmatic; while *rejecting any mystique about measurement*, one is free to make use of techniques selectively and where appropriate. (Ley and Samuels, 1978: 13; emphasis added)

Thirdly, it is also important to note that quantitative methods are not inherently **androcentric** (adopt a male-centred viewpoint) but are

> an outcome of the broader social construction of knowledge and a reflection of rationalist and masculinist dominance in the social and physical sciences. (Moss, 1995: 437)

Finally, revisiting claims about the *status* of quantitative research also means taking a more **reflexive** approach, conventionally associated with qualitative research. This involves the researcher in making their subjective values and assumptions explicit when writing up research. Once again, feminist scholars have outlined an approach to this:

> to be objective in feminist terms means to make one's position *vis à vis* research *known* rather than invisible, and to limit one's conclusions rather than making grand claims about their universal applicability. The call to *limit* and locate one's truth claims is as relevant to researchers who use qualitative methods as to those who [use quantitative methods]. (Mattingly and Falconer-Al-Hindi, 1995: 428–9)

Thus, in using combined research methods you should also adopt a more critical sensitivity to the problems and limitations of quantitative analysis. Think carefully about what is actually being measured through the use of numbers and be aware of the problems of numerical data quality and the limitations of what can be concluded from these. In line with this non-positivistic approach to using quantitative methods, research writing should incorporate the recognition that analytical categories are *constructs*. That is to say, they shape how we see the human and social world as well as reflect it. By using numbers you do not necessarily have to make the *ontological* assumption that universalistic laws govern the human and social world as would be the case in a positivistic framework. Some generalizations *are* possible and different groups *do* have different experiences that can be represented, although imperfectly, through the use of numbers.

Combined methods research in practice: the best of both worlds?

The triangulation of methods

Triangulation of methods entails combining two or more methods in addressing a research question in order to crosscheck results for consistency and to offset any bias of a single research method (see also Chapter 7). The aim is to enhance confidence in the overall conclusions drawn from a study. The concept of triangulating methods is not new. Campbell and Fiske (1959), for example, used more than one *quantitative* method in a psychological study. Triangulation has also been applied to qualitative research methods, such as ethnographies consisting of participant observation and unstructured interviews as well as to combined qualitative and quantitative methods. Box 22.3 gives an example.

The triangulation of methods has come, however, under considerable criticism. The most fundamental criticism is that the approach is based on the 'naive realist' assumption that a single, fixed and coherent reality can be converged on through the use of more than one method (Blaikie, 1991). This approach assumes, for example, that the language used by respondents in research interviews directly reflects (if not perfectly) a

---

Box 22.3   An example of the triangulation of methods

The triangulation of methods was used in a study that examined social scientists' attitudes to media coverage of their research (Deacon et al., 1998). A cross-section of quantitative and qualitative research methods were combined, including a structured mail questionnaire survey and semi-structured interviews. A number of inconsistencies between the quantitative and qualitative components of the study were, however, revealed in the analysis of the data. The quantitative method (the mail questionnaire) suggested that the social scientists were generally positive about how the media covered their work, whilst the more qualitative (semi-structured) interviews revealed their views to be far more negative. Instead of privileging the accuracy of one set of findings over another, the data were re-examined in order to understand the inconclusive results. The study concluded that whilst the social scientists were *generally* satisfied with the media reporting of their research, they were much more critical of *specific* instances in which they felt the media had represented their research in a negative light.

---

reality outside that interview. It fails to recognize that different findings are likely to emerge from each method and that any one individual is likely to interpret data and write research accounts in very different ways. (Seale (1999) calls this the *ethnomethodological critique* of triangulation.) A further criticism of triangulation is that even if research employing different methods generates consistent findings, it is by no means certain that a further method would not reveal different, contradictory findings. (Seale (1999) refers to this as the *philosophical critique* of triangulation.)

It is important, then, to recognize that qualitative and quantitative methods can rarely be used to address exactly the same research question: 'it is highly questionable whether quantitative and qualitative research are tapping the same things even when they are examining apparently similar issues' (Bryman, 1992: 64). It is wise, therefore, to use triangulation exercises either closely to re-examine the data or to open up new lines of inquiry, without imagining that triangulation will produce a definitive account of the 'truth'.

Multiple methods

Triangulation can be distinguished from **multiple methods** research, which is informed by the postmodernist idea that there should be multiple standards for understanding the social world (*epistemological relativism*) and therefore diversity and contradictions should be incorporated

within research accounts. This involves *not* (necessarily) aiming to converge on a single, definitive account: if different methods *do* produce what appear to be consistent results, these results should not be seen as unassailably coherent, fixed and definitive. Denzin (1989) also rejects convergence as a goal for the triangulation of methods, outlining instead *strategies of multiple triangulation:*

> [t]he researcher using different methods should not expect findings generated by different methods to fall into a coherent picture … [t]hey will not and they cannot, for *each method yields a different slice of reality.* What is critical is that different pictures be allowed to emerge … The goal of multiple triangulation is a fully grounded interpretive research approach. Objective reality will never be captured. In-depth understanding, not validity, is sought in any interpretive study. (Denzin, 1989: 246; emphasis added)

In practice, each qualitative or quantitative method has its own strengths and weaknesses and hence can appropriately address different kinds of research question that constitute different facets of an overall research problem. This allows for a broader range of issues to be addressed than might otherwise be possible in using a single method.

One way of applying multiple methods is to

use qualitative approaches to examine small-scale or **micro**-level phenomena that underly the large-scale or **macro**-level regularities that quantitative methods may reveal. Qualitative methods (such as ethnographic methods or unstructured interviews) can be helpful in capturing complexity and processes as well as diversity and contradiction in the human and social world within local settings. Quantitative analysis of official statistics, for example, as often used for *secondary analysis* (see Chapter 26), can be used to highlight aspects of people's lives that are measurable (such as spatial, temporal and socio-economic inequalities in income or health, perhaps at neighbourhood, regional, national or international levels). McLafferty highlights the advantages of combining methods in this way by suggesting: 'By coupling the power of the general with the insight of the particular, such research illuminates people's lives and the larger contexts in which they are embedded' (1995: 440). Qualitative methods are often then effective in interpreting patterns emerging from quantitative analysis.

Box 22.4 shows an example of multiple methods research in which both quantitative and qualitative interviews were carried out to look at different but related research questions. In this example, qualitative interviews helped to explain the broader patterns revealed in the quantitative interview survey.

Multiple method research also involves bringing different perspectives to bear on an overall research problem. Bryman (2001), for example, shows that quantitative and qualitative methods can be used to provide a balance between exploring researchers' and participants' perspectives respectively. Thus quantitative methods (such as structured questionnaires/interviews) can be usefully drawn on in exploring the specific concerns of the researcher. Qualitative methods, such as unstructured interviews and participant observation that tend to be open-ended, are more effective in grounding research in participants' perspectives without filtering these views through researchers' pre-established constructs and categories.

Combining research methods to generalize

For research to influence policy makers or public service providers who often need to make judgements on the spending of resources, the level of generality or relative significance of findings usually needs to be revealed through a quantitative component of a study. The *quasi-quantification* of qualitative research reports in order to suggest the relative significance of phenomena being discussed by using phrases such as 'the majority' and 'very few' is common. Taking this one step further, it is sometimes useful to make the frequencies of phenomena identified explicit in research accounts. This way of combining methods is sometimes known as the **limited quantification** of qualitative studies. It adds a degree of precision to a reader's appreciation of

---

Box 22.4 An example of multiple methods research

A multiple methods approach involving both quantitative and qualitative methods was used in my own research to examine the ways in which pastoral mobility excluded families from health service provision in rural Jordan (Spicer, 1998, 1999). I carried out a structured questionnaire-interview survey to compare patterns of health service and 'traditional' Arabic medicine use between semi-nomadic and settled groups. This approach usefully allowed the broad differences between groups of families to be explored. However, the method provided limited explanation of the patterns it revealed. A number of semi-structured and unstructured interviews were used on a complementary basis in order to draw out far more experiential accounts of health, illness and health care-seeking activities and related family biographies to changing 'lay' discourses of health and illness. The qualitative methods therefore provided an understanding of the broader differences and similarities that the quantitative aspect of the study revealed.

Box 22.5 Limited quantification in a qualitative report

Presenting simple counts of events can help readers gain a sense of how representative and widespread particular instances are. This was shown in a study of 163 elderly people living alone in their last year of life, where relatives and others were interviewed after the deaths of the people concerned. Here is an extract from the report of this study:

> It was very common for the people living on their own to be described either as not seeking help for problems that they had (65 instances covering 48 people), or refusing help when offered (144 instances in 83 people). Accounts of this often stressed that this reflected on the character of the person involved, although other associations were also made. In particular, 33 speakers gave 44 instances where they stressed the independence which this indicated: '[She] never really talked about her problems, was very independent ...'; '[She] was just one of those independent people who would struggle on. She wouldn't ask on her own'; 'She used to shout at me because I was doing things for her. She didn't like to be helped. She was very independent.' Being 'self sufficient', 'would not be beaten', and being said to 'hate to give in' were associated with resisting help. (Seale, 1996: 84)

---

the generality of phenomena being discussed in a research account (Box 22.5).

However, care should be taken in assuming that the precision that comes with using numbers *necessarily* equates to greater accuracy. In particular, you should take care in using numbers *selectively* in research accounts to support a particular line of argument without accounting for contradictions and inconsistencies. Seale (1999) calls this 'counting to mislead' and suggests that 'counting on its own is not enough; it must be supported by a genuinely self-critical, fallibilistic mindset,

involving a commitment to examine negative instances' (1999: 131). As I said earlier in this chapter, it is important that you make explicit in research writing the limitations of what numbers appear to show.

Quantitative methods can also be used to assess whether a specific case or small number of cases studied in-depth using qualitative methods are more generally typical at a wider 'population' level (in other words to assess the **external validity** of a qualitative study). An in-depth discourse or semiotic analysis of selected documents or

---

Box 22.6 An example of the use of quantitative methods to generalize

A study of a community-based initiative in London that piloted a number of innovative models of community participation was conducted by Hewitt, Spicer and Tooke (2003). Unstructured focus group interviews and observational work with young people provided insights into their experiences of a number of selected projects, each of which represented one of the models of community participation from a larger number of projects supported by the community-based initiative. This was complemented with a structured telephone questionnaire survey with project workers from all of the projects in order to gain an appreciation of their perspectives on the effectiveness of the different models of participation as well as to highlight the relative frequency of each of the models. This provided an appreciation of the scale of generality of the issues examined qualitatively. Importantly, care was taken to ensure that the qualitative cases *were* representative of the categories used in the quantitative part of the study. This provided a sound basis for the generalizations made within a well-defined population.

visual images, for example, could be combined with a quantitative content analysis of a wider cross-section of documents or images in order to judge the extent to which the cases examined in depth are representative (for example Bell, 2002). Box 22.6 shows an example of the use of quantitative methods to generalize from a qualitative study.

The facilitative combination of research methods

Qualitative and quantitative methods can also be combined *sequentially*. Qualitative methods can be used as the first stage of a wider researcher project in order to facilitate, inform or prepare the ground for primarily quantitative research. For example:

- Qualitative methods can provide contextual awareness of research settings and subjects and inform the development of analytical categories for quantitative surveys. In this way, analytical categories can be more closely grounded in the perspectives of research subjects.

- Qualitative methods can be drawn on to help generate research questions and hypotheses used in quantitative work. The first example in Box 22.7 shows qualitative methods being used to inform quantitative research in this way.

- Qualitative methods can inform the design of structured questionnaire or interview surveys by giving a researcher greater sensitivity in framing specific interview questions using appropriate language to minimize the possibility of misunderstanding and to avoid sensitive or offensive questions.

Quantitative methods can be used to facilitate qualitative research. For example:

- Quantitative methods can be used in revealing patterns that are subsequently investigated through the use of in-depth qualitative methods.

- Quantitative methods can be used to establish or refine research questions that could be subsequently addressed through the use of in-depth qualitative methods.

Box 22.7   Two examples of the facilitative combination of methods

Qualitative methods facilitate a quantitative study
Qualitative methods were used by Dressler (1991) to inform a quantitative study that looked at the complex relationships between factors such as economic conditions and social support resources that affected depression among African Americans in a community in the southern United States. Exploratory unstructured interviews were used in the first instance to provide insights into the perceptions of community members. These were explored further in a structured interview survey that formed the second stage of the research. The fact the initial interviews were open-ended meant that many of the concepts examined in the quantitative study were grounded in the views of interview respondents.

Quantitative methods facilitate a qualitative study
McLafferty (1995) carried out research into patterns and causes of low birth weights in a number of neighbourhoods of New York City in which the analysis of quantitative data informed the use of qualitative methods. As a first stage of the research she looked at the spatial unevenness in low birth weights and changes in these patterns over time that were apparent through secondary statistical data sources. She was therefore able to pinpoint a number of neighbourhoods in which low birth weights had risen which were therefore appropriate locations for detailed empirical analysis involving qualitative methods in order to identify factors that had caused these localized changes.

Box 22.8   Web pointers for combining methods

The qualitative–quantitative debate
http://trochim.human.cornell.edu/kb/qualdeb.htm

Forum: Qualitative Social Research
A special issue on 'Qualitative and quantitative research: conjunctions and divergences
www.qualitative-research.net/fqs/fqs-e/inhalt1-01-e.htm

Quantitative and qualitative research
http://writing.colostate.edu/references/research.cfm

Visit the website for this book at www.rscbook.co.uk to link to these web pointers.

- Quantitative surveys and the analysis of official statistics can be used to identify groups or geographical settings for qualitative research or to provide profiles of groups or settings for selecting comparative cases for in-depth study using qualitative methods. The second example in Box 22.7 shows this.

Conclusion

In addition to ontological and epistemological issues as well as pragmatic factors, *research questions* should guide your choice of qualitative and quantitative research methods. Philip summarizes this approach:

> Researchers should think beyond the myopic quantitative–qualitative divide when it comes to designing a suitable methodology … I am not trying to say that all research should combine methods, but urge that the *research topic itself* should play a prominent role in leading the researcher to design a methodology … as opposed to a researcher automatically using certain methodologies because their epistemological positioning stresses a particular approach to collecting information and data analysis. (1998: 273–4; emphasis added)

You should therefore not assume that combined methods are inherently better than research based on a single method in all circumstances, but combine qualitative and quantitative methods where appropriate. I would also suggest that you find ways of combining methods that have not been discussed in this chapter: the capacity to innovate lies at the heart of creative research practice.

Further reading

Seale's (1999) *The Quality of Qualitative Research* is very useful further reading on a number of issues that I have touched on in this chapter. He provides a detailed critique of triangulation, explores a number of approaches to generalizing from qualitative research as well as using numbers to improve the quality of qualitative research. He also discusses reflexivity in research writing. Hammersley (1992b) details a number of ways in which conventionally held assumptions about the differences between qualitative and quantitative methods can be destabilized. Bryman (2001) provides a comprehensive classification of approaches to combining qualitative and quantitative methods. See also a special issue of *Professional Geographer* (47 (4): 1995) devoted to this issue.

Student Reader (Seale, 2004): relevant readings

76 John K. Smith and Lous Heshusius: 'Closing down the conversation: the end of the qualitative–quantitative debate among educational inquirers'

77 Alan Bryman: 'Quantitative and qualitative research: further reflections on their integration'

78 Ann Oakley: 'Who's afraid of the randomised controlled trial? Some dilemmas of the scientific method and "good" research practice'

79 Maureen Cain and Janet Finch: 'Towards a rehabilitation of data'

Key concepts

Combined or **multiple methods research**
Deductive *versus* **inductive**
Epistemological relativism

Limited quantification
Micro versus **macro** levels of analysis
Reflexivity
Triangulation

23

Coding and analysing data

Clive Seale

CONTENTS

Social and cultural research involves taking a particular view of the world, choosing a way of seeing a topic that is different from other possible ways. The selection of certain things rather than others to be called 'data' is an important part of this, but once a researcher is faced with a pile of questionnaires, interview transcripts, field notes or tape transcripts, a further selection occurs. Certain parts of the data will be considered more relevant than others. Additionally, the researcher will usually be interested in detecting *patterns* in the data. A pattern demands that things that are similar are identified. **Coding** involves placing like with like, so that patterns can be found.

Coding is therefore the first step towards data analysis. Decisions taken at this stage in a research project have important consequences. The quality of a coding scheme influences the eventual quality of data analysis, for it is in coding schemes that a researcher becomes committed to particular ways of categorizing the world. Coding schemes can be narrow, artificial devices that hinder thought, or they can contain the seeds of creative new insights.

In this chapter I will first describe the coding of data to prepare it for the statistical procedures described in Chapters 24 and 25. This sort of work is largely associated with the social survey (Chapter 13), but can also be applied to other methods where counting is involved. This includes methods that are normally called 'qualitative'. The chapter will then consider the coding of qualitative data of the sort often produced in ethnographic work or other qualitative methods. Throughout, the use of computer software to assist these procedures will be demonstrated (see Figures 23.1 and 23.2).

Coding for quantitative analysis

The data matrix

At the heart of the statistical analysis of social

	npersons	nadults	typaccm	centheat	video	freezer	washmach	drier	dishwash	microwve	phone	cdplyer	computer	b
1	2	2	5	1	1	1	1	1	2	1	1	1	1	
2	2	2	5	1	1	1	1	1	2	1	1	1	1	
3	1	1	1	1	1	1	2	2	2	1	1	2	2	
4	1	1	1	1	1	1	1	1	1	2	1	2	2	
5	3	2	1	1	1	1	1	2	1	1	1	1	1	
6	3	2	1	1	1	1	1	2	1	1	1	1	1	
7	3	2	1	1	1	1	1	2	1	1	1	1	1	
8	1	1	3	2	1	1	1	2	2	1	1	2	2	
9	4	2	3	1	1	1	1	1	2	1	1	1	1	
10	4	2	3	1	1	1	1	1	2	1	1	1	1	
11	4	2	3	1	1	1	1	1	2	1	1	1	1	
12	4	2	3	1	1	1	1	1	2	1	1	1	1	
13	2	2	3	1	1	1	1	2	2	2	1	2	2	
14	2	2	3	1	1	1	1	2	2	2	1	2	2	
15	2	2	3	1	1	1	1	2	2	1	1	1	2	
16	2	2	3	1	1	1	1	2	2	1	1	1	2	
17	1	1	3	2	1	1	1	2	2	2	1	2	2	
18	4	2	3	1	1	1	1	2	2	2	1	1	1	
19	4	2	3	1	1	1	1	2	2	2	1	1	1	
20	4	2	3	1	1	1	1	2	2	2	1	1	1	
21	4	2	3	1	1	1	1	2	2	2	1	1	1	
22	1	1	3	1	2	1	1	2	2	2	1	2	2	
23	3	3	3	1	1	1	1	2	2	1	1	2	2	
24	3	3	3	1	1	1	1	2	2	1	1	2	2	
25	3	3	3	1	1	1	1	2	2	1	1	2	2	
26	2	2	5	2	1	1	2	2	2	1	1	1	1	
27	2	2	5	2	1	1	2	2	2	1	1	1	1	
28	1	1	5	1	1	1	1	2	2	1	1	1	1	
29	2	2	2	1	1	1	1	2	2	1	1	1	2	
30	2	2	2	1	1	1	1	2	2	1	1	1	2	
31	1	1	5	2	1	1	1	2	2	1	1	2	2	

Figure 23.1 *SPSS (www.spss.com/) software for statistical analysis. The Data Viewer showing data from the 1995 General Household Survey (GHS)*

survey data lies the **data matrix,** as is suggested by Catherine Marsh in her definition of the social survey:

> a survey refers to an investigation where … systematic measurements are made over a series of cases yielding a rectangle of data … [and] the variables in the matrix are analysed to see if they show any patterns … [and] the subject matter is social. (1982: 8)

Box 23.1 shows a small data matrix, derived from a hypothetical social survey in which five people were asked four questions: their sex, their age, whether they were working full-time, part-time or not at all, and the extent of their satisfaction with their work. This last question gave people five options, ranging from 'very satisfied' (1) to 'very dissatisfied' (5). These questions become the **variables** in the matrix. In other words, they are qualities on which the *cases* (in this instance cases are people) vary. If you read the section in Chapter 12 in which library catalogue *databases* are described, you will detect similarities.

It will be seen that there is a simple pattern in the matrix, with people beyond conventional retirement age (cases 1 and 5) being out of work. Additionally, the people in work are all females; the people out of work are all male. People out of work were not asked an irrelevant question about job satisfaction, so the *Jobsat* variable for these cases shows data to be missing.

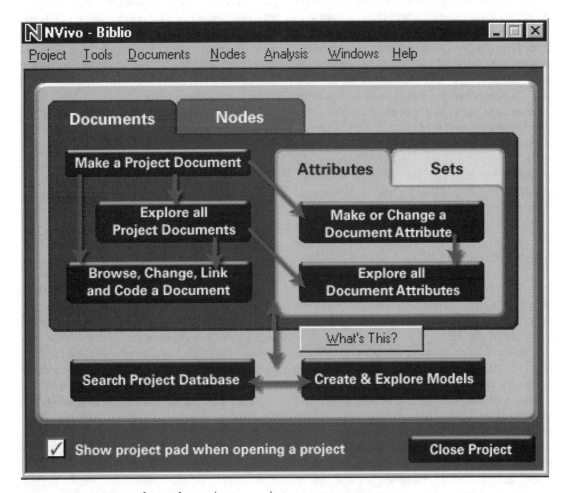

Figure 23.2   *NVivo software for qualitative analysis*
(www.qsrinternational.com/products/nvivo.html). The Project Pad with a project called 'Biblio' opened

Box 23.1 A data matrix

Variables or questions

People	Sex	Age	Working	Jobsat
Case 1	Male	66	No	Missing
Case 2	Female	34	Full-time	1
Case 3	Female	25	Part-time	2
Case 4	Female	44	Full-time	5
Case 5	Male	78	No	Missing

The variable called *Sex* is a **nominal** variable (sometimes also called *categorical*). This means that it applies a *name* to the quality, but that there is no sense of magnitude between the different categories of that quality. In this respect it is different from the *Jobsat* variable, where there is a sense in which the categories of the variable have magnitude. Someone who says they are 'very satisfied' can be understood as having 'more' satisfaction than someone who says they are 'very dissatisfied'. Variables like this, with a sense of rank order or magnitude, are known as **ordinal** variables. *Age* clearly has a sense of magnitude as well, but this is known as an **interval** variable. This is because there is a fixed and equal distance between the points on the scale. Thus the 'distance' between a person who is 25 and another who is 20 years old is the same as that between a 15-year-old and a 20-year-old. The mathematical operations of addition and subtraction 'make sense' with an interval level variable, whereas they do not with an ordinal variable, where the 'distances' between the points of a scale are unknown quantities. The distinction between nominal, ordinal and interval variables becomes important when data analysis begins (see Chapters 24 and 25).

Another feature of the variables in Box 23.1 is that they are expressed in either **string** or **numeric** form. String variables use letters to indicate values; numeric variables use numbers. *Age* and *Jobsat* are numeric; the rest are string. When entering data like these into a computer it is generally advisable to give string variables numeric values. Although most computer packages accept string variables, some place restrictions on the analyses that can be performed with them. The variable *Sex* could be transformed

into a numeric variable by giving 'male' the value of 0, and 'female' the value of 1. The variable *Working* could be transformed by the following: 'none' = 0; 'part-time' = 1; 'full time' = 2. Finally, some variables are **dichotomous** (consisting of only two values). *Sex* is an example of a dichotomous variable. It is not difficult to imagine how the information in Box 23.1 might have been recorded originally on a form or questionnaire for each of the cases, and then transferred from such forms into the data matrix.

Looking carefully at Figure 23.1 (the SPSS **Data Entry** window) is also revealing, since this too shows a data matrix. You may find the appearance of this screen familiar if you have worked with spreadsheet software. Like the data matrix in Box 23.1, the *cases* (also, in this instance, people) are listed down the side and the *variables* across the top. For the person listed first (Case 1) we can learn that two people lived in that household (the variable *npersons*) and that both of these were adults (*nadults*). The accommodation was type '5' (*typaccm*) and a '1' is given for the variables *centheat, video, freezer, washmach* and *drier*.

We can discover what these numbers mean by seeing how each question was coded when it was entered into SPSS. For example, a '1' for the variables concerning central heating, video ownership and so on means 'yes', the household has this; a '2' would have meant 'no'. The **value labels** for the variable *typaccm* are shown in Figure 23.3. These indicate that the number '5' has been assigned to people who live in a purpose built (PB) flat with no lift.

A visit to the *Question Bank* (http://qb.soc.surrey.ac.uk) reveals the original questionnaire used by interviewers on this year of the

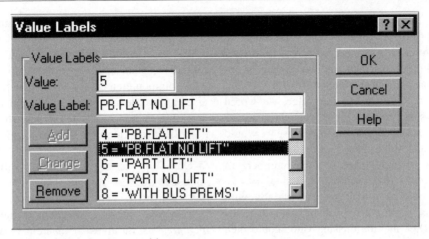

Figure 23.3 *Value labels for the variable* typaccm

GHS. The question used to find out about the type of accommodation is given in Figure 23.4.

Different question formats

Box 23.2 shows some examples of questions in different formats. For each format there are differ-

ent ways of transferring information into a data matrix. Note that the first three questions in Box 23.2 are *closed* and largely *pre-coded* (see Chapter 13), which is to say that they allow answers from a range of pre-specified choices. The fourth question is an *open* one.

Question 1 can easily be transferred to a data

```
ALL HOUSEHOLDS


TypAccm             Type of accommodation occupied by this
                    household.
                    CODE FROM OBSERVATION, BUT IF IN DOUBT, ASK
                    INFORMANT

                    Whole house, bungalow, detached ...............    1
                    Whole house, bungalow, semi-detached ..........    2
                    Whole house, bungalow, terraced/
                        end of terrace ............................    3
                    Purpose-built flat or maisonette
                        in block - with lift .....................    4
                    Purpose-built flat or maisonette
                        in block - without lift ..................    5
                    Part of house/converted flat or maisonette/
                        rooms in house - with lift ...............    6
                    Part of house/converted flat or maisonette/
                        rooms in house - without lift ............    7
                    Dwelling with business premises ..............    8
                    Caravan/houseboat ............................    9
                    Other (SPECIFY AT NEXT QUESTION) .............   10

XTypAccm            Specify type of accommodation
```

Figure 23.4 *Extract from the 1995 General Household Survey questionnaire*

matrix as a numeric variable. What would one do, though, if someone did not know their age in years, or refused to answer, or forgot to answer that question? A missing value would then be entered at that point in the matrix. If 0 or 99 were chosen to represent a missing value, we would have to be sure that there were no newborn babies or 99-year-olds in the sample, otherwise we would have used up a value needed for these people. One solution is to incorporate negative numbers as missing values (for example, 'missing' = –1). Another would be to treat *Age* as a variable with three digits, so that a 99-year-old would be recorded as 099, and the missing value could then safely be allocated a number such as 999.

Question 2 is a bit like the 'job satisfaction' question represented in the data matrix shown in Box 23.1, or the question about the type of accommodation in the GHS (Figure 23.4). People, or cases, can be given a value between 1 and 4 in the matrix to indicate the judgement they made about their state of health. However, as is common on this sort of item, a space was allowed for respondents who wanted to describe their health in terms different from those offered by the question. Managing this at the data entry stage depends on how many people chose this option, and whether the detail of their replies is important in achieving the aims of the research study. If replies are rare and the issue is of low importance, one could simply categorize these people as a 5. Alternatively, one could go through all of the questionnaires where people had chosen this option, and devise a category system to place replies into categories with common elements, each of which would be given a separate number: 5, 6, 7, 8 and so on. This procedure is in fact the same as that which will be described for question 4, the open question, below.

Question 3 is an example of a **multiple response item.** Here, respondents can underline (or tick) as many or as few items as they wish. It is best to treat this as a question containing five *dichotomous* variables. If an item is ticked, for example, one could record the person as saying 'yes' to that question; if an item is not ticked, the person has said 'no'. These could be given *numeric* values ('yes' = 1; 'no' = 2, for example), so that the answer of a person indicating they had a cough and a cold but none of the other conditions might be a row of the following numbers: 1 1 2 2. The first number is the person's answer to question 3(a), the second to question 3(b) and so on.

The fourth question is an open one, asked on an actual interview survey of 9,000 people's health and lifestyles (Blaxter, 1990). Such a question gathers qualitative rather than quantitative data, but it is possible to categorize replies so that quantitative analysis can proceed. In one sense, this is done in *all* quantitative data analysis. The world is

---

Box 23.2   Different question formats

1   What is your age in years?

2   Would you say that your health, for your age, is:

Excellent	1
Good	2
Fair	3
or Poor?	4
Other (please specify)	

3   Please indicate which of the following you have experienced in the past year by under lining the conditions that apply:

    (a)   Persistent cough
    (b)   Cold or 'flu
    (c)   Measles
    (d)   Mumps
    (e)   Rubella

4   At times people are healthier than at other times. What is it like when you are healthy?

Box 23.3 Categorizing qualitative answers to an open question: 'At times people are healthier than at other times. What is it like when you are healthy?'

1 *Unable to answer:*

'I don't know when I'm healthy, I only know if I'm ill'; 'I'm never healthy so I don't know'

2 *Never ill, no disease:*

'You don't have to think about pain - to be free of aches and pains'; 'Health is when you don't have a cold'

3 *Physical fitness, energy*

'There's a tone to my body, I feel fit'; 'I can do something strenuous and don't feel that tired after I've done it'

4 *Functionally able to do a lot*

'Being healthy is when I walk to my work on a night, and I walk to school to collect the grandchildren'; 'Health is being able to walk around better, and doing more work in the house when my knees let me'

5 *Psychologically fit*

'Emotionally you are stable, energetic, happier, more contented and things don't bother you so. Generally it's being carefree, you look better, you get on better with other people'; 'Well I think health is when you feel happy. Because I know when I'm happy I feel quite well'

(*Source:* Blaxter, 1990: 20–30)

---

essentially a qualitative experience; the quantitative researcher imposes categories upon the world and counts them (see Chapter 8). In *pre-coded* items, such as question 2, the categorizing occurs as the respondent answers the question. In question 4, the information can be **post-coded,** that is, coded after the answer has been recorded. This means that respondents are less constrained by the question wording to respond in the researcher's fixed terms, and the researcher has more knowledge about the variety of *meanings* that have contributed to answers and to the development of coding categories. This is likely to improve the *measurement validity* (Chapter 7) of a question though, as with most of the good things in life, better-quality work demands more time and effort. There is always a temptation to opt for a badly designed pre-coded question in order to save the effort required to analyse qualitative data.

Mildred Blaxter devised a coding scheme for replies to the question about health based on a close reading of 200 of the 9,000 interviews in the survey. The categories devised, together with illustrative examples, are shown in Box 23.3, which shows that a five-category variable was derived.

Cleaning data

Once entered into a spreadsheet or into SPSS, the data may need to be **cleaned**. This is because data entry often involves errors. This may, for example, be due to pressing the wrong key. There are ways of setting up SPSS so that this is more difficult – for example, one can 'tell' SPSS only to accept certain values for a particular variable, but mistakes creep in nevertheless. With modern spreadsheets it is often quite a simple matter to run one's eye down a column of figures to check that no 'out of range' values occur. Alternatively, a variety of data cleaning procedures can be helpful in the early stages of analysis. (Chapter 24 contains explanations and examples of the following procedures.) A **frequency count** for a variable will detect out of range values. A **cross-tabulation** can be used to see if people have answered a question which, according to the values of another variable, they should not have done. Additionally, cross-tabulations can show illogical combinations: if someone is aged 25 it is likely to be an error if they are recorded as having a child aged 20.

Coding meaning

Categorizing the qualitative replies to openended questions in a structured interview is one way of turning quality into quantity so that patterns can be detected in data analysis. It is, however, possible to go a step further than this and code material derived from almost any kind of qualitative material, making it available for statistical analysis.

Unstructured interviews (such as those discussed in Chapter 14), where different respondents are asked different questions, or simply encouraged to tell the story of their lives, can be coded in this way. This was done by George Brown and Tirril Harris (1978), in their study of the role of *life events* in causing depression. Brown and Harris rejected what they called the 'dictionary approach to meaning' evident in other researchers' methods for measuring the importance of life events in disrupting people's lives. In such an approach, which relies on people simply reporting whether particular things happened to them in a certain period, different events are given different 'weightings' according to how disrup-

tive the researchers feel the event would be. Thus in one such device (Holmes and Rahe, 1967), researchers gave a weighting of 100 to 'death of a spouse', 73 to 'divorce', 47 to 'dismissal from work' and 11 to 'minor violations of the law' to indicate the severity of each event. The problem with this approach is that an event like 'dismissal from a job' will not have the same meaning in everyone's life. An actor, well accustomed to moving in and out of different jobs, will find this less distressing than a 50-year-old miner, made redundant after a lifetime of work in an area with no alternative sources of employment. Another way of putting this is that Holmes and Rahe's approach demonstrates a low level of **contextual sensitivity** to the variable way in which people constitute the meaning of life events.

Brown and Harris therefore proposed that in order to measure the impact of life events on people it was necessary to gather a great deal of qualitative information about the person's life. This was done in lengthy qualitative interviews in which women were encouraged to talk freely about their circumstances. A group of researchers then read the transcripts of these interviews and rated different aspects of the impact of the various life events reported. Examples of how events were rated according to the long-term threat they posed for people's lives are given in Box 23.4.

Brown and Harris were then able to incorporate the measures into a sophisticated analysis of the social causes of depression. In doing this they were following Durkheim in his study of the effect

---

Box 23.4 Severity of life events in terms of long-term threat

(a) Severe
Woman's father died aged 81. She was married and he had lived with her for 7 years.

Woman's husband was sent to prison for two years; woman was pregnant.

(b) Non-severe
Woman had to tell her husband that his sister had died.

Woman was in a car accident. In a rainstorm a woman 'walked into the car'; her husband was driving. The woman left hospital the same evening as the accident. There were no police charges.

(Source: Adapted from Brown and Harris, 1978)

---

of social structure on rates of suicide (see Chapter 2). Unlike Durkheim, though, who simply guessed at the meaning of events to people (such as religious affiliation), Brown and Harris had specifically *investigated* meanings. Coding at this level involves more than just transferring information from a form into a computer, and is linked with complex issues of measurement validity. This example also shows how to overcome simplistic notions of a quantitative–qualitative divide (see Chapter 22).

Coding for qualitative analysis

You have seen how the replies to open questions in structured interviews can be coded, and how Brown and Harris coded whole interviews to assess the severity of life events. Qualitative data, however, do not emerge only from interviews. Field notes of observations during ethnographic work (Chapter 17), visual images (Chapter 20), published texts (Chapter 27), transcripts of conversations (Chapter 28) and historical documents (Chapter 19) all commonly provide qualitative material for analysis. Sometimes the amount of such material collected during a research project is mountainous, and one purpose of data analysis is to reduce this, by excluding irrelevant material, and grouping together things that are similar. Another reason for coding such material, however, is to develop and test out theories. It is often the case that the coding of qualitative data begins before data collection has finished. Indeed, the development of a coding scheme may determine the sort of data that are collected next in a project, so that *theoretical sampling* (see Chapter 18) can take place. Coding schemes are the creative beginnings of the eventual insights which the researcher hopes to gain by investigating the social world.

Additionally, systematic coding can help in improving the validity of reports of qualitative data. This is done chiefly by presenting *counts* of how many times, and in which circumstances, a thing happens (called *limited quantification* in Chapter 22), and by using coding categories to search for **negative instances** that may contradict, or help to develop, an emerging theory (see Chapter 7). Computer programs, such as NVivo, can help in doing all of these things.

Developing a coding scheme

The initial stage when faced with an interview transcript, or with a set of notes describing observations, or some other qualitative material, is to develop a set of codes that both reflect the initial aims of the research project, and take into account any unexpected issues that have emerged during data collection. That is to say, a coding scheme emerges both **deductively** from pre-existing concerns, questions and hypotheses, and **inductively** from the data itself. Unlike the classical quantitative social survey, where the aims of the research project stay relatively fixed from beginning to end, qualitative research can often be more exploratory, and can end up addressing issues that were not imagined before the project began. For this reason, it may be appropriate to understand **coding** as being also a type of **indexing** (as in the index of a book), whereby the analyst is marking sections of text according to whether they look like contributing to emerging themes. Box 23.5 shows how a coding scheme emerged in a study of nurses' talk.

On this project, then, there were four emerging codes: confessional talk, green issues, touch and stigma. They relate to the initial aims of the research, to unexpected features that emerged during data collection, and potentially to areas of social theory (for example, Goffman's 1968 theory of stigma). Initial coding consists, then, of reading through material and identifying where themes of particular interest are illustrated by data.

Coding schemes like this develop as a research project proceeds. First, the meaning of particular code words can develop as new segments of data prove hard to fit into existing coding categories. It is, therefore, important to record definitions of code words, and any changes to these. Secondly, codes can subdivide, so that a category begins to develop branches. Thus, for example, we might expect the category *green issues* to contain a variety of subtopics as more data are collected. It might, for example, involve strong commitment versus strong rejection of these issues; it might involve commitment to a green diet (vegetarianism), to green politics, or to personal usage of alternative medical therapies. Some people will

313

Box 23.5   Developing a coding scheme

The research project: Nurses' use of alternative therapies in palliative care.

The initial aims:

- To discover whether nurses use these therapies to get patients to engage in intimate, self-revelatory talk.
- To find out whether nurses' use of these therapies was a part of a more generalized commitment to 'green' issues.

The data: Qualitative interviews with nurses involving questioning about these issues.

The initial (deductive) coding of interview transcripts:

- Involved the application of codes called *confessional talk* and *green issues* to segments of text where these topics are discussed.

Later (inductive) coding:

- Unexpectedly, the researcher found that nurses involved in certain sorts of alternative therapy discussed the role of *touch* in expressing a caring relationship, and in helping patients with stigmatized conditions (for example, AIDS or breast removal) to feel better about their bodies and more accepted by other people. Accordingly, two new codes were identified to indicate segments of talk that refer to the topics of *touch* and *stigma*.

Example of data coded as being about 'touch' and 'stigma':

A nurse talking about a patient with AIDS said:

> I have done [massage] with somebody who's got really bad psoriasis and I've been able to massage ... and that's been good for that person psychologically because he had quite a bad body image and he felt like he hadn't been touched and he felt quite repulsed by his skin, so to actually have someone else touch him was quite, it was probably the best thing.

(*Source:* adapted from Garnett, 2000)

---

exhibit particular combinations of codes that others do not.

A coding scheme may be informed by the principles of a particular methodology, such as *conversation, discourse, grounded theory* or *semiotic analysis* (all of which are covered in other chapters of this book). However, a great deal of qualitative analysis is done without particular reference to such specialist methodological approaches and can be termed **qualitative thematic analysis**. An alternative term, *interpretive content analysis*, is used in Chapter 27 to convey a rather similar approach to qualitative analysis. You may wonder why a special term is needed to describe it. The coining of this term is a response to a very common anxiety amongst people starting qualitative analysis for the first time, who often worry that their work will be inadequate unless they can say that their approach has a legitimating name. 'Qualitative thematic analysis' describes what many qualitative researchers actually do, and it often works very well indeed.

Computers and qualitative data analysis

Figure 23.5 shows a transcript of talk between a doctor and the mother of a child brought to the surgery with a cough and a cold. This was part of a research project investigating the prescription of antibiotics (Rollnick et al., 2001). The transcripts were entered using a word processor and then imported into NVivo, from which the extract in

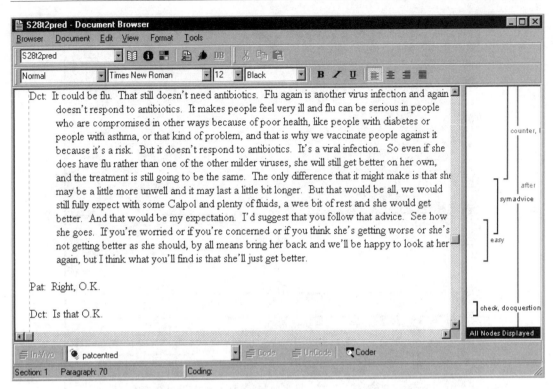

Figure 23.5   *Coded talk in a medical consultation*

Figure 23.5 was taken. On the right hand side of the screen are *coding stripes* – lines with words like 'symadvice', 'easy' and 'check' next to them. These are the names of codes used in the project. Every time a doctor gave advice on symptoms (as this doctor does in relation to the value of Calpol and rest), that section of the text was highlighted and marked with the code 'symadvice'. The code 'easy' occurs when doctors tell patients that they will be happy to see them again if symptoms flare up or do not go away. 'Check' indicates a doctor checking that he or she has been understood, or agreed with.

Using NVivo it is also possible to attach *attributes* to data files, which might be transcripts of naturally occurring talk, or interviews, or almost any other form of text. An attribute might be a characteristic of an interviewee (their gender or their age, for example) or of a data transcript (for example, whether a medical consultation led to a prescription). Attributes can be treated as if they were *variables* and can be exported from NVivo to spreadsheets or SPSS for numerical analysis in support of qualitative analysis.

A number of consultations were taped for this study and the researchers were able to trace the impact of a communication skills training programme on doctors' consultation styles. For example, some doctors after training were more likely to ask patients what they expected of consultations, something that was rarely done before the training. To discover this, a search was done in which an *attribute* was used to first select just those consultations occurring before training. These transcripts were then searched for segments of text coded as being questions about patients' expectations. Then the same search was done on consultations that occurred after training. When compared, the result described above was found. Another result concerned advice on symptoms which, it was found, was more common in consultations where antibiotics were *not* prescribed, suggesting that they might have a 'consolation prize' function.

Figure 23.6 shows the search tool in NVivo. A 'node lookup' search allows the user to find all segments of text coded under a particular code or 'node' (the preferred term in NVivo). A 'text

315

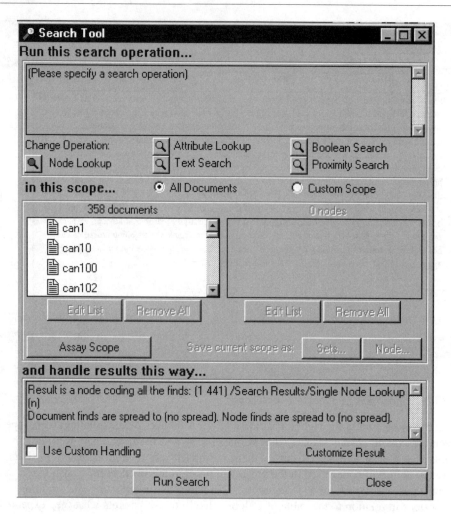

Figure 23.6 *The search tool in NVivo*

search' can also be useful; this allows the researcher to retrieve all instances of a particular word or string of text that occur in data associated with a project, together with surrounding text (the paragraph, for example). Using this feature, for example, it would be possible to retrieve all paragraphs containing the word 'antibiotics'.

'Boolean' searches allow the analyst to combine different kinds of search in a single operation. For example, a search might be made for all paragraphs with the word 'antibiotics' in them occurring in consultations before training happened, comparing these with such paragraphs in consultations after training. Or an attribute like gender might be used to compare whether male or female doctors talk about symptoms in different ways. Chapter 12 contains detailed advice on how to do Boolean searches.

Counting and qualitative research

The use of computers, then, enables the rapid retrieval of information from a mass of otherwise unwieldy transcripts, and is a superior method to manually cutting out segments from the transcript and sorting these into piles. Additionally, computers can help to develop more refined coding schemes. Once a researcher has all the examples of a particular coding category listed in a single document, it is relatively easy to read through

---

Box 23.6 Private and public health care

Out of 42 private consultations, subsequent appointments with the doctor were fixed at the patient's convenience in 36% of cases; in 60% of cases the consultation involved polite small talk about either the doctor's or the patient's personal or professional lives. The corresponding percentages in the 104 public health service clinics observed were significantly smaller (10% and 30%). This supported Silverman's impression that a more personal service was given in private clinics.

(*Source:* Silverman, 1984)

---

these and detect subcategories of existing codes. Computers can also help in producing *counts* of the number of times particular things occur.

Counting in qualitative research can help in reassuring the reader that the researcher has not simply trawled through a mass of data and selected anecdotes to report that support his or her particular bias. This is an aspect of *validity* (see Chapter 7). If phrases such as 'most people felt', 'usually people I interviewed said' or 'it was rarely observed' can be backed up by the actual number of times events occurred in field notes or interview transcripts, then the reader has more confidence in the report. Additionally, counts can be helpful in making comparisons between settings. David Silverman (1984) found this in an observational study comparing medical consultations in private clinics with those in public health service clinics (Box 23.6).

Careers and typologies

Two devices that have often proved useful in organizing qualitative data for analysis are the notions of **career** and **typology**. The first of these helps to explain the progress people make through social settings or experiences; the second of these helps to categorize the sorts of experience they can have. Each of these represents a way in which new theories can be developed to account for observations.

Perhaps the best-known usage of the concept of *career* occurs in Howard Becker's (1963) study of how people come to use marijuana. Here, he argued that individuals passed through three stages in careers that ended in becoming a user. These are described in Box 23.7, together with

code words (not reported by Becker) to describe them.

Other research workers using the concept of career to organize their data include Sally MacIntyre (1977), who interviewed unmarried women who had become pregnant. She mapped their subsequent careers through various events and decision points (whether to have an abortion, whether to marry, whether to offer their baby for adoption and so on) to produce a variety of career outcomes (for example, single motherhood, marriage). Patricia Taraborrelli (1993) describes how she used the idea of career to understand people's experience of caring for spouses who had developed Alzheimer's disease. Figure 23.7 shows her flowchart describing three 'career paths'. People who had had previous experience of caring for chronically sick individuals followed pattern B, whereby at diagnosis they quickly adopted what the researcher termed the 'carer's perspective', involving a practical approach to the problem. Such carers successfully distinguished caring *for* their spouse from caring *about* their spouse. Thus they were willing to seek practical help with care from formal services without feeling that this meant they did not care about the person enough to do the work themselves. Others, however, had to learn this hard lesson, and after a period of 'initial innocence' would follow one of two paths: a 'crisis point' leading to breakdown (pattern C), or a 'turning point' where they successfully adopted the carer's perspective and learned to seek the help they needed (pattern A).

In each of these cases, the researchers will have developed coding categories to identify segments of data illustrating the phenomena they describe (such as the moment a person

---

Box 23.7 Coding careers in a study of marijuana users

1 Learning the technique of smoking to produce effects   *technique*
2 Learning to perceive the effects   *perceive*
3 Learning to enjoy the effects   *enjoy*

A variety of instances in his data illustrate these themes. A numbered version of one extract is produced below:

I didn't get high the first time …	1
The second time I wasn't sure,	2
and he [smoking companion] told me,	3
like I asked him for some of the	4
symptoms or something …	5
So he told me to sit on a stool.	6
I sat on – I think I sat on a bar	7
stool – and he said 'let your	8
feet hang' and then when I got	9
down my feet were real cold you	10
know … and I started feeling it,	11
you know. That was the first time.	12
And then about a week after that,	13
sometime pretty close to it,	14
really got on. That was the first	15
time I got on a big laughing kick,	16
you know. Then I really knew I	17
was on.	18

Lines 1–12 concern *technique,* lines 10–18 concern *perceive* and lines 15–18 concern *enjoy.*

(*Source:* adapted from Becker, 1963)

---

recognized embezzlement as a solution, the 'crisis point' accounts given by Taraborrelli's carers, the decision points described by the women MacIntyre interviewed).

Figure 23.7 shows a flowchart drawn with the *modelling* tool in NVivo. This, as you can see, helps draw diagrams and these can be cut and pasted into other software. Additionally, though, NVivo allows *nodes* and *attributes* to be included in models and these drawing objects are 'live' links to the original data associated with them. Thus, on examining a model such as the one in Figure 23.8, a researcher can click on one of the nodes and retrieve text associated with it. Such a model thus becomes a tool to think with. In this case, the model arises from a project examining the representation of cancer experience in newspapers (described more fully in Chapter 27). Women with experience of breast cancer wrote books about their experience more often than men with cancer or women with other kinds of cancer. These books frequently involved themes of life review, struggle and personal transformation. Many of the authors achieved celebrity status as a result.

Typologies, in contrast to careers, are a means of categorizing events or people without necessarily involving a sense of progression from one event to another. Glaser and Strauss (1966), in their study of dying people, developed a typology of *awareness contexts,* shown in Box 23.8. It will be seen that by incorporating the idea of 'determinants' of particular awareness contexts, the researchers are proposing a causal theory. In

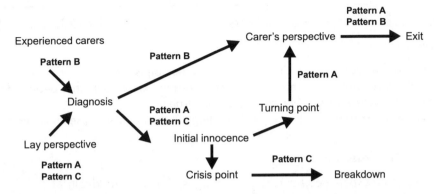

Figure 23.7   *Flowchart showing three career paths for carers.* (Gilbert 1993: 183)

fact, Becker in his study described earlier, does the same thing, claiming that *all* the steps in the career path are needed before the relevant career outcome can be achieved.

We have now moved some way from the relatively simple procedure of coding segments of text into categories in order to show how this can quickly develop into a complex process of **theory building** from data. This is discussed in Chapter 18 on the *discovery of grounded theory*. It is relevant here to note that, in qualitative research, coding and analysis of data are activities that can begin in the early stages of data collection. The ideas that emerge will frequently determine where the researcher next looks for data. Thus, the researcher may be interested in using *theoretical sampling* (Chapter 18) to develop a strategy for data collection. This might involve searching for

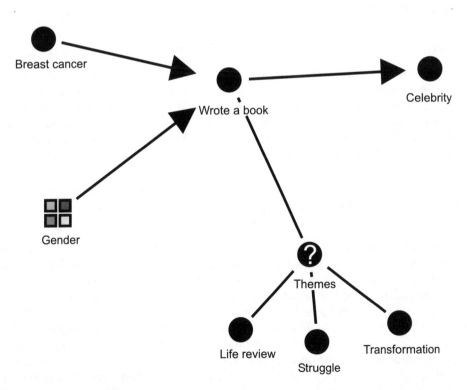

Figure 23.8   *An NVivo model*

> ## Box 23.8   Awareness contexts: a typology and its determinants
>
> *Typology*
>
> 1   **Open awareness**   Everyone knows the person is dying
> 2   **Closed awareness**   The dying person does not know, but other people do
> 3   **Suspicion awareness** The dying person suspects
> 4   **Pretence awareness**   Everyone, including the dying person, pretends that they do
>   not know
>
> *Determinants of closed awareness*
>
> 1   Patients are inexperienced at recognizing signs of impending death
> 2   Medical staff are skilled at hiding the truth
> 3   Staff have a professional rationale that says that it is best to withhold the truth
> 4   The patient has no family allies

negative instances (see also Chapter 7) that contradict an emerging theory, so that a better theory can be developed. Theoretical sampling to search for such variation is described in the account from Glaser and Strauss in Box 23.9, concerning the way in which their typology of awareness contexts was developed.

as well as other studies shown in this chapter are examples of combined qualitative and quantitative analysis. Additionally we have shown that an interaction between data collection, analysis and theory building is appropriate; the creative construction of coding schemes lies at the core of such activity.

Conclusion

This chapter has reviewed methods for coding data in order to prepare them for analysis. Both statistical and qualitative analyses have been covered since an important theme of this book is to encourage the use of both forms of data in research projects. The work of Brown and Harris

Further reading

De Vaus (2002) contains a helpful discussion of coding for quantitative analysis. Coffey and Atkinson (1996) explain and illustrate a variety of approaches to qualitative data analysis, including those based on the sort of coding explained in the chapter, as well as some others.

> ## Box 23.9   Theoretical sampling in developing a grounded theory of awareness contexts
>
> 'Visits to the various medical services were scheduled as follows: I wished first to look at services that minimized patient awareness (and so first looked at a premature baby service and then a neurosurgical service where patients were frequently comatose). I wished next to look at dying in a situation where expectancy of staff and often of patients was great and where dying tended to be slow. So I looked next at a cancer service. I wished then to look at conditions where death was unexpected and rapid, and so looked at an emergency service ... So our scheduling of types of service was directed by a *general conceptual scheme* – which included hypotheses about awareness, expectedness and rate of dying – as well as by a *developing conceptual structure including matters not at first envisaged*.' (Glaser and Strauss, 1967: 59; emphasis added)

Box 23.10   Web pointers for coding and data analysis

An article on different methods for coding occupational and **social status for statistical analysis:**
http://qb.soc.surrey.ac.uk/resources/classification/socintro.htm

Working with text: part of the Atlas website (software for qualitative data analysis) devoted to explaining concepts behind such analysis
www.atlasti.de/worktext.shtml

Qualis Research home page (makers of The Ethnograph, a tool for qualitative data analysis) – click on 'QDA paper' to download an excellent overview of qualitative thematic analysis
http://www.qualisresearch.com/

QSR home page, click on 'resources' for helpful material for learning qualitative data analysis. More information about NVIVO (software for qualitative analysis) can be found here too
www.qsrinternational.com

Visit the website for this book at www.rscbook.co.uk to link to these web pointers.

Student Reader (Seale, 2004): relevant readings

18   A.N. Oppenheim: 'The quantification of questionnaire data'
44   Anselm L. Strauss and Juliet Corbin: 'Open coding'
45   Graham R. Gibbs: 'Searching for text'
46   Udo Kelle: 'Theory building in qualitative research and computer programs for the management of textual data'

Key concepts

Coding

SPSS
  Cross-tabulation
  Data viewer
  Frequency count

Data cleaning
Data matrix
Multiple response item
Nominal, ordinal, interval variables

Pre-coded and **post-coded**
String, numeric, dichotomous variables

NVivo
  Attribute
  Coding stripe
  Modeller
  Project pad

Career
Qualitative thematic analysis
Typology

24

Statistical reasoning: from one to two variables

Alice Bloch

CONTENTS

The use of statistics in social research has a long history, with the production of social statistics being closely tied to programmes of legislation and social reform (see Chapter 8). Research reports in the quantitative tradition often present statistical tables with the author's interpretation of them in the surrounding text. It may be tempting to concentrate on the text rather than 'read' the table and draw one's own conclusions. The purpose of this and the following chapter is to help you to read research reports that include statistical analysis, so that you can understand and then assess whether a researcher's conclusions are supported by the numerical data they present. The chapters will also help you to construct statistical arguments of your own.

This first chapter on statistical reasoning will begin by outlining some key ideas about **univariate** statistics, before going on to **bivariate** statistics. That is to say, it will discuss the presentation of single *variable* analysis before discussing ways in which two variables can inter-

act. This will lead, in the chapter that follows, into a discussion of how statistical reasoning can be used to construct arguments about **causality**, the idea that one variable has caused another variable to vary.

Univariate statistics

As you saw in the previous chapter, the product of a social survey is a *data matrix* that can be analysed, most efficiently, by entering data into statistical software such as SPSS. Figure 23.1 in that chapter showed you an example of some data that had been entered. Figure 24.1 is another image of the SPSS *data editor*, but this time showing 'variable view', a screen which allows you to enter information about variables. Here, the researcher can specify information about each variable and assign numerical labels to each category for the purpose of analysis. Figure 24.1 shows this with **value labels** for the variable *jobsat* showing.

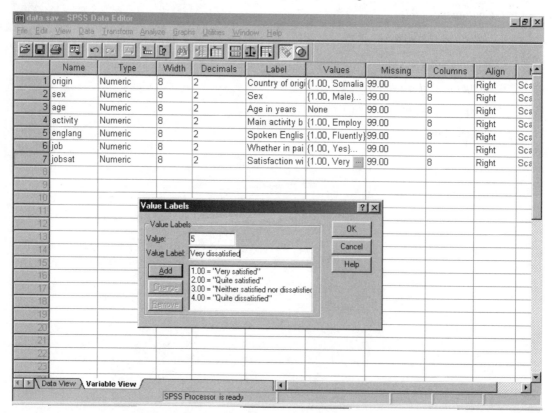

Figure 24.1   *Variable view and value labels dialogue box (SPSS)*

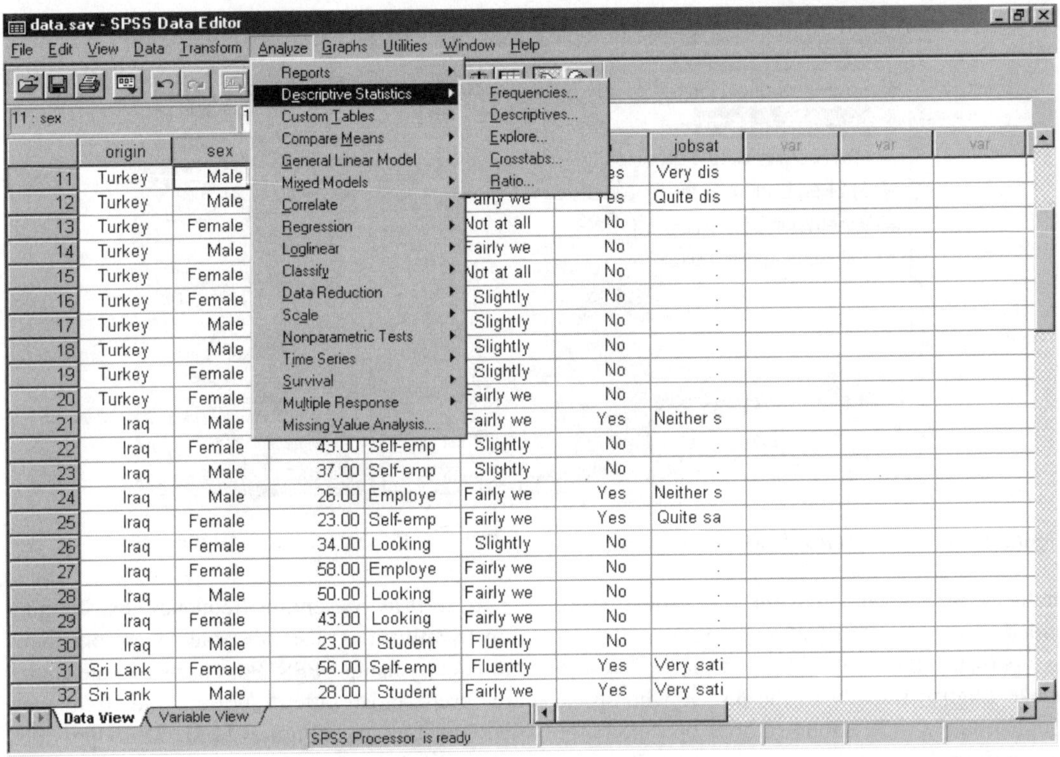

Figure 24.2   *Descriptive statistics with SPSS*

If a raw data matrix such as that in Figure 23.1 were presented in a research report it would be difficult to see the main patterns that exist in the data. Using SPSS makes the analysis of data simple and quick and also provides options for the numerical or graphical presentation of the data.

Univariate statistics are those that present the analysis of a single variable. Such analysis might involve the production of **frequency distributions** – the distribution of data from a single variable showing the number of times each score or value occurs. Using SPSS, the data from a frequency distribution can be presented as both absolute numbers and percentages. Figure 24.2 shows the SPSS commands to open the frequencies dialogue box.

Clicking on 'frequencies' in the right hand menu brings up a frequencies *dialogue box* (Figure 24.3). In order to specify which variables are required for analysis the variables are transferred from the source list (left hand side) to the target variable list (right hand side) by using the arrow in the middle of the dialogue box. In Figure 24.3 the

variable *sex* has been transferred to the target variable list while *age* is highlighted in order to be transferred.

Clicking on 'OK' generates an analysis and SPSS output (see Figure 24.4). The information for the variable *sex* shows that there were 25 men and 25 women in the survey (see 'Frequency' column). Another way of putting this is that 50% were males and 50% were females and this is indicated in the column marked 'Percent'. The column 'Valid percent' excludes *missing values* if there are any (see Chapter 23). The final column is the 'Cumulative percent' and is most useful for *ordinal* and *interval* variables because there is a sense of increase or decrease, which is not the case with *nominal* variables (see Chapter 13).

The distribution for *spoken English at the moment* shows a more complex picture than that of *sex*. It shows that eight people spoke English fluently, which was 16% of respondents or 16.7% of valid respondents. The percent and valid percent differ because two respondents did not answer the question and were therefore not

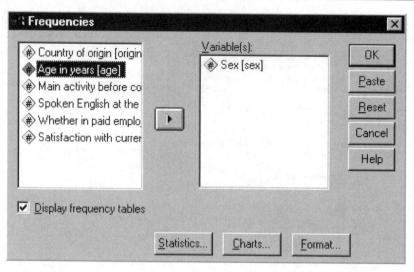

Figure 24.3   *Frequencies dialogue box (SPSS)*

included in the valid percent and instead were coded as missing (99). The final column, cumulative percent, shows that if we add the 16.7% who spoke English fluently to the 33.3% who spoke English fairly well, a total of 50% of valid cases spoke English either fluently or fairly well.

As well as presenting frequency distributions numerically, it is also possible to present them graphically using SPSS. Bar charts and pie charts are used most often. Within the frequency dialogue box (see Figure 24.3), SPSS provides output options including **charts**. Figure 24.5

Sex

		Frequency	Percent	Valid Percent	Cumulative Percent
Valid	Male	25	50.0	50.0	50.0
	Female	25	50.0	50.0	100.0
	Total	50	100.0	100.0	

Spoken English at the moment

		Frequency	Percent	Valid Percent	Cumulative Percent
Valid	Fluently	8	16.0	16.7	16.7
	Fairly well	16	32.0	33.3	50.0
	Slightly	17	34.0	35.4	85.4
	Not at all	7	14.0	14.6	100.0
	Total	48	96.0	100.0	
Missing	99.00	2	4.0		
Total		50	100.0		

Figure 24.4   *Frequency tables for the variables 'sex' and 'spoken English' (SPSS)*

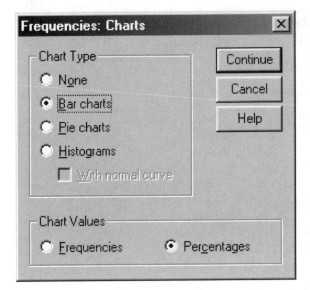

Spoken English at the moment

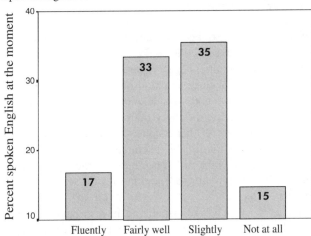

Spoken English at the moment

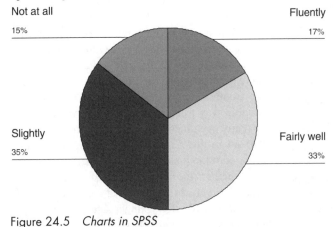

Figure 24.5 *Charts in SPSS*

shows the chart options with 'bar charts' selected and the output that results when, first, **bar charts** and, secondly, **pie charts** are selected for the variable *spoken English at the moment*.

While numerical frequency distributions and graphical representations for ordinal level variables such as English language can be very useful, for interval or ratio level variables there are generally too many categories. Using the example of *age*, which is an interval level variable, one strategy would be to **recode** the variable into age band categories that make it into an ordinal level variable and then use bar charts or pie charts to display the results. This is easily done in SPSS (use the 'recode' button on the drop-down menu at 'transform') and can be useful. However, collapsing categories involves losing information about fine differences between cases. If we wish to keep the details of the raw data then we can summarize the distribution of an interval level variable using **descriptive statistics**: the *mean*, *mode*, or *median*. These are all **measures of central tendency,** which means that they are statistics that help to indicate the central point of a particular distribution. Another statistic, the **range**, measures the distance between the highest and lowest scores. In the frequencies dialogue box there is a submenu that will produce these statistics, shown in Figure 24.6.

The **mean** is the average of the distribution of the variable. The mean is calculated by adding together all the ages (the sum) and dividing by the number of cases. From the output shown in Figure 24.7 we can see that the mean age of respondents in this data is 36.54. The **median** is the number positioned in the middle of a distribution, below which half the values fall: it is 34. The median is more suited to variables measured at ordinal

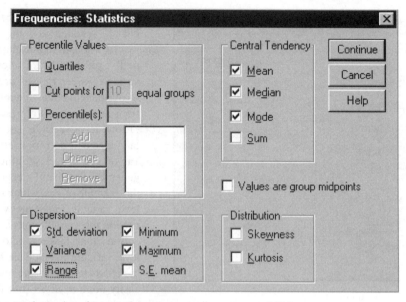

Figure 24.6 *Dialogue box for specifying univariate statistics in SPSS*

level than interval level. The third measure of central tendency is the **mode** and this statistic is normally used for nominal variables, being the most frequently occurring value in a distribution, which in this case is 19.

In addition to these measures of central tendency, you will sometimes find social researchers referring to the **standard deviation** in research reports. This is a statistic which indicates how widely cases are dispersed around the mean. If many of the values of cases are far away from the mean, the standard deviation will be high. If most of the values are close to the mean it will be low. In

Statistics

Age in years

N	Valid	50
	Missing	0
Mean		36.5400
Median		34.0000
Mode		19.00
Std. Deviation		14.0541
Range		46.00
Minimum		18.00
Maximum		64.00

Figure 24.7 *Output of descriptive statistics for the variable 'age in years'*

the case of age the standard deviation (sometimes written as SD) is 14.05, indicating quite a narrow dispersion for age. If a researcher reports the mean and standard deviation of interval variables this tells us a great deal about the variable, even without seeing the raw data that led to them. Another measure of dispersion is the **range**. Figure 24.7 shows that in this example the range is 46. The range is the difference between the highest score or maximum (64) and the lowest score or minimum (18).

One way of visualizing the distribution of interval level variables is to obtain a **histogram** in SPSS. Figure 24.8 shows a histogram produced by SPSS for the variable *age*. Note that SPSS has grouped the data so that patterns can be easily seen. Statistics have been requested, appearing to the right of the histogram, and a **normal curve** has been superimposed onto the data. The normal curve is a theoretical distribution based on an infinite number of cases. If the distribution of this variable was truly 'normal' the curve would be perfectly symmetrical, whereas in fact it is **skewed** in this case. Superimposing the normal curve onto the histogram allows the researcher to see whether the distribution of a variable is skewed. Figure 24.8 shows that the variable *age* is skewed towards the younger age groups or, put another way, is *negatively skewed*.

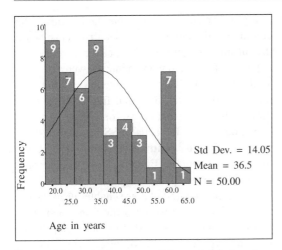

Figure 24.8 *A histogram of the variable 'age'*

Bivariate analysis

Univariate analysis can show us how a single group of people varies on some characteristic, such as sex, age or job satisfaction. However, to really understand data and to think about it theoretically or in terms of policy development or evaluation it is necessary to explore the relationship between two or more variables. **Bivariate**

analysis involves exploration of relationships between two variables. For instance, a researcher might seek to discover the relationship between sex and economic activity, or between country of origin and levels of spoken English. (Where the researcher is concerned with the relationship between three or more variables, **multivariate** statistics are used, covered in the next chapter.)

Contingency tables

The best way to approach bivariate analysis is through the analysis of **contingency tables**, though such analysis can also be presented in graph form. Contingency tables are devices that show the relationships between two variables, each of which has only a few categories. Interval level variables (such as *age in years*), if not recoded, generally have too many values for inclusion in tables, so if they are to be used in tables they are often re-coded into categories.

In SPSS, the production of contingency tables is done using the 'crosstabs' option in the 'descriptive statistics' submenu of the main 'analyze' menu. Figure 24.9 shows the resultant menu, with

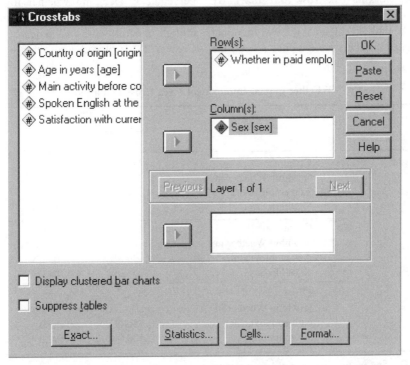

Figure 24.9 *Crosstabulations in SPSS*

two variables selected from the left hand list and pasted into two of the right hand boxes.

The researcher must decide which variable should be the **row variable** (going across the table) and which the **column variable** (going down the table). The third box allows for the selection of a third 'layer' variable, which is used for multivariate analysis (see Chapter 25). You can see, too, that there are options for 'statistics' and 'cells'. Under the 'statistics' menu the researcher can select a number of statistics including *measures of association* and *chi-square tests*. These will be explained in a later section below. Under the 'cells' menu the researcher can choose how the data is displayed in each box or **cell** of the resultant table. This idea is best explained by looking at the output from this procedure in Figure 24.10.

Both these variables are *dichotomous*, which means that within each variable there are two categories. The resultant output is a 2 × 2 contingency table. The 14 in the top left-hand group of numbers, or **cell** as it can be called, represents in this case the number of male respondents in paid employment. Adding the 4 women who were also in paid employment means that a total of 18 people were working (the **row marginal**). By adding 14 to 4 in this way, we are going across the top row of the table to calculate the row marginal of 18. Marginal numbers are the ones around the

'margins' or edges of the table. Going down the columns of the table, we can see that in each case the **column marginal** is 25, since there were equal numbers of men and women interviewed. Conveniently, SPSS prints out the percentage of the total represented by each marginal figure. Thus 18 is 36% of the total, which is 50 (or 100%).

Inside each of the cells SPSS has placed three numbers: first the **count**, as described above, and then two percentage figures. These are, respectively, the **row percentage** and the **column percentage**. The first of these enables us to see the proportion of those who answered in a particular way to the question who were in each group. Thus, we can say that 77.8% of those who were in employment were men compared with 22.2% of women. Of those who were not working, 34.4% were men and 65.6% were women. This is not particularly helpful, as we want a more direct comparison between men and women. Therefore, we should look at the column percentages, which show that 56% (14 out of 25) of men were working compared with only 16% (4 out of 25) of women. If we were using this output to write up results in this case we would use column percentages. Deciding whether row or column percentages are appropriate is sometimes difficult, though generally the *independent variable* (see Chapter 25) is placed across the top of the table

Whether in paid employment * Sex Crosstabulation

			Sex		
			Male	Female	Total
Whether in paid employment	Yes	Count	14	4	18
		% within Whether in paid employment	77.8%	22.2%	100.0%
		% within Sex	56.0%	16.0%	36.0%
	No	Count	11	21	32
		% within Whether in paid employment	34.4%	65.6%	100.0%
		% within Sex	44.0%	84.0%	64.0%
Total		Count	25	25	50
		% within Whether in paid employment	50.0	50.0	100.0%
		% within Sex	100.0	100.0	100.0%

Figure 24.10 *Sex by whether in paid employment*

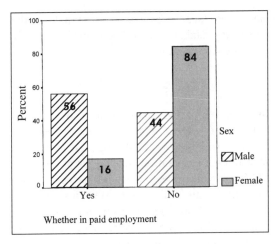

Figure 24.11 *Graphical representation of a contingency table*

and the percentage used when describing the data is the column percentage.

As with univariate statistics, bivariate statistics can be presented in graphical form, often giving them greater impact. Figure 24.11 shows how men and women differed in terms of paid employment by means of a bar chart. The vertical axis (y **axis**) shows the percentage working or not working while the horizontal axis *(x* **axis**) distinguishes between men and women.

Statistical significance

We might stop at this point in our analysis of Figures 24.10 and 24.11 and conclude that men

are more likely than women to be in paid employment. However, this would be a mistake. How can we know whether this result is not simply caused by chance? Perhaps we have, at random, picked an unrepresentative sample. In other words, how likely is it that we can generalize from the sample of 50 to the population from which it is drawn, which in this case are all refugees eligible to work in Britain? Estimation of the likelihood that a sample result is true of the population involves **statistical inference**. A variety of statistics that help to do this are available, but the one most commonly used for contingency tables is known as the **chi-square test**. Using SPSS it is possible to obtain statistics for contingency tables (see dialogue box in Figure 24.9). Figure 24.12 shows SPSS output when a chi-square test is specified.

The information given in the SPSS output is much more detailed than is necessary for basic data analysis and interpretation. The top line of output is all that is needed here. Pearson's chi-square test produces an estimate of the statistical *significance* of the result in the associated table (in this case, the table in Figure 24.10). If the significance value is small (conventionally less than 0.05) then we reject what is known as the **null hypothesis** of no association between the two variables and say that they *are* related. That is to say, as one variable changes, so the other one changes too. A condition of using the chi-square statistic is that the sample has been collected using a *probability sample* (see Chapter 13). In the

Chi-Square Tests

	Value	df	Asymp Sig. (2-sided)	Exact Sig. (2-sided)	Exact Sig. (1-sided)
Pearson Chi-Square	8.681[b]	1	.003		
Continuity Correction[a]	7.031	1	.008		
Likelihood Ratio	9.062	1	.003		
Fisher's Exact Test				.007	.004
Linear-by-Linear Association	8.507	1	.004		
N of Valid Cases	50				

[a]Computed only for 2 × 2 table.

[b]0 cells (.0%) have expected count less than 5. The minimum expected count is 9.00.

Figure 24.12 *Statistical output for chi-square in SPSS*

above example, the significance of the Pearson chi-square is 0.003, which is less than 0.05 so we can say that the result is probably not due to chance and if we had been able to study the entire population of refugees eligible for employment then we would find the same sort of difference between men and women.

The significance of the chi-square value is sometimes known as the **p-value** with *p* standing for *probability*. The value of chi-square is affected by sample size. Intuitively it makes sense because a random sample of 1,000 is going to be more representative of the population than a random sample of 10 where we are more likely, by chance, to have selected atypical individuals that skew the distribution. A statistically significant result (in other words, a low *p*-value) is more likely with large samples. Additionally, the principles underlying chi-square require that the *expected values* in at least 20% of the cells in a contingency table are more than 5. Thus, SPSS (in note b to the output shown in Figure 24.12) has produced a 'minimum expected count' of 9, indicating that it is valid to use the results of chi-square. **Expected values** for particular cells are those that we would expect by chance given the distribution of the *marginal* figures in a table. The expected value for the top left-hand cell is calculated by multiplying the left-hand column marginal (25) by the top row marginal (18) and dividing by the total sample size (50) to get 9. You will see that the actual value (usually called the observed value) in that cell is 14. The calculation of chi-square involves comparing the *observed values* with the *expected values* in cells.

The mathematical calculations that underlie the chi-square statistic are not particularly complex. It is unnecessary to learn them in order to analyse data. The suggestions for further reading at the end of this chapter contain books where these calculations are shown if you wish to take this further. The important thing to grasp is the meaning of statistics such as the chi-square rather than the underlying mathematics.

Finally, the chi-square is not the only test of significance. Others exist for data that are not arranged in contingency tables. However, all have the same underlying purpose of allowing estimates to be made about the likelihood of a sample having produced a chance result. Whatever the underlying statistic, this likelihood is usually expressed as a *p*-value.

Measures of association

In contingency tables statistics can also be used to indicate the *strength* and *direction* of association between variables. Such statistics are known as **measures of association** and they are produced in SPSS using the same dialogue box as the one used for producing chi-square statistics. Output relevant to Figure 24.10 is given in Figure 24.13, showing two of the many tests of association available: *phi* and *Cramer's V*.

Each measure of association has slightly different characteristics, and the choice of which to use is governed by the level of measurement of the variables in the table (for example, whether nominal or ordinal), and by how many cells there are in the table. SPSS gives on-screen help in selecting the test most appropriate for each type of table. For a 2 × 2 contingency table (in other words, a table with two variables each with two categories) the most appropriate statistic to use is *phi*. For larger tables *Cramer's V* is a more appropriate s tatistic and will give a slightly different result where such tables are involved. Association can vary between 0 and +1 or –1. An association can therefore be positive or negative. A perfect **positive association** is indicated by +1, a perfect **negative association** by –1 and the absence of association by zero. An association of 0.417, as shown in Figure 24.13, suggests a moderate positive association between the variables.

You should note that the concept of *association* is the *same* as the concept of **correlation**. 'Association' tends to be used when discussing the analysis of tables; 'correlation' tends to be used

		Value	Approx Sig.
Nominal by Nominal	Phi	.417	.003
	Cramer's V	.417	.003
N of Valid Cases		50	

Figure 24.13 *Tests of association for a crosstabulation produced by SPSS*

when discussing bivariate analysis using interval level data, the subject of the next section. It is very important to distinguish between these two concepts and the very different concept of *significance*. For example, a relationship can show an association or a correlation, but may nevertheless fail to be significant if the sample size is too small.

Although it is good practice to report both a test of significance and one of association when writing up the results of a research project, measures of association are often omitted when considering data in tables. This is because a judgement of strength and direction can be made simply by examining the percentages in the table. Additionally, the various tests of association for tables do not always 'behave themselves'. For a variety of reasons, some do not indicate the direction of associations, or may indicate stronger or weaker associations than really exist. For these reasons they are rather rough-and-ready tools, compared with the more consistent chi-square test.

Using interval variables

When variables have many values, as is often the case with interval variables such as *income*, or as mentioned earlier *age*, they can be recoded into a few categories so that they can be presented in bar charts or tables. However, this represents a loss of information and the raw data can be used graphically and statistically to explore the relationship between variables. Using an example of the *number of hours worked* and *income*, Figure 24.14 shows four graphical representations of possible relationships between the number of hours worked and income.

Scattergrams (or **scatterplots** as they are sometimes known) are produced in SPSS by pulling down the 'graph' menu and choosing 'scatter'. The statistics are produced by pulling down the 'analyze' menu, choosing 'correlate' and then 'bivariate', as Figure 24.15 shows. From the bivariate correlations dialogue box the *Pearson coefficient* and the *two-tailed test of significance* were selected to produce the output in Figure 24.14. By selecting a **two-tailed test** the researcher is making no assumptions about the direction of the correlation – in other words, whether it will be positive or negative.

The first scattergram in Figure 24.14 shows a **positive relationship** between the variables *number of hours worked* and *income*. That means it shows a scatter of points rising from the bottom left corner to the top right. Each of the points represents a person about whom two facts are recorded: the number of hours worked and their weekly income. The first scattergram shows that the more hours people work the greater their income. In other words, as one variable increases, the other variable increases too. This is the defining characteristic of a positive relationship.

The next scattergram demonstrates a **negative relationship**, which means that the more hours worked the less people earn. The defining characteristic of a negative relationship is that as one variable increases, the other one decreases.

The third scattergram demonstrates the absence of a relationship, while the fourth one shows a **curvilinear relationship**. Here, there is an initial increase in income in line with the increase in the number of hours worked. However, after a peak in income at 17 hours a week, the amount of income starts to decrease with an increase in hours.

The line that runs through the points in each of these scattergrams is the **line of best fit** or **regression line**. It is the single straight line that can be drawn through the cluster of points that involves the least distance between it and all the points. It is useful in making predictions. With a scattergram that shows a strong relationship between variables it is possible to predict the values of one variable from the values of another, in this case income and hours worked, by using the points on the regression line. Thus, in the first scattergram, we might reasonably predict that someone working 20 hours a week would earn roughly 100 income units. Predicting income by hours worked where there is no relationship or where there is a curvilinear relationship would be misleading as, in practice, the points are very far away from the regression line. Making predictions only makes sense if there is a positive or negative linear relationship where most of the points are reasonably close to the line.

Below the scattergrams there is also a value for *r* (which is **Pearson's *r***) and a *p*-value, both generated by SPSS. The value of Pearson's *r* is a measure

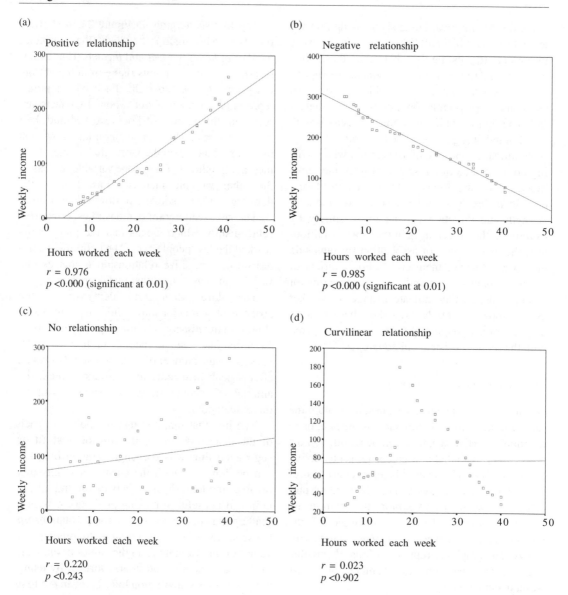

Figure 24.14 *Scattergrams showing different relationships between the number of hours worked and income*

of *correlation* (sometimes called a **correlation coefficient**) and it indicates how close the points are to the line, measuring how *strong* the relationship is. If most of the points are close to the line, this statistic will be close to +1, indicating a *strong positive association*, or –1, indicating a *strong negative relationship*. In fact, if all the points fall on the line, Pearson's *r* is either +1 or –1 exactly. If there is broad scatter of points, as in the third scattergram, Pearson's *r* will be close to

zero, indicating no association. The Pearson's correlation coefficient is an indicator of association suitable for use with two interval variables. Sometimes, *r* is squared; for example, the r^2 for the first scattergram in Figure 24.14 would be 0.976 × 0.976 = 0.953. The advantage of r^2 is that it can be interpreted as the **percentage of variance explained.** Thus we can say that, in the first scattergram, the hours worked per week explains 95.3% of the variability in weekly income.

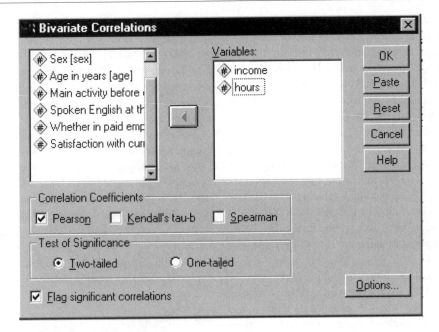

Figure 24.15 *Getting correlations in SPSS*

You will also notice that a *p*-value is given. In the first two scattergrams the SPSS output shows that the relationship between the two variables was significant at 0.01 (which is more significant than the frequently used 0.05). This indicates that the relationship is very likely to hold true in the population, if this is a random sample drawn from that population. In both of the first two cases we would say that the relationship is strong and statistically significant. In the last two we could not say this as $p > 0.05$. You should notice that Pearson's *r* is not suited to indicate curvilinear relationships. Unless we saw the fourth scattergram, we would not be aware that this relationship actually existed.

Comparing the means of two groups

So far, we have considered relationships between two variables measured at the same level. Quite frequently, however, the social researcher is concerned with comparing the average values between two or more groups of people. Thus, we might be interested in how men and women differ, on average, in their incomes. This type of relationship can be understood as one between a nominal variable and an interval variable. One way of ap-

proaching this is to establish whether there is a statistically significant difference between the *means* of the two groups.

Figure 24.16 shows SPSS output from a data set containing 10 men and 10 women who have been asked to indicate their annual income. The value for the *means* (shown under the first bit of output called 'group statistics') shows that women earn more, on average, than men: £14,780 compared with £9,255. The *standard deviations* for each are given, indicating a greater spread of incomes for men. The question that then arises, though, is whether this difference is likely to hold true in the population from which this sample of 20 has been drawn (we assume) at random. This, then, becomes a problem concerning the *statistical significance* of the result, the same problem for which (as you saw earlier) the *chi-square* is used when tables are involved.

The estimation of statistical significance here, though, is based instead on the significance of the *t*-value (this procedure is known as a *t*-test) and two of these are shown: one for *equal* variance ($p = 0.024$) and another for *unequal* variance ($p = 0.028$). (The **variance** is the square of the standard deviation.) Whether the variances are equal is shown by the significance of Levene's test. This

335

helps in deciding which of the two *t*-test results to rely upon. Like a *t*-test, Levene's test sets up a *null hypothesis* of no association (that is to say, that the difference in variance is zero). If Levene's test is significant below the 0.05 level then it is possible to reject the null hypothesis of no association and conclude that variances are significantly different. If $p > 0.05$ then the null hypothesis that the difference between variances is zero is accepted. Since, in this case, the significance of Levene's test stands at $p = 0.017$, indicating that the variances are *unequal*, the second *t*-value ($p = 0.028$) is taken. This indicates that it is likely that this difference between men and women's income holds true in the population from which this sample was drawn.

The statistics shown in Figure 24.16 are obtained in SPSS from a submenu of the 'analyze' menu. Once the 'analyze' box is pulled down, the next step is to click on 'compare means' and then 'independent samples t-test'. The *dependent* variable is placed in the test variable box and the 'grouping' variable – which is the *independent variable* – is placed in the grouping variable box. The 'define groups' box then becomes active and the variable values have to be specified as shown in Figure 24.17. In this case women are coded 1 and men are coded 2.

Sometimes in social research it is important to compare the means of more than two groups. Thus, for example, social class might be measured as upper, middle and lower. If we wished to compare the mean income of groups defined in this way, the *t*-test would be inappropriate, and a related procedure known as the **analysis of variance** would be used. Details of this are beyond the scope of this chapter, but can be explored in further reading.

Conclusion

In this chapter we have moved from the analysis of

Group Statistics

	SEX	N	Mean	Std Deviation	Std Error Mean
INCURV	Male	10	9255.0000	6202.6182	1961.4401
	Female	10	14780.00	3489.9220	1103.6102

Independent Samples Test

	Levene's Test for Equality of variances		*t*-test for Equality of Means							
									95% Confidence interval of the Difference	
	F	Sig	t	df	Sig. (2-tailed)	Mean Difference	Std. Error Difference	Lower	Upper
INCURV Equal variances assumed	6.914	.017	−2.455	18	.024	−5525.0000	2250.6005	−10253.3	−796.6637
Equal variances not assumed			−2.455	14.179	.028	-5525.0000	2250.6005	−10346.3	−703.6631

Figure 24.16 *SPSS output comparing levels of income of men and women*

single variables to a consideration of two-variable analysis. You should by now be familiar with the idea of a frequency distribution and of statistics such as the mean that measure the central tendency of such distributions. You were introduced to the use of the standard deviation to indicate the dispersal of cases around the mean. Further on in the chapter, contingency tables were discussed, followed by a discussion of statistical significance and the way this is indicated for tables by the *p*-value derived from chi-square. It is important to distinguish the idea of statistical significance from the idea of association. The former enables us to judge whether we can infer from a sample to the population from which it is drawn. The latter describes the strength and direction of relationships between variables, regardless of sample size. With large samples even quite weak associations will be significant; with small samples it will be hard to attain significance whatever the strength of association.

The discussion of association moved us

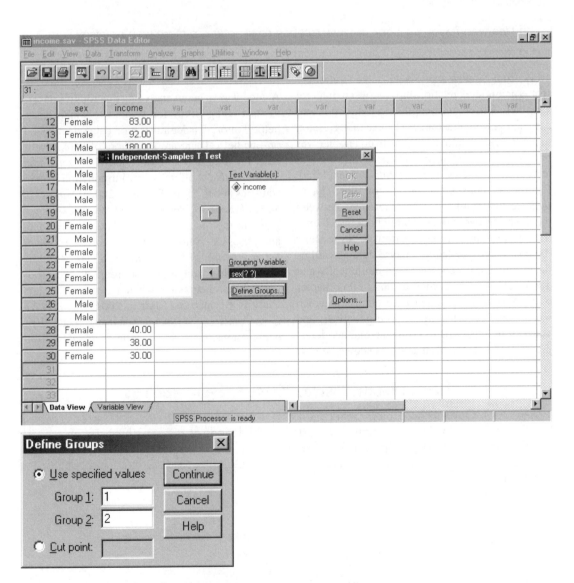

Figure 24.17   *Comparing means and carrying out t-tests in SPSS*

Box 24.1   Web pointers for univariate and bivariate analysis

Tabulating and graphing data
http://glass.ed.asu.edu/stats/lesson1/

Introductory statistics by David Stockburger
www.psychstat.smsu.edu/introbook/sbk00.htm

Online analysis of data (you don't need SPSS to do statistical analysis!)
http://glass.ed.asu.edu/stats/online.htm

De Vaus: Surveys in Social Research (links for Chapters 13 and 14)
www.social-research.org/

Visit the website for this book at www.rscbook.co.uk to link to these web pointers.

---

away from tabular analysis to consideration of scattergrams and relationships between interval variables. Different strengths and directions of association were illustrated. The use of regression to predict values of one variable from another was briefly touched upon, before the application of tests of association to data in tables was explored. Finally, we considered the use of the *t*-test to indicate the significance of differences between the means of two groups. Throughout the chapter there have been screen shots from SPSS to show the commands needed to analyse data as well as the output that is generated both numerically and graphically. Combine your reading of this chapter with some hands-on experience of SPSS (which has superb 'help' facilities if you get stuck) and you will find that you too can generate and interpret the kind of statistical analyses shown here.

Further reading

A good way to begin analysing quantitative data is to start using SPSS for Windows, which has a helpful tutorial, a demonstration data set and good on-line help. There are a plethora of books available. Fielding and Gilbert (2000) *Understanding Social Statistics* offers a clear introduction both to statistics and to SPSS. De Vaus (2002a) *Surveys in Social Research* gives a brief but clearly explained guide to the main principles of quantitative data analysis. De Vaus (2002b) *Analysing Social Science Data: 50 Key Problems in Data Analysis* presents clear and simple solutions to the problems researchers face when carrying out data analysis. Bryman and Cramer (2001) *Quantitative Data Analysis for Social Scientists* relate their explanations of statistical methods to output from SPSS.

Student Reader (Seale, 2004): relevant readings

18   A.N. Oppenheim: 'The quantification of questionnaire data'
19   Paul F. Lazarsfeld: 'Interpretation of statistical relations as a research operation'
20   Morris Rosenberg: 'The strategy of survey analysis'

Key concepts

Bivariate, univariate and **multivariate**
  analysis
Causality
Frequency distribution
Recoding variables
Value labels

Charts
  Bar charts
  Pie charts
  Histogram

Descriptive statistics
  Measures of central tendency
    Mean
    Median
    Mode
  Range
  Standard deviation

Normal curve
Skewed distribution
Variance

Contingency tables
  Cell
  Column marginal
  Column percentage

Column variable
Count
Expected and **observed values**
Row marginal
Row percentage
Row variable

Scattergram or **scatterplot**
  x **axis**
  y **axis**
  Regression line or **line of best fit**

Statistical inference
  Analysis of variance
  Chi-square test
  Null hypothesis
  p**-value**
  t**-test**
  Two-tailed test

Measures of association
  Curvilinear relationship
  Negative association or **relationship**
  Positive association or **relationship**

Correlation
  Correlation coefficient
  Pearson's r
  Percentage of variance explained
  r^2

25

Statistical reasoning: causal arguments and multivariate analysis

Clive Seale

CONTENTS

It was argued in Chapter 4 that the search for causal explanations has often been a part of a *positivist* enterprise, reflecting a desire to generate law-like statements about the workings of society, so that social life is thought of as analogous to a physical structure, or at best a biological organism. Additionally, in Chapter 5, concerning the uses of theory in social research, it was argued, using the example of Moerman's (1974) study of the Lue, that qualitative research is particularly suited to showing *how* people generate meaningful social life. For example, the Lue achieve their ethnic identity by using 'ethnic identification devices' strategically in interactions with, say, visiting anthropologists. (Thus, they claim to like certain foods above others, or to possess certain beliefs, which they say are 'characteristic' of their particular ethnic identity.)

The sociologist Max Weber, who is often associated with the *interpretive* approach to social research aspired to by many qualitative researchers, was interested in causal reasoning too. Weber's criteria for adequate explanations of social life involved explanations adequate at the levels of both cause and meaning (Marsh, 1982). Put in another way, we could argue that as well as asking *how* people achieve various effects (or meanings) in their social lives, we should also be concerned with *why* certain effects are achieved rather than others. Examples of such 'why' questions might be:

- Following Mary Douglas's theory about anomalies (see Chapter 5, Box 5.3), we could hypothesize that more threatened social groups are less likely to tolerate anomalies, this being reflected in the frequencies with which certain foods were eaten.
- We know that male asylum seekers are more likely to be in paid employment than female asylum seekers (see Chapter 24). Could this be because they are better qualified, or is there some other explanation?
- Does getting a good degree result in better pay in the long run?

These are examples of *causal* hypotheses. Quantitative methods can help to establish whether such hypotheses can be supported. Crude beliefs in the

unity of science (for example, that people and molecules are similar classes of being), or a lack of interest in how people actively construct meaningful worlds, are not necessarily involved when pursuing an interest in causal explanations. This chapter will show you how to construct causal arguments with statistics. It depends on a thorough understanding of the concepts introduced in Chapter 24. You should also review parts of Chapter 7 before proceeding, particularly the section on *internal validity*.

Research design

Experiments and quasi-experiments

In natural science, the *experiment* is used to establish causality. For example, let us say that as biomedical researchers we wish to establish whether a new drug is effective. Here, an experimental research design known as the **randomized controlled trial** is very effective in establishing causality. A group of experimental subjects (say 100 people with a given disease) is allocated *at random* to one of two groups: the *treatment* group, who receive the new drug, and a *control* group who do not receive the drug. If the disease is relieved in the treatment group, the drug is judged to be effective. The essential point here is that the people are allocated *at random* to either group. This means that the two groups are unlikely to differ from each other in any systematic way. That is to say, the only variable that is allowed to vary is the issue of whether a person in the experiment receives the new drug or not. Any subsequent difference can then be attributed to the effect of the drug with some confidence. (In fact, other procedures are also usually built into such trials to ensure more complete control of all variables.)

In social research, it is very hard to conduct experimental trials like this, though experiments are not unknown in social science – particularly in social psychology. For the most part, though, it is difficult to manipulate people's social worlds to the extent required in a full experiment. To test the hypothesis that social groups under threat tend to have different views about the consumption of 'anomalous' foods, one would have to randomly allocate people to groups that were either threatened or not threatened. To test the hypothesis that higher education causes income levels to vary, one would have to randomly allocate people to different types of lifetime educational experience. Clearly this is going to be difficult, if not impossible. While it is sometimes possible in social research to use experimental designs, the intervention often changes people's social realities so much that the setting involved becomes artificial (for example, the psychology laboratory), so that generalizing results from the experimental setting to the real world becomes difficult (an issue of the *external validity* of the experiment).

In dealing with data derived from social surveys, therefore, one is usually faced with the necessity to adopt a **quasi-experimental** approach. This involves the manipulation of data so that a causal *argument* is gradually built up from the data, in which associations between variables are demonstrated, arguments for and against the view that these are causal associations are considered, and then further data analysis is done to test out these arguments. There are a variety of ways in which this can be done, but the most accessible of these is to conduct analysis via *contingency tables*. The **elaboration paradigm** is a term used to describe this type of analysis of tables, which was developed by quantitative social researchers in America in the 1940s and 1950s (see Chapter 8 for a historical account of this). Rosenberg's *The Logic of Survey Analysis* (1968) provides a classic account of the approach. The present chapter will focus on explaining the techniques of the elaboration paradigm, though at the end other techniques of multivariate analysis will be briefly illustrated.

Cross-sectional and longitudinal designs

Because *time order* is important in establishing causality (see Chapter 7) it is also important to know whether data arise from a **cross-sectional** study, in which people (or other units of analysis) are studied at a single point in time, or from a **longitudinal** study, in which they are followed over time.

In the example in Box 25.1, a *longitudinal* design would enable time order to be established. If the same people were followed over a long period of time, the reseacher would know when things happened and would treat cases where respiratory illness occurred before the move into damp housing differently.

A *cross-sectional* study could also deal with the time order problem, but with greater difficulty. Questions would have to go into *when* things happened. People's capacity to remember things like the onset of illness is not always very reliable.

Although longitudinal studies have an advantage in controlling time order problems, they also have some disadvantages. They can be expensive, since following people at time intervals involves more visits for data collection and keeping in touch with a large sample can be difficult. People taking part in longitudinal studies may drop out, leading to poor *response rates* (see Chapter 13) at the later follow-up points, or they may start to feel special in some way because they are taking part in a research project and therefore act differently (the problem of *reactivity* – see Chapter 17).

A compromise between cross-sectional and longitudinal designs is the **time series** design, in which a cross-sectional survey is repeated at intervals. At each point the same method for sampling from the population and the same questions are asked, but the people studied are (or may be) different. This enables comparisons and trends over time to be established, but does not necessarily deal with time order problems in causal analysis. The General Household Survey

---

Box 25.1 A problem with time order

Research question: Do damp housing conditions cause respiratory illness?

Variables: Does the person live in damp housing or not? Does the person have a respiratory illness or not?

Time order problem: Did the illness start before moving into the damp housing conditions, or after?

Box 25.2 Three research designs

Cross-sectional: a sample is studied at a single point in time

Longitudinal: a sample is studied at intervals over a period of time

Time series: samples chosen in the same way each time are studied using the same questions at different points in time

---

(see Chapter 26) is an example of a time series study.

The elaboration paradigm

Dependent and independent variables

Before beginning this section, it is worth pausing for a moment to define what is meant by the division of variables into those called **independent** and those called **dependent.** Crudely, one can understand an independent variable as being a *cause,* and a dependent one as being an *effect.* The effect variables 'depend upon' variation in the cause variables. In the examples discussed earlier in this chapter independent variables were:

- The degree to which social groups are under threat
- Being a male or female asylum seeker
- Getting or not getting a good degree

Dependent variables were:

- The frequency with which certain foods are eaten
- Being in paid employment or not
- Level of pay

Establishing whether a variable can be considered dependent or independent is sometimes not straightforward, it may, for example, depend on issues of time order. Take the example of education and income. Clearly it is reasonable to assume that in a sample of middle-aged adults, their income might be determined to some extent by whether they were university graduates or not. But let us imagine that by 'income' we mean the overall wealth of people's family of origin. In this case, many people's 'income' will have been estab-

lished long before they entered the education system. Indeed, it may have been established before they were born! Here, 'income' precedes education and, one could argue, could be considered to be the independent variable (the cause), with education being the dependent variable (the effect). Establishing the point in time at which variables are measured is important in constructing an argument about which can be considered dependent on the other. For this, one needs an understanding of the way in which the data being analysed were originally produced.

Relationships between three variables

Table 25.1 shows a series of tables in which different sorts of relationships between three variables are displayed, below an initial or **zero-order** contingency table. Look first at this top table ((a)(i)), which shows the relationship between educational achievement and income. For simplicity, all the variables in the table are *dichotomous,* that is, they have two values. Thus educational achievement and income are divided into 'high' and 'low'. This is a rather crude measurement of these variables; the ideas of the elaboration paradigm can be applied to more sophisticated measures too.

Within each cell is a *count* and a *column percentage.* In the zero-order table, this indicates that 60% of the 200 people with 'high' levels of educational achievement have achieved a 'high' income, compared with 40% of the 200 people with a 'low' level of education. This is a moderate association, but is a statistically significant result. Phi, a measure of association, has a value of 0.20; gamma, another measure of association, and perhaps the one best suited to this type of table, as it is designed for ordinal variables, gives a value of 0.38. You will recall from the previous chapter that tests of association generally conform to the rule that a

Table 25.1 *Demonstration of the elaboration paradigm: the relationship between education and income, as affected by gender*

(a)(i) *Zero-order table showing an association*

Income	Educational achievement	
	High	Low
High	120 (60%)	80 (40%)
Low	80 (40%)	120 (60%)
Total	200 (100%)	200 (100%)

$p = 0.00006$; phi = 0.20; gamma = 0.38.

(a) (ii) *Replication*

Men

Income	Educational achievement	
	High	Low
High	40 (61%)	26 (39%)
Low	26 (39%)	40 (61 %)
Total	66 (100%)	66 (100%)

$p = 0.01481$; phi = 0.21; gamma = 0.41.

Women

Income	Educational achievement	
	High	Low
High	80 (60%)	54 (40%)
Low	54 (40%)	80 (60%)
Total	134 (100%)	134 (100%)

$p = 0.00149$; phi = 0.19; gamma = 0.37.

(a)(iii) *Spurious or intervening*

Men

Income	Educational achievement	
	High	Low
High	112 (78%)	64 (76%)
Low	32 (22%)	20 (24%)
Total	144 (100%)	84 (100%)

$p = 0.78290$; phi = 0.02; gamma = 0.04.

Women

Income	Educational achievement	
	High	Low
High	8 (14%)	16 (14%)
Low	48 (86%)	100 (86%)
Total	56 (100%)	116 (100%)

$p = 0.93038$; phi = 0.01; gamma = 0.02.

(a) (iv) *Specification*

Men

Income	Educational achievement	
	High	Low
High	90 (60%)	50 (33%)
Low	60 (40%)	100 (67%)
Total	150 (100%)	150 (100%)

$p < 0.00000$; phi = 0.27; gamma = 0.50.

Women

Income	Educational achievement	
	High	Low
High	30 (60%)	30 (60%)
Low	20 (40%)	20 (40%)
Total	50 (100%)	50 (100%)

$p = 1.00000$; phi =0.00; gamma = 0.00.

(b)(i) *Zero-order table showing no association*

Income	Educational achievement	
	High	Low
High	120 (60%)	120 (60%)
Low	80 (40%)	80 (40%)
Total	200 (100%)	200 (100%)

$p = 1.00000$; phi = 0.00; gamma = 0.00.

(b) (ii) *Suppressor*

Men

Income	Educational achievement	
	High	Low
High	20 (67%)	20 (20%)
Low	10 (33%)	80 (80%)
Total	30 (100%)	100 (100%)

$p < 0.00000$; phi = 0.43; gamma = 0.78.

Women

Income	Educational achievement	
	High	Low
High	100 (59%)	100 (100%)
Low	70 (41%)	0 (0%)
Total	170 (100%)	100 (100%)

$p < 0.00000$; phi = -0.45; gamma = -1.00.

value of 0 indicates the absence of association, and a value of +1 or −1 indicates either perfect positive or perfect negative association. The *p*-value, based on chi-square, is 0.00006, way below the level of 0.05 where one normally accepts that two variables are likely to be related in the population from which a sample is drawn.

One can imagine that a researcher might have generated this first table in order to present an argument that gaining educational qualifications tends to cause people to get more highly paid jobs. Initially, it seems, the zero-order table supports this view. But a counter-argument might be that in fact this is a **spurious** result. In other words, the argument would be that although there is a statistical association between these variables, it is in fact caused by some other factor. Gender, for example, may explain the association. Perhaps it is the case that, in the population from which this sample is drawn, boys are encouraged by their parents to do well at school and to think of themselves as high achievers in the job market. This factor of gender-biased parental encouragement may have produced the initial association, suggesting that it is caused by gender (or rather the things associated with gender) rather than representing any real causal relationship between what one learns in the education system and the jobs one can do as a consequence.

In order to *test* this counter-argument the research can break down the initial zero-order table into two tables, first examining the relationship for men, and then that for women. This generates **conditional** or **first-order** tables, showing how the relationship between the variables in the zero-order table looks when considered separately for different values (in other words, male and female) of the third or **test variable. Replication** is said to occur if the original relationship remains, as is the case in the first pair of conditional tables ((a) (ii)). Here, the researcher can conclude that gender does *not* affect the rela-

tionship between educational achievement and income. This is reflected both in the percentages and in the two tests of association, which show little change when compared with the zero-order statistics (although note that the *p*-values are no longer so low, as the sample size has reduced in each of the two tables compared with the size of sample in the zero-order table).

In the next pair of conditional tables ((a) (iii)) you will see that the tests of association are both close to zero in both tables. Additionally, the *p*-value indicates that neither table shows a statistically significant result. If you examine the percentages you can confirm that there is no association between the variables. Educational achievement appears to make no difference to income, once gender is taken into account (or 'controlled for'). If the original relationship disappears once a test variable is entered, as it does here, we may conclude either that the relationship was **spurious,** which is to say that gender has caused the association between educational achievement and income, or that the test variable is an **intervening** one. For a variable to be considered intervening, it must be caused to vary by the independent variable in the zero-order relationship, and in turn must cause variation in the dependent variable (see Box 25.3).

In Table 25.1, though, it is not reasonable to argue that gender intervenes between educational achievement and income. This is because one's level of educational achievement does not cause one's gender to vary! Clearly, gender is largely established by the time one enters the educational system. In fact, the zero-order association is caused by the fact that boys tend to be both high achievers and high income earners, while girls are the opposite. That is to say, gender is independently associated with both educational achievement and income. An argument about *time order,* then, must be generated in order to distinguish between spurious and intervening

---

Box 25.3   An example of an intervening variable

Educational achievement could be seen as intervening in the relationship between people's social class of origin and their eventual social class in adult life. Here, the argument goes, people who are well off provide the type of education that allows their offspring to enter occupations of similarly high status to their parents.

variables. The tables alone will not solve this problem for you.

A further possible outcome when a test variable is entered is that one of the conditional tables will demonstrate an association, whereas another will not. This is known as **specification** because the test variable has specified the conditions under which the original relationship holds true (this is also sometimes called **interaction**). Thus, in the third pair of conditional tables ((a) (iv)) the relationship between education and income is present for men but not for women. Try reading the percentages in the table, and the tests of significance and association, to see how this can be supported. Such a finding may lead the researcher into further theorizing and data analysis. Could it be that men take more vocationally oriented courses than women, for example? Clearly, further data collection and analysis would be needed to explore such a relationship.

Finally, we can consider the idea that a test variable may hide or **suppress** the existence of a relationship in a zero-order table. It is often the case that social researchers faced with a table that suggests the absence of association between two variables give up on their hypotheses at that point, concluding that further reasoning along these lines is inappropriate. It is sometimes said that the presence of association is not enough, on its own, to demonstrate causation. However, it is not often appreciated that *absence* of association is not enough to prove *absence* of causation. Table 25.1 shows how this can occur. The second zero-order table ((b) (i)) suggests that 60% of people have a high income, regardless of their educational achievement. The conditional tables ((b) (ii)),

though, suggest that for men there is a strong positive relationship between educational achievement and income, while for women educational achievement appears to militate against achieving a high income (a negative relationship). Clearly, if such a finding occurred it would be of particular interest, and would justify further argument and data analysis to establish what had led to this pattern.

Notice, too, what has happened to the tests of association (phi and gamma) in tables (b) (ii). In the left-hand table, these are positive values, reflecting the positive nature of the relationship. In the right-hand table, they are negative values. Note too that in the right-hand table gamma gives a value of –1.00, which in theory is supposed to indicate a perfect pure relationship. A glance at the table reveals this to be misleading; it is in fact an artefact of the way in which gamma is calculated that has distorted the value in a table where one of the cells has no cases in it. It is for this sort of reason that it was stated in the previous chapter that tests of association are somewhat crude devices, and that examination of percentages is recommended as well when interpreting tabulated results.

To summarize, the elaboration paradigm is a way in which tabular analysis can be used to assess the adequacy of causal arguments in social research. Through elaborating the relationships found in bivariate analysis by entering third variables as tests of causal propositions, one can gradually build up plausible arguments about what might be going on in an area of social life. One can never, eventually, prove beyond reasonable doubt that one event has caused another. In fact, this

---

Box 25.4 The elaboration paradigm

An initial **zero-order** relationship between two variables, when examined under separate values of a **test variable**, may result in:

- *Replication*: the relationship is maintained
- *Spuriousness*: the relationship disappears and is due to the test variable preceding both of the others in time
- *Intervening*: the relationship disappears and is due to the test variable occurring after the independent variable and before the dependent variable
- *Specification*: the relationship only holds true under some values of the test variable
- *Suppression*: a relationship appears that was previously hidden

method of analysis follows closely the ideas of Popper, who proposed that science proceeded by sustained attempts at *falsifying* theories (see Chapter 2), as well as Campbell (see Chapter 7), who stressed the evaluation of threats to *internal validity* in a similar spirit. When all plausible counter-arguments to a proposition have been tested, progress has been made. On the way, deeper understanding will have been achieved through the fruitful interaction between data and argument that is the characteristic of good data analysis.

Other methods for multivariate analysis

It is a good idea to begin to learn about multivariate analysis by using tables and the elaboration paradigm, since one can see in the cells in the tables, and in the percentages, exactly what happens to each case in the data matrix as variables are entered into the analysis. This helps in retaining a firm grounding in the data; one does not then become detached from it in a self-sustaining technical world of statistical procedures whose meaning and interpretation may be somewhat unclear. However, multivariate analysis with tables has some disadvantages. First, in order to use interval variables one must *recode* them into manageable categories, thus losing information. Secondly, as more variables are entered (and one can go on elaborating first-order conditional tables by entering fourth or fifth variables to produce second-order and third-order tables and so on), retaining a sense of the question one is testing becomes increasingly difficult. Problems also arise with low numbers in each cell, as subtables require the sample to be split up into ever smaller groups. This makes significance testing difficult.

Multiple regression

A popular method of multivariate analysis that preserves interval variables as they are, and which enables the researcher to understand the interactions between quite large numbers of variables simultaneously, is **multiple regression.** This technique preserves the idea that in social statistics one

must often recognize that events have *multiple* causes, rather than *single* ones. If one wishes, for example, to understand what causes people's income to vary, one must recognize that this is down to a number of factors, perhaps including parental income and social class, educational achievement and gender. Discovering the relative *strength* of different variables thought to be causal factors then becomes the task of data analysis. Multiple regression provides the researcher with statistics that enable an estimate of this.

In SPSS multiple regression is fairly easy to do, though interpreting the output can pose some challenges. A sketch of the main points is presented here, but you are recommended to read more detailed treatments if you wish to use this technique. Figure 25.1 shows the SPSS dialogue box that appears once 'linear regression' has been selected using the drop-down menus under 'analyze'. This concerns a data set in which the infant mortality rate (IMR), gross national product (GNP), female illiteracy rate (FIR) and the prevalence of contraceptive usage (PCU) across many different countries are measured. The research question that multiple regression allows us to answer concerns the relative influences of the last three of these on the infant mortality rate. Thus IMR is the dependent variable and the others are all independent variables.

Some of the output from this procedure is shown in Figure 25.2. As is usual in SPSS output, there is a great deal of information, some parts of which is more important than others. The first part of the output tells us that R square is 0.837 (amongst other things). R^2 in multiple regression can be interpreted in the same way as r^2 in simple correlation and regression (see Chapter 24). It describes the percentage of variance explained by the three independent variables. Thus we can say that 83.7% of the variability in IMR can be explained by the three independent variables, leaving very little **unexplained variance** (only 16.3% in fact).

The second part of the output in Figure 25.2 allows us to look at the impact of each independent variable separately, controlling for each of the others. The first column to examine is the first of the two **unstandardized coefficients** columns. **B** allows us to see the impact of a one-unit change in

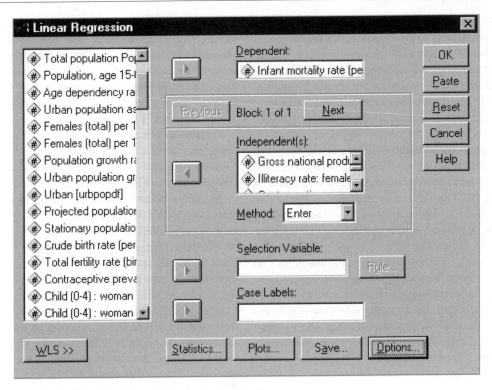

Figure 25.1 *Multiple regression dialogue box (SPSS)*

Model Summary

Model	R	R Square	Adjusted R Square	Std. Error of the Estimate
1	.915[a]	.837	.830	17.7270

[a]Predictors: (Constant), Contraceptive prevalence (% of females 15-49), Gross national product per capita ($US), Illiteracy rate: female (% of females age 15+)

Coefficients[a]

Model	Unstandardized Coefficients		Standardized Coefficients		
	B	Std. Error	Beta	t	Sig.
1 (Constant)	67.567	8.780		7.695	.000
Gross national product per capita ($US)	–1.13E-03	.001	–.074	–1.311	.194
Illiteracy rate: female (% of females age 15+)	.701	.117	.454	6.006	.000
Contraceptive prevalence (% of females 15-49)	–,777	.135	–.469	–5.739	– .000

[a]Dependent Variable: Infant mortality rate (per thous. live births)

Figure 25.2 *Multiple regression output*

each independent variable on the dependent variable (IMR) while controlling for (holding constant) the influence of the other two independent variables. Thus we can say that an increase of 1% in the female illiteracy rate leads to an increase of 0.701 infant deaths per thousand. An increase of 1% in contraceptive prevalence leads to a *decrease* of 0.777 in IMR.

The **standardized coefficients** (Beta) allow different kinds of conclusions to be drawn, relating to the relative importance of each independent variable. The largest impact appears to be the negative one of contraceptive prevalence (–0.469), with the positive impact of illiteracy in raising the rate of IMR close behind (0.454). GNP, rather puzzlingly, appears to have a negligible impact on IMR. To understand this rather counter-intuitive result (after all, surely rich countries are less likely to have high infant mortality rates?) we must turn to **path analysis**, a procedure that allows us to place the results of multiple regression into a **model**, closer to real life.

Path analysis

The implicit 'model' of the world in our multiple regression so far is shown in Figure 25.3. This suggests that each of the three independent

variables has a direct, independent influence on the dependent variable IMR. You will see that the standardized regression coefficients and the estimate of unexplained variance (sometimes also called the **error term**) have been written in next to the path arrows, indicating the relative influence of the independent variables.

A little thought about how things actually work in the real world suggests that this is not a very adequate depiction. When a country has a high GNP it is likely to be quite rich. This wealth tends to produce a better education system and is also associated with a degree of female emancipation. GNP, then, is likely to cause variation in both FIR (the female illiteracy rate) and PCU (the prevalence of contraceptive use). Figure 25.4 shows a more realistic path diagram, reflecting this reasoning.

The standardized regression coefficient for the influence of GNP on FIR was produced using the same SPSS dialogue as before (Figure 25.1), but with FIR as the *dependent* variable and GNP as the only *independent* variable. The influence of GNP on PCU was assessed similarly.

The path analysis and accompanying standardized *Beta* values suggest that GNP does indeed have quite a big impact on both FIR and PCU. In fact, we can say that FIR and PCU are both **inter-**

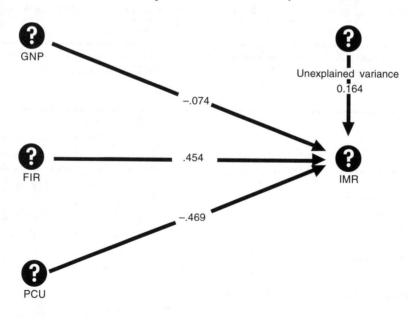

Figure 25.3 *Implied model of influences on infant mortality rate*

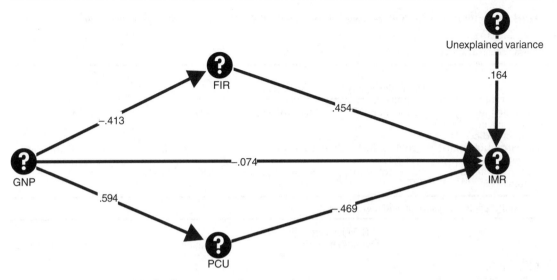

Figure 25.4 *New model of influences on infant mortality rate*

vening variables in mediating the influence of GNP on IMR. Because GNP affects them, and both of them affect IMR, GNP really does influence IMR, but it does so **indirectly** rather than **directly**.

The **direct**, **indirect** and **total** influence of a variable can be calculated from a path analysis diagram like that in Figure 25.4. Table 25.2 demonstrates this. The indirect effects are calculated by multiplying the standardized *Betas* in the relevant path. The total effects are calculated by adding all of the effects together. Reassuringly (perhaps!) for our view of the world they indicate that GNP does indeed have a major impact on infant mortality.

Logistic regression

A technique related to multiple regression is that of **logistic regression.** While multiple regression is

Table 25.2 *Direct, indirect and total effects of GNP on IMR*

Direct effect:		−0.074
Indirect effects		
via FIR:	−0.413 × 0.454 =	−0.188
via PCU:	0.594 × −0.469 =	−0.279
Total effects (direct plus indirect): =		−0.541

suited to estimating the impact of variables upon an *interval* level dependent variable (for example, income measured in units of currency), logistic regression is suitable for assessing the influence of independent variables on a *dichotomous* dependent variable. It has the advantage of producing a statistic whose meaning is intuitively easy to grasp: the **odds ratio.** Here, I will demonstrate the use of this technique in a particular piece of data analysis in order to show the potential of the method. To learn how to use the technique yourself, you will need to consult more advanced texts (see further reading suggestions and web links). You should note, however, that the concepts learned in the elaboration paradigm underlie both multiple and logistic regression.

Table 25.3 presents results from an interview survey of the bereaved relatives, friends and others who knew a sample of people who had died (Seale and Addington-Hall, 1994, 1995a, 1995b). The respondents were asked whether, in their opinion, the person had died at the best time, or whether it would have been better if the person had died earlier than they did. They were also asked whether the person who died had ever expressed a wish to die earlier, or asked for euthanasia. It is commonly said by those who oppose the legalization of voluntary euthanasia that if people are looked after well enough, particularly if they are looked after in hospices devoted to the care of dying people, this

Table 25.3 *Hospice care, euthanasia and the wish to die earlier: bivariate and multivariate analysis*

(a) Bivariate analysis

| | Hospice care | | No hospice care | |
	Domiciliary only	Inpatient		
Proportion of respondents saying better earlier	28% (of 327)	36% (of 312)	26% (of 1179)	$p < 0.01$
Deceased said wanted sooner	26% (of 362)	22% (of 338)	22% (of 1277)	$p > 0.01$ (not sig.)
Deceased wanted euthanasia	7.9% (of 356)	8.8% (of 329)	3.6% (of 1264)	$p < 0.01$

(b) Multivariate analysis (logistic regression)

	Hospice care Domiciliary only	Inpatient	Number of people
Respondent: better earlier	1.4	1.7*	856
Deceased: wanted earlier	1.4	1.0	921
Deceased: wanted euthanasia	2.0	2.1	912

* $p < 0.05$.

Odds ratios have 'no hospice care' as reference category.

(*Source:* adapted from Seale and Addington-Hall, 1995a)

will remove people's desire for euthanasia, as they will learn to accept the benefits of a natural death. The data analysis set out to test this proposition.

Table 25.3(a) shows the proportion of people who said an earlier death would have been better, or who asked for euthanasia, according to whether they had received hospice care. It shows, for example, that of people who received no hospice care, 3.6% were said to have wanted euthanasia. By comparison, 7.9% of the 356 people who received domiciliary hospice care (for example, visits at home by a specialist nurse), and 8.8% of the 329 people who had inpatient hospice care (in other words, who were admitted to a bed in a hospice), were said to have asked for euthanasia. If you look at the percentages given for the 'better earlier' and 'wanted sooner' questions, a somewhat similar pattern is evident. In two cases, the difference between the groups is statistically significant (shown by the *p*-value). Note that we are analysing three separate dependent variables here, represented by the three questions.

One might conclude from this that people who

argue that hospice care reduces the desire for euthanasia have got it wrong. It appears to be the case that the opposite is true: hospice care actually seems to *increase* the incidence of requests. This, however, would be a superficial conclusion. First, there is a potential *time order* problem. The interview did not establish whether requests for euthanasia, or the expression of wishes to die sooner, occurred before, during or after episodes of hospice care. It is possible that some people became so distressed that they made this request, and subsequently entered a hospice where they changed their minds owing to the good care they received. However, this time order problem does not apply to respondents' own views about the desirability of an earlier death, since hospice care had occurred many months before the interviews were done.

Another objection is that a variety of other things are likely to cause people to want to die sooner, or relatives to feel that an earlier death would have been better. People who receive hospice care might be different from people who do not. We cannot conduct a randomized controlled trial here (McWhinney et al., 1994). Perhaps people who enter hospices have more distressing symptoms, or greater levels of dependency. Other analyses of the data (Seale and Addington-Hall, 1994, 1995b) had shown that older people were more likely to want to die sooner, and that respondents who were spouses rather than other types of relative or friend of the person who died were less likely to feel that an earlier death would have been better. Maybe these factors differed systematically between people who received hospice care and people who did not. In other words, a series of plausible reasons as to why the three *zero-order* associations reported in the top half of the table might be *spurious* were considered.

Logistic regression allows the data analyst artificially to hold certain variables 'constant' in order to assess the independent impact of key variables of interest. This impact is represented in terms of *odds ratios*. The odds ratios shown in Table 25.3(b) can be understood by giving a verbal interpretation of one of them: respondents for people receiving inpatient hospice care were 1.7 times more likely than respondents for people not receiving such care (the 'reference category') to say that it would have been better if the person had died earlier. The asterisk indicates that this is a statistically significant result. The odds ratios ensure that like is being compared with like; symptom distress, dependency, age and whether the respondent was a spouse or not, were all held constant in order to make this comparison.

Of course, other potential spurious variables could have caused the association. By thinking through plausible objections to a causal proposition (for example, the rather surprising idea that something about hospice care caused respondents to feel that an earlier death would have been better), measuring the variables involved in these objections, and then including them in multivariate data analysis, a variety of arguments can be investigated.

Conclusion

The ideas of the elaboration paradigm are a useful start in multivariate analysis. A really detailed explanation of more advanced techniques such as multiple or logistic regression are beyond the scope of this book, but the main features of these techniques have been outlined. I hope that this chapter, and the previous one, will have given you an introduction to quantitative data analysis that is sufficient to demystify the procedures involved. Good data analysis proceeds by being constantly aware of the main issues that are being investigated. Statistics are a tool for taking forward an argument. It is unfortunate that technical complexity has sometimes been elevated to an end in itself, so that the researcher loses sight of the basic issues at stake in a piece of data analysis. It has been the aim of these two chapters to show you that these methods are within your grasp.

Box 25.5   Web pointers for multivariate analysis

SPSS tutorials, including regression techniques
http://pages.infinit.net/rlevesqu/spss.htm

Social Sciences Research and Instructional Council: SPSS guide
www.csubak.edu/ssric/Modules/SPSS/SPSFirst.htm

Andy Field's explanation of logistic regression
www.sussex.ac.uk/Users/andyf/teaching/pg/logistic/index.htm

Statnotes: **an online textbook by G. David Garson (includes multiple and logistic regression, path analysis and a host of other topics)**
www2.chass.ncsu.edu/garson/pa765/statnote.htm

Visit the website for this book at www.rscbook.co.uk to link to these web pointers.

Further reading

De Vaus (2002) gives a brief but clearly explained guide to the main principles of quantitative data analysis, including multiple regression. Bryman and Cramer (2001) relate their explanations of statistical methods to output from SPSS. Logistic regression is not often covered in introductory books on statistical analysis. One book that does introduce it in a reasonably accessible way is Field (2000). A good way to begin analysing quantitative data is to start using SPSS for Windows, which has a helpful tutorial, demonstration data sets and plentiful on-line help.

Student Reader (Seale, 2004): relevant readings

19 Paul F. Lazarsfeld: 'Interpretation of statistical relations as a research operation'
20 Morris Rosenberg: 'The strategy of survey analysis'

Key concepts

Quasi-experimental and **experimental design**
Randomized controlled trial
Cross-sectional study
Longitudinal study
Time series study

Independent and dependent variables

Elaboration paradigm
  Conditional or **first-order** tables
  Intervening variable
  Replication
  Specification or **interaction**
  Spurious variable
  Suppression

Test variable
Zero-order table

Multiple regression
  (Beta) standardized coefficient
  R^2
Unexplained variance (or the) **error term**
Unstandardized coefficient (B)

Path analysis
  Direct effect
  Indirect effect
  Model
  Total effect

Logistic regression
  Odds ratio

26

Using data archives for secondary analysis

Clive Seale

CONTENTS

Collecting data for social research can take a lot of time and money. Very frequently, data sets, both qualitative and quantitative, are analysed by their original investigators for certain purposes, but the researchers then move on to other projects. In the past a lot of these original materials were simply thrown away. Fortunately, though, **data archives** now exist in a number of countries to preserve materials so that other researchers can use them – often for purposes unimagined by the original researchers. The main advantage of this, of course, is that the effort that went into assembling the materials does not have to be repeated: research can begin at the analysis stage. As well as such **secondary analysis** by other researchers, data archives have other uses too. This chapter gives a guide to using such resources and will assess the advantages and disadvantages of different approaches to the use of archived data.

Data archives

Such archives exist in a number of countries and most are now easily accessible via the Web. In many cases data can be downloaded from websites in forms readable by standard software packages such as SPSS or NVivo (see Chapters 23–25). In some other cases, though, immediate open access would violate promises made to research participants about confidentiality, so certain paperwork procedures are necessary. Sometimes, too, the supply of data may incur small charges to cover expenses of, say, copying to a CD and posting to the researcher. Box 26.9 contains information about popular data archives and how to find out about others

Official statistics and survey data

A huge range of statistical data sources are available through data archives. These are often derived from surveys done by central government agencies, though researchers from other organizations – such as opinion polling agencies, or academic researchers based in universities – also deposit their data in archives. Box 26.1 lists some of the major surveys available through the UK Data Archive.

Box 26.1   Major surveys in the UK Data Archive

British and Northern Ireland Social Attitudes Surveys
British Crime Survey
British Election Studies
British Household Panel Study
Census of Great Britain
European Community Studies and Eurobarometers
Family Expenditure Survey
Family Resources Survey
Farm Business Survey
General Household Survey
Great Britain Historical Database, 1841–1939
Health Survey for England
Labour Force Survey
National Child Development Study
National Food Survey
National Travel Survey
Survey of Personal Incomes
Time Series Data
Vital Statistics for England and Wales
Youth Cohort Study of England and Wales
Workplace Employee Relations Survey

A survey that is particularly heavily used is the General Household Survey (GHS), and an exploration of this will show you how you can find out more about survey data available in archives.

If you are planning a study on a particular subject and are looking for available data sets it is important to know whether a particular survey contains relevant information. Information about the coverage of archived surveys is normally available on the archive's website. In the case of the GHS, the following summary information is available on the UK Data Archive website:

The General Household Survey (GHS) is a multi-purpose survey conducted by the Social Survey Division of the Office for National Statistics. The survey started in 1971 and has been carried out continuously since then, except for a break in 1997–98 and 1999–2000. The GHS is carried out for a number of government departments providing information for planning and policy purposes and is also used to monitor progress towards achieving targets. Data are collected on housing, employment, education, health, and family information from approximately 9000 households in Great Britain. The GHS has a modular structure and other subjects e.g. elderly, smoking, drinking, contraception, hearing, and childcare are covered periodically, and new topics are introduced from time

to time. (UK Data Archive: www.data-archive.ac.uk/findingData/ghsAbstract.asp)

Clearly, then, it is going to be possible to compare trends over time, going back to 1971, if we examine several years of this survey. It is a very large survey, beyond the resources of most researchers to carry out on their own, which makes it an attractive prospect. But the questions asked, and the way they are asked, may not suit our way of seeing our research problem. Clearly we need to find out more about the actual questions used. It is possible to download full documentation for the GHS questionnaires, including information about how answers were coded and entered onto the computer, from the archive's website. Alternatively, another website exists that is an invaluable guide to UK government surveys. This is the *Question Bank* (http://qb.soc.surrey.ac.uk/), a resource designed for a variety of purposes (including the provision of ready-made items for questionnaires), but also containing the information we need. The full questionnaire for each year of the GHS is reproduced here in a downloadable form.

It can also help to see what other researchers have done with the GHS data sets, and information about this is also available. Over 100 publications by secondary analysts of the GHS are listed on the Archive's website. Box 26.2 shows just four of these, covering issues concerning gender, pensions, housing, smoking and health

---

Box 26.2 Four publications using the General Household Survey data sets

Ginn, J. and Arber, S. (2000) 'Gender, the generational contract and pension privatisation', in S. Arber and C. Attias-Donfut (eds), *The Myth of Generational Conflict: The Family and State in Ageing Societies*. London: Routledge

Dixon, A., Yarnell, A. and Daniel, A. (2001) *Taking Stock: Housing Conditions in the West Midlands Region*. Housing Corporation/Faculty of the Built Environment, University of Central England in Birmingham

Kemm, J.R. (2001) *A Birth Cohort Analysis of Smoking by Adults in Great Britain 1974–1998*, NHS Executive West Midlands Regional Office, Birmingham.

Lahelma, E. et al. (2001) 'The myth of gender differences in health: social structure determinants across adult ages in Britain and Finland', *Current Sociology*, 49 (3): 31–54

inequalities. Further exploration of these articles, books and reports is of great value in evaluating the potential of the data sets.

While this example has concentrated on a single data set in a particular archive, you will find that quite similar procedures for discovering more about data sets are available through other archives. At the University of Michigan archive (see Box 26.9), which I visited for about five minutes between writing this sentence and the last one, I found a data set on the grim topic of 'Capital punishment in the United States, 1973–2000' for example. The description said this:

> This data collection provides annual data on prisoners under a sentence of death and prisoners whose offense sentences were commuted or vacated during the period 1973–2000. Information is supplied for basic sociodemographic characteristics such as age, sex, education, and state of incarceration. Criminal history data include prior felony convictions for criminal homicide and legal status at the time of the capital offense. Additional information is available for inmates removed from death row by yearend 2000 and for inmates who were executed.
> (www.icpsr.umich.edu:8080/ICPSR-STUDY/03667.xml)

I discovered that I could instantly download both the data set and the 'codebook' that describes the original questions and their variables. If I wanted, I could begin my analysis now, using SPSS, by simply clicking on the downloaded data file.

Qualitative data archives

Archives of statistical data are well established, but there is also a growing trend towards the creation of qualitative data archives in a number of countries. A good guide to these across a range of countries is available at the UK Qualidata website (www.qualidata.essex.ac.uk/dataResources/). In the USA a leading archive of this sort is the Murray Research Center (www.radcliffe.edu/murray/). Box 26.3 shows descriptions from the archive of just two of the many qualitative studies deposited there.

Although qualitative data archives often contain data in electronic form, many studies are only available through other means – particularly older studies. Thus a secondary analyst may need to travel to consult original paper documentation, or view and listen to videotapes or audiotapes. This is in part because qualitative data can take many forms (such as videotapes) that may not be easily translated into another medium, but also because electronic analysis of qualitative data only became feasible and popular from the mid 1980s onwards, whereas the analysis of statistical data with

---

Box 26.3   Two qualitative studies archived at the Murray Research Center

Antecedents of Artistic Success: A Study of the Early Lives of Women Visual Artists (1978: Wilton, Nancy)
This study examined the early development and family backgrounds of ... female visual artists, [differentiating] the more successful from the less successful artists. ...
Data were collected in a personal interview session with each participant ... [including] ... a personal data questionnaire, which included typical background and demographic items [and] ... an in-depth interview, which included sections concerning recollections of childhood activities and interests, parents' child-rearing techniques, and the participant's present life situation.

Abortion and the Politics of Motherhood (1980: Luker, Kristen)
The purpose of this study was to explore factors influencing the attitudes of pro-choice and anti-abortion activists and to weigh individual commitments to the abortion debate. The study examines the values and moral beliefs of activists on both sides of the abortion issue. Both pro-choice and anti-abortion activists were interviewed, including men and women between the ages of 19 and 73.

computers started much earlier than this. Early generations of qualitative researchers therefore had no need to store data in electronic form.

An example of this is a study by Professor Hilary Wainwright, deposited in the UK Qualidata archive. This concerned events surrounding the 1984–5 miners' strike in the UK. The research material is described as arising

> from the depositor's personal involvement with organisations supporting striking miners and their families, including 'Women Against Pit Closures' and 'Miners and Families Christmas Appeal'. The deposit provides information on the development of grassroots organisations and the level of public support for miners and includes news-paper cuttings, reports about pit closures, correspondence and organisations' own literature (pamphlets and news-papers). (from: www.qualidata.essex.ac.uk/)

To study this, a researcher must consult the original files, housed at the National Museum of Labour History in Manchester.

On the other hand, another data set in this archive contains some transcripts of qualitative interviews in electronic form. These were done in the 1970s by Paul Thompson, a founder of the archive, for a study of everyday life in Edwardian Britain (1901–1918). They are retrievable either as whole transcripts of each interview or as thematic sections taken from each of several interviews. Themes include topics such as 'School', 'Marriage' or 'Politics'. Box 26.4 shows extracts from two interviews in which different respondents describe the role that meat had played in their diets as children.

Using archived data

Corti and Thompson (2004), in an account of the uses of archived qualitative data that could equally be applied to statistical data, list six main uses for such materials (Box 26.5).

The focus of the present chapter is on secondary analysis, but it is worth saying a little about the use of data sets for 'verification', since some of the problems with this raise important issues for secondary analysts as well. Hammersley (1997) has identified these in relation to archived qualitative data, though once again his discussion has some relevance to statistical analysis too. *Replication* is difficult in qualitative research – probably more so than in research using experimental designs and quantitative data – since time often

---

Box 26.4   Extracts from 'Edwardians Online' at Qualidata: talking about family meals

Respondent 1:
Well – never really did have a lot of meat you know, 'cos she'd make what I – we called a great - a big meat pud – pudding, well there was more pudding than there was meat.

Respondent 2:
Oh we were very lucky with meat. Of course she was a woman who would get stewing beef, rather than steaks, I've known her to get stewing beef for us and make – and rabbit we've had hundreds of rabbits. Of course you can make such good meals, and she was a good cook. She'd either stew a rabbit and make broth and then mince the rabbit up and make sandwiches for your tea, out of it, and perhaps have broth and vegetables for dinner. ... But she did used to have a piece of beef, you know, something like that, occasionally. But we didn't have it very often but I know when she wanted to get me father a bit of something nice she – I've gone across to the butcher, he used to live opposite, almost opposite to us, for a quarter of beefsteak, very tender please. A quarter of beefsteak! That would be me father's. Ours, we've done with these beef soups and stews, but I suppose she'd think he'd get sick of that all the time. She'd done him plenty of vegetables with it. We've lived very well considering we had a big family and not much money.

Box 26.5 Six uses for archived qualitative data

1 *Description:* For example, a study of the City of London business district (Kynaston, 2001) drew on interviews done by other researchers (Courtney and Thompson, 1996) for accounts of working lives. This is rather similar to the use made by historians of data archives (see Chapter 19).

2 *Comparative research, re-study or follow-up:* For example, Franz et al. (1991) used data in the Murray Research Center archive to follow up the children of mothers interviewed in 1951 about their child-rearing practices, comparing this later sample with the earlier one.

3 *Re-analysis or secondary analysis:* For example, Fielding and Fielding (2000) re-analysed data collected by Cohen and Taylor (1972) on men in long-term imprisonment, identifying new themes in the material.

4 *Research design and methodological advancement:* For example, the interview guides of other researchers investigating similar topics can assist a researcher's own development of an interview; the Surrey *Question Bank* (see earlier) can be used to find questions that have worked well in indicating particularly difficult concepts.

5 *Verification:* If a study makes important claims, other researchers can examine its original data to assess the evidence in support of those claims (see the discussion of *auditing* in Chapter 7).

6 *Teaching and learning:* Examining original research materials can be an important resource in learning how to do research. The 'Edwardians Online' (Box 26.4) project has been designed with this purpose in mind. In the field of statistical analysis, special 'teaching data sets' have been prepared from subsets of GHS data, together with suggested lines of inquiry, available from the UK Data Archive.

---

elapses between study and re-study of a setting, in which social change takes place. Another reason for such difficulty is the differing perspective, interests and characteristics of the researcher on each occasion which, in qualitative research, often leads to researchers 'seeing' different things in a social setting. For example, a man studying childbirth in some cultures would simply not get access to certain events that a woman might be allowed to witness.

As a result, *auditing* or 'peer review' (see Chapter 7) has been proposed as a way of generating trust in a study's findings. Here, the original researcher records as much as possible about the methods, decisions and data collected in a study. This body of material is then inspected by other researchers not involved in the project to see whether the links made between claims and evidence seem good. Clearly data and other materials deposited in archives could constitute such an 'audit trail'.

Hammersley, though, points out problems with this use of archived qualitative data. In qualitative research in particular he argues that there is a great deal of room for argument about what counts as adequate evidence for a claim. Additionally, a lot of decisions made by researchers go unrecorded. One researcher, writing about anthropological field notes, has argued that

> [field notes are] ... the anthropologist's most sacred possession. They are personal property, part of a world of private memories and experiences, failures and successes, insecurities and indecisions [...] To allow a colleague to examine them would be to open a Pandora's box. (Bond, 1990: 275)

Hammersley feels that if researchers are aware that their personal diaries and log books, as well as records of data, are likely to be scrutinized by outsiders, they will be 'tidied up' as they are written, in much the same manner as politicians often write their diaries in the certain knowledge that they will one day be published. Thus auditing of this sort will encourage researchers to hide their secrets.

Clearly Hammersley is identifying something very important about the research process: a lot of what goes on in a research project is quite messy and illogical; the final report tends to reconstruct the whole process as more rational than perhaps it really is. He goes on to discuss secondary analysis, drawing on this depiction of the research process, saying that although secondary analysis has many advantages it also has some inherent problems resulting from this informal, messy nature of the research process. This is because research contains a considerable intuitive component. Perhaps qualitative researchers are particularly sensitive to the idea that 'data' are not simply 'given' but are at least in part 'constructed' (see Chapter 2). Hammersley says:

> There is a difference between how ethnographers read the fieldnotes they have produced themselves and how someone else will read them. The fieldworker interprets them against the background of all that he or she tacitly knows about the setting as a result of first-hand experience, a background that may not be available to those without that experience ... The data collected by different researchers will be structured by varying purposes and conceptions of what is relevant. As a result,

users of archives are likely to find that some of the data or information required for their purpose is not available. (Hammersley, 1997: 139)

Clearly, this is a useful warning against using other researchers' data in an uncritical fashion. However, it is not a problem that is new to people who have thought hard about the issues involved in secondary analysis. But secondary analysis developed first in relation to statistical data, and an unfortunate divide has existed between quantitative and qualitative research workers (see Chapter 22 for an assessment of this). Let us see how analysts of statistical material have approached these problems.

Secondary analysis of quantitative data sets

One of the bests texts on this is by Dale et al. (1988), researchers who were at the time based at Surrey University (UK) and had considerable experience of analysing the GHS and teaching the methods involved. They advocate careful inspection of the methods of studies that produced data sets before beginning analysis. Six questions need to be asked (Box 26.6).

It will be seen that, if taken seriously, such questions represent a rigorous assessment of the adequacy of data for analysing issues for which they were not originally intended, taking into account much of the context in which the data were produced. On the other hand, it can be

---

Box 26.6   Six questions to ask about a data set before doing secondary analysis

1   What was the purpose of the original study and what conceptual framework informed it?
2   What information has been collected and is it on subjects relevant to the concerns of the secondary analyst and in the form needed?
3   How was the sample drawn up and what biases in responders and non-responders were evident?
4   What sort of agency collected the data and how adequate were their procedures for ensuring its quality?
5   Which population does the survey represent?
6   When was the data collected and is it still relevant to the circumstances the secondary analyst wishes to investigate?

---

argued that methods for collecting qualitative materials are more dependent on the personal quirks of individual investigators than are quantitative methods. In my view, though, the production of both qualitative and quantitative data ought to be subject to similar levels of critical scrutiny and assessment.

In fact, the broad principles of secondary analysis are similar to those of any researcher engaged in statistical reasoning (Chapters 24 and 25): be aware of the conditions under which data have been produced, and ensure that any generalizations (particularly those that involve causal statements) have been fully exposed to possible counter-arguments. But unlike the researcher who has designed a tailor-made survey, the researcher using officially produced data has little control over the variables measured. Sometimes little can

---

Box 26.7   Construction of a disability index

Coded from answers to six questions: 'Do you usually manage to ...?'
  Get up and down stairs and steps
  Get around the house
  Get in and out of bed
  Cut your toenails yourself
  Bath, shower or wash all over
  Go out and walk down the road

The answers are scored:
  0   On your own without difficulty
  1   On your own, but with difficulty
  2   Only with help from someone else, or not at all

Degree of disability	Scale values	Scale items
None (49%)	0	None
Slight (25%)	1	Has difficulty cutting toenails
	2	Needs help/cannot manage to cut toenails
Moderate (14%)	3	Has difficulty in going up and down stairs
	4	Has difficulty managing to go out and walk down the road
	5	Has difficulty having a bath/shower or wash all over
Severe (7%)	6	Needs help/cannot manage to go out and walk down the road
	7	Needs help/cannot manage to go up and down stairs
	8	Needs help/cannot manage to have a bath/shower or wash all over
Very severe (4%)	9	Has difficulty in getting around the house
	10	Has difficulty in getting in and out of bed
	11	Needs help/cannot manage to get in and out of bed
	12	Needs help/cannot manage to get around the house
100% (3691)		

(*Source:* Arber and Ginn, 1991: 202)

---

be done about this, but at times creative solutions can be found in the transformation of existing variables into **derived variables.** An example of this is found in the work of Arber and Ginn (1991), who draw upon secondary analysis of the 1985 British General Household Survey (GHS) to present a series of compelling arguments about the disadvantages faced by elderly women.

The derived variable generated by Arber and Ginn is shown in Box 26.7. The 'disability index' was created by combining answers from six questions (each of which had three possible answers) to form a scale ranging from 0 to 12, where people with no disability scored 0 and people with very severe disability scored 9 or more. The percentages are the proportion of people aged 65+ in the survey who fell within each broad category of disability. The production of this variable was not the original intention of the people who designed the GHS, but Arber and Ginn found it to have considerable *construct validity* (see Chapter 7). That is to say, as one might expect, scores on the index increased with age and it correlated well with high use of health and welfare services.

Box 26.8 shows how this index of disability was then used to show differences between elderly men and women. It shows, for example, that half (51.9%) of severely disabled elderly women lived alone compared with only a quarter (26.1%) of the men. This meant that more women needed to rely on people from outside their homes for help. Men, on the other hand, were much more likely to be able to rely on their spouse. As well as gender-specific cultural expectations about who should give care, demographic factors lay behind this: on average women live longer than men, and tend to have married men older than them, so are more likely to be widowed. Clearly, qualitative research could be done to show how the broad statistical pictures relate to the finer details of family life.

Conclusion

Secondary analysis of archived qualitative and quantitative data, then, places a method of great potential in the hands of researchers who have appropriate skills. It is always necessary to take account of the conditions of their production, and

---

Box 26.8 Caring contexts for elderly men and women, by level of disability (column percentages)

	Elderly person has:					
	All elderly people		Severe disability (score 6–8)		Very severe disability (score 9–12)	
	Men	Women	Men	Women	Men	Women
All care is extra-resident						
Elderly person lives alone	19.8	47.5	26.1	51.9	14.3	29.2
Co-resident care in elderly person's own household						
Lives with spouse	70.1	36.4	58.5	31.2	69.0	27.4
Lives with others	5.9	8.4	9.2	9.0	7.1	17.7
Co-resident care: elderly person is NOT householder						
Lives with adult children	2.1	4.6	6.1	6.3	4.8	21.2
Lives with others	2.2	3.1	—	1.6	4.8	4.4
Total	100%	100%	100%	100%	100%	100%
N =	(1,477)	(2,155)	(65)	(189)	(42)	(113)

(*Source:* Arber and Ginn, 1991: 145; Table 8.4)

Box 26.9   Web pointers for data archives and places to find more

Some popular data archives
Australia Social Science Data Archive
http://assda.anu.edu.au

The National Archives of Canada – Ottawa, Ontario
www.archives.ca/

The UK Data Archive – University of Essex
www.data-archive.ac.uk/

Economic and Social Data Service (UK)
www.esds.ac.uk

New Zealand Social Research Data Archives
www.massey.ac.nz/~nzsrda//nzsrda/archive.htm

Social Sciences Data Collection, University of California, San Diego
http://ssdc.ucsd.edu/

The Roper Center for Public Opinion Research (USA)
www.ropercenter.uconn.edu/

Inter-University Consortium for Social and Political Research (University of Michigan)
www.icpsr.umich.edu/

Guides to data archives
This page on the University of Toronto Data Library Service website lists links to data archives throughout the world:
www.chass.utoronto.ca/datalib/other/datalibs.htm

See also:
The International Federation of Data Archives (IFDO).
www.ifdo.org

Council of European Social Science Data Archives (CESSDA)
www.nsd.uib.no/Cessda/

Visit the website for this book at www.rscbook.co.uk to link to these web pointers.

---

unwise to assume that the meaning of data is precisely as the original researchers intended. A careful assessment of the conditions under which the original data were produced needs to be made. In statistical secondary analysis, new variables may have to be created from old, and there will be times when the ingenuity of researchers in doing this will face the limits of the original data forms. Nevertheless, this chapter should have given you a lead in identifying the ever-growing range of data sources available for research purposes and may encourage you to search through these when you

plan a research project, so that you can benefit from the time and effort other researchers have put into the collection of research materials relevant to your research problem.

Further reading

Dale et al. (1988) supply an excellent account of the procedures involved in secondary analysis of statistical data, together with a guide to sources of data. On qualitative data, a chapter by Corti and Thompson (2004) provides an up-to-date view.

Student Reader (Seale, 2004): relevant readings

15   Ian Hacking: 'The taming of chance'
16   K. Jill Kiecolt and Laura E. Nathan: 'Secondary analysis of survey data'
17   Angela Dale, Sara Arber and Michael Procter: 'A sociological perspective on secondary analysis'
42   Martyn Hammersley: 'Qualitative data archiving: some reflections on its prospects and problems'

Key concepts

Data archives
Derived variables
Secondary analysis

27

Analysing text and speech: content and discourse analysis

Fran Tonkiss

CONTENTS

This chapter considers the use of written and spoken texts as the basis for social and cultural research. It focuses on two contrasting methods of textual analysis: content analysis and discourse analysis. These techniques provide a critical contrast in representing *quantitative* and *qualitative* approaches to the study of textual data. However, they share a common interest in the use of language in social contexts. Each approach provides insights into the way speech and texts help to shape and reproduce social meanings and forms of knowledge. Methods of textual analysis are relevant to a range of research subjects, in such fields as sociology, psychology, media and communications, history, politics and social policy, cultural studies, socio-linguistics, law, education, management and organization studies.

The discussion begins by outlining content analysis in the study of textual data. I look at different ways of approaching textual content, how this method can be used in conjunction with other forms of analysis, and consider key problems of validity. The second part of the discussion is concerned with discourse analysis. I define the term 'discourse' and explore discourse analysis in relation to three core stages of the research process:

1 Collecting data
2 Coding and analysing data
3 Presenting the analysis

Content analysis

Content analysis is a quantitative method for studying textual data. It seeks to analyse texts in terms of the presence and frequency of specific terms, narratives or concepts. This can involve counting items (specific words or categories) or measuring the number of lines or amount of space given to different themes. Content analysis has a long pedigree in psychology and in communications research (see Berelson, 1952). It is still frequently used in the analysis of media texts – such as newspaper articles, radio and television reports – and is closely associated with the study of visual content in photographic, film and television images (see Chapter 20). In this discussion, however, I am concerned with the use of content analysis in relation to speech and written texts.

The principal strength of this approach lies in the clear and systematic study of textual content as a basis for analysis and interpretation. Content analysis is the primary method used for large-scale and comparative study of textual data. It potentially has a high degree of *validity* and *reliability* in terms of precise sampling, providing clear empirical evidence for research findings, and in allowing for *replication* and *generalization* (see Chapter 7). In grounding analysis on empirical content rather than on interpretive argument, furthermore, this can be seen as one of the most *objective* methods for the study of texts.

Content analysis, however, while it shares many of the advantages of quantitative social research (including, it might be said, certain claims on academic legitimacy), has been subject to a number of criticisms. Chief amongst these is the objection that such analysis is concerned simply with 'crass' content: with *what* is said rather than with *how* it is said; with the description of texts rather than their interpretation, meanings or effects. In this respect, debates over content analysis bear on a central methodological issue in social and cultural research. Content analysis can be placed within a broadly *empiricist* and *positivist* tradition of inquiry, concerned with the analysis of observable features or facts, rather than with less observable and often highly subjective questions of meaning. At the same time, in their focus on texts and speech, content analysts are clearly interested in the production and reproduction of meaning. The method therefore raises quite sharply the question of whether a 'scientific' model of social research can be appropriate to the study of social and cultural objects that are in large part defined by the meanings they hold for social actors. In what follows I examine how content analysis can help to address these questions of qualitative meaning and potential readings.

Content analysis adopts a fairly standard model of research design. Having formulated a research topic, the researcher defines the relevant population of interest and then draws an appropriate *sample* from it (see also Chapter 13). In this case, though, the research will be based on a sample of texts rather than a sample of people. This might come from a number of sources, for example:

- Political debates and speeches
- Media texts
- Policy and legal documents
- Archival sources and other historical documents
- Tourist guides
- Publicity literature
- Press statements

In many instances the potential sample will be vast, given the scale on which texts are produced and circulated. Random sampling is a challenging task even for researchers working on a large scale, and often is not feasible for researchers involved in smaller studies. It is important, therefore, for researchers to delimit their sample very clearly – for example, by:

- Setting time limits, choosing for example:
  - □ television coverage over a one-week period
  - □ three issues of a magazine each year for twenty years
- Defining the type of text as precisely as possible, choosing for example:
- a particular piece of legislation
- presidential speeches or party political broadcasts
- newspaper editorials or front pages

When working with samples of these kinds, the researcher needs to make very clear the rationale for the selection of texts. Moreover, this selection should aim to produce a sample that is *relevant* to the research problem, *representative* of the field of interest, and *manageable* for the researcher to analyse in detail.

Coding content

Counting and analysing textual data can proceed in various ways. A common starting-point is to define categories of analysis and to code the data using these categories. The categories may be pre-set by the researcher in advance of reading the data, or they may be based on an initial reading of the texts. In many cases, coding categories emerge from a combination of these two processes – some will be pre-set to reflect the aims and the theoretical framing of the research, further categories will

arise from detailed reading and coding of textual content. This stage of the research requires intensive work to ensure that coding categories will capture the content of the texts in ways that are clear (reducing ambiguity and overlap) and exhaustive (including all relevant content). A key aim in constructing and applying codes is to limit the margin for interpretation on the part of individual researchers.

The *reliability* of the coding process is an important consideration in content analysis: will different researchers code the data in the same way? Content analysts frequently use tests of **inter-coder reliability** or **inter-rater agreement** to ensure that codes are matched to content in a consistent manner. At the pilot stage of the research, and as a further check in the course of data analysis, a number of researchers will code sample texts using the same set of coding categories and guidelines for their use. The degree of agreement between researchers acts as a test of the reliability of the content analysis as a whole (see Neuendorf, 2002 for a more detailed discussion of validity and reliability in content analysis).

An alternative starting-point for content analysis is for the researcher to compile a simple **keyword** count. This involves beginning analysis with a frequency count of the main items in the text. This often is done using computer searching. There is a variety of software available to assist in content analysis, which will analyse texts in a number of ways, including producing keyword lists and word frequencies, identifying main ideas, analysing patterns of word use, comparing vocabulary between texts, and producing full **concordances** that list and count *all* words that appear in a text (see Figure 27.1). More advanced software uses theoretical frameworks derived from linguistics and psychology to code and analyse textual data. These computer-assisted approaches are extremely useful when researchers are dealing with a large amount of material – the initial 'reading' of the texts is done by computer, measuring the frequency of specific words and providing a broad picture of the texts as a basis for analysis. In this way they organize a large body of data for the researcher in a manageable form. Moreover, this approach can be seen to minimize researcher bias by grounding the initial analysis in

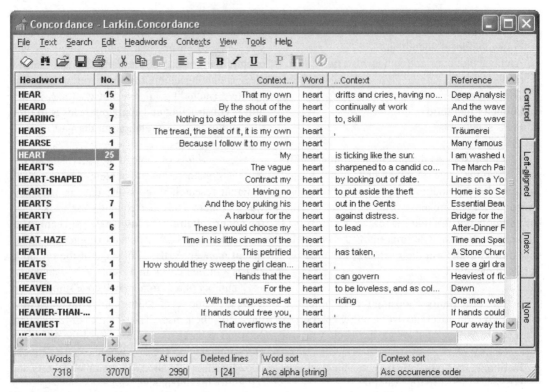

Figure 27.1   *Concordance software showing keywords in context (available at www.rjcw.freeserve.co.uk)*

the **manifest content** of the texts – that is, in the content as it has been written or spoken by the producer, rather than as it has been read by the researcher (sometimes called the **latent content**).

Such techniques are not limited to researchers working on large-scale studies or with extensive resources. More and more textual material is available in electronic form over the Internet and in electronic archives. Newspaper articles, policy documents and political speeches are three key resources that researchers can retrieve at little or no cost, and Internet material in general is a grow-

ing field for analysis. Keyword counts, such as the one shown in Figure 27.1, are commonly used to give a broad-brush account of politicians' speeches (see Box 27.1).

While these counts might look suggestive, they are of course only an 'analysis' in the simplest sense – in terms of sorting and enumerating the data. The context, the meaning and the effect of the speeches remain open to interpretation. A basic counting exercise looking for the term 'abortion' in this debate, for instance, would not capture either the presence or the larger meaning of Bush's

---

Box 27.1   Keyword counting in political speeches

In the first US presidential debate in the run-up to the 2000 election:
- George Bush used the words 'abortion' eight times, 'America' 17 times, and 'taxes' 33 times.
- Al Gore said 'abortion' once, 'America' twice, and 'taxes' 25 times.

(*Source:* Beard and Payack, 2000)

use of 'pro-life' as against Gore's use of 'anti-choice'.

Content analysis and interpretation

This example indicates how the value of content analysis to social and cultural research tends to go beyond simple processes of counting to take in issues of meaning and context. This can work by combining content analysis with other methods, or by using it as a framework for the more interpretive analysis of texts. Two examples illustrate this.

Philo's research is particularly interesting in taking the analysis beyond the counting of manifest content. The content analysis formed part of a larger study that involved audience focus groups with 85 people, and survey questionnaires conducted with 300 17–22-year-olds in Scotland. The aim of these other parts of the study was to examine where people got their information about the Israel/Palestinian conflict, and to explore their understanding and perceptions of what was going on.

This multi-method approach also combined *quantitative* (content and survey) analysis with *qualitative* (focus group) analysis for further exploration of audience interpretation and

---

Box 27.2   A Study of Political Conflict

The research problem

In their study of media coverage of the Israel/Palestinian conflict, Philo et al. (2003; see also Philo, 2001) combined content analysis with *focus group* and *survey* methods. They were interested not only in how the conflict was covered in the news, but also in how the news was 'read' and understood.

Sampling

The content analysis centred on television news reports of the *Intifada* that began in September 2000, based on a clearly defined sample. This was drawn from major news programmes (lunchtime, early evening and late night bulletins) on two British television channels with the largest news audiences (BBC1 and ITN) over an 18-day period from the start of the *Intifada*. The sample yielded 89 reports, which were recorded and transcribed in full.

Coding

Philo et al. then set up a number of themes to code the content of the news stories: including fighting/violence, origins of the crisis and peace negotiations. News content was then analysed in terms of how much coverage was given to these different themes. Here the researchers used the measurement of space as the basis for their content analysis.

Finding from content analysis

They found that, of 3,536 lines of text in the reports, only 17 lines included any account of the history or causes of the conflict. This is in itself a striking finding, based on a fairly straightforward coding and counting exercise: less than 0.5% of the mainstream news coverage in this sample contained information on the background to the conflict.

Finding from audience survey

A survey of 300 young people, involving respondents who said their main source of information was television news, found that many of those questioned knew very little about the origins or character of the conflict. For example, 71% of those surveyed did not know who were 'settlers' and who was occupying the 'occupied territories'; 11% thought that the settlers were Palestinian and the occupation a Palestinian occupation, while only 9% knew that it was an Israeli occupation.

---

understanding. While this did not provide a basis for asserting that the media content *causes* individuals to perceive these issues or events in certain ways, the research did show that a low level of understanding on the part of sample audience groups was paralleled by the limited amount of background information being provided by mainstream media content. Thus the content analysis supplemented and supported the audience study.

A different approach to content analysis is illustrated by Seale's (2002) work on news reports of people with cancer (see Box 27.3). It is important to note the degree of interpretive work being done in Seale's study in assigning content to different codes. How is one to assess, for example, the difference between showing a fighting spirit (a 'good' emotion) and anger (a 'bad' emotion)? These categories are not necessarily clear-cut, and their different meanings will in part come from the *context* in which they are used (see Chapter 5 for a discussion of *contextual sensitivity*). A quantita-

tive content analysis in this way can be used together with a more qualitative analysis of textual meaning to formulate an **interpretive content analysis** (similar to the *qualitative thematic analysis* described in Chapter 23). By looking not only at the number of times different emotional states are mentioned, but also the ways in which they are talked about, Seale developed an interpretive analysis of how gender inflected the representation of cancer in the press. He argues that the texts tended to reproduce ideas of gender difference in stressing 'women's skills in the emotional labour of self-transformation', developing personal resources to deal with their situation, while for men 'cancer is more commonly portrayed as a test of pre-existing character' (2002: 107). The analysis of media content was therefore informed by theoretical perspectives on gender and selfhood, and by the interpretation of textual meanings.

This raises critical questions about the *objectivity* of content analysis. As discussed earlier, the

---

Box 27.3 News reports of people with cancer

The research problem: to discover how news coverage differs in its treatment of men and women with cancer (Seale, 2002).

Sampling: 358 articles published in the English language press during a one-week period.

Counting and coding: In contrast to Philo – who pre-selected categories or themes to code his data - Seale began his content analysis by running a word concordance on the media texts (see Figure 27.1). The text is reorganized so that it reads not as a narrative but as a count of individual words. Such computer searching sorts the text in terms of its quantitative content without the researcher imposing any categories on the initial analysis.

Seale used this basic analysis to identify the different themes and uses of language that were evident in the texts. For example, Seale noted the frequency with which the language of emotions occurred in the news content. He went on to code the texts in terms of the presence of a range of items indicating different states of emotion. Such items as joking or being humorous, feeling supported by others, accepting one's illness or showing a fighting spirit were coded as positive or 'good' emotions. References to fear or anxiety, anger, isolation, misery or depression were coded as negative or 'bad' emotions.

Finding: The content analysis suggested that the emotions of women with cancer were discussed in the news texts more frequently than those of men; this was particularly the case for 'bad' emotions and especially for feelings of fear and anxiety.

(*Source:* Seale, 2002: 110)

validity of this method tends to rest on claims about the neutrality of the researcher's role and the objectivity of the results. There are a number of points to be made here.

1 The 'objectivity' of content analysis can be questioned in that qualitative judgements often underlie the definition of coding categories.
2 Even where researchers use more 'neutral' key-word counts, content analysis will tend to reproduce a repertoire of dominant themes or narratives (for example, in political and media discourse), and therefore can help to reinforce the power of these categories.
3 Content analysis can be seen to assume a shared world of meaning that is accessible in the content of texts. It is not at all clear, how-ever, that statements about content tell us very much about either producers' intentions or con-sumers' interpretations.

It needs to be asked how far the categories used in content analysis reflect the intentions of the author, the understanding of the reader, or merely the perceptions of the analyst. One cannot simply read from intentions via content to audience read-ings: simply, we do not necessarily all read the news in the same way. In these respects, content analysis encounters the problems of meaning that run through all analyses of social texts.

Discourse analysis

The organization of textual meaning is central to discourse analysis. This qualitative approach to textual analysis can sometimes seem a difficult method to pin down because it is used in different ways within different fields (see Hammersley, 2002; Wetherell et al., 2001a). While its origins lie most firmly in the disciplines of linguistics and social psychology, the method has been widely taken up within sociology, media and communi-cations, cultural studies, socio-legal studies, education, management studies, history, politics and social policy. In this discussion I am chiefly concerned with these broadly *social* approaches to textual analysis, focusing on how social cate-gories, knowledges and relations are shaped by discourse. Approaches to discourse analysis

within psychology and linguistics, in contrast, tend to focus more closely on the rhetorical and technical use of language (see Billig, 1987; Fairclough, 2003; van Dijk, 1997).

Discourse analysis takes its place within a larger body of social and cultural research that is concerned with the production of meaning through talk and texts. As such, it has affinities with *semiotics*, which is primarily concerned with visual texts (see Chapter 20) and with *conversa-tion analysis* (see Chapter 28). While approaches to discourse analysis vary, they share a common understanding of language as an object of inquiry. To the discourse analyst, language is not simply a neutral medium for communicating information or reporting on events, but a domain in which people's knowledge of the social world is actively shaped. Anyone who has been in an argument with a skilled or slippery debater will be aware of the way that language can be used to compel certain conclusions, to establish certain claims and to deny others. Discourse analysis involves a per-spective on language that sees this not as *reflecting* reality in a transparent or straightforward way, but as *constructing* and organizing the terms in which we understand that social reality. Discourse analysts are interested in language and texts as sites in which social meanings are formed and reproduced, social identities are shaped, and so-cial facts are secured.

What is discourse?

Discourse can refer to a single utterance or speech act (from a fragment of talk to a private conversa-tion to a political speech) or to a systematic ordering of language involving certain rules, terminology and conventions (as in legal dis-course). This second definition allows researchers to analyse how discourses *inscribe* specific ways of speaking and understanding. Viewed in this way, 'a discourse is a group of statements which provide a language for talking about – i.e. a way of representing – a particular kind of knowledge about a topic' (Hall, 1992: 290). Such an approach is often associated with the work of the French thinker Michel Foucault, and his interest in how discourses help to produce the very categories, facts and objects that they claim to describe

(Foucault, 1972: 49). Discourse, in Foucault's sense, does not refer simply to language or speech, but to the way language works to organize fields of knowledge and practice. Thus, following Foucault, one might ask:

• How is our understanding of sexuality shaped by various moral, medical, legal and psychological discourses?

• How is the concept of deviance (for example, 'mad' or 'delinquent' behaviour) defined and talked about within discourses of psychiatry or criminology?

• How are these discursive constructions linked to social practices, to social institutions, and to the operation of social power?

A good example of this kind of approach is

Box 27.4 Bell's (1993) analysis of discourses on incest

Incest was criminalized in English law in 1908; while it has been criminal in Scotland since 1567, the law was modernized in 1986. Bell bases her analysis on the parliamentary debates surrounding both pieces of legislation (Bell, 1993: 126–7). Her interest is in how incest is defined as a criminal act in ways that draw on particular forms of expertise and evidence, securing certain arguments and excluding others.

Bell identifies three key 'knowledges' that shape the legal discourse about incest.

1 The first of these concerns issues of health – articulated in terms of the dangers of 'inbreeding' in the 1908 debates and 'genetic' risks in the 1980s (Bell, 1993: 130–1). While medical or scientific arguments appear in both debates, Bell points out that they are in themselves insufficient to define the offence of incest. For example, they do not explain why incest would be wrong if there was no chance of conception, they focus on the possible consequence of the act rather than the act itself. At the same time they effectively define incest as a problem in rather limited ways, as referring only to sexual relations between men and fertile women, and to blood relatives rather than adoptive or step-family. The *victim* of incest, furthermore, is understood to be the potential offspring, rather than either of the parties directly concerned. In these terms Bell examines how medical knowledges shape the discourse on incest to produce particular definitions of the problem itself and the subjects it involves.

2 The scientific discourse of genetic harm is supplemented by a second body of knowledges that construct the offence of incest in terms of sexual, psychological or child abuse. Here the speakers in the parliamentary debates are seen to draw on discourses of child protection, social welfare and psychology. Incest is constructed as wrong on the basis of mental harm, coercion and violence, defined in terms of power relations within the family. The victims of incest are represented within these discourses as children or young women who are vulnerable to (especially male) adults. While such a conception of incest might be seen as more in keeping with current understandings, Bell does not claim to assess the 'relative truth' of these competing accounts (1993: 129). Rather she is concerned with the differing ways in which they produce incest as a *legal* fact, defining the problem and the victim in various terms.

3 The third key frame within which incest is constructed in these debates is as a threat to the family as a social institution. This is particularly important for the inclusion of adoptive and step-relations in the definition of incest under Scots law, in contrast to the scientific arguments seen earlier. Here, the offence of incest is construed in terms of a breach of trust within the family, and as violating the family as a social bond rather than simply a genetic one. Such an understanding involves an extended notion of the family unit, as well as its importance to a wider social and moral order.

Bell's (1993) use of discourse analysis to examine how the crime of incest is constituted under English and Scots law (Box 27.4).

Bell's analysis is interesting in showing how the category of incest, while often *naturalized* as a primary human taboo, can be understood as a legal artifact moulded by various discourses. English and Scots law define incest differently; moreover the parliamentary debates that inform these laws draw on contrasting and sometimes conflicting knowledges which go beyond the legal sphere. Incest is constructed as a legal fact via discourses of medical science, psychology, child protection, social welfare, the family and moral order. It follows that legal discourse is neither 'pure' nor disinterested, but is shaped by wider networks of language, knowledge and power. This point goes beyond semantics: discourse – ways of speaking about and understanding an issue – is important here because it helps to shape the practical ways that people and institutions define and respond to given problems.

Discourse in a social context

Perhaps the easiest way to think about discourses as linking language, knowledge and power is to take the model of 'expert' languages. Doctors, for example, do not simply draw on their practical training when doing their job; they also draw on a medical language that allows them to identify symptoms, make diagnoses and prescribe remedies. This language is not readily available to people who are not medically trained.

Such an expert language has a number of important effects: it marks out a field of knowledge or expertise, it confers membership, and it bestows authority.

1 Medical discourse establishes a distinct sphere of *expertise*, setting out the domain of medical knowledge and the issues with which it is concerned. In recent years, for example, there has been a debate as to whether chronic fatigue syndrome or ME should be considered as primarily a physical or a psychological problem, and, to an extent, whether such a condition can be said to exist at all. One way in which this debate plays out is in the language used to describe the condition. The term 'myalgic encephalomyelitis' clearly *medicalizes* the condition, while a term such as 'yuppie flu' does not. The use of language plays a notable part in arguments for recognizing a condition as a 'proper' illness: as a valid object of medical expertise and a suitable case for medical treatment. Medical discourse in this sense helps to delimit a distinct field of knowledge, and to exclude certain facts or claims from this field.

2 Medical discourse confers *membership* in allowing health professionals to communicate with each other in coherent and consistent ways. Language in this sense represents a form of expert knowledge that professionals draw on in their everyday practice and reproduce in their interactions. The internal conventions and rules of medical discourse act as a way of *socializing* individuals into the medical professions, and enabling them to operate competently within them. In this respect, discourse has a role to play in the institutional organization of medical knowledge and its professional culture.

3 Medical discourse *authorizes* certain speakers and statements. Doctors' authority is perhaps most obviously expressed by their access to an expert language from which most of their patients are excluded. On an everyday level, while we may at times be frustrated by the use of medical language to describe our symptoms, we may also be reassured that our doctor is an authority on these matters. More generally, medical authority is asserted in the use of expert discourses to dismiss competing accounts, such as those associated with homeopathic and alternative remedies.

Expert languages provide an obvious and a very fruitful area for research; discourse analysis is, however, by no means confined to this domain. Discourse analysts might study formal policy or parliamentary discourse (as we have seen with Bell, 1993), but also the popular discourses used in politicians' speeches and manifestos (Fairclough, 2000). A researcher interested in the discursive construction of race and racism might analyse political speech and debates (for example Smith, 1994), the news media (van Dijk, 2000; see also van Dijk, 2002), or the everyday language of racism in talk and texts (Wetherell and Potter, 1992). In all cases, the analyst is concerned with examining the way that specific forms of text and speech produce their versions of a social issue, problem or context.

Doing discourse analysis

It is difficult to formalize any standard approach to discourse analysis. This is partly because of the variety of frameworks adopted by different researchers, partly because the process tends to be 'data-driven'. However, while there are no strict rules of method for analysing discourse, it is possible to isolate certain core themes and useful techniques which may be adapted to different research contexts. In the discussion that follows I consider some of these in terms of three key stages of the research process: selecting and approaching data; sorting, coding and analysing data; and presenting the analysis.

Selecting and approaching data

I have stressed the 'special' character of discourse analysis as a method of research – its distinctive approach to language and its resistance to formulaic rules of method. However, the discourse analyst is faced with a common set of questions that arise within any research process. What is the research about? What are my data? How will I select and gather the data? How will I handle and analyse the data? How will I present my findings?

Formulating a research problem can be one of the most difficult moments in social research. Sometimes it can seem like a very artificial exercise – qualitative research frequently is data-led and the researcher cannot be certain quite what the research will be *about* until they have begun their analysis (see also Chapter 11). Discourse analysis often adopts a wait-and-see attitude to what the data throw up. This is underlined by the fact that this form of research is not so much *looking for* answers to specific problems ('What are the causes of juvenile crime?'), as *looking at* the way both the problem, and possible solutions, are constructed ('How is juvenile crime explained and understood within current political discourse?').

Explanations of juvenile crime might draw on accounts of moral decline, poor parenting, the absence of positive role models, inadequate schooling, poverty, lack of prospects, adolescent rebelliousness, and so on. This is not to say that the issue – juvenile crime – does not exist or has no meaning, but asserts that social actors make sense of this reality in various, often conflicting ways. If a dominant understanding of juvenile crime rests on discourses of poor parenting, for example, it is likely that the problem will be tackled in a different way than if it was commonly understood in terms of a discourse of material deprivation.

As with other forms of social and cultural research, discourse analysis often begins with a broad – even vague – interest in a certain area of social life. The way this broad interest becomes a feasible research topic is strongly linked to the choice of research methods (see Box 27.5).

Having set up a problem like the one in Box 27.5 the next step is to collect data for analysis. This will in part be determined by how you are defining the issue. Do you want to look at:

- Immigration policy?
- Immigrant identity?
- Media representations of immigration issues?
- Attitudes towards immigration within sections of the public?

Depending on how you are conceptualizing the research problem, you could collect data from a number of sources. These include parliamentary debates, political speeches, party manifestos, policy documents, personal accounts (including interviews), press or television reports, and campaigning literature. As with textual analysis more generally, a discourse analyst potentially can draw on a very wide range of data. However, the primary consideration in selecting textual material is its relevance to the research problem, rather than simply the number of texts analysed. It is therefore especially important to make clear the rationale for your selection, and how it might provide insights into a topic.

When doing discourse analysis it is not necessary to provide an account of every line of the text under study, as can be the case in conversation

---

Box 27.5   Formulating a discourse analytic project on immigration

There are different ways of approaching research on immigration, and these will influence how the research problem is defined. You might, if you were *not* planning to do discourse analysis,

- explore statistical data relating to the number of people entering a country in each year, their countries of origin, and patterns of change over time;
- select a sample of people who have settled in a place, and use interviews to research aspects of their experiences of immigration, for example: their experience of immigration bureaucracy, of the process of integration, questions of cultural difference, the notion of 'home'.

Using discourse analysis, you might

- choose to examine political debates surrounding immigration legislation;
- analyse press reports on immigration issues;
- investigate anti-immigration literature published by right-wing organizations.

A discourse analyst might be concerned with how immigration is constructed as a political issue, the ways in which immigrants are represented within public discourses, the manner in which certain conceptions of immigration are **warranted** in opposition to alternative ways of thinking – for example, dominant representations of immigration in terms of illegality or 'threat' (see Van der Valk, 2003; see also Philo and Beattie, 1999). A starting point for such a study could be as simple as: 'How is immigration constructed as a "problem" within political discourse?' The analytic process will tend to feed back into this guiding question, helping to refine the research problem as you go along.

---

analysis. It is usually more appropriate and more informative to be selective in relation to the data, extracting those sections that provide the richest source of analytic material. This does not mean that one simply 'selects out' the data extracts that support the argument, while ignoring more troubling or ill-fitting sections of the text. Contradictions within a text (including and perhaps especially those parts that contradict the researcher's own assumptions) can often be productive for the analysis.

Sorting, coding and analysing data

Discourse analysis has been called a 'craft skill' (see Potter and Wetherell, 1994: 55), and has been compared to riding a bike – a process that one picks up by doing, perfects by practising, and which is difficult to describe in a formal way. Doing effective discourse analysis has much to do with getting a real feel for one's data, working closely with them, trying out alternatives, and be-

ing ready to reject analytic schemes that do not work. While it has been argued that discourse analysis is not centrally concerned with 'some general idea that seems to be intended' by a text (Potter and Wetherell, 1987: 168), the overall rhetorical effect of a text provides a framework in which to consider its inconsistencies, internal workings and small strategies of meaning. Potter and Wetherell refer to these as the **interpretive repertoires** at work within a discourse, the ways of speaking about and understanding a topic that organize the meanings of a text.

If there is one rule of method that we might apply to discourse analysis, it would be Durkheim's first principle: abandon all preconceptions! At times it can be tempting to impose an interpretation on a sample of discourse, but if this is not supported by the data then it will not yield an adequate analysis. We cannot *make* the data 'say' what is simply not there. Most discourse analysts would reject the idea that texts are open to any number of different, and equally plausible, readings. Rather, analytical assertions are to be grounded in evidence and detailed argument. In this respect discourse analysis entails a commitment to challenging common-sense knowledge and disrupting easy assumptions about the organization of social meanings.

Discourse analysis is an interpretive process that relies on close study of specific texts, and therefore does not lend itself to hard-and-fast 'rules' of method. Even so, we might take a cue from Foucault (1984: 103), who suggested that one might analyse a text in terms of 'its structure, its architecture, its intrinsic form and the play of its internal relationships'. Put simply, this directs our attention to the organization and the interpretive detail of given texts. Here we can identify some useful pointers for analysis:

1 Identifying key themes and arguments.
2 Looking for variation in the text.
3 Paying attention to silences.

Note that these represent devices or tools for opening up a text, rather than a fixed set of analytic strategies. The tactics that you adopt as an analyst come from engagement with the data themselves, rather than from any textbook approach.

Identifying key themes and arguments

A common starting point for analysis is to locate key categories, themes and terms. Identifying recurrent or significant themes can help you to organize the data and bring a more systematic order to the analytic process. In this way, discourse analysis draws on more general approaches to handling and coding qualitative data (see Chapter 23). The analytic process involves sifting, comparing and contrasting the different ways in which these themes emerge within the data. On a simple level, the repetition or emphasis of keywords, phrases and images reveals most clearly what the speaker or writer is trying to put across in the text. This can provide the basis for a critical interrogation of the data.

• What ideas and representations cluster around key themes?
• What associations are being established between different actors or problems?
• Are particular meanings and images being mobilized?
• How are different subjects spoken about and positioned within the text?

Bell's analysis (Box 27.4), for example, was organized around the three core arguments she identified as shaping the political debates on incest and thereby defining this category as a social and legal problem. Within this frame, she considered the different ways these arguments positioned the *victims* of incest: as potential offspring, as vulnerable children and young people, as the family as a whole. These analytic strategies helped to open up the *interpretive repertoires* – the ways of speaking and modes of understanding – at work in the texts she studied. Reading for key categories and themes can highlight how meanings are attached to abstract or vague formulations that then become difficult to

---

Box 27.6 Analysis of right-wing discourses on immigration

Van der Valk (2003) examines how a notion of 'the people' was mobilized within political debates in France so as to exclude certain groups. She argues that not only did these discourses represent immigrant 'others' in a negative light (especially in terms of criminality), but these negative associations were transferred to those seen as 'allies' of immigrants – specifically, the political left. The invocation of 'the people' works not only to legitimize the anti-immigration discourses of the right, but also to question the legitimacy and the loyalties of the left. References to such abstract notions as 'the people', 'the community' or 'family life' in political discourses are hard to rebut, because they seem to embody values which no one would want to dispute, but at the same time are often imprecise. For these reasons, they can become powerful sites of meaning.

challenge, as is shown in Van der Valk's (2003) study of right-wing French discourses on immigration (Box 27.6).

Looking for variation in the text

Another useful tactic for opening up a piece of discourse is to look for **patterns of variation** within the text. Differences within an account point us to the work that is being done to reconcile conflicting ideas, to cope with contradiction or uncertainty, or to counter alternatives. By paying attention to such variations the analyst disrupts the appearance of a 'smooth' piece of discourse, allowing insights into the text's internal hesitations or inconsistencies, and the way that the discourse aims to combat alternative accounts. Huckin's (2002) study illustrates this (Box 27.7).

In reading for variation in the text, Huckin develops an argument about the way preferred explanations of homelessness are advanced, while alternative arguments are countered. Looking for associations, and reading for variations or contrast, represent two tactics for analysing what Foucault called 'the play of internal relationships' within a text.

The two studies demonstrate each in turn: in her account of right-wing political discourse (Box 27.6), Van der Valk analysed **patterns of association**, showing how these were created between 'the people' and the parties of the right, and between immigrants and the left. In the study of homelessness (Box 27.7), Huckin's *patterns of variation* included inconsistency between the

diagnosis of a problem (mental illness and substance abuse), and the account of practical solutions (charity and policing).

Attending to silences

Huckin's study also points us to the **silences** that run through media accounts of homelessness. He argues that textual silences on issues of racism, domestic abuse and lack of affordable housing support a reading of homelessness as involving individual pathologies and criminal behaviour. Similarly, van Dijk (2000) refers to the 'silence' of ethnic minorities in media coverage of race. Minority voices are seldom heard in mainstream media, he argues, and when they do appear they are often marginal or treated with scepticism.

These kinds of analysis require the researcher to adopt a rather 'split' approach to the text. That is, it is necessary to read *along* with the meanings that are being created, to look to the way the text is organized and to pay attention to how things are being said. At the same time, discourse analysis can require the researcher to read *against* the grain of the text, to look to silences or gaps, to make conjectures about alternative accounts which are excluded by omission, as well as those which are countered by rhetoric. While I have argued that we cannot force our data to say things that are not there, we can as critical researchers point out those places where the text is silent, to think about what remains 'unsaid' in the organization of a discourse. Such a move can help to place the discourse in a wider interpretive context.

Box 27.7 Analysis of media discourse on homelessness

Huckin's (2002) study of media discourse on homelessness draws an example from detailed analysis of a newspaper editorial. He argues that the text emphasizes substance abuse and mental illness as two of the chief causes of homelessness, but does not include strategies for addressing these problems in its discussion of public responses to homelessness. Rather, the text concentrates on charity and voluntary action, on jobs, and on policing and criminalization. There is a mismatch, then, between the textual account of the causes of homelessness, and the account of possible solutions. Huckin reads this mismatch in terms of a conservative political agenda that stresses the role of charity, opportunity and private enterprise over public welfare programmes. Indeed, the public responses highlighted in the text are associated with law and order, which the analysis suggests may be inappropriate to problems of mental illness and substance abuse.

Presenting the analysis

The final stage of the research process involves developing and presenting an argument on the basis of your discourse analysis. It is at this point that the researcher is concerned with using language to construct and **warrant** their own account of the data (that is to say, to back it up with persuasive evidence and authority). This aspect of the process provides a useful context in which to consider the relation of discourse analysis to issues of *validity,* writing and *reflexivity* (see Chapter 29).

Social researchers can think about research validity in terms of both **internal** and **external validity** (see Chapter 7), referring to the coherence and consistency and the evidence base of a piece of research on the one hand, and the generalizability of the research on the other. Discourse analysts have a particular concern with issues of internal validity. Their reliance on close textual work means that they develop arguments on the basis of detailed interpretation of data. One can therefore ask:

• How coherent is the interpretive argument?
• Is it soundly based in a reading of the textual evidence?
• Does it pay attention to textual detail?
• How plausible is the movement from data to analysis?
• Does the researcher bring in arguments from outside the text, and if so how well supported are these claims?

Discourse analysis is concerned with the examination of meaning, and the often complex processes through which social meanings are produced. In evaluating discourse analytic research we should therefore be looking for interpretive rigour and internal consistency in argument. Analytic claims need always to be supported by a sound reading of data. In this sense, good discourse analyses stand up well to the demands of internal validity. However, this is not to say that discourse analysis aims to offer a 'true' or objective account of a given text. The discourse analyst, like other social actors, aims to provide a *persuasive* and well-supported account, offering an insightful, useful and critical interpretation of a research problem. The discourse analyst seeks to open up statements to challenge, interrogate taken-for-granted meanings, and disturb easy claims to objectivity in the texts they are reading. It would therefore be inconsistent to contend that the analyst's own discourse was itself wholly objective, factual or generally true.

Discourse analysts often deal with relatively small data sets emerging from specific social settings. Like much qualitative case study research they are therefore unlikely to support claims of being more widely representative, so raising problems regarding generalization and therefore external validity as conventionally conceived, though their capacity for *theoretical generalization* (see Chapter 7) is likely to be strong.

Discourse analysis involves a commitment to examining processes of meaning in social life, a certain modesty in analytic claims, and an approach to knowledge which sees this as open rather than closed. By adopting such an approach to knowledge, the analyst and the reader may be confident of the internal validity and wider relevance of a particular account while remaining open to other critical insights and arguments. Discourse analysis fits into a broad range of social research methods (for example, conversation analysis) which between them seek to analyse general social patterns through a close investigation of detail.

A critical and open stance towards data and analysis may also be understood as part of a **reflexive** approach to social research (see Chapter 3). In aiming to be reflexive in their research practice, social researchers question their own assumptions, critically examine their processes of inquiry, and consider their effect on the research setting and research findings – whether in terms of their presence in a fieldwork situation, the way they select their data, or how their theoretical framework shapes the process of data collection and analysis. Reflexivity also involves attention to the writing strategies that researchers employ to construct a research account (Chapter 29), and here the insights of discourse analysis are very useful.

Conclusion

In writing this chapter, for example, I have drawn

Box 27.8 Web pointers for content and discourse analysis

***The Content Analysis Guidebook Online*, by Kimberley A. Neuendorf**
http://academic.csuohio.edu/kneuendorf/content

Resources related to content analysis and text analysis
www.content-analysis.de

***Discourse Analysis: A Bibliographical guide*, by Martyn Hammersely**
www.cf.ac.uk/socsi/capacity/Activities/Themes/In-depth/guide.pdf

Discourse analysis online
www.shu.ac.uk/daol

Visit the website for this book at www.rscbook.co.uk to link to these web pointers.

on various discursive strategies in an effort to make my account fit into a methods textbook. I have suggested that, while content analysis is more systematic in its approach to data analysis (although interpretive content analysis breaks free from this to some extent), discourse analysis does not sit easily with hard-and-fast rules of method. At the same time, however, I have drawn on a particular language (data, evidence, analysis, validity) and on particular forms of textual organization (moving from theory to empirical examples, using subheadings, boxes, numbered and bulleted lists) so as to explain discourse analysis in the form of a fairly orderly research process. An attention to the way that language is put to work is a useful tool for any reader or researcher

who wants to think critically about social research processes and to evaluate research findings.

Further reading

Neuendorf (2002) provides a comprehensive guide to content analysis, while Berger (2000) offers a concise introduction to the method in communication research. Wetherell et al. (2001a) collects together pieces by key writers on different approaches to discourse theory, while (2001b) offers a practical guide to discourse analysis; Fairclough (2003) is another extremely useful textbook. For shorter introductions, Gill (1996) and Potter and Wetherell (1994) are clear and very helpful. Both provide detailed examples of the use of discourse analysis in media research.

Student Reader (Seale, 2004): relevant readings

1 Michael Billig: 'Methodology and scholarship in understanding ideological explanation'
14 Robert Philip Weber: 'Content analysis'
45 Graham R. Gibbs: 'Searching for text'
51 Stuart Hall: 'Foucault and discourse'
52 Jonathan Potter and Margaret Wetherell: 'Unfolding discourse analysis'
53 Norman Fairclough and Ruth Wodak: 'Critical discourse analysis'
54 H.G. Widdowson: 'The theory and practice of critical discourse analysis'
55 Catherine Kohler Riessman: 'Strategic uses of narrative in the presentation of self and illness: a research note'

Key concepts

	Keyword
Concordance	**Latent content**
Discourse	**Manifest content**
External validity	**Patterns of association**
Inter-coder reliability or **inter-rater agreement**	**Patterns of variation**
Internal validity	**Reflexivity**
Interpretive content analysis	**Silences** (attending to)
Interpretive repertoires	**Warrant**

28

Analysing Conversation

Key concepts

Concordance
Discourse
External validity
Inter-coder reliability or Inter-rater agreement
Internal validity
Interpretive content analysis
Interactive repertoires

Keyword
Latent content

Patterns of association   Patterns of variation
Reflexivity
Silences unaccountable for
Warrant

Tim Rapley

CONTENTS

At first sight, the idea that an analysis of conversation may be a useful way to make sense of society and culture may seem strange. As part of our everyday life we are bombarded with the obvious truth that talk is 'just talk'. As a child you may have heard the rhyme 'Sticks and stones may break my bones but words can never hurt me.' When we ask someone to account for something they have said they may reply, 'Oh well, it is just something I say.' From this perspective, any focus on conversation may appear to be one of the most trivial of things. However, if you stop and think for a moment, it is not hard to see that conversation – or interaction, for want of a more general description – is potentially *the* central way through which we make friends, have relationships, learn things, do our jobs – as Moerman (1992) explains it: '[T]alk is a central part of social interaction, and social interaction is the core and enforcer, the arena and teacher, the experienced context of social life' (1992: 29).

The analysis of conversation has been undertaken by people working within various theoretical and methodological traditions, including interactional socio-linguistics, the ethnography of communication, discursive psychology and critical discourse analysis (Chapter 27 in this book outlines discourse analysis; Wetherell, Taylor and Yates (2001a) provide an overview.) However, for the purposes of this chapter I am going to outline how the research tradition called *conversation analysis* studies talk and interaction.

Some background to conversation analysis

I want to begin by exploring some of the central issues for conversation analysis. To do that we need to focus on its parent, **ethnomethodology** (see also Chapter 4), and explore a few of the key concerns for this approach to social life. As Melvin Pollner notes:

> One of ethnomethodology's contributions to the understanding of social life is its capacity to produce a deep wonder about what is often regarded as obvious, given or natural. Whether it be the interpretation of

documents, the utterance 'uh-huh' or the flow of everyday interaction, ethnomethodology has provided a way of questioning which begins to reveal the richly layered skills, assumptions and practices through which the most commonplace (and not so commonplace) activities and experiences are constructed. (1987: ix)

There are three things of particular relevance to us in that quote:

- The notion of an attitude of 'deep wonder'
- A focus on 'what is often regarded as obvious, given or natural'
- An appreciation of the practices of social life being immensely 'richly layered'

Conversation analysis and ethnomethodology involves fascination with the **local production** of social reality (that is, its production in particular locations) and explores how it is finely crafted and intimately ordered; it seeks to 'step back' in order to gain purchase on just *how* everyday realities are produced.

Conversation analysis requires researchers to consider how elements of our social life – our talk, tasks and identities – are **locally accomplished** in and through talk and interaction. This approach routinely involves detailed analysis of audio- and video-recorded social interactions. Sometimes it also uses ethnographic fieldwork (see Chapter 17). Harvey Sacks, one of the founders of conversation analysis, outlines the central research strategy for conversation analysis. He 'simply' says: 'Just try to come to terms with how it is that the thing comes off. ... Look to see how it is that persons go about producing what they do produce' (1992a: Fall 64: 11).

To begin to explore Sacks's advice, take the talk in Example 1 (see also the transcription conventions in Box 28.1).

So Sue, in Example 1, wonders out loud about how the person known as 'he' found out about something. I take that most people would hear Fiona as saying 'My *hunch* is that that they found out through work or Kay'. Whether Fiona does in fact know but is unwilling to admit this is open to question. However we can see that she is

---

Example 1

Sue: Wonder how he found out an all that
           (0.4)
Fiona: I:::: I don't know through work or Kay probably

(*Source*: Beach and Metzinger 1997: 569 – simplified transcript)

Example 2

Attorney: Well didn't he ask you if uh on that night that uh::: he wanted you to be his girl
              (0.5)
Attorney: Didn't he ask you that?
              (2.5)
Witness: I don't remember what he said to me that night (1.2)
Attorney: Well you had some uh uh fairly lengthy conversations with the defendant uh did'n
              you? (0.7)
Attorney: On the evening of February fourteenth? (1.0)
Witness: We were all talking.

(*Source*: Drew, 1992: 478–9)

---

displaying or **doing** *uncertainty*. In and through the action of displaying or doing uncertainty, Fiona works to say 'don't hold me accountable for the accuracy of this information'. Let's view another example of this, taken from a trial for rape. We join the sequence as the defence attorney is cross-examining the alleged rape victim.

Again, we can begin to see how the words 'I don't remember' are not necessarily tied to the working of the individual speaker's memory, but rather can be understood as a *social action*. Through the answer 'I don't remember' she avoids confirming the question and so avoids both confirming and disconfirming information that could be potentially damaging or discrediting to her case. The attorney then follows up this line of argument and she answers that 'We were all talking'. In and through displaying her lack of memory or certainty, she displays the lack of importance she gave to the defendant's actions towards her. The defendant's actions, his asking her 'to be his girl' and their 'lengthy conversations', are only unmemorable to her because, at the time, they went unnoticed. The implication is that, at that time, she had no special interest in him or par-

ticular reason to notice him; above all she should not be accused of 'leading him on'.

As with discourse analysis (Chapter 27), conversation analysis does not treat language as a neutral, transparent, medium of communication. Conversation analysis focuses on how social actions and practices are accomplished *in and through* talk and interaction. As the above examples begin to show, apparently mundane, trivial or innocent words like 'I don't know', 'probably' and 'I don't remember' do work for participants – they can work to say (among many other things) 'don't hold me that accountable for what I'm saying'. And this work is *not* tied to individual character, personality or psychology. To be sure, some people might use these words more often than others but the social action that happens in and through the use of these words, in these specific contexts, is independent of individual characteristics.

So conversation analysis looks with wonder at some of the taken-for-granted – seen but unnoticed – ways that we 'do' social life. It seeks to describe the richly layered practices of social life through the close and detailed observation of people's action and interaction. The central source of these observations are recordings of *naturally occurring* talk and interaction.

Recording social life

Schegloff (1999) offers the following story about an aphasiologist (someone who deals with speech disorders caused by dysfunction of the language areas of the brain).

> [W]hile engaged in testing aphasic patients, he would ordinarily use rest periods during which patients had a coffee break to go and check his mail, etc. One day he happened to join the patients in the coffee room during the break and was astonished to hear the patients doing things while talking amongst themselves or with relatives which they had just shown themselves to be 'unable' to do in the preceding test session. (1999: 431)

This story nicely demonstrates the potential benefits of a focus on what people do in the context of their everyday lives. By using observations of *naturally occurring* interactions over, say, experiments, interviews or imagining you already know, you can gain a different perspective on people's actions and interactions.

It is important to note what conversation analysts mean when they say that they prefer to focus on **naturally occurring** interaction. Some people take it to mean that you should only use data that is *not* researcher-led or researcher-prompted. However, what they mean is that you should *try to discover how some action or interaction* – be it a police interrogation or a qualitative interview – *occurs as 'natural', normal or routine*. So, rather than asking a focus group moderator about how they run focus groups, you can gain a better understanding of 'how they run focus groups' through recordings of them actually running focus groups. Equally, rather than asking counsellors about how they counsel, you would want to base your observations on recordings of them actually doing counselling. From this perspective, researcher-led information (from interviews or other sources) is still potentially of use in trying to describe how counsellors do counselling, or how focus group moderators run focus groups, but the primary

source of data would be audio- or video-recordings of what they actually do (see Chapter 16 for advice on how to make and manage recordings).

Sacks (1984) outlines the rationale behind using recording equipment.

> I started to work with tape-recorded conversations. Such materials had a single virtue, that I could replay them. I could transcribe them somewhat and study them extendedly – however long that might take. The tape-recorded materials offered a 'good enough' record of what happened. Other things, to be sure, happened, but at least what happened on tape had happened. I started with tape-recorded conversations ... simply because I could get my hands on it and I could study it again and again, and also, consequentially, because others could look at what I had studied and make use of it what they could, for example if they wanted to be able to disagree with me. (1984: 26)

Audio, and increasingly video, recordings of talk and interactions, although *never a comprehensive record of what's going on*, allow us access to many of the practices of social life.

As Sacks notes, people can only transcribe recordings 'somewhat'; transcripts are by their very nature *translations,* are always partial and selective textual re-presentations. The actual process of making detailed transcripts enables you to become familiar with what you are observing. You have to listen/watch the recording again and again (and again). Through this process you begin to notice the interesting and often subtle ways that people interact. These are the taken-for-granted features of people's talk that without recordings you would routinely fail to notice, fail to remember or be unable to record in sufficient detail by taking hand-written notes as it happened. What is key to remember is that *you base your analysis on the recording*. Transcripts are only, to borrow Spiegelberg's phrase, 'aids for the sluggish imagination' (cited in Garfinkel, 1967: 39); they can help you remember 'what was going on' on the recording. The subsequent benefit of making transcripts is that you can use them in the presentations of your findings.

Box 28.1   Simplified transcription symbols

Symbol	Example	Explanation
(0.5)	that (0.5) is odd?	Length of silence measured in tenths of a second
(.)	right (.) okay	Micro-pause, less than two-tenths of a second
:::	I::::: I don't know	Colons indicate sound-stretching of the immediately prior sound. The number of rows indicates the length of prolonged sound
_____	I know that	Underlining indicates speaker's emphasis stress
[	T: [Well 'at's R: [I mean really	Left brackets indicate the point at which one speaker overlaps another's talK
=	you know=that's fine	Equal signs indicates that there is no hearable gap between the words
WORD	about a MILLION	Capitals, except at beginnings indicate a marked rise in volume compared to the surrounding talk
?	Oh really?	Question mark indicates rising intonation
.	Yeah.	Full stop indicates falling intonation
hhh	I know how .hhh you	A row of h's prefixed by a dot indicates an inbreath, without dot, an outbreath. The number of h's indicates the length of the in- or out-breath.
( )	What a ( ) thing	Empty brackets indicate inability to hear what was said.
(word)	What are you (doing)	Word in brackets indicates the best possible hearing.
(( ))	I don't know ((shrugs))	Words in double brackets contain author's descriptions.

Conversation analysts are often faced with certain dilemmas, including what to record, how to record it, which parts to transcribe and the level of detail of the transcript. There are no definitive answers to any of these questions and most depend on what your analytic interest is. For example, people working with readily available talk (for example, live radio broadcasts) can only use audio recordings and can only transcribe the verbal interaction. For those that focus on interactions that occur in different places at different times (such as nursing work in a hospital ward), a period of *ethnography* may be essential in order to establish what might be relevant to record and what type of recording – audio or video – is feasible and acceptable to the participants.

When it comes to the transcription, most analysts use parts of the transcription system developed by Gail Jefferson for recording verbal interaction (see Box 28.1). This level of technical detail is used to try to re-present the highly dynamic and complex lived interactional work we all engage in when talking to others. Non-verbal interaction, including direction of gaze, gestures, bodily movement and use of artefacts, requires a further layer of description (see Heath and Hindmarsh, 2002).

Exploring a mundane moment in talk

In order to explore some of the ways talk can be analysed, lets focus on a rather 'trivial', ordinary moment of talk.

At first glance this might not be that interesting. However, note *how* John works to display his thoughts about bicycles on campus. Rather than just tell Judy what he thinks about them, he asks Judy a question (1). So John *invites* Judy to offer her thoughts or opinions about bicycles. Judy then *replies*, that she thinks 'they're terrible'. (2). Then, and only then, does John report his *perspective*.

So, why should that interest us at all? What we've got here is some rather lovely work – these people are actively doing something we all routinely do. We can re-produce the opening lines of their talk as follows:

John invites Judy to talk about a topic (1)
Judy talks about the topic (2)
John then gives his perspective on the same topic and his perspective closely fit's with Judy's (3)

Now, it does not take a great leap of imagination to think about a moment when we all do similar work. Think about the times when you leave the cinema or a lecture. Often what happens is, rather than say outright 'I hated that film/lecture' you ask the person you are with a question like 'What did you think', they then tell you that they 'thought is was excellent' and then you may 'fit' your response around what they have just said, 'I liked the start but some of it was quite boring'.

This way of talking, that Maynard (1991) calls the **perspective-display sequence**, can be a wonderful way that we *do caution*. Rather than just giving your opinion 'outright' without knowing whether the other person agrees or not, *once you have heard their opinion* you can then deliver yours in a 'hospitable environment' (Maynard, 1991: 460) as you can tie what they have said into your own report.

This is one example of how people analyse conversations – they focus on *how* speakers interact. A lot of conversation analysis has focused on what Heritage (1997: 162) calls 'the social institution *of* interaction' (author's emphasis) *how* everyday interaction is locally and collaboratively produced. A lot of work also focuses on 'the management of social institutions *in* interactions' (1997: 162), *how* specific institutions, be they law, medicine, education – and institutional activities, be they testimony, consultations, teaching – are *locally* and **collaboratively produced**.

Rather than just offer his perspective at the start of their talk, the doctor delays giving his perspective. Initially the mother just produces 'good' news about her son. She then offers some 'bad' news, which the doctor invites her to elaborate on, which she does. Note how he *only* delivers the 'bad' news diagnosis once the 'hospitable

---

Example 3

1 *John*:   So what do you think about bicycles on campus?
2 *Judy*:   I think they're terrible.
3 *John*:   Sure is about a MILLION of 'em
4 *Judy*:   eh heh

(*Source:* Maynard 1991: 461)

Box 28.2 The interactional management of diagnosis in an institutional setting

Maynard (1992) notes how the *perspective-display sequence* (see Example 3) can occur when doctors deliver 'bad' diagnostic news. He recorded some consultations where parents are given a diagnosis about their child's health.

Example 4

```
1   Dr:   How's Bobby doing.
2   Mo:   Well he's doing pretty good you know
3         especially in the school.
          ...
4         Now [the teacher] thinks he's not
5         gonna need to be sent to another school.
6   Dr:   He doesn't think he's gonna need to be
7         sent
8   Mo:   Yeah that he was catching on a little bit uh
9         more you know like I said I– I– I know that
10        he needs a– you know I was 'splaining to her
11        that I'm you know that I know for sure that
12        he needs some special class or something.
13  Dr:   Wu' whatta you think his problem is.
14  Mo:   Speech.
15  Dr:   Yeah. Yeah his main problem is a – you know a
16        language problem
17  Mo:   Yeah language.
```

(*Source*: Maynard, 1992: 339 – modified transcript)

The doctor asks an open-question about how this mother's child, Bobby, is 'doing' (1). She then replies that he is 'doing pretty good' (2) and goes on to give evidence for this by referring to what Bobby's teacher has been saying (4–5). The doctor asks a question about this (6–7). In the course of replying to his question, she offers her own opinion – that she knows *'for sure* he needs some special class or something'(11–12). The doctor then asks another question, *inviting* her to talk about what she thinks is Bobby's *'problem'* (13). She *replies* that it is 'Speech.' (14). Then, and only then, does the doctor report his *perspective.* He agrees with the mother's understanding 'Yeah.' (15) and then reformulates the problem as 'a *language* problem' (15–16). She then agrees with this and reformulates her description of the problem in alignment with the doctor's terminology (17).

---

environment' of 'bad' news talk has been developed. Also, he delivers the 'bad' news diagnosis as a *confirmation* of what the mother already knows. As Maynard notes, a doctor can use a perspective-display sequence to *co-implicate* or *confirm* a parent's view in the delivery of a 'bad' news diagnosis. In this way, the parent is produced as 'already having some knowledge of their child's condition' and 'good' parents should be experts on their children. Interestingly, the perspective-display sequence can be used by doctors to confirm the parent's own thoughts when they then go on to deliver a diagnosis that is *alternative to* the parent's own thoughts.

Building a case

Maynard's work also shows us something about one of the methods that conversation analysts use. You focus on a single episode of talk to explore in detail how that specific moment of interaction happens. You notice something interesting, something that you think might be an 'organized' way of talking. You then go and look for other examples, in other settings, between different speakers to see if you can find other examples of this type of work. In this way, you attempt to build a case that this organized way of talking is something that people do as part of their everyday lives – that this thing is part of the social institution of interaction. Refusals and disagreements have been investigated in this way.

The social institution of refusal and disagreement

A considerable body of work has been undertaken that collects together many instances of talk where people are either accepting or refusing something, be it an invitation, offers, requests, proposals (Davidson, 1984; Drew, 1984) or agreeing or disagreeing with assessments (Pomerantz, 1984; see also Sacks, 1987). They have documented the routine ways that people do acceptance and refusal and agreement and disagreement in Anglo-American talk.

As you can see acceptance (Example 5) and agreement (Example 6) are routinely done immediately, with no gap in the talk (and sometimes overlapping the other speaker's talk) and are relatively 'forthright', in that they are simple and straightforward. Compare this to how refusals and disagreements are often produced.

The difference is clear. With a refusal or disagreement you routinely get some combination of the following actions:

- Delays – a gap before a response or a gap within a response, a delay before an answer is given
- Hesitations – like 'mm' 'erm' 'uhm' and in-breath or out-breaths
- Prefaces – like 'Well' and 'Uh', agreement tokens like 'Yeah'
- Mitigations – apologies and appreciations
- Accounts – excuses, explanations, justifications and reasons

Interestingly, a lot of the time we say 'no' without ever explicitly saying it and other speakers understand us to be saying 'no' without ever having to hear us say it out loud.

Researchers have documented how we can 'notice' a potential or upcoming refusal or disagreement prior to someone actually producing one. For instance, in Example 10 below, note how speaker Z works to make their invitation more 'inviting'.

Even after the micro-pause (around two-tenths of a second), Z works to **upgrade** their invitation with the 'sweetener' of providing 'beer and stuff'.

Example 5

A: Well, will you help me [out
B: [I certainly will

(*Source*: Davidson, 1984: 116 – simplified transcript)

Example 6

J: It's really a clear lake, isn't it?
R: It's wonderful

(*Source*: Pomerantz, 1984: 60)

Example 7

B: Wanna come down 'n have a bite a' <u>lunch</u> with me?
    I got some beer en stuff.
A: Wul yer real <u>sweet</u> hon, uhm, let-=
B: [D'you have sumpn else?
A: [I have-
A: No, I have to uh call Bill's mother

(*Source*: Pomerantz, 1984: 101)

Example 8

((S's wife has just slipped a disc))
H: And we were <u>wo</u>ndering if there's <u>a</u>nything we can do to help
S: [Well 'at's
H: [I mean can we do any shopping for her or
    Something like tha:t?
    (0.7)
S: Well that's <u>most</u> kind Heather<u>ton</u> .hhh
    At the moment <u>no</u>:. because we've still got the bo:ys at home.

(*Source*: Heritage, 1984: 271)

Example 9

B: I think I'll call her and ask her if she's
    interested because she's a good nurse, and I
    think they would like her don't you?
A: Well, I'll tell you, I haven't seen Mary for
    <u>years</u>. I should – As I remember, yes.
B: Well do you think she would fit in?
A: Uhm, uh, I don't know, What I'm uh
    hesitating about is uh - - uhm maybe she would.
    (1.0)
A: Uh but I would hesitate to uhm - -

(*Source*: Pomerantz, 1984: 73)

In this case, Z has **heard** this pause as a potential refusal and shows the other speaker (and us) what she has taken it to mean. We have seen related work in Example 7. Just after A's appreciative comment 'Wul yer real <u>sweet</u> hon, uhm, let-=' B asks the question 'D'you have sumpn else?'. B's question marks that they have heard A's talk as a preface to an upcoming rejection of the invitation. So we are able to monitor other people's talk for the finest of distinctions.

Through the detailed comparative analysis of instances of talk, conversation analysts have out-

---

Example 10

Z: C'mon down here,=it's okay
    (0.2)
Z: I got lotta stuff,=I got beer and stuff 'n

(*Source*: Davidson, 1984: 105 – simplified transcript)

---

lined how the work of agreeing/accepting and disagreeing/refusing is routinely done. This is not to say they we all behave like robots and that this is *the only* way that people do this work – but rather, when *doing* social life we routinely work with and against this specific **normative interaction order**, or set of obligations and expectations of each other. We only have to think of the multiple ways that a quick and plain 'no' can be interpreted as the speaker being blunt or rude, as someone who holds a heartfelt opinion on that specific topic or as someone who is being mischievous. Note, though, that in some cases, a quick and plain 'no' may be the **preferred** (rather than **dispreferred**) response, say for example when someone makes the self-assessment 'My new hair cut makes me look terrible'.

These two alternative, but non-equivalent, courses of actions – *preferred* actions that are direct and plain responses and *dispreferred* actions that are delayed and embellished responses – document what conversation analysts call **preference organization**. This concept of 'preference' does not refer to inner psychological or subjective experiences of individual speakers. Rather it describes one of the systematic ways that speakers in general, across a range of actions, contexts and situations, work to organize the social institution of talk and interaction.

Before going on to see how conversation analysts have looked at talk in some institutional settings, examine some work (in Box 28.3) which shows the potential insights that can be gained from a detailed focus on *what people actually do*,

---

Box 28.3 'Just say no': conversation analysis and date rape

Kitzinger and Firth (1999) have taken the observation – that in Anglo-American interaction there 'is an organized and normative way of doing indirect refusal' (1999: 310) and begun to question the 'refusal skills' training advocated by many date rape prevention programmes. As you have seen, as part of our everyday lives we routinely understand and orientate to people saying 'no' without them ever having to necessarily say 'no' out-loud. Kitzinger and Firth suggest that

> the insistence of date rape prevention (and other refusals skills) educators on the importance of saying 'no' is counter-productive in that it demands that women engage in conversationally abnormal actions which breach conventional social etiquette, and in allowing rapists to persist with the claim that if a woman has not actually said 'NO' (in the right tone of voice, with the right body language, at the right time) then she hasn't refused to have sex with him. (1999: 310)

As they outline, for a man to claim that because the woman didn't actually say 'no' he 'just didn't understand' or 'wasn't clear whether' she was refusing sex produces him as socially ignorant and interactionally incompetent. It is not that these men are cultural dopes (i.e. don't understand normative interaction order) or that these men just don't understand 'women's ways' of communicating; rather these men do not like being refused sex. As the authors note '[t]he problem of sexual coercion cannot be fixed by changing the way women talk' (1999: 311).

rather than what we imagine they might or should do.

The organization of social institutions in interaction

From the perspective of conversation analysts, institutions are organized and *produced* through action and interaction. At their most extreme, some institutions **pre-allocate** specific talk, tasks and identities to people. Take, for example, courtrooms or the British House of Commons, where, once in session, only specific individuals can speak at specific times. In courtrooms, the judge determines who is 'out of order', who is in 'contempt of court' and directs others to 'answer the question'. Those not allocated the right to talk should, at all times when in session, be silent witnesses to the proceedings. If they do not perform this action, they can, potentially, be removed or incarcerated. However, the social organization of most institutions – be it medicine, education, counselling, news interviews, market research, academic research, sexuality, gender, race, friendship, family, relationships – is not as rigidly fixed and policed in terms of the rights and responsibilities of those involved.

What is of interest to conversation analysts is how specific institutions are locally produced in and through the collaborative actions of people. Let us focus briefly on news media interviews. As Clayman (1988) notes, news interviewers are meant to be

interactionally 'adversarial' while remaining officially 'neutral', that is, to introduce viewpoints that contradict those of the interviewees, not as a matter of personal expression, but as a way of further soliciting interviewees' own views. (1988: 490)

One of the ways that interviewers achieve this is to distance themselves from being heard as 'the author' of any controversial statement. This can be seen in Example 11.

Note how the interviewer (IR) prefaces the question (arrow 1). IR is just following 'up a point the ambassador made', he is *not* to be heard as the 'author' of the question. Again, at arrow 2, he repeats this action; the interviewer is not personally calling someone 'a collaborator', rather he is just following up on something 'the ambassador said'. The interviewee (IE) collaborates in this (arrow 3); the 'target' of his answer, and therefore the person responsible for the content and opinions embedded in the question, is 'The ambassador' and not IR.

Put simply, rather than say something like 'you're an idiot', news interviewers routinely say something like 'Mr Smith says you're idiot' or 'Some people say you're an idiot'. This is just one of the practices that *locally produces* the impartiality of news interviewing and so sustains the impartial status of the institution of news interviews. As Heritage and Greatbatch (1991) note, a question remains: clearly these news interviewers are **doing** impartiality/neutrality but does that mean they are **being** impartial/neutral in any conventional sense?

Such a practice – a speaker distancing themselves from being heard as responsible for the content of a question – does not only occur in news interviewing. Example 12 shows some talk from a pre-test HIV counselling session.

Example 11

> *IR*: Reverend Boesak lemme a pick up a point the ambassador made.   ←1
>   What assurances can you give us that talks between moderates in that
>   country will take place when it seems that any black leader who is willing
>   to talk to the government is branded
>   as the ambassador said a collaborator   ←2
>   and is then punished.
> *IE*: The ambassador has it wrong. It's not the people ...   ←3
>
> (*Source*: Clayman, 1988: 483)

Example 12

1	C:	er: I have to ask you this have you ever injected
2		drugs.
3	P:	No.
4	C:	Because they're the sort of highest ris:k (.)

(*Source*: Silverman, 1996: 155)

The counsellor (C) prefaces their question with 'er: I have to ask you this' (1). This preface works to say 'I would not normally ask such a question and I am only asking it now as this is *part of my job.*' Note the talk that follows the patient's (P) answer, where the counsellor works to further *account* for 'why I asked this question'.

In both cases the questioners try to say 'I'm not wholly responsible for this action'. However, the practical reasoning of doing such work is tied to the *specific* institutional tasks and identities they are engaged with: news interviewers when doing interviewing should be seen and *heard* as impartial; counsellors when doing counselling should try to build rapport. And this is a key point, when studying talk and interaction the idea is not to say 'here's an example of a perspective-display sequence' and 'there's an example of preference organization' but rather to document the work that specific organization of talk does in *locally producing* specific tasks, identities and contexts. To outline what such analysis can look like, I want to look at a study of interaction in a courtroom.

Making sense of evidence in courtrooms

Goodwin (1994) undertook an analysis of the trial of Rodney King. Four white American police officers had stopped King, an African American, and then physically assaulted the man. Unknown to the officers, a man across the street had made a videotape of the incident. How to 'make sense' of the video-record of the police officers' and Rodney King's actions became a central feature of the trial. Example 13 is a transcript from part of the defence's case. We join the talk as the videotape of the incident is being played, stopped and

commented on.

This small fragment contains two sequences (1–7 and 8–16) which share very similar features – the defence lawyer does some description then asks a question about that description, and the expert witness answers that question, and in so doing produces some re-description. What is important to note is how, through their actions, they *collaborate* to build a way of how to 'make sense' of the images on the video.

With the first sequence, the defence lawyer calls out the time of the image 'Four oh five, oh one.' (1) and then describes the image 'We see a blow being delivered=' (2). Note how he describes the action in the image – this is to be seen and understood as *a single blow* – this is not a beating or an attack. He then asks for confirmation of his description, '=Is that correct.' (3). The expert witness confirms this (4) and then re-describes the action in the image. This is not to be seen only as a 'blow', but as a moment when 'The – force has again been escalated … the de-escalation has ceased.' (5–7). With this re-description, the single image of the blow is now to be seen as a precise moment of 'escalation' to a precise 'level' (6) of force. With the second sequence (8–14), similar work goes on, except in this sequence the defence lawyer also uses the description 'the end of a period of, de-escalation' (12) to account for the police officers' actions.

In this example, the defence's case works around coding and highlighting each specific blow on the video ('Four oh five, oh one' and 'four thirteen twenty-nine') as separate, distinct, actions. The multiple strikes to Rodney King's body, that happen seconds apart, are transformed by the interaction between the defence lawyer and the police expert as separate, distinct uses of force.

Example 13

1	*Defence*:	Four oh five, oh one.
2		We see a blow being delivered=
3		=Is that correct.
4	*Expert*:	That's correct.
5		The – force has again been escalated (0.3)
6		To the level it had been previously, (0.4)
7		And the de-escalation has ceased.
		…
8	*Defence*:	And at–
9		At this point which is,
10		for the record four thirteen twenty nine, (0.4)
11		We see a blow being struck
12		and thus the end of a period of, de-escalation?
13		Is that correct Captain.
14	*Expert*:	That's correct.
15		Force has now been elevated to the previous level, (0.6)
16		After this period of de-escalation.

(*Source*: Goodwin, 1994: 617)

This 'individual' strike is *only* to be understood as a moment of elevation or escalation of force, a moment when the period of de-escalation has ceased. The seconds between blows are to be understood as 'an assessment period' (Goodwin, 1994: 617), where the officers are analysing Rodney King's actions for signs of cooperation. As the defence went on to argue, 'Rodney King and Rodney King alone was in control of the situation' (Goodwin, 1994: 618).

One of the things that Goodwin's analysis highlights is how things do not 'speak for themselves' but rather that they are always *spoken for*. In the case of the Rodney King trial, the defence lawyer and the expert police witness collaborated in producing a specific way to 'make sense' of the images on the tape. Throughout the trial, the case for the defence argued that the video tape was an

Box 28.4   Web pointers for Conversation Analysis

Ethno/CA news: information on ethnomethodology and Conversation Analysis
www2.fmg.uva.nl/emca

Charles Antaki's Introductory Tutorial in Conversation Analysis
www-staff.lboro.ac.uk/~sscal/sitemenu.htm

Conversation analysis.net
www.conversation-analysis.net

The International Institute for Ethnomethodology and Conversation Analysis
www.iiemca.org

Australian Institute for Ethnomethodology and Conversation Analysis
wwwmcc.murdoch.edu.au/aiem

Visit the website for this book at www.rscbook.co.uk to link to these web pointers.

objective record of the incident and used the testimony produced with a range of expert witnesses to instruct the jury to understand the video of the beating of King as an example of 'good' police work. The defence argued, successfully in the first court case, that the video displayed that the officers where *only* engaged in 'careful, systematic police work' (1994: 617).

Conclusion

As these examples begin to show, from a conversation analytic perspective, the focus is on *how* institutions are produced in and through the collaborative actions and interactions of people. So what the analysis of conversation allows us to do is to try to document the ways that people organize specific institutions and institutional tasks and identities. Importantly, the analysis is based on what the participants do, to what they themselves are attending within their talk, what outcomes they achieve and is not based on *a priori* assumptions of what the analyst thinks 'should be' going on.

Conversation analysts are constantly preoccupied with describing the *lived work* of talking and interacting. They begin to show us that the work of being an ordinary member of society is made up of masses of tacit, taken-for-granted, knowledges and practices. Such an approach is not going to be for everyone, as it often produces rather modest, descriptive, claims about things we all already just know 'at a glance'. What those researching society and culture can take away from their investigations is that talk is not just a 'trivial' medium for social life, but rather it is *in and through* our talk and interactions that we experience, produce and maintain social life. As Sacks notes:

> [I]n every moment of talk, people are experiencing and producing their cultures, their roles, their personalities. ... [Y]ou and I live lives of talk, experience the social world as motivated talkers and listeners, as tongued creatures of the social order; each with our own bursts of pleasure and pain, each with our proud differences of personal style. (cited in Moerman, 1988: xi)

Further reading

Excellent book-length introductions to conversation analysis have been provided by Hutchby and Wooffitt (1998), and ten Have (1999) and Psathas (1995). Silverman's (1998) account of the writings of Harvey Sacks is a good way into the theoretical background of conversation analysis, as well as giving an account of important methodological procedures.

Student Reader (Seale, 2004): relevant readings

47 David Silverman: 'Harvey Sacks: social science and conversation analysis'
48 Anssi Peräkylä: 'Reliability and validity in research based on tapes and transcripts'
58 Paul Atkinson: 'Transcriptions'

Key concepts

Collaborative production of talk/social life etc.
Doing aspects of social life (e.g. caution, uncertainty, disagreement, neutrality) as opposed to **being** cautious, uncertain, neutral etc.
Ethnomethodology
Hearing (as in interpreting)
Local production/accomplishment

Naturally occurring interaction or data
Normative interaction order
Perspective-display sequence
Pre-allocation of roles, identities etc.
Preference organization
Preferred/dispreferred utterances and actions
Transcription symbols
Upgrading invitations, utterances etc.

29

Reading and writing research

Les Back

CONTENTS

At its most fundamental, the process of doing research involves reading and writing. This seems obvious. Yet, it was not until relatively recently that researchers paid serious attention to the social, linguistic and rhetorical structures of the texts which form the ultimate product of the research act. Beyond this very little has been written about the nature of our audience. We have few insights into the impact of social research on the societies within which it is conducted. Glance at any newspaper and one finds an extraordinary amount of information, and a fetish for social measurement. The appetite for social commentary seems almost infinite. But what place does social science occupy within these circuits of facts and figures? Who is listening and why?

A cynic might reply that the low social standing of some branches of social and cultural research means that no one cares and no one is interested. If this is true, and I must say I am not entirely convinced, then we equally need to ask what has produced a situation where a society, almost pathologically preoccupied with information, demonstrates such little interest in academic research. Writing of sociology, for example, Silverman cautions that 'We do our subject no service if we assume that our low status is simply the result of a cruel world. If in Britain, sociologists are often little more than figures of fun, then the activities of sociologists themselves may have something to do with this' (1990: 1). We therefore need to think carefully about the products of research and how they enter the social world beyond academic circles.

Research is inherently a **rhetorical** activity (Atkinson, 1990). In its common usage 'rhetoric' is often associated with insincere oratory or sloganeering. However, philosophically and historically this notion has another meaning. Here it is defined as the art of persuasion or effective communication, connected with speaking with propriety, elegance and force. Concerns about the lack of status within the social sciences reflect a rhetorical failure on the part of researchers to convince their non-academic audiences of the relevance of research.

This chapter looks in turn at the ways in which social research has been *read* critically and examines new strategies for *writing* research. My aim here is to think through, in a non-programmatic way, a strategy that more closely connects writing with identifying particular audiences. At the same time, the forms of textual critique discussed in the chapter have in common an insistence that forms of power and history affect the process of writing in ways that the authors of research only partly understand and control.

Reading research

One of the core paradoxes of social and cultural research is that the writer or researcher is inside the very thing that she or he wishes to understand, in other words, society and culture. In this sense research texts are social products. This is equally true of the natural sciences; the cool remoteness of scientific papers is in many ways a kind of rhetoric. It is this apparent lack of style that gives scientific accounts their authority. Yet even natural science can be seen as being 'inside' language. Yearley (1981) has shown this through examining the forms of rhetoric found within just one scientific paper and suggests that close scrutiny reveals particular modes of accounting, argument and persuasion. The audience is as much convinced by the rhetoric of scientific texts as it is by the 'facts' that are represented through these means.

Science writing, in both natural and social sciences, attempts to achieve what Latour and Woolgar (1979) refer to as 'literary inscription'. This refers to their success in having the correctness or **facticity** of a given argument accepted as true. Latour and Woolgar point out that this is accomplished when the reader accepts the facts without seeing rhetorical processes at work. The 'scientific message' is composed of conventions of textual performance. I believe that we need to identify and unlock these processes of literary inscription in order to see through the technical mystifications of research texts. In order to achieve this it is necessary to suspend the taken-for-granted assumptions to which readers submit when reading a monograph or research paper. The reader needs to remove prior assumptions and attend to how 'facts' and 'social realities' are constructed through language. This is an attitude towards text rather similar to that of the discourse analyst (Chapter 27).

I will discuss two genres of critical reading that have examined the textual nature of research writing, namely feminist critiques of male bias in social research, and what I will refer to as the *literary turn* in the social sciences. First, I will look at the ways in which feminist writers have criticized the gendered nature of research texts.

Feminism, writing and androcentrism

One of the themes of feminist criticism is that accounts of social life produced by male researchers are presented through a male-centred or **androcentric** viewpoint (see also Chapter 3). Lofland (1974), for example, has argued that the portrayals of women within the American urban studies literature either completely ignore the presence of women or portray them through the eyes of male social actors. She argues that these representations of urban life do not give women a voice or any sense of social agency. This literature presents the men as the generic representatives of the society or subculture as a whole. At the simplest level, this is done by use of the male pronoun ('he') to refer to both men and women. Morgan points out that this also renders significant parts of male social experience invisible: 'men were there all the time but we did not see them because we were looking for mankind' (1980: 93). Missing out the effect of gender on the experience of social life thus disadvantages both sexes.

Feminist responses to this have not been uniform. There are a range of positions on the relationship between research, writing and a political commitment to feminism. Harding, in *The Science Question and Feminism*, identifies a key problem for feminist knowledge:

> The epistemological problem for feminism is to explain an apparently paradoxical situation. Feminism is a political movement for social change. How can such politicized research be increasing the objectivity of enquiry? On what grounds should these feminist claims be justified? (1986: 24)

Subsequently, Harding (1987) outlined a number of broad responses to this paradox. I want to look in detail at what she refers to as **feminist empiricism** and **feminist postmodernism** (see Box 29.1). Both of these broad areas have addressed issues of rhetoric, modes of writing and the role of research.

One of the features of feminist epistemology is the premise that personal experiences should be admissible within feminist knowledge. However, *feminist empiricists* have been sceptical of the way in which this has involved a dismissal of the potential use of reason and objectivity. Thus, with regard to the biological sciences, Birke concludes:

> the association of objectivity with masculinity has sometimes led feminists to reject objectivity and to glorify subjectivity in opposition to it. While it is necessary to revalue the subjective ... we do ourselves a

---

Box 29.1 Two feminist positions on knowledge

The central tenets of **feminist empiricism** are that the existing methodological tools of social science are fundamentally sound. The problem is the issue of male bias and this can be corrected by a stricter, less gender-loaded adherence to the methodological norms of scientific inquiry.

Feminist postmodernism is inspired by French thinkers like Derrida and Foucault and the deconstruction movement (see Chapter 4). This strand within feminist thought is profoundly sceptical about the power of reason and the universalizing claims of scientific discourse. The project of science is seen as fundamentally flawed; the knowledge produced through empirical means is little more than a regime of power and an effect of the desire to know. The rhetoric of social science is viewed as irrevocably harnessed to oppressive ways of knowing and governing people's social experience.
(*Source*: summarized in Harding, 1987)

disservice if we remove ourselves from objectivity and rationality; we then simply leave the terrain of rational thought ... to men, thus perpetuating the system which excluded us in the first place. (1986: 157)

If, as some have argued, scientific rationality is inevitably compromised with male intellectual models, then how do feminist researchers convince a potentially hostile audience of the power of their critique? It is precisely the *rhetorical* power of social science and objectivity that some feminist empiricists have found appealing. Jayaratne and Stewart comment that 'The greatest benefit of apparent objectivity lies in its power to change political opinion. Thus traditional research methods can be used to our advantage to change sexist beliefs or to support progressive legislation' (1991: 100). Sara Arber's work in the secondary analysis of official statistics, described in Chapter 26, demonstrates the appeal of this. Box 29.2 shows another example.

Jayaratne and Stewart conclude that 'Feminist researchers must be critical of both quantitative and qualitative research which is used against women and must be able to marshal the richest and most persuasive evidence in the service of women' (1991: 100). They suggest that the political commitments of feminism are best served by this pragmatic or instrumental approach. Although they do not labour this point, such an approach also subscribes to established forms of research writing which include striving for objectivity, the use of reasoned argument and establishing truth empirically.

The *feminist postmodernist* critique completely breaks with the established conventions of empirical research writing. This is not just a matter of critically engaging with the gender distortion present in male social science; rather, research texts are viewed as little more than the embodiment of male desire, in which power forges representations of social reality through discursive means. The truth-telling power of research texts is reduced to patterns of discourse enshrined in writing. Deconstructivist criticism has been influential in other areas of social thought. Here, I want to look in particular at this perspective as applied to anthropological writing.

'True fictions': the poetics of ethnography

Renato Rosaldo, in his ground-breaking book *Culture and Truth: The Remaking of Social Analysis* (1989), pointed out that classic modes of ethnographic reporting seem farcical parodies when applied to familiar social settings. To demonstrate this, Rosaldo describes a breakfast scene at the home of his prospective parents-in-law (Box 29.3).

This account of the family breakfast is rendered in the present tense favoured in ethnographic writing. It is framed as a drama of generational domination and gender deference, and uses both direct quotes and 'anthropological' categories (such as 'reigning patriarch' and 'ritual praise song'). Yet it reads as a humorous parody and a gross caricature. Rosaldo's in-laws laughed as they listened to him recite his anthropological contemplations. He reflected: 'The experience of having gales of laughter greet my micro-ethnography made me wonder why a manner of speaking that sounds like the literal "truth" when describing distant cultures seems terribly funny as a description of "us"' (1989: 50).

But this is not to say that ethnographic accounts of social life are without merit. They may produce

---

Box 29.2 The persuasive power of statistics

Jayaratne and Stewart (1991) quote an example of a study of maternal death rate conducted in Chicago, which showed a much higher death rate amongst black women than amongst whites. As a result of the research a new programme was initiated by the Illinois health commissioner and the Chicago Health Department allocated $35 million to improve prenatal care. It was precisely the rhetoric of science and the allure of statistical evidence that made the case so compelling.

Box 29.3 American breakfast scene

'Every morning the reigning patriarch, as if just in from the hunt, shouts from the kitchen, "How many people would like a poached egg?" Women and children take turns saying yes or no. In the meantime, the women talk among themselves and designate one among them the toast maker. As the eggs near readiness, the reigning patriarch calls out to the designated toast maker, "The eggs are about ready. Is there enough toast?" "Yes," comes the deferential reply. "The last two pieces are about to pop up." The reigning patriarch then proudly enters bearing a plate of poached eggs before him. Throughout the course of the meal, the women and children, including the designated toast maker, perform the obligatory ritual praise song, saying, "These sure are great eggs, Dad."' (Rosaldo, 1989: 47)

---

insightful observations. The father in his breakfast ritual was approaching retirement and his adult daughters had successful careers. Rosaldo's caricature shows how gender roles were being maintained, even where the 'ruling patriarch's' status was fast being undermined by professional changes in status amongst his daughters. But until recently these modes of anthropological description were taken to be objective characterizations. It is only when one applies them to social contexts with which we are familiar that they strike us as **objectifying** caricatures. This brings into focus the importance of examining the **poetics** of ethnographic writing. Here the notion of poetics means the analysis of the conventions whereby ethnography, or any other form of research, is constructed and interpreted.

The publication in 1986 of *Writing Culture* by Clifford and Marcus marked an important moment in what I want to refer to as the **literary turn** in anthropology. One of the features of this movement is the application of perspectives from literary criticism to ethnographic writing. The book is a collection of essays produced from a discussion forum on the 'making of ethnographic texts' held at the School of American Research in Santa Fe, New Mexico. The fundamental starting point of this collection is that ethnography possesses a rhetorical structure, modes of authority and processes of suppression and omission.

In his introduction to the book Clifford argues that the poetics of ethnography are structured in at least six ways:

1 *Contextual:* It fashions and creates particular social situations and in doing so creates an object of study. In its classical period ethnographers created 'the tribe' as their unit of analysis.

2 *Rhetorical:* Ethnographic writing demonstrates particular conventions of expression. Rosaldo exemplifies one of the most common (the use of the ethnographic present). This way of describing society constructs social relations as if they are enduring facts that are almost timeless.

3 *Institutional:* Ethnographers write within (and sometimes against) specific traditions, disciplines and their audiences. The ethnographic monograph itself is shaped institutionally. It is an unwritten rite of passage that the anthropologist must write long research monographs that provide the space for them to recount the fruits of participant observation.

4 *Generic:* Ethnographies are a particular genre of texts distinguishable from travel writing and other types of research writing.

5 *Political:* This form of writing monopolizes the authority to represent cultural realities.

6 *Historical:* All these conventions and constraints are shifting and changing through time.

These various elements act collectively as ethnographers write. It is as if all of these inherited conventions sit at the shoulder of the writer as he or she commits descriptions, observations and analysis to paper. Clifford uses this analysis to argue that ethnographic truths are inherently partial, committed and imperfect: 'Even the best ethnographic texts – serious, true fictions – are systems, or economies, of truth. Power and history work through them, in ways their authors cannot fully control' (1986: 7). Crapanzano (1986), one of the book's contributors, argues that ethnographers are like tricksters who promise not to lie but on the other hand never tell the whole truth. His point is that their rhetoric of absolute truth both empowers and subverts the message. The task of critical reading is then to read against the grain of the text, to identify the exclusions and the trickery of ethnographic writing and authority. Clifford comments:

'Cultures' do not hold still for their portraits. Attempts to make them do so always involve simplification and exclusion, selection of a temporal focus, the construction of a particular self-other relationship, and the imposition or negotiation of a power relationship. (1986: 10)

The point here is that in order to evaluate ethnographic writing more accurately its *discursive* nature needs to be specified. In simple terms this means posing a number of questions in relation to the text. Who speaks? Who writes? What modes of description are used? What is the relationship between the style of writing and the reality which is represented through these means?

In order to understand the significance of the literary turn one needs to see anthropology in its historical context. In many respects modern anthropology was the child of colonialism. Yet the anthropologists of the 1940s and 1950s were often 'reluctant imperialists' caught between the expectations of colonial bureaucrats and a desire to construct a cross-cultural science (Asad, 1973). With the emergence of independence movements in the 1960s there was a move to reinvent anthropology (Hymes, 1974) and combine the ethnographic enterprise with politicized perspectives drawn from Marxism, feminism and anti-colonialism. The significance of the literary critique developed by people like Clifford is the argument for a reconfiguring of the relationship between the Western anthropologist and the colonial or post-colonial world. Clifford suggests that anthropologists need to share authorship to produce collaborative accounts of the social world. Even so, he warns against the view that such 'cultural insiders' will tell 'the real story'. Accounts from the 'inside' are equally rhetorical performances with conventions and constraints.

Ethnographic writing, though, can allow more than one voice to be represented. This is appropriate because

Culture is contested, temporal, and emergent. Representation and explanation – both by insiders and outsiders – is implicated in this emergence. The specification of discourses I have been tracing is thus more a matter of making carefully limited claims. It is thoroughly historicist and self-reflexive. (Clifford, 1986: 19)

Although these points have been illustrated by arguments from anthropologists, they can be applied equally to other forms of research writing. Atkinson (1990), for example, applies this perspective to sociologists writing ethnographic accounts. Reading any research text from this point of view is helpful in promoting a more reflexive, self-aware style when the time comes to begin writing research for yourself.

Writing research

The literary turn in feminism, anthropology and sociology offers new insights into the processes that affect the textual production of research-based knowledge. What implications does this have for writing research? Atkinson, in his discussion of ethnographic writing in sociology, concludes:

The fully mature ethnography requires a reflexive awareness of its own writing, the possibilities and limits of its own language, and a principled exploration of its modes of representation. Not only do we need to cultivate a self-conscious construction of ethnographic texts, but also a readiness to *read* texts from a more 'literary critical' perspective. Sociologists and their students must cultivate the discipline of reading their own and others' arguments for their stylistic and rhetorical properties. (1990: 180)

The bottom line seems to be that researchers should be aware of their rhetorical strategies because of the tautological notion that self-knowledge is good. There is a real danger, though, that the preoccupation with reflexivity will degenerate into solipsism and self-absorption, where social researchers are continually examining their own discrete and sometimes stale professional cultures. It would be a disaster, in my view, if these insightful perspectives resulted in little more than a self-referential endo-professionalism, where research is reduced to endless textual deconstruction.

Students and young researchers seem to be bewildered by this insistence on complexity and contingency. One of the unintended consequences of the literary turn is that all claims to describe reality are placed in inverted commas. Any kind of research in this scenario appears to be compromised by the fact that it involves a textual practice that can be subjected to the kinds of deconstruction discussed in this chapter. This can result in a kind of intellectual vertigo, where the level of analysis is abstracted to such a degree that the social world with which we are familiar – and which for many provided the basis for an interest in social research in the first place – seems to disappear into a tangle of obfuscating jargon, pathos and uncertainty as to how to write anything at all about social life.

In order to avoid this we might think of ways in which attention to the textual and rhetorical nature of our writing might be used to improve the ways in which we communicate our ideas beyond the boundaries of academia. It is this question that I want to address in the final part of this chapter. Here I want to look at the work of W.E.B. Du Bois and the relationship between research writing, literary form and audience in his early work.

W.E.B. Du Bois, racial terror and social science

William Edward Burghardt Du Bois was an extraordinary intellectual figure. I want to look at his writing career in some detail because he is an example of someone who wrote in a variety of styles depending on the context and audience. Du Bois was a sociologist who both used and broke free from the rhetorical conventions of social science. He was also one of the first African American intellectuals to conduct extensive empirical research. In many respects Du Bois was tackling and resolving some of the issues discussed in this chapter almost 100 years ago. In his work, I would argue, we can find some clues as to how contemporary researchers might develop more creative writing strategies.

He was born on 23 February 1868 and died on 27 August 1963 on the eve of the first civil rights march on Washington. In large part Du Bois has been left out of the canon of American sociology despite the fact that his work and thought influenced figures like Robert Park, Horace Cayton, St Clair Drake and Gunnar Myrdal. He was also a personal friend of Max Weber whom he met while studying in Germany. During his long life he wrote an immense amount, close to 2,000 bibliographical entries which span a wide range of genres including research monographs, social histories, novels, poems, pamphlets and newspaper articles. It is the eclecticism of Du Bois that I want to address, particularly in relation to the way he switched genres in order to make public interventions.

Du Bois was first exposed to the emerging forms of social inquiry that came to be associated with sociology at Harvard and then the University of Berlin. In 1896 Du Bois became the first black person to receive a doctorate from Harvard. This was also the year that he began working on what became *The Philadelphia Negro,* the first serious social investigation of an urban black community. His vision of social science was both utopian and pragmatic: 'The Negro problem was in my mind a matter of systematic investigation and intelligent understanding. The world was thinking wrong about race, because it didn't know. The ultimate evil was stupidity. The cure for it was knowledge based on scientific investigation' (1940: 58).

The Philadelphia Negro was published in 1899. It was met with considerable acclaim and some disquiet from white reviewers. It is an astonishing compendium of quantitative and qualitative information on black life and race relations in Philadelphia. In many respects the book provides a blueprint for the kind of urban sociology that was later developed famously at the University of Chicago under the guidance of Park and Burgess (see Chapter 4). What is striking is the way the text is couched within a rhetoric of pragmatism and scientific method. Equally, there is a strong moral discourse that runs through this text with regard to certain indigent sections of the black community. The book in many ways exemplifies an almost contemptuous scientific fairness and Du Bois subscribed to this way of writing the 'race problem' in a very self-conscious way. At this point in his life reason and science provided the cornerstone of his attack on racism and white supremacy.

By the 1890s a range of black southern educational institutions had started to conduct research into the conditions of rural black communities. After finishing his work in Philadelphia, Du Bois was invited to head a research centre at the University of Atlanta. In his autobiography he reflects that at Atlanta

> I laid down an ambitious program for a hundred years of study ... I proposed gradually to broaden and intensify the study, sharpen the tools of investigation and perfect our method of work, so that we would have an increasing body of scientifically ascertained fact, instead of the vague mass of so-called Negro problems. And through this laboratory experiment I hoped to make the laws of social living clearer, surer and more definite. (1968: 217)

For 18 years Du Bois oversaw the Atlanta studies. It is worth emphasizing that this sophisticated work was conducted in a period when American sociology was in its infancy. Du Bois, at least initially, had a faith that white scholars shared his vision of an intellectual culture that could move beyond the racial divide. He saw the University of Atlanta as having a cultural mission with regard to the politics of academic freedom and social criticism. But in the violent years at the end of the century one incident had a lasting affect on Du Bois's faith in the role of science and reason in achieving social progress. It involved the plight of an illiterate black farm labourer called Sam Hose (Box 29.4).

This experience brought home the barbarism of white supremacy. He could not be a cool, calm and detached social scientist while people like Sam Hose were being lynched, brutalized and starved. The research he was conducting constituted, in his words, 'so small a part of the sum of occurrences'; it was too far from the 'hot reality of real life'. He began to re-evaluate the role of science:

> I regarded it as axiomatic that the world wanted to learn the truth and if the truth were sought with even approximate accuracy and painstaking devotion, the world would gladly support the effort. This was, of course, but a young man's idealism. (1968: 222)

While these experiences shifted Du Bois away from his commitment to science, this was not total. He would return to Atlanta in the 1930s to

---

Box 29.4   Du Bois and the case of Sam Hose

Sam Hose had killed his white landlord's wife. Du Bois set about the task of committing to paper appropriate evidence and the mitigating circumstances of Hose's crime. In *The Autobiography of W.E.B. Du Bois* he describes that:

> I wrote out a careful and reasoned statement concerning the evident facts and started down to the Atlanta Constitution Office, carrying in my pocket a letter of introduction to Joel Chandler Harris. I did not get there. On the way news met me: Sam Hose had been lynched, and they said his knuckles were on exhibition at a grocery store farther down Mitchell Street along which I was walking. I turned back to the University. I began to turn aside from my work. (1968: 222)

Box 29.5   Extract from *The Philadelphia Negro* (1996)

Separating the deaths by the sex of the deceased, we have:

Total death rate of Negroes, 1890 (still-births included)	32.42 per 1,000
For Negro males	36.02
For Negro females	29.23

Separating by age, we have

Total death rate, 1890 (still-births included)

All ages	32.42 per 1,000
Under fifteen	69.24
Fifteen to twenty	13.61
Twenty to twenty-five	14.50
Twenty-five to thirty-five	15.21
Thirty-five to forty-five	17.16
Forty-five to fifty-five	29.41
Fifty-five to sixty-five	40.09
Sixty-five and over	116.49

The large infant mortality is shown by the average annual rate of 171.44 (including still-births), for children under five years of age, during the years 1884 to 1890.

The statistics are very instructive. Compared with modern nations the death rate of Philadelphia Negroes is high, but not extraordinarily so: Hungary (33.7), Austria (30.6), and Italy (28.6) had in the years 1871–90 a larger average than the Negroes in 1891–96, and some of these lands surpass the rate of 1884–90. Many things combine to cause the high Negro death rate: poor heredity, neglect of infants, bad dwellings and poor food. On the other hand the age classification of city Negroes with its excess of females and young people of twenty to thirty-five years of age, must serve to keep the death rate lower than its rate would be under normal circumstances. The influence of bad sanitary surroundings is strikingly illustrated in the enormous death rate of the Fifth Ward – the worst Negro slum in the city, and the worst part of the city in respect to sanitation. On the other hand the low death rate in the Thirtieth Ward illustrates the influence of good houses and clean streets in a district where the better class of Negroes have recently migrated. (Du Bois, 1996: 150–1)

---

write perhaps the definitive history of the Black Reconstruction (Du Bois, 1934). But it was at this point that he became a man of letters, an essayist and a contributor to popular journals. He is thrust into the realm of politics and leadership struggles within the emerging movement for the advancement of black Americans. What is significant for my purpose here is that he did this through *writing*.

On 18 April 1903 the Chicago-based company A.C. McClung published a collection of Du Bois's essays entitled *The Souls of Black Folk* (1989). With the exception of one piece written especially for the book, these articles had appeared in a wide range of popular journals. Between 1903 and 1905 there were no less than six printings of the book. The demand for the work was extraordinary. One of the things that immediately strikes one when reading *The Souls* is its interdisciplinary nature and the variety of genres of writing in the book, which combine fiction, history, sociology and autobiography. The aesthetic of the book is totally engaging and Du Bois's use of language verges on the sublime. This forms a sharp contrast to *The Philadelphia Negro*, which is in the style of a sociological monograph (examples from both books are shown in Boxes 29.5 and 29.6). In the second of these extracts Du Bois is writing about

---

Box 29.6   Extract from *The Souls of Black Folk* (1989)

Blithe was the morning of his burial, with bird and song and sweet-smelling flowers. The trees whispered to the grass, but the children sat with hushed faces. And yet it seemed a ghostly unreal day – the wraith of Life. We seemed to rumble down an unknown street behind a little white bundle of posies, with the shadow of a song in our ears. The busy city dinned about us; they did not say much, those pale-faced hurrying men and women; they did not say much – they only glanced and said, 'Niggers!'

We could not lay him in the ground there in Georgia, for the earth there is strangely red; so we bore him away to the northward, with his flowers and his little folded hands. In vain, in vain! – for where, O God! beneath thy broad blue sky shall my dark baby rest in peace – where Reverence dwells, and Goodness, and a Freedom that is free?

All that day and all that night there sat an awful gladness in my heart – nay, blame me not if I see the world thus darkly through the Veil – and my soul whispers ever to me saying, 'Not dead, not dead, but escaped; not bound, but free.' No bitter meanness shall sicken his baby heart till it die a living death, no taunt shall madden his happy boyhood. Fool that I was to think or wish that this little soul should grow choked and deformed within the Veil! I might have known that yonder deep unworldly look that ever and anon floated past his eyes was peering far beyond this narrow Now. In the poise of his little curl-crowned head did there not sit all that wild pride of being which his father had hardly crushed in his own heart? For what, forsooth, shall a Negro want with pride amid the studied humiliations of fifty million fellows? Well sped, my boy, before the world had dubbed your ambition insolence, had held your ideals unattainable, and taught you to cringe and bow. Better far this nameless void that stops my life than a sea of sorrow for you …

If one must have gone, why not I? Why may I not rest me from this restlessness and sleep from this wide waking? Was not the world's alembic, Time, in his young hands, as is not my time waning? Are there so many workers in the vineyard that the fair promise of this little body could lightly be tossed away? The wretched of my race that line the alleys of the nation sit fatherless and unmothered; but Love sat beside his cradle, and in his ear Wisdom waited to speak. Perhaps now he knows the All-Love, and needs not to be wise. Sleep, then, child – sleep till I sleep and waken to a baby voice and the ceaseless patter of little feet – above the Veil. ['The Veil' refers to Du Bois's notion of the 'veil of colour'.] (Du Bois, 1989: 149–50)

---

the death of his son. It is the combination of fact and moving testimony which stimulated *The Times* reviewer in England to write that *The Souls* 'is an extraordinary compound of *emotions* and *statistics*' (emphasis added).

Gates (1989) has argued that no other text (except possibly the King James Bible) has had more impact on the shaping of the African American literary tradition. Du Bois as a master craftsperson of language manages to rise above the 'veil of colour' to communicate the violence and injustice of segregation and racism to white audiences. Gates suggests that rather than reflecting history, *The Souls* makes history:

How can a work be 'more history-making than historical?' It becomes so when it crosses the barrier between mainly conveying information, and primarily signifying an act of language itself, an object to be experienced, analysed and enjoyed aesthetically. (1989: xvi–xvii)

Clearly, then, Du Bois had made a choice to change the rhetorical nature of his writing, leaving the rhetoric of the sociological monograph and using a whole range of representational strategies to convey social criticism and make social commentary. The literary critique of research writing

---

Box 29.7 Web pointers for reading and writing research

Ethnographic hypermedia environment (follow links on 'writing ethnography')
www.cf.ac.uk/socsi/hyper/ht99/EHE.html

BUBL writing links
http://bubl.ac.uk/link/w/writinglinks.htm

W.E.B. Du Bois papers
www.library.umass.edu/spcoll/manuscripts/dubois_papers/dubois.html

Visit the website for this book at www.rscbook.co.uk to link to these web pointers.

---

points to the quite rigid writing conventions which determine the form of academic research writing. Du Bois shows us the potential for developing a range of rhetorical strategies.

It is beyond the scope of this chapter to suggest in a programmatic fashion what such a multiple writing strategy might look like. But rather than relying on the academic formats of publishing (for example, books, chapters and journal articles) one might think of a variety of ways to disseminate research findings. It still seems to be the case that social researchers view popular genres of writing like journalism to be simplistic, intellectually inferior and somehow beneath them. Yet having dabbled in journalism myself, I realize the skill involved in expressing sometimes complicated arguments in clear and accessible ways. It is my feeling that as researchers we need to be more promiscuous with regard to the genres of writing that we use to convey our message. Equally, autobiographical and fictional modes of writing might be used in productive ways to represent research findings. An attention to the literary critique of social science writing may help in providing rhetorical ways to supplement, rather than replace, the poetics of social research.

Conclusion

Roland Barthes (1977b: 148) once commented that the unity of texts lies not in authorship and writing but in the destination of written work, in other words the creative process of reading. I am not so convinced that as active researchers we should submit completely to this notion of the 'death of the author'. Barthes indicates that one can never control completely the ways in which texts are read. Yet there are possibilities for researchers to exercise a greater influence over how their messages are interpreted. One of the problems in the relationship between social research and wider society is the addiction of some social and cultural researchers to relativistic forms of discourse, and a resistance to making conclusive, absolute statements. This is often interpreted as showing a lack of clarity. The public allure of science and research can itself be used rhetorically in a self-conscious fashion. This point is made well by Jayaratne and Stewart (1991), who offer an instrumental strategy to use the social authority of research, fact and science to achieve feminist outcomes. The literary turn in the social sciences offers us fresh insights into the textual dimensions of social investigation. We must seek to turn these insights into useful tools, whereby we can think again about the way in which we express and disseminate our ideas and findings. Developing the rhetoric of writing will help researchers find new ways of intervening within public life and may enable us to reach wider audiences in a more effective way.

Further reading

Clifford and Marcus (1986) is a classic text which introduced the literary turn to anthropological writing. Atkinson (1990) shows how sociological ethnographies can be understood as deploying rhetorical strategies. Yearley (1981) applies this perspective to the production of texts in natural science.

Student Reader (Seale, 2004): relevant readings

28   John M. Swales: 'Episodes in the history of the research article'
34   Clifford Geertz: 'Being there'
57   James Clifford: 'Partial truths'
60   Laurel Richardson: 'The consequences of poetic representation'
75   William Foote Whyte, Laurel Richardson and Norman K. Denzin: 'Qualitative sociology and deconstructionism: an exchange'

Key concepts

Androcentrism
Facticity
Feminist empiricism

Feminist postmodernism
Literary turn
Objectification
Poetics
Rhetoric

30

Doing a dissertation

Chetan Bhatt

CONTENTS

Students in a variety of social and cultural disciplines are commonly required to write dissertations, often in the final year of an undergraduate degree. This is often seen as an opportunity to integrate and apply your previous learning while developing a personal project of your own. Employers can often look at CVs for evidence of having planned, undertaken and completed an independent project. Doing a dissertation will involve using some of the research methods described in other chapters of this book (or which you have learned about during your degree) and writing up your project as an extended document. Masters degrees also involve dissertations, though these are usually longer, more specialized and more demanding than at undergraduate level.

This chapter will guide you through the various stages of producing an undergraduate or Masters degree dissertation (also offering advice that may assist some PhD students or professional researchers). It necessarily overlaps with many of the other chapters in the book and references to these chapters are made at appropriate points. It is useful, though, to encapsulate in a single chapter the entire research process, from initial conception to final write-up, so that you can see more easily how the various elements of the research process can be combined into a single project

What is a dissertation?

A dissertation is not a long essay, but your own structured investigation or research into an interesting problem or topic. The topic might be chosen by you, or might be set by your tutor (you will need to find out the requirements that apply to you). Writing an extended piece of work on a subject of your own choosing is usually a pleasurable and interesting process; it is also challenging and requires careful thought and planning. In doing the dissertation, you are taking charge in setting your own topic (if allowed), creating your own space, undertaking the relevant reading, planning, organizing and doing your research, and writing up your research. On the other hand you should also listen and respond to the advice and guidance of your supervisor and other advisers. *Both* your ideas and independence *and* listening carefully to advice from your supervisor are important to the

successful completion of a strong dissertation.

A dissertation is normally expected to demonstrate:

- *Knowledge* and *understanding* relevant to a chosen or set dissertation topic or research problem
- Your skills in *planning, organizing, managing* and *undertaking* an independent project
- Your ability to *apply* knowledge and understanding in investigating the topic
- Your ability to *collect* or *produce*, *analyse* and *report on* information or data relevant to the topic
- Your ability to *conclude* your analysis in relation to the initial topic or research problem

You can view dissertations as being of four different kinds:

- *Empirical dissertations* – in which you discover, analyse and report on information you have collected yourself, usually by researching people or objects
- *Dissertations based on secondary analysis* – in which you analyse existing information or data sets that have been created by other (usually professional) researchers
- *Dissertations based on secondary sources* – in which you investigate a problem or topic by collecting other literature, analysing this, and proposing your own interpretation or argument
- *Theoretical dissertations* – library-based dissertations in which you propose your own independent, critical approach or argument in relation to a body of *theoretical* literature from your subject

However, the requirements for undertaking and submitting a dissertation vary across universities and courses. Universities have different regulations about matters such as dissertation length, referencing, style and whether you are required to undertake empirical research (such as interviewing people or doing a social survey). The length requirements can vary from 10,000 to 20,000 words. Because of these differing requirements, your first step in planning a dissertation that you have to submit for assessment must be to:

- gather information about the specific requirements of your institution or course, and
- be aware of the timescale during which you have to plan, produce and submit your dissertation.

Each discipline and course will have a particular view of the *academic contribution* a dissertation is expected to make. Your dissertation might also be assessed on the *transferable* or *employability skills* which are demonstrated within it. It may also be an essential part of the *learning outcomes* of your course or your overall degree that you are able to develop and apply specific research methods and data analysis skills relevant to your discipline. Therefore, familiarize yourself with the learning outcomes relevant to your dissertation and the purpose and the weighting of your dissertation within your degree. You will probably have been allocated a supervisor or tutor for your dissertation work. Meet them as soon as possible. Ensure that you discuss with them any aspects that are unclear in the dissertation guidelines specific to your course. It may also help to look at the dissertations of past students, if that is allowed by your institution. As for any assessed work, not following the expected requirements can affect your final mark, sometimes seriously. Be very clear about what is required from a dissertation in your course.

Dissertation areas

Think about the full scope of your discipline and the range of areas it covers. You can use the latitude of your discipline to develop your approach. You should usually be able to consider any substantive topic or area that you can relate to your discipline as long as you can focus it down into a manageable research problem that can be completed in the time you have available and within the constraints of word length.

If you are doing a combined (joint) degree, you may be required to develop a dissertation that relates to both your disciplines. Many interesting issues emerge at the boundaries of two disciplines. You may need to seek the advice of your supervisor about how best to develop a research topic that addresses and integrates material from two different disciplines.

You should aim to formulate one or more research problems or questions that can be investigated within the constraints of a dissertation and which will provide you with an opportunity to develop and apply discipline-relevant arguments and interpretations. Your supervisor can tell you if you are straying too far from your discipline. You should think carefully how your research topic can be understood from the viewpoint of your discipline and how it can be related to existing

---

Box 30.1 What is the difference between an empirical dissertation and a theoretical dissertation?

Dissertations that involve your collecting information from people (using interviews, questionnaires, focus groups) or analysing items you have collected (such as images, text, film, video) are usually called **empirical dissertations:**

- For example, a dissertation considering racialization in the representation of the body and undertaken through an analysis of magazine advertisements is an empirical dissertation because it involves empirical investigation on your part – in this case, of images in magazines that you have collected.

Library-based dissertations undertaken by critically analysing and engaging with theoretical literature in your discipline are usually called **theoretical dissertations**:

- For example, a dissertation based on theoretical approaches to the racialized body under colonialism would not be seen as comprising empirical research, but might be seen as dealing with a substantive theoretical area, such as the body in colonial discourse, post-colonial theory or social theory. In this type of dissertation, you would be critically engaging with, and providing your own interpretations in relation to, the theoretical literature relevant to the topic.

Box 30.2 Some original approaches to well-worn problems

- If you were to ask young people about their attitudes to water, might it give you more interesting and original results than asking them about their attitudes to alcohol?
- You could analyse the representation of men or women in popular magazine adverts for cosmetics; but would it make for a more interesting project to analyse the contents and state of a bathroom?
- Instead of investigating whether the identities of an ethnic minority group are different from those of majority ethnic groups, would it make for a more interesting project if the research were to investigate whether, and how, the everyday, lived cultures of both are virtually the same?
- You could interview male and female students about their attitudes to sex and sexual relationships; would it make for a more interesting project if you investigated the same issue by analysing graffiti in male and female public conveniences?
- You could ask people about their food choices, shopping and cooking preferences, or you could record the contents of their kitchen.
- You could investigate hybridity in English culture by analysing Asian dance music or the popularity of Bollywood; what other issues might arise if you were to interview people in a local pub and explore the meaning for them of the 'Thai' food they are eating?
- You could investigate men's views of women by using interviews with men; but what about investigating men's views of men, or women's views of women using the same research technique?
- You could investigate associations between education and social class or education and ethnicity using a household survey data set; how about strengthening your dissertation by comparing your findings with published findings from UK labour force surveys, or analyses of ethnicity from the 1991 and 2001 UK censuses?
- You could investigate the experiences of racism faced by African Caribbean and South Asian people in the UK. But what about a more challenging project investigating the experiences of discrimination faced by Romani or Sinti refugee populations from Eastern Europe living in the UK? Or experiences of civil/ethnic conflict *abroad* faced by UK asylum seekers from Central African nations?

knowledge. Chapters 5 and 6 give guidance in the formulation of research questions that relate to broader concerns.

Many dissertations do not *have to* involve *empirical* research (involving you in collecting original data), but nevertheless require engagement with a substantive topic or area (see Box 30.1). Check your local requirements or with your supervisor about this.

You should think carefully about your own creativity and independent critical approach in investigating a social or cultural issue. Examiners often mark dissertations based on, for example, interviews with young people about their attitudes to alcohol, Ecstasy use, sex, music, about their ethnic or cultural identities or their consumer

behaviour. No one will discourage you from doing a dissertation in these areas, but consider more creative approaches that pose a problem in a different and interesting way, or which investigate unexpected, challenging and uncommon questions (see Box 30.2). It can often be useful to think about projects that are concerned with the meanings of objects, identities or spaces that are unfamiliar to you or distant from how you might perceive your immediate identity.

The research process

Irrespective of what your dissertation is about, you will be following many of the stages, and going through several of the phases of a **research**

process (Figure 30.1). It is particularly suited to a dissertation involving empirical work, but many elements also apply to library-based dissertations. Many of these formal stages overlap considerably, and researchers often jump back to earlier stages. Hence, you should use the diagram as a general guide. You may not be expected to develop a formal hypothesis and test it. Nor might you be expected to create new concepts or theoretical terms (but see the next section on how to *combine concepts*). In an empirical dissertation, though, you will usually be expected to:

- Think about an area or interest
- Focus this down to a manageable research problem
- Undertake a literature review in the relevant area, typically using this to refine your research questions
- Consider the strengths and weaknesses of, and apply appropriate research methods to a defined group (or sample) of people or objects
- Analyse your results
- Report the analysis
- Come to a conclusion about your original research problem, possibly also highlighting unresolved areas and debates, or other relevant theoretical or policy implications

Defining your research problem

Students often start thinking about their dissertation by focusing on which research methods to use, together with a general idea of the research area. This is the *least* productive approach. The strength and quality of a dissertation is primarily determined by a fully thought out, tightly focused **research problem** which directly relates to an interest of yours, which you can sustain interest in throughout the process of doing the dissertation, and which you can relate to existing debates, theories, or research in literature from your discipline. You should consider this stage to be the most important stage of the dissertation. Instead of starting off by, for example, thinking: 'I am going to do some interviews to find out why people chat on the Internet', push these ideas aside for the moment, and instead *define and describe clearly a focused research problem*. Here is how you can proceed:

- Consider a strong interest or curiosity you have and which you think you might want to base your dissertation around. The initial curiosity may come from your reading, a lecture, a conversation with friends, the TV, a film, or just your own wandering thoughts. At this stage you can think on a grand scale, and you can think about grand statements. For example, consider the statement: 'We are living in a globalized society'.
- Convert your statement into a question: 'Are we really living in a globalized society?' or 'In what ways are we living in a globalized society?' It is often useful to turn your statement into a 'how' or 'why' question.
- This next step is very important: process and focus your general question into a research problem or question which is in principle *researchable* and which you can undertake to investigate within the time, financial and material constraints imposed on you as a student. Examiners will be looking for how your interests in a general area have been focused down into a manageable research project.
- There are various techniques that you can use to focus down your general interests, but one of the most useful is to spend a couple of undisturbed hours to 'brainstorm' your ideas and make use of visual representations, such as 'spider diagrams', flowcharts and lists. You may have to keep repeating this process until you get a sensible researchable question or topic. Box 30.3 shows how this can occur, using the globalization example.
- You may end up with a research(able) problem that is some way from your original thinking or grand idea. You may decide to repeat the process until you are satisfied that you have a researchable problem which interests you enough to sustain this interest over a lengthy period. But the key point is that you will need to transform an original, perhaps grand scale curiosity, interest or theoretical approach into a manageable, practical research project that you can complete over the allotted timescale. Notice also, in the example in Box 30.1, that the methodology or research techniques have not, strictly speaking, been decided. This is as it should be.

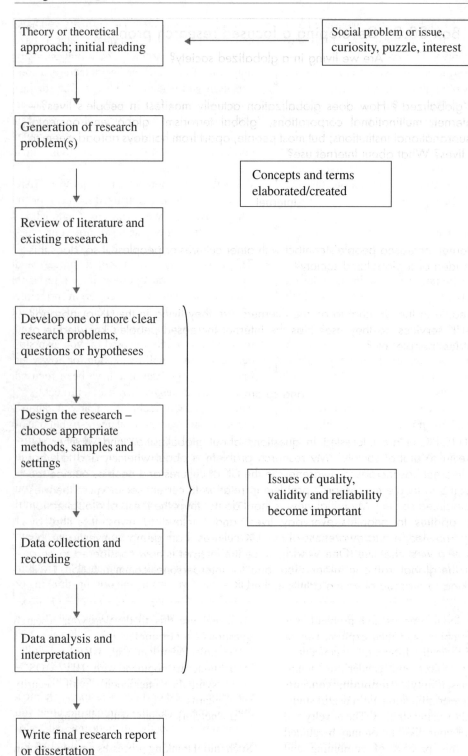

Figure 30.1   *The research process (adapted from Giddens, 1993: 678)*

Box 30.3 Developing a focused research problem

Are we living in a globalized society?

Is the UK 'globalized'? How does globalization actually manifest in people's lives? – brands, Internet, multinational corporations, 'global terrorism', global environmental pollution, supranational institutions; but most people, apart from holidays abroad, seem to live 'local' lives? What about Internet use?

Internet

Has the Internet increased people's contact with other cultures or peoples? If so, does this support the idea of a globalized society?

Who do people in the UK chat to on the Internet? Are they living in the UK or abroad? What non-UK services do they use? Has the Internet increased people's knowledge of other countries, people, etc?

↓

… and so on …

↓

MY DRAFT TOPIC: I am interested in questions about globalization and whether we actually live in a 'global society'. My research problem is about whether, and to what extent, the Internet has increased awareness in the UK of cultures and peoples outside the UK. I am going to locate my research problem in relation to current sociological theories about a globalized society. My initial view is that I do not think the thesis of globalization necessarily applies to people's everyday lives, and I intend to investigate this by considering knowledge and awareness of non-UK cultures. I am going to investigate this empirically at a web chat site (One World), since the Internet is now considered to be a key site for the global traffic in information, and for interpersonal communication. I will also be talking to a group of young adults in the UK.

• In thinking about your research problem, it is useful to combine, and then explore, two or more, often radically different, key concepts – for example, 'power' and 'gender', or 'branding' and 'masculinity'. **Combining concepts** ('interrogative combination') is a useful study, learning and focusing strategy. The novelty and originality of your dissertation may be guided by exactly this process of combining and exploring the relations between two (or more) different conceptual areas. It can also be useful to combine one *theoretical* with one *empirical*

area, and use this to develop your research questions – for example:

- 'postmodernism' with 'Islam'
- 'underdevelopment' with 'HIV/AIDS'
- 'symbolic interaction' with security guards
- 'network society' with 'clothing'.

Such initial thinking processes are important in starting to help you focus your ideas into a practical, manageable project. It is as important to be convinced that this is the research problem you want to investigate. Try not to change your mind about your dissertation area half way through the period you have in which to complete it. You may not have the time to start a new dissertation project afresh. Instead, seek the advice of your supervisor about how you can motivate yourself to make your existing project more suitable and relevant to your interests.

Research design

A research problem can be investigated using a wide range of research methods and techniques. There is no one 'correct' method. For example, use of the Internet can be investigated using depth interviews, semi-structured questionnaires, large-scale social surveys, focus groups, ethnographic methods and observation research. You therefore should be able to make the case that the research methods (techniques) you have chosen are the most appropriate for your research questions, given time limitations and material constraints. Ideally, your research problem would have been formulated so that the research method chosen is clearly (one of the most) appropriate.

In thinking about your research design, it can be useful to distinguish between the **methodology** guiding your dissertation and the research **methods** (techniques) you are using:

- For example, a dissertation using broadly feminist approaches and partially based on statistical analysis of a dataset on marriage and divorce might have a feminist *methodology* and be using quantitative research *methods*.

If you are doing a library-based, theoretical dissertation investigating a substantive area, there is likely to be some overlap between *theory* and *methodology* and you may need the advice of your supervisor:

- For example, a dissertation investigating the changing ways in which the female body has been represented in nineteenth and twentieth century art and literature might be undertaken using, say, Foucauldian social theory (see Chapter 4). In this case, you might want to

also discuss Foucauldian *methodological* approaches (see also Kendall and Wickham (1999) for a guide to applying Foucault's approach).

Whichever research method(s) you select, you should think about the following points.

Strengths and weaknesses You should be able to discuss and justify the research methods you have chosen based on their strengths and weaknesses *in relation to the research problem you are investigating*. You should also, even if briefly, be able to discuss why other methods were rejected, or were not considered appropriate.

Sampling Your sample refers to the *people* you have selected for interviewing or the *objects* (for example, magazine advertisements) you have selected for analysis. How was your sample decided? What are the explicit criteria you have used to decide who or what is, and who or what is not, to be included in your sample? What other characteristics or attributes (age, gender, ethnicity, social class, employment, region, for example) do the members of your sample possess? Chapters 13, 15, 17 and 18 all contain discussions of sampling.

If you are doing small-scale qualitative research you will not be able to claim that your sample represents a larger population. This should be acknowledged when you write up your research, but you should also consider alternative rationales for sampling (for example, *theoretical sampling*, discussed in Chapter 18) that may contribute significantly to the quality of your work.

Note, too, that use of large *representative* samples is quite feasible if you are doing *secondary analysis* of existing quantitative data sets (see Chapter 26). In such a case, you would usually be expected to include discussion about the nature of the sample – for example, the sample size, whether it is a random sample, if it is stratified in some way and the number of relevant missing cases or responses. These matters become especially important in quantitative analysis if you are generalizing your results to (inferring something about) the population from which the sample came.

Box 30.4 Justifying qualitative sampling: an example

Your research may be based on an analysis of six selected issues of a magazine. You should ask:

- To what extent is this kind of magazine representative of 'the media' generally?
- To what extent can the magazine I have selected be considered representative of that subgenre of magazines?
- To what extent can the six issues be considered representative of the magazine?
- What (*purposive*) principles lay behind my selection of *these* six issues? Were these principles related to the research questions of the study, or informed by a search for variety?

Validity, quality and reliability Is your research 'instrument' – the questionnaire, the interview schedule, the focus group topic guide – and your overall research design, including your sample, capable of finding out what you want to discover (for example, supporting your argument that one thing has *caused* another)? Would other people using the same research design get broadly the same research results? Would your research design generate broadly the same results among a different group of research subjects sharing broadly the same characteristics? To what extent, if any, is it possible to generalize from your selected group (sample) to a wider 'population'? If you are doing a secondary analysis of a quantitative data set, you will usually need to address issues of *statistical significance* in your analysis: to what extent can you infer anything about the characteristics of the population from the sample which has been derived from it? These topics are discussed in Chapter 7 where their relevance for both quantitative and qualitative research designs is explored. Note that answering 'yes' to all these questions may not (particularly in the eyes of some 'qualitative' researchers) guarantee quality.

Reflexivity What might be the consequences (actual or potential, intended or otherwise) of the research process on the research results? What might be the consequences of you, your identity and how you undertook the project, on the research process and research results? What are the various reflexive processes at play between you, the research process and your research subjects (see Chapter 3)?

Mixing methods You should also consider more than one method (and in practice, you may well be implicitly using more than one method). For example, you may decide to use semiological methods to analyse some images (Chapter 20) but there is nothing to prevent you also considering a selected focus group's views of those same images (Chapter 15). You might interview individuals (see Chapters 13 and 14) and also analyse policy reports or documents (Chapters 19 and 27) obtained from their organization. Chapter 22 discusses the combination of qualitative and quantitative approaches. Using more than one method can strengthen your dissertation by allowing you to compare the results derived using one technique with those derived using another.

Comparative research You should think about the usefulness of comparative analysis in your research design. For example, you might interview a group of people about dance culture and Ecstasy use, and interview two representatives of a voluntary sector drugs agency. In this case, you are interviewing individuals from two different *groups* ('users' and 'key informants') and two different institutional *sites* ('club culture' and 'the voluntary sector'). It is very common for research questions to focus on documenting the experience of a particular group of people (for example, women). The special nature of a group's experience, though, may be difficult to justify without a comparison with some other group (for example, men). Comparative research therefore requires careful thought about sampling. You can also strengthen your dissertation if you compare your findings with those from relevant published research, or survey and census analysis.

Research methods

You should find out whether your course learning outcomes mean that you are *required* to demonstrate your own skills of data collection in your dissertation. If your research problem requires empirical materials, you need to decide how you are going to gather and analyse these. You should also consider seriously whether you can use existing quantitative or qualitative data sets for your own *secondary analysis* (see Chapter 26). You are unlikely to have the resources to generate for yourself the quantity and standard of materials that teams of professional researchers may have deposited in data archives, particularly where large-scale government social surveys are concerned. If, however, you decide to undertake some small-scale empirical research you need to decide on your method for generating as well as analysing data. A brief review of a range of methods is given here, most of which are described more fully in other chapters of this book.

Depth interviews These are popular with many students and can allow you to explore people's views, perceptions and understandings of an area, often providing you with rich and sensitive material (see Chapter 14). You should develop an *interview schedule* (of usually about six to ten themes or questions) that you want to explore, together with a clear statement of the purpose of your research, a statement on ethical practice, and (if relevant) a guarantee of privacy, confidentiality or anonymity regarding the interview and your tapes or disc files. Pilot your interview schedule with a couple of volunteers, making any changes to the questions as necessary. Plan your interviews to last an hour or so. You can either take notes (which can be distracting for you and your interviewee) or tape and then transcribe the interview. Remember that transcription is very time-consuming, so be realistic about the number of interviews you can do. You should get permission to tape any interviews and follow the advice in Chapter 16 about how to make a good (hearable) recording. Interviews should ideally be conducted

in a comfortable environment. Be prepared to elicit and probe in case of long or uncomfortable silences and monosyllabic answers. If you are researching sensitive areas (for example, violence, sexuality, eating disorders, suicide, drug use, personal relationships), you may need advice from your supervisor. Analysis can take the form of coding and qualitative thematic analysis (see Chapter 23) or content, discourse or conversation analysis (Chapters 27 and 28).

Focus groups These are useful in quickly gathering rich and detailed material around a particular theme or issue, exploring new or 'experimental' areas, or brainstorming ideas. Focus groups can also be used for practical, task-oriented work, such as viewing and discussing a poster or video. Typically, a focus group will have six to eight (but no more) participants. In the focus group, you are aiming to cultivate a strong group dynamic, while having a minimal and facilitating role in guiding the discussion towards your interests and making sure it stays on-topic. A focus group session should not consist of you interviewing a group of people, but the group discussing among itself your themes and questions. Chapter 15 contains detailed advice on how to run focus groups and many of the points made above about the conduct of depth interviews also apply to focus groups.

Ethnographic methods and observational research Ethnography, as is shown in Chapter 17, involves a multitude of methods, including observational research, documentary research, archival research, researching material culture, interviews and textual methods. It can be time- and labour-intensive, though brief episodes of observation can yield surprisingly rich data, particularly if these are electronically recorded and subjected to detailed scrutiny (as in *conversation analysis* – see Chapter 28). Participant observation is a valuable research method that can require considerable skill on the part of the researcher. It can be useful if you want to:

- 'Step back' from the obvious and 'ordinary' and look at the social world and social interactions 'afresh'

- Explore 'extraordinary' or 'unusual' beliefs, behaviours and practices
- Learn about other groups or subcultures
- Learn about how other people view *you*

Observation research requires that you fully and systematically record and analyse your observations, either by keeping a diary or journal or by electronic recording (see Chapter 16). There are important issues regarding both ethics and access when undertaking covert and semi-covert ethnographic research, and your supervisor will be able to advise you further on this.

Semiotics and content analysis Semiotic analysis (Chapter 20) involves a range of powerful methods, based primarily (but not exclusively) on the structural linguistics of Ferdinand de Saussure, the semiology of Roland Barthes and more recently the work of Stuart Hall. This approach is used for the analysis of signs, images, symbols, texts and representations. It is popular with students and is often combined with other methods (such as interviews, focus groups or documentary research). Realistically, using this method you will only be able to fully analyse a few (perhaps 3 or 4) relevant or important images from the ones you initially collect, although if a content analysis is planned (see Chapters 20 and 27) many more images will be involved. It is often helpful to include copies of still images that have been analysed as appendices to a dissertation.

Textual and discourse analysis Discourse analysis refers to a range of techniques, some highly formal, rigorous and systematic, others less so, that are used in the analysis of text, writing and talk (see Chapter 27). Raw materials might consist of small extracts of text, such as selected sections of newspaper reports or an extract from a political speech. Analysis typically focuses on the identification of 'discourses' – widespread systems of knowledge, beliefs or ideas – that speakers or writers draw upon in presenting their versions, particularly in so far as these make their text persuasive, or appeal to certain audiences while excluding others. Content analysis, both qualitative and quantitative, can be a useful adjunct here

when looking for certain themes, phrases and recurring ideas.

Documents Documents are a very useful, somewhat neglected source of data and can be used in conjunction with several of the methods described in this section. You can collect documents that contain material appropriate to your research project, and then analyse them in a variety of ways. Documents can be of many different kinds: annual reports; pamphlets and leaflets; publicity materials; official statistics; policy documents and policy implementation strategies; personal diaries; personal letters; and a wide variety of other published and unpublished documents. You may have to visit a specialist archive (see Chapter 19) or you may simply have to buy a newspaper in order to generate relevant documentary data. There are various techniques for the analysis of documents (including textual and semiological methods). In using them you should consider general questions of authenticity, credibility, authorship, intended audience, representativeness, interpretative context, genre, reliability and coherence (Scott, 1990).

Material culture and artefacts An imaginative analysis of the way that objects are situated in, and move through, space and time can provide an altogether different and enriching perspective on social life. There is a range of methods available for the analysis of material culture, mute objects and artefacts. If used creatively, these can help to provide rich and 'thick' descriptions of social settings (see Kingery, 1998; Miller, 1998). For example:

- Consider looking 'afresh' and objectively at a seminar room in which all the students have gone out for a short break but left their belongings. Think about the placement of the objects (bags, pens, pads, coats, desks, chairs), their styles and design, the colours of the objects, the arrangement of objects on a desk and the 'social symbols' they represent (such as 'barriers', 'enclosures', 'boundaries', 'gates', 'ownership').
- Look at the arrangement of mute objects in a nightclub just after closing time, but before it has been cleaned.

419

- Consider the assisted movement of people through the architecture and design of buildings or public and private spaces.

Archival research Is altogether different from research in libraries (though most archives are deposited in libraries); as Chapter 19 indicates, there is an enormous variety of archives. Archival research needs to be systematic and will be time-consuming. If you are considering archival research, you will most probably (though not necessarily) be conducting historically based research. You can employ a variety of methods in archival research, but there are also important overall considerations regarding archives: access, the history of the objects in an archive, the process whereby the objects and documents have been catalogued by the archivist ('tertiary sedimentation') and hence have forever lost their original associations with each other, incompleteness, issues of contextual interpretation and (usually historically informed) questions of intention and meaning (Hill, 1993).

The social survey Some students choose to undertake a small-scale social survey based on a highly structured questionnaire, and analysed using software such as SPSS (see Chapters 13, 23, 24, 25). If you decide to do this (rather than statistical analysis of an existing data set) be realistic about the sample size you can manage. If you are thinking about generalizing your results to a wider population, you will also need to think about and justify an appropriate random sample size in your research design. Structured interviews will take more of your time than a self-completion questionnaire and hence involve a reduction in the sample size. Survey research requires considerable care in matters of question construction and questionnaire design (Chapter 13). You must also ensure that your questionnaire is directly related to the research problem you are investigating. You would usually be expected to discuss questions of *association* and *statistical significance* in your analysis. You will need to include your questionnaire in an appendix to the dissertation and describe how you undertook your data analysis.

Ethical and practical issues

As a researcher, you have a range of ethical obligations towards the participants in your research project (see also Chapter 10). In some circumstances, you might be required to submit the proposal for your dissertation to an ethics committee, either within your university or outside it, before you can proceed with your data collection plans. It is wise to consult your supervisor and any ethical guidelines produced by the professional authorities in your subject discipline. This is particularly important when:

- Conducting research in sensitive areas
- Interviewing vulnerable people
- In any situation involving direct contact with the service users of hospitals, voluntary sector agencies, charities, schools, or local authority social and care services
- Research involving children or young adults
- Any kind of research that is intended to be covert or semi-covert
- Research involving potentially controversial or politicized themes
- Research involving private information and records (such as personal diaries and documents)

Be clear about your role in emotionally charged or sensitive interview situations – you are not a counsellor, but a social researcher. Any attempt to provide counselling to an emotional or upset person might do more harm than good. It may be best to simply listen, using your human sensitivity, rather than intervene 'directively' or provide advice. Actions that might (though not always) make things worse are:

- Thanking a distressed person and quickly leaving
- Trying to make a distressed person feel better by using platitudes, changing the subject, or minimizing the nature of their difficulties – or conversely, by seeming to agree with them that their difficulties are overwhelming or insurmountable
- 'Over-identifying' with them by telling them

about a similar situation that occurred to you or attempting to 'create empathy' by describing similar or worse situations you know about
• Using your interview subjects to provide counselling or advice to you

If relevant, it is good practice to prepare beforehand and give to interviewees a leaflet providing information on sources of local support or advice related to their difficulties.

When seeking interviews with service users of any voluntary or public sector service, you should write to the director, manager or co-ordinator of the service and get their written permission to approach service users for interview. In some cases, the organization will even arrange the interviews for you. You must always seek the *informed consent* of each individual person you are interviewing, even if the organization has already given you permission. Do not use improper authority (your university's name, the organization's permission to approach people) to attempt to persuade people to give you interviews. Explain clearly that you are a student doing a dissertation, and explain fully the nature and purpose of your research. Similar criteria apply in interviewing employees of commercial organizations.

In conducting a focus group, some participants may disclose personal or sensitive information at that time which they had not originally intended. It is therefore always good practice to have a confidentiality statement and agree an appropriate *ground rule* at the start of each focus group (such as 'information disclosed by everyone stays in the room and should not be discussed outside the group'). Consider also providing research participants and interviewees with a clear statement that their interviews will remain confidential, that you will show them transcripts for their approval or veto, that you will destroy taped interviews after the research is over, or that they can be anonymized in your transcriptions and dissertation.

You should also consider your *own* safety and security. It may not be appropriate to meet interviewees you do not know well or have never met in their private homes. It may be appropriate to be careful before accepting lifts from interviewees. Think of arranging interviews in public places and

consider whether you should give people your home address details and telephone number.

Other practical issues

Interviewing friends and family members Students often ask if they can interview friends or family members. This can have both positive and negative aspects. Your friends may respond by telling you what they think you want to hear about an issue. Conversely, you already have a relationship of empathy with your friends, and so you may be able to explore social issues in greater depth and find it easier to get them to participate in your research. However, you may also take less care and give greater flexibility to them in terms of your research questions than you might in a more formal interview situation. Some students find they get less useful practical data from friends and family, because those you know well may respond less fully to your questions since they assume you already know what they will say. It is important that you fully assess the consequences of your decision to interview friends and family and explain in your dissertation the methodological and reflexive issues involved. Unless your research question is directly related to researching family or friends, consider taking the decision *not* to interview them.

Electronic interviews Some students use email interviews, group posts and electronic chatroom discussions to collect data for their dissertations. This can have a range of positive and negative methodological consequences that vary considerably depending on the type of electronic forum being used to gather your information (see Chapter 21). For example, people may be very forthright about their opinions in, for example, Internet chatrooms and group posts – you may therefore believe you are getting information about their real views. But the same people may be more measured (or express very different opinions) in a face-to-face interview. They might also not respond 'honestly' in an electronic forum, or they might deliberately respond to you in a provocative way. With research subjects found on the Internet, there is an important issue about *verification*. In the web-based chatroom you found on lesbian identity, how do you actually know that you are interviewing a married, bi-curious woman in her mid-40s from Medway, rather than a group of schoolboys from Enfield? Is the very informative reply, from a Hotmail address, to your request for information to alt.culture.indian actually from a Savitri Gupta living in a Delhi suburb?

Planning interviews One of the key reasons why some students do not get to interview the number of people they would like to is poor planning. You cannot expect to telephone a busy voluntary sector organization and ask them for an interview in the next day or so. You also cannot expect that your interview subjects will have free time just when you do. Prepare and plan a timetable and give plenty of notice. Follow up with a letter explaining the purpose of your research, confirming the interview date and thanking the intended interviewee. If they cancel, ask them for another date or plan a telephone interview instead.

- Make sure you have background knowledge about the work and activities of the organization and people you want to interview. If you do not know why the organization was set up or what they do, they in turn may not take your project seriously.
- Start planning your interviews in the early stages of your dissertation.
- Be realistic about who you will be able to get to interview. The chief executive may be flying to a power lunch in Zurich, but her less senior staff might be more amenable.
- Give plenty of notice to the interviewees.
- Provide alternative dates and times.
- Confirm interviews (in writing if necessary).
- Give the arrangement three chances to succeed, or place other realistic time limits on responses.
- Consider alternative or back-up organizations or interviewees.
- Try not to cancel the interview yourself, unless this is really unavoidable – you are unlikely to get the person's cooperation again.
- If you still have difficulty, seek the advice of your tutor and consider changing your research design.

Despite good planning, some students find it difficult in getting interviews or getting interview or focus group subjects to turn up at pre-arranged times (obviously, important for all members of a focus group). They consequently feel they and their research are not being taken seriously. In the public and private sector, people often have busy schedules and other contingencies may arise. Asking them to select appropriate service users and arrange the interview times for you may be the least of their priorities. If you cannot get to see any service users, consider:

- Interviewing a representative of the organization instead (a 'key informant' or 'stakeholder')
- Approaching a different organization
- Asking the organization for their annual reports, other publications, and advice and publicity material (this should be standard practice in any case)
- Undertaking a documentary analysis instead
- Interviewing fellow students or university staff about your topic

Payment to research participants You should not enter into any financial relation or obligation to pay expenses to interviewees (unless your university makes provision, and has guidelines, for this). Make it clear that you are asking them to *volunteer* their time and expertise. Obviously, you may want to make interviewees comfortable, or thank them, by making sure they have tea and coffee. But do not make any other commitments regarding expenses and finance.

Safeguarding your work You must make sure that you save your work regularly, print out your dissertation in good time for the deadline, and anticipate any potential computer problems. The latter may not be accepted as valid reasons for the late submission of your dissertation, and you therefore risk being penalized if your computer decides it wants to give up on you. Ideally, you should keep a copy of your dissertation and all related material – including all your raw materials or data – in two separate places, together with a third backup copy on floppy disk. You can send an ordinary or (if it is very large) a *zipped* attachment of your work and related material from your university email address to your home email address (or vice versa), or to a friend. In this case, you will still have another copy elsewhere if your computer develops problems.

Using libraries and finding appropriate reading
In undertaking a dissertation, you are expected to carry out *independent* research in libraries. In addition to looking for books on your research topic in your university library, you should also search the indexes in relevant journals, carry out index and keyword searches on CD-ROMS, and search the Internet and relevant newspapers, magazines, films and videos (if applicable). Chapter 12 gives helpful guidance on this. You can also approach lecturers other than your supervisor and ask them for their advice or their course handouts. You should also be prepared to explore more libraries than just the one associated with your university if your search leads you to these. Your own university library will tell you about what access rights you have to other libraries, or may be able to negotiate access for you. Make sure that you record the full bibliographic details of the material you come across when you first see it. This will save you time later, when you construct your bibliography.

You may occasionally find that there is very little directly relevant literature in your area. If you face this situation, you should first ask whether this is owing to the way you are thinking about the area, rather than deficiencies in the literature itself. First, you need to be realistic about the literature: there is no point looking for, and getting despondent when you cannot find *the* book on Judith Butler and ice-skating. At the same time, your judgement about relevance may be too narrow. You may not find an article about the impact of network society on personal domestic habits, but you will find literature on changing forms of private and public behaviour and codes in history (for example, by Norbert Elias) or behaviour in 'front stage' and 'back stage' regions (for example, by Erving Goffman) that will contain many relevant insights.

Consider, too, the specialist libraries of relevant voluntary organizations and national charities: these often hold policy reports and other locally published information (*grey literature*)

that may contain a wealth of information relating to your research area. Consider also searches in journals and magazines. If you still find there is very little relevant literature, you must state this in your dissertation, and describe what searches you did actually undertake. It is good practice to explain briefly in your dissertation how you went about finding relevant and appropriate reading.

The structure of the dissertation

You should see the dissertation as your project and, unless your university specifies a particular chapter or section structure, its structure can normally be decided by you, with guidance from your supervisor.

Empirical dissertations

The vast majority of students undertake empirical dissertations and their advantage is that they enable you to explore a particular topic and a body of literature of your choosing, and gain hands-on research and data analysis experience (useful for future careers and employment). *Empirical* dissertations should normally contain the equivalent of:

- An introduction that states clearly your research problem or topic
- A review of the relevant literature (reading) in your dissertation area
- A discussion of methods applied
- Analysis of data and reporting and discussion of results
- Conclusion
- References
- Appendices

Introduction Start with an introduction that establishes clearly and succinctly your research problem or questions, their relation to relevant debates and literature in your disciplines, how you intend to investigate your research problems, and very briefly, the methods used and how you analysed your data. You may also want to include a very brief description of what is covered in each chapter. This provides a signpost for the examiners about the structure of your dissertation.

Literature review Think of your literature review as having some of the following tasks:

- Locating and situating clearly your research problem in the context of the relevant literature and existing debates
- Refining your research problems or questions
- Demonstrating that you have read and understood the literature that is directly relevant to your research problem
- Highlighting areas where there is insufficient literature or debate regarding the problem you want to investigate
- Differentiating your own approach from that of the existing literature
- Providing a theoretical 'grounding' for your dissertation

If you are confused about what you should cover in a literature review, brainstorm your research problem and look at its key concepts (see Box 30.6).

Methodology and methods In your methodology chapter or section, you are expected to discuss and justify your overall research design, the methodological issues related to the research techniques you have used, their strengths and weaknesses, the way you specified and gained access to your sample, how you then generated data (including problems encountered) and how you analysed your data. You should also discuss any issues relating to validity, reliability, quality and reflexivity here.

It is often helpful to include a succinct *narrative description of the research process* itself. This can include information about any false starts or changes in plan or design. For example, if you organized a focus group and no one turned up, make sure you describe this and any subsequent changes in your research design, rather than ignore it as a 'failure' on your part. Similarly, if you were very nervous in conducting your first couple of interviews, describe this, as well as any potential reflexive consequences on the person being interviewed. Such occurrences are part and parcel of real world social research and the examiners are likely to be interested in your critical thinking about such problems. Examiners will also usually be interested in knowing how you might have done your research differently if you were starting again from scratch, or had more time or resources.

Data analysis and reporting your results These chapters or sections should report your main findings. Some of the main areas to consider if your analysis is of qualitative data are:

- The characteristics of your sample. It is good practice to report basic demographic information (age, gender, ethnicity, region, employment or social class) if your sample is one that involves people, and the equivalent if it involves other kinds of sampling (for example, whether a newspaper article is from an American or UK paper; whether it is front page news or from a lifestyle supplement).
- If you used a coding scheme, show this to the reader and describe how it relates to the research questions. Do not report your results according to the order of questions asked in an interview. Organize your reporting thematically and try to organize themes into *major* themes that could be subheadings in your data analysis chapters (see Chapter 18 on developing *grounded theory*).
- Consider which quotations from your interview data work best to illustrate themes, points and arguments. Consider opposite opinions and *negative instances*; consider extreme viewpoints. Show short extracts that disrupt understandings as well as ones that illustrate your claims effectively.
- Do not reproduce long extracts of qualitative material. Be selective and economical, choosing carefully what you think are important extracts. If you have used a coding scheme, you can probably support your presentation of qualitative extracts with counts of the frequency with which particular themes occurred.
- Conclude your data analysis chapters with brief summaries. A certain amount of commentary or interpretation of the significance of your findings can be discussed in the 'results' section of your dissertation (and some disciplines strongly encourage this) but you might want to save your best and 'biggest' points for the concluding chapter.

Box 30.6 What is relevant literature?

Example 1

A dissertation focusing on the representation of women in young men's magazines would be concerned with issues of:

- Representation
- Gender
- Feminism
- Masculinity
- Youth culture

These *keywords* should then guide the searches you make for literature to read and discuss. In this example, you would not expected to provide an assessment of, say, feminist theory, but you would not be expected to provide a discussion of feminist theory *in so far as* it relates to the specific area you are researching: masculinity, representation and so forth.

Example 2

A dissertation based on quantitative analysis of the association between population health and gross national product would be concerned with issues of:

- Development and underdevelopment
- Health and illness
- Political economy

These might be the *keywords* which can be combined to guide your initial literature search. Depending on what else you are investigating, you might also be concerned with some of the following concepts which can be used to refine your search:

- Infant mortality
- Gender
- Urbanization
- Health policy
- Access to clean water

In this example, you would not be expected to provide an assessment of theories of development and underdevelopment, global political economy, the sociology of health and illness, or gender and development, but you would be expected to discuss these areas *in so far as* they relate to and help you refine the hypotheses you are testing.

Conclusion By the time you come to the conclusion, you might be tired of writing – or are rushing to meet a deadline – and so the conclusion can read like a quick summary, or an after-thought tagged on to the end. This is a serious mistake, as it is may be the concluding chapter that an examiner looks to first when seeking to assess the overall message of the work. In planning the writing of your dissertation, you *must* ensure adequate time for a strong, well-written *conclusion*. In this, you might want to:

- Revisit your original research problem in the light of your key or strong findings
- Discuss any implications for the theoretical areas you have explored
- Discuss any implications for practical programmes of action or policy
- Discuss how you might have improved upon the research or changed the research design

425

- Highlight unresolved areas and debates
- Point out areas for further research or debate

Appendices Resist the temptation to use appendices as a way of inflating the length of your dissertation by including more results, analysis and so forth. Appropriate appendices would include:

- A blank questionnaire
- An interview schedule or topic guide
- A letter sent to research participants and (if relevant) the names of organizations approached
- Any visual images analysed in the dissertation
- Brief sections of transcripts to show the level of transcription used

- A coding scheme, perhaps accompanied by a short extract of interview material showing how the codes were applied (but not an entire interview transcript)
- A page of observation fieldnotes to illustrate the technique of data gathering used (but not an entire diary of fieldnotes).

Dissertations based on secondary sources

A dissertation that is based on secondary sources should be distinguished from one based on *secondary analysis*. A **secondary source** consists of evidence which you have not collected yourself, but for which you want to propose a new or

---

Box 30.5 Thinking differently about dissertations based on secondary sources

A dissertation based on a review of secondary sources relating to anti-depressants might make the bold claim that the technical development and marketing of new classes of anti-depressant drugs by pharmaceutical companies precedes, and therefore may cause, the social phenomenon and social category of 'depression'. The relevant literature might be based on the sociology of health and illness, the sociology of mental health, academic literature on Prozac and Seroxat, publicity material from pharmaceutical companies, newspaper reports and epidemiological data. The theoretical approach might be based on 'social constructionist' perspectives on health and illness.

A dissertation on animal rights might argue that animal *welfare* organizations are key organizations responsible for the unnatural deaths of animals in modern societies. The relevant literature might focus on the annual reports and material of the RSPCA, academic work on the sociology of environmentalism and animal welfare, and statistical data on the humane killing by animal welfare organizations of stray and unwanted dogs and cats in Britain. The theoretical approach might be influenced by Weberian ideas about the organisation and consequences of large-scale modern systems of bureaucracy.

A dissertation on 'counter-cultural' new age religious movements might make the claim that they are exemplary of rational, calculating, rigid and systematic methods of organization in modern societies. Relevant literature might include the sociology of new age or new religious movements, and guides and instructions for personal change and transformation from a new age group. The claim might be backed up by Foucauldian theoretical approaches relating to 'technologies of the self'.

A dissertation based on a review of secondary sources relating to the events of September 11, 2001 might start by posing an unusual and controversial argument about the prominence of 'death'-related discourses in a variety of social movements and networks in late modern society, irrespective of religious or ethnic affiliation or identity. The relevant literature might focus on the sociology of death. Secondary sources might include newspaper and magazine articles, websites, political speeches, pamphlets and academic books and articles about the event.

---

different interpretation from your own critical disciplinary position. Again, you must put forward a problem or issue you want to investigate in relation to the secondary literature. Starting with a bold statement (research problem) can often help (see Box 30.5). It is useful when exploring secondary sources to have a clear research problem that helps you stay focused, rather than getting overwhelmed with the amount of secondary material you may find.

Theoretical dissertations

If you are thinking of writing a **theoretical** (or library-based) **dissertation**, you should first think carefully about whether you are comfortable with engaging with and providing your own independent or original interpretations in relation to the existing *theoretical* literature of your discipline. A theoretical dissertation should not simply be an extended essay, but should present and investigate a set of key problems which you have formulated in relation to a specific or substantive area. For example, a dissertation providing an exposition and evaluation of theories of globalization would not in itself suffice. The theme of globalization needs to be related to a key problem which you want to explore (for example,

'existing theories of globalization are inadequate because …'), or which you can relate to a substantive area (for example, 'existing theories of globalization do not address human rights …').

In a theoretical dissertation, examiners are typically looking for evidence of your independent critical judgements and original and creative approaches to the existing theoretical literature. You should not simply summarize, however cogently, existing theoretical debates and literature. You should also remember to discuss *methodological* issues, as relevant. For example, if you are undertaking a critical theoretical analysis of, say, post-structuralist feminism, what is the position from which you are undertaking your reading? What 'theoretical gaze' are you using in order to undertake your critical reading of feminism? Can this therefore be seen as a methodology of reading and analysis? Think broadly about methodological issues in relation to theoretical positions: can postmodern theory be used as a method, as well as a theory?

An ideal structure for a theoretical dissertation would be to have each chapter both dealing with a substantially different area and progressing your arguments and themes forward. You should conclude your dissertation strongly – do not just summarize what you have already covered, but

---

Box 30.7 Typical format for a list of references

Author(s), (Year), *Title*. Place: Publisher. [**Book**]

Author(s), (Year), 'Title', in Editor(s), *Book Title*. Place: Publisher. [**Article in Edited Book**]

Author(s), (Year), 'Title', *Journal Name*, Journal Volume (Journal Number), Pages. [**Journal Article**]

Author(s), (Year), 'Title', *Periodical Name*, Date (where relevant), Page number. [**Newspapers, magazines and other periodicals**]

Author(s), (Year or Date published), 'Title'. <u>Full Internet URL</u>, Type of Internet Document (e.g. 'web page'), Date the document was accessed by you. [**Internet document**]

Author(s), (Year), 'Title'. Place: Publisher. Type of Electronic Medium (e.g. CD-ROM). [**Electronic sources**]

If you are referencing other **material** (films, videos, photographs, pamphlets, leaflets, posters, records, catalogues, CDs/DVDs, artefacts, personal records) or **events** (performances, speeches, installations, exhibitions) ask your tutor for detailed guidance.

conclude properly in relation to the problem you initially started with. You should also refer to unresolved areas and further debates.

Some students doing theoretical dissertations find that they 'get lost in the theory' and cannot bring their dissertation together or conclude it. Remember that you will not find 'an answer' by continuing to read more and more theoretical literature, and possibly getting more confused. You should instead focus on what you initially started with, your own research or theoretical problem and your own critical independent viewpoint. The examiners are interested in this, rather than in the densities of the theoretical literature.

Citations and references

Use a standard recognized format for acknowledging all the sources you have used, both in the body of your dissertation and in a separate reference list or bibliography. Chapter 12 gives guidance on bibliographic software that exports recorded references in various standard formats. In the body of your dissertation and following any quotation, you should typically state the

---

Box 30.8   Examples of dissertation referencing

In the body of the dissertation:

... as argued by Smith (1998: 212) ...

... it has also been argued (Smith, 1998: 212) ...

... this view has also been countered by other writers (for example; Mooley,1996; Gosling, 1999) ...

As Madan has said:

> 'If globalization has allegedly advanced homogeneity, it has also differentiated peoples, ethnicities, cultures and nations in forms unimaginable in the nineteenth-century.' (Madan, 2003: 12)

... was born in 1789, in Malden Grisp, Wokingham (Anonymous, 2002).

... but it has recently been demonstrated that such interventions have clearly failed to 'socially include' groups from other communities (Tyler, not dated).

In the corresponding list of references:

Smith, S. (1998) 'Revisiting "the cyborg": the dynamics of gender and technoculture', *Journal of Sociology & Culture*, 7(3), 198–223.

Mooley, J. K. (1996) 'The economy of social time', in P. J. Holden & T. Matthews eds., *Social Theory Today*, London: Major Publishers.

Gosling, J. (1999) *Social Spaces and Places*, Melbourne: Other Publishers.

Madan, R. (April 2003) 'Globalization and its Discontents', *Students Journal of Social Theory*, volume 1, number 1, www.sjst.com/042003/~mad.html, web page, accessed 01.06.2003.

Anonymous (2002) 'Josephine Bluntley – early life', *Microsoft Encarta 2002*. Redmond, VA: Microsoft Corp. DVD.

Tyler, P. (not dated) 'Social inclusion?', www.anorg.co.uk/poppy/~scu/marginsuk.pdf, pdf document, accessed 24.08.2003.

Box 30.9 Web pointers for doing a dissertation

The Writing Center: thesis writing
www.rpi.edu/dept/llc/writecenter/web/thesis.html

Seven Steps to Effective Library Research
www.library.cornell.edu/okuref/research/skill1.htm

Chemistry Coach: links to a better education
www.chemistrycoach.com/lbe5.htm#Reading%20Textbooks
(Don't be put off by 'Chemistry' in the title of this one; this site is a huge collection of links to resources relevant to all aspects of academic writing, many of which are relevant to social and cultural research.)

Research Methods Knowledge Base
http//trochim.human.cornell.edu/kb/contents.htm

Drew University Writing Program: Web resources
www.users.drew.edu/%7Esjamieso/Webresources.html

Web sites to avoid!
Avoid commercial sites offering ready-made theses and dissertations for sale, or offering 'help' (at a price) in writing your dissertation. There are ways of catching people who use these services and penalties in many universities for such cheating can be severe.

Visit the website for this book at www.rscbook.co.uk to link to these web pointers.

(Author(s), Year: Page number). If citing more than two authors, use (First Author et al., Year: Page number). Your reference list should typically use a format such as that shown in Box 30.7. Box 30.8 shows how references in a dissertation might look.

Plagiarism

Plagiarism is considered to be cheating and is a very serious academic offence. If you do not cite fully your sources, you may end up presenting other people's ideas and work as if they were your own. Copying or closely paraphrasing texts from whatever source without full referencing or acknowledgement of the source is called plagiarism. Copying from the work of other students is a form of plagiarism. Plagiarism also includes copying, closely paraphrasing or not referencing fully and properly:

• Documents from the Internet, including web pages, any other downloaded documents or

files, and any materials obtained from Internet archives and Internet services.
• Other electronic sources, including DVD-ROMs and CD-ROMs, other electronically stored information, electronic magazines and newspapers, electronic journals and any electronic book libraries (e-libraries).

Avoid commercial sites offering ready-made dissertations and theses for sale, offering 'help' in writing your dissertation, or offering 'essay banks'. There are numerous sophisticated ways of identifying people who use these services, or identifying work that has been derived from such services, and the penalties in many universities for this type of cheating can be very severe. You need to be very clear about what is meant by plagiarism and consult your tutor if in any doubt.

Conclusion

Doing a dissertation can be the most fulfilling part of a degree course, enabling you to put together the skills and knowledge you have learned, sometimes over a period of years, in a fully integrated research project that you plan and carry out independently. Using advice from your supervisor wisely (ideally regularly, and from an early stage in the process) is an important way of improving the quality of your eventual dissertation and, in some cases, rescuing you from situations that look as if they are going badly wrong. Using this chapter, in conjunction with the others in this book can help you bring your dissertation to a successful conclusion.

Further reading

Perhaps the best book for advice on how to do an undergraduate dissertation is Walliman (2001). Bell (1999) is also very good, particularly if you are doing educational research. Aimed more at the doctoral student and focused on qualitative research, though still relevant at other levels, is Silverman (1999). Becker's (1998) book is aimed at anyone doing a research project, particularly in sociology, but will be rewarding reading if you are doing an empirically based dissertation.

Key concepts

Combining concepts	**Research problem**
Empirical dissertation	**Research process**
Methodology and method	**Secondary sources**
Plagiarism	**Theoretical dissertation**

31

When things go wrong

Mike Michael

CONTENTS

This chapter is an attempt to present some pointers in coping with what happens when things go wrong in a research project. While there are many methodology books that usefully describe the choice and proper use of particular research methods to answer particular research questions, rather less attention is paid to the variety of routine problems that can arise in any research project. One of the results of this relative neglect is that novice researchers can feel rather inadequate. Everything that goes wrong thus becomes a matter of one's own inexperience, lack of skill, or downright incompetence. This negative attribution to self is unsurprising when what is very often presented is a more or less idealized picture of methodological procedure. A little reflection on the fact that things go wrong even for seasoned researchers would go some way to dispelling the sense of overbearing methodological mystique. To appreciate that even one's supposed intellectual elders and betters have also made mistakes in the process of data collection and analysis can be of considerable reassurance. That is to say, some consideration of the ways that seasoned researchers can 'repair' research that has gone wrong so that eventually interesting and useful things might be said (interesting and useful to the relevant research community or to users such as policy makers), might serve to make the whole research process a little less fraught.

Of course, the phrase 'when things go wrong' covers a multitude of disasters:

- At the grandest level, there might be such huge disparities between the research question posed and the research method chosen that one generates no relevant data.
- At a very practical level there are issues of thwarted access: people simply refuse to speak to you, or do not allow you to speak to those for whom they effectively act as gatekeepers.
- At the interpersonal data-gathering level, there might be respondents who simply do not answer the questions, or who disorient you in some way.

One of the points of this chapter is to suggest that there might still be 'interesting and useful things to be said' about the social world despite this apparent lack of data. As we shall see, this means having a feel for how to judge just what counts as 'interesting' and 'useful', and a *reflexive* sensibility that can help draw out the more general value of one's methodological problems.

So, this chapter is about exploring some of these variants of 'when things go wrong'. It will, of course, not be possible to be exhaustive – things go wrong in many, many surprising and disparate ways. The aim, rather, is to provide a sense of how one can turn a bad situation into a 'do-able' project that can be intellectually interesting. In what follows, I start with some thoughts on what it means to do 'interesting' and 'useful' research in a cultural community of social scientific scholars. After this, I present a catalogue of disasters – well, three anecdotes actually – that draw on my own painful research experience (which has largely been interview-based). In the process, I consider the ways that I managed to get out of what were, in one or two cases, very sticky empirical situations. For example, I suggest that even when it seems self-evident that one has no data, if the research question is properly reformulated, it is possible to discover that one is actually in possession of some fascinating data.

Saying 'interesting' and 'useful' things

Let me start with a brief foray into the doings of science. This is because science is still in many ways the benchmark by which social scientific research is judged, not least in terms of its rigour (if not its forms of explanation). As sociologists of scientific knowledge have shown, the rigour of science is considerably looser than would appear from the outside. For example, Harry Collins (1985) has documented how methods are *always* contestable in science and how, indeed, in a scientific controversy closure or resolution is attained not by simply following methodological rules but by the social processes of argumentation by which other 'opponent' scientists are discredited. To be sure, this might draw on accounts of their methodological strengths or weaknesses, but it will also involve arguments about the quality of opponents' institutional affiliation, assessments of their reputation, and even aspersions about their sanity!

In all this, the resolution of the controversy is, ironically, not decided by the facts of nature as revealed by implementing proper methodological procedure; rather, once the controversy is resolved, that is, once all but one faction in a controversy have been discredited, marginalized or silenced, *then* the facts of nature are known.

There are a number of lessons to draw from this digression into the sociology of scientific knowledge.

1 *Methods are always disputable* and claims about the research 'going wrong' are just part and parcel of the character of science.
2 As such, *methodology is just one form of argumentation* out of several.
3 What makes a fact a fact is crucially *dependent on social and cultural processes*.

Now, one important aspect of these social and cultural processes is the perception that one's work is 'useful' or 'interesting'. That is, if one's findings, ideas, conceptions, frameworks, data and so on contribute to, or in some way enable, colleagues' work, then these are deemed valuable. As Mulkay (1979) noted, whether scientists conform to norms of scientific good conduct is subordinate to whether their work can be judged 'useful' or 'interesting'. The upshot of this is that even when 'things go (disastrously) wrong', if one can find a way of showing how one's work is 'useful' or 'interesting', then it will be seen to be valuable. Inevitably, however, what counts as 'useful' or 'interesting' is difficult to pin down.

Box 31.1 shows the contrary ways, over and above methodological rectitude, in which work can be judged 'useful' or 'interesting' in social science.

These contrasting assessments are rhetorical commonplaces that are constantly drawn upon as a means of congratulating or denigrating peers and colleagues. They are also, as is shown in Chapters 5 and 6, relevant considerations from the outset in planning research. And of course, the *valency* of each commonplace can be reversed. Thus:

* *theoretical sophistication* can be called *ivory tower thinking*;
* *empirical usefulness* can be called *over-simplification*;
* *radicalism* can be called *utopianism*;
* *relevance* can be called *selling out*.

The point is that saying 'interesting' things or staking claims to doing 'useful' work is always a fraught business. Indeed, to complicate matters still further, the capacity to reflect on these different commonplace practices of academic judgement is likewise subject to judgement. As *ethnomethodologists* have long argued (see Chapter 4), there is no time out: none of us moves outside of the criteria of judgement in order to judge them – this very act is subject to judgement. This chapter will be no less subject to such scrutiny than your research reports.

The commonplaces listed above, for all their slipperiness, do nevertheless suggest ways in which it might be possible to recover a research

---

Box 31.1 Two dimensions on which social science may be judged 'useful' and 'interesting'

Theoretical sophistication: for example, does your research demonstrate a thoroughgoing engagement with cutting edge theoretical debates?
   versus
Empirical usefulness: for example, does your research contribute to quality of life, illuminate people's actual social conditions?

Radicalism: for example, does your work 'push the envelope' politically or epistemologically?
   versus
Relevance: for example, does your research contribute to the making of policy or the production of advice?

project even when it has gone horribly wrong. When respondents do not respond, when they do not respond in the expected way, when you realize you have been asking the wrong questions, indeed using the wrong methods, then it might still be possible to say something interesting or useful. In what follows, I will present three anecdotes of research gone wrong with a view to showing how it was, or could have been, turned into something other than mere failure.

- In the first, I relate an interview where everything that could go wrong did go wrong and, to all intents and purposes, no data was collected at all. This episode was in large part due to the 'recalcitrance' of the respondent who simply did not want to talk about the things the interview was supposed to address.
- In the second anecdote, I consider a case where the method was inappropriate and led, once more, to what seemed like a distinct lack of data.
- Finally, in the third anecdote, we found that in focus groups with school students, we were getting data that were not at all what we were expecting, but which, as it turned out, could be

used to raise some interesting and useful questions within the research field as a whole.

Anecdote 1: 'recalcitrant' respondents

In 1989, I was working as a researcher at Lancaster University with Rosemary McKechnie and Brian Wynne looking into the public understanding of science, specifically, ionizing radiation. Most of this research entailed conducting interviews with members of the public to derive the 'mental models' that underpinned their understanding of ionizing radiation. One sample of respondents was drawn from the electoral register. This particular example of a disastrous piece of fieldwork involved an interview with a respondent at her home and is described in Box 31.2.

Now, this was undoubtedly a rather eccentric fieldwork episode. There seemed to be no relevant data that could be salvaged from the interview, even if the recorder had managed to pick up our voices above the cat's activities. For a long time this interview was consigned to a bin in the back of my mind labelled 'put down to experience'. However, more recently I have been reflecting on

---

Box 31.2 A disastrous interview?

This was our second interview. Between this and the first interview, the circumstances of the respondent had changed insofar as she had got a job at Burger King. I was seated on the sofa, the respondent was in an armchair to my right, and the tape recorder was placed on the floor between us. During the preliminary conversation, her pit bull terrier entered the room and made its way slowly over to where I was sitting. It turned itself around and proceeded to sit on my feet. According to the respondent, 'she liked to know where people were'. My main aim in this interview was to get the respondent to talk about how she saw ionizing radiation in a broader context, not least that of the local nuclear power installations at Heysham and Sellafield. However, it very quickly became clear that she would much rather talk about her new job at Burger King. She felt that there were excellent opportunities for rapid promotion. While this conversation was going on, we were joined by her cat, who ambled over to the tape recorder. After a few moments of clawing at the tape recorder, it began to pull it along the ground by its strap, taking it further and further away from the interview. Needless to say, the combination of the pit bull terrier on my feet, the respondent's evident intentness to speak only about the excellent career structure at Burger King, and the disappearing tape recorder all conspired to make this a non-interview. Certainly, I did not feel I could intervene further in this scene of domestic harmony by insisting that we talk about the ionizing radiation. After an hour or so, the 'interview' came to an end and I paid the interviewee and, with considerable relief, left.

the role of non-humans in the production of social ordering. In other words, I have been interested in how entities such as technologies, objects, animals, 'natural' environments of various sorts contribute to what we understand to be more or less routine social events. Suddenly, in the context of this new set of concerns, this 'disastrous interview episode' has become rather interesting.

Re-interpretation of the interview

What it demonstrates is that a whole array of entities need to behave themselves in a particular way, and a peculiar range of relations need to be instituted, in order for there to be 'relevant social data' (in this case, interview material of a specific sort) at all. That is to say, companion animals such as cats and dogs, technologies such as tape recorders and TVs, persons such as interviewees, neighbours, relatives, friends and, of course, interviewers need to be disciplined in such a way that out of their various inter-relations are yielded 'relevant social data'. The 'disastrous interview episode' illustrates what happens when this discipline breaks down. 'Normally' an interview is so organized by both interviewer and, crucially, interviewee, that all manner of possible interruptions are kept at bay.

The obvious upshot is that, if an interview (or, indeed, any form of fieldwork) has gone wrong, one could ask the question: what has *enabled* this to go wrong? In other words, rather than see this as a failure of methodological procedure, one could inquire into the ways in which persons, objects, natures and technologies have started to behave in an 'undisciplined' way such that it becomes impossible to collect 'relevant social data'. As a corollary, one can also begin to examine what has had to be disciplined in order to allow one to collect such data in more successful fieldwork episodes.

Additionally, to say that the 'disastrous interview episode' is an instance of things going wrong is obviously to take the perspective of the interviewer. For the interviewee, this episode might well be characterized as anything from an enjoyable social encounter to a triumphant opportunity to make a particular point. This raises the further issue of how the interviewee interprets

the interviewer. For example, the interviewee in the previous example could be said to be ignoring the topic of ionizing radiation and focusing upon the career prospects of Burger King because she wants to display that she no longer needs the fee that comes with the interview. In other words, she might be interpreting me as a representative of the university and hence elitist or privileged and the source of something like a humiliating largesse (payment for an interview on a topic she is not interested in). Moreover, this interpretation on the part of the interviewee, and the self that is implicated in the 'doing' of such an interpretation, might be partly enabled by the way she is relating to her animals. The point is that one can attempt to re-interpret this disaster as a successful interaction. The question to ask is: how, from the perspective of the 'recalcitrant' respondent, can the 'disastrous' interview be seen to be a 'success'?

Of course, this sort of question generalizes to other situations where respondents, participants, gate-keepers and so on have been 'obstructive' in some way or other. Rather than see such 'obstructions' primarily as a matter of personal failure or incompetence, consider how the 'obstruction' might be reframed as a social encounter that has worked more or less successfully for the 'subject of study'. After all, the scrutiny of everyday social life by a whole host of social and human scientists (some academic, some commercial, some government or charity-sponsored) seems to be becoming comparatively common (Rose, 1999). In such a context, the seeming failure of respondents' engagement can be regarded as an indication of *skilfulness* on their part, as opposed to *skillessness* on the part of the researcher. Another question, then, that one can address is, what sort of social skill has been deployed by the respondent in 'doing' such recalcitrance or accomplishing such obstruction?

The analysis suggested above entails, as it were, 'going meta': it involves interrogating the social arrangements that make the method (e.g. interview) 'work'. In terms of our various criteria for saying interesting or useful things (Box 31.2), one could make the following points.

• The interrogation is **epistemologically radical**

because it has placed on to the sociological agenda (along with various authors such as Latour, 1999 and Haraway, 1997) the role of non-humans in the making of society and social knowledge.

- The interrogation is potentially **politically radical** (and certainly controversial) because it raises, albeit in simplified form, the issue of where agency (the freedom to act and to interpret the meaning of action) and rights lie.

The general lesson, then, is that failures in fieldwork that are precipitated by the 'misbehaviour' of respondents can be recovered when these failures are re-interpreted as an insight into, indeed, an interrogation of, when 'things go right'. See Box 31.3, however, for a reversal of this logic, in which interviews that appeared unproblematic at the time were later seen as quite ambiguous.

Anecdote 2: 'reckless' researchers

In 1987, I took my first research job proper. After finishing my PhD in social psychology, I was hired to do research on the public understanding of science. My main qualification for this was, I suppose, having some (rather limited) experience of interviewing, and an interest in discourse analysis. The project was the same as that mentioned in

Anecdote 1; Box 31.4 describes the source of a new problem with this project.

Rescuing the project

However, in the context of the main studies in public understanding of science, these 'don't know' responses actually proved very interesting. At the time, the majority of studies in public understanding of science tended to be questionnaire-based quizzes which treated any answer of 'don't know' as a simple absence of, or deficit in, scientific knowledge and understanding. In contrast, what we found was that on answering with a 'don't know', respondents would then go on to provide a series of *reasons* for not knowing (for more detail see Michael, 1992, 1996). These included the three 'discourses of ignorance' shown in Box 31.5, each of which reflected a different relationship with scientific authority.

This analysis (albeit rather condensed here), in taking the 'don't know' responses seriously, served as a critical commentary on those questionnaire studies which treated 'don't knows' merely as signs of the absence of knowledge. Indeed, it further suggested that the questionnaires could be used as 'prompts', to get people not so much to answer the questions as remark on the meanings of such questions and their perceived relations to those who would ask or be interested

---

Box 31.3 Coda: problematizing 'successful' interviews

In a series of interviews conducted with scientists about the rights and wrongs of animal experimentation (Michael and Birke, 1994a, 1994b), when we came to interpret our data, we were faced with a problem. While the interviews were, on the whole, very 'successful', the data were interpretable in a number of ways depending on how we interpreted the interviewees' interpretations of us as interviewers. This depended on whether we regarded them as addressing themselves to us as:

- social scientists (both of us were attached to social science departments)
- scientists (my colleague was also a biologist)
- representatives of a science magazine (the research was commissioned by the *New Scientist*)
- pro- or anti-animal experimentation (the funding of the research was provided by both pro- or anti-organizations).

The broader question is, to what extent were the responses addressed to, as it were, the 'wrong' or 'mistaken' versions of the interviewers? Or, to put it another more positive way, *what* has the interviewer been 'constructed as' by the interviewee and to what ends?

Box 31.4 Failure to get relevant data

The project's aim was to unpick people's *mental models* of particular 'scientific' phenomena. At stake was how people understood a phenomenon such as 'ionizing radiation' through particular cognitive representations – images, metaphors, analogies and so on. The procedure was to pose a series of quite difficult, almost technical, questions in order to see what sort of models were applied and how. The further aim was to see whether and how these mental models were shaped by social factors such as people's understanding of, or trust in, the sources of information about those phenomena (for example, the nuclear industry).

In outline, at least, this seemed like a splendid project. I certainly thought so. However, there was one thing that we neglected to register. Many of the existing studies of mental models either applied to social phenomena, or to medical, physical or technological phenomena (such as the common cold, electricity or central heating systems), with which people were generally very familiar. Recklessly, we had generalized this approach to address understandings of ionizing radiation – a phenomenon with which people were, in general, very unfamiliar.

In response to our questions about even the most apparently elementary aspects about radiation (whether it was made up of particles or rays), we were met with a chorus of 'don't knows'. In other words, instead of even the most tenuous effort at answering our questions, our respondents preferred to insist upon their ignorance. It looked as if we had no data from which to derive our mental models. It looked as if the entire research project would prove to be a disaster.

---

in such questions. In terms of saying something 'interesting' or 'useful', this shift of analytic emphasis meant that we could now observe apparent lack of knowledge as something that was itself performed in order to accomplish certain ends. Indeed, the ostensible absence of knowledge, contrary to the then orthodox view in the field of public understanding of science, does not stop people from being effective citizens. Instead of assuming that lack of scientific

---

Box 31.5 Three discourses of ignorance

1 *I can't understand*: 'Ignorance' was said to be a reflection of mental constitution – they did not possess a 'scientific mind' and thus they *could not* understand such knowledge. But in 'admitting' this, they were simultaneously demonstrating that they were aware of the fact, that they were 'rational' about their ignorance. This reflects *subordination* to science.

2 *I don't need to understand*: 'Ignorance' was said to reflect a division of labour: scientists did one thing, other people did other things. Each could not be expected to know the details of the other's job – lay people simply did not *need* to know the science. Indeed, some respondents claimed that such patterns of knowledge and ignorance allowed institutions to work to everyone's benefit. This reflects *functional co-habitation* with science.

3 *I don't want to understand*: 'Ignorance' was represented as a deliberate choice – they did not *want* to come to grips with the scientific knowledge. In these interviews scientific knowledge was consciously bracketed, ignored, jettisoned or avoided because it was perceived as essentially peripheral to, or a distraction from, what the respondent considered to be the real issue at stake. This reflects a *challenge* to science.

knowledge meant that lay people were disabled from contributing to science policy debates, one could say that such a lack of knowledge might be an *expression* of citizenship insofar as it reflected a challenge to, or disaffection with, the very terms of such policy debates. At the time at least, this seemed like an important and useful contribution.

So, from a study that seemed to have generated very little data indeed, a slight shift in perspective meant that a somewhat different set of questions could be formulated which revealed that we were actually in possession of some very good data. This shift of perspective was partly enabled by our knowledge of how others were studying the public understanding of science. Reports about people's ignorance of science were (and still are) a regular feature in the media. Treating ignorance as something that could be rationalized, explained and deployed by lay people allowed us to see how ignorance could also be represented as positive and even productive.

There are a number of broader principles (for want of a better term) that we might draw from the above example.

- First, it is important to go back and examine why a seemingly standard methodology and conceptual framework (in the above case, mental models) failed to generate the expected data. It might be the case that there are limits to the uses of such approaches, and that is itself an important observation.
- Secondly, cultivating an awareness of broader debates within the substantive field or sub-discipline can trigger off a sense of the possible value of one's (lack of) data. One can ask, how would others treat this (lack of) data? Can I say

something interesting about this apparent absence which others have missed?
- Thirdly, do not be discouraged by people's inability or unwillingness to answer your questions (even when you are asking the wrong questions). Being incapable, self-denigration, hostility and so on – all these are social *accomplishments*. One can pose the following questions: *how* have these presentations of self been accomplished and to *what* ends?

Anecdote 3: 'deviant' data

One could say that the 'don't know' responses were 'deviant data' insofar as they were certainly not anticipated. Finding data that one does not expect is, of course, what makes research so exciting. However, sometimes data are gathered which are often difficult to interpret, especially when one begins the research with expectations that are otherwise pretty standard for the research area within which one is working. Chapter 7 in this book discusses a variety of uses to which *deviant cases* or *negative instances* can be put. Box 31.6 shows how this affected another project with which I was involved.

Re-thinking the research problem

This made us re-think what was going on and re-consider our initial expectations, which were grounded in the assumption that such sources of information would be used to inform certain understandings about genetics and illness. In other words, we (and the subdiscipline of public understanding of science) would be expecting to see such sources being treated as if they

---

Box 31.6   Discovery of deviant data

In a research project conducted with Simon Carter, we were aiming, amongst other things, to explore what sources of information (about genetics and illness) were trusted by older school students. In a series of focus groups, we attempted to ascertain the extent to which, for instance, the Web, family members, GPs or medical journals were trusted. Our expectation was that there would be some *consensus* around the, albeit ambivalent, trustworthiness of certain sources. Instead what we found was that as soon as one possible source was mentioned by one participant, another would raise problems with it and suggest another possible source, the trustworthiness of which would, in its turn, be questioned by another student, and so on.

contributed to the emergence of a certain *product* – namely, knowledge (after all, the students were motivated to derive such knowledge, not least for the purposes of passing biology exams). Instead, what we seemed to be witnessing was a *collective performance of contingency and movement*. Against seeing any of these sources as leading to a *product-like* knowledge, the students were engaged in a *process* of picking up, comparing, stringing together and criticizing without necessarily reaching any conclusion or resolution about the trustworthiness of these sources (Michael and Carter, 2001). What looked like 'problematic' data (which perhaps cast aspersions on our ability to conduct focus groups – we could even be accused of letting the focus groups get out of control), could be usefully re-interpreted as raising issues about the very way in which the subdiscipline thought about knowledge and trust. By treating these focus groups as social events, and by shifting our 'take' on the data from 'product' to 'process', we could begin to explore how sometimes it is important for people to evoke a sense of shared scepticism. The social uses of this shared, collectively performed scepticism remain to be studied in detail.

The broader principle that is raised by this final anecdote is that one should not be afraid to innovate. If one's data makes no sense, then it is not necessarily because one has improperly generated or collected that data. It might be the case that the data that have been collected point to the limits of, or poverty of theory within, one's subdiscipline. Even if the punchline to such a study is that there is 'something' further to be investigated, this might still be an 'interesting and useful thing to say'.

Conclusion

In the course of this chapter, I have attempted to deal with three things that can go wrong when doing research:

- When respondents do not 'behave' themselves
- When the researcher has mis-designed the project
- When expectations about the sort of data that should be collected are not met

Obviously, the examples I have offered are but a small selection of what could go wrong. If there is a key lesson to draw, it is 'don't panic'. There are ways and means by which an apparent disaster can be turned around so that 'interesting and useful things' can be said. I have tried to indicate what some of these might be by drawing out some more general principles from the ways my colleagues and I have managed to get out of some tricky situations.

Of course, if such problems do arise, do not feel shy of seeking advice from peers, colleagues and supervisors. At the very least, they might be able to alert you to other concerns and debates within your field to which your data (or 'lack' of it) might be able to contribute. In the end, however, there is a calculation that will need to be made: is the extra work you must do to put yourself in a position to reinterpret your (lack of) data justified, or should you start your project afresh? This is perhaps the thorniest question of all, but it is one that has to be faced: sometimes it is just better to start again from scratch.

There is one final point to make. What counts as 'interesting and useful' is also a matter of *how* one writes. John Law (1994), reflecting on his ethnography of a large physics laboratory, admitted to feeling that wherever he was must be where the action *was not*. In other words, whatever data one is gathering, there is a pervasive sense that the *real* data, the *really good* data, are elsewhere. Conveying a sense of the limits of, and absences in, one's data is not an admission of failure but a sign of **reflexivity** and self-criticism. Properly done, such displays of modesty are an invitation to a dialogue about one's research and one's (lack of) findings: after all, in the end, all research is work 'in progress'.

Further reading

Becker (1998) provides advice and a series of helpful anecdotes from his own research experience, many of which involve the kind of 'lateral thinking' described in this chapter. Janesick (2003) outlines a series of 'stretching exercises' for researchers, designed to feed creativity and loosen trapped thoughts.

Student Reader (Seale, 2004): relevant readings

2 C. Wright Mills: 'On intellectual craftsmanship'
26 Paul Feyerabend: 'Against method'

Key concepts

Epistemological radicalism
Political radicalism
Reflexivity

Part III: Case Studies

32

Representing otherness: collecting and analysing visual data

Thomas Zacharias

CONTENTS

This chapter draws upon my research experience gained whilst conducting an empirical study of *otherness* and its representation in German politics. It provides practical and theoretical guidelines relevant to the gathering of material for visual analysis and relates, in particular, to the methods discussed in Chapter 20.

Initial ideas

During the 2002 German election campaign I noticed a number of political campaign posters for the left-wing party The Greens, which were dealing with the issue of immigration and citizenship, which is a hotly debated topic in German political discourse. Whilst most of the parties positioned in the centre or to the right of the political spectrum were characterized by a strong anti-immigration stance, the liberal Greens were lobbying for a more inclusive approach and voicing a political viewpoint which proposed laxer immigration laws, the drawing up of anti-discrimination laws, and citizenship rights for immigrants. However, I found some of the images and advertisements they were using quite problematic, since the way in which they were depicted drew on an idea of the essential 'other' body and of 'race' and I suspected that their liberal visual discourse was somehow informed by ideas that were present in Nazi representational practices. I doubted that the Greens were aware of these 'echoes from the past' in the way they were depicting those marked as 'other' or that they were using these strategies deliberately, but I nevertheless believed that this was worth investigating.

I decided on a combination of methods, which comprised the collection and *semiotic analysis* of visual data, *discourse analysis* of parliamentary speeches in relation to immigration issues and anti-discrimination laws, and *qualitative interviews* with party spokespersons. Thus, my approach incorporated an investigation of representations with an analysis of the *modalities* of their production (see Chapter 20)

In the early stages of my research, my research question was more of a research idea (How is 'difference' represented in Germany?) and I felt it most appropriate to let the data inform my problem formulation and my research design. It

often happened that, during data gathering, I found particular recurring patterns and similarities in representation, which in turn continued to inform my research question and helped me to focus the direction of my investigations. In this respect I was following an *inductive* logic (see Chapter 2), which is fairly typical of qualitative investigations and, in particular, of *ethnography* (Chapter 17).

Focusing on advertisements and posters

During previous stays in Germany I had noticed numerous advertisements and election campaign posters that, more or less subtly, accentuated the idea of difference and 'race', so I knew that there were data 'out there' to be found. Admittedly, my initial searches were very undifferentiated and I literally gathered everything that was easily accessible. I was informed by my strong interest in German history and culture, in particular the more troubling elements of it, namely the Nazi era and the Holocaust (Box 32.1)

My visual analysis of Green political imagery involved focusing on the idea of *representation*. In its most basic sociological definition, representation refers simply to the production and exchange of meaning between members of a culture (Hall, 1997). The most obvious medium through which this happens is language, but representation can also involve the use of images or signs which, in turn, can consist of written words, pictures, musical notes, film and so on.

Advertising provides an example of representation par excellence. Here, any product, for instance a car, a washing powder, or even a symbol – such as the 'Nike' swoosh – is presented and 'made to mean' to us. As an integral part of modern culture, images or symbols are used to convey meanings, shape our opinions, and create our identities. Leiss et al. (1990) comment that advertisements provide a discourse through and about objects. They form a communication in which individuals send signals to others about their attitudes, expectations and identity. Obviously, the main function of advertising today is to sell status, lifestyles and products. But

---

Box 32.1 Nazi use of propaganda

During the time of the Nazis, Nationalist thinking was at its peak, confounded by an idea of 'race' purity as the basis of citizenship (Linke, 1999). As we now know, the idea of 'race' is a flawed concept without any scientific grounding, but during the time of Nazi Germany it had a powerful allure, propagated through the Nazis' use of newly emerging mass-media technologies such as radio, film and especially postcards and other print advertisements. The Nazis' used these technological tools to create and maintain a distinction between 'self' and 'other'. The 'self' in this case referred to their understanding of an ethnically 'pure' German 'race' and an unwanted, 'impure' 'other' which, for them consisted of anything they perceived as un-German, for instance the disabled, Jews, blacks and gypsies.

In their attempts to expel these 'unwanted elements' and to incite hatred against them in the wider population, the Nazis made use of these new mass-media technologies in emitting their propaganda and published a plethora of writing and images depicting those seen as 'non-German' in a very negative way. They found that the use of images was the most effective means to do that, as images can relay a message very quickly, and the receiver does not have to invest the labour of reading a whole pamphlet but can decode the depicted message very quickly. Thus images and pictures can have a very profound influence on society if, as in the case of the Nazi party, they are used as instruments of ideology to serve the interests of the powerful.

---

advertising can also 'sell' a political message or programme, as in the case of Second World War Nazi ideology cited above.

Developing focused research questions

My research project took a two stage approach. First, I wanted to find out how – in the political climate of the 2002 parliamentary elections – fuelled by moral panic with regard to the issue of immigration – the German Green party depicted and expressed its ideas about immigration and multiculturalism. In particular, I wanted to find out how they represented those 'other' Germans to their potential voter population. In this context, I always kept an eye on the past to see how and if the images were drawing on past conceptions of nationhood and 'race', and whether the advertisements used during the Greens' political campaigns were reproducing *essentialist* concepts in their depiction of 'otherness'. In other words, given that contemporary theorists are arguing against 'race' or 'race-thinking' (Gilroy, 1993, 2000), I wanted to see whether the Greens were in fact – and maybe unwittingly, as they are the only

party in Germany actively speaking out on behalf of 'multiculturalism' – reviving this idea in their representation of German-ness, immigration and citizenship.

Secondly, I wanted to look at groups of people in Germany who found themselves at the societal margins, who had less power to represent themselves and who were actively resisting the Greens' representational strategies. Those 'other' Germans, such as the 'Initiative of Black Germans', 'The Foundation of Turkish Immigrants' and various other grassroots movements concerned with the demands for recognition, anti-racism and equal citizenship, had their own ways of representing themselves and voicing their political views. These views often stand in direct opposition to the diversity-management agenda of the main political parties, who seemed inattentive to the perils of reproducing stereotypical viewpoints and social inequalities and who appeared insufficiently attuned to their historical responsibilities. I thought it imperative to contrast and compare these two inherently different ways of representing the 'other' body. My primary research questions thus were:

1 How do ideas about inclusion, exclusion and citizenship become expressed by the Green party and how is 'difference' conceptualized?
2 How are Germany's 'internal others' represented and how do they represent themselves in the contemporary social milieu?

Collecting data

I did not find preparing for the collection of visual data to be very labour-intensive. The key requirement was to have a clear idea about the topic of my research so that I would not be sidetracked by other images I would inevitably encounter during the data-gathering process. I would offer the following advice to anyone planning such work:

- Get into the routine of always carrying a notepad with you in case you cannot take away certain materials.
- Be prepared to be questioned about your research or your motives by gatekeepers or respondents; being able to give a brief and succinct outline of your research will often convince people who are suspicious.
- Always carry a camera when you are going on research trips because you may discover some material unexpectedly which you will then be able to file. Make sure that a film is loaded and the batteries are in good working order to avoid disappointment of failing equipment in important situations. In addition, I always carry a small dictaphone to be prepared for the eventuality of conducting an ad hoc interview.

When researching visual material, keep in mind that there are no strict rules or guidelines as to how to conduct the data-gathering process. You obviously have to have a relatively clear idea as to what your research topic is and which method you are going to use to investigate that topic. Visual data analysis can be combined with a variety of other qualitative and quantitative methods, and in many instances this can give the study more depth. Once you have settled on a research question, you need to think hard about which sources will provide you with adequate data. Moreover, you need to think about how you can obtain this data. If you are doing a *content analysis* (Chapter 27) of

the representation of women in fashion magazines, for instance, the issue of where and how to acquire the data is less complicated since the data source would consist of a given series of fashion magazines which would be investigated over a predetermined period of time. If, however, you were interested in investigating issues around early twentieth century criminal photography, most of your necessary data would be held in *archives* (see Chapter 19), thus access to and copying of the material would be much more complicated.

Collecting the campaign posters used by the German Green party proved to be quite complicated at times. I first noticed the posters during the 2002 parliamentary elections when they appeared on every street corner and billboard all across Germany. The campaign comprised about 16 images, only four of which were on display in the county that I visited. After an unsuccessful attempt to peel one or two off the displays, which also induced a slight feeling of guilt since I did not want to be held responsible for intervening in the electoral success of the Greens, I paid a visit to the local Greens' headquarters where election assistants were happy to provide me with the images they stocked. I managed to collect another few – which were offered as email greeting cards – in electronic format via the Greens' website, where I also found a contact address. Again, I phoned and inquired about the remaining images only to be told that they had been taken off the site and had not been reprinted. Thus began another phone odyssey and after some calls to the Greens' central office in Berlin I found out that there existed a Green archive in a Berlin suburb which stored all the images ever produced in the context of election campaigns since the founding of the party in the 1980s, mainly those that had not yet been scanned and transformed into an electronic format. Sensing a prime opportunity to gather large amounts of data I got on the train to Berlin the next day and paid a visit to the archive, which was located in a partly refurbished eighteenth-century abattoir.

Working in an archive

Accessing archives can sometimes involve application procedures, which certainly applied in this case. Additionally, this particular archive's opening hours were between 12 noon and 4pm so I had to make several visits over a few days. The archive was set up like a reading room, with three database computers in the middle. These electronic indices contained the image's serial number, the title of the image, the year of production, the political context or election campaign in which it was produced, in some cases the agency responsible for the design, and a brief description of the image. The search operations enabled a topic-based search, so after putting in some *key words* (for example, 'immigration') I was presented with a list of all the images dealing with the topic of immigration. As there were plenty of images produced in this context, the next step was to read through all the short descriptions and select those images which I thought might be useful for my research and to write down the serial numbers. Approximately one hour before closing time I presented the assistant with a list of my selections and she went into the basement storeroom to fetch the posters I had indicated. Once the assistant had put the stack of images on my table, I skimmed through them to see which ones were of use to me. I then took them to a corner table by the window – flash photography was not allowed so I had to get a good source of natural light – and made photographs of the images with the aid of a small tripod, which I adjusted according to the poster size in order to get a full size photograph of them. After a few days of searching the database and taking photos of the posters, all I needed to do was develop the photos to end up with a good collection of miniature size election campaign posters, which I subsequently scanned into my computer to be used for analysis.

In my experience some visual data may be hard to come by, especially those that have been produced in institutional settings or are kept in special storage. Examples of this are pieces of art or photographs, which are kept in museums or archives. Here, the researcher faces the potential problem of accessing as well as reproducing the data since, as in my case, flash photography may be prohibited or the institution may not provide copying facilities. In such cases it may, however, be possible to obtain brochures or catalogues depicting the objects. It is worthwhile to check the websites for certain museums or exhibitions, as some images may appear in their promotions or may even be available to be viewed online. Similar complications may arise when the research requires the viewing or copying of CCTV footage, as this information is normally kept confidential.

Analysing the images
The garden gnomes poster

The 'garden gnome' poster in Figure 32.1 provides a good starting point to show my approach to analysis. Within this image there are several troubling aspects in relation to the representation of others: the latency of 'race' and the underlying theme of 'assimilation'. The garden gnome is a central cultural icon in Germany, a bit like the mythical English 'cup of tea'. The gnomes depicted here are endowed with stereotypical 'racial' characteristics and there is a strong emphasis on the different different skin-colours, an inherently unstable *signifier*, in relation to an assumed German whiteness. The assimilationist idea in the depiction of the gnomes works on two levels: first, they are – despite their differences – absorbed into German-ness through the fact that they all wear a red cap on their heads, that is, the main symbol of the gnome in German cultural representation. Thus, the overriding cultural values are not those of the 'other' but those of the host country.

Secondly, the 'other' gnomes on the left and right do not only subscribe to the unifying red cap but they appear in the essential *form* of the gnome. They *are* already constructed as incorporated into the German whole. They appear to be assimilated through the fact that they have become 'German bodies'. The caption to the image reads Grün Wirkt ('Green Works'), with the subheading 'Bunte Republik Deutschland', which in translation means 'Colourful Republic of Germany' and is a pun on *Bundes*republik (Federal Republic). The emphasis on 'colour' is significant as it runs as a theme through almost all of the images produced in the context of the Greens' politics with regards to 'foreigners' and the ideas of integration and immigration. The fact that the Greens call for a 'colouring-up' of the German

Figure 32.1   *Poster from a Green campaign: garden gnomes*

cultural or ethnic landscape shows the deeply ingrained perception of a homogeneously constituted German body, which needs to be 'revived' through the injection of colour. What is problematic about this is that Germany is encouraging the idea of difference which is expressed solely through the dangerous concept of 'race'.

The containment of cultural difference, in Germany, works through an appeal to 'race'. The Greens are making the mistake of mis-recognizing those perceived as other. In their scenario of a desired rapprochement between self and other, the Greens use representational concepts that aggravate rather than facilitate identity negotiat-

ions, because they construct insurmountable cultural ('racial') boundaries based on stereotypical ascriptions, even as they are unsuccessfully attempting to dissolve them. The relationship between 'self' and 'other' is one of unequally distributed power, first through the fact that the other is 'raced' and, secondly, through the fact that the other is merely a vehicle for the Greens' political ends; it ultimately remains 'inactive' and silenced. This power relationship is further enhanced through an underlying idea of assimilation instead of recognition. Subsequently, the cultural dialogue desired by the Greens turns into a monologue in which only one party speaks and the other is silenced.

Figure 32.2   *Poster from a Green campaign: garden party*

The garden party

The problem with the image in Figure 32.2 is again the reference to a stable 'racial' other (the immigrant) who is a guest, but not an equal, to the German host. This image is geared towards expressing a desire for living with, and incorporating difference, a yearning to move beyond a perceived homogeneity, which however, does nothing for a real integrative project and amounts to nothing more than an adornment of the German body politic with some 'exotic' others, and is furthermore expressive of a particular version of multiculturalism, unconcerned with the redistribution of power or resources.

The principal signification of the poster is about Germans and 'other' Germans who can sit and eat together at a garden party. The danger with the latency of 'race' is, however, that it could be evoked at any point, and turned against the 'invitees': they have been invited to the garden party because of their otherness, which serves the political purpose at this moment in time – but this equally opens up the possibility of rejecting them on precisely the same basis. Once 'otherness' is deployed, irrespective of the motive, it becomes a marker, a stigma, and correspondingly a reason for those groups or persons more interested in the rejection rather than acknowledgement of the people thus marked,

449

to call for their containment, deportation or extermination.

The garden party image is indicative of an assimilationist idea. The posturing of Mrs Roth, the positioning of the people at the table, the central trope of German food, the foregrounded-ness of German-ness and German-dress speak a clear language. In the composition of the picture the table constitutes a clear dividing line between Mrs Roth and her others. Roth's positioning *in front* of everybody else and separated by the table signifies that the cultural boundary, which relocates the extra-nationals to the back – or to the darkness – remains intact and undisturbed. Mrs Roth's husband (seen at the back of the image) is able to transcend the cultural boundaries, to 'cross the line' as a protagonist of the dominant culture, as the others remain in contained isolation behind the table. The dominant power relations remain intact, and it is whiteness which becomes the passport for transgressing into the location of the other.

The clothing, bodily postures and food are also significant in this poster. The batiqued shirt of the 'African' person and the sari and bindi with which the 'Indian' person is adorned are clearly meant to represent 'africanicity' and 'indianicity' res-pectively, geared towards lowest common denominator decoding by the German public. A richly laid table, stacked mainly with exclusively 'German' food such as crusty rye bread, assorted cheeses, and radish and a bowl of fruit represents, in conjunction with her dress, designed in the Bavarian 'dirndl' style, key tropes of German values and culture. An essential German-ness becomes the lens through which the 'other' persons in the picture are read and to which they have to comply. It appears as if the party guests are faced with no alternative but to accept the food they are presented with.

Extending the study

Since I was also interested in how grassroots minority political groups were representing them-selves, it was important to get into contact with groups that were using visual material in their ad-vertisements, their pamphlets or their manifestos. I was aware of the existence of some of those

groups in the cities of Berlin and Frankfurt, so I contacted them via email explaining my research and asking whether they would mind if I met up with a spokesperson for an initial meeting. In most cases, activists were prepared to spend some time in an interview session and to provide me with material that contained visual data.

Another method I deployed was to take long walks in cities that I visited during research periods and to visit cultural centres and areas that I knew were hosting many intercultural events. Since some of these grassroots movements were operating only locally and on relatively small budgets, they resorted to sticking up small posters, stickers or ads in their respective cultural centres, local pubs, or on walls or lampposts within the borough. During these walks my camera became my main research instrument since I simply photographed the material I found, often to the amusement of local residents who seemed puzzled as to why I was taking close-ups of transformer boxes or lampposts. The Internet provided another invaluable resource, since those groups that were using a website usually had some sort of image or symbol on their homepage.

Ethics are an important issue when researching visual material (see Chapter 10). Some people or groups, for instance, are hostile to the idea of researchers using their material, especially if they are working in a volatile political climate. In one of my research settings I was invited to the offices of a grassroots organization that was trying to generate support for a political movement among a particular strand of Germany's ethnic minority population. One of their objectives was to send out their pamphlets and manifestos to so-called ethnic minorities only. It was one of their strategic aims to stay outside of the 'white media' mainstream and thus reduce the risk of distortion of their political message, and of a potential backlash from racist groups. Sitting in one of the offices I noticed some framed examples of their pamphlets and posters hanging on the wall. I asked whether it would be possible to take a picture of them, or receive a copy, but my respondent refused, claiming that he did not want these images published anywhere where dissemination would be beyond his control. After talking for a short while, I was left in the office on my own for a few

---

Box 32.2   Web pointer for case study in visual research

The German Green Party
www.gruene.de

Visit the website for this book at www.rscbook.co.uk to link to these web pointers.

---

minutes as my respondent was making coffee and, having the camera ready in my bag, the thought of taking an illicit snapshot briefly crossed my mind but I decided against it as I could not reconcile this idea with the personal and institutional ethics guiding my research. Instead, I suggested to my respondent that I would merely describe some of the images in my research, but would not attempt an in-depth analysis of these particular images. Unfortunately, in this case I had to sacrifice some very rich material for the price of the research remaining ethical.

Conclusion

In this chapter I have described in some detail how I carried out the collection and analysis of visual images, with research questions and analysis being informed by sensitivity to the politics of 'race' as well as ideas derived from *semiotic* and *discourse analysis*. Clearly, this most obviously relates to Chapter 20, where the use of such material for research purposes is described, and to some extent to Chapter 27, where discourse analysis is discussed. The account of archival work in Chapter 19 is also of relevance. My experiences might also be thought of as a form of *ethnography* (Chapter 17) in which I followed leads in response to emerging research questions and opportunities as they presented themselves to me. As with the other case studies in this section, this should give you an idea of how a variety of methodological approaches may become integrated in a particular research investigation.

33

Embodiment, reflexivity and movement re-education: an ethnographic case study

Jen Tarr

CONTENTS

This chapter will present a case study of an ethnographic project I undertook as part of my PhD in sociology. It provides an example of some of the issues faced by ethnographers (outlined in general terms in Chapter 17) and how these play out in practice. I deal with such issues as choosing ethnography as a research method, gaining access to a field setting, impression management, discomfort within the field and with the role of participant observer, making field notes, and the challenges of using personal experiences as a source of data.

In my PhD studies I was concerned with researching ideas about the body and the notion of 'body wisdom' in the field of movement re-education techniques such as Alexander Technique, Pilates, Feldenkrais, Rolfing and Body–Mind Centring. These are techniques which have developed over the past 125 years in Western societies, with the aim of changing posture and comportment and thereby changing people's mental and emotional states. The techniques claim to be 'holistic' in the sense that they affect both mind and body. I will discuss how they accomplish this in more detail later on in the chapter.

This chapter will focus on my ethnographic research on Alexander Technique specifically. While I did attend a combined body conditioning class that used Alexander Technique and Pilates, and I interviewed people with experience in all of the above techniques, I felt that for the purposes of my research an in-depth study of one technique would provide me with more data and more opportunity for what Geertz (1973) called *thick description* than a comparative study that could only survey each one briefly. I surveyed each of the other techniques for the sake of drawing comparisons to Alexander Technique, rather than claiming to know each of these techniques in detail. Further, as a dancer I had some prior experience in all the other techniques, and chose to focus on Alexander Technique because I felt that this would help give me an appropriate degree of analytic distance, so that I would see this field as *anthropologically strange* rather than from the uncritical perspective of a participant.

My prior experience with these techniques was very useful in enabling me to understand what they were attempting to do and my physical training enabled me to more quickly adapt to what they asked of me. However, it also required me to be *reflexive* about my role in relation to my research; I had to reflect on my values and the ways in which this research was affected by my background and previous experiences. My embodiment was also at issue; how I experienced my body in relation to this research was crucial to the process. It has been argued that ethnography is by its nature an embodied research method (Coffey, 1999), because it requires the bodily presence and involvement of the ethnographer in a way that other research methods do not. Yet my research, because it was about and through the body, required my awareness of bodily presentation to an even greater extent. I was not simply including my body in asides in my documentation; it was literally the topic of much of my writing. Even the interviews I conducted with participants in the Alexander Technique required a constant awareness of my own comportment and the way I was presenting myself to my interviewees; if I slouched in my chair, I wondered, would they take me seriously?

Issues of theory and method

My study emerged out of a curiosity about the way movement re-education techniques looked at bodies and selves. Specifically, I was interested in the concept of 'body wisdom', or the idea that our bodies could not only be keepers of knowledge and 'bodily intelligence', but that ultimately they are the source of truth and know what is best and most healthy for us. In this model, it is bodies that are seen as innately wise and knowing, rather than conscious minds. Implicitly, there is also a conception of what is natural that underlies body wisdom, where social norms are seen as blinding people to the natural wisdom of their bodies. This notion of a 'natural body' is problematic, however, because it tends to be based on some racist ideas about evolution and whose body can be 'natural', as I will explain in more detail later in this chapter. Further, to sociologists, the idea that society corrupts us but that we can overcome this and regain some kind of natural, pre-social state is very questionable, suggesting an *essentialist* view of human nature. From this general research problem, I developed two specific *research questions*:

- First, how does it become possible to think of a 'natural body' that is wise and all-knowing?
- Second, to what extent is this conception of bodies taken up by those who practise movement re-education techniques?

The first of these questions is based on the principles of *post-structuralism*, and is focused on *discourses* and the *social construction* of the world through discourse. It presupposes that there is not an actual 'natural/pre-social body' out there waiting to be discovered, but that this is constructed through certain kinds of social knowledge and ways of speaking about the world. It is therefore *anti-positivist* and *anti-essentialist*. I was not searching for the *essence* of the natural body, but questioning how it has become possible to believe it exists and that we can reclaim it. I believed this was a necessary question to ask because it raised issues about how 'truth' and 'natural body as truth' are formed within a social context.

This first question is also informed by the work of Michel Foucault on subjectivity and particularly what he calls 'techniques of the self' (1985, 1986) or 'techniques of ethical self-formation' (1988). He claims that human subjectivity is shaped through discourse, and that what makes up the human subject at one point in history is not identical to what constitutes it at another point in history (Foucault, 1994: 290). In promising to change both physiology and psychology, Alexander Technique is a *technique of the self*, a way of working or acting upon oneself in keeping with particular ethics and *regimes of truth*. However, Foucault also argues against research approaches that take the subject, or individual person, as central because subjectivity changes throughout history. Most Foucauldians use discourse analysis

as their primary research method because of this, focusing on documents and archives rather than on people (for which see Chapter 27).

I was frustrated with this approach, however, because I felt that while it would give me a good idea what was said about Alexander Technique, it would not give me any idea how its pupils interpreted it and the extent to which they used it and adopted its principles. I would understand the theories and Alexander's 'official line', but not how this was put into practice. This led me to develop the second research question aimed at getting at that experience. I did not see the re-told experiences of my participants as true, authentic accounts of a pre-existing social world, but rather saw them as both sites and sources of the *discourses* around natural bodies and body wisdom, both forming these discourses and being formed by them.

Thus, post-structuralism is not necessarily incompatible with ethnography. It must be added, however, that mixing the two should be approached with caution since post-structuralism questions the conditions of subjectivity and can examine how we become particular kinds of subjects, whereas much *realist* ethnography in the *naturalistic* tradition has taken this subjectivity for granted.

The other reason I chose to do ethnography had to do with the very embodied nature of my topic, which, I felt, needed an equally embodied research method. Alexander and other movement re-educators argued in their books, which I read prior to commencing my research, that *experience* was the only way to truly understand what these techniques were about; that because they were bodily they could not be adequately expressed through words. A discourse analysis that focused

---

Box 33.1 Some other studies that incorporate similar ideas about subjectivity

Martin (1994) is a good example of a multi-site ethnography that uses some broadly Foucauldian ideas yet incorporates the experiences of participants in a wide variety of settings to show how the metaphor of the immune system is constructed and how it is used.

Csordas (1994b) has written an ethnographic study (he calls his approach 'cultural phenomenology') of the phenomenon of charismatic healing in America that also does not take participants' subjectivity as fixed or universally true.

Box 33.2 Background to Alexander Technique

F.M. Alexander was an actor and elocutionist from Tasmania who developed what is now called Alexander Technique in the late 1800s, when he began losing his voice during performances. The story told within the Technique is that doctors were unable to cure his difficulties so he resolved to cure himself. He spent several years in front of the mirror, scrutinizing himself as he recited, realizing that he was restricting his vocal chords by pulling his neck back, and gradually developing a technique to overcome this problem. Having conquered his ailment, he began to teach others his technique, finding it was applicable to a broad range of problems. In the early 1900s he moved to London, where he worked until his death in the mid 1950s. Alexander taught his pupils first to stop and 'inhibit' their reactions to external stimuli, to evaluate these reactions, and then to respond whilst keeping a proper 'head–neck–back relationship', which involved 'allowing the neck to be free' and directing the head to go 'forward and up'. He called this 'correct Use of the Self'. As the term 'self' indicates, he saw his method as holistically affecting not only physical but also psychological health.

However, Alexander also believed that his technique would bring people to a higher stage of evolution, as they became consciously aware of their actions at all times. They would be able to overcome not only most physical ailments, but also broader social problems. His 1910 book *Man's Supreme Inheritance* made explicit ties between his work and the eugenics movement, and was based on some principles of evolution which today are considered very racist, namely the assumption that there are 'savage' cultures and races who are less evolutionarily evolved. In the Victorian era, it was common to fear degeneration of society, which was thought to be demonstrated through the proliferation of poverty and a decline in military prowess, as evidenced by the difficulties of fighting the Boer War and the large numbers of men rejected for military service on the grounds of a lack of physical fitness (Searle, 1973). Eugenic solutions were proposed, such as careful breeding programmes and sterilization of those considered 'unfit'. Eugenics also ranged into areas like hygiene and posture, and Alexander felt that by helping people to stand erect and to consciously consider their actions, he was helping them to evolve. Like many early sociologists and social reformers, Alexander believed that Western societies represented a higher degree of civilization, and that 'man' in his 'savage' state (namely in Africa and Asia) was closer to nature. He believed people in Western society had developed too fast and had lost their natural instincts. Through re-education, the natural body that was lost could be restored, without reverting to the savage lifestyle. In essence, he believed society and civilization had corrupted us, but that it was possible to regain our place in nature through his method of holistic movement re-education.

---

on official texts, then, would surely have led to an impoverished account of what these techniques were about and how they worked.

I discovered the issues outlined in Box 33.2 through an initial *textual analysis* of Alexander's writings. I did this to give me a general idea what the field of Alexander Technique might look like, and how Alexander himself explained the technique. Within my ethnographic research, I was very interested to see whether racist and eugenic

justifications continued to be used by today's teachers, and whether pupils of the technique also adopted them. This formed the basis of some of my questions in *semi-structured interviews*, which I conducted as part of my ethnography (see also Chapter 14). In my case, interviews were the only way to access a field that did not exist in any concrete sense and where there was no way to make contacts with teachers or pupils of the technique other than by deliberately seeking them out.

Finding the field and negotiating access

Some 'fields' exist in a concrete space into which an ethnographer must enter, and some are more loosely constructed. Alexander Technique falls into the latter category. There is no geographically defined community of Alexander teachers, much less of pupils of the Technique. There is a professional regulating body, and within London there are several Alexander centres, where teachers rent space together to give lessons. These centres often run introductory workshops, where one might meet other people interested in the Technique. Other teachers work alone or from their homes. Due to the nature of lessons in Alexander Technique, which are taught individually by a single teacher, it would be very easy to go to and from weekly lessons with little sense that there was any larger community at all. Yet I knew there were some connections between teachers and with the help of my own Alexander teacher, I was gradually able to access other teachers, and through them other pupils. In this way I built up a sense of 'the field'.

Every methods text on ethnography I had read had indicated that *negotiating access* to the field might be a problem, and I was prepared to struggle through a great deal of bureaucratic red tape. There were two facts I had not counted on, however; the first is that I was seen largely as just another pupil and hence another source of income,

and the second is that people perceived me as a source of advertising for the Alexander Technique, and someone who could speak articulately to the outside world about its benefits.

More importantly, perhaps, than the practical help offered by my gatekeeper and sponsor (see Box 33.3) was his non-dogmatic attitude. As a result, the impressions of the Technique that I had gained from reading Alexander's writings shifted. I began to see it as a technique whose meanings and practices, while tied to the views of its founder, were also *negotiated* by the individuals and communities who practised it. I saw that the official discourses of Alexander were not entirely formative of the contemporary Alexander Technique, and that much might depend on the individual teacher.

On one occasion, for example, my teacher explained to me how Alexander Technique could aid people in considering their reactions to stimuli around them, such as chocolate or crisps. He explained that he was very fond of Pringles crisps, and that he might very well eat an entire packet in one sitting. This was a problem, because he did not really need an entire packet; 'it's quite unhealthy.' One solution was to remove the packet, 'but in daily life situations, this is not always possible'. He explained that Alexander Technique could help:

> Okay, we have a whole packet of Pringles and I eat a third of it, then I decide to

---

Box 33.3   Negotiating access with a gatekeeper/sponsor

I began my entry into the field of Alexander Technique with an introductory workshop at a local Alexander centre. I approached the teacher at the end of the workshop to explain my research and my desire to find a teacher who would agree to work with me and who would not mind being interviewed at a later date. When he cheerfully said that he would do this, and that furthermore it was perfectly fine for me to record the lessons on tape, I was taken aback. Anxious to ensure his informed consent, I provided him with a letter detailing my research and its goals and explaining his role in it, which he dutifully read and then filed away. My research was largely a non-issue in my taking Alexander lessons; I fiddled with the tape recorder for a few minutes at the beginning of each lesson and my teacher asked me how the research was going, but that was it. He was in fact delighted to be interviewed and proved to be an invaluable resource in putting me in touch with other Alexander teachers, providing me with articles and books, and explaining the ins and outs of the Alexander Technique and the world around it.

examine whether I really need this or not. What I can decide with Alexander is to examine this and to stop the reaction, to see what's going on inside myself.

However, he acknowledged, there were times when one *did* need an entire packet – for example, during menstruation a woman might need the iron from chocolate. This was an example of the conception of body wisdom I had been looking for in the Alexander Technique, yet it was the kind of thinking not entirely present in the writings of Alexander himself, because of their emphasis on conscious control which did not allow for an unconscious 'bodily knowing'. It was not that the contemporary Alexander Technique (or my teacher) placed less emphasis on conscious control, but that Alexander Technique's meanings and contexts were negotiated and in some cases supplemented by other developments and ways of thinking.

The impressions that Alexander teachers had about my ability to promote the Technique were not wrong, however. It was certainly the case that when I gave academic presentations about my work, people would approach me afterwards, not to ask for clarification on some point I had made but to ask if I knew where they could find an Alexander teacher to take lessons with. This happened whether or not my presentation itself criticized aspects of the Technique. Therefore while I originally felt that perhaps my critiques were a betrayal of the trust of my research participants who believed that I might in fact promote the Technique, I realized that their aims were being realized alongside my own; I was criticizing potentially racist and eugenic aspects of Alexander Technique, yet those who had never heard of the Technique before were also taking away knowledge about it and interest in it. My critiques did not affect the Alexander Technique's credibility as a practice; and this was not my desire, I was occasionally left to wonder whether the critiques made any difference at all. Rather than deconstructing the Alexander Technique and its principles, my goal began to include offering something back to my participants. I wanted them to consider the issues I was raising in relation to their teaching practices, rather than confining my

findings to the academy. Throughout the course of my research I often found myself wondering, as Becker (1967) put it, whose side I was on. Was I criticizing or promoting the Alexander Technique? Could I ever do both? The answers, it seemed, shifted throughout the course of my research.

Managing impressions

Impression management was another crucial issue in my research. Coffey (1999: 65) discusses how dress and personal appearance are crucial to the way we present ourselves in ethnographic settings. How we appear often determines the extent to which participants will trust us and whether they believe we understand the world in which they live. In my field of research, I found that my comportment was crucial. I was in my mid-twenties at the time of undertaking this research, and afraid that my youth and my 'American accent' (I am Canadian) would lead to my not being taken seriously. Wanting to appear professional, I never wore jeans to an interview, although many of my participants did. I was less stringent in how I presented myself to my Alexander teacher, with whom I developed a more long-standing relationship. During the interviewing process, I was extremely conscious of how I sat, stood and drank my tea. I put what I had learned in my Alexander lessons to good use. Often the people I interviewed were more relaxed than I was, yet I felt that if I were to relax too much, I would be taken as a complete outsider who had not yet grasped the 'essence' of Alexander Technique.

Challenges in the field

'The field' is often a place of discomfort. Atkinson (1990) argues that 'the ethnographer's journey of discovery and self-discovery/revelation constitutes an account of personal development. It has features of a *quest* – a sort of voyage of search, adventure and exploration … The ethnographer presents him or herself as anti-hero, blundering and coping in strange and adverse circumstances' (1990: 106). My Alexander Technique teacher and many of the participants I interviewed told me that movement re-education techniques caused major shifts in people's lives, and that often these shifts

---

Box 33.4 Impression management with one interviewee

One man I spoke to was in his seventies and had a reputation within the Alexander community for blunt speech. When he rang me to inquire about being interviewed, he interrogated me about my research and its purpose, accused me of being vague and hiding my real intentions, and demanded to know my methodology, my background in Alexander Technique, and my teacher's name and background. I later learned that the issue of lineage, or who had trained with whom, was a very important one among Alexander teachers. This participant concluded by telling me that I was 'a baby who didn't know what she was getting into', and that he felt my research methods were unlikely to yield the results I was interested in, but then abruptly consented to being interviewed. It was possibly the most gruelling 11 minute phone conversation I had ever been involved in. I approached the interview with a good deal of hesitancy, but found after the first few minutes that I was able to establish a rapport, in part *because of* my youth and inexperience rather than in spite of it. I asked many questions I had been afraid I would not be able to broach. At the end of the interview, he invited me to stay for tea, and introduced me to one of his pupils, who became another research contact for me. He also quizzed me about my love life and whether or not I was having an affair with my Alexander teacher! I said that I definitely was not, but it became clear that no matter what kind of professional distance I tried to construct with dress, comportment and manner, participants sometimes challenged it, and I learned to accept this. When I left this particular interview, the participant told me he had been 'expecting some unfocused, pimply-nosed American', but that I had turned out to be quite all right, and a good listener. His evaluation was both a relief and a source of amusement.

---

were accompanied by tears and emotional upset. This is in keeping with the view that emotions are embedded in ways of holding one's body. One participant told me of a time while training to become an Alexander teacher when she had broken down after a realization about why she was always leaning forward:

> … I remember one Sunday afternoon … I knew I was standing always leaning forward, and I thought why am I doing that, why am I doing that? And suddenly I cried for three hours, and then I remembered I was always rushing. And then I remembered when my mother, she was quite a fast walker, and there was a scene when I said don't walk that fast, don't walk that fast, and she continued walking, and I was really worried I would lose her.

Another Alexander teacher told me she was aware of marriages that had broken down when one partner undertook training in the Alexander Technique. A teacher trainee in the early stages of her training programme explained the tensions, frustrations and difficulties of doing Alexander work on such an intensive level. All participants seemed to indicate that I might eventually go through this type of emotional upheaval myself, yet my own Alexander lessons never bothered me. I was quite comfortable having my body manipulated into various positions and being asked to think of a particular direction or exercise. I reflected that this had to do with my prior experience with other movement re-education techniques and my dance background, which had made me accustomed to such changes. This would surely have been different had I not been working from this background. It was not until I visited an Alexander teacher training school that I began to understand how difficult the work of changing one's comportment could be.

The training school lasted for several hours in the morning. It was held in the living room of two established Alexander teachers who had chosen to set up a school. Ten students stood in front of a circle of chairs, projecting Alexander's directions for 'Good Use of the Self', lengthening their necks and backs and dropping their pelvises toward the floor. Each at their own pace, they sat down slowly, then stood up again, as I had been directed to do in Alexander lessons. Their concentration was palpable. The two established teachers circulated, working on each student individually, guiding their bodies into subtly different positions, here and there giving them a verbal direction as well as a physical one. More advanced students began to work on each other. Both the teachers and I seemed uncertain as to whether I was there as a participant or an observer. I compromised by sitting most of the time, practising my own Alexander directions. My back began to get quite stiff. Eventually, two of the braver students came over and asked if they could work on me. I agreed, but found that their hands were hesitant and both of us were frustrated when I did not understand their directions. There was a mid-morning break with tea, biscuits and presentations of student writing about the Technique. This was followed by a critique and suggestions from the other students.

After the break, the students returned to what they had been doing earlier, except that now they all practised working on each other, with direction from the two teachers. As a new and relatively inexperienced body, the teachers encouraged students to work with me. By the end of the session, I was exhausted, tense and uncomfortable. I had had more Alexander work done on me in a few hours than in any of my previous lessons, and it unsettled me. I sat in a coffee shop eating a sandwich and writing my field notes, unable to lose my erect posture. I felt as if I had been neutralized, shifted, and as if part of myself that I liked had been temporarily taken away from me. It took several more hours for this feeling to wear off, but the memory of that discomfort stayed with me. Although this experience had been uncomfortable, it made me better able to relate to some of the experiences of my interviewees. Thus, my personal experience became an important filter for interpreting fieldwork evidence.

Field notes

I took *field notes* at the end of each lesson, using my tape recording to prompt my memory of what we had done and talked about. I had initially assumed that my field notes would tell a story, yet as the months went by I became discouraged and bored by them. The minute observations about whether we had spent 10 minutes or 20 doing 'table work' that day, or when my teacher asked me to stand, sit, or move my arm in a particular way, seemed incredibly dull and irrelevant. Since I was largely chronicling a set of lessons in a technique about re-educating bodies, I had less sense of 'narrative' than ethnographers doing research in other communities. Much was unspoken, and this could not be captured on tape. Nor would video-taping the lessons have helped. These processes were internal; much of Alexander Technique is taught through touch, and words are associated with this touch only loosely, as pointers and reminders. I could record the words, but the feeling was more challenging.

I knew that, like all ethnographers, I was making editorial choices about what went into the notes, and I began to wonder if I had made the wrong choices, if there was something I was overlooking. Kleinman (1999: 26) points out that ethnographers can never give a complete picture of the field they know: 'We pick and choose, even if our mentors told us to "write everything down".' When I mentioned my dissatisfaction to my supervisor, she told me she was not surprised that I had found these notes dull and lacking in relevant data, and that I would probably find more in them than I had initially imagined. When I went back over them, I discovered that she was right. Far from failing to capture any sense of the Alexander Technique, they did begin to articulate what was in effect a very strange bodily procedure. In how many other environments is one asked to stand in front of the mirror and 'direct the head to go forward and up, back to lengthen and widen?' What process of repetition and experience has to go on for this phrase to be associated with a particular change in comportment? Taken together, my field notes gave a sense of my own progression through the technique, and this was incredibly useful when comparing to the stories of others. I had a sense of the Alexander Technique which, without personal experience or taken without the critical reflection the notes provided, I would not have had. Without this I would not have been able to elicit the same kinds of stories from my participants, nor would I have had the same sense of what to ask them.

What my field notes did not provide was much data on the notion of body wisdom. I was marginally aware of this absence and it was one cause of my dissatisfaction with them, but it was clarified by several interviews with practitioners of the other movement re-education techniques I was looking at for comparison. The emphasis on 'conscious control' in Alexander Technique meant that a kind of subconscious bodily wisdom was not desirable because one was always striving to make one's comportment conscious. This was not the case in other techniques like Feldenkrais or Body–Mind Centring. I came to realize that this was partly historical; that body wisdom itself was foreshadowed in Alexander Technique with the references to naturalness and evolutionary stages, but got a much fuller articulation in the 1960s and 1970s through alternative health and 'New Age' movements. This is where my discourse analysis and sense of historical development became crucial background for my discoveries 'in the field'.

Conclusion

Through my ethnography, I found that within the Alexander Technique traces of the eugenic and racist discourses did persist, but that these varied to a great extent between practitioners. Where one teacher lamented the loss of beautiful comportment among 'black people in Brixton', whom she believed had been corrupted from their natural and savage state by British society, another teacher told me he absolutely rejected the principle that some cultures were more civilized or less natural than others or that it was possible to make developmental comparisons between them. Most participants believed in some kind of natural body, but accounts of what this looked like, or who if anyone possessed it, were variable. Most commonly I was told that children had this natural body, but that through the process of childhood socialization they tended to lose it somewhere between the ages of 4 and 12. This was caused by being asked to deny their natural instincts and conform to the standards of 'civilized society'. Although this was present in the writings of Alexander, it was given a new emphasis by his later followers, and other natural bodies, such as the savage body, were mentioned less. It was clear that Alexander Technique as a discourse had shifted, and that Alexander's original writings were very much negotiated and re-interpreted by later practitioners. This is something that developed because of my choice to use ethnography, and would not have been provided by a strictly textual approach.

Throughout this chapter, I have described some of the challenges and rewards of ethnography in relation to my research. Choosing ethnography as

---

Box 33.5 Web pointers for dance ethnography and Alexander Technique

Alexander Technique in the UK
www.stat.org.uk

Alexander Technique International
www.ati-net.com

The Complete Guide to the Alexander Technique
www.alexandertechnique.com/

Dance ethnography
www.arab-esque.org/ethnography.html

Visit the website for this book at www.rsbook.co.uk to link to these web pointers.

a research method led me to consider my field of study in a very different light than a less embodied approach would have. I became less critical of Alexander Technique, and more sympathetic. Yet I retained a certain distance which was strengthened by my role as both participant and observer. These roles at times seemed contradictory, yet overall they have enabled me to provide a more balanced critique of Alexander Technique.

My embodied experience of Alexander Technique was a necessary resource for interviewing.

Interviewees frequently referred to my experiences, making connections and asking me if I had had similar experiences. The difficulty was in translating these experiences into a written format. Bodily experience, particularly experience conveyed through touch, is often overlooked or ignored in academic texts. In my field notes, I tried to be as specific as possible, knowing that in any attempt to put experience into words, something is lost in translation. Ethnography may be as much a process of *constructing* a social world as it is of *describing* it.

34

My research practice

Clive Seale

CONTENTS

In this case study I illustrate how many of the key concepts and methods outlined in this book have been interweaved with my own research practice over a period of some years. This practice has developed over a number of research projects. I will focus on work that I have done since 1987 in the medical sociology field, largely concentrating on investigations of the experience of approaching death and the way in which people represent these experiences in interviews and in mass media. This work, then, has encompassed survey methods, statistical as well as qualitative analysis, and qualitative thematic analysis of both interviews and mass media texts. I hope in presenting this that you will get a sense of how a research career can develop, the researcher picking up a variety of skills and influences from the surrounding work environment, to form a personal style of craft practice.

Designing a social survey

I began my work in this area when I joined the Institute for Social Studies in Medical Care (a research unit based in London) in the mid-1980s. Until then I had worked in educational research, initially doing an ethnographic observational study of teaching methods in higher education, then moving on to interview, questionnaire and survey work on projects in education and health studies. I came to the Institute to assist Ann Cartwright, its director, in repeating a survey she had done in 1969, called *Life before Death* (Cartwright et al., 1973). This had been a study in which Ann had used death certificates to draw up a

representative national *sample* of deaths occurring in 1969 and employed a team of interviewers to carry out a *structured interview* with people in the community who had known the deceased in order to find out the circumstances people faced in the 12 months before death. A lot had changed since 1969, both in terms of the structure of available services and the demographic profile of elderly people, so a new study that would compare the situation in 1987 with that in 1969 was appropriate. To that end, Ann had formulated a *research proposal* and successfully obtained funding from the Medical Research Council for a repeated study. Thus this new study would be part of a *time series* design, based on a sample selected in the same way as in 1969, asking the same (and some new) questions, so that trends over time could be identified. The aims of the study, in the form in which they appeared in the original research proposal, are shown in Box 34.1.

The advantage of using death certificates as a *sampling frame* is that (unlike almost every other available sampling frame apart from birth certificates) they supply almost complete coverage of the *population* which our sample was designed to represent. The disadvantage, of course, is that the key person who might explain what life was like before death is dead! We therefore had to interview *proxy* respondents who could tell us about the time before death, namely relatives and other people in the community who had known the deceased.

Considerable methodological debate has occurred since that time, as more studies like this were done during the 1990s, concerning the

---

Box 34.1 Aims of the study of 'Life before Death'

1 To describe the last year of the lives of a random sample of adults dying in 1987.
2 To make comparisons with the earlier study and identify changes in the nature and availability of care and in the attitudes and expectations of lay and professional carers.
3 To make some assessment of the influence of the hospice movement on these changes.
4 To describe, in more detail than was done in the 1969 study, the institutional care of people in the year preceding their death.
5 To determine the experiences and views of the doctors and nurses involved in the care of these people in the last year of their lives.
6 To describe the care and support given to close relatives both after and before the death.

adequacy of using proxy respondents rather than interviewing terminally ill people directly (for example, McPherson and Addington-Hall, 2003). Although some differences in views have been found when the accounts of both have been compared, for our project the decision to interview *retrospectively* in this way meant that we were not just finding out about people designated as 'terminally ill' before they died (a group that is actually a minority of people who die). Our sample included people who collapsed and died suddenly without warning, one person who had been murdered, many people who had illnesses from which the possibility of recovery had been in the balance, and quite a few who had just become very old indeed and had breathed their last without necessarily being diagnosed with life-threatening diseases. Because we did not rely on health or social service records to draw up the sample we were able to see who was 'reached' by such official services and who slipped through this net. For example, in two or three cases we interviewed environmental health officers who had cleaned up human remains after an isolated, elderly person had died and lain undetected for some time. No one else had been available to interview since such the relatives of such people were often non-existent, and neighbours knew nothing about the deceased. The deaths of people like this would not have been covered in some *prospective* study of people designated as 'dying'. Additionally, the decision to interview proxy respondents meant that we could find out about the events that happened around the time of death (often very important to the 'quality' of dying) as well as some details of how things were for family members and others after the death.

Sampling and response rates

The sample of death certificates was *clustered* in 10 areas of England. Although we might have chosen the sample from a list of all the deaths in the country that year, we knew that this would involve interviewers travelling all over the country, and that this would be impossibly expensive. Clustering meant that we could employ two interviewers in each local area, whose travel costs would be more reasonable. The areas were chosen from

groupings of electoral wards, *stratified* according to geographical region and the level of provision of hospice services (specialist services for the care of people with terminal illness). They were also selected with a probability proportionate to the number of deaths that occurred in them (so that areas where there were a lot of deaths had a greater chance of being selected than areas with very few deaths). Finally, an extra group of deaths was selected occurring in hospices, since these were rare in the sample overall and we wanted to investigate such deaths in particular detail. Thus, the sample was a *stratified cluster sample*, the clusters selected with a *probability proportionate to size*, with *disproportionate* selection of hospice deaths (these extra deaths being used only in some analyses).

Table 24.1 shows the sample sizes and response rates for the surveys associated with the study, which also involved surveys of doctors and nurses who had attended the people who had died. Consultants and domiciliary nurses were sent postal questionnaires asking for their general views about the adequacy of services in their area, and were interviewed about the specific people in the main study sample for whom they had cared. General practitioners were just sent a postal questionnaire asking about their general views.

In our reporting of the study we did a considerable amount of work to establish whether the *non-response* of some people introduced any *response bias* (Cartwright and Seale, 1990). From the death certificates, for example, we could see whether responders to the main study were different from non-responders on certain key *variables* such as age at death, gender and whether married or not. We found, for example, that deaths of people aged 45–54 were slightly over-represented, but on most variables where it was possible to check, there were no significant biases.

Research questions and interviewing on the main study

The interview was designed as a *structured interview schedule* with some *closed* and *fixed choice* items and some *open-ended* questions. Many of the items were the same as in the 1969 study so that comparisons over time could be made, al-

Table 24.1   *Sample sizes and response rates study of 'Life before Death'*

Survey of:	Sample size	Response (N)
Relatives, friends and others in the community (the 'main study')	800	80% (639)
(with 11 extra hospice deaths)	811	80% (646)
General practitioners (family doctors)	397	62% (245)
Consultants (hospital doctors)		
General	323	65% (211)
Specific episodes	525	43% (226)
Domiciliary (home) nurses[a]		
General	100	92% (92)
Specific	125	90% (113)

[a]The apparently high response rate for domiciliary nurses masks the fact that it was only possible to identify a nurse in 45% of all episodes of care reported by relatives, friends and others.

though there were some new questions. In general, design of the interview schedule was informed by *policy* and *practitioner* considerations rather than social theory. For example, a major area of debate and discussion amongst health care practitioners caring for people with terminal illness had been how much to tell people with terminal cancer about their condition. In professional journals that we had read and conferences we had attended we were aware that there was a widespread belief that telling people and being open was best, this attitude of openness being a reversal of earlier practices in which a 'conspiracy of silence' had often occurred. In the 1950s, for example, it had been common for doctors and relatives to agree that a person with terminal disease ought not to be told that they were dying (Novack et al. 1979; *Lancet*, 1980). We wanted to know if this had changed and, if it had, whether it was a good thing in the eyes of people who had known dying

people. We therefore asked the questions shown in Box 34.2, along with others about who had done any telling and how respondents felt about how it was done.

In addition to circling numbers to indicate responses to the fixed choice questions, interviewers also wrote down verbatim the answers people gave to open-ended questions and were encouraged to write down (both during the interview and after it) as much as possible of what interviewees said, as far as possible in the interviewees' own words. In some cases this amounted to the collection of a great deal of talk (though clearly this was subject to the speed at which interviewers could write, and their interpretations of what was important to record, since none used tape recorders). This *qualitative* material was later to prove an important resource, supplementing and extending the initial statistical analyses of the interview data.

Box 34.2   Questions about telling people about terminal illness

- Did you know, half know, or not know that (deceased) was likely to/might die? (Knew / Half knew / Did not know)
- Did (deceased) know he/she was likely to/might die? (Yes certain / Yes, probably / Probably not / No, definitely)

Ethical issues

We were aware that this was a sensitive topic and that approaches to bereaved people requesting them to talk at length about the illnesses and deaths of their close relatives (often spouses or parents, sometimes their children who had died) could generate a considerable amount of distress. I had personally been concerned about this when I came to be interviewed about the research position and had resolved to inquire closely into the methods of the study in order to ascertain, for myself, that it was going to be well designed. I felt that it was important to ensure that people were not put through harrowing experiences for the sake of a study that was poorly conceived and unlikely to generate benefits. I was reassured by Ann's evident experience in doing social surveys that this worry was unfounded.

However, I was concerned when I heard about how Ann was proposing interviewers ought to approach potential respondents for the main study. She advocated that interviewers simply knock on the door of the residence of the deceased (or the door of the person who had registered the death), introduce themselves and the study and, if the respondent proved willing, go ahead with the interview then and there. I thought this could lead to some vulnerable elderly people feeling pressurized and welcoming people into their homes for an experience they might later regret. Ann (who by that time was close to retirement age herself and who had a lot more experience of working with elderly respondents than I had) did not share these worries. Her argument was that an approach of the sort that I advocated (involving a letter to respondents warning them of the interviewer's pending visit) would raise unnecessary anxieties that the interviewer would not be present to address and result in a lower response rate. Thus the scientific adequacy of the study and its likely capacity to produce results that would help improve services would be diminished.

Ann was the leader of the project, and we went down her route on this issue. It is of interest to note that in a later repeat of the study on a much larger sample (Addington-Hall and McCarthy, 1995), where a preliminary letter was sent, the response rate dropped by 10%. In practice, many interviewees said informally to interviewers that they found the experience of being interviewed helpful (even though it may have involved recollecting painful memories). Only two complaints about the interviewing were made, both by daughters of people who had been interviewed. One of them complained that her mother's memories of poor treatment by the hospital had been stirred up by the experience, so that her mother now planned to complain about it, whereas before her daughter had managed to persuade her not to cause any such trouble.

In order to do the study we had to get clearance from 19 different health authority ethical committees. Seventeen of these gave us clearance; two did not. The story of our mixed experiences of ethical committees has been told elsewhere (Cartwright and Seale, 1990). Respondents were given a letter explaining the study by the interviewer, containing information about how to contact me should they have any further questions about the study after the interviewer had left. They also signed a form indicating their *informed consent* to take part.

Initial data analysis

The main aims of the study could be addressed by statistical analysis and for this we used SPSS. Data were entered from the completed interview schedules and questionnaires twice, the second time being a check on accuracy. Initial analysis was aimed at *cleaning* the data since data entry is not the only point at which errors can occur. The questionnaire was long and complex, with numerous 'skips' and 'routing' instructions to avoid asking interviewees about experiences that they had not had (for example, someone who died instantly in an accident would not be asked questions about illnesses that led to death). If interviewers had made errors in following skip instructions, or had circled the wrong numbers on fixed choice items, illogical combinations of information could occur and could be checked for (for example, a 45- year-old with a 40-year-old daughter).

After cleaning, the majority of our work involved production of *univariate* and *bivariate* analyses in the form of *frequency counts* and *tabulations*. Where tables were produced, the *chi-square* test of statistical significance was applied to see if the *p-value* justified generalizing from the *sample* to the *population* of all deaths. A tabulation, involving comparison of 1990 data with the earlier 1969 survey, is shown in Table 34.2. (Although the 1990 survey was done after the 1987 one (see an account of this in the section below) the tabulation is a good one for showing how trends over time could be identified in these *time series* data; it is also fairly typical of the kind of analyses we did on the 1987 data.)

Have a close look at Table 34.2 and try to say what it is telling you about changes over time. If you have read and understood Chapter 24 in this book and done the associated exercises in Part IV you should be able to 'read' this table for its messages in the same way in which you read ordinary text.

We found that not only were people with terminal illnesses more likely to be said to have known that they were dying in the 1980s compared with 1969, but that this was due (largely) to hospital doctors having told them this directly. Contrary to some press coverage of insensitive communication of such 'bad news' by doctors, analysis of open-ended responses to a question asking about how interviewees felt about the way in which their relative or friend had been told indicated few criticisms and much praise. Thus 47% of the open comments (which were *post-coded* into categories and entered into SPSS) praised the manner of telling; a further 47% simply described the way it was done without offering an evaluation of the manner of telling; only 6% involved criticism of the person who had told.

We wrote up the statistical analyses as a series of papers appearing in academic and professional journals covering different aspects of the survey. Later, these papers were collected together and

Table 34.2 *Prevalence of awareness contexts, by cancer and other causes*[a]

Cancer

Did you know, half know, or not know that (deceased) was likely to/might die?

		Knew	Half knew	Didn't know
Did (deceased)	Yes, certain	50.8 (18.9)	4.4 (0)	2.4 (0.6)
know he/she was	Yes, probably	17.2 (23.3)	5.0 (2.5)	2.8 (1.3)
likely to/might	Probably not	5.9 (8.2)	1.6 (0)	1.5 (0)
die?	No, definitely	4.4 (38.4)	0.5 (1.9)	3.5 (5.0)

1990 N = 1700 (= 100%)
1969 N = 159 (=100%)

Non-cancer

Did you know, half know, or not know that (deceased) was likely to/might die?

		Knew	Half knew	Didn't know
Did (deceased)	Yes, certain	20.8 (18.8)	5.0 (0.9)	3.5 (2.9)
know he/she was	Yes, probably	12.0 (18.8)	8.7 (4.4)	5.4 (1.8)
likely to/might	Probably not	4.6 (9.4)	3.0 (0.9)	6.4 (2.1)
die?	No, definitely	8.5 (22.3)	3.3 (3.2)	18.8 (14.7)

1990 N = 906 (= 100%)
1969 N = 341 (= 100%)

[a]Figures are percentages of the total, with figures for 1969 in parentheses. Relatives and close friends only are included. In 576 cases (18.1%) in 1990 the respondent could not say what their or the deceased's state of awareness was. In 1969 this figure was 211 (29.7%).

appeared, in edited form, as a book (Seale and Cartwright 1994). These reports were largely devoted to providing information about the adequacy of services available to people in the last year of life, the concerns being derived from the immediate concerns of policy makers and health care practitioners.

Multivariate analysis

Very little analysis for these papers and the book involved more than two variables at a time. At most, the *multivariate* analysis that we did involved breaking a tabulation down by the values of some third variable. For example, we might want to see how a relationship between two variables – say, social class and use of hospice services – changed according to whether men or women were involved. Although this is, technically, 'multivariate' (in the sense that it involves three rather than two variables), an analysis like this is not primarily devoted to establishing *causal arguments* in the manner suggested by the *elaboration paradigm*. At the time my research practice in the area of statistics was pretty basic and Ann had spent a career designing imaginative and thorough data-collection exercises, the analysis of which only needed to be simple in order to make important points.

A lot of social research gets done by people working on fixed term contracts, and by the time we came to the end of this three-year study the Department of Health (who funded the core staff of the Institute) had decided to use Ann's retirement to close the Institute. I had to find a job and was lucky enough to be appointed to a lectureship at the University of East London. It was my first permanent job after 10 years of working on a series of fixed term research contracts. As part of my continuing research effort I became involved in helping researchers at University College, London, who wanted to do a similar but larger scale survey in particular health authorities, focusing on cancer deaths in some detail.

It was only after I had been required as a newly appointed lecturer to teach the multivariate techniques that I had never actually used as a researcher, that I began to see how multivariate analysis of this new survey might pay off. I went to a conference at around this time in which representatives of the Voluntary Euthanasia Society (VES) crossed swords with representatives of the hospice movement opposed to the legalization of euthanasia. A central issue in the debate about whether to legalise euthanasia concerned the role which good care (and particularly hospice care) played in reducing the distress that led some people to say that they wanted help with dying sooner, perhaps in the form of a lethal injection from a doctor. Many people believed that hospice care, if provided in a way that was accessible to all, would reduce the incidence of requests for euthanasia since suffering would thereby be relieved. I saw that, with the data available to me, it could be possible to treat this as an empirical, testable proposition in a debate that was otherwise dominated by philosophers, moral entrepreneurs and people speaking from selective, anecdotal evidence.

I have explained in Chapter 25 (see particularly the discussion of Table 25.3) how my colleagues and I used *logistic regression* to analyse the data from the new study. This analysis tested out the robustness of the surprising finding that people receiving hospice services were actually *more* likely to be said to have wanted euthanasia than people experiencing similar levels of dependency and distress who did not receive hospice services. This, and other analyses relevant to the social issue of euthanasia was reported in a series of three journal articles (Seale and Addington-Hall, 1994, 1995a, 1995b). A later analysis (Seale et al., 1997) provided a plausible explanation for this finding: people who receive hospice care tend to be people who like to plan for things. Arranging for hospice care and thinking seriously about euthanasia as an option are part and parcel of this planning mentality. This is something which the social theorist Anthony Giddens (1991) has described as linked to the reflexive formation of self identity that is quite prevalent in societies that he describes as 'late modern'.

Qualitative analysis

When, about two years later, I moved from the University of East London to the Sociology

Department in Goldsmiths College, London I began to change the way I worked. This involved changing emphasis from quantitative to qualitative analysis, and using *social theory* as much as *social policy* concerns to generate research questions. I also became interested in developing a sociological analysis of the place that death has in contemporary society, an interest that was to result some years later in a book on this subject (Seale, 1998). I knew that a wealth of qualitative data lay more or less unused in the handwritten notes on interview schedules from the study. I was lucky enough to get a grant to pay a team of typists to enter this material into a word processor.

Out of this material I did a number of new analyses of the qualitative data from the survey of deaths in 1987 (Seale, 1995a, 1995b, 1996). I will focus here on one analysis in particular, published as an article entitled 'Dying alone' in the journal *Sociology of Health and Illness*.

Dying alone: interview accounts

I got interested in what happened when people died alone for a number of reasons. I was in general aware of arguments within the literature on the sociology of death concerning the apparent 'denial of death' in modern societies which, some argued, meant that elderly people were often neglected and dying people ignored. I knew that a significant contribution of the hospice movement had been to try to reverse this, so that people were never 'alone' when close to death but 'accompanied'. I also started to notice in my local newspaper occasional reports of elderly people who died alone in their homes, only to be discovered days or weeks later. I was interested in the high moral tone that journalists writing these reports adopted, suggesting that such deaths were a reflection of an uncaring, age- and death-denying society where community values were in decline. I tried to find out whether anyone had ever studied this phenomenon and found just one study, by Bradshaw et al. (1977) of the circumstances that had led to the deaths of 203 people 'found dead' in their homes between 1960 and 1977. This report shared journalists' concerns about the issue and aimed to discover the factors that placed people 'at risk' of dying alone in this way. I felt

that Bradshaw's research questions were driven by journalistic and social policy concerns rather than sociological ones. I was more interested in the meaning that these events had for people, and the way such meanings were constructed in talk.

I used Ethnograph, a software program for the management of qualitative data, to implement a *coding scheme* for this work. Initially it was necessary to read through all of the interviews to identify general topics in which I was interested (see Box 34.3a). I then used Ethnograph to retrieve (for interviews where the person was said to have died alone) text that belonged to the coding category DALONE and read it, developing a second coding scheme for this material (Box 34.3b). For material categorized under particular codes in this second scheme I then developed a third and final coding scheme (Box 34.3c).

My report contained both statistical and qualitative material and so is an example of *mixed methods* research. The statistical analysis reported the characteristics of people who died alone (for example, they tended to live alone, be unmarried and to have no living children or siblings), contributing knowledge about what Bradshaw et al. had called 'risk factors' for this event, treating the interview data as a *resource* for discovering such facts. The qualitative analysis was much more oriented towards treating the interview as a *topic* in which speakers created a 'version' of reality and sought both to maintain their moral reputations and to 'repair' the damage to their own basic sense of security that a death like this could produce.

I found that deaths alone were generally said to be regretted by the people who reported on them. If they occurred in hospitals or other institutions they were generally seen as being, nevertheless, 'orderly' and 'managed' deaths. Where deaths alone occurred in private homes, though, there was a greater sense of disruption. The accounts of these deaths often focused on explaining 'what must have happened' in the moments before death, and to 'anaesthetize' the subjective experience of suffering, abandonment and isolation that dying alone might have involved. Box 34.4 contains some quotations that illustrate these themes.

In the article that reported this work I offered an interpretation of the interview talk that was

---

Box 34.3 Developing a coding scheme for analysing accounts of dying alone

(a) Some of the general topic codes
- AGE: How age affected the person, what it is like to be old, what you 'must expect' when old
- LALONE: Living alone – what it is like, how the speaker or the person felt about the person living alone
- DALONE: Dying alone – what led up to it, how it happened, how the speaker feels about it

(Other codes: FRIEND, HELP, HOSTILE, IFONLY, INFO, OBLIG, OPH, PLACE, AWARE, BERAVE, ABUSE, SUFFER, PAIN)

(b) Some of the codes for dying alone (subcategories of DALONE)
- FOUND: How the person was 'found' dead
- LEARN: How the speaker learned that the person had died alone
- MUST: 'What must have happened' to lead to a death alone
- REALLY: Where the status of dying alone is in doubt
- FEELR: How the speaker felt about the person having died alone

(c) Some subcategories of FEELR
- WOULD: What the speaker would have done if only they had known the person was going to die
- BAD: Dying alone was a bad thing
- GUILT: Feelings of guilt about not being there
- BLAME: Blaming someone (usually hospital staff) for a death alone
- FAIR: Feeling it is unfair that the person died alone (for example, 'I visited every day – it was the only day I missed')

---

influenced by the ideas about the meaning of funeral ritual developed by Hertz (1960), whose anthropological work with the Dayak people in Borneo, first published in 1907, had been influenced by the ideas of Durkheim. Hertz (and Durkheim) had suggested that funerals were an opportunity for communities to repair damage to the 'collective conscience' or community spirit that was damaged by the death of a member. Although (sometimes elaborate) funeral rituals in 'primitive' societies had been studied from this point of view by many early anthropologists, it had been assumed by many sociologists that we no longer lived in a society where such ritualized repair was possible. I argued, against this view, that in fact the talk in the interviews could be

---

Box 34.4 What dying alone meant to interviewees

'I wish I had been with him at the end. I know he wouldn't have known I was there, but I wish I had been. We'd been together since schooldays; we neither of us ever went out with anyone else.'

'It must have been sudden. There was half a bottle of whisky and a small glass. The little glass was on the floor but she hadn't managed a drink. The cork was off the bottle as though she was about to have a drink. She wasn't a drinker. I think she was cold as the fire was switched on high. Her hair was scorched at the back.'

---

understood as containing elements of micro-ritual, repeated discursive themes and repertoires that many of the speakers (unwittingly) shared, so that they were participating in a collective organized activity in their talk. In this respect I drew on my knowledge of both *discourse analysis* and *ethnomethodology* which I felt treated talk similarly as deriving from collectively shared resources that might be considered a form of ritualized activity.

Thus I had shifted in my early concerns with *social policy* issues, developed largely through statistical analyses, to an analysis that derived from an interest in certain *social theories*.

Dying alone: mass media accounts

Death is an absorbing topic and I have always felt privileged to have been given the opportunity to think deeply over a number of years about what it means for people in modern society. Eventually, though, I felt that I needed to move on to other things and, apart from writing about methods and methodology, I became interested in how the mass media present health issues (Seale, 2003). In a recent analysis of newspaper accounts (Seale, 2004b) I returned to the topic of dying alone and decided to compare newspaper reports with the interview reports I had analysed. I wondered what part mass media played in constructing the sense of community that I felt I had detected in the interviews. In this respect I was following the lead of Benedict Anderson (1991), who had claimed that the invention and mass distribution of the daily newspaper had been the occasion for the formation of a new kind of community. He called this an 'imagined community', in which people participated without necessarily knowing or having face-to-face contact with other members.

I proceeded with my study of newspapers by drawing on my knowledge of survey research to select a *sample* that was representative of English-speaking newspapers world wide. For this, I simply downloaded articles from a database of (almost all) such newspapers that contained keywords (for example, 'died alone' or 'die alone' or 'dying alone') occurring within a specific time period. I used a *Boolean search*, therefore to retrieve these articles and I described my sample of articles in much the same way as Ann Cartwright had described our sample of people, trying to investigate any potential biases in coverage and so on.

Analysis proceeded, like the *qualitative thematic analysis* I had done of the interview material, by developing a coding scheme. By this time NVivo had become available for managing such qualitative data and I used many features of that software, finding it to be considerably more sophisticated than the early version of Ethnograph that I had previously used.

The main findings of the newspaper study are outlined in Box 34.5. The first two findings describe features of newspaper reports that differ from the interview material. Newspapers in general like to keep readers interested by presenting stories that are unusual and out of the ordinary, so it was no surprise to find this reflected in the media study. The second finding, though, was a little less expected. There had been a very few occasions in the interview material where speakers had criticized the deceased, but these were treated as *negative instances* because they differed from the general pattern of sentiments. People in the interview situation will have been concerned about their own 'reputations' as having

---

Box 34.5 Newspapers and dying alone: some findings

Newspaper reports:

1 Emphasize shocking and unusual causes of death (for example, murder, drug over-dose, suicide).
2 Often stigmatize the people who died as eccentric or selfish, suggesting that they brought it on themselves.
3 Suggest that deaths alone reflect societal failure.

cared appropriately for the deceased; criticizing the character of the person who died alone might have reflected badly on them. Journalists, on the other hand, are well versed in the business of allocating blame to whoever seems like a likely target. The fact that someone is dead just means that this is more feasible, as the victim cannot answer back.

The third and last finding, though, points to an underlying similarity between newspaper accounts and the sentiments of ordinary people describing a death alone. Both kinds of account stress that this is a regrettable event, reflecting on standards of good neighbourliness and community relations. Here, for example, is an American paper waxing lyrical on this theme, following the suicide of an 80-year-old woman:

> Old age holds special terrors, particularly in a society that worships youth ... In North Carolina, many elderly men and women are treated shamefully – abandoned to their own devices or warehoused in nursing homes that put profit before decency. They are left lying in their own waste. They are neglected and abused. They are left to wander off and die in ditches or in stairwells. Other cultures are wiser. They treat their elders with respect and insist they live well ... things unbearable in isolation are bearable shared. There's no need for any of us to die afraid and alone. (*Greensboro News and Record,* 5th October 1999)

I concluded that newspapers amplify and orchestrate themes that circulate in the community at large, although they have somewhat different methods for doing so. Media reflections on community decline are more elaborated than those in interview accounts, which are generally located more within the speaker's own sense of responsibility and guilt about a death alone, but both accounts participate in building an 'imagined community'.

Conclusion

In this chapter I have given an account of several research projects which, together, show the use of a variety of methods in my personal research practice. In particular, the various projects illustrate shifts between *qualitative* and *quantitative* modes of analysis (including some *mixed methods* work) and the differing relationships I have constructed between findings and research questions derived either from *social policy* or *social theory*. I hope that you will have seen that the apparently dry topic of 'research methods' can come alive when it is integrated into a person's research practice. In the end – and we are at the end of this book – I hope that you too will develop a personal research practice of your own and find similar fulfilment in studying and thinking about methods, as I have done.

Further reading

On the methodological front the best 'further reading' you can do is to study the other chapters in this book. I have also developed some of the ideas about how one can integrate the study of method into personal research practice in Seale (1999). A volume that I have co-edited (Seale et al., 2004) contains somewhat autobiographical accounts of researchers using a wide variety of qualitative (but not quantitative) methods. The book on the *Natural History of a Survey* (Cartwright and Seale, 1990) that I wrote with Ann Cartwright gives a blow-by-blow account of the survey that I describe in the first part of the chapter. If you want to know more about the studies I have described, the various references I have made in the chapter to the publications in which they are reported will give you several leads to follow.

Part IV: Workshop and Discussion Exercises

Workshop and Discussion Exercises

Assembled and edited by *Thomas Zacharias*

These exercises are based on the experience of the contributors (and others in the Department of Sociology at Goldsmiths) teaching research methods to students at both undergraduate and postgraduate levels. They are intended to improve understanding of the ideas expressed in the chapters, and give practice in the techniques described. In many cases they are suitable for group work, where students can join together to do the exercises. They are not intended to be wholly prescriptive: they can be modified to suit particular learning needs. In many cases there is no 'right answer', but the exercises will nevertheless enable you to form a deeper and more practical understanding of the material.

Chapter 2: Selected issues in the philosophy of social science

2.1   What, in your view, are the major features of a *science?*

2.2   Explain the arguments for:

(a)   treating social sciences as analogous to natural sciences and

(b)   rejecting the notion of the methodological unity of natural and social sciences.

2.3   What do you understand by the terms *value freedom* and *objectivity?*

2.4   Why do certain theorists (for example, Stanley and Wise, Rosaldo) criticize the idea that emotions are best kept out of social science?

Chapter 3: Politics, identities and research

3.1   Look closely at the linguistic and typographic choices made by the authors of this chapter. For example, the authors place inverted commas around numerous words, such as 'race', 'women', 'cross-cultural', 'black' and 'non-white'. They use words like 'knowledges' instead of 'knowledge', 'knowers' rather than 'researchers' or 'social scientists', 'problematize' rather than 'question' or 'debate'. One of the authors they refer to is bell hooks, who chooses to write her name in this way, rather than Bell Hooks. What are the reasons for these choices? What are they trying to convey? Should all social and cultural researchers write like this?

3.2   Two of the authors of this chapter were concerned that it be made clear that one of the readings in the 'Student Reader' box (No. 74 Martyn Hammersley: 'Hierarchy and emancipation') was *not* a recommendation that they would wish to make, and that it was something placed there by Clive Seale, the editor of the book. Read Hammersley's piece. (It is also available in the original publication from which it was derived, on pages 45–65 of Hammersley, 1995).

Assess whether it is a piece that advances your knowledge of this area of methodology.

3.3 Choose one or more of the case studies of particular research projects in Chapters 32, 33 or 34, or any piece of social and cultural research which you know well. To what extent are the researchers who did these studies sensitive to the issues raised in Chapter 3? Could their practice be improved by further attention to the politics of research knowledge?

Chapter 4: Developments in social theory

4.1 Take each of the following theoretical perspectives in turn: functionalism, action theory, symbolic interactionism, phenomenology, ethnomethodology, structuralism, post-structuralism and postmodernism. Answer the following questions for *each* perspective:

(a) How could researchers working within this perspective use *quantitative* methods (for example, social surveys, official statistics, content analysis, counting events)?

(b) How could researchers working within this perspective use *qualitative* methods (for example, participant observation, qualitative interviews, semiotics, discourse and conversation analysis)?

(c) Are there any theoretical perspectives where it is not possible to think of examples?

4.2 Why is interpretive social theory said to draw upon *idealism*?

4.3 Which theoretical perspectives illustrate a *realist* approach?

4.4 How might Foucault's genealogical method help researchers who want to understand and alleviate social problems?

Chapter 5: Research and social theory

5.1 This exercise asks you to think further about the different research strategies used by Moerman and Douglas.

(a) How far do (i) Moerman and (ii) Douglas make use of the five points listed towards the end of the chapter to help them theorize about data? (These were *chronology, context, comparison, implications* and *lateral thinking.*)

(b) Imagine that you were carrying out a study of a small group already known to you (for example, a family, a friendship group or club). How could you use either Moerman's or Douglas's ideas to help you work out a research problem and to theorize about your data?

5.2 This exercise encourages you to think further about the different ways of conceiving family life. Imagine that you wish to do an observational study of the family. Now consider the following questions:

(a) What are the advantages and disadvantages of obtaining access to the family household?

(b) In what ways may families be studied outside the household setting? What methodology might you use and what questions could you ask?

(c) What might observation tell you about the 'family' in each of the following settings: law courts, doctor–patient consultations, television soap operas?

(d) Either do a study of one of these settings or write hypothetically about all three.

5.3 What does it mean to say you are studying the 'family' (that is, within inverted commas)?

Chapter 6: Research and social policy

6.1 In the context of any social problem you choose (for example, homelessness, racism, sexism), outline what you think to be a relevant research problem. Now discuss the following questions:

(a) How does your research topic differ from the common-sense version of your selected social problem?

(b) If your research topic sticks very closely to this common-sense version of the problem, how does it benefit from the insights of social science?

(c) If your research problem differs from how we usually see this social problem, how can your proposed research contribute to society?

6.2 This exercise gives you an opportunity to think through the various ways researchers have answered Becker's question: 'Whose side are we on?' You are asked to imagine that research funding is available for whatever topic and research design you prefer.

(a) Suggest a research topic and outline a methodology using one or more of the methods set out in Part II of this book.

(b) Justify the topic and methodology from the point of view of (i) the scholar and (ii) the partisan.

(c) Now select any one article which reports research findings in a social science journal. Which of the positions referred to in (b) does it adopt?

(d) Set out how this position might be criticized from the point of view of (i) the other position and (ii) your own views on the relevance of social science research.

Chapter 7: Validity, reliability and the quality of research

7.1 How would you design a study of the causal influence of police crackdowns on driving behaviour that overcame the threats to internal validity listed in Box 7.1 and the threat to external validity mentioned later in the chapter?

7.2 Seek out and read two studies that represent different 'moments' in the history of qualitative research. For example, choose a study that involves grounded theorizing and another where the author situates him- or herself within postmodernism. How do the studies differ in their conception of what makes a good research study? How might each author apply these criteria to the other's work?

7.3 Choose a research study in an area of work where you have some knowledge of existing literature and assess it in the light of the following questions:

(a) How consistent are the findings with what is already known?

(b) What evidence is supplied to support the credibility of the conclusions and how persuasive is this?

(c) What relevance might the study have for political or practical affairs?

7.4 In relation to a specific study, consider whether its quality would be improved by atten-

tion to the issues raised under the 'positivist' headings of measurement validity, internal and external validity and reliability. To what extent could the modified interpretivist criteria outlined in the chapter be applied to the study? Do these lead you to consider different issues from those raised under the 'positivist' headings?

7.5 This exercise requires you to work with others on some qualitative data, such as some interview transcripts.

Without discussing your ideas with others in your group, read one part of the data transcript (for example, a single interview) and draw up a list of key themes you perceive in the data.

Compare the themes you have identified with those of others in your group. What are the similarities and differences?

Take four or five themes from those identified by members of the group and, working individually again, apply them to some new data (for example, a second interview) by marking parts of the transcript which you believe exemplify each theme.

Compare what you have done with others in the group. What difficulties are there in consistently applying the themes? Does inconsistency matter?

Chapter 8: History of social statistics and the social survey

8.1 What were the chief methodological innovations developed by Booth, Rowntree and Bowley?

8.2 In what ways did the surveys of Booth and Rowntree participate in the Victorian social construction of poverty?

8.3 Assess the argument that the production of social statistics is inevitably linked with the mentality of government.

8.4 Explain the difference between descriptive and explanatory social surveys.

Chapter 9: History of qualitative methods

9.1 Examine a report of an early ethnographic study (for example, by Malinowski, Mead or Evans-Pritchard). Compare this with a more recent report of an ethnographic investigation.

How do the reports differ with regard to:

(a) The *subject position* and field relations of the author (his or her authority, assumed relationship with the reader, with people in 'the field' etc.).

(b) The reporting of data or evidence and the extent to which verbatim material is presented and the links between claims and the evidence for them.

(c) The degree to which the author exhibits *reflexivity* about his or her own role in the process.

9.2 Find two research studies from different periods in which interviewing has been an important method. Assess whether the author has *topicalized* the interview, or has treated it as a *resource*. What would have to be done in each study to implement the alternative approach to that which was used?

9.3 Examine Box 9.9. Considering the research practices prevalent in an earlier *moment* in the history of qualitative method (for example, one of the first two moments listed in Box 9.10), to what extent were the 'sensibilities' listed in Box 9.9 possessed by researchers in those days? What methodological sensibilities did researchers possess in past times that are now *not* listed in Box 9.9. You may wish to answer these questions by referring to a particular research study.

Chapter 10: Ethics and social research

10.1 Consider one of the research projects listed in Box IV.1 or a research project in which you are involved. Establish the following things:

(a) How would you gain the freely given informed consent of those studied? Are there circumstances under which it would be right not to seek consent?

(b) In what way might the research harm the interests of the people involved? Are there any circumstances where harming the interests of those studied is justified?

(c) How would you write up and publicize the study in such a way that it preserves the anonymity and confidentiality of those involved? Are there any circumstances in which the preservation of these is not justified?

Chapter 11: Research design and proposals

11.1 This is a group exercise in defining a research project.

(a) Choose a research topic (e.g. homelessness, racism, sexism, identity, family life).

(b) Write a list of the aims of your research. Think of as many as you can which you believe are relevant to the project. When you have done this, consider each one carefully by asking the questions:

1 How will the aim be achieved – methods, resources, skills, time? Is it realistically possible to achieve it?

2 What results are required for it to be achieved?

3 Is the aim central to your study?

4 Are there any overlaps between the aims? Keep them discrete.

5 Is there a sequence or hierarchy which links one aim to another. If so, are they in the correct order?

6 Are there too many aims to be realistically achievable?

7 What settings could you gain access to in order to study this topic?

11.2 This is designed to help you choose methods for a study.

(a) Choose a research project that someone in your group is planning to conduct.

(b) From the list of methods and sources below choose four that could be applied to the topic and say:

(i) What can these methods and sources tell me about the issue; how could they take further the aims and research questions of the project; would they involve generating new aims?

(ii) Which of these methods and sources is most/least feasible to use? What would the practical issues in implementing them be?

List of methods and sources:
Depth interviews
Focus groups
Observation
Ethnography

Box IV.1 Some research topics that could raise ethical issues

1   The causes and consequences of homelessness for single people
2   The effectiveness of community service orders as a means of rehabilitating offenders
3   The way of life of travellers
4   Assessment of the way the police deal with sexual crime
5   How policy is made in a political party
6   How EEG (electro-encephalogram) readings correlate with emotional states
7   Children's reading preferences
8   Students and how they manage their academic work
9   Quality of terminal care of cancer patients
10 Sexual activity in public settings (e.g. public toilets)
11 The experience of trainee nurses
12 School bullying
13 Racism in football
14 Victims of domestic violence
15 Sex discrimination at work
16 Right-wing political groups
17 New age religion
18 The experience of boys in a ballet school
19 Analysis of archived qualitative interviews with elderly people recollecting wartime experiences
20 Analysis of media representations of ideal female body shape
21 Conversation analysis of calls to a computer help line
22 Ethnographic study of an on-line support group for parents of children with disfiguring conditions
23 Comparative analysis of discourse on immigration in US presidential and British prime ministerial speeches

Semiology/semiotics/content analysis
Textual/discourse analysis
Conversation analysis
The Internet
Documentary sources
Material culture/artefacts
Archives
Social survey (plus secondary analysis of existing survey data)
Official statistics

11.3   With a partner or a small group, choose *one* of the following topics: students who are in paid employment; men who stay at home to look after children while wives or partners go out to work; youth crime. (Alternatively, take a topic from Box IV.1.)

Individually draft an outline research proposal in line with the areas discussed in this chapter, paying particular attention to the aims and objectives, method, data analysis and dissemination. You can use any of the methods in the book.

Discuss your outline proposal with other(s), who should ask questions to clarify the reasons for planning a study in this area, what the study aims to achieve, how it will be done, and whether the findings will be useful. Take note of the questions which you would ask others in order to be convinced of their proposal.

Complete a research proposal form provided by a research funding body. For example, you can download one of these, together with instructions for completing the form, from:

http://eforms.esrc.ac.uk/download.htm

481

Chapter 12: Doing a literature review

12.1   For a given research topic (take, for example, one of the topics listed in Box IV.1) explore and compare the coverage of two or more of the following resources for finding academic literature on the subject:

(a)   Your university library catalogue

(b)   A searchable journal database

(c)   An Internet search engine such as Google

12.2   Examine a journal article reporting original social or cultural research on a topic that interests you. Consider answers to the following questions:

(a)   To what extent is the literature review separated from the rest of the report?

(b)   What connections are made between the analysis of data and the literature review?

(c)   Many literature reviews have a funnel structure, with broad concerns being discussed at the outset, narrowing down to specific questions explored in the research study. Is this literature review like this? Identify sections where broad concerns are discussed and where specific research questions are identified.

(d)   In the concluding section of the report, what references are made by the author to the concerns raised in the literature review?

(e)   Try to find an important article or book on this subject that this researcher has failed to spot.

Chapter 13: Doing social surveys

13.1   Pick one or more of the sampling frames listed in Box IV.2. Discuss the adequacy of these lists in covering the populations concerned. What omissions are there likely to be? What problems of access might there be in getting these lists, and in approaching people listed on them? What stratifying factors are likely to be present and useful for each sampling frame?

13.2   The questionnaire in Box IV.3 is routinely distributed to students following courses at Goldsmiths College, University of London. Lecturers are encouraged to allow students 10 minutes or so to complete it in the penultimate week of a course (chosen because of concern that student attendance for final lectures on courses may be low). Lecturers hand in the completed forms for automatic data input, processing and output of results by a machine designed to read the forms and print out frequencies of responses for each question. Printed results are placed in a file in a common staff resource area and lecturers are encouraged to examine the output.

(a)   Assess the adequacy of the questionnaire design.

(b)   Assess the adequacy of the survey exercise as a whole, taking into consideration the way in which questionnaires are distributed and results reported.

(c)   How would you use a social survey to evaluate and improve an educational course?

Box IV.2   Examples of sampling frames

Covering the general population:
Register of electors; telephone directory; birth certificates; death certificates

Covering institutions
Directory of universities, schools or colleges; health services directory; directory of penal institutions

Covering professional groups
Medical directory; registers of psychologists, nurses, osteopaths; register of chartered surveyors

Some other groups
A university department's list of students attending a course; hospital admissions daily log book; a school register of pupils; an employer's records of employees; a solicitor's records of clients

13.3   In a group of three or more, design a short interview schedule, containing some open, some closed and some pre-coded questions. The topic may be anything of which people in the group can reasonably be expected to have some experience (for example, watching or participating in sports events, studying research methods).

One person should use the interview schedule to interview another person in the group, while others observe, considering the following issues:

1 What difficulties were there in doing the inteview?
2 Did the interviewer appear or feel at ease?
3 Did the respondent appear or feel at ease?
4 Did the respondent find the questions unambiguous and easy to answer?
5 Did he or she find them relevant to his/her life experience?

Swap roles, until everyone has had a go at interviewing, replying, and observing. How would you now redesign the interview schedule?

13.4 Imagine that you are engaged in a small-scale interviewing survey, designed to discover how people feel about balancing the demands of home life with those of their work life. You have the resources to interview about 20 people. How would you select people to interview?

13.5   Examine the questions in Boxes 13.2, 13.5, 13.6. How well do they indicate the concepts which they are designed to indicate? Imagine that you are going to do a survey in which you want to use these concepts. Design alternative questions to indicate the concepts and discuss their adequacy with other members of your group.

Chapter 14: Qualitative interviewing

14.1   The aim of this exercise is to produce interview data on students' experiences of studying and thus to experience some of the problems of asking questions and understanding answers in an unstructured interview.
(a)   The workshop should be divided into groups of three or four.
(b)   Each group should draw up a short *topic guide* for unstructured interviews with other students. Focus on a specific aspect of experience (for example, reasons for coming to university, financial problems, reactions to lectures and classes) and work out some questions.
(c)   Each group should choose an interviewer, an interviewee and one or two observers.
(d)   The interviewer should interview the interviewee using the topic guide. The observer should write down as much as they can of what the interviewee says. Then change roles, and do another interview.
(e)   Compare the two interviews and discuss what you have found out. Consider the language of the questions. What do these take for granted? How far is the interviewer sharing understandings with the interviewee? How could the interview be improved?

14.2   Read the transcript of an interview with Joanna, an Australian woman interviewed for a research project concerning mothers' experiences of child day care centres (Box IV.4)
(a)   How would you characterize the relationship between interviewer and respondent?
(b)   What does this interview tell us about what has happened to Joanna and her child? Construct a list of key themes relating to this and say which segments of talk illustrate each theme.
(c)   What does this interview tell us about the person Joanna wants to be, and about the child that she wants Jared to be? Construct a list of key themes relating to this and say which segments of talk illustrate each theme.

Chapter 15: Using focus groups

15.1   Working in small groups, choose a topic that you could explore through focus group research. Such topics might include questions about public attitudes (e.g. attitudes towards immigration), how audiences interpret media (e.g. consumption of news content; 'readings' of different magazines; the influence of violence on television), or the study of meanings and beliefs (e.g. perceptions of national identity).

Having agreed your topic of study, discuss and note down your responses to the following questions:

Box IV.3   Questionnaire distributed to students

As part of its commitment to Quality Assurance, Goldsmiths seeks to take account of students' views of courses and would be grateful if you would complete this form. Please DO NOT write your name on this form. Please hand it in before you leave the class.

Completing the questionnaire. If a question is not applicable please leave blank. The questionnaire uses a 4-1 scale where 4 = High or Strongly Agree, and 1 = Low or Strongly Disagree, plus a category entitled 'none of these apply.'

Programme of Study (e.g. BA Fine Art)...

Course Title..

Year of Study

Yr 1
Yr 2
Yr 3
Yr 4
Other

Personal Details

	Male	Female
Gender	Male	Female
Full-time / Part-time student	F/T	P/T
UK / European Union student	Yes	No
Overseas student	Yes	No
Registered mature student	Yes	No
Visiting exchange student	Yes	No

	Strongly Agree/High			Strongly disagree/Low	None applied
I have put a lot of effort into this course	4	3	2	1	0
My attendance on this course was good	4	3	2	1	0

Course organization (administrative framework)

The course was, on the whole, well organized	4	3	2	1	0
The course information					
• was issued in good time	4	3	2	1	0
• explained the purpose of the course	4	3	2	1	0
• accurately described the content of the course	4	3	2	1	0
• accurately described assessment methods and procedures	4	3	2	1	0
• gave a clear schedule of activities	4	3	2	1	0
• included a useful preliminary reading list	4	3	2	1	0
The workload was heavier than in other courses	4	3	2	1	0
Written work was handed back within a reasonable time	4	3	2	1	0

	Strongly Agree/High			Strongly disagree/Low	None applied
Essential texts were usually available in the bookshop	4	3	2	1	0
An appropriate range of texts was available in the College Library	4	3	2	1	0
Seminar and lecture rooms were satisfactory	4	3	2	1	0
Course tutors were open to suggestions and constructive criticisms	4	3	2	1	0

Course presentation (teaching)

	Strongly Agree/High			Strongly disagree/Low	None applied
The course was, on the whole, well organized	4	3	2	1	0
Sessions started and finished on time	4	3	2	1	0
Handouts were informative	4	3	2	1	0
Audio-visual aids were used effectively	4	3	2	1	0
Lectures were stimulating and effective	4	3	2	1	0
The course of lectures was coherently structured	4	3	2	1	0
Lecturers allowed/encouraged questions	4	3	2	1	0
Lectures and their related classes were well integrated	4	3	2	1	0
Seminars enhanced my understanding of the subject	4	3	2	1	0
Seminars/workshops/classes helped me develop my own views	4	3	2	1	0
Comments on my work were helpful	4	3	2	1	0
I would recommend this course to next year's students	4	3	2	1	0

Practice-based work (for courses with a workshop or studio element)

	Strongly Agree/High			Strongly disagree/Low	None applied
The course was, on the whole, well organized	4	3	2	1	0
I was satisfactorily advised about the organizational aspects of my practical work	4	3	2	1	0
Access to the workshops/facilities was adequate	4	3	2	1	0
Technical support was helpful	4	3	2	1	0
Adequate training was offered to help me carry out the work myself	4	3	2	1	0
The working atmosphere was constructive	4	3	2	1	0
Health and safety precautions were clearly explained to me	4	3	2	1	0

Please write any other comments on the rear of this form.
For example: how could this course be improved? What were the best and worst features?

(*Source*: DRS Data and Research Services and Goldsmiths College)

Box IV.4   Transcript of a qualitative interview

Interview with Joanna, separated, about Jared, aged 18 months, who has been going to a child care day centre for three months

1   *Q*:   How did you feel during the first week or so that Jared was in
2   day care?

3   *Joanna*:   Ah I worried. I worried a lot because he was very young then about
4   three or four months old. Um but then I used to go and visit him say
5   after two because I had a break and I'd go and visit him in between and
6   he wasn't even interested in ..I stopped doing it because I'd go in
7   and after I'd been there an hour and a half two hours to play with him
8   and he was busily involved in something else and um wasn't grizzly
9   enough to want me.

10   *Q*:   You said you were rather worried. What were you worried
11   about?

12   *Joanna*:   Um I was worried that it was going to affect him not
13   being with me – that he wouldn't get the same love and attention – that
14   he'd cry and miss me and but now I think it's ah I worry more about me
15   missing him than him missing me.

16   *Q*:   How long has Jared been in day care now?

17   *Joanna*:   Since he was three months. So about a year and a bit.
18   He virtually been going there really since he was about two months. I
19   have found though that when we shifted from the country up here he didn't
20   go for about eight weeks and he was … used to cry all the time for the
21   first week or two um then I started to take him back to going into
22   creche.

23   *Q*:   You found it difficult leaving him after?

24   *Joanna*:   Yes I found it difficult I don't know if it was a stage he was
25   going through. That clingy stage or whether he just got so used to being
26   with me he didn't want to ..

27   *Q*: Was that hard for you?

28   *Joanna*:   Yes terribly hard. I don't know if I could leave him if he was
29   the type that cried all the time that I left him because I just … it
30   makes me feel sick. I worry about him being away from me the whole
31   time that he is away … so I'm really glad that he's happy and laughing
32   when he walks in.

33   *Q*:   Have your emotions changed since the first weeks Jared was in day
34   care. If so – how?

35   *Joanna*:   Well I think I've got a really positive outlook for it now I really
36   feel that it's a really good thing for him to be going to day care as an
37   only child – he doesn't have any brothers and sisters to mix with – it
38   teaches him sharing and not being the centre of attention. Um and how
39   to get on with other children and I think it's really important. And I
40   think maybe an only child doesn't learn that early enough if they
41   don't go to something where they are mixing with other children so I

42 think really even if I didn't have to he would go at least a couple
43 of times a week into a local child care centre.

44 *Q*: And if you were perfectly free to choose, how would you have arranged
45 your life since the birth of Jared?

46 *Joanna*: I'd have a nanny ... If I was really going to choose anything I'd
47 have a nanny/housekeeper. [*Jared appeared with something that he*
48 *shouldn't have had – mother quickly removed it – Jared started to cry*].
49 I find he get very bored if he's at home with me I usually by ten o'clock
50 have got to go down the street because he get so restless.

51 *Q*: How about in the future if you were perfectly free to choose?
52 *Joanna*: I'd still have him go into a creche maybe not quite as much as he
53 does at the moment um and I think I would prefer to have more help at a
54 night time.

55 *Q*: So you'd still like a nanny?

56 *Joanna*: A nanny/housekeeper. I mean I wouldn't like her to be bringing him
57 up. But I suppose um somebody who could replace because my parents
58 aren't up here. Somebody who would replace his grandmother I suppose.
59 Somebody ah who I could just ... more of a grandmother figure I suppose.
60 Um just somebody who could help out occasionally a bit ... It's very hard
61 when you've got no ... I've got girlfriends up here but none of them
62 have got children so it's very hard to ... yeah some are having children at
63 the moment so it'll be different once they have them. But I wouldn't
64 leave him with someone who didn't have children because it might put
65 them off.

66 *Q*: Is there anything else you would like to add?

67 *Joanna*: Well I actually feel that it doesn't hurt any child going to
68 child care I think it does depend on the child care centre um and I've
69 been really lucky with both centres he's been to they've been really
70 good. Really good in the way that they're brand new. So they have
71 been very clean bright and new facilities bright windows a good
72 playground which is really important. And the staff have all
73 been new so they're all really enthusiastic um and they really like
74 what they're doing and um I've found also that the children that go to
75 them have been really nice types, and that makes a difference. And um
76 I'm not being classist or anything but I'm not sure if I was living in
77 a housing commission area and going to creche there in those areas I
78 would find a difference. But both times he's been in really nice where
79 the parents are nice types and ah it does affect even on really young
80 children you can tell about the parents. In both the creches he's
81 been in there have been no children swearing being naughty they've been
82 taught discipline and I think that's good and actually the creche is good
83 it teaches them a little more discipline than I do in a way.
84 Sitting when he's eating and things like that where as a sole parent I
85 can get a little bit soft on him so it's good that he does have a little
86 stern-ness.

(*Source*: Lyn Richards)

(a) How would you select groups to participate in the study? How does the selection of these groups relate to your research problem?

(b) Are there any methodological or ethical problems you might encounter in researching this topic via group discussions?

(c) Could this study be extended by using other research methods?

15.2 This exercise involves running a focus group to discover students' experience of drug use at university. One person should act as moderator and six to ten others should act as members of the focus group. You may wish to have two observers who can take notes on the interaction and provide an assessment of the effectiveness of the exercise in producing relevant data. The moderator should use the following questions to stimulate discussion and can also make other interventions in the discussion where appropriate:

1 Can you talk about whether or not you feel safe in your university?

2 Do you have some thoughts on how your university is doing regarding alcohol and drug problems with students? Can you describe to me what you know about this?

3 What does your university do to educate you about the use of alcohol and drugs?

4 Do you think drugs or alcohol are easily available to students?

5 What kinds of rules do you have about alcohol and drugs?

6 If you ever had a problem with alcohol or drugs, who would you approach to talk about it? Can you explain your thoughts about your choice of this individual?

7 Can you talk about your thoughts on how alcohol and drugs affect a person, a family, a school or university, a community?

Chapter 16: Making and managing audio recordings

16.1 The following exercise will require you to consider how to overcome recording-related problems that may occur in a classic fieldwork-research situation. Discuss the following scenarios in small groups of three or four:

1 Imagine you are doing covert or undercover research in an industry where your access is restricted to selected people. A relevant conversation arises during a moment when your identity as a researcher needs to remain secret. How would you record it?

2 You are the mediator of a focus group of 12 people (see Chapter 15). The setting is the great hall of the local municipal office building, which is sparsely furnished and has very high ceilings. What do you need to consider when recording in such a setting? How would you organize the seating arrangement and position people in relation to the recording device? Think about the possible effects of using a hand-held rather than a built-in microphone. Which type of microphone, if any, would be the most suitable?

3 Half-way into an interview with a highly significant respondent, he or she suddenly asks you to stop taping the interview. Which other techniques of 'recording' are available to you? Would it be unethical to ask to continue the recording?

16.2 Use the advice in Chapter 16 to make an audio recording of a brief interview. Compare the quality of your recording with that of others in your workshop group, or others that you have made. What factors led to good quality recordings? What would you now adjust in order to make better recordings?

Chapter 17: Doing ethnography

17.1 This discussion exercise involves thinking again about the methods used by Jen Tarr in her study of Alexander Technique (Chapter 33). When you have read her account, try to answer the following questions:

(a) To what extent was she a stranger in this social setting? How did her previous experience influence what she 'saw'?

(b) In terms of Junker's four observer roles, which of these best characterizes the research? What were the advantages and disadvantages of the role adopted?

(c) How did Jen Tarr gain access to the setting? What obstacles did she face? Did she find herself 'sponsored' by anyone? What did her access negotiations reveal about the power relations within the setting?

(d) How did Jen Tarr use her relations in the field as a source of data? What personal strains did this entail? What ethical issues did this raise? Did her 'ascribed characteristics' (for example, her gender), dictate what she observed?

(e) What issues of reliability, validity and representativeness were entailed in the research?

(f) What role did social theory play in the research? Was it generated from data, or did theory guide observation?

(g) Whose 'side' was Jen Tarr on?

17.2 This is a field-based exercise in ethnographic methods using observation techniques.

(a) Choose a social setting where you can act as an observer more than a participant. Examples of suitable settings are: council meetings; student union meetings; libraries; interaction between people providing a service (shop workers, doctors' receptionists and so on) and clients; pubs; launderettes; public transport, waiting rooms.

(b) Record what you see and hear as fully and as neutrally as possible, that is without making inferences about why people are doing whatever they are doing. Note the sequence of events, the frequency, any patterns you can discern as well as groupings and non-verbal behaviour. Briefly describe the physical setting of the room. You may find it necessary to concentrate on a particular group, or person.

(c) Write on-the-spot observations on one side of a double-sided page of a notebook; on the opposite side of the page write down your own thoughts about what is going on so that you separate your observation from your interpretation. Write down any difficulties you experience and note any instances of when your observing seems to be affecting the scene you are observing. If you are doing this with a partner, you may find it interesting to compare notes, looking for any similarities and differences in what you recorded.

(d) Then try to interpret what you have seen. You should be concerned with trying to explain what you have been observing and hearing, and to a degree participating in. Your interpretation should try to understand what has been going on from the perspective of those you have been observing.

(e) Consider whether there are any aspects or themes that seem worth exploring further. Discuss what you have learned about the problems and possibilities of participant observation as a method of data collection.

Some advice: people beginning this sort of research often have difficulty in seeing' the unusual in situations that initially seem pretty routine. To avoid producing a purely descriptive account of 'what happened' try observing two contrasting examples of the setting (for example: compare an academic library with a public one; compare queuing at a bus stop with queuing in a takeaway shop). This can often help you see the underlying rules of interaction that are being used by participants. If you are observing a social situation that is strange to you, see if you can find a person to 'guide' you through it; such an informal sponsor can help by explaining the underlying rules of the situation, as well as showing you how to pass successfully as a member.

17.3 In Box IV.5 is an extract from the field notes of a practising ethnographer, Daniel Miller, who did fieldwork in Trinidad in 1988 (published in Miller, 1994). These sections of the notes contain records of conversations, observations and other techniques relevant to how Trinidadians liked to view and talk about a US-made soap opera, *The Young and the Restless*, which in Miller's words concentrated 'on the domestic life and turmoil of wealthy families in a generalized American city' (1994: 247–8). In his final research report Miller argues that Trinidadians use their viewing of this programme to express a spirit which they call 'bacchanal', which 'can refer to [a] general level of excitement and disorder, [but also involves] the emergence into light of things which normally inhabit the dark ... directed against the pretensions of various establishment forms, revealing their hollow or false nature' (Miller, 1994: 246–7).

Examine these field notes and answer the following questions:

(a) Which of them describe people's actions, and which their words?

(b) What details of the context of actions and words are given? Are there any notes that suggest what Miller was doing? For example, is there any evidence of his having questioned people?

(c) Is any counting involved? Where do the numbers appear to come from, and what do they tell us?

(d) Are there any *analytic memos,* in which Miller reflects on what the observations mean to him?

(e) How objective and representative do these observations appear to be?

(f) How could notes like this be improved?

Chapter 18: Generating grounded theory

18.1 Choose a specific research study and ask of it:

(a) How well are the concepts grounded in data; how adequately are central claims supported by evidence?

(b) Can you identify core categories and subsidiary categories? What are the properties of these categories and what are the relationships between them?

(c) What strategies from grounded theorizing might the researcher have pursued in order to generate a more 'saturated' or 'thick' theoretical account? Consider, here, theoretical sampling decisions that might have been taken, or comparisons that might have been made.

18.2 Grounded theorizing involves an attempt to construct an account that is well defended against threats to its truth status. To what extent does this allow for alternative voices? Is this a desirable feature of qualitative research?

Chapter 19: Doing historical and archival research

19.1 Consider the research topics listed in Box IV.1. Which ones could be investigated (either wholly or in part) by means of archival research? Pick one of them (or do this exercise for a project on which you are working) and consider:

(a) What kinds of *primary* and *secondary* sources might you hope to find?

(b) What kinds of *oral* and *documentary* sources might you hope to find?

(c) How would you gain access to these sources and what problems might you need to overcome in doing so?

(d) Use the index of this book to look up what is meant by the distinction between treating text as a *topic* rather than a *resource*. In relation to the research example that you are considering for this exercise, what would be gained by examining relevant archival material as a topic rather than a resource?

19.2 Find a local or national archive that will allow you to do one of the following:

(a) Reconstruct the history of your house or home, focusing on its occupants or owners.

(b) Study the socio-economic composition of your street at one point in time more than 75 years ago.

(c) Study a major local event, occasion or institution from more than 75 years ago.

Chapter 20: Using visual materials

20.1 In this exercise you will do a semiotic analysis for which you will need to have collected a number of advertisements featuring women. For instance, select from a women's magazine all the advertisements for perfume. The overall concern is to gain knowledge of how meanings about gender are used, organized and produced within visual texts. For example, questions you might ask are: How are women portrayed? How is sexual difference represented? How are relationships between men and women depicted? Use semiotic concepts *(sign, signifier, signified, connotation, denotation)* to consider the following questions for each image (these are suggestions):

(a) What are the elements of the sign (the advertisement)? Look at images of people, settings, products, written text. Consider what they *signify:* what kinds of meanings and associations do they bring into the image? What kinds of codes of meaning do they draw on? How are these elements organized and related to each other (do they support or contradict each other, do they comment on each other)?

(b) How are the different meanings in the text related to the product advertised, and what meaning is thereby given to the product?

(c) Is there an overall ideological structure of meaning which emerges from the advertisement? (For example, what conclusions about gender do you think the advert leads the reader to?)

(d) In comparing the different advertisements,

what can you infer about the range of possible constructions of gender available within advertising?

You can apply this approach to other types of image too – say images of men in cigarette adver-

---

Box IV.5   Field notes extract

507:   Longdenville women, both addicts of Y&R [*The Young and the Restless*], since view it daily, say – it's about young people, about relations between rich and poor, tend always to go back to the first person you loved, e.g. in own family elder sister went with moslem boy, married off by parents to hindu man but she left husband, gone back to first man and had child by him.

614:   result of my survey of all media: note 70% watched Y&R, news just less but then nothing else over 30%, asking who watched (I guess regularly 50% women, 30% men).

622:   even panmen watch Y&R.

641:   Rene: I discuss TV with sister, neighbours or with people in the health centre – have to get back by 12 to see it, when my neighbour gets back from her friends where she watches – we discuss, very exciting right now. Where Brad's first wife taken him away but he doesn't know why he's doing it; people who come from America saw it already.

(Me: most Trinidadians asked to describe the character of their islands in one word would say 'bacchanal' with a smile that suggests affectionate pride triumphing over shame.)

EY18:   Women talk about Y&R: 'I prefer that, you see it is safer to talk about the celebrities business than to talk about people business, you won't get into trouble, nobody won't cuss you if you say Chancellor was with this one's husband you just won't get into trouble. Although it is gossip won't be anybody's personal life ... but it is just bacchanal, all them soaps is just bacchanal ... even if you don't like what is happening on the show you could even admire their earrings or their pearl necklaces; their hairdressing is exotic ... I would copy Brad's wife although I won't like to have a husband like Brad. I like Cricket, I like Tracy and I like Lauren.' Talking about marriage in Trinidad: 'I find it should be 50–50 not 30–70. The woman have to be strong, she have to believe in her vows no matter what ... that make me remember Y&R – Vickie want her marriage to work but Victor is in love with somebody else, but she is still holding on.'

ET21:   Everybody does watch Y&R, 'when they tell me Mamy they like so and so's clothes in the picture, so I would sit down on Friday evenings and watch it to see the style. I don't have ties during the day. If watch it from TV I can copy the style. The last style copied was a style Ashley had – low cut across with a frill and a mini.' It is a black and white TV so she buy a black skirt, don't know what colour it really was. Copied Cassandra's jacket with the gathers on top; got the T shirt from Young and Restless.

(*Source*: Daniel Miller)

tisements, or images of children in clothes cata-logues.

20.2 An exercise in memory work:

Ask some elderly people you know to show you some photographs from their past. Ask some of the questions relating to 'memory work' listed in the chapter on this. Record the replies and discuss the issues that arise from these recollections.

20.3 An exercise in photo elicitation:

Choose some images (still or otherwise) that relate to a controversial topic (for example, racism). Use these materials to prompt discussion in a focus group (see Exercise 15.2 for instruc-tions on how to run a focus group for a project concerning drug usage).

20.4 An exercise in making images:

Using a camera (for still or moving images), record images that relate to an important social division in society. For example, the houses, shops, streets, or vehicles in a rich part of town compared with a poor part; family mealtimes in households of varying economic circumstances; shop fronts in areas with different ethnic or cultural compositions. Write a report, or discuss with others, what these images reveal about social divisions.

Chapter 21: Using the Internet

21.1 Searching for research resources on the Web:

(a) Choose a topic or subject you would like to explore on the Internet.

(b) Use (i) a search engine and (ii) a web direc-tory (see Boxes 21.2 and 21.3) to search for relevant material.

(c) Which approach delivered the best results?

21.2 Take a brief questionnaire that you have de-signed, or that you have access to. Visit a website where you can design your own web question-naire and see if you can turn this into a web questionnaire. Are there any items or features of the questionnaire (for example, instructions to skip some questions if a particular answer is given to one item) that cannot be converted into web versions? Suitable sites for this are:

http://psych.fullerton.edu/mbirnbaum/pro-grams/surveyWiz.HTM

www.createsurvey.com

21.3 Outline the methodological issues involved in doing an ethnographic study of a virtual com-munity, such as an organization in which people with a particular illness or condition contact each other and provide information, self help and mutual support. Consider:

(a) What issues of access and ethics might be involved?

(b) What advantages and disadvantages would there be in making observations of on-line behaviour as opposed to face-to-face behav-iour of the same people in 'real' life?

(c) What materials would you count as 'data' for such a study and what methods of data analy-sis would you use?

21.4 Box IV.6 describes an ethnographic study of the Internet. Read it and answer the following questions:

(a) In what way does this on-line ethnography differ from traditional ethnography?

(b) Are there particular methods and techniques that are appropriate to an on-line ethnogra-phy like this or are any of the methods described in this book suitable for such an investigation?

Chapter 22: Combining qualitative and quantitative methods

22.1 Identify and discuss both the method-ological *differences* and *similarities* between qualitative and quantitative approaches to social research. Is quantitative research *always* positivistic? In what ways might qualitative research adopt the assumptions of positivism?

22.2 Discuss the potential problems of letting the audience of a piece of research determine which methods you use. In particular, think about the differences between research for an academic audience and that for a policy audience.

22.3 Design a research project in which qualita-tive and quantitative methods are combined in an advantageous way. Discuss whether you would use *triangulation* or the *multiple methods* ap-proach in combining the methods and the implications this has for the knowledge you generate from the research.

22.4 Which of the research topics listed in Box

IV.1 would be appropriately investigated using:
(a) Quantitative methods only?
(b) Qualitative methods only?
(c) Combined methods?

Chapter 23: Coding and analysing data

23.1 For this exercise you will need some questionnaire items, some of which are *pre-coded,* others *closed* and others *open.* Examples of these are in Boxes 13.2, 13.5, 13.6, 14.9, 23.2, 23.3. You are also likely to have an interview schedule, and some data, if you have carried out Exercise 13.3.

Having chosen a number of items you will need to generate answers to the questions, either by asking them of at least five people, or by using your imagination. Now you have some data that you can prepare for quantitative analysis.

Draw up a coding scheme which indicates the variable names and the value labels. Using a square grid of boxes, fill in the values of the data matrix. If you are learning SPSS or some other statistical software package you can try entering these data and producing some frequency counts.

23.2 Examine either the transcript of a taped interview in Box IV.4 or the transcript in Box IV.7, taken from a study by Jocelyn Cornwell (1981) Then do the following:
(a) Consider what themes you can find in this extract and use these to make a list of codes for the passage. Mark your transcript with code words that describe the themes on the margin.
(b) Consider what assumptions you have made. What have you found difficult? Are you drawing on a feminist theory of gender? If not, would coding from a feminist perspective affect what you could 'find' in the data?
(c) Are your codes objective? What decisions have you taken in choosing particular codes to characterize particular words or phrases in particular ways? How do you account for similarities and differences in coding between other people in your group who have coded the extract? What has been left out? Can the use of such codes give us agreed interpretations of these data? If codes are not agreed, does this matter?

(d) Report back to the rest of the workshop. Can interviews of this sort be used as a basis for generalizing about the beliefs, practices and feelings of women? Does this interview raise any ethical issues?
(e) If you are using a computer package for analysing qualitative data, such as NVivo, you may find it helpful to enter the data and your codes and use the computer to search for coded segments, or segments where codes overlap.
(f) You could repeat this exercise using the texts used for the exercises for Chapter 27.

Chapter 24: Statistical reasoning: from one to two variables

24.1
(a) Using the data matrix in Table IV.1 (p. 499) draw a frequency distribution for the variable *Working.* Do the same for *Age,* recoding it into three broad categories. Draw a bar chart of these distributions. Calculate the mean, median and mode for each variable.
(b) Construct contingency tables that show the relationship between: *Sex* and *Working; Sex* and *Jobsat; Working* and *Jobsat.* Ensure that each cell contains a count and column and row percentages. Describe the character of the relationships which you find.
(c) Draw a scattergram, plotting *Age* against *Jobsat.* Describe the character of this relationship.
(d) Using the recoded version of *Age* construct contingency tables showing the relationship between this variable and each of the other three variables. Describe the character of the relationships you find.
(e) If you are learning SPSS or another statistical package try inputting these data. You will find it easier to get the computer to do the analyses specified above. You can also generate tests of association and significance and consider the meaning of these. Try using the software to produce output in the form of graphs (e.g. pie charts, histograms).

24.2 Table IV.2 (p. 500) consists of four contingency tables demonstrating different types of relationship between the two variables of social

---

Box IV.6   An Internet ethnography

'The trial of Louise [Woodward] in a Boston court for the murder of a child in her care received much media attention and stimulated a large amount of activity on the Internet. Supporters of Louise who had watched the trial produced their own websites to argue for her release and to campaign on her behalf. In the aftermath of the trial, web users could read up on the trial, register their support, lobby the judge and review the evidence … In this ethnography I make claim to be studying the relationship between offline and online, and yet I have restricted myself for practical reasons to online interactions …

At any time I could explore other traces left in web pages and newsgroup discussions by the person with whom I was in email contact … The activities of newsgroups became the focus of the next phase of research, around the time when the appeal upheld the judge's original ruling and Louise flew home. The first task was to locate the newsgroups where the case was being discussed … Rather than trawling through postings from the very beginning of the case I decided to concentrate on more recent events, and initially I concentrated on one month … Through a combination of the use of the search engine and manual counting and indexing, I drew up a list of the newsgroups which had mentioned Louise that month … The aim was … to track the different manifestations of the Louise Woodward case on the newsgroups and to investigate the ways in which the case was rendered differently within the spaces of different newsgroups …

'Using [a] discourse analytically inflected ethnographic approach it was possible to see that many, although not all, of the interactions on the Internet referring to the Louise Woodward case were organized to promote authenticity [in their actions] … The question that I most frequently asked is … "Why they do it" … because they share a set of understandings which render the production of a web page as a form of social action. Without this set of assumptions the production of a website can seem a bizarre activity to spend large amounts of one's time upon …' (Hine, 2000: 10, 11, 71, 76, 77, 78, 142, 144, 147, 148)

---

class and home ownership. Below each is a P-value and the result of a test of association (Q). For each table, describe the character of the relationship and explain why the *p*-values and tests of association vary.

24.3   This is a structured exercise in reading a statistical table that aims to give you a general strategy for perceiving the main messages of such tables. You could apply this approach to Box 26.8 in this book, or find tables as suggested in Exercise 26.4. You will find that not all of the questions are relevant to every table, but experience has shown that these steps, if followed carefully, enable a deeper understanding of any statistical table.

(a)   Read the title before you look at any numbers. What does this reveal about the content of the table?

(b)   Look at the source: who produced the data, with what purpose? Was it a census or a sample?

(c)   Look at any notes above or below the table. How will they influence its scope and your interpretation?

(d)   Read the column and row titles. They indicate which variables are applied to the data.

(e)   How many variables are there and what are they? Can any be considered independent or dependent?

(f)   How are the variables measured? Are there any omissions or peculiarities in the measurement scale? How else might such a measure have been constructed?

(g)   What units are used – percentages, thousands, millions? If you are dealing with percentages, then which way adds up to 100%?

(h)   Look at the 'All' or 'Total' column. These are

494

Box IV.7   Interview transcript

1 *Jocelyn:* Last time we met, you told me that between the times
2 that we'd seen each other, you'd been in hospital, and
3 had had an operation.

4 *Wendy:* That's right, I had er the hysterectomy done last year.

5 *Jocelyn:* Can you tell me about that, about, take me back to the
6 beginning with what happened. Were you unwell, what
7 happened?

8 *Wendy:* It was mainly cos I'd been on the pill for twelve years,
9 and because of my age and the fact I smoked. I was
10 reaching what they classed as erm a risk barrier, at risk
11 age, and they wanted me to come off the pill. I'd been
12 using the pill mainly to regulate my periods all that time.
13 So I knew that if I come off, I'd be having a lot of
14 problems, and basically the doctor suggested other forms
15 of contraceptive, but it wouldn't have helped me as far as
16 the bleeding was concerned.

17 *Jocelyn:* What was the bleeding about?

18 *Wendy:* My periods had never regulated from the time I'd started,
19 so I used to bleed heavily, and maybe lose for ten, fifteen
20 days at a time. The only thing that really regulated it was,
21 was the pill. But it was getting to a stage that that wasn't
22 easing it off any more.

23 *Jocelyn:* Right.

24 *Wendy:* It was unusual. I used to bleed for just five days while I
25 was on the pill. I used to know exactly when my periods
26 would start. It used to be sort of like 3.30 on a Wednesday
27 afternoon, and then it started to change. I was starting to
28 lose maybe on the Tuesday, heavier and for longer. And
29 I found that strange considering all them years it had
30 stayed the same.

31 *Jocelyn:* Did you talk to anyone about it before you went to see
32 the doctor?

33 *Wendy:* No, no.

34 *Jocelyn:* No one at all?

35 *Wendy:* No, I was just worried myself that there might be
36 something wrong.

37 *Jocelyn:* Did you ever talk about anything of that kind with either
38 Sandra or with your mother?

39 *Wendy:*   No.

40 *Jocelyn:*   No, or with friends?

41 *Wendy:*   No, no. I would, I would tell them after I'd already sorted
42 it out myself. But I would just automatically follow through
43 on something myself. Go to my own doctor, or the family
44 planning clinic.

45 *Jocelyn:*   And did they talk to you about that sort of thing or not?

46 *Wendy:*   No, no, it was never discussed. When I was younger nothing
47 like that was ever discussed. Something that you just ...
48 well I've always dealt with it on my own, I suppose I could
49 talk to my mum about it, I just never did. Something I never
50 spoke to her about.

51 *Jocelyn:*   So you went to see the doctor, and she said, she sent you
52 to the hospital.

53 *Wendy:*   She suggested, well she said it was my body, and it was my
54 choice. Cos, they said I could go on for quite a few years like
55 it. But they did want me off the pill, and that I wasn't willing
56 to do, just come off the the pill and take a chance on what
57 would happen.

58 *Jocelyn:*   Who was it who first mentioned having a hysterectomy then,
59 you or them?

60 *Wendy:*   Me.

61 *Jocelyn:*   You?

62 *Wendy:*   Yes, on the, erm the second occasion when I went to the
63 hospital, that was my suggestion. He asked me what I
64 wanted done and I said I wanted the lot taken away, and
65 he said fine. The first doctor didn't want to know, he
66 said I wasn't old enough. There was nothing they could do.

67 *Jocelyn:*   How old, how old were you?

68 *Wendy:*   About 33, 32 or 33. And then they wasn't willing to do it.

69 *Jocelyn:*   What made you think of that as an option? Were you, you
70 were given other options, were you given the option of
71 being sterilized, or anything like that?

72 *Wendy:*   No, sterilization wouldn't have made any difference to the
73 bleeding.

74 *Jocelyn:*   Right.

75 *Wendy:*   That's just a form of contraception. As far as the bleeding's
76 concerned, it's a matter of trial and testing different drugs.
77 And I know other women that have maybe done that for

78 four years. Tried drugs, don't work. Tried a different one,
79 it doesn't work, try another one, it doesn't work. And they
80 still end up having the hysterectomy done anyway. I don't
81 see why I should go through all that hassle for two, three,
82 four years, just for the same end result anyway. Makes you
83 feel rather like a guinea pig, just testing out the drugs for
84 them to see if they work. It's annoying, most of the
85 gynaecologists are men anyway, so they don't know what
86 you're going through. It's fine for a doctor to sit there and
87 say you can go on for another ten years. He doesn't have
88 that problem every month.

89 *Jocelyn:* You see I think that um a great many people would find it
90 shocking that you chose that as an option.

91 *Wendy:* Well. No not really. I've got my children. If you want to
92 look at it that way, that's what the womb is for. The
93 womb is for reproduction, I've done my bit! I've got my
94 two, I didn't want any more, so it was fine for me to have
95 it taken away.

96 *Jocelyn:* Did you have any idea, have you ever had any idea
97 about why you have always bled so much, why, why your
98 periods haven't ever been regulated?

99 *Wendy:* No, I'd never, from the time mine started when I was at
100 school, I never knew when I would start, I never knew
101 how heavy I would lose. I used to be at home maybe for
102 three or four days in bed. I was that ill. And the only time I
103 wasn't was when I was on the pill. The doctor at the family
104 planning said like they will regulate. I said I'm thirty! If they
105 haven't regulated in fifteen years I said I don't think they're
106 going to now. But she just didn't want me to have it no
107 more cos I smoked. That was it. She wanted me to stop
108 smoking and I wouldn't. So I got my pills from my doctor
109 instead! Just changed.

110 *Jocelyn:* Did she give you any explanation for why you needed to
111 stop smoking that was connected to whether or not she
112 would prescribe the pill?

113 *Wendy:* Because as you get older your blood thickens, you're more
114 thickens the blood. And taking the pill also does the same,
115 so for me I had three factors.
116 *Jocelyn:* Getting older, taking the pill, smoking.

117 *Wendy:* Getting older, taking the pill, smoking. I can't stop getting
118 older! I wanted to stay on the pill, but I could give up
119 smoking, you know what I mean, so that was it, you cut
120 out the smoking and you can keep the pill.

---

121 *Jocelyn:* And what's the consequence of this been? You had the
122 operation a year ago?

123 *Wendy:* Yes, I had it done last year. And I felt fine, never had no
124 problems. Obviously same problems as anyone has after
125 an operation, but nothing drastic.

126 *Jocelyn:* Um, has it made any difference to your sense of yourself?

127 *Wendy:* Err, no. I mean some, some women sort of say they feel
128 less of a woman for it, I don't. Not at all. I'm same as I
129 was before. Just can't have children. That's it. I feel better
130 in myself healthwise, because I don't have them problems
131 every month that I had before.

(*Source:* Cornwell, 1981)

---

usually found on the right-hand column and/or the bottom row (the 'margins' of a table). What do variations in the row or column tell you about the variables concerned?

(i) Now look at some rows and/or columns *inside* the table. What do these tell you about the relationships between variables? What social processes might have generated the trends you find?

(j) Is it possible to make causal statements about the relationship between variables? If so, do any of these involve the interaction of more than two variables?

(k) What are the shortcomings of the data in drawing conclusions about social processes?

(l) What other enquiries could be conducted to take this analysis further?

(m) Finally, consider the issue of whether the table reveals something about social reality, or creates a particular way of thinking about reality.

Chapter 25: Statistical reasoning: causal arguments and multivariate analysis

25.1 Choose any article or book that reports the results of a *qualitative* research study. What sort of causal propositions does the author assume to be true? What sort of causal arguments are contained in the text? How could these be tested in quantitative data analysis? What would the independent and dependent variables be?

25.2 Table 25.3 and the discussion that accompanies it suggests that hospice care may cause people to want euthanasia. What plausible objections might there be to this causal argument? How could they be tested in further research? How could qualitative research be used to investigate this proposition?

25.3 Take Table IV.2(a) to be a zero-order table. Draw hypothetical conditional or first-order tables that you might expect to find by entering the test variable of *income,* measured as low or high. The pairs of tables should, in turn, illustrate (a) the existence of a *spurious* or *intervening* relationship between social class and home ownership; (b) *replication* of the original relationship; (c) *specification* of the original relationship; (d) *suppression* of a stronger relationship.

25.4 Use SPSS to analyse a statistical data set. Chapter 26 has web pointers to data archives, from which such data sets can be downloaded. The website for this book (www.rscbook.co.uk) contains links to data archives and data sets. Use data transformations (e.g. Compute or Recode) as well as univariate, bivariate and multivariate statistical procedures to investigate the data. Try to pursue an argument, hypothesis or research question in your analysis, considering counter-arguments to yours and dealing with these, where possible, with further data analysis.

Table IV.1: *A data matrix*

	Variables or questions			
	Sex	Age	Working	Jobsat
Case 1	Male	66	No	Missing
Case 2	Female	34	Full time	1
Case 3	Female	25	Part time	2
Case 4	Female	44	Full time	5
Case 5	Male	78	No	Missing
Case 6	Male	40	Full time	2
Case 7	Male	33	Full time	1
Case 8	Male	16	No	Missing
Case 9	Female	35	Full time	1
Case 10	Female	45	Full time	2
Case 11	Male	30	No	Missing
Case 12	Female	56	Part time	4
Case 13	Male	79	No	Missing
Case 14	Male	60	Part time	4
Case 15	Female	55	Part time	4
Case 16	Female	54	Part time	5
Case 17	Male	55	Full time	1
Case 18	Male	17	No	Missing
Case 19	Female	23	Full time	3
Case 20	Female	20	No	Missing

Chapter 26: Using data archives for secondary analysis

26.1 If you are planning a research project involving data collection, see if you can find a data set in a data archive on the Web that will help you answer your research questions. Investigate its adequacy for this purposes. The questions in Box 26.6 might help you do this. If you are not currently working on a research project, try doing this for one of the following research problems, or for a research problem that you invent:

(a) In what ways does ethnic origin affect life chances?

(b) How do American (US) attitudes towards world affairs compare with the attitudes of people in other countries?

(c) How do people use home entertainment technology (e.g. VCRs, home computers, hi-fi, television)?

26.2 Go to the 'Edwardians Online' website: http://www.qualidata.essex.ac.uk/edwardians/search/transcripts.asp

Use the various ways of searching these interviews ('Browse themes' or 'search') to investigate specified topics, comparing what each interviewee has to say about the topic.

Alternatively, you can copy and paste the full transcripts into a word processor such as Word. Either print it out and analyse it 'manually', or save each transcript as a 'rich text format' file and import it into NVivo (see Chapter 21) or a similar qualitative analysis package. You can then code and search the transcripts for themes.

26.3 Go to the ICPSR (Inter-University Consortium for Social and Political Research) website:

http://www.icpsr.umich.edu/access/index.html Click on 'Online analysis using the DAS'.

There are over 90 different studies there, containing statistical data on a wide range of topics. You can analyse them 'online' without having any statistical software on your computer. Find out about how you can do this for a particular survey data set that interests you by clicking on relevant links on the website (for example, you will need to look at the study's 'codebook' for

Table IV.2   *Tables showing different relationships between social class and home ownership (column %)*

(a)

Home ownership	Social class		
	Lower	Middle	Upper
Owner	20	30	50
Private, rented	30	40	30
Council, rented	50	30	20

$p < 0.01, Q = 0.6.$

(b)

Home ownership	Social class		
	Lower	Middle	Upper
Owner	60	40	3
Private, rented	35	35	45
Council, rented	5	25	52

$p < 0.01, Q = -0.8.$

(c)

Home ownership	Social class		
	Lower	Middle	Upper
Owner	33	32	36
Private, rented	30	28	33
Council, rented	37	40	31

$p < 0.05, Q = 0.04.$

(d)

Home ownership	Social class		
	Lower	Middle	Upper
Owner	56	10	59
Private, rented	23	20	22
Council, rented	21	70	19

$p < 0.01, Q = -0.02.$

information about the variable names). Produce some frequency counts, tables or other data displays and comment on what they tell you about the social and cultural processes involved.

26.4 Choose a topic of interest to you, for example, ethnicity, gender differences, class inequalities, educational inequalities, family structure, health differences. Find some tables of official statistics on your chosen topic in the reference section of your library. Do not choose data that are already presented in graph form. Some examples of UK statistical series that you are likely to find are: *Social Trends; General Household Survey; Annual Abstract of Statistics; Population Trends; Mortality Statistics; Decennial Census; Marriage and Divorce Statistics.*

Present an analysis of up to four tables of data from such publications relevant to your chosen topic. Consider questions like: What do the tables tell you about the topic? What might explain the patterns you see? How might the way in which the statistics were collected affect the conclusions that can be reached? How would the tables need to be modified (in other words, broken down by other variables) in order to take your inquiry further? What further data would need to be collected in order to take your inquiry further?

You may find it relevant to recalculate and re-present data in simpler or graph form to clarify the main messages of the tables analysed. Speculate on the links between the tables chosen: conduct an *inquiry* into the topic by analysing the data from the various tables. Make sure you consider critically the measurement validity of the variables involved.

Chapter 27: Analysing text and speech: content and discourse analysis

27.1 This exercise involves doing a content analysis of dating advertisements. Your raw materials will be a page or two of such advertisements taken from a newspaper or other publication containing such advertisements. The focus of the analysis will be on documenting the way in which gender and sexual preference are constructed in the advertisements.

(a) *Defining categories:* Look through the advertisements and discuss them with others with whom you are doing this analysis. Develop a list of categories and keywords which describe the main attributes that people seek for in partners (for example, words that relate to physical appearance, to character, to social status, to expectations of the desired relationship).

(b) *Assigning categories:* Once your list is complete, go through each advertisement indicating whether each category applies to each one. Where there are disagreements over the assignment of categories, discuss these. Keep a tally of how many advertisements are assigned to each category.

(c) *Analysis:* Look at the overall distribution of advertisements across the various categories and try to draw some conclusions about the attributes sought for in partners. Which attributes predominate? How do the attributes vary according to whether men, women, heterosexual or homosexual partners are sought for? Why do you think this is? Have your categories worked well? What different story would other categories have told? Do you think your findings can be generalized to other magazines or media that contain such personal advertisements?

(d) You can apply this process to a variety of other media and to topics other than personal ads. It is often illuminating to make statistical comparisons of different media, or to compare a medium in the past with the same genre today.

27.2 The extract in Box IV.8 is from a 1994 British parliamentary debate concerning a move to lower the age of consent for homosexual intercourse from 21 to 16 years of age, which is the age of consent for heterosexual intercourse. You should read it and consider the following questions.

(a) Consider the different *discourses* that are being drawn upon to construct the speaker's arguments: for example, which moral, medical, 'expert' and political theories and ideas are being mobilized in order to support the speaker's position?

(b) How does the speaker construct a particular 'identity' or 'authority' for himself?

(c) How does the speech use variation and patterns of emphasis to create its rhetorical effect?

(d) Note the instances where the speaker draws on abstract ideals that are difficult to challenge, for example 'wisdom' or 'justice'. Are there alternative ways in which these ideals could have been drawn upon to create an argument *against* equalizing the age of consent?

Chapter 28: Analysing conversation

28.1 This is a task designed to help you familiarize yourself with the transcription conventions used in conversation analysis. As a consequence, you should start to understand the logic of transcribing this way and be able to ask questions about how the speakers are organizing their talk.

Tape-record no more than five minutes of talk in the public domain. One possibility is a radio call-in programme. Avoid using scripted drama productions as these may not contain recurrent features of natural interaction (such as overlap or repair). Do not try to record a television extract as the visual material will complicate both transcription and analysis.

Now go through the following steps:

(a) Attempt to transcribe your tape using the conventions in Box 28.1. Try to allocate turns to identified speakers where possible but don't worry if you cannot identify a particular speaker (put ? at the start of a line in such cases).

(b) Encourage a friend to attempt the same task independently of you. Now compare transcripts and listen again to the tape recording to improve your transcript.

(c) Using the chapter as a guide, attempt to identify in your transcript any features in the organization of the talk (for example, preference organization, institutional talk, upgrading of invitations or utterances, perspective-display sequences, strategies used to appear neutral and so on).

28.2 Examine Examples 1 and 2 on p. 503 (drawn from Atkinson and Drew, 1979: 52 and discussed in Heritage, 1984: 248–9):

(a) Why does Heritage argue that these extracts demonstrate that 'questioners attend to the fact that their questions are framed within normative expectations which have sequential implications' (1984: 249)?

Box IV.8 Extract from a speech made in the House of Commons

1   **Mr Neil Kinnock** (Islwyn): I shall do my best to respond positively to your appeal,
2   Mr Morris, in the interests of the Committee and in defiance of my record.

3   I support new clause 3, moved by the Hon. Member for Derbyshire, South
4   (Mrs Currie), and I pay tribute to the way in which she has worked to ensure
5   this debate. I hope that she will have the reward of achieving a necessary reform
6   to the law.

7   I support the new clause, which provides for an age of consent for sexual
8   relations common to both men and women, on three main grounds. First, it
9   is equitable to treat both sexes the same. Secondly, it is rational to legislate for
10 equal treatment, in terms of both sexual orientation and enforcement of the
11 law. Thirdly, it is wise to decriminalize consensual sexual activity above the age of
12 16 at a time when the fearful disease AIDS has to be fought with all the
13 information, counselling and promotion of greater safety in sexual relationships
14 that we can muster or bring to bear as a consequence of our activities in the House.

15 I shall develop each of those arguments, but I must first emphasize an
16 essential general principle: all that I say and all that is said by everyone who
17 favours reform, whatever the age and the amendment that they prefer, refers
18 to consensual sexual relations. The essential purpose of supporting change in the
19 law is to remove the threat of prosecution and punishment for engaging in
20 sexual activity, which to them is natural, from homosexual males above the age of
21 16. The purpose is emphatically not to provide any opportunity or excuse to anyone
22 – heterosexual or homosexual – who seeks to impose his or her sexual will on
23 anyone else.

24 I arrived at the decision that I should support the new clause and the common age
25 of consent of 16 in two stages. It became obvious to me, as it did to many
26 Hon. Members, that the age of consent, which was fixed at 21 in 1967, has long
27 failed to deal with the realities of sexual orientation and civil liberties. There
28 are significant difficulties in enforcing the law credibly and injustices and
29 dangers inherent in continuing a system that criminalizes male homosexuals
30 before the age of 21.
31 Having reached that conclusion, I was faced with the question, 'What is the
32 most appropriate age of consent if it is not 21?' The compromise of 18
33 automatically suggested itself. It is the age of majority and the age at which
34 young men seem most able to decide for themselves about their sexual orientation.
35 In short, it is not only the legal age of majority, but the biological age of maturity.
36 It seemed to me to be a view that was sensible as an alternative to the current
37 legal provision, liberal in terms of the accommodation of personal convictions
38 and sexual orientation and realistic in terms of an individual's right to privacy.

39 Then, just when I was comfortable with that, the facts began to intervene. I had
40 made the assumption that young men and young women were somehow more able
41 to determine their sexuality at 16 if they were heterosexual. Because of that,
42 I assumed that the heterosexual age of consent could reasonably remain lower
43 than the homosexual age of consent. On reflection, however, it became difficult

44 for me to convince myself that there was a difference in the capacity to decide
45 among 16-year-olds.

46 If I and the majority of other heterosexual men knew our sexual orientation by the
47 age of 16, why should not homosexuals be equally sure of their sexual
48 orientation? The evidence has long existed to prove that people are sure, as the
49 Hon. Member for Derbyshire, South said. The Wolfenden report, published 37
50 ago, concluded: 'The main sexual pattern is laid down in the early years of life
51 and ... usually fixed by the age of 16.'
52 More recently, the Royal College of Psychiatrists reported its long-held view:
53 'there is no developmental reason to treat young men and young women
54 differently' in the law relating to the age of consent. Project Sigma, jointly
55 financed by the Department of Health and the Medical Research Council,
56 proffered strong evidence that homosexual orientation was fixed and understood
57 by homosexuals by their mid-teens. The British Medical Association holds the
58 same view.

59 That evidence and other reliable, responsible material persuaded me that it would
60 be wrong to continue to discriminate in the law between men who are
61 homosexual and those who are heterosexual. It would also be wrong to continue
62 to discriminate in the law between young men who are homosexual and
63 young women who are heterosexual.

64 As a father, I must say that I was equally exercised about the prospect of my
65 daughter and son engaging in heterosexual relations at 16. No father could
66 think otherwise. Frankly, I just hope that had it been the case that either of
67 my children had proved to be of homosexual orientation, I could have shown
68 them the love, and understanding, as their parent, as several parents already do
69 to their children in similar circumstances. I was not offered that test, for which
70 I frankly give thanks. Faced with that prospect, however, as children grow up,
71 who could conclude that we should discriminate in the law between different kinds
72 of young people of different sexes on the basis of sexual orientation? How could
73 we do that when we know that heterosexual relationships carry at least as
74 much danger, as much menace and as much threat to young people's moral values
75 as homosexual relationships?

(*Source: Hansard*, 1994: 81–2)

Example 1

1 *A:* Is there something bothering you or not?
2 (1.0)
3 *A:* Yes or no.
4 (1.5)
5 *A:* Eh?
6 *B*: No.

Example 2

1 *Child*: Have to cut the:se Mummy.
2 (1.3)
3 *Child*: Won't we Mummy?
4 (1.5)
5 *Child*: Won't we?
6 *M:* Yes.

(b)   In Example 2, what are the consequences of *Child* naming the person to whom his utterance is addressed? Why might children often engage in such naming?

Chapter 29:   Reading and writing research

29.1   The two extracts from Du Bois's writing in Boxes 29.5 and 29.6 discuss the issue of infant mortality within African American life. The first is taken from his sociological monograph *The Philadelphia Negro* and the second is an excerpt from his autobiographical essay 'On the passing of the first born' taken from *The Souls of Black Folk*. Here Du Bois writes about the death of his son and its significance to him as a black man living under segregation and racism. Compare and contrast the narrative voice, textual quality and 'empirical facts' in these two extracts. How, in each case, does the writer achieve authority and persuasiveness? What are the rhetorical aspects of each extract?

29.2   Choose articles reporting two research studies, one largely quantitative, the other largely qualitative. If possible, they should be on similar subjects. How do they compare in terms of structure (look at the subheadings) and rhetorical devices to persuade the reader of the author's point of view?

Chapter 30: Doing a dissertation

There are no exercises associated with this chapter

Chapter 31: When things go wrong

There are no exercises associated with this chapter

Chapter 32:   Representing otherness: collecting and analysing visual data

32.1   Who were the *gatekeepers* controlling access to the settings and material that Thomas Zacharias wanted to study? How was access negotiated with these people?

32.2   Assess the adequacy of the sampling and data-recording strategies employed for this study.

32.3   Which of the different methods for analysing images described in Chapter 20 and elsewhere in this book were used to analyse the material collected on this study? Could others have been used? What might they have revealed?

32.4   What ethical issues did the study raise?

32.5   What is the relevance of this research for (a) social policy and (b) social theory?

Chapter 33: Embodiment, reflexivity and movement re-education: an ethnographic case study

33.1   What aspects of this account show *reflexivity* in action?

33.2   What aspects of the research demonstrate *anti-essentialist* or *social constructionist* perspectives?

33.3   What role did (a) social theory and (b) relevance to dance education practice or social issues play in the research study?

33.4   What philosophical perspective was adopted by the author?

33.5   How could methods other than the ones employed have been used to find out about this topic? What would the practical issues in using these have been? Would these have revealed different things from the ones that the author actually used?

Chapter 34: My research practice

34.1   Which aspects of these linked research projects addressed social policy concerns? Which aspects addressed social theoretical concerns?

34.2   How could methods other than the ones employed have been used to find out about these topics? What would the practical issues in using these have been? Would these have revealed different things from the ones that the author actually used?

34.3   What aspects of your own research practice would you most like to develop? How are you going to do this?

Glossary

Action theory: social theory in which action, its purposive nature and its meaning to people, is taken to be of central importance. Action theory is often associated with the name of Max Weber, who developed the interpretive tradition in social science.

Analysis of variance or **ANOVA:** a method for analysing the relationship between two or more variables where the dependent variable is interval-level and the independent variable(s) is or are nominal. It proceeds by testing the significance of any differences between the mean values of the dependent variable within the different groups described by the independent variable. ANOVA is useful where the independent variable has three or more categories, and can then be understood as an extension of the logic of the t-test.

Androcentrism: ideas or methods of research which prioritize men's views of the world, excluding the experience of women.

Anthropological strangeness: the art or mental trick of making a social setting and behaviour within it appear as if the observer is encountered as a stranger. If applied to mundane 'taken-for-granted' events, this can lead to unusual and original insights.

Anti-essentialism: see **essentialism**

Archives: repositories of a variety of materials, such as documents, photographs and films, often of an historical nature, catalogued and filed for the use of researchers, scholars and other investiga-

Association: see **correlation**

Bias: A realist approach to bias depicts this as consisting of any systematic error that obscures correct conclusions about the subject being studied. Typically, such bias may be caused by the researcher, or by procedures adopted for data gathering, including sampling. The concept makes little sense from a relativist standpoint, though provision of a reflexive account of the research process can help in addressing issues of trust that the concept of bias was intended to resolve.

Boolean searches: searches for material (such as references or segments of coded text) using combinations of keywords linked by operators such as 'and', 'or' or 'not'. Databases (for example, library catalogues) and qualitative analysis software (such as NVivo) commonly support such searches.

Bracketing: used in semiotics to indicate the suspension of interest (for analytic purposes) in the relationship between signs and their referents. The term is also helpful in understanding the mental attitude required when doing discourse analysis or any analytic approach that treats text as a topic rather than a resource. Instead of considering the claims made in texts about reality outside the text, bracketing forces the analyst to consider the 'reality' the text constructs.

Career: used, primarily, by symbolic interactionists and ethnographers to describe a person's progress through a social setting, as stages in learning how to experience the drug, or mental patients pass through a series of institutional settings.

Case study: the study of a single 'case' – for example, a person, an institution, an event. How 'caseness' is defined depends on the logic of the particular research inquiry. For example, a nation might be thought of as a 'case' for certain purposes, even though a nation contains many people, each of which might be understood as a 'case' in some other inquiry.

Census: a count of the characteristics of every member of a given population (as opposed to a survey of a selected sample from that population).

Coding: this is done when observations, segments of text, visual images or responses to a questionnaire or interview are collected into groups which are like one another, and a symbol is assigned as a name for the group. Data may be 'coded' as they are collected, as where respondents are forced to reply to fixed-choice questions. Alternatively, the coding of qualitative data can form a part of an interpretive, theory building approach.

Comparative method: the comparison of people's experiences of different types of social structure or social setting in terms of historical points in time, or across cultures at a single point in time. This is an approach which can shed light on the particular arrangements of both sides of the comparison. (See also **constant comparison** in index)

Connotation: used in semiotics to indicate the interpretive meanings of signs, which may be ideological. Thus a picture of a soldier saluting a flag connotes nationhood and patriotism as well as the more straightforward things such as 'soldier' and 'flag' that it denotes.

Constructionism: see **social constructionism**

Content analysis: normally used in methods texts to refer to the quantitative analysis of texts or images, content analysis is in practice often combined with *qualitative thematic analysis* to produce a broadly interpretive approach in which quotations as well as numerical counts are used to summarize important facets of the raw materials analysed.

Contingency table: a table of numbers in which the relationship between two variables is shown. Contingency tables can usefully be broken down into rows and columns. Percentages placed in the cells of the table, giving the proportion which each cell contributes to the sum of particular rows or columns, are often helpful in detecting the strength and direction of relationships.

Correlation: in social statistics this term means the same as **association**, referring to a situation where two variables vary together. Amongst other things an association or correlation may be positive (in which case the two variables rise together) or negative (where one goes down the other goes up). Correlation coefficients (or tests of association) exist to indicate the strength and direction of linear relationships like this.

Cultural scripts or texts: terms used by those concerned to analyse cultural objects, such as pictures, films, sports events, fashions, food styles, to indicate that these can be viewed as containing messages in a manner comparable to a piece of written text.

Data: is the plural of datum, which refers to a record of an observation. Data can be numerical (and hence quantitative) or consist of words or images (hence qualitative). A distinction is sometimes made between naturally occurring data – such as tape recordings of conversations that would have occurred whether a researcher was present or not – and data generated in research settings, as in interviews or on questionnaires. Quantitative data are often arranged in a data matrix for ease of analysis.

Data archives: can be distinguished from the more general term 'archive' in that they contain quantitatively coded material from surveys, or qualitative material collected as part of social research studies, made available through the archive for secondary analysis.

Deconstruction: is an approach to social analysis that undermines claims to authority by exposing rhetorical strategies used by social actors, including the authors of research reports themselves. It has been promoted in particular by the postmodernist Derrida.

Deduction: see **hypothetico-deduction**

Dependent variable: see **variable**

Determinism: is the view that everything that happens is caused. When applied to human action, it suggests that our perception of having a free will is an illusion, and that the task of social research is to expose the true causes of action.

Discourse: has come to refer, under the influence of Foucault, to systems of knowledge and their associated practices. More narrowly, it is used by discourse analysts to refer to particular systems of language, with a characteristic terminology and underlying knowledge base, such as medical talk, psychological language, or the language of democratic politics.

Elaboration paradigm: a structured approach to the exploration of causal relationships between variables through the examination of contingency tables. By introducing third variables to bivariate tabulations, arguments about causal direction and spuriousness are tested. The logic of this approach underlies most multivariate statistical analysis.

Empiricism: the view that knowledge is derived from sensory experience, for example visual observation. More loosely, it has been used to describe research that contains little in the way of reflection or theory, preferring to report 'facts' as they appear to be (as in the term 'abstracted empiricism').

Epistemology: refers to the philosophical theory of knowledge, consisting of attempts to answer questions about how we can know what we know, and whether this knowledge is reliable or not. Debates about the adequacy of empiricism, for example, are epistemological debates.

Essentialism: is now increasingly used in order to explain why anti-essentialism is preferable, though in more purely philosophical discussion the term has greater usefulness. Amongst social and cultural researchers, anti-essentialism involves the rejection of a scientific quest for universal essences, such as the discovery of a universal psychological makeup, or generally applicable sex differences, in preference for a view that human 'nature' is a social construction.

Ethnocentrism: refers to the practice of judging a different society by the standards and values of one's own. This is seen, particularly by ethnographers, as inhibiting understanding of other ways of life.

Ethnomethodology: involves the examination of the ways in which people produce orderly social interaction on a routine, everyday basis. It provides the theoretical underpinning for conversation analysis.

External validity: see **validity**

Facticity: is the process whereby certain perceptions or phenomena achieve the status of uncontroversial fact. Phenomenological analysis attempts to reduce facticity, as does the method of deconstruction, by exposing the social practices that generate it. Achieving facticity may involve both the objectification and the naturalization of something as a fact.

Frequency distribution (or frequency count): a count of the number of times each value of a single variable occurs. Thus, the proportion of the population fitting into each of six categories of social class may be given as a frequency distribution. The distribution can be presented in a variety of ways, including, for example, a raw count, percentages or a pie chart.

Functionalism: is an approach to explaining social phenomena in terms of their contribution to a social totality. Thus, for example, crime is explained as necessary for marking the boundary of acceptable behaviour, reinforcing social order. Prominent functionalists include Durkheim and Parsons.

Genealogy: Foucauldian term involving the metaphor of a family tree to indicate an interest in the historical and social roots of ideas, systems of knowledge or discourses. Foucault suggested in a further metaphor that an *archaeological* approach towards the elucidation of these be adopted.

Grounded theory: a term coined by Glaser and Strauss to describe the type of theory produced by their methods of ethnographic data collection and analysis. The approach emphasizes the systematic discovery of theory from data, by using methods of constant comparison and theoretical sampling, so that theories remain grounded in observations of the social world, rather than being generated in the abstract. This they propose as an inductive alternative to hypothetico-deductive approaches.

Hypothetico-deduction: is the view that science proceeds by deriving hypotheses from theories, which are then tested for truth or falsity by observation and experimentation. It is the opposite of induction, which proposes that theories can be derived from observations.

Idealism: often opposed to realism, this term describes the view that the world exists only in people's minds.

Independent variable: see **variable**

Internal validity: see **validity**

Interpretive content analysis: see **content analysis**

Interpretivism: refers to approaches emphasizing the meaningful nature of people's participation in social and cultural life. The methods of natural science are seen as inappropriate for such investigation. Researchers working within this tradition analyse the meanings people confer upon their own and others' actions.

Intersubjectivity: the common-sense, shared meanings constructed by people in their interactions with each other and used as an everyday resource to interpret the meaning of elements of social and cultural life.

Intertextuality: The explicit or implicit echo of one text in another text. This may take the form of explicit cross-references, or implicit, latent themes.

Linguistic repertoire: a term used in discourse analysis to refer to the resources (discourses, intersubjective meanings, etc.) on which people draw in order to construct accounts.

Logistic regression: see **regression**

Malestream knowledge: see **androcentrism**

Marginality: used to describe the typical position of the ethnographer, who exists on the margins of the social world being studied, in that he or she is neither a full participant nor a full observer. Also used to describe groups of people living outside mainstream culture.

Measures of central tendency: statistics such as the mean, median or mode which in various ways indicate the central point in a frequency distribution.

Methodology: concerns the theoretical, political and philosophical roots and implications of particular research methods or academic disciplines. Researchers may adopt particular methodological positions (for example, concerning epistemology or political values) which establish how they go about studying a phenomenon. *Method*, on the other hand, generally refers to matters of practical research technique.

Multiple regression: see **regression**

Multivariate analysis: analysis of the relationships between three or more variables (as opposed to bivariate analysis, which involves two variables, or univariate analysis which involves one).

Naturalists: take the view that the methods of the natural sciences are appropriate to the study of the social and cultural world. This should be distinguished from another meaning of the term *naturalism* or *naturalistic* which is sometimes used to refer to the claim of ethnographers to collect naturally occurring data.

Naturalizing: is the process whereby matters that are in fact socially constructed and were once fluid and changeable come to be perceived as a part of the natural order and therefore fixed, inevitable and right. Social researchers often wish to denaturalize phenomena (such as sexual identity for example) by exposing the human processes whereby they are constructed.

Ontology: a branch of philosophy concerned with what can be said to exist. This can be distinguished from *epistemology* which concerns how we may know what exists.

Operationalization: the process of developing indicators for concepts. Thus a concept such as 'alienation' might be indicated by questions on a questionnaire about powerlessness, isolation or moral deviance. The adequacy of operationalization is an aspect of measurement validity, but can also be applied usefully to assess the adequacy of links made in qualitative research between ideas and examples.

Paradigms (Kuhnian): the overall conception and way of working shared by workers within a particular discipline or research area. In this view, paradigm shifts occur from time to time as scientific communities experience revolutions of thought.

Participant observation: used to describe the method most commonly adopted by ethnographers, whereby the researcher participates in the life of a community or group, while making observations of members' behaviour.

Path analysis: a procedure associated with *multiple regression* involving a diagram indicating the strength and direction of influences between several variables, enabling calculation of direct and indirect causal pathways.

Plagiarism: presentation of someone else's work as if it were your own. This can be done by direct copying without citation of the original work, or by summarizing another person's ideas and presenting them as if they were your own. *Self plagiarism* occurs when a person presents or publishes the same piece of work more than once without indicating the first source. Plagiarism is generally used to indicate the idea of copying, although failing to acknowledge another person's contribution to a work that is being presented or published for the first time may be considered plagiarism: it is certainly a dishonest practice. Other forms of cheating include fabrication of quotations, data and other results, although the concept of 'fabrication' depends on certain epistemological assumptions.

Positivism: in its looser sense has come to mean an approach to social inquiry that emphasizes the discovery of laws of society, often involving an empiricist commitment to naturalism and quantitative methods. The word has become almost a term of abuse amongst social and cultural researchers, losing its philosophical connotations where its meaning is both more complex and precise.

Postmodernism: a social movement or fashion amongst intellectuals centring around a rejection of modernist values of rationality, progress and a conception of social science as a search for overarching explanations of human nature or the social and cultural world. By contrast, postmodernists celebrate the fall of such oppressive grand narratives, emphasizing the fragmented and dispersed nature of contemporary experience.

Post-structuralism: see **structuralism**

Primary sources: see **secondary sources**

Qualitative thematic analysis: analysis based on the identification of themes in qualitative material, often identified by means of a coding scheme. A widely used approach to qualitative analysis, generally treating accounts as a *resource* for finding out about the reality or experiences to which they refer, this is similar to *interpretive content analysis.*

Quasi-experimental design: involves control of spurious variables by means of statistical operations at the analysis stage, rather than the design stage (as occurs in randomized controlled trials). The approach is often used to analyse survey data, or in situations where strict experimental designs may be impractical or unethical.

Randomized controlled trial: an experimental method whereby subjects are randomly allocated to either a group receiving a 'treatment' or another which acts as a control', so that the effects of the treatment can be established. The method is effective in ruling out spurious causation.

Reactivity: the reactions of people being studied to the presence of an observer, seen by some to be a source of bias, in that behaviour may become artificial as a result.

Realism: is the view that a reality exists independently of our thoughts or beliefs. The language of research is seen to refer to this reality, rather than purely constructing it, though more subtle realists recognize constructive properties in language as well.

Reductionism: the identification of a basic explanation for a complex phenomenon. Thus sexual identity may be explained by reference to genetic determinants alone, or social life explained in terms of economic relations alone.

Reflexivity: in its broad meaning this is used to refer to the capacity of researchers to reflect upon their actions and values during research, whether in producing data or writing accounts. More narrowly, ethnomethodologists use the term to describe a property of language, which reflects upon actions to make them appear orderly.

Regression: a statistical technique for using the values of one variable to predict the values of another, based on information about their relationship, often given in a scattergram. Multiple regression involves the prediction of an interval-level variable from the values of two or more other variables. Logistic regression does this too, but predicts the values of nominal or ordinal variables.

Relativism: can be epistemological (or 'conceptual'), cultural or moral. The first of these involves the rejection of absolute standards for judging truth. The second suggests that different cultures define phenomena in different ways, so that the perspective of one culture cannot be used to understand that of another. The third implies that perceptions of good and evil are matters of social agreement rather than having universal validity.

Reliability: the capacity of a measuring device, or indeed of a whole research study, to produce the same results if used on different occasions with the same object of study. Reliability enhances confidence in validity, but is insufficient on its own to show validity, since some measurement strategies can produce consistently wrong results. Establishing *intercoder* or *interrater reliability* may be important in some studies where unambiguous meanings for codes in a coding scheme are at stake, so that exercises in which the same material is coded by more than one person and the results compared for consistency may be carried out.

Replication: is closely linked with reliability, involving the repetition of a study to see if the same results are obtained on both occasions. (The term has a narrower meaning within the context of the elaboration paradigm.)

Rhetoric: the linguistic strategies used by speakers or authors of text to convey particular impressions or reinforce specific interpretations, most commonly in support of the authority of the text to speak the truth.

Sampling: the selection of units of analysis (for example, people or institutions) for study. Sampling can involve attempts to statistically represent a population, in which case a variety of random or *probability* methods are available. Alternatively, sampling can be opportunistic, or formed by emerging theoretical concerns of a researcher.

Secondary analysis: analysis of data by researchers unconnected with the original purposes of the data collection, as where academic researchers use data sets gathered as a part of government social surveys.

Secondary sources: analyses or restatements of primary sources (records of events as they are first described or original data) by other authors or researchers. Secondary sources might take the form of research reports, news articles, biographies, documentaries or history books) used to gain an understanding of a topic. Primary sources might be poems, raw tabulations of census data, video recordings or other records of observation. The use of secondary sources should be distinguished from *secondary analysis* of other researchers' original data (a primary source).

Social constructionism: the view that the phenomena of the social and cultural world and their meanings are created in human social interaction. Taken further, social constructionism can be applied to social research itself, prompting debates about whether social research and fiction differ. The approach often, though not exclu-

sively, draws on idealist philosophical orientations.

Social facts: regularities of social life that appear to have an independent existence, acting to determine or constrain human behaviour. Norms of conduct or religious rules are examples. The concept is of particular importance in relation to functionalism and positivism.

Social structure: ordered interrelationships that are characteristic of particular societies, such as its class structure or system of economic or political relations.

Standpoint models: involve the assumption that different social positions produce different experiences and therefore lead to different types of knowledge. Because of this researchers often engage with the experiences of socially oppressed and marginalized groups. The knowledge derived from this is felt to provide a more valid account of the social world than adopting an apparently 'neutral' or 'objective' stance.

Statistical inference: the generalization of findings from a sample to the broader population from which the sample has been randomly drawn. A variety of statistical tests, such as the chi-square, help in estimating the level of probability that such inferences about the population are true, given the sample size. This is expressed as the statistical significance of the finding.

Structuralism: the view that behind the social and cultural realities we perceive, such as clothes or food fashions, kinship organization and even language itself, deep structures exist which, through combinations of their elements, produce the surface complexity of the relevant phenomena. *Post-structuralism* retains elements of structuralism (its interest in surface signs for example) but abandons the quest for deep structures.

Symbolic interactionism: a body of theory that emphasizes the organization of everyday social life around events and actions that act as symbols to which actors orient themselves. Interactionists frequently study this through observation of face-to-face interaction and a preferred method for doing this is ethnography.

Text: although this term includes the kind of thing we usually mean by 'text' (e.g. a written document), under the conditions of the literary turn, structuralism and post-structuralism the term can be applied to almost any object in the world. Semioticians, for example, have considered items as diverse as wrestling matches and Coca Cola cans as 'texts', worthy of analysis for their cultural connotations.

Theoretical sampling: choosing a sampling element (e.g. a person, a social setting) on the basis of its likely contribution to a (grounded) theory emerging during the course of a study.

Thick description: a term adapted by the anthropologist Clifford Geertz to convey the essence of his semiotic approach to ethnography, based on intensive observation of social life from which interpretations of cultural signs can be generated, as for example in the many layered meanings of a Balinese cock fight.

Topicalizing an account: refers to an analytic approach to texts (such as an interview) in which the focus of interest is the world constructed in the text and the methods by which the text achieves this. This involves *bracketing* the truth claims of the text, refusing (at least temporarily) to treat it as a *resource* for discovering truths about some reality outside the text.

Triangulation: a metaphor derived from surveying and navigation to indicate the convergence of two or more viewpoints on a single position or, in social research, truth. A triangulation exercise might, for example, involve seeing whether the results of a questionnaire are repeated in observational data. Associated with a realist approach and, largely, with early qualitative discussions of validity, triangulation is treated with scepticism by non-realists who reject the view that revelation of a single truth is the object of a research account.

Validity: at its most simple this refers to the truth status of research reports. However, a great variety of techniques for establishing the validity of measuring devices and research designs have been established, both for quantitative and qualitative research. More broadly, the status of research as truth is the subject of considerable philosophical controversy, lying at the heart of the debate about postmodernism. A convenient way of categorizing concerns about validity is to divide these into *internal* and *external*. The former refers to the internal design of a study (for example, can it prove causality?); the latter refers to the generalizability of a study (for example, does the sample represent a population adequately?).

Variables: qualities on which units of analysis vary. Thus, if a person is the unit of analysis in, say, a social survey, examples of variables might be their social class, gender, attitudes to politics, and so on. Variables can be measured at a variety of levels, according to which they can be subjected to specific mathematical operations. In considering relationships between variables it is important to define which is a causal (or independent) variable, and which is an effect (dependent) variable.

Verstehen: Max Weber used this word to describe the study of *intersubjectivity*, involving an attempt to understand the meaning of social action from the actor's viewpoint.

References

Abel-Smith, B. and Townsend, P. (1965) *The Poor and the Poorest.* London: Bell.

Abrams, P. (1968) *The Origins of British Sociology, 1834–1914.* Chicago: University of Chicago Press.

Abrams, P., Deem, R., Finch, J. and Rock, P. (eds) (1981) *Practice and Progress: British Sociology, 1950–1980.* London: Allen & Unwin.

Addington-Hall, J. and McCarthy, M. (1995) 'Regional study of care for the dying: methods and sample characteristics', *Palliative Medicine,* 9: 27–35.

Alasuutari, P. (1996) *Researching Culture: Qualitative Method and Cultural Studies.* London: Sage.

Alasuutari, P. (2004) 'The globalization of qualitative research', in C.F. Seale, D. Silverman, J. Gubrium and G. Gobo (eds), *Qualitative Research Practice.* London: Sage.

Alderson, P. (1995) *Listening to Children: Children, Ethics and Social Research.* Ilford: Barnardo's.

Ali, S. (2003) *'Mixed-Race' Postrace: Gender, New Ethnicities and Cultural Practices.* New York and Oxford: Berg.

Anderson, B. (1991) *Imagined Communities: Reflections on the Origin and Spread of Nationalism,* 2nd edn. London: Verso.

Antaki, C. and Rapley, M. (1996) ' "Quality of Life" talk: the liberal paradox of psychological testing', *Discourse and Society,* 7 (3): 293–316.

Arber, S. and Ginn, J. (1991*) Gender and Later Life: A Sociological Analysis of Resources and Constraints.* London: Sage.

Asad, T. (ed.) (1973) *Anthropology and the Colonial Encounter.* London: Ithaca Press.

Atkinson, J.M. and Drew, P. (1979) *Order in Court: The Organisation of Verbal Interaction in Judicial Settings.* London: Macmillan.

Atkinson, P. (1990) *The Ethnographic Imagination: Textual Constructions of Reality.* London: Routledge.

Atkinson, P. and Coffey, A. (1997) 'Analysing documentary realities', in D. Silverman (ed.), *Qualitative Research: Theory, Method and Practice.* London: Sage.

Atkinson, P., Coffey, A., Delamont, S., Lofland, J. and Lofland, L. (eds) (2001) *Handbook of Ethnography.* London: Sage.

Back, L. (1996). *New Ethnicities and Urban Culture. Racisms and Multiculture in Young Lives.* London: UCL Press.

Baez, B. (2002) 'Confidentiality in qualitative research: reflections on secrets, power and agency', *Qualitative Research,* 2 (1): 35–58.

Barbour, R.S. and Kitzinger, J. (eds) (1999) *Developing Focus Group Research: Politics, Theory and Practice.* London: Sage.

Barnes, C. (2003) 'What a difference a decade makes: reflections on doing emancipatory disability research', *Disability and Society,* 18 (1): 3–17.

Barthes, R. (1977) *Elements of Semiology.* New York: Hill and Wang.

Barton, A. and Lazarsfeld, P.F. (1955) 'Some functions of qualitative data analysis in sociological research', *Sociologica,* 1: 321–61.

Baudrillard, J. (2001) *Jean Baudrillard: Selected Writings.* London: Polity.

Bauman, Z. (1987) *Legislators and Interpreters.* Cambridge: Polity.

Beach, W.A. and Metzinger, T.R. (1997) 'Claiming insufficient knowledge', *Human Communication*

Research, 23: 562–88.

Beard, R. and Payack, P.J.J. (2000) 'Presidential debates mirror long-term school decline'. http:// www.yourdictionary.com/library/presart1/html.

Beauchamp, T.L. (1994) 'The "four-principles" approach', in R. Gillon (ed.), *Principles of Health Care Ethics.* Chichester: John Wiley and Sons Ltd.

Beauchamp, T.L., Faden, R.R., Wallace, R.J. and Walters, L. (eds) (1982) *Ethical Issues in Social Science Research.* Baltimore, MD: Johns Hopkins University Press.

Becker, H.S. (1958) 'Problems of inference and proof in participant observation', *American Sociological Review*, 23 (December): 652–60. Reprinted in Becker, H.S. (1970) *Sociological Work: Method and Substance.* Chicago: Aldine. pp. 25–38.

Becker, H.S. (1963) *Outsiders: Studies in the Sociology of Deviance.* New York: Free Press.

Becker, H.S. (1967) 'Whose side are we on?', *Social Problems*, 14: 239–48.

Becker, H.S. (1970) *Sociological Work: Method and Substance.* Chicago: Aldine.

Becker, H.S. (1998) *Tricks of the Trade: How to Think about Your Research While You're Doing It.* Chicago: University of Chicago Press.

Becker, H.S. and Richards, P. (1986) *Writing for Social Scientists: How to Start and Finish your Thesis, Book or Article.* Chicago: University of Chicago Press.

Becker, H.S., Geer, B., Hughes E.C. and Strauss, A.L. (1961) *Boys in White: Student Culture in a Medical School.* Chicago: University of Chicago Press.

Bell, J. (1999) *Doing your Research Project: A Guide for First-time Researchers in Education and Social Science.* Buckingham: Open University Press.

Bell, P. (2002) 'Content analysis of visual images', in T. van Leeuwen and C. Jewitt (eds), *Handbook of Visual Analysis.* London: Sage.

Bell, V. (1993) 'What's the problem? The construction and criminalisation of incest', in *Interrogating Incest: Foucault, Feminism and the Law.* London: Routledge. pp. 126–49.

Benetar, S. and Singer, P.A. (2000) 'A new look at international research ethics', *British Medical Journal,* 321: 824–46.

Berelson, B. (1952) *Content Analysis in Communication Research.* Glencoe, IL: Free Press.

Berger, A.A. (2000) 'Content analysis', in *Media and Communication Research Methods: An Introduction to Qualitative and Quantitative Approaches.* London: Sage.

Berger, P. and Luckmann, T. (1966) *The Social Construction of Reality.* New York: Doubleday.

Berners-Lee, T. (2002) *The World Wide Web – Past Present and Future.* www.w3.org/2002/04/Japan/ Lecture.html

Best, S. and Kellner, D. (1991) *Postmodern Theory: Critical Interrogations.* New York: Guilford.

Bhaskar, R. (1989) *Reclaiming Reality.* London: Verso.

Birke, L. (1986) *Women, Feminism and Biology.* New York: Methuen.

Blaikie, N.W.H. (1991) 'A critique of the use of triangulation in social research', *Quality and Quantity,* 25: 115–136.

Blaxter, M. (1990) *Health and Lifestyles.* London: Routledge.

Bloch, A. (2002) *Refugees' Opportunities and Barriers in Employment and Training.* Research Report 179, Department for Work and Pensions, Leeds.

Bloch, A. (1992) *The Turnover of Local Councillors.* York: Joseph Rowntree Foundation.

Bloch, A. and John, P. (1991) *Attitudes to Local Government.* York: Joseph Rowntree Foundation.

Bloor, M. (1983) 'Notes on member validation', in R. Emerson (ed.), *Contemporary Field Research: A Collection of Readings.* Boston, MA: Little, Brown.

Bloor, M. (1997) 'Techniques of validation in qualitative research: a critical commentary', in G. Miller and R. Dingwall (eds), *Context and Method in Qualitative Research.* London: Sage.

Bond, G.C. (1990) 'Fieldnotes: research in past occurrences', in R. Sanjek (ed.), *Fieldnotes.* New York: Cornell University Press.

Booth, C. (1902–1903) *Life and Labour of the People in London* (17 volumes). London: Macmillan and Co.

Bowley, A.L. and Burnett-Hurst, A.R. (1915) *Livelihood and Poverty: A Study in the Economic Conditions of Working-Class Households in Northampton, Warrington, Stanley and Reading.* London: Bell.

Bowley, A.L. and Hogg, M.H. (1925) *Has Poverty Diminished? A Sequel to 'Livelihood and Poverty'.* London: Ling.

Bradley, P. (2001) *The Advanced Internet Searcher's Handbook.* London: Library Association.

Bradshaw, J. Clifton, M. and Kennedy, J. (1977) 'Found Dead'. University of York, Department of Social Administration and Social Work, Social Policy Research Unit, working paper.

Brannen, J. (1992a) 'Combining qualitative and quantitative approaches: an overview', in J. Brannen (ed.), *Mixing Methods: Qualitative and Quantitative Research.* Aldershot: Avebury.

Brannen, J. (1992b) (ed.) *Mixing Methods: Qualitative and Quantitative Research.* Aldershot: Avebury.

British Sociological Association (2002) *Statement of Ethical Practice.* http://www.britsoc.org.uk/about/ethic.htm

Brown, G. (1973) 'Some thoughts on grounded theory', *Sociology,* 7: 1–16.

Brown, G. and Harris, T. (1978) *Social Origins of Depression.* London: Macmillan.

Brown, R.H. and Davis-Brown, B. (1998) 'The making of memory: the politics of archives, libraries and museums in the construction of national consciousness', *History of the Human Sciences: Special Issue 'The Archive'* 11 (4): 17–32.

Bryan, B., Dadzie, S. and Scafe, S. (1985) *The Heart of the Race: Black Women's Lives in Britain.* London: Virago.

Bryman, A. (1988) *Quantity and Quality in Social Research.* London: Unwin Hyman.

Bryman, A. (1992) 'Qualitative and quantitative research: further reflections on their integration', in J. Brannen (ed.), *Mixing Methods: Qualitative and Quantitative Research.* Aldershot: Avebury.

Bryman, A. (2001) *Social Research Methods.* Oxford: Oxford University Press.

Bryman, A. and Cramer, D. (2001) *Quantitative Data Analysis for Social Scientists.* London: Routledge.

Buckingham, R.W., Lack, S.A., Mount, B.M., Maclean, L.D. and Collins, J.T. (1976) 'Living with the dying: use of the technique of participant observation', *Canadian Medical Association Journal,* 115: 1211–15.

Buckland, T. (ed.) (1999) *Dance in the Field: Theory, Methods and Issues in Dance Ethnography.* Basingstoke: Macmillan; New York: St. Martin's.

Bulmer, M. (1991) 'W.E.B. Du Bois as a social investigator: The Philadelphia Negro 1899', in M. Bulmer, K. Bales and K.K. Sklar (eds), *The Social Survey in Historical Perspective.* Cambridge: Cambridge University Press. pp. 170–88.

Bulmer, M., Bales, K. and Sklar, K.K. (eds) (1991) *The Social Survey in Historical Perspective.* Cambridge: Cambridge University Press.

Bury, M. (1996) 'Disability and the myth of the independent researcher: a reply', *Disability and Society,* 11 (1): 111–13.

Busfield, S. (2000) 'Irving loses Holocaust libel case', *Guardian,* 11 April 2000.

Butler, J.P. (1990) *Gender Trouble: Feminism and the Subversion of Identity.* New York and London: Routledge.

Cairncross, F. (1997) *The Death of Distance: How the Communications Revolution will Change Our Lives.* Boston, MA: Harvard Business School Press.

Campbell, D.T. (1969) 'Reforms as experiments', *American Psychologist,* 24: 409–29.

Campbell, D.T. and Fiske, D.W. (1959) 'Convergent and discriminant validation by the multitrait-multimethod matrix', *Psychological Bulletin,* 56 (2): 81–105.

Cantor, M.G. and Pingree, S. (1983) *The Soap Opera.* London: Sage.

Cartwright, A. and Seale, C.F. (1990) *The Natural History of a Survey: An Account of the Methodological Issues Encountered in a Study of Life before Death.* London: King's Fund.

Caplan, P. (ed.) (1987) *The Cultural Construction of Sexuality.* London: Routledge.

Carby, H. (1982) 'White women listen! feminism and the boundaries of sisterhood', in Centre for Contemporary Cultural Studies (ed.), *The Empire Strikes Back: Race and Racism in '70s Britain.* Birmingham: University of Birmingham Centre for Contemporary Cultural Studies. pp. 212–35.

Cartwright, A. (1964) *Human Relations and Hospital Care.* London: Routledge and Kegan Paul.

Cartwright, A., Hockey, L. and Anderson, J.L. (1973) *Life before Death.* London: Routledge and Kegan Paul.

Cartwright, A. and Seale, C.F. (1990) *The Natural History of a Survey: An Account of the Methodological Issues Encountered in a Study of Life before Death.* London: King's Fund.

Cerulo, K.A. (1997) 'Reframing social concepts for a brave new (virtual) world', *Sociological Inquiry,* 67 (1): 48–58.

Chakrabarty, D. (1989) *Rethinking Working-Class History.* Princeton, NJ: Princeton University Press.

Chambliss, W. (1975) 'On the paucity of original research on organized crime', *American Sociologist,* 10: 36–39.

Chandler, D. (2001) *Semiotics: The Basics.* London: Routledge.

Christie, B. (2000) 'Doctors revise Declaration of Helsinki', *British Medical Journal,* 321: 913.

Cicourel, A.V. (1968) *The Social Organization of Juvenile Justice.* New York: Wiley.

Clayman, S.E. (1988) 'Displaying neutrality in television news interviews', *Social Problems,* 35: 474–92.

Clayman, S.E. (1992) 'Footing in the achievement of neutrality: the case of news-interview discourse', in P. Drew and J. Heritage (eds), *Talk at Work.* Cambridge: Cambridge University Press.

Clifford, J. (1986) 'Introduction: partial truths', in J. Clifford and G.E. Marcus (eds), *Writing Culture: The Poetics and Politics of Ethnography.* Berkeley, CA: University of California Press.

Clifford, J. and Marcus, G.E. (eds) (1986) *Writing Culture: The Poetics and Politics of Ethnography.* Berkeley, CA: University of California Press.

Code, L. (1991) *What Can She Know? Feminist Theory and the Construction of Knowledge.* Ithaca, NY: Cornell University Press.

Coffey, A. (1999) *The Ethnographic Self: Fieldwork and the Representation of Identity.* London: Sage.

Coffey, A. and Atkinson, P. (1996) *Making Sense of Qualitative Data: Complementary Research Strategies.* London: Sage.

Coffey, A., Holbrook, B. and Atkinson, P. (1996) 'Qualitative data analysis: technologies and representations', *Sociological Research On-line,* 1 (1) http://www.soc.surrey.ac.uk/socresonline.

Cohen, S. and Taylor, L. (1972) *Psychological Survival: The Effects of Long-term Imprisonment.* London: Allen Lane.

Collins, H.M. (1985) *Changing Order: Replication and Induction in Scientific Practice.* London: Sage.

Collins, R. (1994) *Four Sociological Traditions.* Oxford: Oxford University Press.

Coomber, R. (1997) 'Using the Internet for Survey Research', *Sociological Research On-line,* 2 (2) www.socresonline.org.uk/socresonline/2/2/2.html.

Corbin, J. (1987) 'Women's perceptions and management of a pregnancy complicated by chronic illness', *Health Care for Women International,* 84: 317–37.

Cornwell, J. (1981) *Hard Earned Lives.* London: Tavistock.

Corsaro, W. (1981) 'Entering the child's world: research strategies for field entry and data collection in a pre-school setting', in J.L. Green and C. Wallats (eds), *Ethnography and Language in Education Settings.* Norwood, NJ: Ablex.

Corti, L. and Thompson, P. (2004) 'Secondary analysis of archived data', in C.F. Seale, G. Gobo, J.F. Gubrium and D. Silverman. (eds), *Qualitative Research Practice.* London: Sage.

Courtney, C. and Thompson, P. (1996) *City Lives.* London: Methuen.

Crapanzano, V. (1986) 'Hermes' dilemma: the masking of subversion in ethnographic description', in J. Clifford and G.E. Marcus (eds), *Writing Culture: The Poetics and Politics of Ethnography.* Berkeley, CA: University of California Press.

Csordas, T. (ed.) (1994a) *Embodiment and Experience: The Existential Ground of Culture and Self.* Cambridge: Cambridge University Press.

Csordas, T. (1994b) *The Sacred Self: A Cultural Phenomenology of Charismatic Healing.* Berkeley, CA: University of California Press.

Dale, A., Arber, S. and Proctor, M. (1988) *Doing Secondary Analysis.* London: Unwin Hyman.

Davidson, J.A. (1984) 'Subsequent versions of invitations, offers, requests, and proposals dealing with potential or actual rejection', in J.M. Atkinson. and J. Heritage (eds), *Structures of Social Action: Studies in Conversation Analysis.* Cambridge: Cambridge University Press.

De Vaus, D.A. (2002a) *Surveys in Social Research.* London: Routledge.

De Vaus (2002b) *Analysing Social Science Data: 50 Key Problems in Data Analysis.* London: Sage.

Deacon, D., Bryman, A. and Fenton, N. (1998) 'Collision or collusion? A discussion of the unplanned triangulation of quantitative and qualitative research methods', *International Journal of Social Research Methodology,* 1: 47–63.

Deleuze, G. and Guattari, F. (1988) *A Thousand Plateaus: Capitalism and Schizophrenia, Volume II.* London: Athlone.

D'Emilio, J. (1981) 'Gay politics and community in San Francisco since World War II', in M.B. Duberman, M. Vicinus and G. Chauncey (eds), *Hidden From History: Reclaiming the Gay and Lesbian Past.* Harmondsworth: Penguin. pp. 456–73.

Denscombe, M. (2002) *Ground Rules for Good Research: A 10 Point Guide For Social Researchers.* Buckingham: Open University Press.

Denzin, N.K. (1970) *The Research Act in Sociology.* London: Butterworth.

Denzin, N.K. (1978) *The Research Act: A Theoretical Introduction to Sociological Methods,* 2nd edn. New York: McGraw-Hill.

Denzin, N.K. (1988) 'Qualitative analysis for social scientists', *Contemporary Sociology,* 17 (3): 430–32.

Denzin, N.K. (1989) *The Research Act: A Theoretical Introduction to Sociological Methods* 3rd edn. Englewood Cliffs, NJ: Prentice-Hall.

Denzin, N.K and Lincoln, Y.S. (eds) (1994) *Handbook of Qualitative Research.* Thousand Oaks, CA: Sage.

Denzin, N.K and Lincoln, Y.S. (eds) (2000) *Handbook of Qualitative Research,* 2nd edn. Thousand Oaks, CA: Sage.

Derrida, J. (1996) *Archive Fever: A Freudian Impression.* Chicago: University of Chicago Press.

Dingwall, R. (1977) *The Social Organisation of Health Visitor Training.* London: Croom Helm.

Dingwall, R. and Murray, T. (1983) 'Categorisation in accident departments: "good" patients, "bad" patients and children', *Sociology of Health and Illness,* 5 (12): 121–48.

Doucet, A. and Mauthner, M. (2002) 'Knowing responsibly: linking ethics, research practice and epistemology', in M. Mauthner, M. Birch, J. Jessop and T. Miller (eds), *Ethics in Qualitative Research*. London: Sage.

Douglas, M. (1975) 'Self-evidence', in M. Douglas (ed.), *Implicit Meanings*. London: Routledge.

Dressler, W.W. (1991) *Stress and Adaptation in the Context of Culture: Depression in a Southern Black Community*. Albany, NY: State University of New York Press.

Drew, P. (1984) 'Speakers' reporting in invitation sequences', in J.M. Atkinson and J. Heritage (eds), *Structures of Social Action: Studies in Conversation Analysis*. Cambridge: Cambridge University Press.

Drew, P. (1992) 'Contested evidence in courtroom cross-examination: the case of a trial for rape', in P. Drew and J. Heritage (eds), *Talk at Work: Interaction in Institutional Settings*. Cambridge: Cambridge University Press.

Du Bois, W.E.B. (1934) *The Black Reconstruction*. New York: Harcourt, Brace.

Du Bois, W.E.B. (1940) *The Dusk of Dawn*. New York: Henry Holt.

Du Bois, W.E.B. (1968) *The Autobiography of W.E.B. Du Bois: A Soliloquy on Viewing my Life from the Last Decades of its First Century*. New York: International Publishers.

Du Bois, W.E.B. (1989) *The Souls of Black Folk*. New York: Bantam (first published 1903 in Chicago by A.C. McClung).

Du Bois, W.E.B. (1996) *The Philadelphia Negro: A Social Study*. Philadelphia: University of Philadelphia Press (first published 1899).

Durkheim, E. (1915) *The Elementary Forms of the Religious Life: A Study in Religious Sociology*. London: Allen and Unwin.

Durkheim, E. (1970) *Suicide: A Study in Sociology*. London: Routledge and Kegan Paul (originally published 1897).

Durkheim, E. (1972) *Selected Writings* (ed. A. Giddens). Cambridge: Cambridge University Press.

Durkheim, E. (1982) *The Rules of Sociological Method*. London: Macmillan.

Ereaut, G. (2004) 'Qualitative market research', in C.F. Seale, D. Silverman, J. Gubrium and G. Gobo (eds), *Qualitative Research Practice*. London: Sage.

ESRC (Economic and Social Science Research Council) (2003) *ESRC Mission Statement*. http://www.esrc.ac.uk/esrccontent/postgradfunding/mission.asp.

Evans-Pritchard, E.E. (1940) *The Nuer*. Oxford: Oxford University Press.

Fairclough, N. (2000) *New Labour, New Language?* London: Routledge.

Fairclough, N. (2003) *Analysing Discourse: Text Analysis for Social Research*. London: Routledge.

Fay, B. (1996) *Contemporary Philosophy of Social Science*. Cambridge, MA: Blackwell.

Featherstone, M. (1991) *Consumer Culture and Postmodernism*. London: Sage.

Feyerabend, P. (1975) *Against Method*. London: New Left Review.

Feyerabend, P. (1978) *Science in a Free Society*. London: New Left Review.

Feyerabend, P. (1981) 'How to defend society against science', in I. Hacking (ed.), *Scientific Revolutions*. Oxford: Oxford University Press.

Field, A. (2000) *Discovering Statistics using SPSS for Windows*. London: Sage.

Fielding, N. (1981) *The National Front*. London: Routledge and Kegan Paul.

Fielding, N. and Gilbert, N. (2000) *Understanding Social Statistics*. London: Sage.

Fielding, N. and Fielding, J. (2000) 'Resistance and adaptation to criminal identity: using secondary analysis to evaluate classic studies of crime and deviance', *Sociology*, 34 (4): 671–89.

Fielding, N. and Lee, R. (eds) (1991) *Using Computers in Qualitative Research*. Newbury Park, CA: Sage.

Finch, J. (1984) '"It's great to have someone to talk to": ethics and politics of interviewing women', in C. Bell and H. Roberts (eds), *Social Researching: Politics, Problems, Practice*. London: Routledge.

Finnis, J. (1983) *Fundamentals of Ethics* Washington, DC: Georgetown University Press.

Fisher, B., Margolis, M. and Resnik, D. (1996) 'Surveying the internet: democratic theory and civic life in cyberspace', *Southeastern Political Review*, 24 (3): 399–429.

Flick, U. (1998) *An Introduction to Qualitative Research*. London: Sage.

Fontana, A. (2002) 'Postmodern trends in interviewing', in J.F. Gubrium and J.A. Holstein (eds), *Handbook of Interview Research: Context and Method*. Thousand Oaks, CA: Sage. pp. 161–76.

Foucault, M. (1972) *The Archaeology of Knowledge*. London: Tavistock Publications.

Foucault, M. (1977) *Discipline and Punish*. Harmondsworth: Penguin.

Foucault, M. (1979) *The History of Sexuality: Volume 1*. Harmondsworth: Penguin.

Foucault, M. (1980) *Power/Knowledge: Selected Interviews and Other Writings 1972–1977*. New York: Pantheon.

Foucault, M. (1982) 'The subject and power', in H. L.

Dreyfus and P. Rabinow, *Michel Foucault: Beyond Structuralism and Hermeneutics*. Brighton: Harvester.

Foucault, M. (1984) 'What is an author?' in P. Rabinow (ed.), *The Foucault Reader*. Harmondsworth: Penguin.

Foucault, M. (1985) *The Use of Pleasure: The History of Sexuality, Volume 2*. New York: Pantheon.

Foucault, M. (1986) *The Care of the Self: The History of Sexuality, Volume 3*. New York: Pantheon.

Foucault, M. (1988) 'Technologies of the Self', in L.H. Martin, H. Gutman, and P.H. Hutton (eds.) *Technologies of the Self*. London: Tavistock.

Foucault, M. (1994) 'The ethics of the concern for self as a practice of freedom', in P. Rabinow (ed.), *Ethics: Subjectivity and Truth*. London: Penguin.

Foucault, M. (2000) 'Lives of infamous men', in *Essential Works of Foucault, 1958–1984, Volume III: Power*. London: Penguin.

Frankenberg, R. (1993) *White Women, Race Matters: The Social Construction of Whiteness*. London: Routledge.

Franz, C., McClelland, D. and Weinberger, J. (1991) 'Childhood antecedents of conventional social accomplishment in midlife adults: a 36-year prospective study', *Journal of Personality and Social Psychology*, 60 (4): 586–95.

Garfinkel, H. (1967) *Studies in Ethnomethodology*. Englewood Cliffs, NJ: Prentice–Hall.

Garnett, M. (2000) 'Out of This World: An Exploration Into the Use of Complementary Therapies by Those Who Nurse the Dying'. PhD thesis, University of London.

Gates, H.L. (1989) 'Darkly, as through the veil', introduction to W.E.B. Du Bois *The Souls of Black Folk*. New York: Bantam.

Geer, B. (1964) 'First days in the field', in P. Hammond (ed.), *Sociologists at Work*. New York: Basic Books.

Geertz, C. (1973) *The Interpretation of Cultures*. London: Fontana.

Geertz, C. (1988) *Works and Lives: The Anthropologist as Author*. Stanford, CA: Stanford University Press.

Gerth, H.H. and Mills, C.W. (eds) (1948) *From Max Weber: Essays in Sociology*. London: Routledge and Kegan Paul.

Giddens, A. (1991) *Modernity and Self-Identity: Self and Society in the Late Modern Age*. Cambridge: Polity Press.

Giddens, A. (1993) *Sociology*. Cambridge: Polity Press.

Gilbert, N. (1993) *Researching Social Life*. London: Sage.

Gill, R. (1996) 'Discourse analysis: methodological aspects', in J.E. Richardson (ed.), *Handbook of Qualitative Research Methods for Psychology and the Social Sciences*. Leicester: British Psychological Society.

Gilroy, P. (1993) *Small Acts*. London: Serpent's Tail.

Gilroy, P. (1993) *The Black Atlantic: Modernity and Double Consciousness*. London: Verso.

Gilroy, P. (2000) *Between Camps*. London: Allen Lane/Penguin.

Glaser, B.G. (1978) *Theoretical Sensitivity: Advances in the Methodology of Grounded Theory*. Mill Valley, CA: Sociology Press.

Glaser, B.G. (1992) *Emergence versus Forcing: Basics of Grounded Theory Analysis*. Mill Valley, CA: Sociology Press.

Glaser, B.G. and Strauss, A.L. (1964) 'The social loss of dying patients', *American Journal of Nursing*, 64 (6): 119–21.

Glaser, B.G. and Strauss, A.L. (1966) *Awareness of Dying*. London: Weidenfeld and Nicolson.

Glaser, B.G. and Strauss, A.L. (1967) *The Discovery of Grounded Theory: Strategies for Qualitative Research*. Chicago: Aldine.

Glaser, B.G. and Strauss, A.L. (1968) *Time for Dying*. Chicago: Aldine.

Goffman, E. (1959) *The Presentation of Self in Everyday Life*. New York: Doubleday Anchor.

Goffman, F. (1968) *Stigma: Notes on the Management of Spoiled Identity*. Harmondsworth: Pelican.

Goldthorpe, J.H., Lockwood, D., Bechhofer, F and Platt, J. (1969) *The Affluent Worker in the Class Structure*. Cambridge: Cambridge University Press.

Goodman, N. (1982) 'The fabrication of facts', in M. Krausz and J.W. Meiland (eds), *Relativism: Cognitive and Moral*. Notre Dame, IN: University of Notre Dame Press.

Goodwin, C. (1994) 'Professional vision', *American Anthropologist*, 96 (3): 606–33.

Gray, A. (1997) 'Learning from experience: cultural studies and feminism' in J. McGuigan (ed.), *Cultural Methodologies*. London: Sage.

Guba, E.G. and Lincoln, Y.S. (1994) 'Competing paradigms in qualitative research', in N.K. Denzin and Y.S. Lincoln (eds), *Handbook of Qualitative Research*. Thousand Oaks, CA: Sage. pp. 105–17.

Gubrium, J. (1988) *Analyzing Field Reality*. Newbury Park, CA: Sage (Qualitative Research Methods Series No. 8).

Gubrium, J. and Holstein, J. (1987) 'The private image: experiential location and method in family studies', *Journal of Marriage and the Family*, 49: 773–86.

Gubrium, J. and Holstein, J. (1997) *The New Language of Qualitative Method*. New York: Oxford University Press.

Gubrium, J. and Holstein, J. (eds) (2002) *Handbook of Interview Research: Context and Method*. Thousand Oaks, CA: Sage.

Guha, R. (1997) 'Chandra's death', in R. Guha (ed.), *Subaltern Studies Reader, 1986–1995*. Minneapolis, MN: University of Minnesota Press.

Hacking, I. (1990) *The Taming of Chance*. Cambridge: Cambridge University Press.

Hall, S. (1980) 'Encoding/decoding', in S. Hall (ed.), *Culture, Media, Language*. London: Hutchinson. pp. 128–38.

Hall, S. (1992) 'The West and the rest', in S. Hall and B. Gieben (eds), *Formations of Modernity*. Cambridge: Polity Press.

Hall, S. (1997) *Representation: Cultural Representations and Signifying Practices*. London: Sage.

Hallam, E. and Street, B. (eds) (2000) *Representing Otherness*. London and New York: Routledge.

Hammersley, M. (1992a) 'On feminist methodology', *Sociology*, 26 (2): 187–206.

Hammersley, M. (1992b) 'Deconstructing the qualitative–quantitative divide', in J. Brannen. (ed.), *Mixing Methods: Qualitative and Quantitative Research*. Aldershot: Avebury.

Hammersley, M. (1992c) *What's Wrong with Ethnography: Methodological Explorations*. London: Routledge.

Hammersley, M. (1995a) *The Politics of Social Research*. London: Sage.

Hammersley, M. (1995b) 'Theory and evidence in qualitative research', *Quality and Quantity*, 29: 55–66.

Hammersley, M. (1997) 'Qualitative data archiving: some reflections on its prospects and problems', *Sociology*, 31 (1): 131–42.

Hammersley, M. (2002) 'Discourse analysis: a bibliographical guide', http://www.cf.ac.uk/socsi/capacity/Activities/Themes/In-depth/guide.pdf.

Hammersley, M. and Atkinson, P. (1995) *Ethnography: Principles in Practice*, 2nd edn. London: Routledge.

Hansard (1994) *Criminal Justice and Public Order Bill*. House of Commons, 21 February. London: HMSO.

Hansen, E.C. (1977) *Rural Catalonia under the Franco Regime*. Cambridge: Cambridge University Press.

Haraway, D. (1991) 'A cyborg manifesto: science, technology, and socialist-feminism in the late twentieth century', in *Simians, Cyborgs and Women: The Reinvention of Nature*. London: Free Association Books.

Haraway, D. (1997) *Modest Witness, Second Millenium: FemaleMan Meets OncoMouse: Feminism and Technoscience*. London: Routledge.

Harding, S. (1986) *The Science Question and Feminism*. Bloomington, IN: Indiana University Press.

Harding, S. (ed.) (1987) *Feminism and Methodology*. Milton Keynes: Open University Press.

Harding, S. (1991) *Whose Science? Whose Knowledge?: Thinking From Women's Lives*. Milton Keynes: Open University Press.

Harding, S. (1998) *Is Science Multicultural?: Postcolonialisms, Feminisms, and Epistemologies*. Bloomington, IN: Indiana University Press.

Harper, D. (1998) 'An argument for visual sociology' in J. Prosser (ed.), *Image-based Research: A Sourcebook for Qualitative Researchers*. London: Falmer Press. pp. 24–41.

Harris, C. (1991) 'Configurations of racism: the Civil Service, 1945–60', *Race and Class* 33 (1): 1–29.

Hart, C. (1998) *Doing a Literature Review: Releasing the Social Science Research Imagination*. London: Sage.

Hart, C. (2001) *Doing a Literature Search: A Comprehensive Guide for the Social Sciences*. London: Sage.

Have, P. ten (1999) *Doing Conversation Analysis: A Practical Guide*. London: Sage.

Heath, C. and Hindmarsh, J. (2002) 'Analyzing interaction: video, ethnography and situated conduct', in T. May (ed.), *Qualitative Research in Action*. London: Sage.

Hempel, C. (1966) *Philosophy of Natural Science*. Englewood Cliffs, NJ: Prentice-Hall.

Heritage, J. (1984) *Garfinkel and Ethnomethodology*. Cambridge: Polity Press.

Heritage, J. (1997) 'Conversation analysis and institutional talk: analysing data', in D. Silverman (ed.), *Qualitative Research: Theory, Method and Practice*. London: Sage. pp. 161–82.

Heritage, J. and Greatbatch, D. (1991) 'On the institutional character of institutional talk: the case of news interviews', in D. Boden and D.H. Zimmerman (eds), *Talk and Social Structure: Studies in Ethnomethodology and Conversation Analysis*. Berkeley, CA: University of California Press.

Hertz, R. (1960) *Death and the Right Hand*. Glencoe IL: Free Press (first published 1907).

Hesse, M. (1972) 'In defence of objectivity', *Proceedings of the British Academy*, LVIII: 275–92.

Hewitt, R. (1996) *Routes of Racism: The Social Basis of Racist Action*. Stoke on Trent: Trentham Books.

Hewitt, R., Spicer, N. and Tooke, J. (2003) *Projects, Participation and Partnerships: An Analysis of LSL HAZ Activities*. London: Goldsmiths, University of London.

Hey, V. (1994) 'Telling tales: methodological issues arising from doing research on decision making and the frail elderly', in P. Alderson (ed.), *Sharing Health and Welfare Choices with Old People*. London: SSRU Consent Series no 7. pp. 46–56.

Hill, M.R. (1993) *Archival Research Strategies and Techniques*. London: Sage.

Hill Collins, P. (1990) *Black Feminist Thought: Knowledge, Consciousness and the Politics of Empowerment*. London: Harper Collins Academic.

Hine, C. (1988) 'Virtual ethnography'. Paper presented at a 'Research and Information for Social Scientists' conference held 25–27 March 1998, Bristol, UK. http://www.sosig.ac.uk/iriss/abstracts/iriss16.htm.

Hine, C. (2000) *Virtual Ethnography*. London: Sage.

Hirschi, T. and Selvin, H.C. (1967) *Delinquency Research: An Appraisal of Analytic Methods*. New York: Free Press/Collier-Macmillan.

Hodge, D.C. (1995) 'Should women count? The role of quantitative methodology in feminist geographic research', *Professional Geographer*, 47 (4): 426.

Hoffmaster, B. (1994) 'The forms and limits of medical ethics', *Social Science and Medicine,* 39 (9): 1155–64.

Holdaway, S. (1982) 'An inside job: a case study of covert research on the police', in M. Bulmer (ed.), *Social Research Ethics: An Examination of the Merits of Covert Participant Observation*. London: Macmillan.

Holland, J. (1991) 'Introduction: history, memory and the family album' in P. Holland and J. Spence (eds), *Family Snaps: The Meanings of Domestic Photography*. London: Virago. pp. 1–14.

Holland, J. and Ramazanoglu, C. (1994) 'Coming to conclusions: power and interpretations in researching young women's sexuality', in M. Maynard and J. Purvis (eds), *Researching Women's Lives from a Feminist Perspective*. London: Taylor and Francis.

Hollis, M. (1994) *The Philosophy of Social Science: An Introduction*. Cambridge: Cambridge University Press.

Holmes, T.H. and Rahe, R.H. (1967) 'The social readjustment rating scale', *Journal of Psychosomatic Research*, 11: 213–18.

Holstein, J.A. and Gubrium, J.A. (1995) *The Active Interview*. Thousand Oaks, CA: Sage.

Homan, R. (1991) *The Ethics of Social Research*. London: Longman.

hooks, b. (1994) *Teaching to Transgress*. London and New York: Routledge.

Huckin, T. (2002) 'Textual silence and the discourse of homelessness', *Discourse and Society*, 13 (3): 347–72.

Humphrey, L. (1970) *Tearoom Trade: A Study of Homosexual Encounters in Public Places*. London: Duckworth.

Hunt, P. (1981) 'Settling accounts with the parasite people', *Disability Challenge*, 2: 37–50.

Hutchby, I.R. and Wooffitt, R. (1998) *Conversation Analysis: Principles, Practices and Applications*. Cambridge: Polity Press.

Hyman, H. (1955) *Survey Design and Analysis*. New York: Free Press.

Hymes, D. (1974) *Reinventing Anthropology*. New York: Vintage.

Jackson, B. and Marsden, D. (1962) *Education and the Working Class*. London: Routledge and Kegan Paul.

Jagose, A. (1996) *Queer Theory*. Carlton South, Victoria: University of Melbourne Press.

Janesick, V. (2003) *'Stretching' Exercises for Qualitative Researchers*, 2nd edn. Thousand Oaks, CA: Sage.

Jayaratne, T.E. (1983) 'The value of quantitative methodology for feminist research', in G. Bowles and R. Duelli Klein (eds), *Theories of Women's Studies*. London: Routledge and Kegan Paul.

Jayaratne, T.E. and Stewart, A. (1991) 'Quantitative and qualitative methods in the social sciences: current feminist issues and practical strategies', in M.M. Fonow and J.A. Cook (eds), *Beyond Methodology: Feminist Scholarship as Lived Research*. Bloomington and Indianapolis, IN: Indiana University Press.

Jeffery, R. (1979) 'Normal rubbish: deviant patients in casualty departments', *Sociology of Health and Illness*, 1 (1): 90–107.

Jones, J.H. (1993) *Bad Blood: The Tuskegee Syphilis Experiment*. New York: Free Press.

Jones, S. (1999) *Doing Internet Research: Critical Issues and Methods for Examining the Net*. London: Sage.

Junker, B. (1960) *Fieldwork*. Chicago: University of Chicago Press.

Kaplan, A. (1991) 'Gone fishing, be back later', in W.B. Shaffir and R. Stebbins (eds), *Experiencing Fieldwork*. Newbury Park, CA: Sage.

Keddie, N. (1971) 'Classroom knowledge', in M. Young (ed.), *Knowledge and Control*. London: Collier-Macmillan.

Kelle, U. (1997) 'Theory building in qualitative research and computer programs for the management of textual data', *Sociological Research Online*, 2, 2: http://www.soc.surrey.ac.uk/socresonline.

Kelman, H.C. (1982) 'Ethical issues in different social science methods', in T.L. Beauchamp, R.R. Faden, R.J. Wallace and L. Walters (eds), *Ethical Issues in*

Social Science Research. Baltimore, MD: Johns Hopkins University Press.

Kendall, G. and Wickham, G. (1999) *Using Foucault's Methods.* London: Sage.

Kendall, L. (1999) 'Re-contextualising "Cyberspace"; methodological considerations for on-line research' in, S. Jones (ed.), *Doing Internet Research: Critical Issues and Methods for Examining the Net.* London: Sage.

Kent, R.A. (1981) *A History of British Empirical Sociology.* Aldershot: Gower.

Kingery, W.D. (1998) *Learning From Things: Method and Theory of Material Culture Studies.* Washington, DC: Smithsonian Institute.

Kirkwood, J. (1993) 'Investing ourselves: use of researcher personal response in feminist methodology', in J. deGroot and M. Maynard (eds), *Women's Studies in the 1990s: Doing Things Differently?* Basingstoke, Macmillan.

Kitzinger, C. (2000) 'Doing feminist conversation analysis', *Feminism and Psychology*, 10: 163–93.

Kitzinger, C. and Firth, H. (1999) ' "Just say no?" The use of conversation analysis in developing a feminist perspective on sexual refusal', *Discourse and Society,* 10 (3): 293–316.

Kitzinger, J. (1994) 'Focus groups: method or madness?', in M. Boulton (ed.), *Challenge and Innovation: Methodological Advances in Social Research on HIV/AIDS.* London: Taylor and Francis. pp. 159–75.

Kleinman, S. (1999) 'Essaying the personal: making sociological stories stick', in B. Glassner and R. Hertz (eds), *Qualitative Sociology as Everyday Life.* London: Sage.

Krathwohl, D.R. (1988) *How to Prepare a Research Proposal: Guidelines for Funding and Dissertations in the Social and Behavioural Sciences*, 3rd edn. Syracuse, NY: Syracuse University Press.

Krauss, R. (1990) 'A note on photography and the simulacral', in C. Squiers (ed.), (1991), *The Critical Image: Essays in Contemporary Photography.* London: Lawrence and Wishart. pp. 15–27.

Krueger, R.A. and Casey, M.A. (2000) *Focus Groups: A Practical Guide for Applied Research*, 3rd edn. London: Sage.

Kuhn, A. (1995) *Family Secrets: Acts of Memory and Imagination.* London and New York: Verso.

Kuhn, A. (2000) 'A journey through memory', in S. Radstone (ed.), *Memory and Methodology.* New York and Oxford: Berg. pp. 17–25.

Kuhn, T. (1970) *The Structure of Scientific Revolutions*, 2nd edn, enlarged. Chicago: University of Chicago Press.

Kynaston, D. (2001) *The City of London, IV: A Club No More, 1945–2000.* London: Pimlico.

Lancet (1980) 'In cancer honesty is here to stay', *Lancet*, ii: 245.

Laslett, P. (1979) *The World We Have Lost.* London: Methuen.

Latour, B. (1999) *Pandora's Hope: Essays on the Reality of Science Studies.* Cambridge, MA: Harvard University Press.

Latour, B. and Woolgar, S. (1979) *Laboratory Life: The Production of Scientific Facts.* Princeton, NJ: Princeton University Press.

Law, J. (1994) *Organizing Modernity.* Oxford: Blackwell.

Lawrence, E. (1982) 'In the abundance of water the fool is thirsty: sociology and black pathology', in Centre for Contemporary Cultural Studies (ed.), *The Empire Strikes Back: Race and Racism in '70s Britain.* Birmingham: University of Birmingham Centre for Contemporary Cultural Studies. pp. 95–142.

Lawson, V. (1995) 'The place of difference: examining the quantitative/qualitative dualism in post-structural feminist research', *Professional Geographer*, 47 (4): 449–57.

Layder, D. (1994) *Understanding Social Theory.* London: Sage.

Lazarsfeld, P.F. and Rosenberg, M. (1955) *The Language of Social Research: A Reader in the Methodology of Social Research.* Glencoe, IL: Free Press.

Lechte, J. (1994) *Fifty Key Contemporary Thinkers: From Structuralism to Postmodernity.* London: Routledge.

Leiss, W., Kline, S. and Jhally, S. (1990) *Social Communication in Advertising: Persons, Products and Images of Well-Being*, 2nd edn. London: Routledge.

Leitsch, Dick (1969) 'Police raid on N.Y club sets off first gay riot', in C. Bull (ed.) *Witness to Revolution: The Advocate Reports on Gay and Lesbian Politics, 1967–1999.* Los Angeles: Alyson. pp. 11–15.

Lévi-Strauss, C. (1969a) *Totemism.* Harmondsworth: Penguin.

Lévi-Strauss, C. (1969b) *Elementary Structures of Kinship.* London: Eyre and Spottiswood.

Ley, D. and Samuels, M.S. (eds) (1978) *Humanistic Geography: Prospects and Problems.* London: Croom Helm.

Lincoln Y.S. and Denzin, N.K. (2000) 'The seventh moment: out of the past', in Denzin, N.K. and Lincoln, Y.S. (eds), *Handbook of Qualitative Research*, 2nd edn. Thousand Oaks, CA: Sage. pp.

521

1047–65.

Lincoln, Y.S. and Guba, E. (1985) *Naturalistic Enquiry*. Beverly Hills, CA: Sage.

Linke, U. (1999) *German Bodies – Race and Representation after Hitler*. London: Routledge.

Lipstadt, D. (1993) *Denying the Holocaust: The Growing Assault on Truth and Memory*. New York: Free Press/ Macmillan.

Lister, M. (ed.) (1995) *The Photographic Image in Digital Culture*. London: Routledge.

Little, D. (1991) *Varieties of Social Explanation*. Boulder, CO: Westview.

Livingston, E. (1987) *Making Sense of Ethnomethodology*. London: Routledge.

Llobera, J. (1998) 'Historical and comparative research', in C.F. Seale (ed.), *Researching Society and Culture*. London: Sage. pp. 72–81.

Lofland, J. (1971) *Analysing Social Settings: A Guide to Qualitative Observation*. Belmont, CA: Wadsworth.

Lofland, L. (1974) 'The "thereness" of women: a selective review of urban sociology', in M. Millman and R.M. Kanter (eds), *Another Voice: Feminist Perspectives on Social Life and Social Science*. New York: Anchor.

Lomax, H. and Casey, N. (1998) 'Recording Social Life: Reflexivity and Video Method-ology', *Sociological Research Online*, 3 (2) www.socresonline.org.uk/socresonline/3/2/1.html.

Lunt, P. and Livingstone, S. (1996) 'Rethinking the focus group in media and communications research', *Journal of Communication*, 46 (2): 79–98.

Lyotard, J.-F. (1984) *The Postmodern Condition: A Report on Knowledge* (trans. G. Bennington and B. Massumi). Minneapolis: University of Minnesota Press.

MacDonald, S. (2001) 'British social anthropology', in P. Atkinson, A. Coffey, S. Delamont, J. Lofland and L. Lofland (eds), *Handbook of Ethnography*. London: Sage. pp. 60–79.

MacIntyre, S. (1977) *Single and Pregnant*. London: Croom Helm.

Malinowski, B. (1922) *Argonauts of the Western Pacific: An Account of Native Enterprise and Adventure in the Archipelagoes of Melanesian New Guinea*. London: Routledge and Kegal Paul.

Malinowksi, B. (1929) *The Sexual Life of Savages*. London: Routledge and Kegan Paul.

Malthus, T. (1798) *An Essay on the Principle of Population, As It Affects the Future Improvement of Society, With Remarks on the Speculations of Mr Godwin, M. Condorcet and Other Writers*. London,

printed for J. Johnson, in St Paul's Churchyard.

Mann, C. and Stewart, F. (2000) *Internet Communication and Qualitative Research. A Handbook for Researching Online*. London: Sage.

Margolis, E. (2000) 'Class pictures: representations of race, gender and ability in a century of school photography', in *Education Policy Analysis Archives*, 8 (31), 4 July 2000. http://epaa.asu.edu/epaa/v8n31/.

Marris, P. (1958) *Widows and their Families*. London: Routledge and Kegan Paul.

Marsh, C. (1982) *The Survey Method: The Contribution of Surveys to Sociological Explanation*. London: Allen and Unwin.

Marsh, C. (1984) 'Problems with surveys: method or epistemology?', in M. Bulmer (ed.), *Sociological Research Methods*. London: Macmillan.

Martin, E. (1994) *Flexible Bodies: The Role of Immunity in American Culture from the Days of Polio to the Age of AIDS*. Boston, MA: Beacon Press.

Martin, M. and McIntyre, L.C. (eds) (1994) *Readings in the Philosophy of Social Science*. Cambridge, MA: MIT Press.

Marx, K. (1976) *Capital: Volume I*. London: Penguin.

Mason, J. (1996) *Qualitative Researching*. London: Sage.

Mason-John, V. (ed.) (1995) *Talking Black: Lesbians of African and Asian Descent Speak Out*. London and New York: Cassell.

Mattingly, D.J. and Falconer-Al-Hindi, K. (1995) 'Should women count? A context for the debate', *Professional Geographer*, 47 (4): 427–35.

Mauthner, M (1998) 'Bringing silent voices into a public discourse: researching accounts of sister relationships', in J. Ribbens and R. Edwards (eds), *Feminist Dilemmas in Qualitative Research: Public Knowledge and Private Lives*. London: Sage.

Mauthner, M., Birch, M., Jessop, J. and Miller, T. (eds) (2002) *Ethics in Qualitative Research*. London: Sage.

May, T. (1996) *Situating Social Theory*. Buckingham: Open University Press.

Maynard, D.W. (1991) 'On the interactional and institutional bases of asymmetry in clinical discourse', *American Journal of Sociology*, 97: 448–95.

Maynard, D.W. (1992) 'On clinicians co-implicating recipients' perspective in the delivery of diagnostic news', in P. Drew and J. Heritage (eds), *Talk at Work*. Cambridge: Cambridge University Press.

Maynard, M. and Purvis, J. (eds) (1994) *Researching Women's Lives from a Feminist Perspective*.

London: Taylor and Francis.

McCall, G.J. and Simmons, J.L. (eds) (1969) *Issues in Participant Observation: A Text and Reader.* Reading, MA: Addison-Wesley.

McLafferty, S. (1995) 'Counting for women', *Professional Geographer,* 47(4): 436–42.

McPherson, C.J. and Addington-Hall, J.M. (2003) 'Judging the quality of care at the end of life: can proxies provide reliable information?', *Social Science and Medicine,* 56 (1): 95–109.

McWhinney, I.R., Bass, M.J. and Donner, A. (1994) 'Evaluation of palliative care service: problems and pitfalls', *British Medical Journal,* 309: 1340–42.

Mead, M. (1942) *Growing up in New Guinea: A Study of Adolescence and Sex in Primitive Societies.* Harmondsworth: Penguin (first published in 1930).

Mercer, K. (1994) 'Reading racial fetishism; reading the photographs of Robert Mapplethorpe', in *Welcome to the Jungle: New Positions in Black Cultural Studies.* London and New York: Routledge.

Merton, R.K. (1987) 'The focused interview and focus groups: continuities and discontinuities', *Public Opinion Quarterly,* 51: 550–66.

Michael, M. (1992) 'Lay discourses of science: science-in-general, science-in-particular and self', *Science Technology and Human Values,* 17: 313–33.

Michael, M. (1996) 'Ignoring science: discourses of ignorance in the public understanding of science', in A. Irwin and B. Wynne (eds), *Misunderstanding Science? The Public Reconstruction of Science and Technology.* Cambridge: Cambridge University Press. pp. 105–25.

Michael, M. and Birke, L. (1994a) 'Animal experimentation: enrolling the core set', *Social Studies of Science,* 24 (1): 81–95.

Michael, M. and Birke, L. (1994b) 'Accounting for animal experiments: credibility and disreputable "others"', *Science Technology and Human Values,* 19 (2): 189–204.

Michael, M. and Carter, S. (2001) 'The facts about fictions and vice versa: public understanding of human genetics', *Science as Culture,* 10 (1): 5–32.

Milgram, S. (1974) *Obedience to Authority.* New York: Harper and Row.

Miller, D. (1994) *Modernity: An Ethnographic Approach.* Oxford: Berg.

Miller, D. (1998) *Material Cultures: Why Some Things Matter.* London: UCL Press.

Miller, E.J. and Gwynne, G.V. (1972) *A Life Apart.* London: Tavistock.

Mitchell, J.C. (1983) 'Case and situational analysis', *Sociological Review,* 31 (2): 187–211.

Moerman, M. (1974) 'Accomplishing ethnicity', in R. Turner (ed.), *Ethnomethodology.* Harmondsworth: Penguin.

Moerman, M. (1988) *Talking Culture: Ethnography and Conversational Analysis.* Philadelphia: University of Pennsylvania Press.

Moerman, M. (1992) 'Life after CA: an ethnographer's autobiography', in G. Watson and R.M. Seiler (eds), *Text in Context: Contributions to Ethnomethodology.* London: Sage.

Morgan, D. (1980) 'Men, masculinity and the process of sociological enquiry', in H. Roberts (ed.), *Doing Feminist Research.* London: Routledge and Kegan Paul.

Morgan, D. (1993) *Successful Focus Groups.* London: Sage.

Morgan, D. (1997) *Focus Groups as Qualitative Research,* 2nd edn. London: Sage.

Morley, D. (1980) *The 'Nationwide' Audience.* London: British Film Institute.

Moser, C.A. and Kalton, G. (1971) *Survey Methods in Social Investigation,* 2nd edn. Aldershot: Gower.

Moss, P. (1995) 'Embeddedness in practice, numbers in context: the politics of knowing and doing', *Professional Geographer,* 47 (4): 442–49.

Moss, S. (2000) 'History's verdict on Holocaust upheld: historians claim victory after rigorous courtroom test', *Guardian,* 12 April 2000.

Moya, P.M.L. (2002) *Learning From Experience: Minority Identities, Multicultural Struggles.* Berkley, CA: University of California Press.

Mulkay, M. (1979) *Science and the Sociology of Knowledge.* London: Allen and Unwin.

Mulvey, L. (1975) 'Visual pleasure and narrative cinema', *Screen,* 16 (3): 6–8.

Myhill, A. and Allen, J. (2002) *Home Office Research Study 237: Rape and Sexual Assault of Women: The Extent and Nature of the Problem. Findings from the British Crime Survey.* London: Home Office Research, Development and Statistics Directorate.

Najman, J.M., Morrison, J., Williams, G.M. and Andersen, M.J. (1992) 'Comparing alternative methodologies of social research: an overview', in J. Daly, I. McDonald and E. Willis (eds), *Researching Health Care: Designs, Dilemmas, Disciplines.* London: Routledge.

Nelson, B. (1984) *Making an Issue of Child Abuse: Political Agenda Setting for Social Problems.* Chicago: University of Chicago Press.

Neuendorf, K.A. (2002) *The Content Analysis Guidebook.* London: Sage.

Newton-Smith, W.H. (1981) *The Rationality of Science.* London: Routledge.

Novack, D.H., Plumer, R., Smith, R.L., Ochitill, H., Morrow, G.R. and Bennett, J.M. (1979) 'Changes in physicians' attitudes toward telling the cancer patient', *Journal of the American Medical Association*, 241: 897–900.

Oakley, A. (1981) 'Interviewing women: a contradiction in terms?', in H. Roberts (ed.), *Doing Feminist Research*. London: Routledge.

Oakley, A. (1989) 'Who's afraid of the randomised controlled trial? Some dilemmas of the scientific method and "good" research practice', *Women and Health*, 15 (4): 25–59.

Odum, H.W. and Jocher, K. (1929) *An Introduction to Social Research*. New York: Holt.

Oevermann, U., Allert, T., Konau, E. and Krambeck, J. (1979) 'Die Methodologie einer "objektiven Hermeneutik" und ihre allgemeine forschungs-logische Bedeutung in den Sozialwissenschaften', in H.G. Soeffner (ed.), *Interpretative Verfahren in den Sozial-und Textwissenschaften*. Stuttgart: Metzler. pp. 352–433.

Oliver, M. (1999) 'Final accounts and the parasite people', in M. Corker and S. French (eds), *Disability Discourse*. Buckingham: Open University Press. pp. 183–91

Parmar, P. (1990) 'Black feminism: the politics of articulation', J. Rutherford (ed.), *Identity: Community, Culture Difference*. London: Lawrence and Wishart. pp. 101–26.

Parsons, T., Naegele, K., Pitts, J. and Shils, E. (eds) (1961) *Theories of Society* (2 vols). New York: Free Press.

Passerini, L. (1991) 'Memory', *History Workshop Journal*, 15 (Spring) 1983.

Passey, A. (1999) *Civil Society in the New Millennium*. Report to the Commonwealth Foundation. London: National Council for Voluntary Organisations.

Pawson, R. and Tilley, N. (1997) *Realistic Evaluation*. London: Sage.

Pearce, J. (2003) 'Being Young and Keeping Safe: Young People, Space and Safety'. PhD thesis, University of London.

Pearson, G. (1983) *Hooligan: A History of Respectable Fears*. Basingstoke: Macmillan.

Philip, L. (1998) 'Combining quantitative and qualitative approaches to social research in human geography – an impossible mixture?', *Environment and Planning*, 30: 261–76.

Philo, G. (1990) *Seeing and Believing: The Influence of Television*. London: Routledge.

Philo, G. (2001) 'Bad news from Israel: media coverage of the Israeli/Palestinian conflict.' Glasgow University Media Group. http://www.gla.ac.uk/departments/sociology/Israel.pdf.

Philo, G. and Beattie, L. (1999) 'Race, migration and media', in G. Philo (ed.), *Message Received*. London: Longman.

Philo, G., Gilmer, A., Rust, S., Gaskell, E. and West, L. (2003) 'Television coverage of the Israel/Palestinian conflict', in D.K. Thussu and D. Freedman (eds), *War and The Media: Reporting Conflict 24/7*. London: Sage.

Phoenix, A. (1994) 'Practising feminist research: the intersection of gender and "race" in the research process', in M. Maynard and J. Purvis (eds), *Researching Women's Lives from a Feminist Perspective*. London: Taylor and Francis. pp. 49–70.

Phoenix, A. (1987) 'Theories of gender and black families', in G. Weiner and M. Arnot (eds), *Gender Under Scrutiny*. London: Hutchinson. pp. 50–63.

Pink, S. (2001) *Doing Visual Ethnography: Images, Media and Representation in Research*. London: Sage.

Platt, J. (1996) *A History of Sociological Research Methods in America*. Cambridge: Cambridge University Press.

Platt, J. (2002) 'The history of the interview', in J.F. Gubrium and J.A. Holstein (eds), *Handbook of Interview Research: Context and Method*. Thousand Oaks: Sage. pp. 33–54.

Pollner, M. (1987) *Mundane Reason: Reality in Everyday Life and Sociological Discourse*. Cambridge: Cambridge University Press.

Pomerantz, A. (1984) 'Agreeing and disagreeing with assessments: some features of preferred/dispreferred turn shapes', in J.M. Atkinson and J. Heritage (eds), *Structures of Social Action: Studies in Conversation Analysis*. Cambridge: Cambridge University Press.

Popper, K.R. (1957) *The Poverty of Historicism*. London: Routledge and Kegan Paul.

Popper, K.R. (1963) *Conjectures and Refutations*. London: Routledge and Kegan Paul.

Popper, K.R. (1972) *Objective Knowledge*. Oxford: Clarendon Press.

Popper, K.R. (1994) *The Myth of the Framework*. London: Routledge.

Poster, M. (2000) 'Postmodern virtualities', in M. Featherstone and R. Burrows (eds), *Cyber Space, Cyber Bodies, Cyber Punk; Cultures of Technological Embodiment*. London: Sage.

Potter, J. and Wetherell, M. (1987) *Discourse and Social Psychology: Beyond Attitudes and Behaviour*. London: Sage.

Potter, J. and Wetherell, M. (1994) 'Analyzing discourse, in A. Bryman and B. Burgess (eds), *Analyzing Qualitative Data*. London: Routledge.

Price, R. and Price, S. (1991) *Two Evenings in Saramaka*. Chicago: University of Chicago Press.

Priestley, M. (1997) 'Who's research?: a personal

audit', in C. Barnes (ed.), *Doing Disability Research.* Leeds: The Disability Press. pp. 89–107.

Psathas, G. (1995) *Conversation Analysis: The Study of Talk-In-Interaction.* Thousand Oaks, CA: Sage.

Punch, K.F. (2000) *Developing Effective Research Proposals.* London: Sage.

Punch, M. (1986) *The Politics and Ethics of Fieldwork: Muddy Boots and Grubby Hands.* Newbury Park, CA: Sage.

Radway, J. (1987) *Reading the Romance: Women, Patriarchy and Popular Literature.* London: Verso.

Ramazanoglu, C. and Holland, J. (2002) *Feminist Methodology: Challenges and Choices.* London and New York: Sage.

Rayner, G. and Stimson, G. (1979) 'Medicine, superstructure and micropolitics: a response', *Social Science and Medicine,* 13A: 611–12.

Reinharz, S. (1992) *Feminist Methods in Social Research.* New York: Oxford University Press.

Renzetti, C. and Lee, R.M. (1993) *Researching Sensitive Topics.* London and New York: Sage.

Ribbens, J. (1989) "Interviewing – an 'unnatural situation'?" *Women's Studies International Forum,* 12 (6): 579–92.

Richardson, L. (1997) *Fields of Play: Constructing an Academic Life.* New Brunswick, NJ: Rutgers University Press.

Riessman, C. (1987) 'When gender is not enough: women interviewing women', *Gender and Society,* 1 (2): 172–207.

Riessman, C.K. (1993) *Narrative Analysis.* Newbury Park, CA: Sage.

Rollnick, S., Seale, C., Rees, M., Butler, C., Kinnersley, P. and Anderson, L. (2001) 'Inside the routine general practice consultation: an observational study of consultations for sore throats', *Family Practice,* 18 (5): 506–10.

Rosaldo, R. (1989) *Culture and Truth: The Remaking of Social Analysis.* London: Routledge.

Rose, G. (1982) *Deciphering Social Research.* London: Macmillan.

Rose, G. (2001) *Visual Methodologies: An Introduction to the Interpretation of Visual Materials.* London: Sage.

Rose, N. (1999) *Powers of Freedom: Reframing Political Thought.* Cambridge: Cambridge University Press.

Rosenberg, M. (1968) *The Logic of Survey Analysis.* New York: Basic Books.

Rossman, G.B. and Wilson, B.L. (1994) 'Numbers and words revisited: being "shamelessly eclectic"' *Quality and Quantity,* 28: 315–27.

Rowntree, B.S. (1901) *Poverty: A Study of Town Life.*

Basingstoke: Macmillan.

Rowntree, B.S. (1941) *Poverty and Progress: A Second Social Survey of York.* London: Longmans.

Rowntree, B.S. and Lavers, G.R. (1951) *Poverty and the Welfare State: A Third Social Survey of York Dealing Only with Economic Questions.* London: Longmans.

Sacks, H. (1974) 'On the analyzability of stories by children', in R. Turner (ed.), *Ethnomethodology.* Harmondsworth: Penguin.

Sacks, H. (1984) 'Notes on methodology', in J.M. Atkinson and J. Heritage (eds), *Structures of Social Action: Studies in Conversation Analysis.* Cambridge: Cambridge University Press.

Sacks, H. (1987) 'On the preferences for agreement and contiguity in sequences in conversation', in G. Button and J.R.E. Lee (eds), *Talk and Social Organisation.* Clevedon: Multilingual Matters.

Sacks, H. (1992a) *Lectures on Conversation, Volume 1.* Oxford: Blackwell.

Sacks, H. (1992b) *Lectures on Conversation, Volume 2.* Oxford: Blackwell.

Sacks, H., Schegloff, E. and Jefferson, G. (1974) 'A simple systematics for the organization of turn-taking in conversation', *Language,* 50 (4): 696–735.

Saussure, F. de (1974) *Course in General Linguistics.* London: Fontana.

Schegloff, E.A. (1999) 'Discourse, pragmatics, conversation, analysis', *Discourse Studies,* 1: 405–36.

Schutz, A. (1962) *Collected Papers, Volume 1.* The Hague: Martinus Nijhoff.

Schutz, A. (1964) *Collected Papers, Volume 2.* The Hague: Martinus Nijhoff.

Schutz, A. (1970) 'Concept and theory formation in the social sciences', in D. Emmet. and A. MacIntyre (eds), *Sociological Theory and Philosophical Analysis.* London: Macmillan.

Schütze, F. (1977) 'Die Technik des narrativen Interviews in Interaktionfeldstudien, dargestellt an einem Projekt zur Erforschung von kommunalen Machstrukturen'. Manuskript der Universität Bielefeld, Fakultät für Soziologie.

Scott, J. (1990) *A Matter of Record: Documentary Sources in Social Research.* Cambridge: Polity Press.

Scott, S. (1984) 'The personable and the powerful', in C. Bell and H. Roberts (eds), *Social Researching: Politics, Problems, Practice.* London: Routledge.

Seale, C.F. (1995a) 'Dying alone', *Sociology of Health and Illness,* 17 (3): 376–92.

Seale, C.F. (1995b) 'Heroic death', *Sociology* 29 (4): 597–613.

Seale, C.F. (1996) 'Living alone towards the end of life', *Ageing and Society,* 16: 75–91.

Seale, C.F. (1998) *Constructing Death: The Sociology of Dying and Bereavement.* Cambridge: Cambridge University Press.

Seale, C.F. (1999) *The Quality of Qualitative Research.* London: Sage.

Seale, C.F. (2002) 'Cancer heroics: a study of news reports with particular reference to gender', *Sociology,* 36 (1): 107–26.

Seale, C.F. (2003) *Media and Health.* London: Sage.

Seale, C.F. (ed.) (2004a) *Social Research Methods: A Reader.* London: Routledge.

Seale, C.F. (2004b) 'Media constructions of dying alone: a form of "bad death"', *Social Science and Medicine* 58: 967–74.

Seale, C.F. and Addington-Hall, J. (1994) 'Euthanasia: why people want to die earlier', *Social Science and Medicine,* 39 (5): 647–54.

Seale, C.F. and Addington-Hall, J. (1995a) 'Euthanasia: the role of good care', *Social Science and Medicine,* 40 (5): 581–87.

Seale, C.F. and Addington-Hall, J. (1995b) 'Dying at the best time', *Social Science and Medicine,* 40 (5): 589–95.

Seale, C.F., Addington-Hall, J. and McCarthy, M. (1997) 'Awareness of dying: prevalence, causes and consequences', *Social Science and Medicine,* 45 (3): 477–84.

Seale, C.F. and Cartwright, A. (1994) *The Year before Death.* Aldershot: Avebury.

Seale, C. and Silverman, D. (1997) 'Ensuring rigour in qualitative research', *European Journal of Public Health,* 7: 379–84.

Seale, C., Gobo, G., Gubrium J.F. and Silverman D. (eds) (2004) *Qualitative Research Practice.* London: Sage.

Searle, G.R. (1973) *The Quest for National Efficiency: A Study in British Politics and Political Thought, 1899–1914.* Oxford: Blackwell.

Shaffir, W.B. (1985) 'Some reflections on approaches to fieldwork in Hassidic communities', *Jewish Journal of Sociology,* 27 (2): 115–34.

Shakespeare, T. (1996) 'Rules of engagement: doing disability research', *Disability and Society,* 11 (1): 115–19.

Sherman, C. and Price, G. (2001) *The Invisible Web: Uncovering Information Sources Search Engines Can't See.* Medford, NJ: Information Today, Inc.

Silverman, D. (1975) 'Accounts of organisations – organisational structures and the accounting process', in J.B. McKinley (ed.), *Processing People: Cases in Organisational Behaviour.* London: Holt, Reinhart & Winston. pp. 269–302.

Silverman, D. (1984) 'Going private: ceremonial forms in a private oncology clinic', *Sociology,* 18: 191–202.

Silverman, D. (1985) *Qualitative Methodology and Sociology.* Aldershot: Gower.

Silverman, D. (1987) *Communication and Medical Practice: Social Relations in the Clinic.* London: Sage.

Silverman, D. (1990) *Sociology and the Community: A Dialogue with the Deaf?* Inaugural lecture, Goldsmiths College, University of London, 24 October.

Silverman, D. (1993) *Interpreting Qualitative Data: Methods for Analysing Talk, Text and Interaction.* London: Sage.

Silverman, D. (1996) *Discourses of Counselling: HIV Counselling as Social Interaction.* London: Sage.

Silverman, D. (ed.) (1997) *Qualitative Research: Theory, Method, Practice.* London: Sage.

Silverman, D. (1998) *Harvey Sacks.* Cambridge: Polity Press.

Silverman, D. (1999) *Doing Qualitative Research: A Practical Handbook.* London: Sage.

Silverman, D. (2001) *Interpreting Qualitative Data,* 2nd edn. London: Sage.

Silverman, D. and Jones, J. (1976) *Organisational Work: The Language of Grading and the Grading of Language.* London: Collier/Macmillan.

Singer, P.A. and Benatar, S.R. (2001) 'Beyond Helsinki: a vision for global health ethics', *British Medical Journal,* 322: 747–48.

Skeggs, B. (1994) 'Situating the production of feminist ethnography', in M. Maynard and J. Purvis (eds), *Researching Women's Lives from a Feminist Perspective.* London: Taylor and Francis.

Slater, D.R. (1998) 'Analysing cultural objects: content analysis and semiotics', in C. Seale (ed.), *Researching Society and Culture* London: Sage. pp. 233–44.

Smart, B. (1993) *Postmodernity.* London: Routledge.

Smith, A-M. (1994) *New Right Discourse on Race and Sexuality.* Cambridge: Cambridge University Press.

Smith, D. (1987) *The Everyday World as Problematic.* Toronto: University of Toronto Press.

Smith, M.J. (1998) *Social Science in Question.* London: Sage.

Song, M. (1998) 'Researching Chinese siblings', in J. Ribbens and R. Edwards (eds), *Feminist Dilemmas in Qualitative Research: Public Knowledge and Private Lives.* London: Sage.

Spicer, N.J. (1998) 'Sedentarization and accessibility to health services', in R.W. Dutton, J.I. Clark and A.M. Battikhi (eds), *Arid Land Resources and Their Management: Jordan's Desert Margin.* London:

Kegan Paul International.

Spicer, N.J. (1999) 'Pastoral mobility, sedentarization and accessibility of health services in the northeast Badia of Jordan', *Applied Geography,* 19 (4): 299–312.

Stacey, J. (1988) 'Can there be a feminist ethnography?', *Women's Studies International Forum*, 11 (1): 21–27.

Stanley, L. (1990) *Feminist Praxis: Research, Theory and Epistemology in Feminist Sociology.* London and New York: Routledge.

Stanley, L. and Wise, S. (1993) *Breaking Out Again: Feminist Ontology and Epistemology.* London: Routledge.

Stein, S. (1999) *Learning, Teaching and Researching on the Internet: A Practical Guide for Social Scientists.* Pearson Education: New York.

Stockdale, A. (2002) 'Tools for digital audio recording in qualitative research', *Social Research Update*, 38. www.soc.surrey.ac.uk/sru/SRU38.html.

Strauss, A.L. (1987) *Qualitative Analysis for Social Scientists.* Cambridge: Cambridge University Press.

Strauss, A.L. and Corbin, J. (1990) *Basics of Qualitative Research: Grounded Theory Procedures and Techniques.* Newbury Park, CA: Sage.

Strauss, A.L. and Corbin, J. (eds) (1997) *Grounded Theory in Practice.* Thousand Oaks, CA: Sage.

Strong, P. (1979) 'Sociological imperialism and the profession of medicine', *Social Science and Medicine*, 13A: 199–215.

Strunk, W. and White, E.B. (1979) *The Elements of Style*, 3rd edn. Boston, MA: Allyn and Bacon.

Sudnow, D. (1965) 'Normal crimes: sociological features of the penal code in a public defender's office', *Social Problems*, 12: 255–76.

Sudweeks, F. and Simoff, S. (1999) 'Complementary explorative data analysis: the reconciliation of quantitative and qualitative principles', in S. Jones (ed.), *Doing Internet Research: Critical Issues and Methods for Examining the Net.* London: Sage.

Swales J.M. (1990) *Genre Analysis: English in Academic and Research Settings.* Cambridge: Cambridge University Press.

Tagg, J. (1988) *The Burden of Representation: Essays on Photographies and Histories.* Basingstoke: Macmillan Education.

Taraborrelli, P. (1993) 'Becoming a carer', in N. Gilbert (ed.), *Researching Social Life.* London: Sage.

Taussig, M. (1987) *Shamanism, Colonialism and the Wild Man.* Chicago: University of Chicago Press.

Taylor, C. (1994) 'Interpretation and the sciences of man', in M. Martin and L.C. McIntyre (eds), *Readings in the Philosophy of Social Science.* Cambridge, MA: MIT Press.

Taylor, S. (2001) 'Locating and conducting discourse analytic research', in M. Wetherell, S. Taylor and S. Yates (eds), *Discourse as Data: A Guide for Analysis.* London: Sage. pp. 5–48.

Taylor, S.J. and Bogdan, R. (1984) *Introduction to Qualitative Research Methods*, 2nd edn. New York: John Wiley.

Thomas, B. and Williams, R. (1999) *The Internet for Schools: A Practical Step-by-step Guide for Teachers, Student Teachers, Parents and Governors.* Plymouth: Internet Handbooks.

Thompson, E.P. (1966) *The Making of the English Working Class.* London: Vintage.

Thompson, P. (1988). *The Voice of the Past. Oral History*, 2nd edn. Oxford: Oxford University Press.

Tonkiss, F. and Passey, A. (1999) 'Trust, confidence and voluntary organisations: between values and institutions', *Sociology*, 33 (2): 257–74.

Townsend, P., Corrigan, P. and Kowarzik, U. (1987) *Poverty and Labour in London.* London: Low Pay Unit.

Trochim, William M. The Research Methods Knowledge Base, 2nd edn. Internet WWW page, at URL: www.trochim.human.cornell.edu/kb/index.htm (version current as of 2 August 2000).

Tyler, S.A. (1986) 'Post-modern ethnography: from document of the occult to occult document', in J. Clifford and G. Marcus (eds), *Writing Culture: The Poetics and Politics of Ethnography.* Berkeley, CA: University of California Press. pp. 122–40.

UPIAS (1976) *Fundamental Principles of Disability.* London: Union of Physically Impaired Against Segregation. http://www.leeds.ac.uk/disability-studies/archiveuk/UPIAS/UPIAS.pdf.

Van der Valk, I. (2003) 'Right-wing parliamentary discourse on immigration in France', *Discourse and Society*, 14 (3): 309–48.

Van Dijk, T. (ed.) (1997) *Discourse Studies: A Multidisciplinary Introduction.* London: Sage.

Van Dijk, T. (2000) 'New(s) racism: a discourse analytical approach', in S. Cottle (ed.), *Ethnic Minorities and the Media.* Buckingham: Open University Press. pp. 33–49.

Van Dijk, T. (2002) 'Discourse and racism', in D. Goldberg and J. Solomos (eds), *The Blackwell Companion to Racial and Ethnic Studies.* Oxford: Blackwell. pp. 145–59.

Van Zoonen, L. (1994) *Feminist Media Studies.* London: Sage.

Vidich, A.J. and Lyman, S.M. (2000) 'Qualitative methods: their history in sociology and anthropology', in N.K. Denzin and Y.S. Lincoln (eds), *Handbook of Qualitative Research*, 2nd edn. Thousand Oaks, CA: Sage. pp. 37–84.

Waitzkin, H. (1979) 'Medicine, superstructure and micropolitics', *Social Science and Medicine*, 13A: 601–09.

Walliman, N. (2001) *Your Research Project: A Step-By-Step Guide for the First-Time Researcher*. London: Sage.

Ware, V. and Back, L. (2001) *Out of Whiteness: Color, Politics, and Culture*. Chicago: Chicago University Press.

Warren, C.A.A. (2002) 'Qualitative interviewing', in J.F. Gubrium and J.A. Holstein (eds), *Handbook of Interview Research: Context and Method*. Thousand Oaks, CA: Sage. pp. 83–102.

Weber, M. (1930) *The Protestant Ethic and the Spirit of Capitalism*. London: Allen and Unwin.

Weber, M. (1946) 'Science as a vocation', and 'Politics as a vocation', in H. Gerth and C.W. Mills (eds), *From Max Weber*. Oxford: Oxford University Press.

Weber, M. (1949) *The Methodology of the Social Sciences*. New York: Free Press.

Weber, M. (1978) *Economy and Society*, 2 vols. Berkeley, CA: University of California Press.

Wells, A.F. (1935) *The Local Social Survey in Great Britain*. London: Allen and Unwin.

Wengraf, T. (2001) *Qualitative Research Interviewing: Biographic Narratives and Semi-Structured Methods*. London: Sage.

West, P. (1990) 'The status and validity of accounts obtained at interview: a contrast between two studies of families with a disabled child', *Social Science and Medicine*, 30 (11): 1229–39.

Wetherell, M. and Potter, J. (1992) *Mapping the Language of Racism: Discourse and the Legitimation of Exploitation*. London: Harvester Wheatsheaf.

Wetherell, M., Taylor, S. and Yates, S.J. (eds) (2001a) *Discourse Theory and Practice: A Reader*. London: Sage.

Wetherell, M., Taylor, S. and Yates, S.J. (eds) (2001b) *Discourse as Data: A Guide for Analysis*. London: Sage.

White, J. (1980) *Rothschild Buildings*. London: Routledge.

White, J. (1986) *The Worst Street in North London: Campbell Bunk, Islington, Between the Wars*. London: Routledge.

Whittaker, J. (2002) *The Internet: The Basics*. London: Routledge.

Whyte, W.F. (1943) *Street Corner Society: The Social Structure of an Italian Slum*. Chicago: University of Chicago Press (3rd edn 1981).

Whyte, W.F. (1955) *Street Corner Society: The Social Structure of an Italian Slum*, 2nd edn. Chicago: University of Chicago Press.

Wiener, C.L. (1975) 'The burden of rheumatoid arthritis: tolerating the uncertainty', *Social Science and Medicine*, 9: 97–104.

Williams, M. and May, T. (1996) *Introduction to the Philosophy of Social Research*. London: UCL Press.

Winch, P. (1970) 'Understanding a primitive society', in B.R. Wilson (ed.), *Rationality*. Oxford: Basil Blackwell.

Wittig, M. (1992) *The Straight Mind and Other Essays*. Boston, MA: Beacon Press.

Wolcott, H. (1990) *Writing Up Qualitative Research*. Newbury Park, CA: Sage. (Qualitative Research Methods Series No. 20.)

Wrong, D. (1961) 'The oversocialized conception of man in modern sociology', *American Sociological Review*, 26: 183–93.

Yearley, S. (1981) 'Textual persuasion: the role of social accounting in the construction of scientific arguments', *Philosophy of Science*, 11: 409–45.

Young, L. (1996) *Fear of the Dark: 'Race', Gender and Sexuality in the Cinema*. London: Routledge.

Young, M. and Cullen, L. (1996) *A Good Death: Conversations with East Londoners*. London: Routledge.

Young, M. and Willmott, P. (1957) *Family and Kinship in East London*. London: Routledge and Kegan Paul.

Zorbaugh, H. (1929) *The Gold Coast and the Slum*. Chicago: University of Chicago Press.

Index